Ireland's History

Ireland's History

Prehistory to the Present

KENNETH L. CAMPBELL

Bloomsbury Academic
An imprint of Bloomsbury Publishing Plc

BLOOMSBURY

LONDON • NEW DELHI • NEW YORK • SYDNEY

Bloomsbury Academic
An imprint of Bloomsbury Publishing Plc

50 Bedford Square
London
WC1B 3DP
UK

1385 Broadway
New York
NY 10018
USA

www.bloomsbury.com

BLOOMSBURY and the Diana logo are trademarks of Bloomsbury Publishing Plc

First published 2014
Reprinted by Bloomsbury Academic 2014

British Library Cataloguing-in-Publication Data
A catalogue record for this book is available from the British Library.

ISBN: HB: 978-1-4411-1576-8
PB: 978-1-4411-0378-9
ePDF: 978-1-4725-6782-6
ePUB: 978-1-4725-6784-0

Library of Congress Cataloging-in-Publication Data
A catalog record for this book is available from the Library of Congress

Typeset by Deanta Global Publishing Services, Chennai, India
Printed and bound in Great Britain

CONTENTS

PREFACE

This survey of Irish history is not intended as a definitive, much less a comprehensive, history of Ireland. Despite the availability of a number of other surveys of Irish history, it is meant to fill a gap and to serve several purposes. There are longer, more detailed accounts of the Irish past, most notably, the multivolume *New History of Ireland* series published by Oxford University Press. Yet, it is doubtful that many people, much less undergraduate students or general readers, would sit down and read this set from cover to cover. Here, I have attempted to strike a balance between some excellent texts, such as Thomas Bartlett's *Ireland: A History*, that is more appropriate as a graduate-level introduction, primarily because of the length rather than the reading difficulty, and shorter surveys that especially tend to skim over the earlier periods of Irish history. Even Bartlett covers the period from 1159 to 1541 in a single chapter. The format of my book, consisting of 14 chapters of moderate length, plus an introduction and a conclusion, is intended to be conducive to a college semester. It is hoped that those who read this book will be inspired to read further on Irish history in the sources mentioned within, those found in the bibliography and notes, and the suggested readings on the accompanying web site.

This book, then, is intended to be a general, introductory survey of Irish history that is accessible to students taking their first course on the subject and to general readers who wish for a broad overview of a reasonable length. The book includes the major themes that any history of Ireland must address, beginning with prehistoric times and continuing down to the present day. Readers will encounter discussions of the emergence of Celtic Christianity; the influence of the Vikings and of the Norman conquest; the Reformation and Ireland's role in the religious and political turmoil that affected so much of Europe during the sixteenth and seventeenth centuries; Irish migration; the 1798 rebellion and the impact of the French Revolution; the Act of Union and the rise of Irish nationalism; the Great Famine and the Land War; the Easter Rising and the Anglo-Irish Treaty of 1921; the partition of Ireland in the twentieth century; the Troubles in Northern Ireland and the history of the Republic of Ireland; Ireland's relationship with the European Union and rapprochement with the United Kingdom; and some consideration of Irish social and cultural systems for each of the periods throughout its history.

In addition, this book pursues several themes and topics that will provide the text with some coherence and distinguish it from other general books on the subject. First, the book does not treat Irish history in a vacuum, but rather considers the ways in which that history is reflective of changes that have helped to shape the modern world in general. Special attention is given to connections and comparisons with British history. Second, at several points in the text Irish literary sources will be discussed as reflective of broad changes in Irish culture and society. Third, this book will not attempt to put forth a single narrative, but rather to weave together several narrative strands that represent different political perspectives and reflect class and religious differences, each of which could significantly alter the narrative and meaning of Irish history if taken separately.

In other words, this book will not adopt a nationalist perspective—or any monolithic, much less moralistic—perspective on the past. At the same time, however, it will not ignore those who have taken or would take such a perspective because those who have done so have greatly influenced the history that is discussed here and are a part of it. In addition, the text will balance treatment of social and economic history with political, cultural, and religious history. These approaches overlap much more than is sometimes acknowledged and so I will explore the interconnections among them when it is appropriate. Finally, this text will encourage readers and students to think critically about the past and invite them to consider how a study of Irish history might inform and influence their understanding of history in general.

This book would not have been written if Beth Gilmartin and Stan Green had not proposed beginning an Irish Studies program at Monmouth University. Stan has been especially supportive, lending me key books at the start of the project and allowing me to accompany him on a trip to Ireland in March 2012. I am also appreciative of Brian Sexton, Brian Rice, and Claudia Green for the insights and guidance that each provided in their own way on that trip. Gretta Byrne provided an excellent tour at Céide Hill and was nice enough to send me a copy of the preliminary report of the work done in the excavations at Céide Hill, Behy, and Glenulra in County Mayo. Monmouth University awarded me a sabbatical for the fall of 2012, which allowed me the time to finish writing and for which I am extremely grateful. I also received a Grant-in-Aid in Creativity from Monmouth that helped to finance my trip to Ireland while I was working on the book. Joan Manzo read each chapter as it was completed. I cannot thank her enough for her suggestions and corrections and for sharing her own extensive knowledge of and enthusiasm for Irish history. I am grateful to the anonymous reviewers who first provided feedback on my proposal for this book. I am especially thankful for the many valuable suggestions and insightful comments from the anonymous reviewer who read early drafts of Chapters 6, 10, and 14, which deal with three of the most controversial periods in Irish history, and then the entire text when it was finished. Stan Wakefield looked over the proposal at an early stage and was instrumental in bringing it to the attention of my editor at Bloomsbury, Claire Lipscomb, who has been a joy to work with and incredibly encouraging throughout the project. Thanks also to Rhodri Mogford, who assisted with the illustrations, and to my outstanding copyeditor, Subitha Nair. Finally, I owe my deepest gratitude to the support and encouragement I have received from my wife Millie and the rest of my family, especially Ermalee, Tracy, Caleb, and Stephanie, all of whom have been incredibly supportive and understanding of my desire to write this book and the time needed to do so.

Kenneth L. Campbell
Perryville, Maryland

A NOTE ON GEOGRAPHY AND CLIMATE

Before beginning our examination of Irish history, I thought it might be helpful to begin with a brief overview of Irish geography. Ireland's geography, in fact, has its own history. Geologists believe that Ireland was once much larger than it is now because for eons it was composed of mostly ice. Ireland today is what was left after all of the ice melted away. A relatively small island, measuring about 300 miles at its longest and about 170 miles at its widest and comprising about 32,000 square miles, Ireland is located between 52° and 53° N latitude. Every location in Ireland is within 100 miles of the coast. It has a moist climate brought about by winds from the ocean; Irish souvenirs representing its four seasons show rain falling in spring, summer, fall, and winter. The Island receives a mixture of cold air from the north and warm air from the currents associated with the jet stream that come from the south. The warm air tends to predominate, giving Ireland a temperate climate.

Ireland has a quite varied landscape for an island of its size. It is more mountainous near the coasts than it is inland, with the exception of a stretch of coast that runs about fifty miles north of Dublin. This is a factor that influences the drainage of water, which contributes to the bogs and the frequently saturated fields of the lowlands. The mountainous areas are much better suited to animal grazing than they are to arable farming, but significant portions of the lowlands are not well suited to grain cultivation either. In general, the east is more easily cultivable than the west, with the River Shannon as the dividing line, but fertile land is interspersed with wild rocky or boggy areas throughout the island. One might think that a territory the size of Ireland would have easily become a unified political entity early in its history, but partly because of its topography this has proved problematic throughout its history. One main problem was that Ireland lacked a central location that was easily accessible to all and easily supported by an abundance of fertile land. But this does not mean that the conception of Ireland as single cultural or political entity did not exist; during the early stages of its history the people of the island shared a common language and literary culture.

The movement and recession of glaciers has left Ireland with a series of bogs, lakes and gently sloping hills called "drumlins" in the northern and western parts of the lowlands.[1] About one-sixth of the Irish land, a total of

3.31 million acres, consists of bogs.[2] The bogs sit now where glacial lakes used to be. For centuries bogs have provided Ireland with its main source of fuel, in the form of turf, which comes from the top layer of the peat, or decomposed vegetation that makes up the bogs. The peat is cut and dried to form turf. Only recently, in 2010, has legislation been passed in the Republic of Ireland to protect the bogs. That legislation, phased in over several years, covers a number of bogs in which famers will be prohibited from cutting turf. One of the reasons that the Irish have relied so heavily on turf for fuel is a relative lack of other kinds of heating material. Ireland lacks any significant amounts of oil or coal and has a relative scarcity of timber. Kevin Whelan has estimated that the Irish Republic currently contains 2.4 billion trees covering only about 10 per cent of the land, compared to a European average of 30 per cent. Northern Ireland has even less, about 6 per cent.[3]

Ireland's location off the far northwestern coast of Europe has also played a key role in its history. This can be seen, for example, in the important fact that Ireland never became part of the Roman Empire, which extended as far as what is now England and southern Scotland. Ireland's relative isolation has affected its history in both positive and negative ways. The sea that could at times isolate Ireland from other parts of Europe at other times could more readily bring people from foreign lands to its shores.

There is one other important aspect of Irish geography—historically perhaps the most important aspect. Ireland, of course, is also part of a group of islands, the largest of which we know as Britain. For a time, Ireland was even connected to Britain before the sea levels rose at the end of the last Ice Age. Because Britain is the largest of the islands, the entire chain is known as the British Isles, much like Hawaii or the Hawaiian Islands derive their name from the largest of that chain, known locally as simply the "Big Island." I should point out that there is a trend in recent scholarship away from using the term "the British Isles" because it is seen as privileging Britain over Ireland. I am not sure if substitutes such as the "Atlantic Archipelago" or the "Atlantic Isles," which have problems of their own, will become standard usage or that readers will automatically know what is meant by these terms, so I have chosen not to use them in this text. I have, however, used "British Isles" sparingly out of respect for those who find the term objectionable and because this is a history of Ireland. Still, as will be apparent throughout the text, at many points the history of Ireland cannot be discussed without reference to its relationship with Britain. That is as much a product of geography as it is of history.

---

[1] F. H. A. Aalen (2011), "The Irish Landscape: Synthesis of Habitat and History," in F. H. A. Aalen, K. Whelan and M. Stout (eds), *Atlas of the Irish Rural Landscape*, 2nd edn. Cork: Cork University Press, p. 8.

[2] F. H. A. Aalen, K. Whelan and M. Stout (eds), *Atlas of the Irish Rural Landscape*, 2nd edn. Cork: Cork University Press, p. 168.

[3] Kevin Whelan (2011), "Facing the Future," in F. H. A. Aalen, K. Whelan and M. Stout (eds), *Atlas of the Irish Rural Landscape*, 2nd edn. Cork: Cork University Press, p. 126. There is an interesting page on the deforestation of Ireland at: http://www.forestryservices.ie/history.

LIST OF ILLUSTRATIONS

Civilization survey texts. Second, Ireland's history provides an understanding of how the people of one land have navigated the relationship with an imperial power, whether Ireland was officially designated as a colony or not. A related theme centers on the choice between conformity and rebellion and the basis on which that choice is made. Irish history provides insights into the advantages and disadvantages of both. Irish history also provides a telling case study of the power of history to influence both the present and the future at any given time. This is what has made Irish historiography (the writing of Irish history) so important. Historians have been helping the Irish people to find meaning in their past ever since the epic tales that were first told in prehistoric times. Many people in Ireland consider their history sacred and cling to a particular version of it that appeals to them. That is a subject worthy of study and analysis in its own right.

Even the very recent history of Ireland has much to teach the world at large. For example, the violent conflict in Northern Ireland known as *the Troubles* and the peace process there have much to teach about the nature of both conflict and conflict resolution. The history of the Republic of Ireland is in many ways a remarkable success story involving the creation of a new nation that changed and adapted over the course of a complex and rapidly changing era. The Republic of Ireland has not only successfully managed its own affairs as an independent country, but it has also exercised leadership in the European Community disproportionately to its size and was elected to the United Nations Human Rights Council in November 2012. But there have been failures, problems, and missed opportunities in the history of the Republic that can be instructive as well. In addition, there are lessons to be learned from Ireland's rise as an economic power during the "Celtic Tiger" years of the late 1990s and early twenty-first century and its precipitate decline after 2007.

Another dimension of great importance to Irish history is the phenomenon of migration. A large number of people have left Ireland for other lands. As they have done so, they have taken their culture, their memories, and, frequently, their love for their homeland with them. Ireland always had its own language and its own culture that remained distinct from that of Britain and the rest of Europe. The Irish people have managed to cultivate and preserve not only their culture but also a certain image of Ireland and its past that contains a strong emotional appeal for those who are ambivalent about the modern industrial and postindustrial worlds. Nor is that image entirely imaginary, since Ireland has produced a prolific amount of literature and music that have had a universal appeal. The works of Jonathan Swift, Maria Edgeworth, James Joyce, Samuel Beckett, and Elizabeth Bowen, just to name a few, would appear on any reading "bucket list" of great novels. The people of Ireland have overcome negative stereotypes imposed upon them by the British to become a source of cultural pride for people of Irish descent around the world.

But Irish history is not a monolithic tale of the triumph of good over evil—it is far more interesting than that. In each period of Irish history, as in that of any land, one can find positive and negative aspects. The past was never a golden age where all was good; the present is never as bad as it seems from watching the news or reading the newspaper. Writing a history of Ireland that includes both the Republic and Northern Ireland does not need to be taken as a political statement that the island should be politically unified—or that it should not. In this history, I have tried to balance both sides of that argument and to place the issue in historical perspective. To some degree, the inclusion of both is necessary because the history of the North and the South is very much intertwined, whatever differences exist between them. In addition, however, it is hoped that those primarily interested in the history of Northern Ireland will learn more about and become more aware of the importance of the history of the Republic and vice versa.

Why a new history of Ireland?

I realized in the course of writing this book that, with all of the information available, I could easily have written a thousand pages. But that would have defeated the purpose for which the book is intended. As I stated in the preface, it is meant to be a brief, up-to-date survey that is accessible to the reader who has no prior knowledge of the subject. The explosion of books and articles on the subject of Irish history is actually one reason why it is necessary for a new history to be written periodically. In a survey of Irish history written twenty-six years ago, Liam de Paor commented on the phenomenon of increased specialization in the field:

> We are informed, as never before about ether-drinking in nineteenth-century Derry, about the genealogists of minor eighth-century dynasts, about the subinfeudation of thirteenth-century Meath, about seasonal migration as a prelude to permanent emigration, and about a thousand other topics.[1]

The number of writings on Irish history has increased exponentially since then, so much so that it would probably be impossible for a person to read in a single lifetime all that has been written on Ireland in just the past 26 years. The author of a survey text like this can only hope to bring some sense of the current state of thinking and knowledge in the field based on the works of specialists who have absorbed much of the literature within their

---

[1] Liam De Paor (1986), *The Peoples of Ireland: From Prehistory to Modern Times*. London: Hutchinson, pp. 11–12.

own particular area of expertise. This is especially true for the history of the twentieth century.

Another justification for a new book on Ireland's history is that the history of the island has changed in significant ways just within the past 10 years. The events in the past do not change, but our perspective on them does and that is important. History is not a subject to be undertaken for its own sake, but because we find it useful, instructive, or interesting—in other words, because it means something to us in the present. It is the present that always calls us to re-examine the past because we continue to discover where that past history has led, which has the capacity to change the story. A history written in the 1970s or 1980s might have seen the Troubles as the culmination of Ireland's history; now peace in Northern Ireland has changed that narrative. But this also cautions us not to regard the current state of affairs as definitive or the end of history. Finally, in the past 20 years the teaching and writing of Irish history has continued to move away from the ideological perspective through which it had been seen in the nineteenth century and the early part of the twentieth. If this text brings your attention to some of the recent works by many fine historians and encourages you to read even some of them, then this book will have served a valuable purpose. (Suggestions for further reading on each of the topics included in the text are included in the online resources that are available at http://www.bloomsbury.com/irelands-history-9781441103789)

Irish historiography

People's views on history matter almost as much as what has actually happened in the past. In the seventeenth century some writers began to think of Ireland as a separate unified kingdom. At that point whether or not Ireland ever had been a unified kingdom became less important than the fact that people thought that it had been one. In the eighteenth century, interest in Irish history increased significantly as certain educated Irish writers began to envision a different future for Ireland. But the real dividing line in the writing of Irish history is the Rebellion of 1798. After that fateful year, Irish history tended to be written much more from a nationalistic perspective, a trend that dominated in the nineteenth century and for much of the twentieth. In the nationalistic version of Irish history, the British were always the villains exploiting the good Irish people, who had been engaged in a centuries-long struggle for freedom from British dominance. In the twentieth century, however, Irish history as an academic field has exploded, as has the entire historical profession. As a result, people have begun to learn and think differently about the Irish past.

There have certainly been exceptions prior to the twentieth century of Irish historians who tried to take a more objective approach to Irish history. For example, W. E. H. Lecky, whose multivolume *History of Ireland in the*

Eighteenth Century, appeared toward the end of the nineteenth century, produced a work that was largely free from the partisan biases of his times, even though the author was an Irish Protestant. Historians, beginning in about the 1930s, started to look at history from a variety of perspectives, including social, economic, and cultural. Robert Dudley Edwards and T. W. Moody were particularly influential in helping to bring about this shift. Edwards produced a number of notable books on Irish history from the sixteenth to the nineteenth centuries and founded, along with Moody the journal *Irish Historical Studies*. That journal became associated with revisionist Irish history, which moved it out of the political arena. Irish historians also began to challenge past stereotypes about Catholics and Protestants. Irish history as "morality tale," in the words of Roy Foster, has been eschewed for more complex levels of analysis and detailed investigations into specific topics.[2] Foster's own survey, *Modern Ireland, 1600–1972* (1988), was one of the most important general histories of Ireland to challenge this older interpretation. Foster did not so much attempt to provide a rival interpretation, however, as he sought to explore other aspects of Irish history through a nonnarrative format. There have been many attempts at synthesis since then, with the result that no single version of Irish history is accepted in the academic world today.

In moving away from the familiar narrative and aspects of the history of Ireland, these historians have provided a great stimulus to students and scholars of the subject. The *New History of Ireland* series, published by Oxford University Press, is a tremendous accomplishment that represents the topical, specialized approach to Irish history. This comprehensive multivolume work contains contributions from leading scholars in every field of Irish history, broken down into its component parts. Much recent work has focused on race, class, ethnicity, and gender, popular and important topics that downplay the importance of narrative political history. But there is still a need for an introduction that makes newcomers to the subject aware of some of those familiar story lines, while at the same time introducing them to some of the more nuanced interpretations that operate within a more thematic framework.

Of course, aspects of the older nationalist tradition still survive. Tim Pat Coogan's recent book on the Great Famine, *The Famine Plot: England's Role in Ireland's Greatest Tragedy* (2012), revives the charge anew that the British were culpable in the deaths of the Famine victims in the mid-nineteenth century. The Great Famine remains a controversial touchstone for academic and popular historians alike. The Irish War for Independence remains another. In his book on the subject, *The Irish War of Independence* (2002), Michael Hopkinson wrote that the "IRA guerilla warfare and Black and Tan [British] reprisals have rivaled the issue of the British government's

---

2 Roy Foster (1988), *Modern Ireland, 1600–1972*. London: Allen Lane, p. viii.

culpability for the Great Famine as the most emotive subject in modern Irish history."[3] Hopkinson, who attempted to look at the events from a more objective perspective, wrote about the difficulty of challenging the nationalist approach to the events that followed the Easter Rising of 1916. That topic has more recently undergone critical scholarly analysis by D. M. Leeson in *The Black and Tans: British Police and Auxilliaries in the Irish War of Independence, 1920–1921* (2011). Leeson takes a more nuanced approach to understanding the soldiers who were sent to Ireland to defend British authority from IRA attacks than has been the case in the past.

The focus on other topics besides religion and nationalism, while needed, can also produce its own distortions. Mary Kenny wrote in her preface to *Good-bye to Catholic Ireland* (1997) that she had written her book because "the culture of Catholic Ireland . . . seemed to have been so overlooked in Catholic studies."[4] Ireland does have a unique history and the attempt to write Catholicism or nationalism out of it in seeking to make Ireland seem more typical of the Western experience would be as misleading as any history that would simply perpetuate the stereotypes based on a Catholic or nationalist historiography alone.

Irish historiography thus has recently fallen into two camps, a nationalist school that has now mainly become the province of more popular historians and a more "liberal" or "revisionist" school that downplays the importance of nationalism as the central thread of Irish history. It should be pointed out, however, that anticolonialism has been a prominent theme in historical studies in general, one in which the British are still portrayed as being on the wrong side of history. When writing about the history of Ireland, it can be challenging to balance conflicting and competing viewpoints. Although this book represents an attempt at synthesis, I recognize that, in the end, it is yet another individual perspective on the Irish past.

Value of understanding earlier periods

Another premise of this book is that each period of the past has something to teach us beyond a consideration of the ways in which it has helped to shape the world that we inhabit today. Therefore, the reader will find here a greater concentration on earlier periods of Irish history than appears in many surveys. Earlier periods are no less important as part of the Irish or human experience than later periods—in some ways they are of greater

---

[3] Michael Hopkinson (2002), *The Irish War of Independence*. Montreal and Kingston: McGill-Queen's University Press, p. xvii. The auxiliary military forces sent to Ireland to restore order by the British were called "Black and Tans" after the colors of their uniforms.

[4] Mary Kenny (1997), *Goodbye to Catholic Ireland: A Social, Personal and Cultural History from the Fall of Parnell to the Realm of Mary Robinson*. London: Sinclair-Stevenson, p. xiii.

importance. One of the reasons that it is important to study and understand earlier periods on their own terms is because the past can be misused in the present. For example, many people today still view the relationship between Britain and Ireland as defined by events that occurred during and after the seventeenth century. But the relationship between Ireland and Britain did not begin in the seventeenth century; it actually dates back to prehistoric times. Certainly one of the most important events in Irish history was the mission of St Patrick, who came from Britain to convert the Irish to Christianity. Views of the relationship between Britain and Ireland would be significantly different if the seventh century were to be used as a frame of reference rather than the seventeenth. Thomas Cahill's book, *How the Irish Saved Civilization: The Untold Story of Ireland's Heroic Role from the Fall of Rome to the Rise of Medieval Europe* (1995), was an attempt to find contemporary relevance in the distant recesses of Ireland's historical past.

This is not to suggest that developments in later periods are less important—quite the contrary. The modern history of Ireland cannot be understood without knowing something about the Protestant Reformation and English colonization in Ireland in the sixteenth and seventeenth centuries, both of which have left legacies that are still with us today. The rebellion of 1798 and the Irish response to the Act of Union in 1801 would make no sense without some knowledge of the history of the previous three centuries. Furthermore, myths and legends of the past are a part of history. History is not just about disentangling what people believed from what was "really true." First, what was "really true" is an extremely problematic concept. Second, what people believed tells us much about them and is just as, if not more, important in shaping the history of subsequent generations than actual events.

Responses open to Ireland throughout history—resistance versus accommodation— and the role of history and literature in influencing those choices

It is historically important that Ireland has been invaded and occupied for a large portion of its history since prehistoric times. Although it was one of the few places that the Romans did not invade and conquer in Western Europe, Ireland underwent subsequent invasions from the Vikings, the Anglo-Normans, and the English on a number of occasions. In each instance the Irish people have had to respond—collectively and individually. Usually, their choices have been narrowed down to two: resistance or accommodation. Deciding when to conform and when to rebel is one of the most important and difficult choices in the life of people in groups and as individuals. In the nationalistic version of Irish history, of course, it is always rebellion that is celebrated. Accommodation or conformity is seen as nonheroic at best and perverse disloyalty or treason at worst. But is one always right and one always wrong?

Throughout history that has been a difficult question to answer and it is no less so for the historian. This book will not attempt to answer that question definitively, but it will raise the question and try to assist the reader in furthering her or his own personal response to it. History and literature have helped influence those choices in the past and will continue to influence people who have to make them in the future. The historical memory of the Rebellion of 1798, the Great Famine, and the Land War influenced the Easter Rising of 1916. Protestant commemorations of the Battle of the Boyne have been a source of pride for Protestants and a sore point for Catholics down to the present day. Popular novels such as Leon Uris's *Trinity* (1976) and histories such as Coogan's *Famine Plot* help to keep anti-British sentiment alive in the present. Whether this is a good thing or not is for each person to decide. But this in turn raises some other questions. If anti-British novels and histories keep old grievances and hatreds alive, can nonnationalistic novels or histories help to defuse them? Is this a legitimate role for history or literature?

Generally, the role of literature has not been to proselytize for a political cause, although there have certainly been works of literature that have done that. It is worth noting that Ireland's two greatest writers, James Joyce and William Butler Yeats, both rejected political nationalism. Joyce also rejected the Catholic heritage that has been such an important part of the Irish nationalist ethos. It is perhaps significant that the Irish literary revival coincided with the end of the political career of the nationalist leader Charles Stewart Parnell and a lull in the Irish campaign for Home Rule. Yeats wrote that "the modern literature of Ireland . . . began when Parnell fell from power in 1891."[5]

There is a reason why literature has been so important to the Irish and why Ireland has produced, and continues to produce, so many great writers. In a society where great minds do not have the same outlet for their creativity in politics or other fields, they frequently turn to literature as a means of expression. This would help to explain why czarist Russia produced a cluster of the greatest writers ever, including Gogol, Turgenev, Dostoevsky, and Tolstoy and how the Soviet period could produce a Pasternak and a Solzhenitsyn, whose training was in mathematics and physics. Many examples could be provided from Mexico and Latin America, as well as other colonized or oppressed peoples, but an extended discussion would stray too far from the topic of Irish history and literature. The point is that both history and literature can show the strengths and weaknesses of

[5] Quoted in Ibid., p. 8.

resistance on the one hand and accommodation on the other. Because this dichotomous choice has been such an important theme in Irish history, it makes the treatment of that history all the more important.

One thing is clear: one cannot understand contemporary Ireland without some understanding of its history. A case can also be made that one cannot understand Ireland and its history without knowing something about its literary and historiographical traditions. For example, without some knowledge of these subjects, one cannot understand the differences between North and South, why the island is politically divided, or why divisions remain within Northern Ireland.

In her book, *Dangerous Games: the Uses and Abuses of History* (2009), the historian Margaret Macmillan makes the point that people select from the past to create an image of it that appeals to them or explains what they think is happening, or what they want to happen in the future. Macmillan discusses the advantages of getting the truth about the past out in the open where wrongs have been committed and where apologies and redress are warranted. She gives as examples the Swiss banks that profited from the confiscation of Jewish property during the Holocaust and the efforts at reconciliation after the end of Apartheid in South Africa. But she also wonders about the efficacy of politicians apologizing for events that happened in past centuries under belief systems very different from those of today, giving as examples the pope's apology for the Crusades and Tony Blair's apology for the nineteenth-century potato famine in Ireland (see Chapter 10).

Macmillan says that the danger of focusing on past evils is that doing so takes away from focusing on current problems. She cites as an example how focusing on slavery and demands for reparations does nothing to address educational standards that empower African-American communities or employment rates among African-American males. She also points out that in the Republic of Ireland students today are taught a much fuller version of history than the one that previous generations had been taught because of political pressures: a tale of eight centuries of oppression followed by the triumph of Irish nationalism that ignored anything that might have complicated the story, such as the civil war between the nationalists themselves in the early 1920s.

Macmillan's point is that, although we cannot find in history a blueprint for how to act because each historical situation is different, we can find useful examples and information that make us ponder those decisions. For example, she discusses the long and checkered history of politicians citing the policy of appeasement practiced by the British prime minister, Neville Chamberlain, before World II when they wished to justify going to war with an intransigent enemy. She questions whether it is always wrong to talk to one's enemies in an attempt to broker peace—even whether it was wrong for Chamberlain and his allies to do so in the 1930s in an attempt to avoid another war, even though we know in retrospect that Hitler was not willing to stop at Germany's natural boundaries.

Applying this premise to Irish history, there are certainly a number of times when historical precedents have been used to justify actions or policies in the present. The Rebellion of 1641 shaped the attitudes toward Catholics in Ireland and the policies implemented by William III and the Protestant Ascendancy after the Revolution of 1688. In his 2012 novel *The Dream of the Celt*, the Peruvian writer Mario Vargas Llosa has found in Roger Casement—who became an Irish nationalist after working for the British in the Congo and Peru—an example to inspire anticolonial sentiment in the present. The inspiration for action in the present does not even need to come from recent history. Declan Kiberd says of the Easter Rising that "many of the young men who joined the rebels of 1916 did so in the belief that they were re-enacting the sacrifice of Cuchularn, that ancient Celtic hero who defended the Gap of the North against all comers, even unto death."[6] Many of the leaders of the Rebellion of 1798, such as Theobald Wolfe Tone, were Protestant. Many of the leaders of the Irish cultural revival of the late nineteenth century, such as Standish O'Grady, were Protestant. And yet both the Rebellion of 1798 and the Irish cultural revival have been adopted in the service of a version of an Irish nationalism that is essentially Catholic.

Irish history thus presents a number of challenges to the student and the historian. These challenges have the potential, however, to make Irish history even more interesting and rewarding. It is easy to watch a film like *Michael Collins* (1997) and get caught up in the romantic and heroic aspects of Irish history, in the same way that Mel Gibson's film *Braveheart* (1996) inspired a new generation of Scottish nationalists and sympathizers. The challenge is to enjoy those films and also be inspired by them to learn more about the complicated history with which they deal instead of just accepting them at face value. If this book assists the reader in learning more about Irish history and inspires him or her to look even more deeply into it, it will have served the main purpose for which it was intended.

---

[6] Declan Kiberd (1989), "Irish Literature and Irish History," in R. Foster (ed.), *The Oxford Illustrated History of Ireland*. Oxford: Oxford University Press, p. 278.

CHAPTER TWO

Prehistoric Ireland

It is necessary always to remember that although the flint tools, pots, tombs, house plans and decoration so frequently illustrated in archaeological text-books are important, they are important primarily as documents of social history—as clues to how their makers and users eked out a precarious living or enjoyed a lavish life-style.

– LAURENCE FLANAGAN, *Ancient Ireland: Life Before the Celts*, 1998

Who are the Irish?

The Celts, the people to whom the modern Irish have tended to trace their cultural identity, seem to have arrived in Ireland about 2,500 years ago, although no one is quite sure about exactly when and how they arrived. The Celts themselves, insofar as they were even an identifiable people, were probably more unified by culture and language than by blood or tribal identity; medieval historians such as Patrick Geary have debunked the notion that the tribal groups to which the Romans (and later historians) assigned names constituted some kind of pure ethnic identity.[1] Group membership was far more fluid in the past; those who belonged to a particular tribe did not necessarily think of themselves in the same terms as outsiders such as the Romans did. *Celts* is a convenient term for people with similar cultures and

---

[1] Patrick J. Geary (2002), *The Myth of Nations: The Medieval Origins of Europe*. Princeton: Princeton University Press. Geary was dealing with a later period, but the same principle applies here.

languages that substitutes for making distinctions among the various groups of people who come under that designation. More than one Celtic tribe settled in Ireland, but it was one, the Everni, who gave the Irish people their name. We know them as the *Érainn*, thanks to later references by Christian writers.

At the time of their arrival, Ireland had already been settled for at least 7,000 years. Archaeological evidence suggests, contrary to what some scholars have argued in the past, that the earliest settlers lived throughout the island instead of just residing in the northeast. Of these earliest settlers, we know that they inhabited circular huts that were arranged in close proximity to one another. Other than that, we know very little about the people who inhabited Ireland in the Mesolithic period, which lasted from about 7,500 BCE to about 3,500 BCE.

Even the manner of the arrival of the people who settled in Ireland is a mystery. Ireland became an island because of the global warming that caused the seas to rise at the end of the last ice age—probably about 12,000 BCE. Some scholars have suggested that the first settlers followed animals that had previously migrated across the land bridge from Britain to Ireland when Ireland was still a peninsula physically connected to Britain,[2] but more recent specialists such as Richard Bradley have disputed this notion.[3] However the original settlers got there, another population shift took place about 6,800 BCE with the arrival of new immigrants who are identified by their use of different kinds of implements.

The Neolithic period that began about 3,500 BCE is associated with the coming of settled agriculture, a process that had transformed civilization in southwest Asia, China, and India several thousand years earlier. The next stage of prehistory is the Bronze Age, so called obviously because of the introduction of bronze tools and weapons, which began in Ireland about 2,000 BCE, but which is itself subdivided into phases. The Later Bronze Age began about 1,200 BCE. Bronze swords, shields, crescent-shaped collars called lunulas, drinking vessels, and even musical instruments like horns and trumpets have been found in Ireland from this period; some of these artifacts are of types completely unique to Ireland. Although ancient writers tended to portray Ireland as backward because it was located outside of what was considered the civilized world, archaeological discoveries indicate that Bronze-Age Ireland contained a surprising amount of wealth. The Bronze Age lasted until the beginning of the Iron Age about 500 BCE. The big question surrounding each of these transitions is whether or not they occurred internally or were brought about by new arrivals on

---

[2] Michael J. O'Kelly (2005), "Ireland before 3000 BC," in D. Ó Cróinín (ed.), *A New History of Ireland: Volume I: Prehistoric and Early Ireland*. Oxford: Oxford University Press, p. 57.

[3] Richard Bradley (2007), *The Prehistory of Britain and Ireland*. Cambridge: Cambridge University Press, p. 9.

the island. It hardly matters in an assessment of prehistoric Ireland how derivative its art, culture, or social practices were; cultural borrowings and the infusion of new ideas and traditions always enrich a culture and make it more interesting. This does not mean that the peoples of prehistoric Ireland contributed nothing original; nothing quite like the sun window at Newgrange (see below) has been found anywhere else during the period in which it was conceived.

The later treatment of Irish prehistory down to the twentieth century was heavily influenced by the *Lebor Gabála Érenn*, also known as the *Book of Invasions*, which portrayed the settlement of the island by the Gaídil, as if they had brought their rule and culture to a barren land. Based on earlier sources, this book was probably not written down until the eleventh century. Whoever they were, the Gaídil or the Celts did not simply come in and take over the island; in fact, it is more likely that they benefited from the thriving Bronze Age civilization that they found upon arrival. What we think of as Celtic culture was undoubtedly heavily influenced by those people already living on the island. The answer to the question of who are the Irish will depend on the definition of the person asking it, but the people who inhabited the island in the Mesolithic, Neolithic, and Bronze Ages are as much a part of the story of Ireland as those who came after them.

Settled agriculture versus hunting and gathering

The earliest settlers in Ireland were certainly hunters, who had learned to make knives, scrapers, and arrow tips out of flint. Numerous leaf-shaped flint tools have been discovered throughout Ireland, including thousands near the River Bann in Northern Ireland, leading archaeologists to call them *Bann flakes*, otherwise known as *butt-trimmed flakes*. Early Irish hunters pursued a more narrow range of wildlife than that which existed on the European continent or even in Britain; they mainly hunted wild boar and squirrels, though other potential prey included game birds, hares, pine martens, and even bears. But too much can be made of the distinction between hunters and gatherers on the one hand and practitioners of settled agriculture on the other. Hunter-gatherer societies coexisted with farmers on the European continent for thousands of years. Most societies were probably hybrids that tended to practice one to a greater degree but not to the total exclusion of the other.

Archaeological evidence supports this overlap for Ireland as well. In fact, the date for the beginning of settled agriculture in Ireland is now estimated to be much earlier than had been previously thought; cattle bones discovered at Ferriter's Cove in County Kerry have been dated to 4,500 BCE. What distinguished Neolithic people from their Mesolithic forerunners was not just the fact that they farmed but their use of different technologies to do so and the extent of forest clearance that they undertook in order to open more land for cultivation. They also had hearths for cooking inside of their dwellings, located in the center so as to reduce the risk of the walls catching on fire. However not all of the technology was new; for example, at the earlier Mesolithic sites of Lough Boora and Mount Sandel, archaeologists have found stone axes of the type that would have been used to cut down trees. Furthermore, hunting and gathering did not disappear with the coming of settled agriculture; the Beaker people seem to have been great hunters who had refined their arrow tips and wore wrist guards that allowed them to use more powerful bowstrings.

Scientists studying elm pollen levels preserved in the decaying vegetation that makes up the Irish bogs, in combination with radiocarbon dating, have been able to ascertain the approximate date of certain settlements and the extent to which they engaged in agricultural activity. (The preservative quality of the bogs has proved a real boon to those interested in the prehistory of Ireland, most sensationally in the discovery of several well-preserved bodies of prehistoric men that are now on display in the National Museum of Ireland). Reduced levels of elm pollen in the layers of decayed vegetation that coincide with a certain period indicate the clearing of forests that consisted primarily of elm trees during that time. Tree clearance was not restricted to a single region of the island; evidence of a significant reduction in elm pollen has been found in both the northeast and the southwest between roughly 3,865 and 3,590 BCE. Not all scholars have accepted the elm pollen thesis as entirely convincing; some have suggested that climate change could also help to explain the reduction in trees. It is also possible that the devouring of new elm shoots by domesticated cattle would have reduced pollen levels independent of arable farming.[4] However, the existence of settled agriculture is not really in dispute, and it is surely no coincidence that a reduction in elm pollen is generally accompanied by an increase in pollen associated with grains and grasses.

Even if the transition to settled agriculture was gradual and incomplete, it still represented an extremely important change in Ireland, as elsewhere. The excavations at the site of Ballynagilly in County Tyrone by Arthur ApSimon in the late 1960s provided evidence for a very early Neolithic settlement there that dated to between 3,600 and 3,800 BCE.[5] The site of Lough Gur in County Limerick has been an equally valuable source of information, suggesting that these early farmers knew something about how to test soil quality, since this is an especially fertile location. In addition,

---

[4] Michael O'Kelly (1989), *Early Ireland: An Introduction to Irish Prehistory*. Cambridge: Cambridge University Press, p. 33.
[5] Database of Irish Excavation Reports. http://www.excavations.ie/Pages/Details.php?Year=&County=Tyrone&id=5440.

Lough Gur, which was first excavated by Sean O Riordáin in the 1940s, contained evidence of wood houses similar to that which ApSimon found at Ballynagilly. Lough Gur also contains examples of the pottery known as *Beakerware* that identifies it as a site of location by the Beaker people. The Beaker people seem to have migrated from Britain and settled in Ireland at the beginning of the Bronze Age. The name *Beaker people* has been given to them as a result of the numerous examples of their pottery, which are shaped so similar to beakers that at first it was assumed that the objects were used for drinking even though they lacked handles. Beaker pots are generally characterized by an inverted bell shape and were probably used for a variety of purposes that could have included the smelting of copper, which was in use during this period. Beaker pottery in Ireland has been found, among other places, at Newgrange, Lough Gur, and Knowth.

Other significant Neolithic sites include: Céide Hill and Belderg Beg in County Mayo, where archaeologists have been able to determine the layout of the field system; Newtown in County Meath, one of several sites containing evidence of rectangular dwellings; and Lambay Island in County Dublin, the site of a prehistoric axe factory. At Céide Hill, archaeologists have discovered 5,000-year-old plow marks, "visible as narrow dark peaty bands in the lighter soil,"[6] in fields surrounded by stone walls next to a well-planned village. The Neolithic farmers who lived there cultivated wheat and barley and raised sheep and cattle.

Archaeological excavations at places such as Lough Gur and Céide Hill have therefore begun to tell us something about the transition to settled agriculture and the way of life of the people who cultivated the fields of Ireland in Neolithic times. They lived in round or rectangular peat houses built with frames of wood. The houses were fairly close together in settlements of perhaps 2,000 people. Communal agriculture allowed for larger, more permanent settlements; hunter-gatherer groups tend to remain smaller since they are entirely dependent on what nature provides. It is likely that inhabitants of one village had connections with other members of the same tribe who lived elsewhere. The burial sites at Céide Hill that date from after about 3,700 BCE and the nearby court tomb at Behy reveal the spiritual side of the people who lived there, while the constructions that still stand today required considerable engineering skill and planning to quarry and transport the stones that were used in them. The presence of animal bones at key sites tells us that these farmers kept goats and pigs, in addition to sheep and cattle. We do not know where these domesticated animals came from, but, like the wheat and barley crops to which arable farming was devoted, these animals, with the possible exception of pigs, were brought into Ireland

---

[6] Seamus Caulfield, Gretta Byrne, Noel Dunne and Graeme Warren (2011), *Excavations on Céide Hill, Behy & Glenulra, North Co. Mayo, 1963–1994*, preliminary report, courtesy of Gretta Byrne.

from elsewhere. Sheep, goats, and cattle were unknown in Ireland before the late-Mesolithic, early Neolithic periods. This has led to the conclusion that a significant influx of new settlers arrived in Ireland between about 4,500 and 3,500 BCE.

The transition to settled agriculture in Ireland proved problematic in one respect. Since Ireland is a relatively small island and its fertile lands somewhat limited, early farmers who did not know about soil exhaustion or the value of manure as a fertilizer may have found it difficult to sustain their way of life once their lands failed to produce the requisite number of crops. This may have led them to once again rely more on fishing, hunting, and gathering; some may have simply died out as a result of malnutrition. Surely, prehistoric farmers were not immune to crop failures, which would prove devastating as late as the nineteenth century. An increase in elm pollen after the period associated with the beginning of settled agriculture in Ireland could be explained by the abandonment of exhausted land or the decimation of early farming communities by disease or famine.

Ritual sites and prehistoric religion

The only insights that we have about prehistoric religion in Ireland are those that can be gleaned from the ritual sites known as *passage tombs*, the most famous of which are found at Newgrange, Knowth, and Dowth, all of which are located in the Boyne River Valley. In the eighteenth century, Thomas Pownell (1722–1805) found inscriptions which he identified as Phoenician;

FIGURE 2.1 *Newgrange Burial Chamber. Photo by Jimmy Harris.*

he used them to argue for outside influence upon Celtic civilization.[7] Similarities with passage graves in Brittany have led others to suggest that the tombs may have been built by settlers with connections to that region who may have recently arrived in Ireland, but such speculation is still provisional. In recent times, Newgrange has gained a reputation among those interested in Irish prehistory comparable to that possessed by Stonehenge, the site of giant megalithic stones located on Salisbury Plain in England. The tomb at Newgrange dates from about 2,500 BCE, approximately the same period in which Stonehenge was built.

Like Stonehenge, Newgrange has become a highly controversial site. As it turns out, sunlight infuses the inner chamber of the tomb at Newgrange only during the winter and summer solstices. It is perhaps a myth, as Clive Ruggles has suggested in a 1999 book, that ancient peoples possessed some secret astronomical scientific knowledge to which we no longer have access that makes them somehow more advanced in that area than we are. Ruggles also questioned whether the horizons at locations such as Stonehenge and Newgrange have remained the same since prehistoric times and whether such sites were primarily intended for the observations which modern people are so fond of celebrating.[8] However, it might be a mistake to dismiss the astronomical knowledge of the prehistoric builders of these monuments too quickly. For example, in one study, 23 of 37 prehistoric sites in Ireland were found to have "significant astronomical orientations," with 21 of them oriented to either the east or the west.[9] Even taking Ruggles's caveats into consideration and without pretending to his mathematical expertise, from a layperson's perspective, the exact timing of the days on which sunlight floods the tomb at Newgrange does seem too coincidental to be insignificant, especially when one considers how far the light needs to travel (over sixty feet) to achieve this effect.

In his 2004 book, *Newgrange: Temple to Life*, Chris O'Callaghan stresses that Newgrange must have combined a strong set of spiritual beliefs with astronomical knowledge and engineering skill on a scale to which the simple term *passage grave* does not do justice.[10] He counters Ruggles by suggesting that "it seems very unlikely that the designer of the monument left the spot, where the first rays of the winter solstice sun would touch the Newgrange

[7] Peter Rowley-Conwy (2007), *From Genesis to Prehistory: The Archaeological Three Age System and Its Contested Reception in Denmark, Britain, and Ireland.* Oxford: Oxford University Press, p. 179.

[8] Clive Ruggles (1999), *Astronomy in Prehistoric Britain and Ireland.* New Haven and London: Yale University Press.

[9] Ann Lynch (1981; 1994), "Astronomical Alignment or Megalithic Muddle," in D. Ó Corráin (ed.), *Irish Antiquity: Essays and Studies Presented to Professor M.J. O'Kelly.* Dublin: Four Courts Press, p. 25.

[10] Chris O'Callaghan (2004), *Newgrange: Temple to Life.* Cork: Mercier Press, p. 10.

ridge, to random chance."[11] Furthermore, he argues that the entire monument was built around the sun window, and its location chosen on that basis, suggesting that it *was* the primary purpose for which it was built in the first place, thus making *passage grave* an inadequate name for the site.

A number of other passage graves have been discovered in Ireland, some of them in circular cairns as small as 8 meters (8.75 yards) in diameter.[12] (In comparison, the large stones that surround Newgrange have a diameter of over 100 meters (109.4 yards). Many of them are located in the Boyne Valley where Newgrange is found. In some of the graves, large stones were covered by a round mound whereas others had a rectangular shape. The mound at Newgrange is higher than 12 meters or 40 feet. These passage graves seem to have been constructed over a period of about five centuries, thus representing a particular phase of Irish prehistory, but megalithic stone monuments in Britain and Ireland span a period of about three millennia.

It seems safe to say that the builders of the Irish passage tombs, like the engineers who constructed Stonehenge, came from a sophisticated society that possessed a high level of knowledge and that it is likely that these monuments carried some religious significance. In addition, these societies invested an enormous amount of time, effort, and resources to construct these monuments, providing a sense of their priorities and indicating the existence of powerful political or religious leaders who could galvanize their people to invest in such massive projects. It is reasonable to assume that only very important individuals were buried in the passage graves and that objects placed there, such as javelin heads, had some purpose in assisting the deceased in the afterlife. It is possible, however, that some of the graves were intended not for a single individual but perhaps for an extended family or even a whole community.

Connections between the peoples of Ireland and the rest of the Isles

Another important question that has concerned specialists in prehistoric Ireland has been the nature of the relationship between the people of Ireland and those who lived at that time in Britain and the smaller nearby islands. The peoples of Britain and Ireland in prehistoric times used such similar technology, which is our main means of identifying them, that it is sometimes hard to determine the exact nature of the relationship among them. Axes found in Ireland are virtually indistinguishable from those found in Britain during the Middle Bronze Age, which means that they could have

---

[11] Ibid., p. 23.
[12] Michael J. O'Kelly (2005), "Neolithic Ireland," in D. Ó Cróinín (ed.), *A New History of Ireland: Volume I: Prehistoric and Early Ireland*. Oxford: Oxford University Press, p. 89.

been exported from Ireland to Britain or simply that they used the same technology. Either way, it shows a close relationship between the islands at this time. Mallory and McNeill have challenged the earlier interpretation that the first settlers came from what is now Scotland because microliths found in Ulster can also be found in the Irish midlands, particularly at the site of Lough Boora in County Offaly.[13] Richard Bradley, however, sees a connection between the material remains in Britain and Ireland down to about 6,000 BCE but no strong correlation between them thereafter.[14] His assessment has been supported by the variety of stone tools and piles of shells (known as *shell middens*) found from the later Mesolithic period that suggest a greater emphasis on fishing than can be found in Britain at that time.[15] This theory is reinforced by the fact that most settlements in Ireland from this period were found along coasts or rivers. Isolation from Britain did not necessarily mean isolation from the European continent, however.

Additional connections between Ireland and Britain occurred during the Iron Age. The style associated with what is known as *La Tène culture* dates to the period from about 200 BCE to about 100 CE. Here, we see a strong connection between the material remains from Britain and Ireland during what is also known as the *Celtic period*. This evidence suggests that the Celts migrated to Ireland from Britain, probably from what is now Scotland, which at that time was inhabited by people known to the Romans as the *Picts*. The continued similarities of artistic styles, as they evolved over a period of time, suggest continued cultural contact and not merely one as derivative of the other. The most famous examples of this style, which is mainly characterized by spiral-shaped designs, include the Turoe Stone in County Galway and the Battersea Shield in the British Museum. However, similar designs can be found on numerous objects such as the sword scabbards found at Lisnacrogher in County Antrim. The curved patterns of La Tène art—including "palmettes, lyre, waves, spirals, s-scrolls, and leafy tendrils"—are thought to have originated in the Mediterranean and represent a movement away from purely geometrical forms and patterns.[16] Gold collars, some of which included chevrons and other designs, and war trumpets are among the other objects prominently associated with this period. In addition, similarities in language have been noted; both Welsh and Irish descended from a proto-Celtic language, which some scholars have divided into P-Celtic and Q-Celtic branches. As a result, many similar words appear on both sides of the Irish Sea; for example, the Irish word for river

---

[13] J. P. Mallory and T. E. McNeill (1991), *The Archaeology of Ulster from Colonization to Plantation*. Belfast: The Institute for Irish Studies, p. 20.

[14] Bradley, *op. cit.*, pp. 9–10.

[15] Gabriel Cooney (2000), *Landscapes of Neolithic Ireland*. London and New York: Routledge, p. 13.

[16] Barry Raftery (2005), "Iron-Age Ireland," in D. Ó Cróinín (ed.), *A New History of Ireland: Volume I: Prehistoric and Early Ireland*. Oxford: Oxford University Press, p. 139.

FIGURE 2.2 *The Turoe Stone, County Galway. Courtesy of Getty Images.*

abhainn appears in Welsh as *afon* and in Cornish as *avon*. Their religious sensibilities also seem to have been connected by a common devotion to springs and rivers and the particularly gruesome cult of the severed head, evidence for which has been found on both islands.

Finally, in 2006, a medical geneticist at the University of Oxford named Stephen Oppenheimer put forth the argument based on DNA evidence that the Irish and British have too many genetic similarities to be considered separate people. In fact, he argues that it is likely that they are descended from the same basic group of people who migrated from the European continent, primarily Spain, between 13,000 and 5,500 BCE. Oppenheimer contends that the genetic makeup of the people of the Isles has been changed relatively little by the later influx of the Celts or the Romans, or by those who subsequently migrated from Germany, Scandinavia, and Normandy.[17] If he is correct, his discovery has the potential to challenge the way in which the people of Ireland and Britain have viewed themselves and each other for centuries, as well as the whole notion of a "Celtic invasion" of Ireland.

Archeology—ring-forts

Probably the most characteristic archaeological find in Ireland dating from the prehistoric and later periods is the Irish ring-fort, the subject of a recent book by Matthew Stout. Ring-forts were circular-shaped areas surrounded by an earth or stone barrier behind a ditch. The majority of Irish ring-forts that have been found date from the medieval period, but it is clear that the structure has its origins in Irish prehistory, especially the Later Iron Age that lasted from the end of the first to the fifth-century CE. The ring-forts were not military structures, but their rise did somewhat coincide with the decline of the great hill-forts at Tara and Emain Macha, also known as *Navan Fort*. Ring-forts consisted of stone barriers used by farmers to protect their homes and livestock from attacks or raids by animals or people.

Ring-forts arose because Irish farmers in the later prehistoric and early Christian period did not congregate in villages but spread out across the land. Irish ring-forts are not protected by perimeter defenses nor are the entranceways particularly strong. In Ulster, Mallory and McNeill have found no evidence that the banks of the ring-forts were strengthened after erosion began to decrease their steepness.[18] However, in 27 of 46 ring-forts studied by Stout, the houses associated with them were located in the center of the fort at the farthest possible place from the boundary. In 71 per cent of Stout's ring-forts, the houses faced to the east, which was both toward the entrance and away from the prevailing winds.[19] Ring-forts varied in size from about 15 meters to over 50 meters in diameter.[20] Not all of the examples that Stout studied provided evidence of human occupation, but since most dwellings were built of wood, this does not necessarily mean that the absence of evidence proves that they were not there. On larger sites, of course, more than one human dwelling would have been present.

The ring-forts are not uniform in size. Some may not have been intended for defense at all but simply to mark a boundary or to keep cattle confined. Evidence of farming has been discovered in association with most ring-forts. One of the real advantages of the ring-forts as archaeological finds is that

---

[17] Stephen Oppenheimer (2006), *The Origins of the British: A Genetic Detective Story: The Surprising Roots of the English, Irish, Scottish and Welsh*. New York: Carroll and Graf.

[18] Mallory and McNeill, *op. cit.*, p. 197.

[19] Matthew Stout (2007), *The Irish Ringfort*. Dublin: Four Courts Press, p. 32.

[20] Pat Dargan (2011), *Exploring Celtic Ireland*. Dublin: The History Press Ireland, pp. 15–16.

they still exist in the exact form in which they were used before they were abandoned. One of the largest and most spectacular of the ring-forts is Navan Fort in County Armagh. Other prominent ring-forts include the one at Ardagh in County Limerick and the Danetown ring-fort in County Meath, although these date from a later period. The Turoe Stone was originally located in a ring-fort in County Galway known locally as the *Rath of the Big Man*.

In addition to ring-forts, archaeologists have studied a number of hill-forts, which were also in use in early Christian Ireland but have their origins in the late Bronze Age. There are many more ring-forts than hill-forts, however, perhaps attesting to a relatively peaceful island without much pressure on land from a growing population. Navan Fort, which is built on a hill surrounded by a large ring barrier, could be considered a ring-fort or a hill-fort. A third type of construction from this period was the crannóg, a man-made island located in a lake or a marsh that was also used for defensive purposes. These fascinating dwellings were usually constructed in a shallow part of a lake that could be accessed from shore by a stone or wood causeway. Their builders used a variety of materials in their construction, including peat, wood, stones, and anything else that came to hand. They must have been effective; the earliest date from the Neolithic period, but they remained quite common in the early centuries of the Christian era.

FIGURE 2.3 *Crannog, Fair Head, County Antrim. Photo by Katharine McMillan.*

Earliest literary sources

The earliest Irish literary sources were not written down until the centuries following the coming of Christianity, but there is little doubt that they originate in the preliterate days of Celtic Ireland at the end of the prehistoric period. Oral traditions survived until even as late as the tenth and eleventh centuries when they were written down; until very recently, Irish Gaelic bards were reciting lengthy epics that dated from centuries earlier and had never been written down. The strongest connections between early Irish literature and the prehistoric period come from the literary references to and descriptions of actual prehistoric sites, especially those associated with kingship such as Emain Macha, Tara, Crúachain, and Dún Ailinne, all of which date from the Later Bronze Age. These were probably not the sites of ancient royal residences but rather the locations of tribal assemblies at certain times of the year. Each of them appears in early Irish literature. Emain Macha or Navan Fort is the site associated with the most famous early Irish literary epic, the *Táin Bó Cúailinge*. Also known as *The Cattle Raid of Cooley*, the emphasis on the importance of cattle in the story dovetails nicely with the evidence from the ring-forts that were likely built to protect them.

The basic plot of the *Táin* revolves around the desire of Queen Medb of Connacht for the prized Brown Bull of Cooley. Her wish to acquire the bull originated over pillow talk with her husband, Aillil, who started boasting about how lucky Medb was to have married such a rich and royal man. Medb took this as an insult, insisting that she was just as wealthy and had a comparable royal lineage. The discussion degenerated into a contest to see whose possessions outshone the other's. From the lowliest household items to the most magnificent jewels, however, they could find no difference that made one superior to the other. It was only when they compared cattle that Aillil could claim superiority based on a bull that had left Medb's herd to join his because he did not want to be owned by a woman. Medb ordered a search for a bull to rival that of her husband's. When she is informed about the bull of Cooley, which was the possession of Emain Macha, Medb at first attempts to make a deal to borrow it, but when that falls through, she decides to take the animal by force. The lengthy poem then recounts the war that resulted from her attempt to steal the Brown Bull. The popularity of the story suggests that cattle possession conferred greater social prestige than mere farming. It also has provoked interest because of the Irish obsession with the landscape that is the setting for the poem. Fr. Tom O'Connor has actually attempted to trace the route that Queen Medb took from Connacht to Emain Macha. He suggests—based on a study of place names—that she traveled on a straight line between Athenry and Athlone.[21]

---

[21] Fr. Tom O'Connor (2003), *Turoe and Athenry: Ancient Capitals of Celtic Ireland*, edited by Kieran Jordan. Midleton: Litho Press, pp. 165–6.

The *Lebor Gabála Érenn* or *The Book of the Taking* refers to a time in the
mythological past when "Ireland was an unbroken forest" and kings with
difficulty divided the land among them.[22] These early tales reflect a warrior
society that is further illuminated by the ancient weaponry on display at the
National Museum of Ireland in Dublin. A chain-link collar dated from 900
to 500 BCE does not look too dissimilar from the chain-mail armor worn
by the Normans and other medieval warriors in the eleventh-century CE.
A magnificent bronze shield dates from the same period.

These stories provide information about everyday life in addition to the
heroic tales that they preserved. One might question the reliability of sources
written down centuries after the conditions and events they describe, but
used in conjunction with archaeological evidence they assist in a tentative
reconstruction of a world that is largely lost to us. They may in fact be
closer approximations of a reality that predated the Christian era than
times closer to their written composition. O'Connor has noticed a strong
correlation between place names in Galway and those that appear in the
collection of early Irish written documents known as the *Dindsenchas*.[23] A
study of place names located near the bend of the River Boyne has yielded
strong correlations with those that appear in Irish mythological literature.
For example, a tenth-century poem by Ó hArtagain includes a reference to
a cemetery at a place called Brug at a site with the ancient name of Brug na
Boinde (palace by the Boyne).[24]

In addition, La Tène war accoutrements have mainly been discovered
in Connacht and Ulster, the two areas that went to war in the *Táin Bó
Cúailinge*. Barry Raftery has argued for a strong correlation between the
construction of the monumental hill-forts at Navan Fort and Dún Ailinne
and the capacity for collective undertakings described in the *Táin*.[25] James
Carney observes that the society described in the *Táin* and other examples of
early Irish literature "seems basically similar to those of pre-Roman Britain
and Gaul."[26] This was also the view of Kenneth Hurlstone Jackson, who
regarded early Irish literature as providing "a window on the Iron Age."[27]
The society depicted in the story does not closely resemble the society of
the seventh century that it purports to describe; for example, no seventh-
century warriors fought in chariots as those in the Táin did. Exactly how

---

[22] R. A. Stewart MacAlister (ed. and trans.) (1938–), *Lebor Gabála Érenn: The Book of the
Taking of Ireland*. Dublin: Irish Texts Society, III, p. 77.

[23] O'Connor, *op. cit.*, p. 26.

[24] Geraldine Stout (2003), *Newgrange: The Bend of the Boyne*. Cork: Cork University Press,
p. 62.

[25] Raftery, *op. cit.*, pp. 168–9.

[26] James Carney (2005), "Language and Literature to 1169," in D. Ó Cróinín (ed.), *A New
History of Ireland: Volume I: Prehistoric and Early Ireland*. Oxford: Oxford University
Press, p. 469.

[27] Kenneth Hurlstone Jackson (1964), *The Oldest Irish Tradition: A Window on the Iron Age*.
Cambridge: At the University Press.

much the written tales preserved of their original form is still open to debate, but in the absence of other written evidence, scholars have found them very useful. The ways in which the tales connect to other evidence inspire some confidence that they reflect something of the ancient society that predated the coming of Christianity to Ireland.

Going back even earlier, one of the oral myths that has been passed down into Irish history through the *Lebor Gabála Érennis* is associated with the Tuatha De Danann or "the people of the goddess Danu," who were believed to have magical powers and thrived in Ireland until their defeat by Celtic invaders about 2,000 BCE. If this tribe did exist, they have passed into the realm of legend, but in this instance, the *Lebor Gabála* may be passing along a distant memory that was preserved in Celtic culture that also says something about their own beliefs and traditions.

Assessment of prehistoric culture and society

Even specialists in Irish prehistory hesitate to make grand pronouncements evaluating the cultures and societies that flourished in Ireland during prehistoric times. The progression from Mesolithic to Late Mesolithic to Neolithic to the Bronze and Iron Ages occurred over thousands of years. These periods overlapped and there are no sharp dividing lines; for example, people used iron before the end of the so-called Bronze Age. Nor were these periods monolithic; at the end of the Bronze Age, jewelers and weapon-makers became much more adept at their craft than their counterparts in the early Bronze Age. Furthermore, there are sometimes significant geographical variations in Ireland within each period that indicate a diversity of prehistoric cultures even in such a small land. Despite painstaking research and archaeological field work, our understanding of the prehistoric period is still extremely limited compared to our knowledge of later periods. For the La Tène period, we know much about their art but little about their housing arrangements or social organization. By contrast, we know more about the material lives of earlier inhabitants, but their culture and religion are almost completely lost to us. In this chapter, I have given some highlights of what specialists in the field have had to tell us in recent decades and the questions that concern them. To sum up:

First, prehistoric culture in Ireland was not static but evolved and changed over a long period of time. It is likely that sometimes these changes resulted from an influx of new people from Britain or the European continent and that at other times newcomers learned from those already living on the island. The artifacts that have remained from the prehistoric period suggest that in each period people were capable of sustaining life through various means. The existence of passage graves, of the spectacular monument of Newgrange, the abstract spiral designs associated with La Tène art, and the discovery of musical instruments all demonstrate that they had other concerns as well. Geometrical artistic designs predated the La Tène period, though discovering their symbolic meaning now is probably impossible. It is hard to know why society moved on from the building of passage graves, but standing stones continued to be used to mark grave sites after the period associated with the passage graves was over. These included dolmens, structures in which one large rock was placed horizontally on top of two vertical standing rocks.

Socially, in Ireland, prehistoric people made the transition from hunting and gathering to settled agriculture, although this was not a unilateral change where one meant the exclusion of the other. Even though agricultural communities tend to be larger than those of hunter-gatherers, in Ireland, these communities were still fairly small and were probably still based on kinship. They developed systems of organization such as that employed at Céide Hill in the far west of Ireland. They successfully mined flint and built impressive stone walls and buildings using only levers, ropes, and rollers. They lacked knowledge about fertilizers, but demonstrated knowledge of soil that was naturally fertile and took steps to clear forests in desirable locations. We do not know much about their spiritual life, but we know that they had one and that they buried their dead, sometimes in elaborate passage graves to assist their journey to the afterlife. Artistic designs have been found on many of the stones associated with the passage graves of the Neolithic period.

The one major deficiency of prehistoric culture from the modern point of view was the absence of writing, unless one counts the rudimentary linear ogham symbols that may have been in existence before those on stone carvings that date from the early Christian period. Ogham characters were marked on stones, usually around the edges. They do not seem to contain the kind of grammatical elements that would allow scholars to decipher them as an early version of Irish. One theory suggests that they represent the names of important individuals and are intended as a kind of genealogical record. But, though they lacked writing, the people of prehistoric Ireland had art and music that indicate the capacity for abstract thought. Twenty-six bronze horns have been discovered in one Bronze Age hoard at Dowris in County Offaly, along with 58 objects that appear to be a primitive kind of maraca. Laurence Flanagan describes the two basic types of horns found at Dowris:

> End-blow, shaped like cow-horns, where the air is applied through a fairly small aperture at the end of the horn, and side-blow, where the air is applied through a fairly large aperture on the side of the horn.[28]

Even though only one has been passed down to us, the four large bronze trumpets discovered near Emain Macha in 1798 reinforce the importance of

---

[28] Laurence Flanagan (1998), *Ancient Ireland: Life before the Celts*. Dublin: Gill and Macmillan, p. 224.

music in prehistoric Ireland as do the better preserved and more sophisticated instruments found at Ardbrin in County Down.[29]

Legacy of prehistoric Ireland

One twentieth-century scholar has gone so far as to suggest that the slower progress made toward civilization in prehistoric Ireland, perhaps a result of its relative isolation as an island on the northwestern fringe of Europe, might be connected to the slower pace of life in Ireland that has survived into the modern age and helped Ireland to preserve more of its prehistoric traditions than other places.[30] Irish mythology and folklore, stretching back into the prehistoric age, does seem to have played a larger role in Irish history than in many other cultures. The Celts, being the most recent people to settle and transform the culture of Ireland before the beginning of the early Christian period, of course had the most immediate influence. Perhaps, the largest legacy from the prehistoric Celts to modern times comes in the survival of the Celtic languages that are still being kept alive in Wales, Ireland, and Scotland. As elsewhere, elements of pagan religion became adapted or transformed by Christianity. For example, the popularity of St Brigid in Ireland could have something to do with the Celtic goddess of the same name; Saint Ellen was previously known as *Sidh nEthlena*, who takes her name from a place near Athenry in County Galway.[31] In addition, the Iron-Age ring-forts remained a dominant type of settlement in Ireland well into the medieval period.

One general legacy of those people who settled in Ireland in prehistoric times was their ability to identify certain prominent places that lent themselves to settlement. Many of the same places were reoccupied after they had been previously abandoned.[32] In this way, the Celts built on the legacy left by earlier people and passed that legacy down to their descendants. Finally, the political boundaries of decentralized kingdoms that had their capitals at Tara and Navan Fort seem to have survived as well. It seems that even the separation of Ireland between the kingdoms centered on Ulster in the north and those in the southern part of the island can be traced to defenses separating the two that were constructed during the Iron Age.[33]

---

[29] Raftery, *op. cit.*, pp. 156–7.
[30] Peter Harbison (1988), *Pre-Christian Ireland: From the First Settlers to the Early Celts.* London: Thames and Hudson, p. 195.
[31] O'Connor, *op. cit.*, p. 163.
[32] Gabriel Cooney (2000), "Reading a Landscape Manuscript: A Review of Progress in Prehistoric Settlement Studies in Ireland," in Terry Barry (ed.), *A History of Settlement in Ireland.* London and New York: Routledge, pp. 30–1.
[33] Mallory and McNeill, *op. cit.*, p. 165.

CHAPTER THREE

Irish Christianity and early medieval Ireland

Unlike the other Celts, the Irish of the Roman period were not to be made ashamed of an old culture, they were not awkwardly to bend their minds to foreign ways of thinking, they were not to be the colonized people aping even the worst aspects of a well-organized well-fed industrialized, and matter-of-fact civilization.

– MICHAEL RICHTER, *Ireland and Her Neighbours in the Seventh Century*

Political context for early medieval Ireland

Politically, early medieval Ireland was divided into numerous kingships (perhaps as many as 150), which were frequently interlocked with one another by ties of blood and dependency. Given that written evidence for this period does not predate the seventh century, we can only form a general idea of political life in earlier centuries, but there seems to have been a rough equilibrium of power among the various kings. Some were inevitably stronger than others, and there was at least a conception of a "high king" who would have been considered as somehow superior to the others even if his rule was still geographically limited. This would have been similar to the position of the bretwalda in Anglo-Saxon England; there, the bretwalda was a designation given to the most powerful of the seven kings that combined to form what scholars refer to as the heptarchy. Irish literary sources refer to a pentarchy of five main kingdoms, which Dáibhí Ó Cróinín has speculated might have corresponded to the regions of Ulster in the north, Leinster in the southeast, Munster in the south, Connacht in the west, and Meath in the center.[1] But even if the literature preserves an actual memory of such a division, it had ceased to exist by the fifth century.

In both Anglo-Saxon England and early medieval Ireland, all kings exercised authority over their people and territory and ruled independently of one another. Like their Anglo-Saxon counterparts, Irish kings also seem to have made alliances with one another that could sometimes lead to much larger federations, such as that of the Ulaid in the north, which declined in the early fifth century only to give way to another large federation that covered much of the northern half of Ireland from Donegal to the southeastern lowlands.[2] It was more common, however, for each king, known in Gaelic as a *rí tuaithe*, to rule over a tribe of several thousand people known as a tribe or *túath*, though larger tribes might have several kings. Each king generally ruled over people who lived within a 10- to 15-mile radius. Kings were expected to look out for the interests of their people, both internally and externally. If they failed to do so, they could definitely be subject to challenges from their own kin, or from neighboring kings who were always on the lookout for weakness in their rivals.

At their courts, each king was surrounded by members of his nobility, starting with members of his own family. Since royal blood was defined rather broadly, this meant that each king had a large number of potential rivals in his immediate family. In addition, each kinship group had a representative known as an *aire tuise* who served as a liaison between his people and the king and maintained a personal presence at court. Poets also played a key role within the courts of these kings; St Patrick was said to have converted a young poet at the court of Tara who eventually became a bishop. The king did not have many public responsibilities, but he generally would have held an annual assembly to deal with legal and administrative matters. The dispensation of justice in an equitable manner was one of the main duties of a king in Irish society. Each king drew his support from a system that included a number of his clients and could require the adoption of foster children to ensure loyalty. The relationships established through the practice of fosterage forged bonds that could be stronger than those of biological kinship. The number of clients that a king had went a long way toward determining the amount of power that each king possessed. As in later feudal society, clients would be granted a living—in Ireland either through land or livestock, generally cattle—in exchange for their loyalty and a portion of their annual income. The king would also provide "hospitality"

[1] Dáibhí Ó Cróinín (2005), "Ireland, 400–800," in D. Ó Cróinín (ed.), *A New History of Ireland: Volume I: Prehistoric and Early Ireland*. Oxford: Oxford University Press, p. 187.
[2] Liam De Paor (1986), *The Peoples of Ireland: From Prehistory to Modern Times*. London: Hutchinson, p. 42.

for his clients, who in turn would have been expected to perform military service if required. The adoption of a client's child by the king would have been one way to help ensure the loyalty of that client.

Social context for early medieval Ireland

Irish society, then, was an aristocratic one in which wealth was based primarily on ownership of land and livestock. Because political power was so completely decentralized, there were no administrative centers and town life was virtually nonexistent. The capitals of powerful early kings, such as those who resided at Cashel or Tara, were generally castles or palaces with a surrounding village rather than cities. A large number of people would have congregated around these centers of activity, including not only poets, but also musicians and magicians or anyone who thought they could make a living off the king's largesse. But the basis of the early medieval economy was a blend of agricultural and pastoral pursuits, with dairy products making up a substantial proportion of the daily diet, supplemented by meat more than the other way around. In addition to cattle, the Irish also kept pigs and sheep, the latter more valued for their wool than anything else.

Ireland's social structure before the coming of Christianity consisted of a traditional division into aristocracy, priests, and those free men who worked the land or tended the livestock. Tenants who worked the land but did not owe military service should be distinguished from those clients of the king who made up the aristocracy. These tenants did not have the same rights as clients to possession of the land. Their work in the countryside would have been supplemented by slaves who were sometimes captured from adjacent kingdoms or on raiding parties across the Irish Sea to Britain. The position of women in Irish society depended on their class, but women did not have some of the inherent disadvantages under the law that existed in many societies; women had more freedom to obtain a divorce if they so desired, for example. However, women could hardly claim equal status with men. Inheritance laws strongly favored male heirs, with women's inheritance being restricted to "moveable goods, gifts of property, or life interest in the family land."[3]

The biggest influence on Irish society in the earliest centuries of Ireland's recorded history was the conversion of the Irish people to Christianity by the end of the fifth century. But the triumph of Christianity cannot be understood without some knowledge of the political and social context in which the new faith was allowed to flourish. For example, Ireland was not a centralized state where the conversion of one king would ensure the conversion of the

---

[3] Lisa M. Bitel (1998), *Land of Women: Tales of Sex and Gender from Early Ireland*. Ithaca: Cornell University Press, p. 92.

entire island, but the aristocracy was well established, and their conversion would greatly enhance the strength of a new faith; without their support, no religious change would have been possible. It is no wonder that the Irish church became so decentralized, with monasteries and churches sometimes, though not always, under the control of individual kings.

Other conditions affected the early history of Christianity in Ireland as well. Ireland had a well-established social structure that was unaffected by Roman expansion and was removed from the wave of migrations that brought so much instability to Britain and continental Europe. Many of the political and social traditions of early medieval Ireland, then, were probably rooted in traditions that had evolved over a long period of time. Christian missionaries needed to work with these traditions and present their faith in a way that was consistent with them if they were to have success. In addition, Ireland had a justice system that favored victims' compensation for crimes instead of blood feuds or capital punishment, making it more consistent with Christian ideals. Ireland also must have had an educational system in place that predated Christianity in order to account for the poets, judges (brehons), and Druid priests who were all so important in early Irish society. An ollam was an individual who had achieved the highest degree or educational designation possible in the schools run by the Druid priests, one that was only attainable after intense study for a period of a dozen years.

Finally, Christianity arrived at a time when Ireland was prospering, judging from the evidence that population was increasing beginning in the fourth century. Pollen samples indicate an increase in agricultural activity about this time for reasons that are not entirely clear to us. Agricultural methods were improving, thanks to the use of the moldboard plow, which enabled farmers to turn over cut sod and utilize longer strips of land for cultivation.[4] A flourishing economy would also have contributed to a stable society and cut down on the number of wars and incidences of violence. Still, after all of these factors have been taken into account, the triumph of Christianity in Ireland cannot be understood without attention to the individuals most involved in the conversion process, especially the legendary St Patrick.

The first Christian missions

The story of Christianity in Ireland begins before the arrival of St Patrick from Britain in the fifth century. Not only did Christians exist in Ireland before the missionary efforts of Patrick, but in fact Ireland already had a bishop by the name of Palladius, who may have come from Auxerre in

---

[4] Michael Richter (1999), *Ireland and Her Neighbours in the Seventh Century*. New York: St. Martin's Press, p. 21.

northern Gaul. The problem is that no evidence exists to tell us the date of the first Christian missions to the island, and historians have only been able to guess at the numbers of Christians in Ireland before Patrick. Irish historians of early Christianity have concentrated so much on Patrick largely because so little is known about Palladius and the extent of his authority in Ireland. We do know that Palladius arrived in Ireland in 431, according to the Chronicle of Prosper of Aquitaine, but not much else. Prosper refers to him as *the first bishop of the Scots* (meaning the Irish). Palladius may in fact deserve more attention than he receives, but it is highly unlikely that at this point any new evidence will come to light to remedy that historical injustice. Kathleen Hughes believed that he brought Christianity to the southern half of the island, but this was as much as she was willing to say.[5] Nonetheless, it is clear that Patrick, unlike many other contemporary and later-day missionaries, was not bringing Christianity to a place that was completely unfamiliar with it.

Patrick's first visit to Ireland was not as a Christian missionary, however, but as a slave forcefully brought there from his home in what is now northwestern England when he was about 16 years old. In time, Patrick came to count this as a blessing in disguise, even saying that he and his fellow captives deserved their fate because they had turned away from God and refused to keep his commandments.

But at the time, this must have come as a terrible shock to a youth brought up in what seems to have been a comfortable household. With the collapse of Roman authority in 410, Britain became subject to invasions, which were often little more than organized raids. Slaves were in demand in Ireland, mostly to tend livestock, and Patrick was a victim of one of these raiding parties. Patrick managed to escape from Ireland after about 6 years as a slave, returning to Britain having already undergone a conversion to Christianity. But instead of remaining in his homeland, he became inspired to return to Ireland to spread his new-found faith among the native inhabitants there.

Unlike Palladius, Patrick provided us with some idea of his experience in Ireland in the few writings that he left behind. He tells us, for example, that in the course of his travels he spent 2 months in captivity; as to how he escaped, he only says cryptically that "the Lord delivered me from their hands."[6] He had confessed his former sins at one point only to have them thrown back in his face 30 years later, making him the subject of scandal and ridicule. But he persevered and gave God credit for the numerous converts that he said he made in Ireland. As a bishop, he had the authority to ordain priests and was responsible for laying the foundation for an expansion of the Irish church,

[5] Kathleen Hughes (2005), "The Church in Irish Society, 400–800," in D. Ó Cróinín (ed.), *A New History of Ireland: Volume I: Prehistoric and Early Ireland*. Oxford: Oxford University Press, p. 303.

[6] St Patrick, "Declaration," in A. B. E. Hood (ed. and trans.) (1978), *St. Patrick: His Writings and Muirchu's Life*. London: Phillimore, p. 21.

even if he exaggerated his own role as its founder. Furthermore, whereas Palladius's mission was probably confined to the south, Patrick gives the impression of having traveled extensively throughout the island and having met with many kings and people who had obviously been untouched by Palladius's mission, though most modern scholars believe that he worked mostly in southeastern Ulster and never actually made it to Mayo. Patrick attracted followers from among the royal aristocracy, but he catered to all; having once been a slave, he was particularly empathetic, as Jesus had been, to slaves, women, and the common people.

Patrick's few short writings provide some insight into his theology and spirituality. He believed that God held humans accountable on judgment day, which, like many religious leaders throughout history, he believed was imminent. But he also exhibited a profound sense of God's mercy and testified to the grace which he received, first when he was rescued from his sinful life through slavery and then when he was released from captivity and given the opportunity to serve God by bringing the Christian message to the land to which he had been delivered by destiny. In his *Letter to Coroticus*, Patrick wrestled with the earthly injustice of seeing many of his Christian converts carried into slavery by the soldiers of Coroticus, a British king who was taking advantage of the absence of Roman authority in Britain. Here he reflects again on the ways in which he felt called to fulfill God's purposes, writing that

> ...I have a share with those whom He called and predestined to preach the gospel right to the ends of the earth in the midst of no small persecution, even if the enemy shows his resentment through the unjust rule of Coroticus, who does not fear God or His priests whom He has chosen and endowed with the supreme, divine power that those whom they bound on earth should be bound in heaven also.[7]

Patrick's missionary efforts in Ireland occurred during a century in which Christian missionaries were just beginning to expand their efforts at the northern outreaches of the declining Roman Empire in Western Europe. For example, Bede, the famous historian of English Christianity who wrote in the eighth century, attributed the sixth-century conversion of the southern Picts, who inhabited the borderlands between what later became Scotland and England, to a missionary named *Ninian*, who may have originally come from Wales. Irish missionaries also did much to bring Christianity to Britain well before Pope Gregory the Great dispatched a missionary named *Augustine* to bring Roman Christianity to convert the Jutes of Kent at the end of the sixth century. Patrick's mission to Ireland began a process of

---

[7] St Patrick, "Letter to Coroticus," in A. B. E. Hood (ed. and trans.) (1978), *St. Patrick: His Writings and Muirchu's Life*. London: Phillimore, p. 56.

conversion that involved religious missionaries traveling from Britain to Ireland and back again that did much to forge a common religious culture across the Irish Sea. When Columba (521–97), also known by his Irish name of *Colm Cille* ("dove of the Church"), set out for northern Britain in 563, he, like Patrick earlier, was going to a location that had already been exposed to Christian missions. But he went because missionary efforts had become a huge part of Irish Christianity. Irish monks, who did not face much in the way of persecution in Ireland, frequently sought what has been described as a *white martyrdom*, which consisted of a self-imposed exile from their native land in harsher, more remote environments abroad. By contrast, those monks who sought isolation in the wilds of Ireland itself were practitioners of what was called *green martyrdom*.

Irish missions

Thus, when Columba departed for the western coast of north Britain, he initiated a pattern of missionary activity on the part of Irish monks who were intent on taking their brand of Christianity beyond their own shores. Patrick, who exhibited a strong streak of asceticism and sponsored the growth of the first Irish monasteries, had already contributed to the monastic nature of early Irish Christianity. Bede tells us that Columba received the island of Iona as a site on which to build a monastery from a powerful king of the Picts named *Bride* as a result of Columba's successful preaching and the good Christian example that he set for the king's subjects. Columba did not permanently remain in Iona, although he would use it as a base for his journeys and died there. He continued his missionary activity on other islands and the Scottish mainland and, according to Bede, established many other monasteries in Britain in addition to those, such as Durrow and Kells, which he is credited with founding in Ireland.

Iona became the center of Celtic Christianity because of the personal prestige and saintly reputation of Columba. In his biography of Columba, Adomnán records an incident in which the saint restored the life of the dead son of Christian parents as just one of his many miracles. In another example of a miracle that imitated one attributed to Jesus in the New Testament, Adomnán tells us that Columba changed water into wine. Columba was also credited with the gift of prophecy and the ability to see events that were taking place far away from his presence "because although absent in the body, he was present in spirit."[8] He foresaw ordinary events, such as a ship arriving from Ireland carrying a man who had committed a crime but whose sincere remorse Columba also sensed. At a certain place, he stopped

---

[8] Adomnán (1991), *Life of Columba*, edited by Alan Orr Anderson and Marjorie Ogilvie Anderson. Oxford: Clarendon Press, pp. 17–18.

abruptly to tell his companions that a pagan man would be baptized and die on the very spot where he stood, which we are led to believe ultimately came to pass. Adomnán does not reveal the source of these miraculous powers, but he does say that on occasion Columba received visits from angels. Columba's spiritual powers did not stop there. His spiritual presence was once felt by a group of monks traveling on Iona, a feeling that Adomnán describes as "marvelous and strange." In short, Columba was a highly revered figure, one whose visit late in life to Clonmacnoise aroused such excitement among the monks that Columba had to be protected from those swarming to be near him by four men holding a wooden trellis. Columba is also famous for his reported encounter with the Loch Ness Monster, the first written reference to the legendary beast in history. According to Adomnán, Columba tamed the beast and frightened it into retreat after it had killed a man and terrified the local population.

Columbanus (c. 543–615) traveled much farther afield than did Columba, driven by an even more intense desire for "white martyrdom" than that which had led Columba to Iona. Having studied hard in his youth and having spent many subsequent years in an Irish monastery, Columbanus was inspired to travel abroad, according to his biographer Jonas, by God's command to Abraham to "get thee out of thy country, and from thy kindred, and from thy father's house, into a land that I will show thee." Columbanus's journeys took him to Gaul and eventually to northern Italy, where he founded an abbey at Bobbio, one of the most famous monastic establishments of the medieval period. While in Gaul, he became embroiled in royal politics, which were frequently quite turbulent and even violent under the ruling Merovingian dynasty. When on good terms with the royal family, Columbanus faced opposition from bishops anxious to preserve their influence and authority within the Frankish church. When out of favor at court, Columbanus simply traveled eastward to convert Germanic peoples such as the Swabians. Jonas records that Columbanus was inspired to go to Italy by a vision from an angel, who told him, "Go to the right or the left where you will, that you may enjoy the fruits of your labors."[9]

Like Columba—and indeed all medieval saints—Columbanus had miracles and special spiritual powers attributed to him that were intended to impress both a pagan and a Christian audience. Jonas tells of one instance in which Columbanus caused a cask of beer intended as an offering to the pagan god Wodan (whose day we still acknowledge every week during our "Wednesday") to shatter to pieces just by breathing on it. One does not need to accept the literal truth of all of the miracles attributed to Columba and Columbanus in order to recognize how historically significant they

---

[9] Jonas (1975), "Life of St. Columbanus," in W. C. McDermott (ed.), *Monks, Bishops and Pagans: Christian Culture in Gaul and Italy, 500–700*. Philadelphia: University of Pennsylvania Press, p. 110.

were in the history of early medieval Christianity. The central importance of Iona, Bobbio, and St Gall, another monastery founded by Columbanus that was named after his traveling companion, to the cultural life of this period make them central figures in the spread of Christianity, the monastic movement, and the preservation of learning. The main difference between these two seminal figures is that Columba represents the continued evolution of Celtic Christianity as a dynamic religious movement in its own right, while Columbanus bridges the Celtic and the Roman world and represents the larger context in which Ireland and early medieval Europe belonged to the same unified church. This did not mean, however, that Columbanus lessened his devotion to the Irish tradition in which he had been raised. For example, he continued to insist on the Irish dating of Easter, which was calculated differently than in the Roman Church.

Distinctive features of Irish Christianity

Many historians have recently called into question the use of the term *Celtic Christianity* on the bases that all Celtic peoples were never unified under a single religious system and that no completely independent Celtic church ever existed separate from the Christian church centered on Rome.[10] Both of these points are well taken, as far as they go. For example, St Patrick was a bishop who appointed other bishops in Ireland, setting up an ecclesiastical hierarchy similar to that emanating from Rome; he certainly never wished to establish his own church independent from the rest of Christendom. However, Irish Christianity did look different in many ways from that practiced on the Continent where Rome had more direct authority. First and foremost, monasticism played a much larger role in Irish or Celtic Christianity, with abbots tending to wield greater authority than bishops (though bishops did not cease to exist). Monasticism dominated largely because of sheer numbers—it has been estimated that 800 monasteries had been established in all areas of Ireland before the year 600. Irish monasticism also differed significantly from the vast majority of monasteries in Western Europe that followed the rule established by St Benedict of Nursia (c. 480–c. 547). One main difference was that, instead of being concentrated in a single large residence, Irish monks generally inhabited single-person dwellings shaped like a beehive. Irish monasteries frequently stood at the center of a larger community and tended to be more closely integrated with the life of the people than their Benedictine counterparts.[11]

---

[10] See, for example, M. P. Bryant-Quinn (2002), Review of Oliver Davies (trans.) (1998), *Celtic Spirituality* (New York: Paulist Press) in *Mystics Quarterly*, 28, 37–40.
[11] For more on this topic, see Lisa M. Bitel (1994), *Isle of the Saints: Monastic Settlement and Christian Community in Early Ireland*. Ithaca: Cornell University Press.

The relative equality of women in Irish society carried over into the Irish church where women played a prominent role as heads of monasteries and in ministering to the needs of the people. At Killeedy in the sixth century, St Ida ran a school that educated St Brendan. According to the medieval text, *The Voyage of St. Brendan*, Brendan crossed the Atlantic in a leather boat, reaching land far to the west. The British adventurer Tim Severin (b. 1940) reenacted Brendan's alleged voyage in 1977 to demonstrate that such a feat was possible, given the level of knowledge and craftsmanship at the time. St Brigid, Ireland's most revered female saint whose popularity is only outstripped by that of St Patrick, elevated her monastic church at Kildare to a high level of prominence within the Irish church. She also lived an independent existence as a missionary in which her travels seem to have been in no way dictated or inhibited by any male superiors. It is more likely that male clerics came to her, and other women, to seek their guidance and support.

Much has been made of the more liberated attitude toward sex and the more favorable attitude toward marriage taken by the leaders of Irish Christianity in comparison with the leading fathers of the Roman Church, such as St Augustine and St Jerome. It seems that monks in some Irish abbeys were actually allowed to be married, while in others lay married couples were part of the monastic community in a way that would have been inconceivable on the Continent. It is this spirit of independence and freedom to improvise practice within the general framework of Christianity that is the most distinctive aspect of Irish Christianity. The spirit of Irish Christianity is still apparent at early monastic sites such as Clonmacnoise, one of several preeminent examples that included Bangor and Clonard as well.

FIGURE 3.1 *Clonmacnoise. Courtesy of Getty Images.*

Located in central Ireland on the Shannon River, Clonmacnoise was a flourishing community at a major crossroads between east and west that participated in Irish politics and became a center of trade, but there is no doubt that as a spiritual center it influenced the life of the wider community as much as it was affected by its participation in worldly affairs. Clonmacnoise was also a center of learning, which was another prominent characteristic of early Irish monasticism.

Christianity and culture

Since Ireland had never been part of the Roman Empire, Latin culture came there rather late, allowing the island to preserve much more of its native culture than did other areas of northern and Western Europe where peoples had succumbed to Roman rule and influence centuries earlier. This could help to explain why the Irish began writing in their language before the appearance of other vernacular languages throughout Europe. Some historians have asserted that Patrick brought Roman culture with him to Ireland on the basis of a legend that he had studied in Gaul for a period of years, but other scholars dispute this based on Patrick's apparent ignorance of Latin. St Patrick prefaced his *Confession* by saying that he had hesitated to write because "I was afraid to expose myself to the criticism of men's tongues, because I have not studied like others . . ."[12] In his *Letter to Coroticus*, he described himself as "unlearned," but insisted that he wrote the letter "with my own hand." Patrick is now considered to be a much more sophisticated and stylish writer than previously thought.[13] Latin culture came to exercise a great influence over Ireland, including the introduction of a written tradition in the seventh century that led to the preservation of much of the Celtic heritage. Writing was not only taught in the monasteries, but it became one of the primary activities associated with monastic life. Irish monks copied numerous manuscripts and produced beautifully illuminated copies of the Gospels, such as the famous *Book of Kells* and the less well known but equally beautiful *Book of Durrow*, both of which date from about the late eighth century. The achievement of the Irish monks in preserving the learning of classical antiquity is all the more impressive when one considers that Ireland was not a part of the Roman world before the fall of the western half of the empire in the fifth century and had no previous exposure to its Latin culture.

Classical culture had long been embraced by Christians, who by and large rejected the attempt to invalidate pagan learning by early church fathers such as Tertullian, who famously asked "What has Jerusalem to do

---

[12] St Patrick, "Declaration," in Hood, *op. cit.*, p. 42.
[13] I am grateful to my anonymous reviewer for pointing this out to me.

with Athens?" Augustine had made frequent use of classical writers in his works and saw nothing wrong with using classical learning in the service of the Christian faith. Essentially, the same attitude can be found in the writings of Adomnán and the teachings of Columba and Columbanus. Columbanus enjoyed poetry and seems to have had a decent knowledge of classical culture. His letters were written in good Latin grammar, while he and Columba were both educated interpreters of the Bible. They had clearly received a good education that was obviously already available in Ireland in the sixth century. They would not have received such an education had it not been for the efforts of Christian monks not only to preserve classical learning but also to teach it and pass it along. However, as much as they embraced classical learning, Irish clerics did not completely reject their own culture nor did they fail to develop their own writing style. Many of them came from aristocratic backgrounds and would have been well versed in their native culture, while also having access to artists and craftsmen who likely created nonreligious works for kings and princes.

Irish Christianity, then, owes much of its distinct nature to the blending of Latin culture with the Celtic heritage of the early Irish Christians. Most of the writings of this early period dealt with religious themes. In addition to the biblical commentaries and sacramental guidebooks that were a necessary part of the effort to educate and train the clergy, there were also the hagiographies of the Irish saints and other writings in prose or poetry that dealt with Christian themes. However, other literary works, such as "The Voyage of Bran," reflect more secular themes that were simply infused with Christian references. For example, this particular epic includes the prophecy that:

A noble salvation will come
From the King who has created us,
A white law will come over seas,
Besides being God, He will be man.[14]

The oldest surviving manuscript of this work dates from the tenth century, but it was copied down at that time from a seventh-century source. The Irish seem to have embraced Christianity without doing as much damage to their traditional culture as occurred elsewhere. For example, the illuminated manuscripts, crosses, ogham stones, and other works of art all bear the unmistakable influence of native Irish culture. Ogham stones were thin stones with Irish writing inscribed on them that stood upright at many of the early monastic sites, especially in southern Ireland. In addition, crosses were engraved on stone slabs before giving way to the traditional "Celtic

---

[14] "The Voyage of Bran," edited by Kuno Meyer in Charles W. Jones (ed.) (1950), *Medieval Literature in Translation*. New York: David McKay, p. 100.

cross" consisting of a cross on the top of a pillar surrounded by a circle. In many respects, a unique Christian tradition had developed in Ireland, northern Britain, and the coastal islands in the region that was characterized by independent abbeys that did not belong to an order that had a fixed hierarchy and that retained many elements of indigenous culture; as Thomas O'Loughlin puts it, "whether we call it 'Celtic Christianity' or 'Christianity in Celtic lands' or 'insular Christianity' will largely be a matter of emphasis."[15]

The Synod of Whitby and the decline of Irish Christianity

The most famous showdown between Celtic Christianity and Roman Christianity occurred at the Synod of Whitby in northern England that met in the year 664. The impetus for this assembly, according to Bede, was the concern on the part of King Oswy of Northumbria that all members of his household observe Easter on the same date since they all worshipped the same God. But Bede notes that this was already a recurring controversy in Kent and Gaul that had been brewing for some time prior to Whitby. Columbanus referred to it in one of his letters and seemed quite intent on defending the Celtic tradition. Although some scholars now downplay the importance of the controversy as affecting relatively few people, Columbanus saw great symbolic significance in attempting to ensure that the moon rise on time in order to prevail over darkness because "the festival of the Lord's resurrection is light, and there is no 'communication of light with darkness'."[16]

The technical details of the controversy do not need to detain us here; what is important is that for some, the controversy had come to symbolize the relative independence of a part of the church, whether it is called the Celtic church or not, to the point where it had its own timing for the holiest day in the Christian calendar. The English historian Bede placed so much emphasis on it because, as a loyal adherent of the papacy and the Roman Church, he thought it a significant moment in the triumph of Roman Christianity in Britain. In fact, the southern half of Ireland had already accepted the Roman date for Easter in 631, leaving the Celtic date isolated to the northern half of both Britain and Ireland. Still, the decision of the Irish representatives at the Synod of Whitby to acquiesce and accept the Roman date for Easter in order to preserve harmony within the church was a significant turning point that

---

[15] Thomas O'Loughlin (2000), *Celtic Theology: Humanity, World and God in Early Irish Writings*. London and New York: Continuum, p. 1.

[16] Columbanus. Letter 1, in *Letters*, translated by G. S. M. Walker, electronic edition compiled by Ruth Murphy, http://143.239.128.67/celt/published/T201054/index.html.

brought the northern Irish church more under the control of bishops. By this time bishops and archbishops represented Rome more than the independent abbots and abbesses who in the past had enjoyed greater prestige and authority. The acquiescence of the Irish representatives at Whitby was a willing surrender rather than a hostile takeover, but it still marked a decline in the distinctiveness of Celtic Christianity. It should be noted, however, that Ireland retained some independent monasteries until most were gradually absorbed by outside orders during the High Middle Ages.

Did the Irish save civilization?

When Thomas Cahill published his book *How the Irish Saved Civilization* in 1995, he found a large and receptive popular audience. His argument was twofold: first, that Irish monks had preserved classical literature and learning at a time when political order was collapsing with the fall of the Roman Empire in the West at the beginning of the so-called *dark ages* when learning was not respected and people had other things to worry about; second, that the Irish monks had provided a different model for Christianity than that emanating from Rome that had a more positive outlook on this earthly life and was more accepting of nature, the world, and the human body. In regard to the first part of his argument, it is true that Irish monks did not discriminate as much as their counterparts on the European continent in regard to the many texts that they preserved, including more apocryphal religious texts dating to the time of the Gnostic gospels than survived elsewhere.[17] As for the second part of his argument, his message that the Irish Christianity of the early Middle Ages still has something of value to offer us in the contemporary world fit in well with the late twentieth-century revival of interest in the Celtic past. Many people had come to believe that great insights could be gained by exploring Celtic spirituality, for which the early centuries of Christianity in Ireland were considered a golden age. In addition, St Patrick's condemnation of slavery, which receives much praise from Cahill, resonates well with modern values. Cahill also praised Patrick for his "emotional grasp of Christian truth" and for his ability to see the good in human nature, an attitude many might find more comforting than Augustine's stress on original sin.[18]

Like all controversial arguments, Cahill's contain a good deal of truth, but they also need to be qualified. On the first part of his argument

---

[17] Muireann Ní Bhrolcháin (2009), *An Introduction to Early Irish Literature*. Dublin: Four Courts Press, p. 14.

[18] Thomas Cahill (1995), *How the Irish Saved Civilization: The Untold Story of Ireland's Heroic Role from the Fall of Rome to the Rise of Medieval Europe*. New York: Doubleday, p. 115.

regarding the preservation of classical culture, whatever contribution that the Irish made to this they did not do alone; the Byzantine Empire and, after the eighth century, the Arabs deserve a great deal of credit as well, just to cite two examples. On the second part of his argument, even if we are to treat the Irish Church and the Roman Church as separate entities (which they were not), the contrast is not as stark as Cahill (and others) have made them out to be. The theology of St Augustine may have been among the more dominant in Western Christianity, but it was not unchallenged, nor was his thought so consistent as to favor a monolithic following. Augustine's challenges to Pelagius (a British monk whose teachings were condemned by the church because they placed too much emphasis on free will in matters of salvation) and his writings on the absolute power of God favor an interpretation of Augustine as a supporter of predestination. This was certainly not the primary emphasis in the teachings on salvation that predominated in the medieval church. Furthermore, St Patrick condemned Pelagius as well, and a strong strain of Christian asceticism exists among the Irish monastic founders of the fifth and sixth centuries that would be just as foreign to most modern sensibilities as the traditions of Benedictine monasticism. There were some married abbots in the Irish church and Irish monasteries accepted married couples as part of their community, but plenty of Irish monks and abbots chose to be celibate. None of the above is intended to discourage readers from finding spiritual consolation wherever they choose or to say that the early Irish church has nothing to offer to the spiritual seeker today. To the extent that Irish Christianity is regarded as taking a more positive attitude toward the natural world, its teachings will continue to have value in addition to whatever spiritual renewal it might bring to its devotees. In that sense, Cahill may be right in suggesting not only that the Irish saved civilization in the Middle Ages, but also that they might still do so in the twenty-first century.

CHAPTER FOUR

The impact of the Vikings and the Norman conquest

Fierce is the wind tonight.
It ploughs up the white hair of the sea.
I have no fear that the Viking hosts
Will come over the water to me.

Mid-ninth century, translated by F. N. ROBINSON

Government, law, and social order before the Vikings

In the centuries immediately following the coming of Christianity, Ireland retained the same basic decentralized political structure consisting of a number of kings, many of whom ruled over their local areas with the assistance of relatively small retinues. Resources were limited and a significant amount of them went to the church. Much money was put into the founding and support of monasteries, which frequently had close relationships with the political authorities, as was mentioned in Chapter 3. Increasingly, however, significant differences began to emerge among Irish kings; by the eighth century, it becomes gradually more difficult to view Ireland as being governed by a collection of roughly equal petty despots as some kings began to acquire additional power. Some historians have attempted to distinguish among different categories of kingship in Ireland; for example, the Irish word for king (*rí*) had several variants such as *rí túathe* and *rí cóieid*, with the latter implying rule over a larger area. But it can be very difficult to harmonize theory and practice when it comes to medieval Irish politics.

By the eighth century, however, some kings had broken out of even these categories to assume a wider power over larger portions of the island. One example would be Áed Oirdnide mac Néill, who ruled in the North from 797 to 819. Mac Néill managed to assert his claims at the expense of the kings of Leinster, who were the main rivals of the Uí Néill for political power in Ireland during the eighth century. Eventually, claims to rule all of Ireland started to be asserted; by the tenth century, such an individual came to be known as a *high king* or an *ard-rí*, a term which originally was applied only to God. This process began even before the arrival of the Vikings, but in Ireland, as in England, the Viking invasions of the ninth and tenth centuries encouraged greater political unity. In England, the late-ninth-century king of Wessex, Alfred the Great (r. 871–99) reclaimed territory from the Vikings and expanded his power to the point where he could be considered king of England, even though the Danes still controlled a significant amount of territory in the north around York (Viking *Jorvik*). In Ireland, claims to the high-kingship culminated in the success of Brian Boru (c. 926–1014) (see below). However, unlike in England, the concept of a single king for Ireland was not sustained during the succeeding centuries. By the twelfth century, greater power was attributed to Brian Boru and earlier Irish *high kings* than they actually possessed, largely as a way of celebrating their victories over the Vikings and adding to the prestige of their descendants.

Irish kings were not only the military leaders of their people, but also the final arbiter in the enforcement of laws that were agreed upon by people elected to an assembly, which was called an *oenach*. Written Irish law codes date from the seventh and eighth centuries. The church encouraged written law codes along with the spread of Christianity because its leaders had a vested interest in maintaining social order and protecting its own personnel and property. The establishment of law schools followed closely upon the existence of written laws, which in Ireland mostly took the form of books used for training experts in the law known as *brithen*. In these books, elements of traditional practice among the Irish coexisted with Christian influences. Codes such as the late-seventh-century "Bretha Comaithchesa" dealt mainly with property rights, reflecting their great importance within Irish society. Irish laws from this period also put a great emphasis on distinguishing between relationships within a family and those that existed among people who were not related, showing the importance of kinship as an organizing factor for this society.

Although royal authority and laws were important, social order in early medieval Ireland was mostly dependent on a structured set of relationships that was determined by social status. A person's status derived from a combination of wealth and lineage rather than from occupation, although learning could play a role in heightening one's position. The basic social distinction was between nobles and commoners, though among commoners there was an important difference between those who were free and those who were not. Freemen had the right to vote for members of the assembly and had a higher legal status that made their word more valuable as trial witnesses or in legal contracts.

Most of the country consisted of a patchwork of small farms that included pasture lands, as well as fields dedicated to the growing of grain. In Ulster, livestock were supported through the winter by grazing on lands set aside for that purpose instead of through stored hay or feed. More prosperous farmers surrounded their lands with ring-forts, which consisted of circular barriers made of earth, the diameters of which averaged about 30 meters (see Chapter 2). Elsewhere, fenses separated the lands of relatives and neighbors. Archeology has confirmed a good deal of order in the arrangement and management of these farmlands. Some of these lands were hereditary lands that belonged to or were overseen by a king or tribal chieftain. Private property that could be bought and sold did exist, but for the most part, property was conceived of as belonging to a family and not an individual. Landowners often had an obligation to provide not only for their immediate family but also for first or second cousins. Every family had a patriarch who generally ensured that such obligations were met, thus contributing to the overall stability of Irish society. In addition, a significant amount of land belonged to the church; monasteries frequently oversaw the farms in their immediate vicinity. This had the effect of further spreading the influence of Christianity over the rural population and providing additional social order. But the stability of society and the position of the church were both shaken in the ninth century by the impact of the Viking invasions.

Viking invasions and Scandinavian expansion

In 795, the Vikings invaded an island that the sources identify as Rechru, which some scholars identify as Lambay and others as Rathlin Island. Either way, this attack began about a three-decade period in which Ireland could generally count on at least one significant raid per year. These raids were part of a larger pattern of invasion of the entire British Isles and northwestern Europe about this time; the Vikings had sacked the English monasteries at Lindisfarne and Jarrow in Northumbria in the 2 years that preceded the attack on Rechru. In 806, they murdered 68 residents of the monastic community at Iona, causing the successors of St Columba to move 20 miles inland to Kells. Other monks took off for the Continent; many more would follow them during the Viking age. The following year, the Vikings sacked Roscommon on Galway Bay and set fire to the monastery on Innishmurray Island off the coast of County Sligo. By then, it was clear that these were not isolated incidents but a part of a series of large-scale planned invasions of the entire region by different Viking leaders who were beginning to coordinate increasingly larger forces. The *Annals of Ulster* record an attack on E'tar in 821, in which a number of women were taken captive. Additional attacks are recorded for 823, 824, and 825, before the "heathens" suffered a costly defeat at the hands of the Ulaid; then, in the half-century between 830 and 880, the raiding actually accelerated, with 83 known raids during that period.[1] There was an especially high concentration in the period from 830 to 849.

Norwegians conducted most of the earliest Viking raids in Ireland, probably because of their close proximity to the island. The causes of Norse expansion are a matter of debate, but probably resulted from a confluence of circumstances that included their ability to raid and the availability of wealth in the monastic centers along the coasts of the British Isles. The Vikings benefited from their expertise in shipbuilding, especially their ability to construct ships that were sturdy enough for sailing on the rough waters of the North Atlantic but narrow and light enough to traverse inland waterways, even those where the water was only 3-feet deep. The Vikings were attracted to lands that possessed wealth in the form of gold and precious metals, which was the main reason why churches and monasteries were usually their most frequent targets. Churches and monasteries used gold and silver to make their chalices and other liturgical items and often studded their crosses with jewels. In addition, laymen frequently stored their wealth at monasteries, which became something like the banks of the Middle Ages. Their wealth had made monasteries objects of attack by Irish kings as well, but Irish attacks did not cause near the amount of death and destruction that the Vikings did.

In 840, for the first time, Vikings stayed in Ireland throughout the entire year, the first sign that they would become a permanent presence on the island. Earlier raids, although violent and destructive, were temporary and ended with the Vikings leaving as soon as they had pillaged and looted to their heart's content. Permanent residence did not at first mean peaceful coexistence; the earliest Viking settlements in Ireland were fortified bases from which they could carry out raids further inland. But at some point in the ninth century, the focus shifted from invasion to settlement, though these were certainly not mutually exclusive. Raiders and settlers were not necessarily the same people; some came in search of land, willing to take advantage of the protection afforded to them by pirates, just as many peaceful settlers migrated to the American West in the nineteenth century looking to own land while benefiting from the US Army's decimation of the Indians. Even so, Viking settlements in Ireland remained largely confined to coastal regions, unlike in England. Once established in Ireland, Viking

---

[1] Kathleen Hughes (2005), "The Irish Church, 800–c. 1050," in D. Ó Cróinín (ed.), *A New History of Ireland: Volume I: Prehistoric and Early Ireland*. Oxford: Oxford University Press, p. 638.

rulers began to assert their influence throughout the region. The Anglo-Saxon poem *The Battle of Brunanburh* suggests an alliance between the Viking king of Dublin, the king of the Scots, and the king of Strathclyde in what is now southern Scotland, perhaps in opposition to English expansion into Celtic lands. The kings of Dublin also made alliances with Welsh and Cornish rulers on occasion. Dublin's trading contacts may have been even more important than its political alliances, though the two were probably closely connected.

Trade and assimilation

Many scholars have attempted to revise the negative reputation that the Vikings have had historically by pointing out their many creative contributions to European history and the lands where they eventually settled. Other historians have challenged this revision and continue to emphasize their total insensitivity toward the people they killed and the amount of destruction they caused. In his 1999 essay on "The Effect of Scandinavian Raiders on the English and Irish Churches: A Preliminary Reassessment," Alfred P. Smith emphasizes that a true measure of the impact of the Viking raids cannot be attained by simply counting the number of attacks in a given period, but only by the psychological impact that these raids had, including the intense fear of the possibility of a raid at any moment, even in years when they did not occur.[2] Edward Rutherfurd includes a withering description of a typical Viking raid in his novel about English history, *Sarum* (1987) that leaves no doubt about which side he is on in this historical debate. The negative effects of the Viking impact upon Ireland and Europe were certainly real, and no attempt will be made here to discount it. In Ireland, the Vikings had a deleterious effect upon learning, religion, the economy, and political life through their conquests, raids, destruction of monasteries, books, and works of art, and the encouragement their raids gave to the further militarization of Irish society. It is true, no doubt, that Irish society would have changed anyway during this period, but this is largely a moot point because the Viking attacks did occur and they did have a large impact. However, it should at least be noted that while some Scandinavians were interested in plunder, others were interested in trade, even at the time of the first invasions. The shipping towns of Birka in Sweden, Hedeby in Denmark, and Kaupang in Norway all date from about that time. Vikings interested in more peaceful pursuits such as trade brought with them an expertise in shipbuilding and metalworking, among other skills.

---

[2] Alfred P. Smyth (1999), "The Effect of Scandinavian Raiders on the English and Irish Churches: A Preliminary Reassessment," in Brendan Smith (ed.), *Britain and Ireland, 900–1300: Insular Responses to Medieval European Change*. Cambridge: Cambridge University Press p. 33.

FIGURE 4.1 *Ruins of Dunseverick Castle, County Antrim, scene of Viking attack. Drawn by W. H. Bartlett, engraved by R. Wallis. From* The Scenery and Antiquities of Ireland *by N. P. Willis and J. Stirling Coyne. Illustrated from drawings by W. H. Bartlett. Published London c. 1841. Courtesy of Getty Images.*

The history of Dublin illustrates the two different sides of the Viking enterprise; first founded as a base for further raids and some trade in the 840s, the city was founded a second time about 917 as a permanent settlement with walls constructed for the defense of the population. The gap in Dublin's history is attributed to the expulsion of the Norwegians who had settled there about 902 by the combined force of several Irish kings. The Scandinavians returned 15 years later with a determination to make the settlement stick.[3] It is also worth noting that Viking Dublin could not have sustained itself without supplies from the surrounding countryside, which benefited economically from the emergence of the city. Trade would have included luxury and manufactured goods as well as food supplies. Local merchants also gained permission to trade in Dublin in exchange for products that included malt, salt, firewood, meat, and candles.[4]

Interestingly, the towns that the Vikings founded, which in addition to Dublin included Limerick, Waterford, and Wexford, are all in the southern half of the island as opposed to the north, which was closer to their homelands. Although it has been suggested that the Vikings settled in the south to be closer to the European continent for purposes of attack or

---

[3] Patrick F. Wallace (2005), "The Archaeology of Ireland's Viking-Age Towns," in D. Ó Cróinín (ed.), *A New History of Ireland: Volume I: Prehistoric and Early Ireland*. Oxford: Oxford University Press, p. 815.

[4] Ruth Jackson (2004), *Viking Age Dublin*. Dublin: Town House, p. 71.

trade, this was not entirely by choice.[5] In Ireland, the strongest native rulers happened to reside in the north, specifically, the Uí Néill and the Ulaid, who were even strong enough to contest with the Vikings at sea. In England, conversely, the Vikings settled in the north—in the area that became known as the Danelaw—largely because Alfred the Great, the most powerful ruler in England, resided in the south. Still, the location of the Viking towns in Ireland did facilitate close cultural and economic contact with Britain and the Continent and contributed to their dominance in the region, which lasted until at least the mid-eleventh century. Cork was founded perhaps as early as the mid-ninth century, while the first settlement at Waterford dates closer to the early tenth century. As these towns developed in the eleventh and twelfth centuries, their layout and housing structures bear such a strong resemblance to those of Dublin, according to Maurice Hurley, that the common Scandinavian cultural provenance is unmistakable.[6] The Viking presence in Ireland was not confined to the southeast, however, as they also settled, at least temporarily, on the western shores of Donegal, Sligo, and Galway and infiltrated the interior parts of the country as well.

Without question, the Vikings, for all the riches they stole, brought or recirculated a great deal of wealth within Ireland. Viking treasures discovered by archaeologists in Ireland provide some clues about the history of their presence on the island. Some hoards contain coins, providing evidence of trade, while others, such as the hoard discovered at Carrick in County Westmeath, consist of considerable amounts of gold and silver. The site at Carrick contained the largest amount of wealth found in Ireland—about 60 huge silver ingots weighing about 31.8 kilograms or about 70 pounds. Since the size of both the treasure and of the individual ingots was atypical of Scandinavian hoards during the period, archaeologists have concluded that this was actually an example of Irish wealth that was perhaps acquired in the process of trading with the Vikings. Evidence from coins shows that trade within Ireland had certainly begun by the tenth century; the largest hoard of coins discovered to this point seems to have been that found at Drogheda in June 1846 with an estimated date of 905.[7] Another valuable find located at Dunmore Cave in County Kilkenny has been seen by Kristin Collins as indicative of an economy that was making a transition toward one based more on trade and monetary exchange.[8] Kilkenny occupied a

---

5 F. J. Byrne (2005), "The Viking Age," in D. Ó Cróinín (ed.), *A New History of Ireland: Volume I: Prehistoric and Early Ireland*. Oxford: Oxford University Press, p. 619.

6 Maurice F. Hurley (2010), "Viking Elements in Irish Towns: Cork and Waterford," in John Sheehan and Donnchadh Ó Corráin (eds), *The Viking Age: Ireland and the West*. Dublin: Four Courts Press, pp. 154–64.

7 James Graham-Campbell (2011), *The Cuerdale Hoard and Related Viking-Age Silver and Gold from Britain and Ireland in the British Museum*. London: The British Museum, p. 6.

8 Kritin Bornholdt Collins (2010), "The Dunmore Cave [2] Hoard and the Role of Coins in the Tenth-Century Hiberno-Scandinavian Economy," in John Sheehan and Donnchadh Ó Corráin (eds), *The Viking Age: Ireland and the West*. Dublin: Four Courts Press, pp. 19–46.

central location in the Irish kingdom of Ossory along navigable trade routes that led to Dublin, Limerick, and Waterford. In the absence of native mints, foreign coins circulated freely in this transitional phase of the Irish economy that dates from about the mid-tenth century.

However destructive and long-lasting the Viking raids may have been, in the end, those Scandinavians who settled in Ireland did assimilate somewhat with the native population. Exactly how much assimilation occurred is a matter of debate. Historians have not noticed many cross-cultural artistic influences during the early phase of Viking settlement before the tenth century. Eventually, as in other parts of the British Isles, the Vikings intermarried with the native population and around the twelfth century became virtually indistinguishable from the Irish. It is the period in between—the tenth and eleventh centuries—that is most in dispute. The two populations lived separately for a long time and the Norse continued to use their own language into the eleventh century, when they were still referred to by the Irish as *foreigners*. The most important example of cross-cultural influence in this period was the conversion of the Vikings to Christianity. The process of the Christianization of the Vikings in Ireland is more mysterious than the conversion of other pagan groups in Europe from this period precisely because the populations did live so separately.[9] But the Vikings did become Christian—in the case of Dublin, by about the mid-tenth century—and when they did, they stopped looting and started donating to the church. As the Vikings began the process of assimilation into Irish society in the tenth and eleventh centuries, the church began to recover and to gradually increase its wealth again. Christ Church in Dublin, for example, was founded by the Viking king, Sitric Silkenbeard in conjunction with Bishop Dúnán in about 1030. But the conversion of the Scandinavian rulers to Christianity did not stop Irish kings from trying to recapture land and power from those that they still regarded as heathen intruders.

Irish responses

The Irish medievalist Máire Ní Mhaonaigh has provided an excellent discussion on the mystery of why there were not more Irish literary responses to the Viking invasions beyond the brief poem that appears at the beginning of this chapter. She explains this lack partly in reference to existing traditions in Irish literature, which tended to focus on a heroic age containing mythological ancestors that predated the arrival of the Vikings. But Ní Mhaonaigh also alludes to the use that clerical writers made of the

---

[9] Lesley Abrams (2010), "Conversion and the Church in Viking-Age Ireland," in John Sheehan and Donnchadh Ó Corráin (eds), *The Viking Age: Ireland and the West*. Dublin: Four Courts Press, pp. 1–10.

Viking attacks, which some viewed as punishment sent from God to people who were disobeying his commandments, particularly the one dedicated to maintaining the Sabbath.[10] In most writings that do refer to the Vikings from this period, fear is the dominant motif, however.

The Vikings were not the only ones worthy of blame for the violence and threat of destruction that characterized this period of Irish history. Irish kings who struggled for power—such as those representing the Cené nEógain and the Clann Cholmáin—were just as capable of inflicting destruction as the Vikings. It was not unknown for Irish rulers to carry out their own attacks on monasteries and churches, though they did so less frequently than the Vikings. Ní Mhaonaigh points to *The March Roll of the Men of Leinster* as an example of a source from this period that condemns native Irish rulers rather than the Vikings.[11]

The Vikings do not start to appear in Irish literature in a significant way until the twelfth century, when sources such as *The War of the Gaedhil with the Gaill* portray the savagery of ninth-century Viking kings such as Turgesius as a way of celebrating the achievements of Brian Boru for the sake of his descendants:

> There came Turgeis, who [brought] a fleet upon Loch Rai, and from there plundered Midhe and Connacht; and Cluan Mic Nois (Clonmacnoise) was plundered by him, and Cluian Ferta of Brenann, and Lothra, and Tirdá-glas, and Inis Celtra [monasteries of Meath and Connaught], and all the churches of Derg-dheirs, in like manner; and the place where Ota, the wife of Tureis, used to give her audience was upon the altar of Cluan Mic Nois . . . .[12]

Another early twelfth-century source, the *Lebor na Cert*, or *The Book of Rights*, simply treats the Vikings in Dublin as among other regional powers subject to the kingdom of Leinster.

In general, the more powerful and ruthless the Vikings were portrayed as being from the safe distance of the twelfth century, the more glorious the victories of the Irish over them could be made to appear.[13] But it is also possible that Irish literature of the earlier period might sometimes deal with the Viking invasions metaphorically rather than literally. This interpretation would fit well with Alfred Smith's point about the psychological impact of

---

[10] Máire Ní Mhaonaigh (1998), "Friend and Foe: Vikings in Ninth- and Tenth-Century Irish Literature," in Howard Clark, Máire Ní Mhaonaigh and Raghnall Ó Floinn (eds), *Ireland and Scandinavia in the Early Viking Age*. Blackrock: Four Courts Press, pp. 381–402.

[11] Ibid., p. 400.

[12] David Willis McCulloch (ed.) (2000), *Wars of the Irish Kings: A Thousand Years of Struggle from the Age of Myth through the Age of Queen Elizabeth I*. New York: Crown, p. 88.

[13] Ibid., p. 401.

the Viking terror. For example, the following lines could be read as referring to the times through which the ninth-century author was living rather than literally to the time of year:

> Winter has come with scarcity,
> Lakes have flooded on all sides,
> Frosts crumble the leaves,
> The merry wave mutters.[14]

The enslavement of Irish captives by Vikings in the ninth century would have contributed to the bleakness of the period in the minds of those who lived through the raids. Even if this were not the most prominent reason for the raids, the enslavement of native Irish, such as the 700 who were reported taken in one raid on Armagh, would have added an element of terror to the loss of life, theft of wealth, and destruction of property most often associated with the Viking attacks.

By the mid-tenth century, the Vikings had well established their sphere of influence in Ireland, but they never conquered the entire island. They were never even unified among themselves; the Danes and Norwegians fought at least one war in Ireland in which the Danes actually claimed to have the blessing of St Patrick![15] But their presence reinforced the need for strong military leadership among the native population. The practice of overlordship increased whereby certain kings gained authority over lesser lords as part of a military alliance that closely resembled the French practice now known as feudalism. Furthermore, the prior experience of war among Irish kings had already equipped them to deal better with the Vikings than many of their European counterparts. The Irish had some success against the Vikings, as evidenced by a report in a Frankish chronicle from 848 that mentions an Irish victory over Norse invaders.[16] Even during the invasion period, Irish rivals still quarreled for control of lands not under siege from the Vikings. In some cases, Irish kings even enlisted the support of Viking allies against their Irish enemies, as Brian Boru himself was known to do. Overall, the times favored the most powerful rulers, leading to greater centralization of power and a widening of the gap between military leaders and the rest of society.

Eventually, Irish kings vied over the title of high-kingship itself, which the Uí Néill had revived in the ninth century. Domnall ua Néill seems to have begun the practice of stationing troops in areas to maintain power beyond

---

[14] Translated by Kenneth Jackson. David H. Greene (1954), *An Anthology of Irish Literature*, Volume I. New York: New York University Press, p. 18.

[15] McCulloch, *op. cit.*, p. 86.

[16] Francis John Byrne (2001), *Irish Kings and High-Kings*, 2nd edn. Dublin: Four Courts Press, p. 262.

his hereditary lands.[17] The title of high king carried with it aspirations of ruling over the areas dominated by the Vikings themselves. Such was the focus of Brian Boru when he wrested power from the Uí Néill in 1002. Brian Boru had risen to power from a relatively obscure royal lineage, beginning with his victory over the Vikings at the Battle of Sulcoit in Limerick in about 968. However, his main enemies were his Irish rivals, who murdered his brother in 976. Brian temporarily made peace with the Vikings and began to consolidate his power at the expense of his Irish enemies. By 985, he had begun to expand his authority and had troops stationed in County Waterford. Within 10 years, he had expanded his authority throughout Munster. In 998, Brian won another major victory over the Vikings, still referred to in the sources either simply as *foreigners* or *heathens*. The Vikings responded by plundering Kildare, which prompted Brian to enter Dublin in 999 where "he remained . . . a whole week and carried off its gold and its silver and many captives, and burned the fortress, and banished the king, Sitric son of Olaf."[18] The Vikings returned to Dublin in 1000, giving hostages to Brian to guarantee their compliance with his rule.

In 1002, Brian Boru turned his attention to the north, mustering men to move against the Ulaid. The following year, he deposed the king of Laigin and took hostages from the people there. He then undertook a circuit of the north with an army composed of both Irishmen and "foreigners," taking additional hostages to ensure allegiance to his royal title. After assuming the role of high king, Brian Boru continued his onslaught on his enemies, primarily the king of Leinster. With some Vikings fighting on his side, he defeated a combined army of Vikings and Leinstermen at the battle of Clontarf on 23 April 1014. This was not the battle for supremacy of Ireland between the Vikings and the Irish that it is often portrayed as being, but it did represent part of a sustained attempt on the part of native rulers to maintain their power. Brian Boru's victories, though, may have had the short-term effect of furthering Viking assimilation and concentration on trade at the expense of their quest for political power in Ireland. They also contributed to the emergence of the great provincial kingships of Munster, Leinster, Ulster, and Connacht, all rivals for the position of high king in the eleventh and twelfth centuries. Brian himself successfully established a dynasty that continued to rule Munster for the next century and a half, close to the time when Ireland experienced yet another invasion, this time from the east. The Norman invasion of Ireland in 1170 bore little resemblance to the Viking onslaught that flooded Ireland in the ninth century but it was to be just as important in the shaping of Ireland's history.

---

[17] Charles Doherty (1998), "The Vikings in Ireland: A Review," in Howard Clark, Máire Ní Mhaonaigh and Raghnall Ó Floinn (eds), *Ireland and Scandinavia in the Early Viking Age*. Blackrock: Four Courts Press, p. 326.

[18] *The Annals of Tigernach*, http://www.ucc.ie/celt/published/T100002A/index.html.

The Norman invasions of England and Ireland

In England, the Scandinavian presence still made itself felt as a political force in the eleventh century to the point where King Canute of Denmark actually became king of England in 1016. Canute's Anglo-Danish empire had the potential to become a great power for centuries and orient England more in the direction of the North Sea and away from the English Channel. However, power in the eleventh century was still more of a personal than an institutional matter, and when Canute died in 1035, followed shortly thereafter by his two young sons, England looked elsewhere for a royal candidate capable of ruling the country. In 1042, a descendant of the most recent Saxon king was crowned; he is known to history as King Edward the Confessor (r. 1042–66). Edward had resided in Normandy during the reign of Canute and his sons and brought a strong Norman influence to his rule once he took possession of the English throne. But he married the daughter of Godwin, the earl of Wessex, thus cementing an alliance with the strongest member of the English nobility. When Edward died without heirs in 1066, three men claimed the English throne. Harold Hardrada, the king of Norway, launched an invasion that could have potentially brought England back into the political orbit of Scandinavia. Harold of Wessex, the son of Godwin and his successor as the most powerful English ruler, had the support of the leading men of the kingdom who served in an informal advisory council known as the Witan. He also ostensibly had the deathbed blessing of his father-in-law, Edward, which counted for a good deal in medieval succession disputes. The third claimant was William, duke of Normandy, who was distantly related to Edward and had the backing of the papacy.

William partly based his claim to the English throne on such factors as hereditary right, a prior commitment of support made by Edward when both men were younger, and even on a pledge of allegiance made by Harold on a visit to Normandy 2 years before the invasion. However, in many ways, the Norman Conquest of England fit a larger pattern of Norman expansion in the eleventh and twelfth centuries that included the conquest of Sicily and the acquisition of territory in the Middle East following the launching of the First Crusade in 1095. In the end, William became the king of England by virtue of conquest following his military defeat of Harold at the Battle of Hastings in October 1066. In the aftermath of that victory, William cowed the inhabitants of England through a strong military presence supported by the construction of castles throughout the land. He divided the land among his leading military men, who became barons entrusted with power in local areas but who owed allegiance and military service to the king alone. He thus strengthened royal power in England and paved the way for a more centralized and organized monarchy. William then made use of existing Anglo-Saxon laws in order to enforce his authority throughout his kingdom. Finally, he conducted a comprehensive census, the information from which became compiled in the famous *Domesday Book*, which was to be used in determining the assessment of taxes. For a time, the Anglo-Saxons chafed under Norman rule but there was little that they could do about it.

Although it could not have been known at the time, the Norman Conquest of England would eventually have serious consequences for Irish history as well. At this time, the papacy, after a prolonged period of decline and corruption in the tenth century, was beginning to recover its prestige and authority, thanks to a major reform initiative in Rome that was launched in the mid-eleventh century. Pope Alexander II (r. 1061–73) and his retinue, which included the intense and ardent reformer, Hildebrand, were looking to extend papal influence throughout Europe. They supported the Norman Conquest in the hope that William would favor papal influence over clerical appointments in England. In 1070, William appointed an Italian cleric, a former Benedictine monk named Lanfranc (c. 1005–89), as his archbishop of Canterbury. Lanfranc and his successor, another Italian known as Anselm of Bec (1033–1109), asserted their control over the English church. Lanfranc brought in Norman clerics to replace Anglo-Saxon ones whenever possible. Lanfranc also began to extend his influence over the church in Ireland, beginning in 1074, following the death of Dúnán, the first bishop of Dublin who had been appointed to his see in 1038. Lanfranc's new appointee, Patrick, was asked to pledge obedience to the see of Canterbury prior to his consecration. In 1096, Anselm consecrated two English-educated clerics named Samuel and Malchus as bishop of Dublin and bishop of Waterford, respectively. Lanfranc and Anselm both concerned themselves with ecclesiastical affairs in Ireland; both wrote letters to the king of Munster expressing their concern that bishops were not being appointed in the proper manner.[19]

Given the expansionist policies of the Normans and the interest of Anglo-Norman clerics in the Irish church, perhaps, it was only a matter of time before the Anglo-Norman kings conceived the idea of the conquest of Ireland. But William's immediate successors, William II (r. 1087–1100) and Henry I (r. 1100–35) concentrated on consolidating their power in England and Normandy. The reign of Henry I was followed by a civil war in which rival claimants to the throne found it difficult enough to maintain their hold on England, much less concern themselves with Ireland. Henry II (r. 1154–89), conversely, was one of the most powerful kings of the High Middle Ages, ruling over a third of France, including the prestigious territories of Anjou, Normandy, and Aquitaine, in addition to England and Wales. Nevertheless, the conquest of Ireland in 1170 was not actually Henry's idea. The chain of events that led to it began in Ireland with the overthrow

---

[19] Marie Therese Flanagan (2010), *The Transformation of the Irish Church in the Twelfth and Thirteenth Centuries*. Woodbridge: The Boydell Press, pp. 39–40.

of the king of Leinster, Diarmaid Mac Murchú (Dermot MacMurrough) (1110–71) by an alliance led by Tigernán Ó Ruairc (Tiernán O'Rourke) (r. c. 1124–72), the king of Breifne, and Ruaidhrí Ó Conchobhair (Rory O'Connor) (r. 1156–83), the king of Connacht in 1166. Diarmaid traveled to the English port city of Bristol in search of aid for his efforts to regain his lands in Ireland. A number of English and Welsh soldiers volunteered to support him in his quest to regain his lands. Diarmaid returned to Ireland and conquered Wexford in May 1168. However, Dublin refused to support Diarmaid, recognizing his rival, Ruaidhrí, as high king instead. In 1169, a fleet was assembled in England to sail for Ireland that included "seventy heroes, dressed in coats of mail," according to the *Annals of the Four Masters*. Gerald of Wales is more specific regarding the invasion fleet, which he says consisted of "thirty men-at-arms . . . together with sixty men in half-armour, and about three hundred archers and footsoldiers."[20] The most prominent among them was an earl, Richard Fitzgilbert, known as Strongbow, who was to be rewarded with Diarmaid's oldest daughter, Áine, and lands in Ireland. Henry II did not accompany the initial invasion fleet. Neither did Diarmaid, who sent his illegitimate son, Duvenald, aboard the first fleet, which landed in Ireland in May 1170. Meanwhile, Diarmaid made his own way to Ireland with an additional 500 men, thinking that he could make himself high king of Ireland. Henry at first gave his blessing to anyone who wanted to go, but then rescinded it, displaying a degree of ambivalence toward the initial invasion.

A series of military victories by the invaders followed. Waterford fell on 25 August 1170. Dublin followed on 21 September. At Gillemaire, 700 men were killed, including the lord of the Deisi, Ua Faelain, and his son.[21] The king of Ath-chiath, Axall Mac Torcaill, was killed by the invaders. Then, in May 1171, Diarmaid Mac Murchú died, reportedly unrepentant and without having received the Eucharist. Upon Diarmaid's death, the infighting between his natural son Domnall Cáemánach and rival claimants for Leinster began almost immediately. Domnall had been left in a weakened position because his father had been unable to realize his ambition of becoming high king. Prior to the Anglo-Norman invasion of Ireland, internal warfare among Irish kings was common, and the title of *high king* of Ireland was still in play. Things were about to change.

Henry soon launched his own invasion, accompanied by 240 ships (according to the *Annals of Ulster*). He landed near Waterford on 17 October 1171. According to the renowned historian Robin Frame, Henry came "not primarily out of a desire to extend his dominion westwards, but because he was anxious to impose control upon a process of conquest that was taking

[20] Gerald of Wales (1863), *The Historical Works of Giraldus Cambrensis*, edited by Thomas Wright. London: H.G. Bohn, p. 189.

[21] *The Annals of the Four Masters*, http://www.ucc.ie/celt/published/T100005B/index.html.

place almost despite him."[22] The English king spent 2 days at Waterford before making his way to Dublin, which had already been subdued by the invaders. Henry demonstrated his control over the situation first by awarding Leinster to Strongbow instead of to Domnall. Meanwhile, Tigernán Ó Ruairc, Ruaidhrí Ó Conchobhair, and Murchadh Ó Cearbhaill (O'Carroll), the king of Airgialla, prepared to resist the invasion and defeat Strongbow's forces. *The Annals of the Four Masters* says that, after 2 weeks of minor battles, Ó Conchobhair "went against the Leinstermen, with the cavalry of Breifne and Airgialla, to cut down and burn the corn of the Saxons."[23] What followed was also a civil war in which some Irish fought alongside the Anglo-Normans and others opposed them.

Irish kingship and the response to the Anglo-Normans

Several explanations have been offered for the success of the English invasion of Ireland. First, the church in Ireland, which already had a strong Norman influence, viewed Henry favorably. Second, following the argument of Robin Frame, Henry had come to impose order on the conquest, which had originally been undertaken on behalf of the Irish king, Diarmaid Mac Murchú. Knowing this, some Irish chieftains took Henry's side or at least did not take up arms against him. According to the *Annals of Ulster*, the leading men of Munster and Meath immediately pledged their allegiance, as did the men of the Ui-Briuir and Airgialla of Ulidia. Even Diarmaid's enemies in Leinster were not unified, despite their shared opposition to him. Henry certainly did not face unified opposition from the Irish. Third, for a long time, it was a given that the invaders simply possessed military superiority, following the contemporary explanation offered by Gerald of Wales. On this last point, however, Marie Therese Flanagan has argued that there was no marked distinction between Anglo-Norman warfare and that practiced by the Irish before the invasion. The supposed superiority of the English was said to have consisted of better professional training, superior defensive armor, greater reliance on cavalry, and their facility for constructing castles. Furthermore, she points out that there was no clear demarcation between Anglo-Norman and Irish forces since the Irish fought on both sides. Henry's army, in fact, seems to have conquered Ireland not so much because of its military superiority, but rather from a general lack of organized military opposition.[24]

---

[22] Robin Frame (1981), *Colonial Ireland*. Dublin: Helicon, p. 11.
[23] *The Annals of the Four Masters*, http://www.ucc.ie/celt/published/T100005B/index.html.
[24] Marie Therese Flanagan (1996), "Irish and Anglo-Norman Warfare in Twelfth-Century Ireland," in Thomas Bartlett and Keith Jeffery (eds), *A Military History of Ireland*. Cambridge: Cambridge University Press, pp. 52–75.

In 1172, Tigernán Ó Ruairc was beheaded by the Anglo-Normans and their allies, after which his body was hung upside down as a warning to other potential challengers to Anglo-Norman rule. Still, not all of the Irish had completely given up or become reconciled to domination by the foreigners. One source reports that in 1173, 200 English soldiers died at Uí Cheinneslaig in an attack by Domnall Cáemánach Mac Murchú, Diarmaid's son. An alliance between Ruadrí Ó Conchabhair and the king of Munster, Domnall Ua Briain (O'Brien) (r. 1168–94) invaded Ossory in 1173, while Ruadrí's son attacked Strongbow's motte-and-bailey castle at Kilkenny that same year. Domnall MacGillapatrick of Ossory abandoned his territory and took refuge in Waterford, along with many of the residents of Kilkenny. In response to rumors of an assault on Munster, they met an English army at Thurles in 1174, where the Irish won a decisive victory. Few English soldiers were said to have survived the battle, which resulted in a reported 1,700 dead among the defeated army. Ruadrí followed this triumph with additional victories over the English at Meath and west Leinster.

Other kings, however, remained compliant and accepted Henry's authority in Ireland. Resistance faded after Ruadrí failed to take Dublin and decided to retreat west to the Shannon. The death of Domnall Mac Murchú in 1175 effectively brought the rebellion against English rule to an end. English nobles were granted lands in Ireland. In addition to Strongbow, those receiving lands included prominent English nobles such as Hugh de Lacy, who was rewarded with Meath, and lesser soldiers of the king such as Gilbert Popard and Bertram de Verdon, whose grants were located in Louth. Henry and his successors would still face challenges in Ireland. Power changed hands rapidly in twelfth-century Ireland, and Henry could not necessarily count on even the support of sons whose fathers had pledged allegiance to him. Still, a dividing line had been crossed in Irish history. Just as the Norman Conquest of England in 1066 had brought England into closer relationship with the French world politically and economically, Henry II's invasion of Ireland solidified the close connection between Ireland and England. Ireland would not formally regain its legislative independence until the adoption of the Statute of Westminster in 1931.

The Irish church and the Normans

Like William the Conqueror in his invasion of England, Henry II had sailed for Ireland with the blessing of the pope, at least according to Gerald of Wales, whose claim is now generally accepted by historians. In the aftermath of the rebellions against Henry's authority, the papal legate, Gilla Críst Ua Connairche, reinforced papal support for Henry II by encouraging Irish kings who had sworn loyalty to Henry II to keep their oaths or face excommunication by the church.[25] Pope Alexander III (r. 1159–81) personally wrote to Henry in September 1172 reinforcing his support for the king's claim to rule Ireland. Alexander sent separate letters at the same time conveying the same message to Connairche and the Irish kings. Geoffrey Keating in his seventeenth-century history of Ireland credited the Anglo-Normans with doing "much good in Ireland in building churches and giving church lands to clerics for their support . . ."[26] The immediate effects of the Anglo-Norman invasion of Ireland on the church were not altogether salutary, however. Strongbow was accused of committing many acts of theft and sacrilege against the church, in addition to the plunder that he acquired at the expense of the people.

The Anglo-Norman invasion did not bring about a complete change in direction in Irish church history, however. The Synod of Ráth Breasail of 1111 had already imposed a diocesan organization on the Irish church, establishing a parish structure that was already in place before Henry's arrival. Some reform of the diocesan structure took place at the Synod of Kells in 1152, but the basic organization of the Irish church was reaffirmed. St Malachy (1094–1148) promoted the reform of the Irish church as archbishop of Armagh, bishop of Down, and papal legate to Ireland. Mutual interest in reform helped to prepare the way for the cooperation of the Irish clergy with the English church after the Norman invasion.

Monastic reform, in particular, characterized this period and featured the founding of half a dozen major new orders and hundreds of new monasteries and nunneries. New abbeys had already started to flourish in Ireland before the arrival of the English. In this respect, the founding of new nunneries by wealthy Anglo-Irish patrons represented a continuation of a movement, not a new departure in Irish religious history. An increase in formal women's piety was among the important religious changes occurring in the twelfth century in general. In fact, Dianne Hall in her important book, *Women and the Church in Medieval Ireland*, views the nunneries founded following the Anglo-Norman invasion as the third of four distinct periods of new women's religious foundations in Ireland during the Middle Ages.[27] Most of these new foundations were associated with the Augustinian, Benedictine, and Cistercian orders and were not even founded until the second generation of Anglo-Normans in Ireland in the early thirteenth century. Even older monasteries received new life, reflected in the new crosses, carved doorways, and other decorative flourishes that were sometimes added to their

---

[25] Flanagan, *Transformation of the Irish Church*, p. 181.
[26] Keating Geoffrey, *History of Ireland*, http://www.ucc.ie/celt/published/T100054/index.html.
[27] Dianne Hall (2003), *Women and the Church in Medieval Ireland, c. 1140–1540*. Dublin: Four Courts Press, p. 63.

churches.[28] According to Hall, most of the donations for the renovations came from native Irish families. She views the foundation of new abbeys as part of the Anglo-Norman colonization process.

Of the Irish clergy, Gerald of Wales—hardly an unbiased source—praised them for their piety, for performing "with great regularity the services of the psalms, hours, lessons, and prayers," and for employing "their whole time in the offices to which they are appointed." He also made note of their "attention to the rules of abstinence and a spare diet." However, he undermined these complimentary comments by informing his readers that "you will scarcely find one who, after his devotion to long fastings and prayers, does not make up by night for his privations during the day by the enormous quantities of wine and other liquors in which he indulges . . ."[29] Gerald, of course, does not tell the whole story. Some members of the clergy, and their patrons such as the O'Briains in Munster, showed an interest in reform that predated and was separate from the agenda of Rome or Canterbury. Irish clergy preached against violence and often served as mediators between warring parties. Whatever the strengths and weaknesses of individual clerics, or even of the clergy as a whole, the Irish church played an important role in Irish society both before and after the Anglo-Norman conquest.

But the Anglo-Norman conquest did have both short-term and long-term consequences for Ireland. Perhaps most importantly, foreign invasion had once again, as had happened following the Viking invasions, encouraged some Irish leaders to think of Ireland as a single political and cultural entity in need of unified leadership. Whether or not the period that followed represents the birth of Irish nationalism is the opening topic of the next chapter.

---

[28] Françoise Henry (1970), *Irish Art in the Romanesque Period (1020–1170 A.D.)*. Ithaca: Cornell University Press, p. 26.

[29] Gerald of Wales (1863), "The Topography of Ireland," in Thomas Wright (ed.), *The Historical Works of Giraldus Cambrensis*. London: H.G. Bohn, p. 141.

CHAPTER FIVE

Ireland in the high and late middle ages, ca. 1172–ca. 1485

The Scots enemies of the lord king arrived in this land, since whose arrival the Irish of the Leinster mountains, manifestly unable to restrain themselves, put themselves at war against the lord king, just as the other Irish in this land did, and they hostilely invaded, burned, and totally destroyed the aforesaid lands and tenements of the lord king at Bray and indeed all other lands and tenements of divers lieges of the lord king in those parts.

– A WICKLOW COLONIST, ca. 1316[1]

The beginnings of Irish nationalism?

After the occupation of Ireland by the English King Henry II in 1171–72, the next foreign invasion occurred in 1315, when Edward Bruce of Scotland arrived on the island seeking to overthrow English rule and establish his own. His invasion appeared to have a good chance of success. A century and a half of Anglo-Norman rule had not endeared the English to the Irish or vice versa. Though Bruce most likely undertook this enterprise on his own initiative,[2] he quickly gained the support of a number of Gaelic chieftains

---

[1] Quoted in Seán Duffy (2002), "The Bruce Invasion of Ireland: A Revised Itinerary and Chronology," in Seán Duffy (ed.), *Robert the Bruce's Irish Wars: The Invasions of Ireland, 1306–1329*. Stroud, England: Tempus, p. 32.

[2] A. A. M. Duncan (1988), "The Scots' Invasion of Ireland," in R. R. Davies (ed.), *The British Isles, 1100–1500: Comparisons, Contrasts, and Connections*. Edinburgh: John Donald, p. 104.

and was crowned king of Ireland in 1316. The chronicler Father John Clyn recorded that "almost all of the Irish of the land adhered to [the Scots] with only a very few keeping faith and fealty [with the English]."[3] Irish forces joined the Scots in raiding and plundering Anglo-Norman towns, churches, and monasteries, most notably the town of Dundalk, an important frontier town north of Dublin that had been established by Henry II. The invading troops also burned the town of Athlone in north-central Ireland, putting an end to what had been an important medieval Anglo-Norman outpost. At the time, it seemed as if the Scots—who had just secured their own independence at the Battle of Bannockburn under Edward's brother, Robert Bruce, in 1314—were destined to assist their Celtic counterparts across the Irish Sea in their own liberation from English rule. Robert personally came to the assistance of his brother's cause in Ireland in the winter of 1316–17, leading his troops into the heart of Munster in the southwest.

Some Irish chieftains did oppose the Scots, while some Anglo-Norman lords left for England to reaffirm their loyalty to King Edward II (r. 1307–27). However, it was the landing at Youghal in County Cork of Edward II's lieutenant and royal justiciar, Roger Mortimer, along with a thousand English troops, on Holy Thursday in 1317 that marked the beginning of the end of the brief reign of Edward Bruce in Ireland. Mortimer arrived with the express purpose of driving the Scots out of Ireland. At the Battle of Faughart in 1318, an Anglo-Irish army destroyed Bruce's forces, killing the Scottish leader in the process. But the success of Mortimer's invasion did not so much demonstrate the strength of the English position in Ireland as Bruce's short-lived reign demonstrated its weaknesses. The widespread recognition that Bruce's coronation had received and the support of Domnal O'Neill, the king of Ulster whose grandfather had held the title of High King of Ireland, were clear warning signals of deep-seated resistance to English rule. Furthermore, combined with the defeat that English forces had suffered in Scotland, Bruce's assault on the English position in Ireland was emblematic of the general weakness that would characterize the reign of Edward II. Finally, the Bruce invasion came at the beginning of a century of war, plague, and economic difficulties that would render Ireland of peripheral concern to the English monarchy.

Although Bruce's invasion falls in the middle of the period covered by this chapter, it is a useful starting point because it reflects much about the previous 150 years and anticipates much about the century and a half that followed it. In the immediate aftermath of Henry II's military occupation, only Connacht and Ulster had held out from submitting to Henry's authority. In those areas under Henry's control, Irish chieftains essentially became Norman-style vassals, holding their lands as fiefs from the king.

---

[3] *The Annals of Ireland by Friar John Clyn* (2007), edited and translated, with an Introduction by Bernadette Williams. Dublin: Four Courts Press, p. 162.

They became subject to the accompanying feudal obligations of rendering military service when necessary as well as paying an annual tribute for the use of their lands. Henry III (r. 1216–72) reinforced the legal claims of the English crown to Irish territory in a 1254 charter that clearly delineated the principle that Ireland belonged to the English king in perpetuity. Henry II's invasion had therefore profoundly altered the course of Irish history, even though the full effects of his conquest would not begin to show up until almost a century later. In fact, the Anglo-Norman Conquest of Ireland was followed by a period of relative peace and stability. But, again, a real dividing line had been crossed nonetheless. In addition to the submission of the Irish chieftains, Anglo-Norman noblemen, such as Richard Clare or Richard Fitzgilbert, arrived to occupy certain lands in the name of the king. In the areas directly controlled by these noblemen, the Anglo-Normans introduced a more centralized form of feudalism similar to that which William I had imposed on England in the eleventh century.

Henry's successor, Richard the Lionhearted (r. 1189–99) was preoccupied with the attempted reconquest of the Holy Land in what was known as the King's Crusade, but his younger brother and successor John (r. 1199–1216) took a strong interest in Ireland. John had made his first visit to Ireland in 1185, arriving in Waterford on 25 April and returning to England 8 months later. Unlike Richard, John was a secular-minded monarch who sought to centralize and extend his authority over his kingdoms. He insisted on his full rights as overlord of the territories that had been conquered by his father, including the right to issue common law writs in Meath over the head of his justiciar, William Marshall. John was determined to follow in his father's footsteps in asserting royal authority at the expense of the feudal nobility in both Ireland and England. In fact, John was so determined to attack the power of the leading feudal lords, that he was willing to make concessions to the church, the towns, and even native Irish chieftains in order to gain their support. He pursued many of his father's policies, such as granting town charters, as he did for Limerick sometime around 1197.

In 1210, John sent a register of writs to Ireland, bringing his territories there under the jurisdiction of English Common Law, which had already been introduced there in the 1190s. Itinerant justices—which had been central to the expansion of royal justice under Henry II—were now to travel throughout Ireland to hear the most serious criminal cases. John had gained English baronial approval for this measure, but he wanted to weaken their authority in both Ireland and Wales as well. In short, John wished to extend his authority over as much of Ireland as possible. But in the end, John's efforts in Ireland foundered on his difficulties in England, which led him to accept the Magna Carta (Great Charter) in 1215. Faced with a baronial uprising under the leadership of the archbishop of Canterbury, Stephen Langton, John made significant concessions toward the ancient feudal privileges of the nobility. In Ireland, badly in need of allies, he restored the kingdom of Meath to Walter de Lacy (d. 1241) 5 years after he had declared the lands

of Walter and his brother, Hugh (d. 1242) forfeited. He also abandoned his
claims to issue common law writs there.

Throughout the reign of John's successor, Henry III (1216–73), Anglo-
Norman rule and culture continued to coexist with their Gaelic counterparts.
In the medieval period, political success in both England and Ireland could
wildly vary according to the personal qualities of individual rulers. In his
entry for the year 1224, the author of the *Annals of Connacht* described the
king of Connacht, Toirrdel bac Ó Conchobair, as "the king who carried out
the most plundering and burnings against Galls and Gaels who opposed
him" and "who most blinded, killed, and mutilated rebellious and disaffected
subjects," but also as "the king who best established peace and tranquility
of all the kings of Ireland" and "who most comforted clerks and poor men
with food and fire on the floor of his own habitation."[4] That the annalist
could also describe him as "perfect in every good quality" is an indication
not to accept these hyperbolic generalizations at face value, but we are
still left with the impression of a ruler who had, for better or worse, made
a significant difference in the lives of those who lived under his control.
A succession crisis in Connacht opened the door to greater Anglo-Norman
influence, but rival claimants to the throne there made this anything but
a smooth process, as when Fedlimid Ó Conchobair smashed the castles
built by Richard de Burgh in 1232. Hugh de Lacy fought the Anglo-Irish
government to a standstill and forced it to recognize his possession of Ulster,

FIGURE 5.1 *Ruins of an Anglo-Norman Castle, Clonmacnoise. Photo by Millie
Campbell.*

---

[4] *The Annals of Connacht* (1970), edited by A. Martin Freeman. Dublin: The Dublin Institute
for Advanced Studies, p. 3.

at least until his death in 1242. The powerful ruling families of Connacht and Munster both recognized Brian O Neill as high king of Ireland in 1258, only 4 years after the charter that unequivocally made Ireland the property of the English crown. Henry III found this extremely presumptuous, but at the time, there was little he could do about it. He did send his son Edward to represent his interests there, but his presence alone was not enough to bolster royal authority in Ireland.

Brian O Neill was a strong force to be reckoned with in the north, determined as he was to resist the spread of English authority. Fortunately, for Henry and for English rule in Ireland, O Neill died, along with a number of other Irish nobles from Connacht, at the Battle of Downpatrick in 1260. Unfortunately, for Henry, he soon had his hands full with rebellious barons in England, led by Simon de Montfort, who captured Henry at the Battle of Lewes in May 1264. That same year, his son Edward secured the support of a powerful ally in Ireland when he awarded Walter de Burgh, the powerful Lord of Connacht, with the additional title of earl of Ulster, thus combining two important ancient kingdoms in the hands of a single individual. In 1264, the powerful Geraldine family, whose main lands were in Leinster and Munster, waged a particularly destructive war with de Burgh. They succeeded in capturing and imprisoning the justiciar of Ireland, Richard de la Rochelle and other leading figures of the opposition. De Burgh, however, had taken control of a number of manors and castles that belonged to the Geraldines in Connacht. Meanwhile, in just the very next year, Edward—benefiting from Irish baronial support—defeated Simon de Montfort at the Battle of Evesham, after which he became de facto ruler of England and Ireland.

When Henry died in 1272, Edward inherited not only the throne of England but royal claims to authority in Wales and Ireland as well. At his accession, some areas of Ireland remained under royal control while others were in the hands of vassals of the crown. As a king, Edward I (r. 1272–1307) spared no expense in bringing Wales under English control in the years from 1282 to 1284. Edward was no less a secular, aggressive, and domineering monarch than John had been, but he had already learned that Ireland presented special problems. A century had passed since Henry II's invasion and Ireland was far from being pacified, as the recent war in Connacht had demonstrated. Not enough settlers had come from England to occupy the entire island. If Edward knew that the heavy-handed approach he tried in Wales would not work in Ireland, this knowledge did not stop him from trying to permanently alter England's state of affairs there. Furthermore, he did have some advantages in Ireland, compared to in Wales, such as the precedent of the introduction of English common law there. Edward began his reign in Ireland by appointing as justiciar his friend Geoffrey de Geneville, who had been accompanying the king on a crusade to the Holy Land at the time. This act demonstrates the importance that Edward attached to Ireland. The role of the justiciar, a position that dated to the twelfth century, was that of the "military chief of the colony, the head of its civil administration and its supreme judge."[5] In England, the justiciar for all intents and purposes ruled in the king's absence; in Ireland, he was equally powerful. Geneville served 3 years in the position, with mixed success, but by about 1290, it had appeared that Edward had gotten the situation in Ireland under control, allowing him to derive economic support from the Anglo-Norman lordships that were now more secure from attacks by Gaelic chieftains. Such stability proved to be extremely short-lived because Edward's troubles in France and Scotland created new opportunities for those in Ireland seeking to break free from English influence. When Edward's Italian bankers, the Riccardi, went bankrupt in Lucca in 1294, he found himself in desperate financial straits that threatened to undo each of his colonial and foreign policy objectives. English colonists put pressure on Edward to address their concerns about the vulnerability of their position in Ireland at an Irish Parliament in 1297. Edward, anxious "to establish peace more firmly" in Ireland, included a particularly wide representation from the Irish community.[6] Confronted with rebellion in Scotland and war in France, Edward had little choice but to appease the Anglo-Norman leaders of Ireland. Legislation of that year authorized the formation of private armies in Ireland, but only in those frontier territories considered most at risk. One such territory was the county of Kildare, which was on the southwestern border of the areas on the east coast of Ireland directly under English control that later became known as the *Pale*. In 1297, Kildare was granted to the Anglo-Norman Fitzgerald family, which subsequently became one of the most powerful families in Ireland. Two additional powerful earldoms extended Anglo-Irish authority further in the direction of the southwest. The earldom of Ormond separated Kildare from the earldom of Desmond, which extended to Ireland's southern coast.

Following Edward's death, the political weakness of Edward II encouraged the rebellions led by the Bruce brothers in Scotland and Ireland. Even after Edward Bruce's defeat, Irish chieftains learned the lesson of Anglo-Norman vulnerability and sought to challenge it at every opportunity, even if they had not all supported Bruce's invasion. English lords in Ireland found themselves increasingly vulnerable and their position was not significantly strengthened by several English military expeditions in the second half of the fourteenth century. The English became increasingly subject to raids from the Wicklow Mountains south of Dublin, while Roscommon (east of Connacht) reverted to Gaelic rule after a six-decade occupation. English interest in Ireland diminished as involvement in the Hundred Years War with France, which began in 1337 and was fought intermittently until 1453,

---

[5] A. J. Otway-Ruthven (2008), "The Chief Governors of Medieval Ireland," in Peter Crooks (ed.), *Government, War and Society in Medieval Ireland: Essays by Edmund Curtis, A.J. Otway-Ruthven, and James Lydon*. Dublin: Four Courts Press, p. 79.

[6] James Lydon (1997), "Parliament and the Community of Ireland," in J. Lydon (ed.), *Law and Disorder in Thirteenth-Century Ireland*. Dublin: Four Courts Press, p. 125.

took priority. The Dublin administration was frequently left to fend for itself and faced challenges from Gaelic leaders such as the O'Kellys of Ui Maine and Art MacMurrough Kavanagh (ca. 1357–1416), the King of Leinster.

For their part, the English continued to regard the Irish, even their leading chieftains, as barbarians who did not follow the normal rules of protocol or civilized behavior and thus were not deserving of their own autonomy. In 1366, the English Statutes of Kilkenny prohibited intermarriage between the English and the natives of Ireland, while also declaring the Irish ineligible to receive church benefices. In 1388, Richard II (r. 1377–99) had spared the lives of a number of disaffected nobles in England—mainly as a result of the pleading of his wife Anne according to the chronicler Henry Knighton—and settled on presumably the next worst punishment after death: exile to Ireland with no possibility of return.[7] Richard placed restrictions upon their travel and divided them into pairs as he dispersed them to their new locations. But the vast majority of English nobles who held possessions in Ireland were now absentee landowners with little direct knowledge of the local population. This problem had increasingly troubled Edward III (r. 1327–77), who was concerned about the potential consequences of a lack of direct representation in Ireland. Not all English landlords had abandoned Ireland in the fourteenth century, but some had decided to cut bait and sell their lands before invasion or economic depression ruined them. Edward actually encouraged some of them to do so, preferring more reliable vassals, even if he had to promote new families to the Irish ruling class.[8]

Richard II led a new expedition to Ireland aimed at reasserting royal authority in 1394, the first English king to set foot on Irish soil in almost 200 years—since John's visit in 1210. The English found it necessary to educate Irish kings scheduled to be knighted by Richard II in forms of behavior appropriate to an audience before the English king.[9] But any gains made in Ireland were undercut just a few years later by more difficulties back in England. In 1399, Richard II was actually deposed by his cousin, Henry Bolingbroke, and died in captivity shortly thereafter. Richard's downfall had significant implications for Ireland, because Bolingbroke, now King Henry IV, would have to fight to solidify his claim to the English throne and was forced to abandon Richard's Irish project.

To what extent did these developments, particularly the support given to Edward Bruce's Scottish invasion, reflect or give rise to the beginnings of Irish nationalism? Shortly after landing in Ireland, Edward Bruce and Domnal

[7] Henry Knighton (1995), *Knighton's Chronicle, 1337–1396*, edited and translated by G. H. Martin. Oxford: Clarendon Press, p. 503.

[8] Brendan Smith (2007), "Lordship in the British Isles, c. 1320–c. 1360: the Ebb Tide of the English Empire?," in Huw Price and John Watts (eds), *Power and Identity in the Middle Ages: Essays in Memory of Rees Davies*. Oxford: Oxford University Press, p. 161.

[9] David Carpenter (2003), *The Struggle for Mastery, 1066–1284*. Oxford: Oxford University Press, p. 24.

O'Neill recounted the history of Ireland as an independent territory prior to the Norman invasion in a Remonstrance sent to the Pope, now resident at Avignon just outside French territory. They sought papal support against the English and appealed on what might seem to be nationalistic grounds. However, when Richard II visited Ireland in 1394–95, he received great respect from the Gaels who seem to have regarded him as a great king. After Richard's expedition, he was said to have gained "power and honor from all Irishmen."[10] This impression, however, did not long survive Richard's 1399 expedition—and neither did Richard. It is clear that English rule in medieval Ireland was highly problematic and was anything but uniformly accepted or successful. Still, it is difficult to speak of a coherent nationalism in medieval Ireland because of the lack of political unity among the native rulers and people. This does not mean, however, that traces of nationalist sentiment were nonexistent, particularly in the literature of the period.

Medieval Irish literature

Among the numerous effects that the Anglo-Norman invasion had upon Ireland was the influence that it had upon the culture of the island. But continuities were as important as the appearance of new trends, particularly, the political role that literature, especially poetry, had occupied in the Irish past. In the Gaelic areas of Ireland, poets composed elegies to support the dynastic claims of their patrons. Throughout early medieval Ireland, professional poets known as *fili* preserved and passed down the history and genealogy of their regions. These traditions survived the Norman Conquest and continued to dominate Irish literary culture until the end of the Middle Ages. But at the same time, the pervasive influence of the Normans, as seen through the construction of so many new castles and churches, had its influence on Irish literature, too. In addition, the introduction of new religious orders, particularly that of the Franciscans in the thirteenth century, changed Irish literary culture significantly. Nor was Ireland completely isolated from the cultural revival that medieval scholars refer to as the Twelfth-Century Renaissance.

Despite these new factors influencing the culture of medieval Ireland, almost all scholarship and literature were expected to adhere to and further previously established traditions. *The Yellow Book of Lecan* and *The Great Book of Lecan* both helped to preserve a collection of literary and historical materials that testify to the strength and vitality of letters in medieval Ireland. *The Yellow Book of Lecan* contains 17 sections that reflect the predilections

---

[10] Anthony Goodman (2006), "The British Isles Imagined," in Linda Clark (ed.), *The Fifteenth Century VI: Identity and Insurgency in the Late Middle Ages.* Woodbridge: The Boydell Press, p. 10.

of the authors and compilers, who were associated with the MacFirbisigh family, with one part probably written by Gilla-Iosa, son of Donnchad Mór MacFirbisigh, in 1380. Gilla-Ioss MacFirbisigh and others wrote *The Great Book of Lecan* around 1416.[11] Earlier, the mythological narrative, the *Táin Bó Cúainge* (The Cattle Raid of Cooley), appeared in a newly-written version in *The Book of Leinster* in the early twelfth century. Yet the same author seems to have added a new heroic myth entitled *Cath Ruis na Ríg* or *The Battle of Rosnarec*.[12] In short, old traditions were infused with new material, while some literary tropes made their first appearance after the Norman Conquest.

Traditional Irish narratives are generally divided into four separate cycles, all of which were transmitted and some of which were added during the High Middle Ages. These included the Ulster Cycle, the Mythological Cycle, the Historical Cycle, and the Finn or Fianna Cycle. The Finn Cycle could almost be considered a new twelfth-century addition because of the paucity of stories that belonged to it prior to this later period. This cycle centers on legends associated with Fionn mac Cumhaill (Finn MacCool) and his loyal warriors known as the Fianna. The magical folktales associated with Finn date back to the eighth century, but it was not until the early thirteenth century that his cycle achieved something like an equal status to the *Táin*.[13] Like the legendary King Arthur in Britain, he even appears in some of the early historical accounts by medieval authors. Perhaps because the other three cycles were more fully developed, twelfth-century authors were able to take greater liberties with Finn, just as authors such as Chretien de Troyes and Geoffrey of Monmouth were inventing new aspects of the Arthurian legends. In addition to the four Irish cycles, twelfth-century Irish authors converted stories from Greek and Roman mythology, such as the destruction of Troy (*Togail Troí*), the wanderings of Ulysses (*Merugud Ulix*), and the civil war of the Romans (*In Cam Cathorda*) into their native language.

The fact that Gaelic literature not only survived but also continued to flourish to the end of the fifteenth century despite the extensive Anglo-Norman cultural influence testifies to an intense and lasting cultural pride on the part of the Irish. Poets were seen as central to that cultural mission. The Abbot of Boyle, Donogh Mor O'Daly (d. 1244) was known as the Ovid of Ireland. O'Daly's poems included "In Praise of the Blessed Virgin Mary," "On the Vanity and Instability of Human Life," and "On the Goodness of God, and the Merits of Heaven," any of which might have been written by St Bernard of Clairvaux a century earlier. As often happens when cultures meet, the older tradition is revitalized and transformed by the influence of

---

[11] J. E. Williams and Patrick K. Ford (1992), *The Irish Literary Tradition*. Cardiff: University of Wales Press, p. 123.
[12] Eleanor Knott and Gerard Murphy (1966), *Early Irish Literature*. New York: Barnes and Noble, p. 154.
[13] Williams and Ford (1992), *The Irish Literary Tradition*, p. 126.

the new, even as it seeks to retain its own identity. Religious poetry emanating from the monasteries of Ireland that predate the Norman period contributed an important strain to the literary tradition of the High Middle Ages. It is not surprising that many poems from the period would deal with religious themes since most educated poets would have received their education from the church, which also served as a patron for their works. For example, poems petitioning Mary or the other saints to intercede with her Son were not uncommon.

Still, the dominant form of poetry in medieval Ireland was known as bardic poetry, which celebrated the deeds of its subjects, usually the poet's patrons or the members of the patron's dynasty. One example would be the 168-verse poem written by Tadhg Mor O'Higgin to celebrate Magnus O'Conor, the king of Connacht in the late thirteenth century. The poets or *fili* of medieval Ireland frequently inherited their positions from their fathers, so family connections between bard and patron often ran deep. The most prominent of the *fili* could achieve virtual noble status themselves, especially those who achieved the rank of ollamh, the highest to which a bard could aspire. Ollamhs generally achieved their status by vote of those already holding the title. The main difference between a *fili* and an ordinary bard was in their level of education; the *fili* were considered scholars as well as poets, whereas bards were frequently illiterate. But the distinction between them was waning in the High Middle Ages and they would have appeared indistinguishable to the Anglo-Irish residents of the island. In medieval Ireland, the secular bards actually came closest to expressing sentiments that resemble modern Irish nationalism. This certainly helps to explain the animosity that English authorities had toward Gaelic poetry, even though it did not reflect specifically anti-English sentiment at that time. Moreover, the Irish literary cycles, such as the Finn Cycle, did not contain anything resembling contemporary political analysis.

Even so, the English authorities in Ireland not only failed to encourage the perpetuation of this native literary tradition, but also actively sought to restrict it. The 1366 Statutes of Kilkenny not only outlawed Irish-English marriages and restricted church benefices, but also forbade the use of the Gaelic language by those of English or Anglo-Irish descent. As it turned out, however, the statute proved unenforceable and Gaelic literature continued to flourish even in those areas nominally under English authority. The Anglo-Irish poet and landowner Gerald Fitzgerald (1357–98) even incorporated some of the heroic tales of Gaelic Ireland into his own poetry.[14] Perhaps for this reason, Irish literature during the Middle Ages does not come across as being specifically anti-English or anti-Norman. Furthermore, the Norman version of the French language had its own influence on Irish letters, just as it had in England since 1066. It would be some time before the English

---

[14] Paul F. State (2009), *A Brief History of Ireland*. New York: Checkmark Books, p. 80.

would effect the virtual destruction of the literary traditions of medieval Ireland, but in the meantime the Anglo-Norman conquest continued to have a profound impact on the Irish.

The impact of the Anglo-Normans

The most visible impact of the Anglo-Normans in Ireland was the widespread appearance of motte-and-bailey castles that dotted the land and served as the main symbols of military occupation there, as they had in England. The initial stage of the conquest, as such tend to be, was quite violent as Henry's nobles grasped as much of the land and wealth of the conquered territory as they were able to. But the English influence on Ireland—as was often the case in the Middle Ages when one group of people expanded into another's territory—came more from the people who migrated to their new lands than from the soldiers who had paved the way for that to happen. Robert Bartlett regards Ireland as part of the French "aristocratic diaspora" that saw nobles of French descent occupy lands and establish new dynasties throughout Europe and the Middle East beginning in the eleventh century.[15] But they did not come to their new territories alone. Almost the entire eastern seaboard of Ireland had been settled and occupied by a large number of English agricultural laborers, craftsmen, and clergymen who had found new opportunities across the Irish Sea in the first half century after Henry II's invasion.

The Anglo-Norman occupation swallowed up Meath in the north-central region and Limerick in the southwest and encompassed the southern half of Ulster in the northeast as well. At their northernmost outpost of Carrickfergus, the English built a 90-foot-high castle keep that would serve as a constant reminder of their presence there. The conquerors made no apologies for the conquest, which was accepted as bestowing rights upon the victors according to the political ideology that prevailed during this period. In Ireland, at least, native rulers were generally invited to retain their power if they would swear allegiance to their new overlord. But the Anglo-Norman conquest of Ireland was an ongoing process by which, beginning with John in the early thirteenth century, English monarchs sought opportunities for territorial expansion whenever time and circumstances permitted. John pushed the English boundary past the Shannon as far as Killaloe in the west. Whenever territorial expansion did occur, English military and ecclesiastical architecture generally followed. But it should be pointed out that historians of medieval Ireland have concluded that what it meant to fall under Anglo-Norman lordship could vary widely from place to place. In Ireland, English authority could

---

[15] Robert Bartlett (1993), *The Making of Europe: Conquest, Colonization, and Cultural Change, 950–1350*. Princeton: Princeton University Press.

be very loose and vague indeed, especially in the claimed areas farthest from Dublin. Subinfeudation, or the process of dividing fiefs among a number of vassals, became common, particularly in the midlands such as Leinster and Meath, allowing for the chiefs of smaller tribes to continue to exercise authority over their lands. It made a difference that the ruling government for Ireland had its center in England and that its rulers had widespread lands and interests in France as well, leaving them continually distracted.

The Anglo-Norman conquest of Ireland would be as transformative as had been the Norman conquest of England during the preceding century. But this does not mean that it was identical or that the political arrangements that governed the relationships between rulers and ruled were exactly the same. For example, the Normans incorporated many Anglo-Saxon legal and political traditions in developing a common law and administration for their new English kingdom. In Ireland, the assumption from the beginning was that English common law would be transferred wholesale to Ireland. In addition, Norman government of England had meant the development of a common law that applied to the entire country. In Ireland, John's register of writs applied mainly to the English settlers in the lands that were already directly under royal control, despite a 1246 letter that declared the king's intention that common law apply equally in England and Ireland.

One of the most powerful men to rule Ireland was William Marshall (c. 1146–1219), a leading knight and royal official whose service to the crown spanned the reigns of four kings. Yet, Marshall only spent 5 years in Ireland (1207–12) and also had extensive lands in England and Wales to claim his attention. Furthermore, John himself encroached upon Marshall's authority by insisting that all appeals in Leinster and Meath be made directly to the king. Yet, as determined as John was to rule Ireland, troubles at home prevented him from exercising his full authority—even in the lands under Anglo-Norman control. Nonetheless, by the end of John's reign, Ireland had irrevocably become a part of the larger Anglo-Norman sphere of influence that dominated Western Europe at that time.

Although the tendency today is to condemn any territorial conquest as imperialistic, the Normans did provide a measure of political stability in most lands that they occupied, as well as a measure of defense against wanton raids from rival kingdoms. As the Normans had done in France, Sicily, and England, the English established a new ruling aristocracy in Ireland that carried with them their own air of authority. As elsewhere, they would become transformed even as they were creating a new political and cultural dynamic. But in Ireland, the positive benefits of these changes were offset at least in part by the levels of discrimination employed against the native inhabitants of the island. Furthermore, the relative lack of focus placed upon Ireland by Henry II and his successors after the conquest prevented Ireland from enjoying long periods of peace and stability. Finally, the incomplete nature of the conquest meant that significant parts of Ireland would not experience whatever benefits did derive from Anglo-Norman rule.

The English impacted the church and Christianity in Ireland in several ways as well. Immediately after the conquest, allegiance to Rome was proclaimed by a council of leading churchmen (ensuring that church services in England and Ireland would be identical). However, nowhere would the discrimination against native Irish inhabitants be more pronounced than in the case of the church. Not a single native Irishman occupied the archiepiscopal see of Dublin after 1180; most who did were English appointees of the crown. A royal proclamation disseminated in 1217 went so far as to reserve all Irish bishoprics for Anglo-Irish officials. Even though a subsequent compromise preserved one-third of the bishoprics for Irish clerics, the Irish never got over their resentment of the original proclamation. There is no questioning the pervasive impact of the English on Ireland, but there is also no denying the creative native impulses that responded to that influence. The English built numerous churches, but ecclesiastical construction flourished during the same period in those parts of the island that lay beyond Norman control. If the Normans did not bring institutional education to Ireland, they did not prevent members of the Irish clergy from seeking education abroad at the new universities of Oxford, Cambridge, and Paris. Though the Franciscan and Dominican orders established themselves in Ireland in the thirteenth century, they did not become part of the system of land ownership and so tended to identify with the interests of the Gaelic inhabitants. Thus, even the influence of the Church had varying results depending on the particular circumstances in different regions.

The influence of the Church

During the High Middle Ages, the church in Ireland was drawn closer into the orbit of churches that revolved around Rome, and therefore subject to increasing concerns emanating from the Holy See about the exercise of church authority over the morals and spiritual lives of its inhabitants. No sooner had Henry II invaded Ireland in 1171 than Irish bishops were called to Cashel to meet that November to discuss issues of church reform. But it was not as if the Irish Church had neglected these concerns, or that it would later ignore them in areas not under Anglo-Norman control. In fact, the bishops responded quite positively to Henry's initiative and sent a letter to the pope acknowledging their desire to bring their church into conformity with Rome. Not only that, but the Irish church had already been restructured along diocesan lines prior to Henry II's invasion in 1171. As recently as 1152, the Synod of Kells had doubled the number of Irish archbishops to four and restructured diocesan organization in Ireland. Furthermore, the commitment of the Irish church to ecclesiastical reform even predated the papal-sponsored Gregorian Revolution of the eleventh century. But as far as the papacy was concerned, or Henry II for that matter, the Irish church still represented too much of an entity unto itself that needed to be brought in line with the continental church. Fortunately, for them, the momentum building toward reform prior to 1171 continued after the invasion and was sustained well into the thirteenth century. The shared desire for reform led to a general harmony between Norman and Irish clergy during this period.

It should therefore come as no surprise to find that the Irish were willing participants in the movements of monastic reform that swept through Europe in the eleventh and twelfth centuries. This movement was perhaps best embodied by the Cistercian order, founded by an Englishman, Stephen Harding, who helped establish a monastery in the remote French woods of Citeaux so that he and his fellow monks would far remove themselves from the distractions and temptations of the civilized world. It was this order that would have the greatest impact on a reformed Irish monasticism. Having never fully recovered from the destruction of their monasteries at the hands of the Vikings, the Irish welcomed the foreign impetus that promised a strong sense of renewal. After the coming of the Normans, however, Irish monasticism fell under the auspices of orders that originated on the European continent. Instead of reviving the monasteries from the golden age of Celtic Christianity, the new monasteries in Ireland were another product of Anglo-Norman colonialism. If monasticism was revived in Ireland during the High Middle Ages, it was as a part of a new political and religious order shaped by the Anglo-Norman occupation. It should be noted, however, that the first Cistercian abbey in Ireland, Mellifont Abbey in County Louth, was founded in 1142 prior to the invasion, the impact of which should not be exaggerated.

As with the law, the English envisioned no difference between the English and the Irish churches. This vision of unification drew strong support from the papacy, as was reflected in Pope Alexander III's (r. 1159–81) denunciation of the Irish as "uncivilized and undisciplined."[16] In their desire to conform to Roman Christianity, the leaders of the Irish church had unwittingly distanced themselves from their native traditions. At least in this regard, they had aligned themselves with the interests of the conquerors. The bishops who met at Cashel viewed Henry as a valuable ally of the church. This bears a certain amount of irony, given his struggles with his own archbishop of Canterbury, Thomas Becket (1118–70). Becket had been murdered by vassals of the king only the year before Henry arrived in Ireland after a prolonged struggle over the relationship between church and state. As in England, Irish clerics enjoyed the "benefit of the clergy," which gave them the right to be tried in the notoriously more lenient ecclesiastical courts instead of being brought to justice in secular courts, even for crimes against common law. This had been one of the main issues of contention between Henry and Becket—one on which Henry was forced to back down after Becket's assassination, the timing of which worked to the advantage of the Irish clergy.

---

[16] Quoted in Robin Frame (1998), *Ireland and Britain, 1170–1450*. London and Rio Grande: The Hambledon Press, p. 133.

In the thirteenth century, a new wave of reform gained support from the papacy in the form of the establishment of two new orders: the Dominicans and the Franciscans. Francis of Assisi (d. 1226) had gained papal support for his order of mendicant friars from Pope Innocent III (r. 1198–1216), who saw an opportunity to channel Francis's commitment to the poor and downtrodden in the service of the Church. A highly educated priest from Spain named Dominic (d. 1221) became the inspiration for the Dominican order, which focused more on defending orthodox Catholicism through education and the persecution of heretics. By 1225, the Dominicans had already entered Ireland, and the Franciscans followed by 1232. They were followed by the Carmelites in 1270 and the Augustinian friars in 1282. Of all of these orders, the Franciscans became the most predominant in Ireland with houses established both along the coast and at interior sites such as Athlone, Castledermot, and Kilkenny.[17] But the Dominicans had 25 houses in Ireland themselves by the end of the thirteenth century.[18] As previously mentioned, both orders had a reputation for being sympathetic to the native people of Ireland.

These orders did much to revitalize Christianity in Ireland, but when the church began to experience serious problems on the Continent, these affected the church in Ireland as well. From the height of the papacy under the assertive and domineering former canon lawyer Innocent III to the pontificate of the irascible and confrontational Boniface VIII (r. 1294–1303), thirteenth-century popes had insisted on their rights to veto the election of bishops and abbots and to exempt the clergy from secular taxation. These principles had been affirmed by leading churchmen in Ireland. However, Boniface's death following a brief period of captivity under the French king Philip IV left the papacy in crisis. When a Frenchman, Raymond Bertrand de Got, was elected pope in 1305, he took the name Clement V (r. 1305–14). A few years later, he relocated the papacy to Avignon, a town on the Rhone River just outside French territory at the time. Avignon remained the new papal capital until 1378, a period known at the time as the "Babylonian Captivity of the Church." This phrase implied that the papacy no more belonged in Avignon than the Jews had belonged in Babylon in biblical times. When Europe became divided between two rival popes—one in Rome and one in Avignon—during what became known as the Great Schism (1378–1417), the Irish people suffered along with the rest of Europe. The Schism created uncertainty about the validity of their sacraments, which now depended upon whether their leaders had backed the true pope. What made the situation even worse in Ireland was the existence of a number of people who supported the French

---

[17] A. J. Otway-Ruthven (1968), *A History of Medieval Ireland*. London: Ernest Benn, p. 137.
[18] Michael Richter (1988), *Medieval Ireland: The Enduring Tradition*. New York: St. Martin's Press, p. 129.

popes in Avignon out of hostility to the English, who supported the Roman pope because of their wars with the French.

The cumulative effect of these developments, of course, was the further weakening of papal authority. For example, the English parliament had responded to the residence of the papacy at Avignon with legislation designed to limit appeals outside of the country (the Statute of Praemunire, 1353) and to restrict the right of the papacy to make ecclesiastical appointments in England and, by extension, Ireland (the Statute of Provisors, 1351). Despite the attempt of the English to enforce these measures in Ireland, by the late fourteenth century, anti-English feeling there actually led to support for papal candidates, at least in the areas outside English control. The refusal of the English government in Dublin to recognize these candidates caused additional confusion within the church and among its members. Bishops outside of Anglo-Norman-controlled areas needed the support of the Gaelic kings within whose territories there dioceses lay. They therefore faced the problem of conflicting allegiances. Throughout the Middle Ages, such conflicts had posed serious problems for the church, especially for leading church officials such as bishops and abbots who were frequently appointed more on the basis of their political allegiance than for their moral or spiritual qualifications. The issue of laymen controlling clerical appointments, which was known as lay investiture, was at the center of the Gregorian reform movement of the eleventh century. In the later Middle Ages, the crisis of the fourteenth-century papacy gave way to still more troublesome problems confronting the church in the fifteenth, when abuses such as absenteeism, pluralism, and simony continued and further eroded people's confidence in the church as an institution. These centuries were also characterized by population decline and economic hard times, during which men became priests and men and women often entered religious orders without a true spiritual vocation. Professor Otway-Ruthven has called attention to the abundant evidence of negligence on the part of both the regular and the secular clergy toward their spiritual duties in fifteenth-century Ireland.[19] These conditions spawned yet another reform movement, this time focusing on the argument that church councils held greater authority than the papacy and ought to be called upon to fix the church's problems and restore its reputation.

Still, whatever anyone might have thought of Rome or the papacy, the Roman Church played a critical role in the lives of the people throughout Europe, including Ireland. For example, the church was the main source of education for those who wished or could afford to receive it. When the earl of Ulster proposed the founding of a new chantry at either Loughrea or Ballintubber, the accompanying educational opportunities were cited as an additional benefit.[20] However, Ireland did not get its first university

---

[19] Otway-Ruthven, *History of Medieval Ireland*, p. 141.
[20] Ibid., p. 143.

until Pope Clement V authorized the establishment of one at St Patrick's Cathedral in 1311, which had an uneven reputation until it closed for good during the 1530s at the time of the Reformation. So opportunities for higher education at home were nonexistent in the High Middle Ages and extremely limited in the fourteenth and fifteenth centuries. But the Irish with a religious vocation were not lacking for opportunities to join religious houses, which outnumbered those in Wales and Scotland together by more than two to one.[21] Furthermore, additional reorganization of the church along parochial lines in the thirteenth century provided a greater measure of stability and must have given the laity a stronger sense of identification with their parish, at least in those areas under Anglo-Norman control. Some bishops and abbeys also owned huge tracts of land, which would have placed large numbers of serfs and tenants directly under them. Both monasteries and bishoprics derived income from the parishes that were located within their dioceses.

A defining characteristic of the church in Ireland was its role in the relationship between ruler and ruled. As supporters of Norman rule in Ireland, Irish clerics had a profound impact on the degree of acceptance that it received among the native populations. When Edward Bruce invaded Ireland in 1315, support from the clergy greatly increased his chances of success and indicated the extent of disenchantment with English rule at that time. In 1317, the Irish king Domnal O'Neill sent a letter to Pope John XXII that became known as the "Remonstrance of the Irish Princes." O'Neill recounted to the pope a variety of complaints about the English in Ireland in an effort to gain papal sanction for Edward Bruce's authority in Ireland. His list of grievances included their failure to adhere to the terms of the 1155 papal bull, "Laudabiliter," which had granted Henry II control over the Irish church. The situation of the church in Ireland demonstrates that developments in late medieval Ireland must be seen in a larger context. This is also true because Ireland did not exist in isolation from the other components of the Isles, as Bruce's invasion so well demonstrates.

Irish society in the high and late middle ages

In the meantime, a dividing line in Irish social history occurred in August 1348 with the outbreak of bubonic plague, subsequently referred to as the Black Death. This epidemic, which swept throughout Europe in 1348–49, had entered the continent in 1347 via flea-infested black rats that brought the disease with them aboard ships sailing from the Black Sea region of central Asia. In Ireland, Friar John Clyn estimated that 14,000 died of the plague in Dublin alone between August and Christmas. He reported that "the disease

---

[21] Bruce M. S. Campbell (2008), "Benchmarking Medieval Economic Development: England, Wales, Scotland, and Ireland, c. 1290." *Economic History Review*, 61, 900.

entirely stripped vills, cities, castles and towns of inhabitants of men, so that scarcely anyone would be able to live in them."[22] The numbers of deaths in towns and the more populated Anglo-Norman areas were perhaps more conspicuous, but many died in the countryside as well, including members of the native ruling class. The *Annals of Connacht* describe "a great plague in Moylurg and all Ireland" in 1349 and record the deaths of several prominent figures, including at least one king, Risderd O Raigillig of East Brefne.[23] An estimated 40 per cent of the population of Europe died in the first wave of this pandemic; Ireland suffered proportionately and its population seems not to have recovered by the end of the fourteenth century. The reduction in population meant less need for agricultural produce, leading to lower prices and lower rents, leaving the nobility faced with both a decline in income and a serious shortage of labor. Mortality from the plague was even higher in the towns, where the Anglo-Irish population suffered disproportionately to the native Irish who lived in the countryside.

This was true in both England and Ireland, but by the 1360s, the English nobility had almost totally lost interest in their Irish lands, leading to an increase in the number of absentee landlords that threatened to undo English power there. Those who did remain, like the de Burghs, an ancient Norman family, increasingly adopted Gaelic practices, took Irish spouses, and underwent a transition from Anglo-Norman to Anglo-Irish. This provides an important part of the context for the Statutes of Kilkenny in 1366, which sought to reinforce the distinction between the English and the Irish in Ireland. The Black Death thus reduced the wealth and power of the nobility and saw a decline in Anglo-Norman influence. What it did not do was alter the basic structure of Irish landed society or the key differences between the Anglo-Norman nobility and the native princes of Gaelic Ireland.

As in the rest of Europe, land ownership and family status became the two markers of social distinction, with the latter being influenced by military prowess in addition to the size of one's territorial possessions. These two factors coalesced in Anglo-Norman lands to reinforce the custom of primogeniture, which ensured that familial lands held together by passing them all down to the eldest son. The introduction of English common law further solidified this practice. In Gaelic Ireland, or the lands not under Anglo-Norman control, territorial possession actually counted for less because of the success that native dynasties had in perpetuating their power. They owed this success to their ability to disperse their property as they saw fit, allowing them to empower those most worthy to succeed them based on their military competence rather than their birth status. However, even before the arrival of the Normans in 1171, land patterns and social relationships had taken on many aspects of feudalism. When the Normans arrived, their particular

---

[22] *Annals of Father John Clyn*, pp. 248, 250.
[23] *The Annals of Connacht*, p. 303.

brand of feudalism—which was extremely hierarchical and emphasized a single overlord of the kingdom—made its mark throughout Ireland.

R. R. Davies has identified three important distinctions that existed at this time between the English aristocracy and the Anglo-Norman nobility in Ireland.[24] The Anglo-Norman nobility in Ireland had a greater degree of freedom with which to exercise their feudal rights since they were farther away from their overlord, the king. In addition, the Anglo-Norman nobility in Ireland tended to be more militaristic than their English counterparts, given their presence on the frontier of English rule with still over half the island not secured under royal authority. Therefore, the nobility in Ireland had to take local circumstances into greater account and display greater flexibility in their exercise of power. However, some commonalities existed as well; for example, they operated under the same set of laws and regulations, and both the English and the Irish nobility tended to subdivide their lands among more supporters than they actually needed. For example, Leinster was subdivided among 180 knights despite only being responsible for providing the king with 100, while about 120 knights held fiefs in Meath, which had responsibility for only 50.[25]

As in England, the Irish peasantry was divided into a number of subcategories, ranging from the free tenants who paid rent for the lands that they worked to cottars or cottiers, who had no lands of their own to work aside from the odd vegetable garden on a small patch outside the cottages for which they were named and any newly cultivated land (known as assarts) that they might cultivate out of the common lands or woodlands. These distinctions among the peasantry would not have always been apparent to the naked eye, particularly as those belonging to different categories frequently lived side by side on the manors that belonged to members of the feudal nobility. Even among the peasantry, land and family status counted for much, however, meaning that they certainly would have been aware of the social level to which they belonged. The so-called military tenants would perhaps have stood out the most in a society that still placed so much value on war. A step below knights, military tenants shared with them the obligation to provide military service—unless they substituted a monetary payment known as scutage—in exchange for land. This was one of the reasons why, particularly in Ireland, female inheritance of land was regarded as out of the question, especially among the nobility and the classes that owed military service. Another important distinction existed between free tenants and farmers, who held shorter leases and did not enjoy the privilege known as *land tenure* that free tenants shared.

---

[24] R. R. Davies (2009), *Lords and Lordship in the British Isles in the Late Middle Ages*, Edited by Brendan Smith. Oxford: Oxford University Press, p. 24.

[25] Otway-Ruthven, *History of Medieval Ireland*, pp. 104–5.

Finally, Ireland did have some town life outside of Dublin in the Middle Ages, with at least 56 known boroughs having been confirmed by archaeological evidence.[26] Some villages were so populated that, although not quite the size of towns, they received their own charters and were designated as rural boroughs. Towns multiplied after the Conquest, particularly in Anglo-Norman areas of eastern and southeastern Ireland. Henry II extended his practice of granting royal charters for towns in England to his newly conquered territory, beginning with a charter to Dublin in 1171. Towns tended to fall into certain categories, ranging from ports such as Galway and Youghal to market towns, including Clonmel and Navan, while others, such as Athlone, Carrickfergus, and Kilkenny, were founded as military outposts. As in England, market towns served to link surrounding areas of the countryside and existed in a symbiotic relationship with them. But in a sense, all towns had some sort of market and all of them were fortified with walls and gates for defensive purposes. From the English perspective, the towns mostly served as outposts of Anglo-Norman civilization in a colony that many in England still considered to be a foreign and barbarian land.

Connections to and comparisons with the rest of the Isles

The impact of the Anglo-Normans varied to some degree across Ireland, Scotland, and Wales, but some important similarities existed as well. The biggest difference between Ireland and Scotland, of course, was the degree of Scottish independence that was maintained in the twelfth and thirteenth centuries and successfully defended at the beginning of the fourteenth. However, although Gaelic culture was preserved in Scotland to a large extent, the same was true in Ireland since some parts of the island had remained outside direct Norman control. Conversely, it was also true that Scotland did not completely escape Anglo-Norman influence despite its political autonomy. Scottish kings accepted at least the nominal lordship of England's Norman rulers and patterned themselves after them to a large degree. For example, David I (r. 1124–53) adopted some aspects of Anglo-Norman feudalism in his political organization of Scotland. David had benefited from the instability caused by civil war in mid-twelfth-century England, but later kings would gradually encroach upon the autonomy of the Scottish monarchy. For instance, Scottish nobles in the Lowlands came to hold fiefs from the English king as well. This situation led to conflicting loyalties among these nobles, even during the wars of independence.

---

[26] Joseph Brady (2003), "Urbanization," in B. Lalor (ed.), *The Encyclopedia of Ireland*. New Haven and London: Yale University Press, p. 1104.

Wales and Ireland both succumbed to English sovereignty, while Scotland successfully defended its independence until 1707, and even then it retained a surprising degree of autonomy. But in both Wales and Ireland, conquest was a gradual process and was not accomplished in a single stroke. Wales and Ireland had more internal divisions of political leadership than did the relatively unified kingdom of Scotland. Their histories follow a similar pattern because the English kings, such as Edward I, who were interested in subjugating one territory, were usually equally interested in the submission of the other. Likewise, during periods of weakness in the English monarchy, such as during the reign of Henry III, the native nobility of Wales and Ireland both gained in strength and autonomy. Even after occupation, Ireland and Wales provided problems for the English that England had not for the Normans, leading to the construction of even bigger and stronger castles, especially in Wales. Both Wales and Ireland were transformed, however, by the introduction of Anglo-Norman patterns of lordship, as English kings rewarded their courtiers with newly conquered lands.

A shared allegiance to the Roman Church was one unifying factor among England, Ireland, Scotland, and Wales in the Middle Ages, aside from the period of the Great Schism in the late fourteenth and early fifteenth centuries. In Wales, as in Ireland, the church was reorganized into a diocesan structure under the auspices of the Roman Church, with Welsh bishoprics being established at Bangor, Llandaff, St Asaph, and St David's. Yet ecclesiastical differences continued to exist among the regions of the Isles; for example, English bishops wielded more power and authority over their people than did their Irish or Welsh counterparts who remained somewhat more isolated from those within their dioceses. Furthermore, monasticism continued to have a much stronger appeal in England, Wales, and Ireland than it did in Scotland, perhaps because of the more political role that abbeys tended to play in Scotland as supporters of the crown.

Anglo-Norman rule at least had the potential to unify Scotland, Ireland, and Wales against England, though, of course, this never happened—at least not completely. The Irish provided supplies to the Scots in their wars of independence, but many Irish soldiers fought in English armies as well. Edward Bruce's invasion of Ireland provides another example of mutual Scots-Irish collaboration against Anglo-Norman hegemony.

But connections among the territories threatened by English dominance offer only one model for interpreting the history of the Isles from the twelfth to the fifteenth century. Another model involves the connections established between England and the constituent parts of its empire during the same period. In addition to the Anglo-Normans who actually settled in Ireland, a wide range of merchants, clergymen, and aristocrats traveled back and forth between England and Ireland on a regular basis. The port city of Bristol particularly benefited from the closer connections with Ireland after the twelfth-century invasion. Historians have long assumed that the ties between the two islands became weaker during the fourteenth and fifteenth centuries, but that assumption is no longer taken for granted. For example, Henry Crystede, who was born in Ireland, moved to Bristol in the 1360s with his wife, the daughter of a native chief, to find himself in the midst of a community of people who could converse with him in Irish. In the 1390s, Crystede found himself back in Ireland as a translator for Richard II in his dealings with the local chiefs.[27]

If Richard's journey to Ireland in the 1390s shows that the English had not lost interest in their control of Ireland, it is significant that Richard still came in the role of a conquering king asserting his territorial rights. Richard would not have gone if he had not thought that those rights were being threatened, however. The exodus of English landlords from Ireland in the late fourteenth century had been accompanied by those lower down the social scale who returned to England in search of better economic opportunities. When Richard embarked for Ireland in 1394, he sought to force those refugees who had been born in Ireland to return there, though he made an exception for over 500 known individuals who were permitted to stay in England.[28]

The extent of English colonialism before the Reformation

English colonial government in Ireland could only be as strong as the ties that bound it to the home country. These could be quite erratic and complicated. Throughout the Middle Ages, however, the English always conceived any connections with other regions in the Isles from a vantage point of English dominance. Henry II conquered Ireland at the time when his empire covered England and much of France. From the time of Edward I, English kings regularly attempted to reestablish the Angevin Empire by recovering lands squandered during the reigns of John and Henry III. The extent to which Ireland figured in those plans varied in different reigns and at different times, but Ireland's colonial status was never in doubt. The extent of English colonization there, however, was always an open question because of the lack of a definitive dividing line between those areas controlled by Gaelic kings and those under Anglo-Norman jurisdiction. An attempt was made to rectify this situation in the 1420s when Dublin, Kildare, Louth, and Meath were grouped together for administrative purposes.[29] Collectively, these four shires became known as the *Pale* in 1495, the area that was considered obedient to

[27] See for example, Brendan Smith (2011), "Late Medieval Ireland and the English Connection: Waterford and Bristol, ca. 1360–1460." *Journal of British Studies*, 50, 565.

[28] Robin Frame (2006), "The Wider World," in Rosemary Horrox and W. Mark Ormond (eds), *A Social History of England, 1200–1500*. Cambridge: Cambridge University Press, p. 449.

[29] S. J. Connolly (2007), *Contested Island: Ireland, 1460–1630*. Oxford: Oxford University Press, p. 41.

English authority. The boundaries of the Pale shifted over time according to the amount of territory directly controlled by the English. The name came from a general word for any territory with an established set of boundaries.

Moreover, English colonization in Ireland from the twelfth to the fifteenth century was never just a matter of establishing political authority because of the thousands of people of all social classes, including numerous British peasants, who migrated there. They were drawn to Ireland, as is the case with most immigrants to all lands, in search of a better life and greater economic opportunities. Many of these individuals continued to seek the protection of English legal authority, reinforcing colonial power in the process. But Ireland was certainly not the top priority of English rulers most of the time. Even when it was, the basic situation remained virtually unchanged. For all of his pretensions to expanded authority, Edward I never bothered to change his title from "lord of Ireland." Furthermore, by the time of Edward's reign, English colonists in Ireland, now several generations removed from the first settlers, were no longer thought of—and no longer thought of themselves—as fully English.[30] Ireland had begun to acquire a new identity in the immediate centuries following the Anglo-Norman conquest, but it was still its own identity. The notorious Statutes of Kilkenny failed completely at preserving a marked distinction between English and Irish in Ireland.

In conclusion, if Ireland was an English colony in the Middle Ages, it was one in which native rulers could still enjoy a great deal of autonomy if they gave some recognition to the legitimacy of English lordship. But it was also a colony that by the mid-fifteenth century had become a significant source of revenue for England, primarily from the ports on the eastern and southeastern coast. At times, the English had pushed the extent of settlement farther than others, with varying degrees of success. In the third quarter of the fifteenth century, English authority had reached something of a low point. The end of the Hundred Years War was accompanied by the growing mental instability and weakness of King Henry VI (1422–61). His decline precipitated an aristocratic bloodbath in England known as the Wars of the Roses. As rival claimants from the Houses of York and Lancaster vied for the throne, those aristocrats who managed to survive the carnage increased in power and autonomy. This was true of Anglo-Irish aristocrats in Ireland as well, although Edward IV made some efforts to curb their pretensions. By the time that a prince with a tenuous title to the throne named Henry Tudor claimed the crown after a military victory over King Richard III at the Battle of Bosworth Field in 1485, the reestablishment of royal authority in Ireland and a clearer definition of its relationship with England had become necessities if the island was to remain a part of the English Empire.

---

[30] Robin Frame (1998), "'Les Engleys Nées in Irlande': The English Political Identity in Medieval Ireland," *Ireland and Britain, 1170–1450*. London and Rio Grande: The Hambledon Press, p. 131.

CHAPTER SIX

Ireland and the Reformation

. . . it is in vayne to speake of planting of laws, and plotting of policies, till they [the Irish] are altogether subdued.

– EDMUND SPENSER, *A View of the Present State of Ireland*, 1596

Divisions within Irish society

When the Reformation came to Ireland, as it did to the rest of Europe, in the sixteenth century, it came to two separate Irelands, both of which were in a state of transition. This fact was not officially recognized by English authorities; in 1541, the English Parliament made no such distinction when it bestowed the title of king of Ireland upon Henry VIII (r. 1509–47). Such a measure had become necessary after Henry VIII broke with the papacy because England's prior claim to rule Ireland had been based on a papal grant. Nor did the Irish parliament place any geographical restrictions on the title when they recognized it a year later. But anyone who knew anything about Ireland knew that the Anglo-Irish areas were in fact quite distinct from those parts of the island that remained part of the Gaelic world and operated under different social and political realities. The dividing line between these areas was not fixed and both were in fact susceptible to strong influences from the other. Gaelic culture influenced even the highest members of the Anglo-Irish aristocracy, while, on such a small island, Anglo-Irish influence extended to some of the most remote regions. Gaelic rulers were not averse to imitating their Anglo-Irish counterparts whenever it served their purposes. Nonetheless, an understanding of the social and political divisions between and within these distinct parts of the island is necessary to comprehend the Irish world to which the Reformation came and the impact that it had on that world.

Sixteenth-century Ireland was sparsely populated, numbering approximately 750,000 people throughout the period, though some estimates place the population as low as 500,000 at the beginning of the century. The small population perhaps contributed to the retention of traditional social structures in Ireland at a time when much of Europe was experiencing a population boom and undergoing significant social change. Gaelic Ireland still operated under a clan system of social and political leadership that decentralized power and was distributed among approximately 60 local chieftains.

If Gaelic Ireland remained more traditional because it was less populated, the Anglo-Irish areas of settlement were more populated, giving rise to a different kind of society. Farmers in these regions made greater and more efficient use of agricultural cultivation, whereas the Gaelic rural economy remained more pastoral. As had occurred elsewhere in the High Middle Ages, agricultural surpluses allowed for the growth of towns and cities, primarily in southeastern Ireland. Not only did half a dozen sizeable towns emerge in this area, but also the Anglo-Irish areas contained approximately 40 market towns, similar to those scattered throughout England that were so important to its economy in the early modern period. In the Anglo-Irish areas, large landowners could decide how best to use their land and get their tenants to cooperate. The de Burgh family in southern Connacht has been noted for its adoption of Gaelic customs to the point where they might have been confused for Gaelic chieftains.[1]

In Gaelic areas, land was considered the corporate property of the clan, underwent frequent changes of possession, and was viewed more statically rather than as a potential source of economic progress. The latter was typical of traditional rural societies throughout Europe. Anglo-Irish areas differed from their Gaelic counterparts in that in the former, a class of elite landholders was not incompatible with the presence of prosperous tenants. In Gaelic Ireland, a greater divide existed between property owners and an impoverished class of landless laborers. This led to the availability of numerous soldiers who could earn a living supporting the political and military ambitions of the local lord. These soldiers contributed to the chaotic and violent character of life "beyond the Pale." Even if Anglo-Irish lords admired certain aspects of Gaelic laws and customs, they did not seek to replicate the social and political divisions that characterized those parts of the island beyond their jurisdiction.

In a situation where central authority was entirely lacking, peace could only be maintained by agreements among a number of rival chieftains. However, the temptation to seize the lands or property of others could prove too great if one neighboring leader was significantly stronger than another or if he found himself with more children to provide for. Such was the case

---

[1] Nicholas Canny (1989), "Early Modern Ireland, c. 1500–1700," in Roy Foster (ed.), *The Oxford Illustrated History of Ireland*. Oxford: Oxford University Press, p. 106.

of the Ma'g Uidhir (or Maguire) prince who had 11 sons spanning the late fifteenth and early sixteenth centuries. Some of the other dominant families that emerged in the course of the sixteenth century were the McMahons, O'Donnells, O'Neills, O'Reillys, and O'Rourkes. Eóghan O'Neill attacked both Gaelic and Anglo-Irish lords in his campaign through the midlands in 1430. A century later, the O'Neills suffered a devastating defeat at the hands of the O'Donnells at the Battle of Knockavoe in 1522, which greatly strengthened the position of the O'Donnells in Ulster. The O'Neill chiefs of Tyrone were not even averse to enlisting military assistance from the Anglo-Irish earls of Kildare if it helped them cope with their Gaelic rivals.

In Gaelic Ireland, social divisions tended to be based more on prestige and status than on wealth, with the main dividing line in society being simply between those who owned land and those who did not. These clan leaders, unlike their Scottish counterparts, did not acknowledge the landless portion of the local population as their kin. In the sixteenth century, the Mc Giolla Padraig rulers in Ossory were still requiring free labor service, transportation of goods, and maintenance of their servants, horses, and hounds from the commoners who lived in their territory.[2] But the extent of the wealth or power of these individuals should not be exaggerated. The frequency of cattle raids and the intense local rivalries reflect the financial insecurity of local chieftains. Their resources could not compete with those of their wealthier English counterparts or with those of the nobility elsewhere in Europe. They could not extract as much labor from their tenants either and their living conditions did not radically differ from those below them on the social scale. The practice of the ballybetagh, which involved land allocation on the basis of clientship at the expense of economic considerations, shows that there were other ways in which the Gaelic chiefs sought to maintain their power and prestige. Life in Gaelic Ireland was largely self-sufficient: they wove their own clothes, grew their own grain, and made their own dairy products. Peasants in Gaelic Ireland depended heavily on a pastoral economy, which allowed them some mobility, but they still came under the authority of local lords.

Another consequence of the slow rate of population growth in Ireland, however, was a fair amount of stability in land rents and tenant obligations. Without a heavy demand for land, landowners were in no position to enforce higher rents or to impose new service obligations on their tenants. In England, long leases were granted by lords to tenants as the population was plummeting during the demographic crisis of the fourteenth and fifteenth centuries. These leases were expiring in the sixteenth century, and lords began adjusting their rents upward and granting shorter leases to reflect the recovery of the population and the inflationary economy. A similar process

---

[2] David Edwards (2001), "Collaboration with Anglisation: The MacGiollapadraig Lordship and Tudor Reform," in P. J. Duffy, D. Edwards and E. Fitzpatrick (eds), *Gaelic Ireland, c. 1250–c. 1650: Land, Lordship and Settlement*. Dublin: Four Courts Press, pp. 83–4.

occurred in Anglo-Irish Ireland on a smaller scale. In Gaelic Ireland, the rural population still remained poorer than those in Ireland under English landlords as a result of the undeveloped nature of the economy as a whole. During the fifteenth and sixteenth centuries, the economic situation was not helped by the decentralized political structure or the ability of the most powerful chieftains to simply confiscate lands on the rather thin pretense of offering protection for the clans who occupied them.

In the course of the sixteenth century, the English would use this situation to justify their attempt to extend their authority over the entire island. Their efforts did not improve conditions in Gaelic Ireland, but instead encouraged Gaelic lords to increase their authority and military might in order to resist such encroachments. These efforts at resistance culminated in the alliance between Hugh O'Neill, Hugh O'Donnell, and Hugh Maguire in 1595 at the beginning of what became known as the Nine Years War. In the late sixteenth century, Gaelic lords increasingly turned to Scottish mercenaries, which they could only afford by imposing additional burdens on the rural population. The use of these *galloglass*, a term based on an Irish word for *foreign soldiers* that dates from the medieval period, contributed to the comparatively advantageous position of Gaelic tenants of English landowners, despite their shorter leases, higher rents, or increased services. It is perhaps important to point out here that most of the tenants of English landlords were native Irish, although there were some English tenants who had come to Ireland to take advantage of lower rents than those being imposed in England.

This survey does not quite do justice to the diversity or complexity of social divisions within sixteenth-century Ireland. Some tenants in Gaelic Ireland could be quite prosperous if they had the support of a powerful clan leader, while others might lose their land and descend into the ranks of landless laborers. But increasingly in the course of the sixteenth century, the fortunes of the Irish population were shaped by war and English efforts to extend their authority and to further colonize the island.

Political divisions

At the beginning of the sixteenth century, Ireland was distinctly divided into those areas under English administration and those that were not. If anything, Gaelic Ireland was becoming more politically decentralized at that time. The number of lordships was actually increasing, thanks to the divisions of some territories, such as Annaly, which was held by the O'Ferrall clan.[3] However, this did not mean that political and administrative order was

---

[3]   D. B. Quinn and K. W. Nicholls (1976), "Ireland in 1534," in T. W. Moody, F. X. Martin and F. J. Byrne (eds), *A New History of Ireland III: Early Modern Ireland 1534–1691*. Oxford: Clarendon Press, p. 25.

entirely lacking, even if it was relatively unsophisticated. Chieftains were themselves elected according to custom by all male descendants of the clan within four generations of a common male ancestor.[4] Presumably, the title generally fell to those candidates who already possessed the most power and prestige following the time-honored concept in warrior societies of throne-worthiness. In addition, these chieftains commonly sought to strengthen their claims by hiring poets/scholars to trace the history and lineage of the family. This was an ancient practice similar in intent to the bardic poems that were composed celebrating the lineage of a new ruler in the Middle Ages. The powerful Geraldine earls of Desmond, for example, routinely employed such individuals from the O'Daly, O'Hifernain, O'Maobchonaire, and Mac Bruaieadha families to affirm the legitimacy of their rule over Munster.[5]

Furthermore, within each territory, the brehon was still charged by the ruling lord with enforcing justice and defending his interests. The parties who appeared before the brehon would have agreed to a kind of binding arbitration before meeting with him. This was probably recognized as in the interest of both parties, since they did not have the same recourse to common law that those in Anglo-Irish Ireland did. In Gaelic Ireland, such law and order as did exist could be employed by lords as a means of oppression. This situation led some landowners to offer their allegiance and services to more powerful lords who might afford greater protection.

The system as a whole resembled that of fifteenth-century England during the Wars of the Roses, the dynastic struggle that created a high level of political instability between 1455 and 1485. Lords relied on monetary payments to armed retainers in lieu of the traditional feudal bonds that were supposed to be based on the concepts of homage and fealty. In England, these bonds had broken down during the Wars of the Roses because of the relative weakness of the English crown and the preoccupation of those who held it with establishing or consolidating their position in England. In Gaelic Ireland, a similar situation resulted from the absence of royal authority, in contrast to the English-controlled areas where traditional feudal bonds continued to be recognized, including those of allegiance to the crown. It is important to realize that the English did not successfully assert their authority even in all areas in Ireland nominally under English control, especially during the chaotic fifteenth century. However, as royal authority recovered under the Tudor dynasty following the end of the Wars of the Roses, its prestige revived in Ireland as well.

In 1500, then, the preconditions for the extension of English power existed in Anglo-Irish Ireland. These conditions included a local aristocracy that

---

4 Steven G. Ellis (1998), *Ireland in the Age of the Tudors, 1447–1603: English Expansion and the End of Gaelic Rule.* London and New York: Longman, p. 41.
5 Anthony M. McCormack (2005), *The Earldom of Desmond, 1463–1583: The Decline and Crisis of a Feudal Lordship.* Dublin: Four Courts Press, p. 45.

spoke English and was dependent upon English support and the previous Anglicization of law, government, and administration. The challenge for the Tudors was going to involve consolidating English control not only over Gaelic Ireland but also in places such as Kilkenny and Tipperary that had only partially adopted English law and institutions. In order to do so, English monarchs would need to co-opt the support of the most powerful nobles in Ireland.

Surveying the political realities of the island as a whole, two dominant Anglo-Irish families stand out above the rest: the noble dynasties of Ormond and Kildare. Of these, the earls of Kildare had emerged as the most powerful by the sixteenth century. The Ormond family had suffered during the Wars of the Roses, the fifth earl, James Butler, having been executed by Edward IV after the Battle of Towton in 1461. The earls of Ormond could still wield immense influence, but as absentee landlords, they did not do so as consistently as did the Fitzgerald earls of Kildare. The earls of Kildare thus had the potential to be the king of England's greatest allies—or his greatest enemies. Like the nobles appointed to rule the borderlands of Wales and Cornwall in Britain, the earls of Kildare enjoyed greater autonomy and might be tempted to align themselves with others who opposed encroachments of royal authority. They serve as a reminder that local rulers in the English-controlled areas of the island could be just as powerful and autonomous as their counterparts in Gaelic Ireland. These individuals had enjoyed greater power during the Wars of the Roses, which had weakened royal authority as the English kings became even more preoccupied with events in England. This might explain why the Fitzgerald earls of Desmond and Kildare sought to prolong the civil war in England by supporting Perkin Warbeck, who asserted his claim to the throne by pretending to be one of the young sons of Edward IV (r. 1461–83) who had mysteriously disappeared during the reign of Richard III (r. 1483–85).

Although a sharp division existed between Gaelic and Anglo-Irish Ireland, Anglo-Irish acceptance of Gaelic culture and identification of Anglo-Irish settlers with the local population always posed the potential threat of something like a unified resistance to further encroachments of English royal authority. During the sixteenth century, a chief governor appointed by the king exercised that authority. The problems inherent in this arrangement prompted a major realignment in England's relations with Ireland in the course of the sixteenth century. The Tudor policy of consolidating and strengthening royal authority in England animated their policy in Ireland as well. The Tudors found that they would be able to take advantage of the political divisions that existed in Ireland and the frequent infighting among Gaelic chieftains. Tudor rule would mean significant changes for Ireland, even if none of the Tudor monarchs fully achieved their objectives there. These changes included—but also predated—the effects of the Protestant Reformation.

Tudor policy toward Ireland under Henry VII and Henry VIII

The triumph of Henry Tudor in the Wars of the Roses proved one of the most decisive turning points in English history. Recent historiography has tended to emphasize the continuity of English history in this period; historians such as Christine Carpenter have viewed Henry's reign as belonging to the period encompassing the wars rather than as a dramatic departure from them.[6] While there is some merit in this interpretation, it can still be argued that, in retrospect, Henry VII (r. 1485–1509) did initiate a new kind of Renaissance monarchy. The new king introduced changes that would have long-term effects on both England and Ireland and prepare the way for the reign of his son, Henry VIII. Of particular note was Henry's ability to eliminate private armies in England, a fact that was recognized by Parliament's passing the Statute of Liveries in 1504. If Henry VII had not successfully ended the Wars of the Roses and established his authority in England, Henry VIII would never have thought of expanding his authority in Ireland, where private armies remained a standard feature of the political landscape. Henry VII's main concern with Ireland was mainly to keep it quiet enough not to pose a threat to his rule in England. To that purpose, he turned to Gearóid Mór, better known as Gerald Fitzgerald (1456–1513), the powerful earl of Kildare, for assistance.

Since 1479, Fitzgerald had served as governor of Ireland under the Yorkist king, Edward IV. The Wars of the Roses had continued into Henry's reign in the form of challenges from pretended Yorkist claimants to the throne, such as Lambert Simnel. Simnel, posing as one of the missing sons of Edward IV, received the crown from Yorkist supporters in Ireland, including Kildare, who refused to reconcile himself to the reign of someone whom he regarded as a usurper. To Kildare's credit, he came to recognize that he had backed the losing side and eventually realigned himself with Henry VII; to Henry's credit, he accepted Kildare into his service despite his past associations and actions that Henry would have considered treasonous. But Henry's handling of Kildare was consistent with the shrewd policies he employed toward his former opponents in England. In 1487, 2 years after he had won the crown at the Battle of Bosworth Field in August 1485, Henry had gotten the English Parliament to pass an Act of Treason that made everyone who had fought against him in that battle guilty of treason. Yet, Henry spared the lives of his enemies, choosing to levy fines instead. In the process, he earned their gratitude and increased his treasury at the

---

[6] Christine Carpenter (1997), *The Wars of the Roses: Politics and the Constitution in England, c. 1437–1509*. Cambridge: Cambridge University Press.

same time. He even married Elizabeth of York in an effort to unify the two rival dynasties. Henry was nothing if not pragmatic, as further evidenced by his future treatment of Fitzgerald. In 1494, Henry removed Fitzgerald from office temporarily to allow Sir Edward Poynings (1459–1521) to consolidate the king's authority over his Irish administration. Henry then turned around and reappointed Fitzgerald as his deputy as soon as Poynings had accomplished his objective.

Poynings is primarily associated in Irish history with the law that bears his name. Poynings' Law, passed by an Irish parliament at Drogheda in 1494, was more a response to Henry's immediate situation in Ireland than a result of any long-range plan for the governing of the island. In 1487, the earl of Kildare had secured the approval of an Irish parliament for the coronation of Henry's rival, the pretender Lambert Simnel. This obviously struck a direct blow at Henry's authority in Ireland, but it also set a precedent for a parliament in Ireland to act independently of the English parliament. Henry VII understandably wanted to ensure that such an act would not recur during his reign. Poynings' Law, which was not repealed until 1782, stated that no parliament could meet in Ireland without the king's consent and that the king and his council had to approve any bills before they could be passed in Ireland. Poynings' Law set the parameters that accompanied the reappointment of the earl of Kildare as Henry's Deputy Lieutenant in Ireland in 1496. From that point forward, relations between the two men remained stable, and Kildare served the king faithfully and effectively. He even married the king's cousin, Elizabeth St John. It is not clear what Henry would have done if he had not been able to rely on the earl's fidelity.

His foremost biographer determined that Henry VII never actually brought the Irish parliament under his control and, furthermore, that he had no intention of doing so.[7] While Henry at least began the process of extending royal authority beyond the Pale, he mainly wanted to keep Ireland quiet as opposed to making it an English colony. This was one of the reasons why he chose to convert Fitzgerald from an enemy to an ally, despite the role that the earl had played in the Simnel conspiracy and suspicions that he had backed another pretender named Perkin Warbeck in the 1490s. Henry did not have, or at least did not wish to spend, the resources necessary to conquer Ireland on his own. He therefore could not afford the permanent alienation of the most powerful earl on the island. Until the end of his reign, Henry VII was more concerned with preserving the power that he had gained as king of England than he was with extending that power throughout the Isles.

When Henry VIII succeeded Henry VII in 1509, he immediately set out to distance himself from his father's policies and establish his own identity as king. Whereas Henry VII had paid shrewd attention to his finances and built up a sizeable surplus in the royal treasury, Henry VIII spent lavishly

---

[7] S. B. Chrimes (1972), *Henry VII*, Berkeley: University of California Press, p. 268.

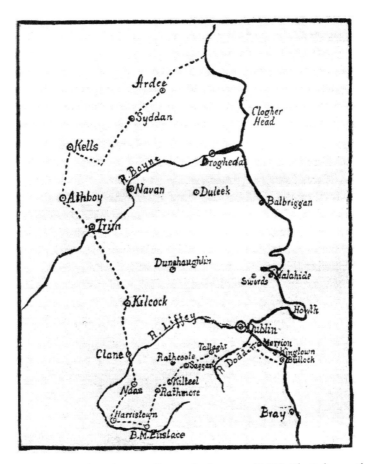

FIGURE 6.1 *Map – The Pale according to the Statute of 1488. The Pale was the area that was under direct English control. From Weston St John Joyce,* The Neighborhood of Dublin. *Dublin: M.H. Gill and Son, 1921.*

and quickly wiped out the savings he had inherited. Whereas Henry VII fought only out of necessity once he had gained the crown, Henry VIII sought the glory that came from war and reopened ancient conflicts with France and Scotland shortly after his succession. Whereas Henry VII utilized the energetic lawyers Richard Empson and John Dudley to reclaim royal lands that had been alienated from the crown during the Wars of the Roses, Henry VIII had the two men executed as a means of endearing himself to those who had been their legal victims. In Ireland, whereas Henry VII made no special effort to extend his personal authority there and relied heavily on the earl of Kildare, Henry VIII, when he finally turned his attention to Ireland in 1519, decided to abandon reliance upon the earl and to rule on his own. Each one of these shifts in policy caused Henry trouble, in the long run if not immediately. Yet, none of these changes compared to the religious shift that Henry would undertake when he oversaw England's break with Rome and the beginnings of the Protestant Reformation in England in the 1530s.

The Reformation was a complicated religious movement that from the start had serious political ramifications. Its beginnings are usually traced to the German reformer, Martin Luther (c. 1483–1546), who was excommunicated by the Catholic Church in 1520 because he challenged the efficacy of most of the church's religious sacraments—retaining only Baptism and Holy Communion—and because of his argument that human beings were saved by God through faith alone rather than through a combination of good works and faith. Luther objected particularly strongly to the sale of indulgences, which were essentially written statements acknowledging forgiveness for sins in exchange for a cash payment. Luther initially defended the papacy and did not seek a break from the church. But once he was excommunicated, Luther became increasingly vehement in his attacks on the pope, whom he started to regard as the antichrist. At first, Henry VIII was repulsed by the teachings of Martin Luther. In 1521, the king published a work under his name entitled *The Defense of the Seven Sacraments* defending Catholic doctrine and practices.

Henry's motivations for breaking with Rome about a decade later, like most important human decisions, did not derive from a single consideration. On a personal level, he desired to divorce his first wife, Catherine of Aragon, and marry Anne Boleyn, with whom he had fallen passionately in love. On a political level, he desired a legitimate male heir to ease concerns about the succession and prevent the recurrence of civil war. On an administrative and financial level, he sought to gain the kind of control over the English church and its revenues that the Catholic kings of France and Spain had already negotiated from the papacy. On a religious level, he was at first mainly concerned that he had violated both canon law and God's will when he received a papal dispensation to marry his deceased brother's widow.

It is very difficult to characterize the Reformation of the church undertaken by Henry VIII. On the one hand, the Henrician Reformation brought about some significant religious changes, including the dissolution of the monasteries, the translation of the Bible into English, and the elimination of papal authority, which made all clerics directly subject to the authority of the king. On the other hand, the Protestant Church of England, and its counterpart, the Church of Ireland, retained many religious practices, some of the dogma, and the diocesan administrative organization of their Roman Catholic predecessor. Henry's Reformation was a long and tortuous process conducted in fits and starts and characterized by sudden reversals that were influenced by international as well as domestic considerations. Henry's changes were often associated with his frequent change of marital partners and the religious views of his wives' families. They created instability and uncertainty in England, and in Ireland.

In Ireland, the potential dangers of the might accrued by the Fitzgeralds exploded into reality in June 1534. The Kildare rebellion occurred just as

Henry was engaged in the beginnings of the English Reformation and seeking support for his second marriage—to the upstart, Anne Boleyn, whom many believed had bewitched the king. According to the *Annals of Ulster*, Henry had summoned the ninth earl of Kildare, Gerald Fitzgerald to answer charges of illegal and unjust actions against his people and had promptly locked him in the Tower of London "in anticipation of his ruin."[8] Gerald's son, "Silken Thomas," also known as Lord Offaly, rebelled in protest. (Thomas's nickname derived from the silk fringes on the helmets of the 140 horsemen that accompanied him to Dublin in June 1534 to launch his rebellion.) A larger background cause of the rebellion derived from opposition to the governmental changes that had been introduced by Thomas Cromwell (c. 1485–1540), Henry's leading minister. Furthermore, Henry's break with the Catholic Church provided additional religious motivations among the rebels, many of whom opposed the Reformation. The rebels were alleged to have boasted that "they were of the pope's sect and band, and him they will serve against the king and all his partakers," reflecting the Catholic rhetoric used to support the rebellion. The fear of a Spanish invasion—it was rumored that 12,000 Spanish troops were ready to support the rebellion—and the rebels' condemnation of Henry as a heretic made the rebellion especially menacing in the eyes of those in charge of the Tudor government.[9]

Catholicism had remained strong within the Pale in the decades leading up to the Reformation. It had become fused with other social and political traditions to become an important component of the area's cultural identity. A number of churchmen who remained loyal to the king fled Ireland for England "for fear and for great dread of the son of the Earl putting them to death in revenge of his father."[10] Replacing papal authority with the royal supremacy in Ireland was going to be no easy task. Yet, this was not an issue on which Henry was willing to compromise.

At first, supporters within and immediately beyond the Pale rallied to Thomas Fitzgerald's cause, while his representatives sought financial support from Henry's main enemies—the pope, the Holy Roman Emperor Charles V (the nephew of Henry's first wife, Catherine of Aragon), and King James V of Scotland. The initial support for the rebellion was a testament not only to sympathy for the earl, but also to widespread discontent under the Tudor regime. The rebels placed Dublin Castle under siege in July and Thomas succeeded his father as earl of Kildare when Gerald died in September. Foreign assistance was not forthcoming, however, and the siege ended on 4 October. The Kildare stronghold of Maynooth Castle, which had been in the Fitzgerald family since 1176, surrendered to the Lord Deputy of Ireland,

---

[8] *The Annals of Ulster*, http://www.ucc.ic/celt/published/T100001C/index.html.
[9] Colm Lennon (1995), *Sixteenth-century Ireland: The Incomplete Conquest*. New York: St. Martin's Press, pp. 108–9.
[10] *The Annals of Ulster*, op. cit.

Sir William Skeffington, in March 1535. Thomas was beheaded in London on 3 February 1537, along with five of his uncles, dealing the Geraldine clan a crushing blow.

The collapse of the Kildare rebellion disrupted local politics in Ireland severely and left a power vacuum into which Henry VIII was only too happy to step. Even in Anglo-Irish Ireland, political allegiance was generally directed to the lord, on whom all property rights within his area ultimately depended, instead of the king. The defeat of the earl of Kildare diminished the authority of the lord, but did not mean the end of lordship or remove all obstacles to an extension of royal authority. Later, English writers would use the extent of power held by the lords over their tenants to help justify the attempted conquest of the island. Henry's first step, however, was to have an Irish parliament establish the Protestant Church of Ireland under Henry's headship. This meant that from this point forward, Henry and his successors—with the exception of the Catholic Queen Mary in the mid-1550s—would simultaneously face political resistance from the Anglo-Irish lords and clerical resistance, even within the diocese of Dublin.[11] This is not to mention the potential resistance of powerful Gaelic lords such as those who headed the O'Donnell, O'Neill, and O'Reilly clans. Henry needed a basis for expanding his power if he wanted to achieve his goals of having his authority over church and state recognized in Ireland.

The constitutional change of 1541 making Henry VIII king of Ireland (replacing the title of lord of Ireland) was a major turning point in Irish history. Henry formally staked his claim to rule over the entire island. What made this claim so significant, however, was that it followed on the heels of the beginnings of the English Reformation. In breaking from Rome, Henry had redefined the relationship between church and state. The Act of Supremacy of 1534 had made him the "Supreme Head" of the Church of England. By extension, Henry's claims to rule Ireland in its entirety placed the English king at the head of the Church of Ireland as well. Henry had no intention of rejecting papal authority in one realm and acknowledging it in another. He sought to bring about the same kind of constitutional change in Ireland that he had achieved in England in which his authority over both church and state would be recognized by his subjects in both kingdoms.[12] Ireland, in other words, was to become an extension of the Tudor state.

But what the act did not do is as historically significant as what it did. The act did not attempt to unify the two kingdoms, thus preparing the way for a later historical tradition that emphasized the autonomous nature of

---

[11] James Murray (2009), *Enforcing the English Reformation in Ireland: Clerical Resistance and Political Conflict in the Diocese of Dublin, 1534–1590*. New York: Cambridge University Press.

[12] Brendan Bradshaw (1979), *The Irish Constitutional Revolution of the Sixteenth Century*. New York: Cambridge University Press.

the kingdom of Ireland.[13] Interestingly, the independent nature of the Irish kingdom was reinforced by the pope, who declared Ireland a kingdom in 1555 when England was under the rule of Henry's Catholic daughter, Mary I (r. 1553–58). This illustrates the complex interaction of politics and religion during this period, since Pope Paul III's excommunication of Henry VIII in 1538 had undermined the king's claim to Ireland. But Paul IV wanted to legitimize Mary's royal title in Ireland and did so in a papal bull recognizing Mary as Queen of Ireland.

The position of Ireland in relation to England, Scotland, and Wales

It is important to understand that the policies of the first two Tudors in Ireland were consistent with those that they pursued in Britain. The establishment of the royal title for Henry VIII in Ireland had been preceded by only a few years by the Act of Union, which had conjoined England and Wales in 1536. Because it was the earliest of the acts of Union—one with Scotland would follow in 1707, with Ireland not until 1801—Wales became more closely bound to England and experienced less conflict with its more powerful neighbor in the succeeding centuries than did either Scotland or Ireland. Wales did retain some of its own legal traditions, but England imposed a great measure of cultural uniformity upon Wales. For example, the Act of Union stipulated that Welshmen needed to speak English in order to hold any official positions in their native land. But if the expansion of English hegemony was less successful in Scotland or Ireland than it was in Wales, it was not for lack of trying.

English kings had actually claimed Scotland as part of their inheritance since the thirteenth century, though prior to the Tudor period Scotland had successfully defended its independence, at times with great difficulty. Earlier in Henry's reign, English encroachments upon Scotland had provoked his brother-in-law, James IV, to invade England with 26,000 men. Henry launched an invasion of Scotland in 1542, only one year after becoming king of Ireland. He was determined to end—or at least render moot—Scotland's alliance with France.

The Scottish kings faced their own problems, with the country divided along lines similar to those in Ireland. Neither Scotland nor Ireland was unified politically or economically. Gaelic culture prevailed in the north and west of Scotland, much as it did in Ireland. Scottish kings tried to expand their authority throughout their kingdom, just as the English monarchs were

---

[13] Bernadette Cunningham (2010), "Seventeenth-century Constructions of the Historical Kingdom of Ireland," in Mark Williams and Stephen Paul Forrest (eds), *Constructing the Past: Writing Irish History.* Woodbridge: The Boydell Press, p. 11.

doing in Ireland, efforts that in both places would eventually lead to wars of conquest. Such efforts were supported by a certain attitude that regarded the Gaelic inhabitants of Scotland and Ireland as uncultured barbarians who needed to be civilized. However, there were important differences between Scotland and Ireland as well, starting with the fact that Scotland shared in the rise in population that occurred in the sixteenth century more than did Ireland; population growth in Scotland has been estimated at around 50 per cent compared to Ireland's relatively stable numbers. In addition, the Scottish parliament was stronger than the Irish parliament, the latter hampered as it was by Poynings' Law. In Scotland, parliament played a role in limiting royal power as well as in the country's ability to resist the designs of the English upon Scottish independence. Queen Elizabeth I (r. 1558–1603) benefited from an alliance with the Protestant reformer John Knox (c. 1513–72). Knox worked with the Scottish parliament to restrict the influence of the Catholic Mary Queen of Scots (1542–87) over religious matters during the 1560s.

The English tended to ignore cultural distinctions among both the Scottish and Irish peoples and thought of both places as unities, reinforced by the 1541 act that made Henry king of Ireland. By contrast, the Stewart kings of Scotland held the official designation "king of the Scots," as opposed to "king of Scotland." Henry VII had even made a clear distinction between English and Irish coinage and ordained that Irish coins be marked on one side with the sign of the harp, a Gaelic symbol.[14] The main purpose was to keep devalued Irish coinage out of England, a goal that was reemphasized later during Mary's reign when the queen forbade use of an Irish coin called the "rose pence" in England.[15] During the sixteenth century, the Irish appeared more and more as an alien race defined by their differences from their English counterparts.

Ireland did, in fact, come to differ more from Britain, Scotland, and Wales, but mainly as a result of the changes in each region brought about by the Reformation in the course of the sixteenth century. Yet, Irish historians have tended until recently to give short shrift to the Reformation as if Ireland had remained largely untouched by it.[16] As previously mentioned, Henry VIII very much intended for the religious changes implemented in England to

---

[14] Paul L. Hughes and James F. Larkin (eds), (1964), *Tudor Royal Proclamations: Volume I: The Early Tudors (1485–1553)*. New Haven and London: Yale University Press, p. 293.

[15] Paul L. Hughes and James F. Larkin (eds), (1969), *Tudor Royal Proclamations: Volume II: The Later Tudors (1553–1587)*. New Haven and London: Yale University Press, p. 314.

[16] That this has begun to change is reflected in books such as those by W. Ian P. Hazlett (2003), *The Reformation in Britain and Ireland: An Introduction*, London. T&T Clark and Felicity Heal (2003), *The Reformation in Britain and Ireland*. New York: Oxford University Press. Hazlett observed that general surveys of the Reformation period tend to ignore Ireland; my research has confirmed that this has not changed since the date of the publication of his book.

pertain to the rest of his dominions, including Wales and Ireland. The desire to unify their kingdoms politically and religiously would prove an important but elusive goal for the Tudor and Stewart dynasties of the sixteenth and seventeenth centuries. Beginning with the Reformation Parliament of the 1530s, there was always an assumption that its legislation applied throughout the lands controlled by the English king. The financial resources at the king's disposal constituted the material background to this assumption as it applied to Wales and Ireland. When Silken Thomas rebelled in 1534, he offered both the Catholic Emperor Charles V and the pope lordship over Ireland as possible replacements for the king, who was now regarded as a heretic. There was a precedent for this, as King John had accepted Ireland as a fief from Pope Innocent III in the early thirteenth century. The Reformation would change the entire dynamic of the relationship among all four major territories of the Isles, especially that between Ireland and England.

The impact of the Reformation

Henry VIII took important strides toward establishing royal English control over Ireland politically, but he had much greater difficulty securing allegiance to his authority over the Irish church. Prior to the Reformation, Britain and Ireland shared at least a common religious culture that centered on the sacraments of the Catholic Church, the Eucharist first and foremost. Henry, and his chief minister, Thomas Cromwell, tried to keep it that way and even to extend religious uniformity to an even greater degree throughout the Isles. The Geraldine Rebellion of the 1530s and the Pilgrimage of Grace, a popular, religiously conservative uprising that occurred in northern England in 1536, altered both their strategies and their perceptions about how easy it would be to achieve their goals. These rebellions did not, however, lessen Cromwell's intention to dissolve the monasteries and to make available the English translation of the Bible nor did they decrease Henry's commitment to the Act of Supremacy. The reason that Henry went through the English parliament to carry out his revolutionary changes was to give royal authority a force of law that would be recognized by his people. The king and Cromwell had every intention of having that law respected in Ireland as well.

At first, it appeared as if the Irish would at least outwardly conform to the new religious injunctions, especially in southern and western Ireland. However, only within the Pale were Henry VIII's religious reforms successfully enacted. As a result, the Reformation altered the dynamics of the relationship among the different parts of Ireland as well. One effect of the Reformation was to reinforce the contrast between conditions in the Pale and those areas outside it by adding a religious dimension to the differences between them. People who no longer felt bound together by sacraments that made them part of the same religious community were less likely to identify with one another or to be thought of in the same way by outsiders. At the same time, however, the surprisingly large numbers of the Anglo-Irish population within the Pale who retained their allegiance to the Catholic Church in the sixteenth century now had more reason to identify with the people of Gaelic Ireland. This is not to say that Anglo-Irish Catholics did not retain their cultural snobbery or that a shared religion bridged the ethnic divide between them and their Gaelic coreligionists. But the divide between the Anglo-Irish and the English was widened. Henry may have exacted outward allegiance among the Anglo-Irish, but his Reformation did not win many converts to the reformed faith. The king was himself a religious conservative, even though he had rebelled against the pope, and he did not exactly encourage the spread of Lutheranism. Only 40 per cent of the religious houses of Ireland had been dissolved by 1540 and many monks and friars simply continued to go about their business.[17] By the end of Henry's reign in 1547, the Protestant Reformation was nowhere fully established in Ireland, thanks to a combination of Henry's conservative religious agenda, his willingness to settle for outward conformity so as to avoid trouble, and, no doubt, the continued appeal of the old faith to many Irish people.

It is easy to exaggerate the differences between Catholics and Protestants in the Reformation period, especially given the long history of conflict between them that followed and that has continued in Northern Ireland into recent times. Historians of the Reformation have tended to focus on that history of conflict at the expense of the numerous examples of Protestants and Catholics learning to live together. Sometimes, they even shared the same worship space, albeit at different times of the day.[18] Furthermore, even Catholics recognized the need for serious church reform by the early sixteenth century; this was as true in Ireland as it was elsewhere. Ireland shared with much of Catholic Europe examples of clergy who did not take preaching seriously and monks and nuns who lacked a true religious vocation. Of course, there were also bishops, priests, and monks who took their spiritual calling seriously and encouraged devotion among their fellow Christians, as Henry Jefferies argues was the case with the pre-Reformation archbishops of Armagh.[19] Also, by the early sixteenth century, the Franciscan order in Ireland had experienced significant growth, especially in Gaelic lands, just one sign pointing to a vital religiosity in late medieval Ireland.[20]

The immediate result of Henry's attempt to impose the Reformation on Ireland was the destruction of some monasteries and many objects of religious devotion. Other than that, the Reformation in Ireland remained a fairly

---

[17] Colmán N. Ó Clabaigh (2002), *The Franciscans in Ireland, 1400–1534: From Reform to Reformation.* Dublin: Four Courts Press, 2002, p. 78.

[18] Benjamin J. Kaplan (2007), *Divided by Faith: Religious Conflict and the Practice of Toleration in Early Modern Europe.* Cambridge, MA: The Belknap Press of Harvard University Press.

[19] Henry A. Jefferies (1997), *Priests and Prelates of Armagh in the Age of Reformation, 1538–1558.* Dublin and Portland, OR: Four Courts Press.

[20] See Ó Clabaigh (2002), *The Franciscans in Ireland, 1400–1534.*

conservative affair, with no ardent reformers being appointed to ecclesiastical positions. Irish bishops uniformly opposed the attempts of the reform-minded John Bale (1495–1563), who was appointed by Edward VI (r. 1547–53) as Bishop of Ossory in 1552, to introduce the English *Book of Common Prayer* to Ireland. The Dean of Dublin protested at Bale's ordination ceremony when Bale successfully insisted that the Roman ritual not be used. The majority of the laity, including the Anglo-Irish landlords, sympathized with the old faith and went along with Henry's changes reluctantly, if at all.

The changes of Henry's reign had created an uncertain future that the next ten years did little to clarify in England or in Ireland. The young Edward VI was brought up as a sincere Protestant and his ministers strongly supported the Reformation. But his short 6-year reign was marked by rebellion in England and did not provide enough time to firmly establish the new faith on either side of the Irish Sea. Queen Mary, the daughter of Henry VIII and Catherine of Aragon, attempted to return her dominions to the Catholic faith after she ascended the throne in 1553. Her reign stopped whatever momentum the Reformation had achieved under Henry and Edward, although a number of Protestants would flee to Germany and Switzerland. There, they would become exposed to the influence of the French reformer, John Calvin (1509–64), who had established something of a Protestant theocracy in Geneva. In Ireland, what little success the reforms of Edward had achieved was halted and Catholic-minded bishops in the Church of Ireland breathed a collective sigh of relief. But Mary's reign was even more short-lived than that of Edward, and soon the royal supremacy and a moderate version of the English prayer book were approved by the English Parliament under Elizabeth I (r. 1558–1603).

Tudor policy toward Ireland under Elizabeth I

According to Myles Ronan, we can only be certain of 7 of a minimum of 27 bishops in Ireland in 1560 who accepted the new Act of Supremacy and only 5 who accepted the new Act of Uniformity, which were both passed at the beginning of Elizabeth's reign.[21] Yet, even members of the church hierarchy who were unwilling to introduce ecclesiastical reforms remained in their positions—such as the archbishop of Tuam, Christopher Bodkin and the bishop of Clonfert, Roland Burke.[22] This is indicative of the caution with which Elizabeth proceeded in her efforts to further the Reformation.

---

[21] Miles V. Ronan (1930), *The Reformation in Ireland under Elizabeth, 1558–1580*. London: Longmans, Green, and Co., p. 24.

[22] Thomas G. Connors (2001), "Surviving the Reformation in Ireland (1534–80): Christopher Bodkin, Archbishop of Tuam and Roland Burke, Bishop of Clonfert." *Sixteenth Century Journal*, 32, 335–55.

This did not mean, however, that the new queen was not fully committed to preserving the Reformation in her lands. In England, Elizabeth's moderate course gradually allowed Protestantism to become firmly established among the people. Even a large number of Catholics known as Church-papists outwardly conformed and attended Church of England services. In Ireland, most Catholics remained committed to the church of their birth, which further distanced itself from the Reformation in the anti-Protestant decrees adopted by the Council of Trent (1545–63). Thus, in the course of Elizabeth's reign, the religious differences between England and Ireland became much more apparent. Irish Catholicism later received reinforcements in the seventeenth century, when an aggressive, foreign-educated Catholic clergy brought the Counter-Reformation to Ireland.

From the late sixteenth century, a strange religious situation existed within the Pale where the region outwardly owed allegiance to the Church of England but had a population and a clergy that continued to practice the Catholic liturgy and retained allegiance to Rome. The Reformation in England was a slow, ongoing process that succeeded not because the monarchs forcefully compelled belief but because it was given enough time to gain acceptance. The Reformation encountered greater difficulties in Ireland, at least in part because people tend to resist changes imposed from outside authorities. In addition, the Tudor government did little positively to promote the Protestant faith through active preaching while insisting on political obedience, while the Catholic Church was about the launch a Counter-Reformation focused more on the spiritual life of the Irish people.[23]

By the end of the sixteenth century, the Protestant Reformation in Ireland had failed to capture the majority of the population. The expansion of the Franciscan order is evidence of the appeal of pre-Reformation Catholicism. The Franciscans even attracted a number of laymen who joined the order as tertiaries, individuals who took religious vows but could remain in the world and even be married. Among their other contributions, they provided religious education for boys and assisted the clergy with their parochial responsibilities. But the Reformation had provoked a change in Irish Catholicism that helped the Catholic Church to evolve as an institution. According to John Bossy, before the Reformation, the church in Ireland had "possessed little in the way of real practical structure and performed erratically in religious observance and sacramental practice."[24] Religious missionaries helped to revitalize and reshape Catholicism in Ireland, just as they inspired renewed commitment from the declining Catholic minority in late-sixteenth-century England. In addition, the increase in religious instruction that accompanied the Counter-Reformation may also have

---

[23] Canny, "Early Modern Ireland," *op. cit.*, p. 118.
[24] John Bossy (1970), "The Counter-Reformation and the People of Catholic Ireland, 1596–1641," *Historical Studies*, 8, p. 157.

helped to curb kinship rivalries and the Irish devotion to the medieval custom of blood feuds.

This did not mean that the Protestant Reformation in Ireland was a total failure or a historically insignificant movement, however. The Church of Ireland served a dedicated Protestant minority and established Trinity College, Dublin in 1592 to educate those interested in serving it. The Protestant community became tight-knit and acquired a distinct identity by virtue of its status as a religious minority. The cathedrals of St Patrick's and Christ Church in Dublin became Protestant churches, with many of their Catholic accoutrements removed by order of Elizabeth in 1559. Historians, like journalists, tend to focus on the instances of violence and rebellion, ignoring the decades-long periods of peaceful coexistence between Protestants and Catholics. In Ireland, Protestants needed to be able to negotiate a way to live in peace with the Catholic majority, even in areas where the Reformation was "enforced" by English authorities. They frequently found a way to do so, thus ensuring their own survival. At the same time, Irish Protestant thinkers, such as the seventeenth-century archbishop of Armagh, James Ussher (1581–1656) made significant contributions to Protestant thought on the basis of the need to defend his faith in a relatively hostile environment.

Still, in Ireland, Catholicism remained the religion of the majority. The survival of Catholicism in Ireland certainly complicated English rule and made things more difficult for Elizabeth. The basic religious and political situation described earlier in the chapter had not changed substantially by the beginning of her reign, despite the royalist claims put forth by Henry VIII or the official religious policy that had made the English monarch the head of the Church of Ireland. The Gaelic lords in particular retained their open allegiance to the papacy. Indeed, in the first decade of her reign, even Archbishop Bodkin and Bishop Burke continued to recognize the authority of both Elizabeth and the pope.[25] Since Elizabeth had herself retained cordial relations with the papacy in the first decade of her reign, this could hardly have seemed too objectionable. However, another Catholic rebellion in Northern England in 1569 changed relations between the England and Rome. Pope Pius V excommunicated Elizabeth in 1570 in the papal bull *Regnans in Excelsis*.

After 1570, Elizabeth thus felt the need more keenly to reduce the territories within her dominions that remained committed to the pope. Henry VIII had already claimed jurisdiction over the entire island and attempted to extend his authority throughout Ireland. During the later part of his reign, he had attempted to secure the cooperation of the Irish chiefs in converting the erratic pattern of Irish landholding into a more stable system based on English rights of land tenure, with mixed results. During the mid-sixteenth century, the regents of Edward VI initiated efforts to conquer the

---

[25] Connors (2001), *op. cit.*, 337.

parts of Ireland not under English control. The native population was now treated simply as an obstacle to be removed. A new military commander, Edward Bellingham, led a successful campaign against the chief of Offaly, Brian O'Connor. Bellingham then imposed a harsh and watchful rule over the areas that he controlled. Policy shifted again after Mary assumed the throne in 1553. Under the influence of her husband, King Philip II of Spain, whose country had acquired lucrative colonies in the Americas, Mary viewed Ireland as a colonial venture that called for simple expropriation of the land, if necessary. Historians refer to the process they used as one of "surrender and regrant," whereby Irish clan leaders accepted English royal jurisdiction over their lands in exchange for having those lands restored to them by the Crown. A number of leaders submitted to this process, but the efforts of Tudor statesmen under Edward and Mary also provoked further opposition in Gaelic Ireland, particularly in the figure of Shane O'Neill (1530–67), who won a civil war with the help of Scottish mercenaries. O'Neill murdered or banished members of his own family. Elizabeth therefore had stepped into an extremely difficult situation, one that made her sick just thinking about it.

One of the reasons that Elizabeth did not push a Protestant agenda in Ireland was because she knew that she would have enough trouble bringing Ireland under English control as it was. In Ireland, Elizabeth faced problems that she did not have in England or Wales. Her father and grandfather had successfully brought the latter two kingdoms under their control, but Ireland remained something of a wild card, especially since most of its inhabitants now shared the same religion as England's Catholic enemies. In the 1560s, while Shane O'Neill continued to stir up trouble in Ulster, the earls of Desmond and Ormond fought for control of Munster, making life unpleasant for the English and Scottish who attempted to settle there.[26]

Elizabeth therefore found herself resorting to brute force in an attempt to quell social and political turbulence throughout the kingdom—increasingly as her reign wore on. This was not her first choice as she did not wish to spend the money that warfare and conquest entailed. In fact, she preferred not to think about Ireland at all.[27] In addition, Elizabeth was not an aggressive ruler. She generally fought only when she had no other choice. Throughout her reign, she usually followed the path of least resistance in an effort to retain her precarious perch upon the English throne. But she did fight when she needed to. She put down rebellions at home, such as the Northern Rebellion

---

[26] On Shane O'Neill, see Ciaran Brady (1999), "Shane O'Neill Departs from the Court of Elizabeth: Irish, English, Scottish Perspectives and the Paralysis of Policy, July 1559 to April 1562," in S. J. Connolly (ed.), *Kingdoms United? Great Britain and Ireland since 1500: Integration and Diversity*. Dublin: Four Courts Press, pp. 13–28.

[27] On Elizabeth's attitudes toward Ireland, see Hiram Morgan (2004), "'Never Any Realm Worse Governed': Queen Elizabeth and Ireland". *Transactions of the Royal Historical Society*, Sixth Series, 14, 295–308.

of 1569. She sustained a lengthy war with Spain that lasted from 1587—when Philip II declared war on her—until the end of her reign. She also sponsored military activity on behalf of Protestants in France and the Netherlands when it became clear that to do so was in her own best interest. In Ireland, she did not have much choice other than to approve a policy of conquest and colonization if she was going to keep Ireland under Tudor control. She needed to prevent Ireland from forming an alliance with Spain similar to the "Auld Alliance" between Scotland and France that had been a thorn in England's side for so long. The Spanish had designs upon Ireland, which they viewed as a suitable launching site for an invasion of England. Then, in 1579, James Maurice Fitzgerald attempted to reprise the Geraldine uprising of the 1530s. The Baltinglass Rebellion of 1580, led by the third viscount of Baltinglass, James Eustace, had strong support from the Gaelic population in Leinster. The Gaelic chief Fiach MacHugh O'Byrne thrashed an English army in Leinster on 25 August 1580.[28] Eustace, who was a representative of the English elite on whom Elizabeth was counting to maintain order in Ireland, illustrated the dangers of Tudor policy there. His rebellion showed the extent to which Ireland had become the most dangerous threat to Tudor rule.

English colonization

In addition to the policy of the sword in Ireland, a number of individuals had begun to contemplate English colonization and settlement of the island as a solution to the perceived barbarism and potential disloyalty of the native population. The first plantations in Ireland, those in Laois and Offaly, occurred during the reign of Mary. As Nicholas Canny has pointed out, the treatment of Ireland as a land inhabited by uncivilized savages problematically ignored just how many people of English descent were already living there.[29] Some writers solved this problem by treating Ireland as such a barbaric land that the English settlers had become corrupted just from living there. The Pale was already regarded as thoroughly English and even its Gaelic inhabitants were thought of as more civilized as a result of close contact with English culture and language. But related to this belief was the conviction that the English who had settled outside the Pale had become less civilized as a result of intermingling with the native population and adoption of Gaelic traditions and manners. The bishop of Ossory, John Bale, made such an argument in his *Vocacyon*, the main purpose of which was to defend his Protestant beliefs. In 1552, the English writer

---

[28] Chistopher Maginn (2004), "The Baltinglass Rebellion, 1580: English Dissent or a Gaelic Uprising?". *Historical Journal*, 47, 205–32.

[29] Nicholas Canny (1988), *Kingdom and Colony: Ireland in the Atlantic World, 1560–1800.* Baltimore: Johns Hopkins University Press, 1988, p. 35.

Edward Walshe had written of the need to bring the barren country of Ireland the fruits of civilization to rescue it from barbarism.[30] Englishmen such as Sir Thomas Smith set their sights on colonizing Ireland with the firm intention of civilizing the native population, a desire that appealed to Queen Elizabeth. English colonization in Ireland received a literary justification from the poet Edmund Spenser whose unfinished *Faerie Queene* (1590; 1596) instructed its readers that violent conquest could be morally justified when it served a higher purpose. Spenser turned that sentiment into a formal policy recommendation in his 1596 work, *A View of the Present State of Ireland*. Spenser saw the Irish situation as potentially destabilizing in England, with opposition to the Tudors there going back to the Wars of the Roses. But he also blamed the English government for its failed policies there, which had not brought about a stable and peaceful environment in which Ireland could thrive and flourish. This was to be achieved, in his view "by a strong hand" and "the soldier, being once brought in for service into Ulster, and having subdued it and Connaught, I will not have him to lay down his arms any more till he have effected that which I propose."[31]

English writers also justified the colonization of Ireland on economic grounds in terms of the search for profitable colonies that others were finding overseas. Such concerns would also provide the basis for the founding of the first English North American colony—not counting the "lost colony" of Roanoke—at Jamestown in the early seventeenth century. Thomas Smith had seen Irish colonization as an outlet for English population growth and as a source of landed estates for the younger sons of the nobility. In 1571, Smith attempted to entice colonists from among the gentry by offering large tracts of land at extremely low prices. One of the foremost proponents of English colonization in America, Sir Walter Raleigh, proposed a plan for the colonization of Ireland as well. But the nature of the English colonial experience in Ireland would be shaped by events on the ground. The actual experience of colonization would be more important than plans based on a preconceived goal of transforming Ireland from barbarity to civilization.

Attempts at colonization did not bring immediate success or attract large numbers of settlers. The English did manage to create new plantations in southwestern Ireland at Munster. Some English Catholics went to Ireland for religious reasons, but found themselves as much resented by the native Catholic population as any Protestant settlers. The political situation in Ireland was too unstable at the beginning of Elizabeth's reign. It was not until 1603 that the island would become pacified and the last major rebellion of the sixteenth century defeated. But the English were determined at this

---

[30] Andrew Hadfield (1993), "Translating the Reformation: John Bale's Irish *Vocacyon*," in B. Bradshaw, A. Hadfield and W. Maley (eds), *Representing Ireland: Literature and the Origins of Conflict, 1534–1660*. Cambridge: Cambridge University Press, p. 51.

[31] Edmund Spenser (1970), *A View of the Present State of Ireland*, edited by W. L. Renwick, Oxford: Clarendon Press, p. 140.

point to spread their influence outside of the Pale, even though doing so meant encroaching on the territories of Gaelic chiefs who were determined to resist. English colonization of Ireland was only going to be accomplished by force, and it was not going to be easy.

James Maurice Fitzgerald, a cousin of Gerald, the fifteenth earl of Desmond, led a rebellion in 1569, while the earl was being held in London. He attracted enough support that he held off the English until 1573 in what is known as the First Desmond Rebellion. In the 1570s, the English imposed martial law on Munster and executed hundreds in order to bring the region under control. The Second Desmond Rebellion, also known as the Munster War, lasted from 1579 to 1583 and resulted in the deaths of an estimated 10 per cent of the Irish population. The English government struggled to keep its troops in Ireland provisioned, resulting in numerous hardships for those stationed there. In January 1586, Sir Francis Walsingham, Elizabeth's secretary of state, received word from Ireland that English soldiers were dying of starvation while Irish soldiers were proving capable of practically superhuman feats, marching "24 miles through water up to his neck clad in rags."[32]

Nonetheless, English power in Ireland reached a new high-water mark during the reign of Elizabeth. The final struggle of her reign came during the Nine Years War that lasted from 1594 to 1603. The alliance of the O'Neills, the O'Donnells, and the Maguires provided a strong challenge to English authority, but they mostly fought a defensive war until the arrival of Spanish ships in Kinsale in 1601. When they were fighting in their own lands, they harassed the English; Cormac O'Neill and Hugh Maguire defeated an English army at the famous "Ford of the Biscuits" near Enniskillen in August 1594, killing 56 English soldiers in the process. Other Irish victories included the Battle of Clontibert in 1595, the Battle of the Curlew Mountains in 1599, and the battle of the Yellow Ford in 1598, the last of which resulted in the death of about 2,500 English soldiers out of an army of more than 4,000. But the Irish leaders could not sustain their success outside of their territories; Hugh O'Neill suffered a significant defeat when he marched south to join the Spanish forces at Kinsale and the war dragged on until Elizabeth's death in 1603.

The end of medieval Ireland

In the sixteenth century, Ireland had remained predominantly Catholic, but that simple fact masks the enormous changes that had occurred there that accompanied the Reformation period. Ireland was no longer a medieval

---

[32] *Calendar of State Papers Related to Ireland, of the reigns of Henry VIII, Edward VI, Mary. . . .* http://www.archive.org/stream/1887calendarofstatep03greauoftpage14/mode/2up.

land and Catholicism in Ireland was no longer medieval Catholicism. Furthermore, Ireland was not entirely a Catholic country, but had an important Protestant minority that was as committed to the Reformation as their coreligionists elsewhere. Nor were Catholics a monolithic religious entity. Some Catholics in Ireland accepted the reality of the new Church of Ireland and were content to live peacefully with it as long as they had access to their old parish church. Others were more strident in their hostility to the English and more ardent in their commitment to the Counter-Reformation. Despite the ability of many Catholics and Protestants to live in peace, Ireland had become drawn into the conflict between Reformation Protestantism and Counter-Reformation Catholicism, whether the Irish people liked it or not. The defeat of the earl of Tyrone in the Nine Years War (1594–1603) only increased the appeal of the Counter-Reformation to those individuals who sought religion as at least one way to resist English colonization. Though the English had not succeeded in spreading the Reformation much among a hostile population, they had effectively subordinated the recalcitrant territories and ended the political arrangements that had long characterized medieval Ireland.

To suggest that the sixteenth century marked the end of medieval Ireland is not to say that traditional ways of thought and life did not continue to flourish. Historians no longer view the past as shaped entirely by linear processes and regard the Reformation itself as a long-term movement that reinforced and coexisted with traditional patterns of thought in complex ways.[33] For example, belief in magic and the supernatural survived the Reformation of the sixteenth century, the Scientific Revolution of the seventeenth, and the Enlightenment of the eighteenth century. Such beliefs particularly survived in the rural areas of Britain and Ireland until at least the late nineteenth century, as evidenced by the English novels of Thomas Hardy and the eerie case of the village murder of Bridget Cleary in late-nineteenth-century Ireland on the grounds that the woman who was burned to death was a fairy changeling who had taken the place of the real Bridget.[34]

When the English did settle and establish plantations in Ireland, they frequently isolated themselves from the native population, precisely because of the preconceived notions of their barbarity and incapacity for civilization that had helped to justify conquest and colonization in the first place. Within a short time, however, the English colonists who settled in Ireland ceased to be purely English and began to take on an Irish, or at least a mixed, identity of their own. Benjamin Myers argues that Edmund Spenser was attracted by the rugged nature of the Irish wilderness, even though it had benefited those rebels who used it to their advantage in their guerilla warfare against the

---

[33] See especially Alexandra Walsham (2008), "The Reformation and 'The Disenchantment of the World' Reassessed." *Historical Journal*, 51, 497–528.

[34] Angela Bourke (2001), *The Burning of Bridget Cleary*. New York: Penguin.

English.[35] Spenser believed, as an Englishman, that one of the major causes of disorder in Ireland was the failure of English captains to prosecute the war against the rebels with sufficient vigor, as if they did not want to subdue the enemy.[36]

In 1587, Richard Stanyhurst (1547–1618) wrote that Ireland under English rule had been improved on a daily basis, thanks to the establishment of good laws, the suppression of rebellions, and the substitution of civility for rudeness. This may have been wishful thinking, especially in 1587, but Stanyhurst had summed up the English hopes for Ireland in this assessment. By the seventeenth century, these hopes had been expanded to include commercial development based on a stable and productive landowning class and the introduction of more fairs and markets to recently conquered territories such as Ulster. In 1603, James VI of Scotland succeeded Elizabeth as James I of England, thus unifying the crowns of the three countries. During the first half of the seventeenth century, James would seek to unify his kingdoms politically, while his son, Charles I would seek to impose religious unity. But even in Elizabeth's reign, political rebellion had acquired religious overtones; so in fact, these two causes would always be linked in the minds of many Irish Catholics. In 1594, the Irish had rebelled under the leadership of Hugh O'Neill, the earl of Tyrone, forcing Elizabeth to send the Earl of Essex to put it down. In 1641, the Irish would rebel again.

---

[35] Benjamin Myers (2006), "'Such is the Face of Falshood': Spenserian Theodicy in Ireland." *Studies in Philology*, 103, 383–416.

[36] Edmund Spenser (1997), *A View of the State of Ireland*, Andrew Hadfield and Willy Maley (eds), From the printed edition of 1633, Oxford: Blackwell, pp. 88–9.

CHAPTER SEVEN

Seventeenth-century Ireland

*Ireland is part of the Dominion of England and a kingdom
subordinate to it . . . Without the subjection of Ireland,
England cannot flourish and perhaps not subsist.*

– RICHARD COX, *Aphorisms Relating to the Kingdom of Ireland*, 1689

Ireland under James I

Queen Elizabeth I died without heirs on 24 March 1603, marking the end of
the Tudor dynasty. The English Parliament recognized the slovenly 37-year-
old king of Scotland, James VI (1566–1625), as king of England—and, by
extension, Ireland—signaling the beginning of the Stuart dynasty. James I,
as he was known in England and Ireland, was the son of Elizabeth's cousin,
Mary Queen of Scots, and a direct descendant of Henry VII through his
daughter Margaret, who had married King James IV of Scotland in 1503.
James was an enigmatic and controversial king. He was a mature man who
had two decades of experience as a ruling monarch before he became king
of England and who wrote voluminously on matters of politics and political
theory. Yet, he struggled to maintain a good relationship with the English
parliament, spent profligately, and mostly garnered criticism and discontent
for his policies and ruling style. He wrote intelligently on theology, yet
lacked common sense to the degree that he was branded with the sobriquet
"the wisest fool in Christendom." James alienated some of his subjects by
reversing Elizabethan foreign policy, especially toward England's arch-foe
and religious nemesis, Spain. In addition to ending the Spanish war in 1604,
he cultivated a good relationship with Spain throughout his reign and
even tried to forge a Spanish marriage for his son, Charles, despite deep

public antipathy toward the match. James was tolerant of Catholics, despite a Catholic conspiracy to assassinate him and his family in 1605. He was less so of Puritans, yet he appointed Calvinists to high positions within his church. And these are just a few of the aspects of his reign that have led to shifting interpretations of it in the succeeding centuries.[1]

James's reign in Ireland mirrors his reign in England. He essentially continued the colonial policies of Elizabeth. He was certainly capable of asserting his right to rule; in fact, that was the one thing at which James was consistently good. Yet, he was glad that the Nine Years War had ended before he took the throne and generally tried to avoid further trouble. He kept the penal laws in place and forbade public worship among Catholics, but he did not overly trouble himself with enforcement and made little effort to suppress private worship. Seminary priests and Jesuits were banned from Ireland (as they were from England), but mainly for fear that they would stir the Catholic nobility to political disobedience, which was James's primary concern. At the end of the Nine Years' War, Hugh O'Neill, the earl of Tyrone (1550–1616) managed to retain some power as part of the terms of his surrender. Yet, when O'Neill, Rory O'Donnell, and about 100 other leading landowners left Ireland in September 1607, James took the opportunity to seize their lands. This "flight of the earls" provided the opportunity in 1609 to open Ulster further to plantation by English and Scottish settlers who would be loyal to the Crown, to which they owed the claim to their estates. Under James, who was generally risk-averse, for the first time, all of Ireland was brought under the political control and legal jurisdiction of the British.

James rewarded the English swashbuckler Sir Arthur Chichester (1563–1625) for his military service during the Nine Years War by appointing him Lord Deputy for Ireland in 1605. Chichester was among the "New English" who were now gaining control of the kingdom and were determined to safeguard their interests. It behooved the people now known as the "Old English," who had been born in Ireland, to take part in government in order to look out for their own interests. Anglo-Irish Protestants still retained a good deal of the authority to run a government that was now primarily expected to serve the interests of England.

The main cornerstone of those interests involved the continuation of the plantation system in which new lands were granted to settlers who were expected to remain loyal to the Crown and contribute to its economic prosperity through productive use of their lands. The Crown could not afford to finance these plantations, however, which were semiprivately funded through the merchant companies of London. Plantations were

---

[1] For a good overview of the historiography of James VI and I, see Ralph Houlbrooke (2006), "James's Reputation, 1625–2005," in R. Houlbrooke (ed.), *James VI and I: Ideas, Authority and Government*. Aldershot: Ashgate, pp. 169–90.

not just founded in Ulster, but in Munster as well. It has been suggested that English settlers were more attracted to Munster because of its resemblance to England, whereas Scottish settlers were drawn to Ulster because of similarities between it and their native land. These plantations did provide economic opportunities for those willing to take a risk on one. The first earl of Cork, Richard Boyle, for example, made a fortune after taking up residence on his plantation in Munster in the year of the Spanish Armada, 1588.

In 1613, James granted a charter to some merchant companies from London giving them the right to inhabit the city of Derry, which the English started to refer to as Londonderry. In exchange for the charter, these companies were expected to protect the city and ensure that it remained under English control. To do so, they built a wall around the city, as it had been common practice for urban merchants to do since medieval times. The wall that they built, however, was not very strong and not overly well defended with artillery. This indicates that there was no great fear of a foreign attack, a notion reinforced by the lack of strong English forts along the coast of Ulster.[2] Grants did not just go to London merchants, but also to English soldiers and officers, enterprising Scots, and even some native Irish who had remained loyal to the English during the Nine Years War. However, the native Irish were generally given some of the worst lands; in fact, more than half of the 3,800,000 acres allotted for the settlement of Ulster were largely infertile.

More settlers were migrating from England to Ireland in the reigns of the first two Stuarts than were moving to North America. Jane Ohlmeyer estimates that about 100,000 people moved from Britain to Ireland by 1641, compared to the approximately 14,000 individuals who left for Massachusetts and Virginia in the same period. The migrants contributed to the overall population growth, which Ohlmeyer estimates to have expanded from about 1.4 million in 1600 to 2.1 million in 1641.[3] Of those who went to Ireland, about 30,000 were Scots who mainly settled in Ulster. Many of the immigrants to Ulster became financially successful, especially those merchants who sold timber to the Dutch and the English, who were experiencing a fuel shortage at this time. Iron-smelting led to an early industrial boom in Ireland in the first half of the seventeenth century. Ireland was shifting to more of a market economy under English rule in the seventeenth century. The English continued to think of themselves as bringing civilization to a backward and barbaric land. Yet, little consideration was given to the local

---

[2] J. P. Mallory and T. E. McNeill (1991), *The Archaeology of Ulster from Colonization to Plantation*. Belfast: The Institute for Irish Studies, p. 307.

[3] Jane H. Ohlmeyer (1998), "'Civilizing of those rude partes': Colonization within Britain and Ireland, 1580s–1640s," in Nicholas Canny (ed.), *The Oxford History of the British Empire: Volume I: The Origins of Empire: British Overseas Enterprise to the Close of the Seventeenth Century*. Oxford: Oxford University Press, p. 139.

Irish inhabitants of the region, who were apparently expected to just fall in line and accept the new plantations and settlers. At least for a time, they seemed to do just that.

But the Catholic peasantry did not generally share in whatever economic success the settlers brought to Ireland. The new settlers did not assimilate well with the native Irish. Nor did they make much of an effort to do so. The English government did not trust the Catholics and actively sought to replace Catholic landowners with Protestants to assure Ulster's loyalty in the future. Here, they ran up against the ambitions of the Counter-Reformation papacy, which was determined not to allow any additional lands to fall away from the Roman Church; in fact, in the first half of the seventeenth century, Catholic religious and political leaders made a determined effort to regain some of the lands lost to the Reformation in the sixteenth century. In Ireland, the Catholic Church was committed to at least providing spiritual support for the Irish Catholics to keep them within the Roman fold.

In short, Ireland was a different place at the end of James's reign in 1625 than it had been in 1600, especially Ulster. Many of its leaders had gone into exile after the Nine Years War, while others tried to accommodate themselves to the new realities. For example, while Owen Roe O'Neill (c. 1590–1649), the nephew of Hugh, left Ireland with his family, Sir Phelim O'Neill (1605–53) had been brought up in Ireland as part of the land-owning class and remained on friendly enough terms with the English aristocracy that he would become a justice of the peace. Despite their different upbringings, however, both men would play key roles in the next outburst against the English, which erupted with great force in 1641.

The Irish rebellion of 1641

In the decades that followed the end of the Nine Years War, the English considered rebellion in Ireland to be a possibility based on history, religion, and the ongoing efforts at colonization. On 22 October 1641, their worst fears were confirmed when Irish Catholics led by Sir Phelim O'Neill began an uprising in which Catholic forces seized control of the town of Dungannon and Charlemont castle in Ulster. The following day, they extended their control over Moneymore, Portadown, Tandragee, and Newry. A plan to take Dublin castle failed—much to O'Neill's disappointment—but the rebellion was succeeding spectacularly in Ulster. Events, however, quickly spiraled out of O'Neill's control. In November, Rory O'More led an uprising in which his men massacred a large number of English and Scottish Protestant settlers in revenge for taking their land and subjecting them to all kinds of religious discrimination. Violence or neglect of human necessities during imprisonment would eventually claim the lives of about 12,000 in the course of the rebellion.

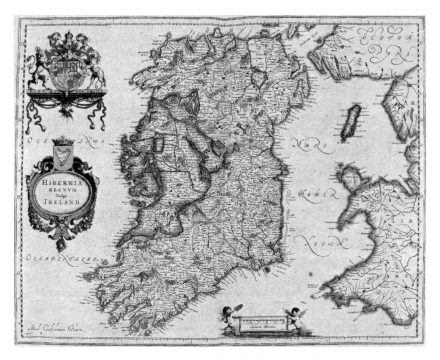

FIGURE 7.1 *Seventeenth-century Map of Ireland. From Willem (1571–1638) and Joan Blaeu (1596–1673),* Theatrum Orbis Terrarum sive Atlas Novus . . ., *1635. Courtesy of Getty Images.*

The immediate chain of events that led to the Irish rebellion began in 1631 when Charles I appointed Thomas Wentworth (1593–1641) lord deputy for Ireland, although Wentworth did not actually arrive in Ireland until July 1633. Along with Charles's archbishop of Canterbury, William Laud (1573–1645), Wentworth had been instrumental in introducing a policy of "Thorough" in England, designed to give the king complete authority over church and state. Now, he hoped to further strengthen the king's hand in Ireland. This meant reducing the power of the Anglo-Irish landowners and their English and Scottish tenants as much as expanding his authority over the native inhabitants. In 1629, Charles had made the decision to rule in England without Parliament, with whom he had bitterly quarreled during the first few years of his reign. Wentworth therefore needed to make sure that money flowed from Ireland to help ensure that Charles had the financial resources necessary to rule without going to Parliament for money. Wentworth engineered a new land settlement in Ireland that caused a great deal of resentment among landowners. Charles ended up recalling Wentworth to London in September 1639, but this was because of the difficulties he was having in suppressing a Scottish rebellion and was not because of his dissatisfaction with Wentworth's rule in Ireland. In fact, the king commanded the earls of Antrim and Ormond to keep Wentworth's army together and to replenish the ranks as soon as possible in order to further strengthen royal authority there.

In 1641, the Irish rebels followed an early modern formula of claiming that they were not rebelling against the king but rather against the abuses of his government. At the beginning of the uprising, O'Neill proclaimed that the purpose of the rebellion was the defense of Catholic liberties, not the infliction of harm upon the king or his subjects. The rebels maintained that they were really acting in the king's best interests. Depositions taken from the rebels after the rebellion reflected their hopes for the establishment of a Catholic kingdom under Charles I. They denied that they sought the downfall of English rule in Ireland; in fact, they insisted that they believed—based on the advice of their leaders—that the king approved of their actions.[4] They hoped for a quick triumph that would allow them to put their terms before the king from a position of strength.

The rebellion met with immediate success as the rebels quickly gained control of Ulster. But the rebellion quickly got out of hand. Catholics massacred Protestants not only in Ulster, but also in Sligo, Roscommon, and Galway. Protestant ministers quickly came under attack in Wexford and Wicklow, where Catholic resentment against the exactions of the established church was particularly strong. Catholic priests and some of the leaders of the rebellion, such as Sir Phelim O'Neill sought to restrain the vengeful violence that many Catholic rebels had begun to inflict upon their Protestant neighbors. By December, Catholic landowners had started to join the rebellion, largely because royal authorities failed to distinguish between Catholics who had remained loyal and those who had not. Whatever the reason, the participation of the Catholic landowners meant that the uprising would be more religiously motivated than class-based. Protestants had also started to retaliate against Catholics and the situation degenerated into one of the worst episodes of religiously inspired violence of the seventeenth century, with atrocities committed on both sides. The situation was reminiscent of the 1572 St Bartholomew's Day Massacre in France; in fact, Protestant descriptions of the atrocities sometimes bore striking resemblances to those that had occurred earlier in France. These similarities have led to suspicions about the accuracy of those accounts, some of which were given by people who had been absent from the scenes of the actual events that they described.[5]

As devastating as the rebellion was, the reports that reached England in its immediate aftermath were even worse. The pamphleteer John Temple claimed

---

[4]   Nicholas Canny (1995), "What Really Happened in Ireland in 1641?," in Jane H. Ohlmeyer (ed.), *Ireland From Independence to Occupation, 1641–1660*. Cambridge: Cambridge University Press, p. 29.

[5]   Martyn Bennett (2000), *The Civil Wars Experienced: Britain and Ireland, 1637–1661*. London: Routledge, p. 48.

that the Catholics had massacred 300,000 people, even though there were only about 100,000 Protestants then living in Ireland! An early pamphlet from 1641 published in England told the story of a pregnant Protestant women being raped by Catholic soldiers who then ripped the baby from her womb, burned the mother and the child, stole what they wanted, and set the house on fire as they left, all after the woman's husband had offered them his hospitality.[6] Temple's was just one of a number of pamphlets published in England in 1641 and 1642 that portrayed such violence, not as random acts of war but as entirely characteristic of the nefarious designs of Catholics toward Protestants as a whole.[7] But the reality of the rebellion was bad enough, without the need to resort to exaggerations or stereotypes. The Protestant William Clarke of Agralohoe in County Armagh reported in a deposition taken in July 1642 that he had been imprisoned with at least 100 men, women, and children, during which time he witnessed tortures that included "strangling and halfe hanging and many other cruelty [sic]." This was before the prisoners were forced into a river at the point of swords and pikes that led to the drowning of some and the shooting of others who managed to swim successfully to shore.[8] Most of the depositions taken after the rebellion were given by Protestants, so we know more about Catholic atrocities than we do about Protestant ones.

As for the course of the rebellion, the rebels needed to win some victories beyond Ulster if they were going to place themselves in a strong position for negotiations with the king. Some rebels marched west to Leitrim and Mayo, while others went south toward Dublin. The southbound force besieged Drogheda in late November. Yet, even as they sought to expand the rebellion beyond Ulster, they never gained complete control of Ulster itself, thanks to intervention from the Scots. Meanwhile, the murderous attacks on Protestants and the stories of other atrocities, both real and imagined, had inflamed not only the Protestants of Ireland but also Protestant sentiment in England. Ireland was about to become embroiled in a much larger contest that would bring about entirely unforeseen consequences.

The "three kingdoms approach": Ireland and the *British Civil Wars*

When word of the outbreak of the Irish rebellion reached England, it came in the midst of perhaps the gravest political crisis of England's long history.

---

[6] *A Bloody Battell: Or the Rebels Overthrow, and Protestant Victorie* (1641). London: Joseph Greensmith. http://bluehawk.monmouth.edu:2213/openurl?ctx_ver=Z39.88-2003&res_id=xri:eebo&rft_id=xri:eebo:image:125544.

[7] Ethan Shagan (1997), "Constructing Discord: Ideology, Propaganda, and English Responses to the Irish Rebellion of 1641." *Journal of British Studies*, 36, 8.

[8] Deposition of William Clarke, 7/1/1642. http://www.1641.tcd.ie/index.php.

During his so-called *Personal Rule*, Charles I ruled without Parliament from 1629 to 1640. He had alienated some of his subjects because of the increased intrusion of royal government into local affairs. Others were disturbed because of his refusal to call Parliament and his desire to challenge what they regarded as an "ancient constitution" by ruling on his own. Many people were upset because of the religious reforms carried out by William Laud, which seemed in the eyes of many people to be moving the Church of England in the direction of Roman Catholicism. When Charles did reconvene Parliament in April 1640 to ask for assistance in dealing with a crisis with Scotland (see below), he was met with numerous grievances that led him to dismiss the assembly after only three weeks. However, a second military defeat at the hands of the Scots necessitated reconvening Parliament once again in November. Charles now had no choice but to capitulate to some of Parliament's demands. For example, in February 1641, Parliament passed a Triennial Act, which stipulated that Parliament be called at least every three years. On 10 May, Parliament bypassed royal prerogative by passing an act that called for its own continuance until such time as its members would vote for dismissal. Perhaps most notably, Charles exhibited a sense of defeatism in acquiescing to the trial of Wentworth, (now the earl of Strafford), who was put to death on 12 May.

But as spring moved into summer, Charles began to gain in strength and determination, partly out of a sense of guilt at his betrayal of Strafford. What had once seemed a unified opposition to the king now seemed to be fragmenting over religious and political differences. Charles made peace with the Scots, while most members of both houses of Parliament left London to avoid the plague. The Scottish nobility, for all the trouble that they had caused Charles, had no wish to see his political authority replaced by that of the English parliament. At this point, they were quite content to negotiate a deal with the king. Scotland was dividing along lines similar to those that were forming in England—between royalists and parliamentarians. In England, Parliament, after further usurping some of Charles's powers while the king was in Scotland, adjourned for a six-week recess on 9 September. When Parliament reconvened on 20 October, John Pym (1584–1643), the leader of the opposition, was in an angry mood and determined to confront the king once again about his abuse of power related to an alleged plot to kidnap two Scottish leaders while he was in Edinburgh. It was in this heated atmosphere that news of the Irish rebellion arrived in London on 1 November.

Neither king nor Parliament was content to sit idly while rebellion raged in Ireland, but leading parliamentarians feared that a royal army used to crush the Irish rebellion could potentially be redeployed to England to annihilate parliamentary opposition and support Charles's claims to absolute authority. Yet, for the king to consider granting Parliament control over an army was unthinkable. The Irish rebellion had brought the two sides to an impasse. Compromise seemed impossible and negotiations broke down.

Both king and Parliament prepared to raise their own army, but that now meant defeating not only the Irish rebels but also each other and thus the possibility of a civil war in England.

Historians now tend to use the term *British Civil Wars* in preference to *English Civil War*, although even this term is somewhat restrictive because it could be taken as excluding the civil war in Ireland. In Scotland, royalists took up arms in support of Charles I and later fought their own civil war. England, of course, was divided between supporters of the king and supporters of Parliament, with armies representing both sides fighting conventional battles, occupying territory, placing hostile towns and cities under siege, and recruiting/drafting soldiers to serve in them. We have already seen the intense religious strife that was tearing Ireland apart. Use of the term *British Civil Wars* simply acknowledges that the civil war experience was not just confined to England during the 1640s.

In addition to employing the terminology of *the British Civil Wars*, the English historian Conrad Russell is primarily responsible for a historiographical trend dealing with the period known as *the three kingdoms approach*. The three kingdoms approach reflects the historical reality that the main events in any of the kingdoms of England, Scotland, and Ireland during this period cannot be understood without reference to developments in the other two. The three kingdoms approach also has the advantage of encouraging the integration of the England, Scotland, and Ireland in treatments of this period and elevating the importance of events in Ireland and Scotland to an equal position alongside those occurring in England. Proponents of this approach advocate a truly integrated history of the three kingdoms, not, in S. J. Connolly's words, "an occasional invocation of the Celtic periphery to illuminate a primarily English narrative."[9]

The three kingdoms approach is not without its problems, particularly when used as a causal explanation for the outbreak of the civil wars. Peter Lake has argued that such a causal explanation does not replace traditional explanations for the wars because it fails to address the internal dynamics that led, for example, to the Irish rebellion in the first place. In other words, to suggest that the Irish rebellion caused the English Civil War merely raises the further question of what caused the Irish rebellion.[10] The same could be said for Scotland in terms of the Bishops' Wars that created the immediate crisis that led Charles to call the Short Parliament in April 1640. The causes of these events are certainly complex and subject to varying interpretations. But once this caveat is taken into consideration, it is hard to ignore the role

---

[9] S. J. Connolly (2009), Review of Alan Ford, *James Ussher: Theology, History, and Politics in Early Modern Ireland and England. Journal of British Studies*, 48, 202.

[10] Peter Lake (1996), "Retrospective: Wentworth's Political World in Revisionist and Post-Revisionist Perspective," in J. F. Merritt (ed.), *The Political World of Thomas Wentworth, Earl of Strafford, 1621–1641*. Cambridge: Cambridge University Press, pp. 252–83.

that developments in both Scotland and Ireland played in precipitating the Civil War in England.

In order for a true "three kingdoms approach" such as that envisioned by Professor Connolly to work, then, the historian would need to take into consideration the importance of developments in England for precipitating events in Scotland and Ireland, while also taking into account how developments in Scotland and Ireland affected events in England without giving precedence to any of the three kingdoms. As an example of how events in different countries impacted the others in mutually important ways, it is hard to argue that the English Civil War did not have at least its immediate origins in Scotland, but that was only because Charles I, in one of the most ill-considered decisions ever made by a reigning monarch, attempted to force the Presbyterian Scots to adopt the English Book of Common Prayer and the episcopal system of church government. Why did Charles do this? In addition to a general desire to see his kingdoms unified religiously, Charles may have feared that in the future the Presbyterians in Scotland and Ireland would form an alliance with his religious critics at home. This did come to pass in the 1640s, though Charles's actions unwittingly helped to bring it about. The Scots formed the National Covenant and steeled themselves to resist Charles's religious instructions. Wentworth, whose high-handed manner and determined support of Charles's absolutist policies had already alienated the king's subjects in England and Ireland, now drew the ire of the Scots by encouraging Charles not to back down and by arranging for an army to crush Scottish resistance. Charles rewarded Wentworth's loyalty by making him earl of Strafford, as well as his principal advisor. Strafford's advice backfired, however, leading to the Scots' hatred of him and their resentment toward the king. The Scottish rebellion thus had occurred within a specifically Scottish context related to its religious and political history, which clashed with the designs of Charles and Strafford in the late 1630s. The Scots' success at fending off the king had repercussions in England, but only because the English parliament was having its own problems with the king at the same time.

The Irish situation provided another variable on the events in and the relationship between England and Scotland. Like the Bishops' Wars, the Irish rebellion had both immediate and long-range causes. But the English response to the rebellion was conditioned by immediate concerns that were inflamed by the pamphleteers who portrayed the Irish rebellion as a Protestant Armageddon.[11] Yet, the Irish rebellion actually became a secondary concern for Parliament, once its leaders determined that they might need to fight the king. Before long, Parliament would see Ireland largely as a source of land to be sold for money to pay its army or to be granted as a reward for its supporters. Ireland never fulfilled this promise and the cost of conquering

---

[11] Shagan, *op. cit.*, esp. pp. 5–6.

Ireland has been estimated at £3.5 million.[12] Like the Irish, the English and the Scots both discovered that their actions and decisions came with numerous unintended consequences.

The conflict in Ireland had reached a stalemate by the end of 1641. The English stronghold of Drogheda in County Louth was under siege by Catholic rebels led by Phelim O'Neill. However, in March 1642, English reinforcements from Dublin lifted the siege and the rebels retreated back to Ulster. In April 1642, a Scottish army of about 2,500 men arrived in the seaport of Carrickfergus northeast of Belfast to put an end to the Irish rebellion and reestablish Protestant control. But they had to contend not only with the Catholic rebels but also with a royal army led by James Butler (1610–88), the earl of Ormond. Thus in Ireland, for a brief time, there were three conflicting armies trying to gain control. However, given that two of them were hostile to the Scots and the English parliament, it was perhaps inevitable that they would join forces. Anxious to add Irish recruits to his army, in September 1643, Charles instructed Ormond to begin negotiations with the Irish Catholics. Charles had not benefitted greatly from Irish support, even though some of Strafford's former soldiers were dispatched from Ireland to serve in the king's army, and he was sorely in need of it. But Charles's pandering to the Irish discredited him further in the eyes of many of the English people. Meanwhile, given that the English parliament and the Scots had the same enemies it was perhaps inevitable that they would become allies. Parliament financed the addition of another 8,000 Scottish troops to be sent to Ireland by the end of the year.

Moreover, in 1644, a desperate Parliament negotiated an alliance with the Scots that was called the "Solemn League and Covenant," in which the Parliamentarians promised to make England a Presbyterian nation in exchange for Scottish military support. The Scots were no longer merely content to safeguard their religion at home, but were looking to protect and expand the Presbyterian faith in Charles's other kingdoms as well. In fact, they had already begun doing so in Ulster, where, for example, the Scottish Presbyterian ministers Robert Blair and John Livingstone were evangelizing in Down.[13] The commitment that Parliament had made to the Scots was far from universally popular in England. The entry of the Scots into the English Civil War made it likely that if Parliament were victorious in England, then Ireland would become part of the Scottish agenda to spread Presbyterianism as well. Within a few years, the Scottish alliance would cause a serious rift within the parliamentary forces as well as between Scotland and the English parliament. Charles, meanwhile, continued to look to Ireland for support,

[12] Derek Hirst (1999), *England in Conflict: 1603–1660*. London: Arnold, p. 262.
[13] Allan I. MacInnes (2000), "Covenanting Ideology in Seventeenth-Century Scotland," in J. H. Ohlmeyer (ed.), *Political Thought in Seventeenth-Century Ireland: Kingdom or Colony*. Cambridge: Cambridge University Press, p. 196.

asking Randall MacDonnell, (1609–83), the marquis of Antrim to raise an army in Ireland for a planned invasion of western England.

The emergence of Oliver Cromwell (1599–1658) as the head of Parliament's New Model Army was a turning point in the history of the British Civil Wars and the three kingdoms. Cromwell was a wild card, a minor politician who had risen to prominence as a result of the war. He inclined more toward the Independents than to the Presbyterians; thus, his rise from the very beginning threatened to undermine the relationship between Parliament and the Scots. The Independents were the heirs of the English Congregationalists, religious separatists who believed that each congregation should have its own autonomy to follow the word of God as it saw fit. They were skeptical of any larger national church organization that would uniformly impose a set of rules on its churches. The English Independents, with the support of Cromwell, were beginning to gain control in the New Model Army. They also had their counterparts in Ireland. The Irish Independents had the support of Viscount Lisle, the lord-lieutenant of Ireland who had been appointed by the English parliament. Patrick Little has shown that Independents in England and Ireland formed an international alliance in opposition to the English and Scottish Presbyterians.[14] The alliance did not last, but at least some Irish Protestants had looked to England for a closer alliance, which Cromwell was going to provide in the 1650s, whether the Irish liked it or not.

Ireland was a divided kingdom, with the Catholic Confederacy neither subdued nor triumphant. Rome, seizing upon the opportunity to support the Catholic faith in Ireland, had dispatched Giovanni Battista Rinuccini (1592–1653), the archbishop of Fermo, as a papal nuncio to Ireland in October 1645. At the same time, the papacy was negotiating with Queen Henrietta Maria, the Catholic wife of Charles I, to find a way to support Catholics throughout the three kingdoms. The pope promised 30,000 crowns to support an Irish army to assist the king in winning the war and making this possible. O'Neill went so far as to offer his army to Rinuccini to help put the pope's plans into effect. But the reestablishment of papal authority in Ireland had not been on the agenda of many supporters of the rebellion whose main goal was simply to achieve toleration for their beliefs and public worship. Rinuccini's mission thus exacerbated a division within the Catholic Confederation that had already started to occur over the issue of clerical influence over the rebellion.

Charles had been somewhat hampered in what he could do for the Catholics of Ireland. A number of conversions to Catholicism by prominent members of his court and his marriage to the French Catholic, Henrietta Maria, had led many in England to suspect Charles of involvement in a plot to bring England back into the arms of the Catholic Church. Given Charles's

---

[14] Patrick Little (2001), "The Irish 'Independents' and Viscount Lisle's Lieutenancy of Ireland." *The Historical Journal*, 44, 941–61.

suspected sympathies toward Catholicism and the overt plotting of Henrietta Maria, any move in favor of the Catholics from the king would be viewed as a step in the direction of popery, which his Anglo-Irish supporters had no desire to see happen. If toleration for the Catholics was going to come at all, it would have to come from Cromwell and the Independents, whose Protestant credentials were impeccable. Cromwell would get that opportunity because he gained control first of the New Model Army and then of the country after Parliament defeated Charles I.

The tide against the Royalists began to turn in 1645. In May 1646, Charles surrendered to the Scots, but they returned him to England to deal with Cromwell and the representatives of Parliament. As soon as it had become clear that Parliament would win the English Civil War, Cromwell began thinking about Ireland, where the Catholics still controlled much of the country and which had done so much to bring about the conflict in the first place. On 5 June 1646, Owen Roe O'Neill and his Catholic army inflicted a decisive defeat on the Scots at the Battle of Benburb, which took place in the vicinity of Armagh. The Catholics were on the verge of securing their military hold on Ulster. Cromwell's concern was partly with the future of Protestantism in Ireland and partly with his own financial security because of investments he held there.[15] On 19 March 1642, the English Parliament had passed the Adventurers' Act, a fund-raising measure that promised 1,000 acres of land in Ireland for every £200 contribution to the war effort in Ireland. Cromwell had invested heavily and wanted to make sure that he got a return for his money. He was prevented from intervening sooner by the outbreak of a second civil war in England in 1648 when Charles I raised another army, this time with the aid of his former foes, the Scots. But once the king was executed on 30 January 1649, Cromwell could turn his intention to Ireland in earnest. The royalist army had been disbanded and Parliament was in complete control of England.

On 20 April, Cromwell announced his intention to go to Ireland. The Council of the Army began to determine which regiments to send with him. After selecting the regiments by lots, it was reported that the officers selected to go "expressed much cheerfulness at the decision," but that the common soldiers were "by no means all of that humor."[16] Having won the war in England, they were probably looking forward to peace and the new society that was promised to follow their victory. Now they were going to Ireland resenting their leaders for sending them there, but resenting even more the Irish rebels who in their eyes had made additional fighting necessary.

---

[15] Patrick Little (2009), "Cromwell and Ireland before 1649," in P. Little (ed.), *Oliver Cromwell: New Perspectives.* New York: Palgrave Macmillan, p. 121.

[16] Oliver Cromwell (1904), *The Letters and Speeches of Oliver Cromwell with Elucidations by Thomas Carlyle,* edited by S. C. Lomas. London: Methuen, p. 437. http://openlibrary.org/books/OL7102295M/The_letters_and_speeches_of_Oliver_Cromwell.

Cromwell and Ireland

Cromwell is the bête noire par excellence of Irish history. Tour guides in Ireland still speak of him with derision, and his reputation there is still so strongly associated with the nationalist version of Irish history that he is spoken of in terms usually reserved for such villains of history as Hitler, Stalin, or Genghis Khan. Malachy McCourt, in his eccentric popular history of Ireland, writes of wanting to exclude Cromwell altogether from his book, saying that he "left an indelible gash on the historical landscape of the country." McCourt sums up Cromwell's legacy in a single phrase borrowed from a friend: "he out-Heroded Herod."[17] But Cromwell was a complex individual who, like Napoleon, has produced many varying and conflicting accounts of his historical legacy. Whatever one thinks of him, that legacy, even for Ireland, certainly cannot be reduced to a single phrase. Dealing with Cromwell's legacy in Ireland, however, provides a real test of the historian's ability to set aside stereotypes and reductionism in an effort to understand the past in all of its complexity.

It is in dealing with Cromwell that the three kingdoms approach is perhaps most illuminating. For example, R. Scott Spurlock has considered Cromwell's role in Ireland from the larger perspective of what Cromwell did in each of the three kingdoms. Spurlock argues that Cromwell's actions in Ireland cannot be understood as simply a result of either anti-Irish or anti-Catholic prejudice. In England, the focus of Cromwell's government, according to Spurlock, both during the Commonwealth (1649–53) and the Protectorate (1653–58), was not on making life difficult for ordinary Catholics. He points out that the government mainly took action against those suspected of the crime of harboring priests, which made them guilty of treason in the eyes of the law. Cromwell and the Independents were better disposed toward religious toleration in general than were the Presbyterians. Cromwell negotiated an agreement with English Catholics in 1647 granting a measure of toleration in exchange for Catholics' willingness to recognize limits on papal authority in the temporal sphere.[18] Even those Independents who supported Cromwell's invasion of Ireland saw it more as an enterprise intended to civilize the barbarous elements among the Irish instead of as a religious crusade against the Catholics.[19]

---

[17] Malachy McCourt (2004), *Malachy McCourt's History of Ireland*. Philadelphia: Running Press, pp. 149–50. The friend's name is Tom McGuire.

[18] R. Scott Spurlock (2010), "Cromwell and Catholics: Toward a Reassessment of Lay Catholic Experience in Interregnum Ireland," in M. Williams and S. P. Forrest (eds), *Constructing the Past: Writing Irish History, 1600–1800*. Woodbridge: The Boydell Press, pp. 170–4.

[19] Norah Carlin (1993), "Extreme or Mainstream?: the English Independents and the Cromwellian Reconquest of Ireland, 1649–1651," in A. Hadfield and W. Maley (eds), *Representing Ireland: Literature and the Origins of Conflict, 1534–1660*. Cambridge: Cambridge University Press, 1993, p. 210.

Cromwell's decision to intervene in both Ireland and Scotland reinforces the importance of the three kingdoms approach since their fates during the civil wars were inextricably intertwined. For Cromwell and his Puritan supporters, there could be no question of simply ruling England and letting Ireland go, for three reasons. First, Catholicism could not be allowed to triumph in Ireland. Whatever their attitudes toward individual Catholics, as committed Protestants, they would not have been willing to leave Ireland to its own devices and risk Ireland becoming a Catholic nation right next to Protestant England. Second, Cromwell's national economic policy was expansionist and Ireland was still viewed as a valuable colony that could provide land for English settlers and potential revenue for England. Third, Cromwell, although he refused the Crown and the title of king, regarded himself as the successor of Charles I in all three of his kingdoms.

Cromwell arrived in Dublin in August 1649 "with 12,000 veterans from the New Model Army, with a powerful siege train and a war chest of £100,000."[20] In Dublin, accounts of the massacres that had accompanied the 1641 rebellion were reprinted at the request of the English Council of State. Cromwell immediately placed the port town of Drogheda, located on the Boyne River in County Louth, under siege. Upon the surrender of Drogheda on 11 September, he had most members of the royal garrison there slaughtered. It is important to remember that Cromwell's victory in Ireland was not assured at this point. He was becoming exasperated with the continued resistance of the rebels and was determined to put an end to it.

Cromwell's lenient treatment of Catholics in Scotland has led Professor Spurlock to argue that Cromwell had them killed because they were royalists, not because they were Catholics. It should also be noted that Cromwell did not make a distinction between Catholic and Protestant loyalists when he seized the lands of Irish royalists; if you were a royalist, you lost your land. But this was not the way in which the massacre was perceived at the time. Just as Protestant propaganda had transformed the Catholic rebellion and its accompanying atrocities in 1641 as religiously motivated and entirely in keeping with Catholic intentions toward all Protestants, Catholic propaganda would portray Drogheda in the same light. Protestant intentions toward all Catholics were called into question. In reality, there were also Protestants among those slain at Drogheda and Cromwell knew it. Furthermore, significant numbers of Irish Catholics served in Cromwell's army, apparently with little to no resentment on the part of the Protestant soldiers from the English army.[21] Catholics in Ireland had been divided over the rebellion for quite some time, the beginning of what would become

---

[20] Jane Ohlmeyer (1996), "The Wars of Religion, 1603–1660," in T. Bartlett and K. Jeffery (eds), *A Military History of Ireland*. Cambridge: Cambridge University Press, p. 168.

[21] Spurlock, *op. cit.*, p. 177. See also Mícheál Ó Siochrú (2008), *God's Executioner: Oliver Cromwell and the Conquest of Ireland*. London: Faber and Faber, pp. 204–10.

a familiar pattern in Irish history. However, subsequent events provided more ammunition to the propagandists. Following the siege of Wexford in October, Cromwell's troops massacred more Irish people. They did so less systematically and without the same orders from above, but the slaughter was equally devastating.

Cromwell swept through Ireland, victory following upon victory. After he returned to England in 1650, his forces completed the conquest of Ireland with the surrender of Galway on 12 April 1652. The 1652 Act of Settlement exiled Catholic landowners to Connacht and County Clare; when asked where those Irish displaced by his conquest should go, Cromwell had allegedly replied, "to hell or Connacht." Many did not take his advice and instead chose to continue to harass Cromwell's troops through guerilla activity. Cromwell may very well have viewed the war in Ireland through the eyes of a military commander rather than as a religious fanatic, but this did not stop his actions from being portrayed as a crusade against Catholics. It did not help that Protestants such as the Presbyterian minister Patrick Adair viewed the fate of the rebels as "the righteous judgment of God," even though he thought that their treatment had been carried out by "unjust hands."[22] There were certainly other Protestants—both Presbyterians and Independents, as well as more radical groups like the Fifth Monarchists and the Baptists—who viewed the conflict in Ireland as something of a religious crusade. But the Presbyterians in Ireland did not really welcome the rule of the Independent Cromwell any more than the Presbyterians in Scotland did, seeing his victories in both places as a test of their own faith.

Like his royal predecessors, Cromwell appointed lord lieutenants and their deputies to rule over Ireland. On 26 June 1657, the Act for the Attainder of the Rebels in Ireland formally declared an end to the rebellion and authorized the seizure of lands held by the heirs of those who had participated in it to be redistributed and settled. Additional plantations followed, continuing the policy followed by the first two Stuart kings. The New English settlers who had arrived under Elizabeth or earlier in the seventeenth century were confirmed in the possession of their lands.

The black legend of Oliver Cromwell in Ireland is based on his alleged religious fanaticism and hatred of Catholics. Yet, in Scotland, it was the Presbyterians who feared his rule the most. Scottish Presbyterians even worried about what Cromwell might do to their coreligionists in England and Ireland.[23] After attempting to secure the safety of Protestants in Ireland, he proceeded to secure the safety of religious minorities, including Catholics, from the religious tyranny of the Presbyterian Church in Scotland. With the

---

[22] Quoted in Kirsten M. MacKenzie (2009), "Oliver Cromwell and the Solemn League and Covenant of the Three Kingdoms," in P. Little (ed.), *Oliver Cromwell: New Perspectives.* New York: Palgrave Macmillan, p. 155.

[23] Ibid., p. 142.

threat of the Catholic rebellion in Ireland ended, Cromwell was prepared to be more lenient toward Catholics in all three kingdoms, including Ireland.[24] He did not view all Catholics as the same nor did he base his policy on the assumption that they were. This is not to suggest that Cromwell did not see himself as a Protestant or that his religious views were completely divorced from his political and military career. It should come as no surprise if he viewed Catholics in Ireland differently than those in England and Scotland given their role in the Irish rebellion. It is only to suggest that he blamed them more for being rebels than he did for being Catholics, as his treatment of Catholics in the other kingdoms demonstrates. Historians differ as to the extent to which Catholics in Ireland enjoyed the same measure of toleration under Cromwell as did their coreligionists in England and Scotland. Toby Barnard, for one, has argued that they did not, nor could they, given the deep divisions that the rebellion had carved in Irish society and the strong religious overtones that it carried and that had accompanied Cromwell's intervention.[25]

Divisions within Ireland

In 1622, Sir James Perrot, a Welsh politician who had been sent to Ireland on a commission of inquiry, wrote to Lionel Cranfield, who at the time was serving as Lord High Treasurer in England, speculating on whether or not Catholics in Ireland could be expected to remain loyal to the English state given the discontent caused "by the diversity of their religion from ours, by loss of their livings, [and] supposed injustice or some other heavy pressures."[26] In order to portray the rebellion when it did happen as particularly treacherous, Sir John Temple in his account of the Irish rebellion painted quite a different picture. According to Temple, "the two Nations had lived together 40 years in peace, with great security and comfort, which had in a manner consolidated them into one body, knit and compounded together with all those bonds and ligatures of friendship, alliance, and consanguinity as might make up a constant and perpetual union betwixt them."[27] In the seventeenth century, Ireland remained divided on the basis of religion and geography. Ireland, like England and Scotland, was roughly divided geographically between

---

[24] Spurlock, *op. cit.*, p. 175. See also R. Scott Spurlock (2007), *Cromwell and Scotland: Conquest and Religion, 1650–1660*. Edinburgh: Birlinn Ltd.

[25] T. C. Barnard (2004), *Irish Protestant Ascents and Descents, 1641–1770*. Dublin: Four Courts Press, pp. 12–13.

[26] "Sir James Perrot to Cranfield," in Victor Treadwell (ed.), (2006), *The Irish Commission of 1622: An Investigation of the Irish Administration, 1615–1622, and its Consequences, 1623–1624*. Dublin: Irish Manuscripts Commission, p. 54.

[27] Sir John Temple (1698), *The Irish Rebellion*. Dublin: Andrew Crook, p. 14. http://bluehawk.monmouth.edu:2213/openurl?ctx_ver=Z39.88-2003&res_id=xri:eebo&rft_id=xri:eebo:image:47155.

southern lowlands that consisted of arable farmland and a northern region that was wilder and rockier and contained soil that made it better suited to a pastoral economy. The difference was that in Ireland the northern region was the Protestant stronghold, whereas in England and Scotland, the Protestant faith predominated in the south and Catholicism had a stronger appeal in the north.

There was also an important religious difference between the Presbyterian Protestants in Ulster who identified with Scotland and members of the established church who maintained their political and religious allegiance to England. In 1672, the political economist William Petty estimated that there were 800,000 Catholics in Ireland and 300,000 non-Catholics, including 100,000 Scottish Presbyterians. Petty further estimated that 100,000 belonged to the established church, leaving an additional 100,000 divided among religious minorities such as the English Presbyterians, Independents, Baptists, and Quakers. Then, there was the division between the Old English and the New English, which sometimes reflected divisions within the established church itself. For example, the archbishop of Armagh, James Ussher, the most influential voice within the established church, was a Calvinist who worried about the conservative direction in which Laud was taking the Church of England. The Old English, who were mostly concentrated within the Pale, staked their hopes of remaining dominant on the royalist cause in the civil wars, despite their own grievances against Wentworth and the rule of Charles I. The Old English thus emerged from the war in a weakened position.

But religious divisions in Ireland were not absolute. For example, a Catholic landlord named Philip MacMulmore made an effort to aid Protestants during the 1641 rebellion even though he had relatives among the rebels themselves.[28] The rebellion seemed to reaffirm to some the desirability of uniting the Irish people under a single religion. Vincent Gookin expressed this hope in 1655, optimistically believing that in time—with gentle persuasion and by not permitting public worship in the Catholic faith—most Irish Catholics could be won over to Protestantism. Gookin saw this as the only option for ending the religious divide in Ireland because he could not conceive "what temptations may invite Protestants to turn Papists."[29] Gookin also thought that the rebellion had only made it that much less likely that Irish Protestants would ever convert to the Catholic faith, while he believed that many Catholics had actually been alienated from their religion by all of the violence perpetrated by their coreligionists. Some Catholics did convert to Protestantism during the 1650s, much to the dismay of the priests and

[28] Joseph Cope (2003), "The Experience of Survival in the 1641 Irish Rebellion," *The Historical Journal*, 46, 295–316.

[29] Vincent Gookin (1655), *The Great Case of Transplantation in Ireland Discussed*. London: I.C., p. 2. http://bluehawk.monmouth.edu:2213/openurl?ctx_ver=Z39.88-2003&res_id= xri:eebo&rft_id=xri:eebo:image:197848.

bishops who resumed their positions after the death of Cromwell in 1658. Gookin ignored, however, the strong feelings of anti-Catholicism that existed among Protestants, including Ussher who was known for his anti-Catholic sermons in the 1620s, and the discrimination that had helped to provoke the rebellion in the first place.

Finally, there were social divisions related to the great disparity between the poor and the wealthy. The level of economic inequality is perhaps best exemplified by Petty's claim that 160,000 families in Ireland had no fixed hearth, while 24,000 families had one chimney and only 16,000 families enjoyed residences with more than one chimney. It is safe to say that with all probability, a majority of those families without a chimney were Irish, while a disproportionate number of those with one or two chimneys were English or Anglo-Irish. These divisions are critical to understanding Ireland's history moving forward, starting with the period in which it attempted to recover from the devastation of the civil wars.

The aftermath of the civil wars

Old English and New English Protestants came together in Dublin in February 1660 to discuss the future of Ireland after Cromwell. They denounced the execution of Charles I, but in the same declaration affirmed Ireland's right to legislate for itself. On 14 May 1660, they officially proclaimed Charles II (r. 1660–85), who had been restored to the English throne days before, king of Ireland. Hoping to gain sympathy for Ireland, the Galway-born loyalist John Lynch assured the restored King Charles II that the Irish rebellion had been the work of "a rabble of men of ruined fortunes or profligate character, that were hurried on for a moment by delirious madness."[30]

William Petty estimated that there were 616,000 fewer people in Ireland in 1664 than there were in 1641 as a result of the rebellion and the events that followed. Of that number, he calculated that about 504,000 had died between 23 October 1641 and 23 October 1652 by "sword, plague, famine, hardship, and banishment."[31] In addition, perhaps 80,000 property owners had lost their land[32] to be replaced in many instances by additional settlers from England and Scotland in what S. J. Connolly has called "a revolution in land ownership."[33] One of the big questions that accompanied the restoration

---

[30] John Lynch (1848), *Cambrensis Eversus*, Vol. I, translated and edited by Matthew Kelly. Dublin: Celtic Society, p. 13.

[31] William Petty (1672), *The Political Economy of Ireland*, p. 18.

[32] T. C. Barnard (1998), "British Settlement, 1650–1700," in Nicholas Canny (ed.), *The Oxford History of the British Empire: Volume I: The Origins of Empire: British Overseas Enterprise to the Close of the Seventeenth Century*. Oxford: Oxford University Press, p. 310.

[33] S. J. Connolly (1992), *Religion, Law, and Power: The Making of Protestant Ireland, 1660–1760*. Oxford: Clarendon Press, p. 13.

of Charles II in Ireland was what was going to become of the Cromwellian land settlement. Charles had no wish to relive the religious and political strife that had brought about the downfall and death of his father and his own exile. He was mostly content to affirm the status quo, and he promised to uphold the Cromwellian settlement. But he also issued a declaration in November 1660 promising that Catholics who had remained loyal during the rebellion and the civil wars would regain their lands. It was unclear how those who had received land grants under Cromwell were going to keep their lands if some of those lands were to be restored to Catholic royalists, but these seemingly incompatible pledges were essentially what Charles had promised. As if that were not enough, the Old English were demanding compensation for losses as well.

Those Cromwellian settlers who did lose their land to Catholics deemed worthy of restoration received additional land carved out of the estates of other settlers from the 1650s. According to a deal between the Irish government and the court of claims reached in 1664, most landowners who had received grants from Cromwell were to give up one-third of their estates for that purpose.[34] In other cases where Protestant settlers and loyal Catholics had claims to the same land, Catholics were simply granted different estates in compensation. Those who had gone into exile with the king received top priority. Land grants were also a handy way to reward royalist soldiers whose pay was in arrears rather than taking the money directly out of the depleted royal treasury. Some Catholics did regain their lands, but the 20 per cent of land owned by Catholics in Ireland after redistribution was still only about a third of the amount owned by Catholics in 1640.[35] The further seeds of discontent among Catholics were thus sown into the land settlement for Ireland that accompanied the Restoration.

Charles's lord lieutenant, Ormond, while supporting the landed interests of the Protestants, did try to appease the Catholics by granting them a measure of religious toleration on the condition that they disavow in writing their belief in the deposing power of the papacy. But even these plans fell by the wayside when Ormond faced opposition from Protestants. Catholics in Ireland were not actively persecuted for practicing their faith and they were better off than they had been under Cromwell, but no additional concessions were made to them. Charles could not do enough for the Catholics, but neither could he please the Protestants, some of whom resented that any land was being given back to Catholics. Catholics remained in a kind of legal limbo for the rest of Charles's reign.

In all three of his kingdoms, the Restoration largely turned back the calendar to 1640. Royal authority was restored, along with the king's privy

---

[34] David Dickson (2000), *New Foundations: Ireland, 1660–1800*. Dublin: Irish Academic Press, p. 8.
[35] Connolly, *Religion, Law, and Power*, p. 15.

council and the bishops in the established church. In England, the king's government did take some steps to limit the role that religion could play in politics. These measures were incorporated into a series of acts that are collectively known as the *Clarendon Code*, named after Charles's chief minister, Sir Edward Hyde (1609–74), the earl of Clarendon. Among the main components of the Clarendon Code were laws making membership in the established church a prerequisite for holding municipal offices, requiring clergy to conduct services according to the *Book of Common Prayer*, and placing limits on the number of people who could attend religious services that were not Anglican.

Charles's approach varied somewhat in each of his kingdoms, based on what political expediency seemed to demand. Scotland had its own parliament and judiciary restored. In Ireland, Charles struck something of a balance, more out of neglect than planned policy. For instance, the king made no immediate moves to replace Cromwell's appointees. A viceroy was appointed for Ireland to replace Cromwell's lord deputy, though the extent of his power was still dependent on the whims of the king. He also continued the policy of sponsoring English plantations in Ireland, choosing to ignore the role that these had played in the origins of the 1641 rebellion, while giving lip service to toleration for Catholics. In each of his kingdoms, he largely alienated Protestants without doing much of significance to benefit Catholics. He fought two wars against the Protestant Dutch at a time when Catholic France was emerging as the most powerful nation in Europe. In 1670, Charles concluded a secret Treaty of Dover with Louis XIV of France, promising military assistance against the Dutch in exchange for French subsidies. Charles also attempted to suspend all laws discriminating against Catholics and Protestant dissenters in a Declaration of Indulgence in 1672. The conversion of his brother, James, the duke of York, to Catholicism about the same time only added to Protestant discontent, as did a rumored plot to assassinate Charles and place James on the throne in 1678. The Popish Plot turned out to be a hoax, albeit one that cost several dozen English Catholics their lives in the hysteria that accompanied it. Finally, when Parliament attempted to pass an Exclusion Bill to prevent James from inheriting the throne—which seemed likely since Charles had no legitimate children—Charles in defiance dismissed Parliament several times over the issue. After dismissing Parliament in 1681, he did not call another one for the final four years of his reign.

In Ireland, the reign of Charles II coincided with an era of general peace and prosperity and can even seem like something of a golden age compared to the periods that came before and immediately after it. His pro-Catholic foreign policy and his attempts to secure toleration for Catholics contributed to a relatively high level of support among the Catholic population of Ireland, while the Irish Protestants did not dare challenge his authority after all that had transpired in the 1640s and 1650s. After Charles dismissed Ormond in 1669, Irish Catholics found it easier to hold offices and to circumvent other legal restrictions. Irish peasants benefited from an end to the services owed to the nobility as a condition of their inheritance and occupancy of their land. The Catholic Church began to recover from the devastations of the wars and a number of Catholic exiles even returned from the European continent. However, the general relationship between England and Ireland remained the same, Ireland's halfway position between a kingdom and a colony intact and unresolved. Economically, Ireland still suffered from English restrictions on its trade, including a prohibition of exporting Irish cattle and restricting the export of Irish wool to England only. Yet, this was a relatively prosperous time for Ireland, largely sustained by English demand for its beef and dairy products and some illicit trade with the European continent. Ireland might not have been benefitting from its connection with England, but under Charles, the atmosphere was relatively peaceful. However, in 1688, the pitfalls of sharing a king with England would be revealed again when the English staged another revolution against Charles's successor, his younger brother James II (r. 1685–88).

The impact of the revolution of 1688 and the Battle of the Boyne

James came to the throne in 1685 a Catholic and a Stuart, who had been conditioned by the political ideology of his father, the religion of his mother, and the experiences and example of his royal brother to believe that he had a right and a duty to follow his conscience and rule as king in what he saw as the best interests of all of his subjects. Political expediency would have counseled him to avoid calling attention to his faith, given the strong anti-Catholic sentiments that still prevailed among Protestants in his kingdoms, especially in England. He did just the opposite.

James's efforts to obtain religious toleration for Catholics are often misconstrued as part of a larger plan to forcefully impose Catholicism on the rest of his Protestant subjects. Even if James dared to dream that someday England might once again become a Catholic nation, it is difficult to see how he hoped to achieve that in his lifetime, given that about 95 per cent of the English population was Protestant and James was 53 years old when he ascended the throne. Protestants particularly objected to James's willingness to allow Catholics into the army and to serve in local government in violation of the Test Act, which imposed a "test" on office holders that consisted of taking communion in the Anglican Church.

In Ireland, Catholics and Protestants entered into power-sharing arrangements in Dublin and Belfast, providing some hope that James could maintain the support of both groups there. At the beginning of his reign, James made the Protestant Clarendon his lord lieutenant in an effort to appease Irish Protestants. However, James gave authority over the army in Ireland to the Catholic Richard Talbot (1630–91), the earl of Tyrconnell.

Clarendon's attempts to reassure Irish Protestants could not counteract Tyrconnell's heavy-handed style, which he employed to benefit Irish Catholics. Tyrconnell aggressively pursued Catholic interests in Ireland, thus alienating Irish Protestants and further angering the critics of the king in England. He not only tried to place Catholics in the army, but also tried to get Protestants out of it. In September 1686, two-thirds of the soldiers were Catholic, as were 40 per cent of the officers, and those numbers went up from there.[36] He followed a similar policy with regard to the Irish administration as well. Tyrconnell was an experienced soldier, who had fought against Cromwell at Drogheda and served in the royalist army thereafter. He was determined to modernize the Irish army, raising suspicions about what James might plan to use it for. In 1687, James appointed Tyrconnell as Clarendon's replacement, though as lord deputy rather than lord lieutenant in deference to Clarendon and his supporters at court.

As much as the policies of James in England and Tyrconnell in Ireland alienated Protestants, the king's age and the fact that his two daughters, Mary and Anne, were both Protestant suggested that those policies would only be temporary. However, the situation changed dramatically when James's second wife, the Italian Catholic, Mary of Modena, gave birth to a son that no one expected in June 1688. (James and Mary had married in 1673 and had no previous children.) The birth of the new prince raised the prospect—at least in the minds of some Protestants—that England might be facing a long line of Catholic kings who over time could erode the country's Protestant faith. More importantly, the birth of the prince provided James's political enemies, who objected to his efforts to erode their power at court and in the country by making his own partisan appointments, the opportunity to stir up opposition against the king and to plot his overthrow. Not wishing to relive the turbulence of the civil war years that had accompanied the downfall of Charles I, however, they chose to invite William of Orange (1650–1702), the ardent Protestant military leader of the Netherlands and husband of James's daughter Mary, to invade England and wrest the throne from James by armed might. On 5 November, William landed in England with approximately 15,000 soldiers ready to stake his claim to the English throne.

The issue of the three kingdoms was brought into play again on 23 December 1688 when King James fled England for France, ostensibly leaving a vacancy on the thrones of England, Scotland (where he was known as James VII), and Ireland, even though James had not actually abdicated in any of his kingdoms. The struggle for the thrones of all three kingdoms between James and his Dutch son-in-law was to have particularly profound repercussions for Ireland. The conflict between William and James had very little to do with either Scotland or Ireland and yet both were forced to take

---

[36] Barry Coward (2003), *The Stuart Age: England, 1603–1714*, 3rd edn. London: Longman, p. 338.

sides in the conflict between them. James continued to act as if he were the legitimate king in both Scotland and Ireland, hoping to hold on to them until he could defeat William and return to England as king. Buoyed by financial and military support from France, James sailed for Ireland, arriving in Kinsale on 12 March 1689. He called an Irish parliament in May 1689, which as king of Ireland it was his prerogative to do. The vast majority of those who attended this parliament were Catholic. James catered to them by granting religious toleration and the restoration of their lands. Irish Catholics in turn staked their future interests and the preservation of their land holdings on the Stuart cause.

The stage was set for a battle in Ireland for the thrones of all three kingdoms. On 16 April, James's army placed under siege the city of Derry, where Protestant forces had already gathered Jacobite forces. The lifting of the siege on 12 August became an important anniversary for Irish Protestants, but its failure was probably inevitable since the Jacobite army lacked the strength and experience to take the town. Thomas Bartlett has called it "the most inept siege in the history of modern warfare."[37] William arrived in eastern Ulster in June 1690. His army advanced toward Dublin, while James's army marched north to meet him. On 1 July, they clashed along the banks of the Boyne River about 3 miles west of Drogheda, which

FIGURE 7.2 *King William III at the Battle of the Boyne, nineteenth-century print. Courtesy of Getty Images.*

---

[37] Thomas Bartlett (2010), *Ireland: A History.* Cambridge: Cambridge University Press, p. 135.

is just above where the river meets the Irish Sea. Although it became perhaps the most famous battle in Irish history, the Battle of the Boyne involved relatively few casualties, about 1,500 between both sides combined. After the battle, James fled to Waterford. On 4 July 1690, the defeated and dejected king sailed for France. Once again, James had a failure of nerve and decided to leave for the Continent rather than to stay and fight for his crown. The victory at the Boyne cleared the way for William to occupy Dublin, which gave him a real advantage from this point forward.

But William's victory was not yet complete. The Jacobites fought on in their leader's absence, led by Patrick Sarsfield, who had fought for James in England in 1685 and 1688. This was no longer simply a battle of kings; once again it was Irish fighting Irish over the future of their land. Informal guerilla forces supplemented the fighting done by the regular armies. But the war also continued because Ireland had become at this point simply another battleground in the Dutch wars against Louis XIV, with soldiers from France fighting soldiers from England, the Netherlands, and other Protestant members of the coalition put together by William.

The final battle of this conflict took place at Aughrim in County Galway on 12 July 1691. Despite facing French-trained soldiers and experienced French commanders on loan from Louis XIV, William's army once again proved superior in organization and tactics. William was an experienced military commander and many of his troops were well seasoned on the battlefields of Europe. Pádraig Lenihan has estimated that at least 4,000 Irishmen were killed or captured at the Battle of Aughrim.[38] The Jacobites' last hope resided in Limerick, whose sympathetic population had previously survived an unsuccessful siege by William's army following the Battle of the Boyne in 1690. William placed Limerick under siege for a second time following his victory at Aughrim. The second Siege of Limerick ended on 23 September 1691 when its Jacobite defenders agreed to negotiate with William. William had defeated James, defended his kingdoms in England and Scotland, and won Ireland. William's army then withdrew to be replaced by Protestant militia.

But what did it mean for William to become king of Ireland? For one, it meant that a kingdom with a large Catholic majority would be ruled by a Protestant king. The terms of surrender as stated in the Treaty of Limerick, signed on 3 October 1691 called for a restoration of the land and religious settlement as it existed under Charles II, including freedom for Catholics to practice their religion "as are consistent with the laws of Ireland." This did not prevent, however, a drastic reduction in the amount of land owned by Catholics or a wave of anti-Catholic legislation in the last decade of

---

[38] Pádraig Lenihan (2011), "The Impact of the Battle of Aughrim (1691) on the Irish Catholic Elite," in Brian Mac Cuarta (ed.), *Reshaping Ireland, 1550–1700: Colonization and its Consequences: Essays Presented to Nicholas Canny*. Dublin: Four Courts Press, p. 304.

the seventeenth century and the first decade of the eighteenth century (see Chapter 8). Catholics lost about a third of the land that they had owned before the war.

William's victory also meant that the political and religious divisions in Ireland would continue, made more bitter by the war and yet another land settlement that favored Protestants. The Protestants now justified their privileged position by reference to the history of Catholic rebellion; to many Protestants, the events of 1641 and those of 1690 were part of a pattern of Catholic treachery. Protestant writers such as Michael Jephson, who in 1690 had referred to the "natural barbarity" of the Catholics, continued a line of thought that held that Catholics could never be trusted because they would always try to destroy Protestants and Protestantism whenever they had the chance.[39]

William's victory also meant the continuation of English claims to dominate Ireland and subordinate the Irish to the English parliament, at least in theory. Richard Cox, one of William's Anglo-Irish supporters, seemed to recognize this in the 1689 pamphlet quoted at the beginning of this chapter, even though he was probably trying to curry favor with William at the time when he wrote it.[40] In fact, the Irish parliament seized the opportunity to assert its power by refusing to cooperate with the legislative agenda prepared by the king's ministers for 1692. The House of Commons rejected bills that would have given more power to the army and the militia. Parliamentary leaders then proceeded to initiate an investigation into charges of corruption on the part of the officials responsible for the land settlement that followed the dispossession of James's supporters. The new government was accused of treating the Catholic population too harshly in the aftermath of the war, even though William had forbidden illegal searches of Catholic homes in order to prevent additional reprisals from being taken by angry Protestants. He had not wanted those who had remained loyal to be at the mercy of private vendettas. When Parliament met again in 1695, it agreed to allow William to present a money bill to raise £14,000, but the remaining £200,000 requested by William was to be the product of Irish-initiated legislation.[41] Many Protestants feared another Catholic insurrection, which led to the passage of some of the penal laws that placed further legal restrictions upon Catholics. Furthermore, divisions among Protestants came to the forefront as Anglicans worried about Presbyterians gaining too much influence under the new regime as increasing numbers of them flooded into Ulster. In the

---

[39] Richard Ansell (2010), "The Revolution in Ireland and the Memory of 1641," in M. Williams and S. P. Forrest (eds), *Constructing the Past: Writing Irish History, 1600–1800*. Woodbridge: The Boydell Press, p. 74.

[40] David Armitage (2000), "The Political Economy of Britain and Ireland after the Glorious Revolution," in J. H. Ohlmeyer (ed.), *Political Thought in Seventeenth-Century Ireland: Kingdom or Colony*. Cambridge: Cambridge University Press, p. 232.

[41] Connolly, *Religion, Law, and Power*, pp. 75–6.

following century, Presbyterians faced similar restrictions to those that the Irish penal laws placed on Catholics. The Anglicans, not the Presbyterians, were the true beneficiaries of William's victory in Ireland.

James had left Ireland, but he was not dead and he had a son. The Treaty of Limerick even allowed for any officers of soldiers who were willing to go overseas to leave Ireland on ships that were designated to transport them; the numerous officers and soldiers who left for France became known as the *Wild Geese*. This provision had raised concerns among some Protestants about how committed William was to protecting Ireland from foreign invasion.

William died on 8 March 1702, having lost the favor of even many who had supported him in his war with James. In retrospect, the Battle of the Boyne seems a decisive turning point in Irish history and is still celebrated as such by Irish Protestants. Indeed, by the time of his death, William seemed to have effectively conquered and subdued Ireland, cementing English dominance there in the process. The situation at the time, however, was considerably more complex. The Irish parliament had started to meet more regularly and was on its way to becoming a more permanent part of the constitutional relationship between England and Ireland. The Irish parliament was a Protestant-dominated affair, however, which approved additional laws discriminating against the Catholics. The eighteenth century therefore opened with the threat of another Jacobite invasion lingering. The Revolution Settlement had once again reinforced religious differences in Ireland, but Catholics now had an outlet for their discontent in their support for Jacobitism. James II seemed resigned to his fate to die in exile, but his son would soon come of age and the supporters of his cause had not given up. Ireland carried its past into the new century even as new cultural forces were starting to emerge that pointed to the possibility of a brighter future.

CHAPTER EIGHT

Eighteenth-century Ireland

The atmosphere of Anglo-Ireland from the early eighteenth-century cannot adequately be represented by the correspondence of the great ladies at houses like Carlton, Castletown or Delville, reading Candide, *building shell-houses, and even (in the Duchess of Leinster's case) considering Rousseau as a tutor for their children*

– ROY FOSTER, *Modern Ireland, 1600–1972* (1988)

I think it highly inconvenient for England to assume this Authority over the kingdom of Ireland: I believe there will need no great Arguments to convince the wise Assembly of English Senators, how inconvenient it may be to England to do that which may make the Lords and People of Ireland think that they are not well used and may drive them into Discontent.

– WILLIAM MOLYNEUX, *The Case of Ireland's Being Bound by an Act of Parliament in England, Stated* (1698)

New cultural forces at work

Ireland's reputation as a cultural backwater during the age associated with the European Enlightenment belies the extent to which new cultural forces were at work in Ireland, including the spread of Enlightenment thought to the island and the contribution of Irish writers to it. The negative stereotypes about Ireland were largely the result of an inherent bias against Ireland as a predominantly Catholic society at a time when Enlightenment thought, rightly or wrongly, is associated with hostility to revealed religion in general and the Catholic Church in particular. If the English still largely regarded the thought and literature of Scotland, one of the leading lights of the eighteenth-century Enlightenment, with disdain in comparison with their own, they were even less likely to take Irish thought at all seriously. But, in the area of political philosophy in particular, Irish thought was often quite sophisticated as a result of its anomalous position within the British Empire as both a kingdom and a colony, the basis for the title of an important book by Nicholas Canny.[1] Whereas in Scotland, the Act of Union in 1707 brought the two countries together to form the nation of Great Britain, the political unification of Great Britain and Ireland would not occur until almost a century later. In the meantime, Ireland wrestled with the disadvantages of being tied to Britain without the benefits that were supposed to accrue to Scotland as a result of the union.

The fact that many Scots did not feel that these benefits were materializing fast enough, at least for the first half of the eighteenth century, did nothing to assuage Irish discontent or to stop attempts by Irish thinkers and politicians to define their own political position vis-à-vis a newly unified British commonwealth. William Molyneux, the author of *The Case of Ireland's Being Bound by an Act of Parliament in England, Stated* (1698), was associated with a group of thinkers headed by Robert Molesworth (1656–1725) who was an early advocate for union between Ireland and England as an answer to Ireland's economic problems and second-class status. From an economic perspective, Ireland was as much a part of the British Empire—with its economic interests as subordinated to the mother country—as any other colony. Molyneux objected to Ireland's subordinate position in relation to England. He was mostly concerned, however, with redressing the imbalance in the relationship rather than with either union or outright independence, particularly with regard to trade, although he did favor greater autonomy for Ireland. The Navigation Acts, comprising several laws passed since 1651, aimed at benefitting English shipping at the expense of foreign competitors such as France and the Netherlands by restricting trade in and out of its colonies. Thirty years after Molyneux's treatise, Jonathan Swift (1667–1745) also attacked the harmful effects of English rule on the Irish economy in *A Short View of the State of Ireland*, written in 1728. His proposed model of two separate but equal kingdoms was the one favored by most Irish advocates of independence for over a century.

Swift towers over all others in many areas of Irish thought and culture during the first half of the eighteenth century. After some time pursuing

---

[1] Nicholas Canny (1988), *Kingdom and Colony: Ireland in the Atlantic World, 1560–1800.* Baltimore: Johns Hopkins University Press.

FIGURE 8.1 *Portrait of Jonathan Swift (1667–1745), Satirst, 1709/16. Studio of Charles Jervas, Irish, c. 1675–1739. Oil on canvas. 76.3 × 63.5 cm. Photo © National Gallery of Ireland. NGI.177.*

a literary career in England, where he became embroiled in politics and was reduced to writing propaganda for the Tory government, Swift took occupancy of St Patrick's Cathedral in Dublin, where he served as dean from 1714 to 1745. From there, he defended Irish interests and the encroachments of the British government upon Irish fiscal independence both in his writings and through his attempts to promote a thriving print industry that would make the book an important weapon in the Irish struggle for greater autonomy.[2] Swift saw this as an issue that had the potential both to unite the Anglo-Irish politically and to serve as a catalyst for the development of a distinctive Anglo-Irish literature. The number of

---

[2] See Sean D. Moore (2010), *Swift, the Book, and the Irish Financial Revolution: Satire and Sovereignty in Colonial Ireland*. Baltimore: Johns Hopkins University Press.

editions of books reprinted in Dublin written by authors associated with the Scottish Enlightenment testifies to the existence of such an industry and the demand for Enlightenment works in Ireland.[3] Many of these works were published illegally as Dublin printers were not always scrupulous about obtaining permission from the authors or the original publishers of the Scottish books that were rolling off their presses.

Aside perhaps from *Gulliver's Travels*, a social satire in the form of an adventure novel, Swift is best known for *A Modest Proposal for Preventing the Children of Poor People in Ireland from Being a Burden to their Parents or Country, and for Making them Beneficial to the Public*, written in 1729. This satirical work, written in the midst of one of the worst famines of the eighteenth century lasting from 1727 to 1730, famously proposed that cannibalism was a solution to the numbers of excess children whose mothers were reduced to begging for alms in the streets and at cabin doors. "I have been assured by a very knowing American," Swift informs his readers (one must assume that Swift thought his readers would have been more willing to believe this information coming from an American), "that a healthy young child well nursed is at a year old a most delicious, nourishing, and wholesome food, whether stewed, roasted, baked, or boiled." Swift facetiously suggested that reducing the population in this way would solve a number of problems, including freeing Irish women burdened with numerous children to become more productive members of society since they would no longer need to resort to begging or thievery in order to support themselves and their children. It would also reduce the number of criminals in society who tended to be bred in early conditions of poverty and hardship. Swift was a keen observer of Irish society who risked alienating the Anglo-Irish ruling class by pointing out how untenable was their position on many issues in the early eighteenth century. He was such a talented writer that much of his satire in works like *Gulliver's Travels* went over the heads of his contemporary readers, but the biting criticisms of *A Modest Proposal* were hard to miss and indicated that he had committed himself to Ireland and that he had given up hopes of a political career in England. Of Swift, himself a member of the dominant Anglo-Irish ruling class, it was said:

Had he but spared his tongue and pen,
He might have rose like other men:
But, Power was never in his thought;
And, wealth he valued not a groat . . .[4]

---

[3] See Richard B. Sher (2007), *The Enlightenment and the Book: Scottish Authors and Their Publishers in Eighteenth-Century Britain, Ireland, and America*. Chicago: University of Chicago Press.

[4] "Verse on the Death of Dr. Swift," in A. Norman and Peter Van De Kamp (eds), (2006), *Irish Literature in the Eighteenth Century*. Dublin: Irish Academic Press, p. 91.

Swift's influence spread to other members of the aristocracy through mutual contacts; his friend Mary Delaney presided over the Irish equivalent of a French salon that included Letitia Bushe (c. 1705–57), the daughter of a lesser landlord whose letters are the subject of an interesting study by S. J. Connolly. One of the most interesting aspects of Bushe's own correspondence remarked upon by Connolly is the relative absence of anti-Catholic prejudice that is assumed to be a characteristic of the Protestant ruling class in Ireland.[5] Delaney's own correspondence also gives us a sense of the cultural climate of Ireland in the first half of the eighteenth century, especially that of Dublin. In spite of the existence of poor beggars and the slums that were characteristic of any large city, even in the eighteenth century, Dublin was becoming a more cosmopolitan and attractive city during this period. In 1731, Mary Delaney described Dublin as "delightful," its "narrow streets and dirty-looking houses" notwithstanding.[6] Delaney also found access to all of the latest cultural fashions there, including a night of French dancing at Dublin Castle in celebration of the anniversary of the coronation of King George II in October, even if she later stated a personal preference for country dances over what she described as "hideous minuets."

The dominant cultural position of France in eighteenth-century Europe was also evident in Ireland from the growing interest in French literature and culture, as well as an increase in the number of educated people there who spoke French. A diverse group of Irish men and women were inclined to learn French for a wide variety of reasons, including those in high society who did so for reasons of prestige, members of the clergy of the Church of Ireland who might have wanted to understand or refute the arguments of the French philosophes, Catholic clergy who wished to study abroad, Catholic refugees who traveled to France to join the court of the Stuart Pretenders, and those with scientific interests who needed to read the latest works emanating from the Paris Academy of Sciences. Protestant merchants who did business with French Huguenots, some of whom had taken refuge in Ireland after the Revocation of the Edict of Nantes by Louis XIV in 1685, also had reason to learn at least some French.[7]

A growing interest in Irish history also manifested itself over the course of the eighteenth century, culminating in the establishment of the Irish Academy in 1785, which became the Irish Royal Academy in 1786. Examples of works that reflected this interest included the chronology

---

[5] S. J. Connolly (2000), "A Woman's Life in Mid-Eighteenth-Century Ireland: The Case of Letitia Bushe." *Historical Journal*, 43, 433–51.

[6] Mary Delany (1879), "Letter from Mary Granville Pendarves Delany to Anne Granville Dewes, October 9, 1731," in S. C. Woolsey (ed.), *The Autobiography and Correspondence of Mrs. Delaney, Volume I*. Boston: Roberts Brothers. http://bluehawk.monmouth.edu:3369/cgi-bin/asp/philo/bwld/getdoc.pl?S1305-D047.

[7] David J. Denby (2005), "The Enlightenment in Ireland," *Eighteenth-Century Studies*, 38, 385–6.

provided by James Eyre Weeks in *The Gentleman's Hour Glass* (1750), Charles O'Conor's *Dissertations on the Ancient History of Ireland* (1753), and Sylvester O'Halloran's antiquarian *Insula Sacra* (1770). These writers fought against English prejudice against the conception that Ireland had its own separate history that was worthy of attention. Irish history was not a subject that was taught in schools in Ireland, where students learned much more about classical history, British, or European history than their own past.[8] O'Halloran made a further—and more successful—attempt to combat the prejudice against Irish history in his *General History of Ireland* (1774), which was sympathetic to Irish Catholics and served as a foundation and inspiration for nineteenth-century writers interested in the subject. O'Halloran particularly tried to challenge the image of the Irish people as uncivilized and barbaric, which still remained as a holdover from the English propaganda of the late Middle Ages.

There were other cultural forces at work that contributed to Ireland becoming a more literate and educated society aside from the influence of Enlightenment thought and the importation of French culture by the aristocratic elite. The founding of the School of Medicine at Trinity College in Dublin in 1711 coincided with the completion of the Anatomy School Building there. This development ushered in a new age in Irish medicine that would eventually place it at the forefront of medical education in Europe. In 1731, the Dublin Society was formed to encourage technological progress in agriculture and industry. What was most notable about this organization was the encouragement of innovation and native styles in architecture it gave to Irish landlords; the society displayed a distinct lack of sympathy for those Irish estate owners known as absentee landlords who chose to reside elsewhere.[9] This encouragement seems to have paid off, given the increase in profits enjoyed by Irish landlords in the middle decades of the century.

Finally, in his travels through Ireland in 1775, Richard Twiss made note of the establishment of the penny post office and the abundance of stage coaches that combined to enhance communication and travel, two important elements in the spread of culture and ideas. Twiss also commented positively on the level of comfort to be found in Irish inns, and the relative absence of thieves and highwaymen in comparison with England, as well as the conditions of the Irish roads, which he found to be of an equal quality to those in the vicinity of London.[10] Eighteenth-century Ireland was a much more civilized, cultured, and comfortable place than it had been in the

---

[8] T. C. Barnard (2010), "Writing in Publishing Histories in Eighteenth-century Ireland," in M. Williams and S. P. Forrest (eds), *Constructing the Past: Writing Irish History, 1600–1800*. Woodbridge: The Boydell Press, p. 111.

[9] Roy Foster (1988), *Modern Ireland, 1600–1972*. London: Allen Lane, p. 184.

[10] Richard Twiss (2008; 1776), *A Tour of Ireland in 1775*, edited by Rachel Finnegan. Dublin: University College Dublin Press, p. 28.

previous century. But underneath the cultural changes that were shaping Ireland during this period, Irish society was also undergoing significant changes, not all of which were as promising for the island's future.

New social forces at work

The biggest social change that occurred in Ireland in the first half of the eighteenth century was the shift from a country to which immigrants came to a country from which emigrants left. At the beginning of the century, immigrants were still coming into Ireland from Scotland, especially to Ulster in the north. Ireland continued to attract immigrants from continental Europe as well. But economic opportunities there were already beginning to dry up. Only a relatively few investors in land or industry could hope to succeed or find new opportunities, while many more people began leaving the country. North America was becoming an increasingly attractive destination, including for those who would become known as the Scots-Irish who had settled in Ireland from Scotland before moving on to the American colonies, particularly North Carolina and Pennsylvania. The foremost authorities on Irish migration place the number of those leaving Ireland for North America between 1700 and the beginning of the American Revolution at somewhere between 100,000 and 250,000.[11]

However, not all Irish migration occurred overseas; a good deal of internal migration also resulted both from the desire of individuals to seek better economic opportunities in Dublin and smaller towns and from the encouragement offered by landlords who sought to attract more reliable and hardworking tenants. In the first half of the century, migration to urban settings led to a modest increase in the percentage of people in Ireland living in towns, at mid-century up 2 per cent from 1700 to a total of about 7 per cent.[12] The famines that occurred in the late 1720s and again in the late 1730s and early 1740s provided additional impetus for internal as well as external migration. In the second half of the century, internal migration was facilitated by the favorable condition of Irish roads commented upon by Twiss, as well as by the improved system of drainage that made the Shannon River navigable as a result of a bill passed in the Irish Parliament in 1716.

Class divisions also became more palpable over the course of the eighteenth century. In Ireland, class divisions were reinforced by religious differences between Catholics and Protestants, especially in the countryside. In the cities, a Catholic middle class could thrive and take advantage of the relative blindness that commerce and industry showed to one's religion. However, in

---

[11] Patrick Fitzgerald and Brian Lambkin (2008), *Migration in Irish History, 1607–2007.* London: Palgrave Macmillan, p. 114.
[12] Ibid., p. 117.

the aftermath of the Revolution of 1688 and the triumph of William III over James II in the late seventeenth century, Catholic landownership declined from an already disproportionately small 22 per cent to a paltry 14 per cent as early as 1703.[13] By 1778, Catholic landownership in Ireland had plummeted to an estimated 5 per cent.[14] Catholics represented approximately 75 per cent of the population as a whole. Furthermore, the control that the Protestant landholding class—many of them English who often functioned as absentee landowners who were only concerned about the income that they could derive from their estates—held over the Irish debt further widened the perception of social and economic injustice toward Ireland, which was one of Swift's main grievances against the Protestant Ascendancy.

This did not mean that there were not some successful Catholic landowners among those who did retain their own estates. In fact, a number of them were quite prosperous, especially in Munster and Leinster.

Meanwhile, Ireland had started to undergo a shift in the direction of what historians call *proto-industrialization*, a term for the early stages of industrialization in which industrial processes are increasingly undertaken for commercial purposes to serve a wider market, even if much of the actual work was still being done in cottages and on small family farms. The weaving, spinning, dyeing, and other processes associated with textile manufacturing were not exclusively done by women in most places where protoindustrialization occurred, but in Ireland, women did predominate in the linen industry for which Ireland would become known in the eighteenth century. In this system, sometimes referred to as the "putting-out system," enterprising merchants purchased the raw materials and put them out to various workers in their homes for different stages in the production process. This led to specialization or a division of labor that is often associated exclusively with the factory system. Different regions began to acquire their own specializations, such as spinning or weaving, for example. Linen production predominated in Ireland partly because the government encouraged it; a Linen Board was formed in Ireland in 1711 for precisely this purpose.

Protoindustrialization is understood as an important part of the background to the Industrial Revolution that occurred in eighteenth-century England, but so is population growth. In England, population increased rather dramatically in the course of the eighteenth century, while Ireland, like Scotland, experienced a very low average growth rate of between 0.2 and 0.4 per cent per year from 1687 to 1755. But these numbers are misleading for Ireland because years of more substantial growth were negated by periods of famine, the worst coming between 1727 and 1730 and from 1739 to 1741. When famine subsided in the second half of the century, Ireland's

---

[13] Ibid., p. 123.
[14] Jürgen Kramer (2007), *Britain and Ireland: A Concise History*. London: Routledge, p. 112.

population grew three times as fast as Scotland's.[15] Research from one linen weaving parish in Ulster from 1771 to 1810 has confirmed that women wed young, thus ensuring that they were married for a high percentage of their childbearing years. In this particular case, half of the women in the parish were married before the age of 21, and 22 years was the mean age of marriage for women compared to 26 for men.[16]

The effects of population growth were not consistent throughout Ireland, however. Northern Irish ports such as Belfast and Derry/Londonderry prospered over the course of the eighteenth century, reflecting a further widening of the North-South divide. The Irish linen industry was centered in the north; for the rest of Ireland, the same lack of economic opportunities that led to increased migration also led to the first efforts at poor relief, starting with the Dublin Workhouse Act of 1704. But as Dublin tended to attract a larger number of people migrating from the countryside in search of work during hard economic times, this act did little to end the problem of poverty, as the famines of the late 1720s and early- to mid-1740s and Swift's *Modest Proposal* attest. This internal migration also had the effect of tipping the balance of the population in Dublin, the center of English Protestant rule, in favor of the Catholics in the second half of the century.

The impact of the English Ascendancy

By the end of the eighteenth century, the term *Protestant Ascendancy* had come into common usage in Ireland, although what the term really meant was *English Ascendancy*, no matter how much some landlords had come to identify their interests as distinctively Irish. The two terms have become virtually synonymous, largely because even those members of the elite who thought that their interests as Irish landlords were distinct from those of the British parliament were disturbed by the lenient enforcement of the penal laws against Catholics, one of their main grievances. This concern was felt most keenly in areas such as Connacht, where Protestants were more isolated from an overwhelmingly predominant Catholic majority. Nonetheless, however much leniency existed in the enforcement of them, the penal laws set Ireland apart from England and much of the rest of Europe, which was moving in the direction of greater levels of religious toleration in the eighteenth century.

The term *penal laws* had come into use by the end of the seventeenth century. The term was actually coined by Irish Catholics who preferred it to "popish" or "papist" laws, which carried derogatory overtones. Collectively,

---

[15] R. A. Houston (1992), *The Population History of Britain and Ireland, 1500–1750.* Houndmills: Macmillan, p. 30.
[16] Ibid., p. 38.

these laws placed restrictions upon the Catholics' rights to worship, own land, participate in politics, or serve in the military. They provide a striking reminder, along with Louis XIV's decision to end toleration for the Protestant Huguenots in 1685, that religious intolerance and discrimination were still powerful forces at the beginning of the eighteenth century. But what distinguished religious discrimination in Ireland, even from Louis XIV's persecution of the Huguenots, was that the Irish penal laws were applied against a large majority of the population.

In fact, new penal laws were still being added to the books in the late seventeenth and eighteenth centuries that had profound repercussions on Irish society. Legislation in 1695 further restricted the right of Catholics to bear arms and attempted to inhibit their ability to study abroad at Catholic universities. The 1697 "Act to prevent Protestants intermarrying with Papists" required any Protestant male to obtain written permission from his minister, bishop, and local justice of the peace if he wished to do so. The act further stipulated that from that point forward, any man who married a Catholic woman would be considered a papist and subject to other penal laws that prohibited his sitting in parliament or occupying any position in the civil government or the military unless his wife converted to the Protestant faith and the bishop was convinced of her sincerity. Another act passed in 1697 called for all members of religious orders and Catholic bishops, among other Catholic Church officials, to leave Ireland before the first of May of the following year. Those who did not leave voluntarily would be subject to deportation, while those who left and then returned were subject to the death penalty.

In addition, a 1709 act called for the inheritances of Protestant children with a Catholic parent or parents to be sequestered by the state to be distributed by the chancery court only upon verification from the bishop that the child was a member of the Church of Ireland in good standing. Furthermore, since Catholics could not be expected to enforce the penal laws, a 1715 act barred Catholics from serving as constables throughout Ireland. Although Catholics were prohibited from sitting in either the British or the Irish parliament, a 1728 law deprived Irish Catholics of the right to vote as well.

The penal laws did not go unchallenged in eighteenth-century Ireland. Catholic attorneys, who nominally conformed to the Church of Ireland in order to practice law, were among those who challenged them in defense of their Catholic clients.[17] Others developed ideological arguments against them, such as James Arbuckle, an Irish writer born in Belfast who became a member of Swift's intellectual circle in Dublin in the 1730s. Arbuckle argued that:

> . . . in those states where Men are obliged by penal laws to be of one Faith, and one Mind, there is little to be met with among the common

---

[17] Ó Ciardha, "The Stuarts and Deliverance," p. 83.

People, but Barbarity and gross Ignorance . . . and the soil wherein they live . . . everywhere wearing a face of Poverty and Desolation, except about the Palaces of Princes, and the Retirements of the Clergy . . .[18]

What is significant about Arbuckle's critique is that he was a Protestant Whig who significantly toned down his critique of Catholicism and disassociated contemporary Irish Catholics from the history of the Catholic Church. Increased sensitivity among the Whig governing class can also be seen in the increased use in the eighteenth century of "Roman Catholic" in place of the more politically charged designation of Catholics as "papists." The more civilized discourse on matters of religious difference was in keeping with the spirit of the Enlightenment and suggested at least the possibility that Irish Catholics and Protestants might eventually resolve their differences and enter into a common political culture at some point in the future. As it turned out, the penal laws persisted into the nineteenth century and, by the time they were repealed in 1829, many Catholics had become too embittered to believe that such a culture was possible.

If a decrease in the hostility between Catholics and Protestants was one prerequisite for Ireland to emerge as a sovereign country, a change in the position of the Irish parliament was another. Ireland had a parliament that generally met at least every other year during the eighteenth century, but it was an entirely Protestant affair. Furthermore, its relationship with the British parliament was ill-defined, although there was no question that executive authority continued to reside with the British. What was also clear was that British legislation took precedence over Irish legislation, leaving the Irish parliament, whatever its prerogatives, in an inferior position. This principle had been established ever since the passage of Poynings' Law in 1494. The Declaratory Act of April 1720 reaffirmed this principle and formalized the supremacy of the British parliament over the Irish parliament. This act granted authority to the parliament in Westminster to pass laws for Ireland; in addition, all appeals now ended in the House of Lords in Westminster, not in Dublin.

The function of the Irish parliament in the eyes of the British was mainly financial since it was expected to approve additional taxes as needed to contribute to the running of the kingdom. Still, in comparison with the past, in the eighteenth century, the Irish parliament did play a larger role in governing Ireland. The accumulation of more power and greater autonomy was reflected in the reference to the designation of the Anglo-Irish ruling class as the "ascendancy." The desire for greater autonomy by the ascendancy

---

[18] Quoted in Richard Holmes (2011), "James Arbuckle: A Whig Critique of the Penal Laws," in J. Bergin, E. Magennis, L. Ní Mhunghaile and P. Walsh (eds), *New Perspectives on the Penal Laws: Eighteenth-Century Ireland/Iris an dá chultúr, Special Issue* No. 1. Dublin: Eighteenth-Century Ireland Society, p. 106.

would receive redress in reform legislation that accompanied the American crisis of the 1770s (see below), which significantly altered the relationship between the English and Irish parliaments and could be seen as presaging even greater independence for Ireland in the future.

In addition to their political demands, the members of the Anglo-Irish ruling class sought to demonstrate their equality with their English counterparts through the construction of both private residences and public buildings in an architectural style that reflected their political and social status as well as their cultural refinement. By the late eighteenth century, Dublin had begun to undergo a significant transformation aided by the creation of a Wide Streets Commission, which engaged in urban planning to make the capital's architectural splendor more visible. The growth and renovation of Dublin in the eighteenth century provided additional jobs and contributed to the increase in population that came from the expanding numbers of those migrating to the capital from the surrounding area. But Dublin became more the preserve of the ruling Protestant aristocracy than the emerging Catholic middle class, members of which were more likely to set up businesses in Cork, for example. This situation is also in contradistinction to Scotland, where Edinburgh, more than Dublin, had become more of a commercial center with a thriving middle class.

But any dichotomy between a distinct Anglo-Irish ruling class and their English counterparts can be somewhat misleading. Many Irish landowners had estates in England, where a great many chose to reside, thus making them absentee landlords in Ireland. A smaller number of aristocrats who owned estates in both places resided in Ireland. Moreover, a number of those members of the ruling class who did live in Ireland, including Swift in the early stages of his career, sought political careers in England and split time between the two kingdoms. In a sense, then, there was no marked difference between the English and Irish ruling class, in either personnel or principles.

In fact, the Whig Party dominated politics in both places from the start of the Hanoverian period in 1714 until the American crisis of the 1770s. During this period, the Whig Party was less based on a common ideology than it was on the common interests of its members in preserving and sharing power and influence in the government, while reaping the rewards of political patronage. The Whigs were broadly committed to supporting commercial interests and economic expansion, preserving the privileged position of the Church of England/Ireland, and keeping a Roman Catholic off the British throne. Jacobitism (see below) provided an alternative ideology for those disenchanted with the Whig ascendancy, but not one that was capable of challenging the Whigs for supremacy in either the English or the Irish parliament. In general, the ruling classes of both countries, despite some tensions between them, tended to work together and shared a common political ideology. However, the relationship remained problematic for two reasons. First, Britain could not allow Ireland to develop—much less implement—its own foreign policy and matters of military defense remained totally under the control of the British. Second, the problem for Ireland's economic situation was that, whereas the British aristocracy was generally supportive of the commercial interests of the merchant class because of what they meant to the economic success of the nation as a whole, Ireland's subordination to English interests meant that the Irish aristocracy was incapable of doing the same for their merchant class, even if they had wanted to.

Ireland's participation in British trade and its position in the British Empire

Keeping in mind that Ireland was not yet a part of the United Kingdom, its trading position within the British Empire in the first half of the eighteenth century resembled more closely that of the American colonies than it did either Scotland and Wales, which were both included in the newly created nation of Great Britain. The measure of legislative independence that belonged to Ireland did not prevent the British parliament from passing protectionist measures that favored English trade and industry at the expense of the Irish. As mentioned above, any illusion that Ireland would have final authority over its own affairs was dispelled by the Declaratory Act of 1720 that formalized the supremacy of the British parliament over the Irish parliament. This supremacy carried over into the area of commerce, where Ireland did not have the same rights of free trade as Scotland after the Treaty of Union. Here, the right of the British parliament to legislate for Ireland had important consequences as evidenced by the restrictions that were placed on the export of Irish woolen goods in the British Woolen Act of 1699 as a means of protecting the British textile industry.

The Woolen Act virtually destroyed the Irish woolen industry, along with the spinners and weavers who had made their living from it. Representatives of the woolen industry in towns like Manchester had put pressure on Parliament to give them precedence over Ireland. Since the English had removed import duties on plain linen in 1696, Ireland turned increasingly to linen production instead. The Irish linen industry benefited further when duties were removed on linen going to the English colonies in North America in 1704.

Linen manufacture was largely restricted to Ulster, where it had been fostered by Huguenot immigrants from France following the Revocation of the Edict of Nantes. The industrious Scots and Huguenots who had settled there, having discovered that flax grew rather easily in the land and climate of Ulster, took advantage of connections with Scottish immigrants in Pennsylvania, which became the main source for the flax seed needed by the Irish linen manufacturers. They benefited from the heavy reliance of the

British navy on Irish linens, one of the reasons why the British decided to encourage that industry at the expense of the wool industry in Ireland in the first place. But, even if the overseas sale of Irish cloth was restricted, this did not mean that there was not a home market for clothing produced by Irish manufacturers who continued to put out quality work; Martyn Powell has shown that, in fact, they took affront when dignitaries visiting from Britain did not purchase Irish textiles.[19]

Molyneux's treatise, *The Case of Ireland's Being Bound by an Act of Parliament in England, Stated,* had originally been written in direct response to the British Woolen Act. It is important to remember that Ireland was not wholly under British control during this period and that fact should not be obscured by the knowledge that this was about to change at the end of the eighteenth century. But Molyneux had regarded the restrictions placed upon Ireland's trade as a great infringement upon the rights and liberties of the Irish people. The author of the preface that was added to this work when it was reprinted in 1770 stated that "Commerce . . . and the Desire of thereby procuring the comforts of Life, are the ruling Principles of the present Age . . ."[20] In his opinion, Ireland was being prevented from benefiting from the great expansion of commerce during the eighteenth century, despite how little it had cost the British and how much Britain had benefited from its control of the island over the centuries. In his eyes, the English were making the Irish people starve—a charge that would be leveled again in the mid-nineteenth century—by restricting Irish trade and not allowing them to take advantage of the natural resources of their land or the industry of its people.

Irish trade was not only hurt by restrictions imposed by Britain but also by the fact that the products that it produced were generally readily available and thus not much in demand in the rest of Europe. Yet, economic historians no longer regard the state of Irish commerce in the eighteenth century as totally sluggish. For example, animal products became valuable export commodities, even if the trade in live cattle had declined. We have already mentioned the linen industry, which grew consistently in the course of the eighteenth century. It was just that those industries that did flourish did not negate the hardship that occurred in the decline of other industries; nor did the existence of some prospering industries mean that the Irish economy would not have been much better off if England had not put its own economic interests before that of Ireland.

---

[19] Martyn J. Powell (2005), *The Politics of Consumption in Eighteenth-Century Ireland.* Houndmills: Macmillan, p. 157.

[20] William Molyneux (1770; first published 1698), *The Case of Ireland's Being Bound by an Act of Parliament in England, Stated, with a New Preface.* London: J. Almon, Preface. http://oll.libertyfund.org/index.php?option=com_staticxt&staticfile=show.php%3Ftitle=1769&layout=html.

Furthermore, it seemed that when hard times came and famine stalked the land, it was the Irish Catholics who suffered disproportionately to the Irish Protestants. Those who belonged to the Protestant Ascendancy suffered even less. A hundred years later, when an even worse famine hit than those that began in 1726 and 1739, this situation had not changed. This does not mean, however, that Irish history in the eighteenth century was static. In the second half of the century, the American crisis and the French Revolution would have profound repercussions for Irish history and provide an inspiration for political expression in Ireland, while agrarian unrest would combine with Enlightenment notions of liberty and equality to threaten British hegemony. Meanwhile, in the first half of the century, Ireland was not immune from the appeal of the political and ideological phenomenon of Jacobitism, which provided the inspiration to several outbreaks of rebellion in Scotland and threatened to overthrow the newly established Hanoverian dynasty in England.

Ireland and the Jacobites

In his *Modest Proposal*, Jonathan Swift added that one benefit of reducing the population of Ireland would be the lower number of Catholic children who grew up to join abroad the supporters of the Stuart pretenders to the English throne. This is a reference to the political movement known as Jacobitism, which in essence centered on support for the exiled Stuart claimants to the English throne—James II and his descendants—following the Revolution of 1688 and James's defeat at the hands of William of Orange at the Battle of the Boyne in 1690. It did not take long for William to alienate his new subjects in England and Scotland, largely as a result of the expenses incurred through his constant wars with Louis XIV, which were seen as mainly benefiting the Dutch. In the course of the eighteenth century, however, Jacobitism acquired deeper ideological overtones that went beyond loyalty to the Stuart dynasty. In Ireland, Jacobitism represented an ideology to which other forms of discontent could easily be attached. The Stuarts provided an alternative for anyone in England, Scotland, or Ireland who held grievances against those who ruled in their stead and the aristocracy who supported those rulers. In Ireland, it was very seldom that those who did not belong to the Protestant ruling class did not have grievances against their English and Anglo-Irish rulers.

The first Jacobite rebellion occurred in Scotland in 1708 and can be directly linked to discontent with the Treaty of Union that had unified Scotland and England the year before. The failure of this rebellion did not quench interest in the Jacobite cause. Jacobite sentiment grew stronger in both Scotland and Ireland with each year that passed as a result of the desire to prevent the succession falling to the German Hanoverians upon the death of Queen Anne (r. 1701–14). During this period, a number of Irishmen, prevented from service in the British army by the penal laws, enlisted in military service abroad; those who went to France very likely did so in the hopes of helping to ensure the succession of James Francis Stuart, the son of James II, after Anne's death. Significantly overweight and in poor health in the later years of her life, Anne passed away in 1714. Her death provided the catalyst for the second major Jacobite rebellion in Scotland and, with hindsight, the one that had the greatest possibility of success.

Those chances of success would have been even greater had French support been forthcoming, but France had just concluded a peace treaty with England at Utrecht in 1713 in which it acknowledged acceptance of the Hanoverian succession. A younger Louis XIV might have broken the treaty and gone back to war if he perceived the Jacobite rebellion to have a chance at success, but the elderly king died on 1 September 1715, just days after John the earl of Mar had summoned a meeting of clan chiefs and less than a week before he signaled rebellion by raising the standard of the Stuarts at Braemar. With the French monarchy in transition, the Jacobites would have to proceed without French assistance.

In the end, no help was forthcoming from Ireland either. Nonetheless, a good deal of optimism still accompanied the beginning of the 1715 rebellion in Scotland. Both the Lowlands and the Highlands of Scotland supported the rebellion, as did significant numbers in northern England. The Scottish Presbyterian Church was not implacably opposed to it. But ineffective leadership on the part of Mar and poor military strategy led to a decisive defeat. The Jacobite army in England surrendered following the Battle of Preston on 14 November—one day after Mar had failed to crush a vastly outnumbered Hanoverian army at Sherrifmuir in Scotland. However, once more, the failure of a Jacobite rebellion in Scotland did little to diminish enthusiasm for the Jacobite cause in Ireland or among Irish exiles on the Continent.

The launching of the Jacobite rebellions from Scotland has obscured how important a cultural and political force Jacobitism was in Ireland in the first half of the eighteenth century. That no Irish revolt occurred which was comparable to the multiple uprisings in Scotland in support of the Jacobite cause has been explained as the result of lack of outside aid from the Stuarts themselves, which rendered an isolated rebellion hopeless if pitted against the Irish army.[21] Still, one could make the case that if the Irish had rebelled—even in 1745—their efforts might have diverted troops away from England that were needed to crush the rebellions there. In the 1745 rebellion, the Jacobite forces under the grandson of James II, Prince Charles Edward Stuart, penetrated as far south as Derby. Some consider Bonnie Prince Charlie's decision to retreat a tactical mistake that eventually

---

[21] Jacqueline Hill, "Convergence and Conflict in Eighteenth-Century Ireland." *Historical Journal*, 44, 1041.

led to the ignominious defeat of Scottish Jacobite forces at Culloden in the Scottish Highlands in April 1746.

Éamonn Ó Ciardha has made the case that the popularity in Ireland of such blatantly Jacobite songs as "Charlie come over the water," "Over the hills and far away," and "The King shall enjoy his own again" testifies to more than just a literary interest in poetry on the part of the elite classes.[22] Jacobite poetry, in fact, makes up a very high proportion of the surviving poetry in Irish from the eighteenth century. Ó Ciardha points out that the authorities took this poetry seriously enough to prosecute at least three poets for treasonous intent and to frighten others who managed to avoid arrest.[23] One can understand why the authorities did this when poets like John O' Tuomy were writing lines such as these in support of James III, while referencing King Philip V of Spain:

> King Philip and James, and their marshalled hosts,
> A brilliant phalanx, a dazzling band,
> Will sail full soon for our noble coast,
> And reach in power Inis Eilge's strand . . .
> They will drive afar to the surging sea
> The sullen tribe of the dreary tongue,
> The Gaels again shall be rich and free;
> The praise of the Bards shall be loudly sung![24]

Thus, even if Jacobite leaders were not interested in Ireland, Ireland still remained interested in the Jacobite cause for much of the eighteenth century. Jacobitism provided an important outlet for political discontent, which helps to explain its continued appeal in Ireland even after the failure of Bonnie Prince Charlie's rebellion in 1745–46. It might seem strange that Irish political discontent would manifest itself in the form of support for the exiled kings of England who were themselves of Scottish descent. But this is precisely why it is important to understand that Jacobitism evolved into a complex ideology that meant a great deal more than just support for the Stuarts out of some kind of antiquated medieval notion of personal allegiance.

First, the deposed James II was a convert to Catholicism, while his son, James Francis, known as the Old Pretender, and his grandson, Charles Edward (the Young Pretender) both persevered in the Catholic faith. Irish

---

[22] Éamonn Ó Ciardha (1999), "The Stuarts and Deliverance in Irish and Scots-Gaelic Poetry, 1690–1760," in S. J. Connolly (ed.), *Kingdoms United? Great Britain and Ireland since 1500*. Dublin: Four Courts Press, p. 81.

[23] Ibid., p. 83.

[24] C. P. Meehan (ed.) (1884), *The Poets and Poetry of Munster: A Selection of Irish Songs*, translated by James Clarence Mangan, 4th edn. Dublin: James Duffy and Sons, p. 76. http://archive.org/stream/poetspoetryofmun00manguoft#page/76/mode/2up.

support for the exiled Stuarts therefore had strong religious overtones. In one Jacobite poem, "The Reply to the Lady of Alba's Lament," John Clarach MacDonnell stated that Charles's triumph would mean that:

> ... Rome shall hold her ancient reign,
> Her laws and lore shall aye remain, ...
> The priest that hides by cave and fen,
> Shall raise his honour'd hood again—
> And to the sky shall hymns arise,
> From harp, and choir, and minstrel men![25]

Poetry was a powerful means of expression that lent itself to memorization and recitation and had the ability to reach even the lower levels of society. Many of the anonymous Jacobite poets may very well have been members of the Catholic clergy. Those poets who were not members of the Catholic clergy were very likely heavily influenced by them.

The presence of the Stuarts in France, which was increasingly looked upon by Irish Catholics as a potential ally, strengthened the appeal of the Jacobite cause in Ireland. However, Irish Jacobites on the Continent had a much more difficult time making their way to the center of the Jacobite court than did their English or Scottish counterparts. In fact, the Irish really had their own Jacobite community that was practically independent from that which surrounded the Stuarts themselves. Irish Jacobites lacked the clout or the patronage to influence strategy plotted at the Jacobite court, which certainly helps to explain why no support for an Irish rebellion was forthcoming. Moreover, at times, overt hostility was displayed by Jacobites of different nationality toward one another. This was probably why Irish Jacobites tended to remain in France even after the Stuart court relocated to Rome in 1718. But this somehow did not seem to lessen support for the Jacobite cause in Ireland.

Furthermore, strong connections remained between those Irish who had fled to France and those Jacobites who had remained in Ireland. Irish Catholic merchants traveling back and forth between Ireland and the European continent served as useful messengers between the two communities. Irish students who traveled abroad to study at Catholic universities or seminaries also developed strong connections between Ireland and the Continent. Messages could be transported back and forth by "fishermen, ship captains, and Franco-Spanish privateers."[26] Dublin served as the center for Irish Jacobitism, but Jacobites could be found in a number of other parts of

---

[25] In John O'Daly (1844), *Reliques of Irish Jacobite Poetry*. Dublin: Samuel J. Machen, p. 39. http://archive.org/stream/reliquesirishja00odagoog#page/n51/mode/2up.

[26] Éamonn Ó Ciardha (2002), *Ireland and the Jacobite Cause, 1685–1766: A Fatal Attachment*. Dublin: Four Courts Press, p. 126.

Ireland as well, including Derry/Londonderry, Galway, and Kilkenny. These people took heart from the numbers of Irish soldiers serving in regiments abroad that might one day arrive home as part of a contingent intended to liberate the island. Poets kept informed and kept people informed of the political situation while also keeping the Jacobite tradition alive in Ireland. The agrarian rebels known as the Whiteboys (see below) were known to sing Jacobite songs during their heyday in the 1760s. One kind of rebellious activity could have easily prepared the way for the next stage.

Eventually, the French Revolution and the rise of nineteenth-century nationalism inaugurated by Daniel O'Connell would replace Jacobitism as political ideologies, rendering Jacobitism obsolete. If the Irish clung to any hope of a Stuart restoration after 1746, it would seem to have been out of sheer desperation or the lack of any conceivable alternative, because for all intents and purposes, the cause was dead after the 1746 Battle of Culloden. However, since Jacobitism in Ireland was primarily expressed in poetry, it formed part of an Irish literary tradition that survived even into the nineteenth century long after the last Stuart heir had died. This certainly reinforces the idea that Irish Jacobitism meant more than personal allegiance to the descendants of James II. It was associated with a profound discontent that sometimes found expression in overt Jacobite songs and poems and sometimes took a more allegorical form. But the first stage in a new kind of political awareness in Ireland occurred when the Irish people woke up to the possibilities suggested by the American crisis that began in the 1760s and culminated in the American War for Independence that began in 1775.

Ireland and the American crisis

The American Revolution would have profound effects in Ireland, as it did in much of the rest of Europe. The American crisis of the 1760s and 1770s came at a time when increasing literacy and the availability of cheaper newspapers, books, and other publications had already produced a more politically conscious populace in both Britain and Ireland. The controversy in England over John Wilkes, a British journalist turned politician, who was denied his seat in Parliament in 1764 despite having been elected as MP for Middlesex, had done much to raise political awareness and to divide the English ruling classes. By 1771, the brewing conflict with the American colonies contributed to an even greater level of politicization among the members of the voting classes in England and Ireland, many of whom were sympathetic to the Americans. These years saw the formation of a Patriot Party in Dublin, formed by men who were alarmed by what they perceived to be the growth of royal absolutism emanating from London. The Patriot Party sought to gain greater independence for Ireland and to prevent the British from infringing on their rights as they had so cavalierly done to their American colonies. To the Patriots, whose leaders all belonged to the

Church of Ireland, the British simply did not have the right to countermand legislation passed in Ireland pertaining to Ireland. Much to the dismay of Irish nationalists, however, the Irish Parliament consented in November 1775 to contribute 4,000 Irish troops to the British imperial army as the American crisis evolved into war and rebellion. This contradicted much prevailing sentiment in Ireland, expressed in newspapers, pamphlets, and public speeches, in favor of the American cause. It also produced an immediate protest from six members of the Irish House of Lords who defended the right of the American colonists to rebel in the face of illegal taxation and because of the precedent that the Revolution of 1688 had set for the right to challenge arbitrary authority. The Society of Free Citizens in Support of the Colonists was founded in Dublin and issued a number of public statements to raise awareness for their position. The Dublin common council, along with the merchants and sheriffs, also backed the Americans and opposed the war.

Presbyterian Scots-Irish, many of whom had relatives who had recently gone to North America, were also inclined toward support for the colonies. The Scots-Irish had contributed significantly to the upward trend in migration out of Ireland in the first half of the eighteenth century. Those Protestants who remained in Ireland became incensed at the prospect of Irish Catholic soldiers being dispatched to help put down the rebellion in America. In his nineteenth-century novel, *Barry Lyndon*, set in this period, William Thackeray refers to the presence of recruiting parties in Ireland even at the time of the Seven Years War (1756–63) to enlist men for service in America and Germany. In the novel, Barry Lyndon, an Irish ne'er-d-well, who eventually rises to the ranks of the Anglo-Irish aristocracy, explains that "King George was too much in want of men to heed from whence they came" and that "most of the fellows who enlisted with myself were, of course, Papists."[27] The decision of the British government to enlist Catholics for military service in the colonies provoked a wave of hostile editorials and public pronouncements against the evils of this practice.

On this matter, the Protestants of the North and many of the leading Catholics of Dublin were in perfect accord, though for different reasons. A British embargo imposed in February 1776 on Irish exports that were not destined for Britain or its colonies, excepting the 13 rebellious colonies in North America, also did little to endear the war to the Irish, whether Catholic or Protestant. The British government was cognizant of these expressions of support for their rebellious colonies and wary that the contagion of rebellion might spread eastward across the Atlantic to Ireland. When news reached Ireland that the English army had suffered a defeat at the hands of the colonists at the Battle of Saratoga in 1777 and that France was to join

---

[27] William Makepeace Thackeray (1984), *The Memoirs of Barry Lyndon, Esq.*, edited by Andrew Sanders. Oxford: Oxford University Press, pp. 62, 67.

the war in support of the Americans, they naturally questioned what these developments might portend for them. For example, if the French supported the Americans against their common British enemies, might they not do the same for the Irish? The fact that the British had been forced to remove most of the 12,000 British soldiers that were usually stationed in Ireland to ensure its political quiescence did nothing to reassure British leaders who feared Irish disloyalty.

Such were the considerations behind the decision of Lord North to appease Ireland by pushing through measures to improve the position of the Irish Catholics. England could scarcely afford an Irish rebellion on top of the one in North America, and it was entirely plausible that the oppressed Catholic majority might seize the opportunity to cause problems for their oppressor. In fact, on 17 June 1778, North had received a message from Lord Amherst, writing from Geneva, stating that:

> I have acquired a piece of information here, concerning a plot for a revolt in the west of Ireland among the Roman Catholics, with a view to overturn the present Government, by aid of the French and Spaniards, and to establish such an one as prevails in this country [Switzerland]. I mean the Cantons, by granting toleration to the Protestants.[28]

Those fears became exacerbated once France joined the war against the British. In October 1779, North received another report, this one in a letter from John Beresford, who was serving in the Irish administration, stating that Ireland was on the brink of revolution. A number of measures were enacted by the government in response to these threats, whether real or imagined. North removed the greatest obstacles to land ownership by Catholics in 1778. England experienced a wave of anti-Catholic violence in the famous Gordon Riots that occurred in London in 1781. The background to those riots included the feeling that the British government had become too accommodating to Catholic interests, particularly when Parliament voted in 1778 to remove some of the penalties on Roman Catholics that had been imposed in the seventeenth century.

Such feelings were not assuaged when Parliament in the very next year passed the Catholic Relief Act of 1782, which removed some of the restraints on Catholic worship and the Catholic clergy. Catholic schools were now permitted, as were Catholic bishops. Having been allowed to bequeath land to a single heir and to sign leases for up to 99 years in 1778, Catholics were now granted the right to purchase land in the 1782 act. In the same year, the British government repealed the Declaratory Act and passed another measure (Yelverton's Act) that modified Poynings'

---

[28] Quoted in James Anthony Froude (1895), *The English in Ireland in the Eighteenth Century*, II, p. 232.

Law for the first time since 1494. All of these measures went a long way toward showing the Irish Patriots that British policy in Ireland was going to be substantially different from that which had provoked the American colonists into rebellion.

Those who remained loyal to Britain now expected something in return for their loyalty. Lord Nugent, who sat in both the Irish House of Lords and the British House of Commons, pushed for looser restrictions on Irish trade in several proposals that he put forth in the summer of 1778 in the face of an ailing economy. Nugent advocated for an end to the law prohibiting Ireland from exporting glass and also to the taxes that inflated the price of Irish cotton goods in Britain. He argued for free trade for the Irish in British colonies, allowing for some exceptions such as woolen textiles and tobacco. Nugent's proposals, however, were temporarily derailed by opposition from British merchant interests from Glasgow to Bristol. Nugent's proposals preceded a more intense campaign in support of Irish free trade in 1779, but the British government approved only a few modest measures in that direction, despite the extent to which Britain needed Ireland's support in the midst of the American war.

The measures taken to appease the Irish did not stop the Dublin Volunteers, a recently formed militia, from standing in the streets outside of the Irish Parliament as it met in October 1779. Ostensibly organized for purposes of defense with so many of the troops normally stationed in Ireland dispatched to North America, the Volunteers adopted as their main objective pressuring the British into granting further political concessions to Ireland. Since Catholics were prevented from bearing arms by the penal laws, all of the Volunteers were Protestant; still within a year, their numbers had reached about 40,000.[29] Against this background, in April 1780, Henry Grattan (1746–1820), one of the leaders of the Patriot Party along with Henry Flood and the earl of Charlemont, delivered a speech in the Irish Parliament in favor of legislative independence for Ireland, a demand that he repeated to the same assembly in February 1782. The Irish Parliament that conducted its own legislative business between 1782 and 1800 subsequently became known as "Grattan's Parliament." When Grattan's speeches appeared in print, they reflected many of the arguments for independence that Molyneux had made at the end of the seventeenth century. Grattan's proposal reflected a growing dissatisfaction with the British response to Ireland's support and political quiescence since the beginning of the war. But, even though many Irish writers had recognized the similarities between the American situation and their own, sympathy for the American Revolution did not lead to rebellion in Ireland. Perhaps

---

[29] John O'Beirne Ranelagh (1983), *A Short History of Ireland*. Cambridge: Cambridge University Press, p. 81.

this was because the Americans reacted quickly to what they perceived as a new imperial system that was imposed in the 1760s, although in many cases, the English were just enforcing existing laws such as the Navigation Acts that had been on the books since 1651. Irish Catholics had long been inured to the penal laws and even saw some hope of release as a result of the conciliatory attitude of Lord North during the American crisis. Despite much public opposition to the war, many Catholics had remained loyal to the British government and some had willingly enlisted to serve in the British army overseas. The Irish Catholic middle class had no desire to see widespread rebellion in Ireland and their support for the administration of the earl of Carlisle when he took over as lord-lieutenant in December 1780 did much to help stabilize the situation there. As for the Protestant ruling class, it had gained a greater degree of independence in the eighteenth century and still hoped for more. Furthermore, not all Irishmen supported the American Revolution.

Still, when in the end the United States had gained its independence from Great Britain as a result of its rebellion, this must have stirred the blood of many Irishmen and women who desired the same for their country. A comparison between the grievances of the colonists and those held by the Irish was inevitable, as was speculation about the possibility that a rebellion in Ireland might achieve the same result. The ineffectiveness of the Patriot Party to achieve any of its goals spurred a reaction among those not willing to give up and convinced them that more radical measures might be in order. Nor had those in Ireland who had remained loyal during the crisis been granted the kind of concessions for which they had hoped. But Ireland was still dominated by a ruling class that had close ties with England that they were reluctant to cut since they were Protestant, and the overwhelming majority of the Irish population was Catholic. It was against this ruling class that social discontent had begun to manifest itself even before the American crisis. But there are no straight lines in Irish history. Conflicting and competing movements coexist, along with reflection upon them and Ireland's state by its authors and poets. Therefore, before continuing with the history of social unrest in eighteenth-century Ireland, we pause to consider the literature of the period.

Eighteenth-century literature

The main distinction to be made when discussing eighteenth-century Irish literature is one that is not exclusive to this period: the division into works written in Irish (Gaelic) and those composed in English. As one might expect, literature in the native Irish language frequently, but not always, carried political and nationalist overtones. For example, Art MacComhaigh lamented the triumph of William III over James II at the Boyne in 1690 and

Aughrim in 1691, after which Ireland would never be the same. He writes in the poem "Úirchillan an Chregáin":

> It stabs me to know
> The Gaels of Tyrone are gone.[30]

An excellent example of a nonpolitical poem in Irish from this period would be Brian Merriman's (c. 1749–1805) "The Midnight Court," which treats gender relations in the eighteenth century as seen through the eyes of a group of fictitious women in a way that is reminiscent of Boccaccio's Renaissance masterpiece, *The Decameron*. Though entirely different from one another in form, both address themes such as the immorality of the clergy, the sexual incompatibility between older men and their much younger brides, and the stigma attached to illegitimate children, leading one to reflect on the similarities between fourteenth-century Italy and eighteenth-century Ireland. The theme of unhappy marriages comes up again in Thomas Amory's novel written in English, *The Life and Opinions of John Buncle, Esq.* (1755; 1766), although the protagonist protests against the prevailing sentiment that marriage equals misery. In fact, he claims never to have had a single unhappy hour through a succession of seven wives! This is in contrast to Jonathan Swift's Gulliver, who confesses that he could not stand to eat in the same room with his wife and children after returning from his travels.

Most literature in both Irish and English was written by men, although there are some notable exceptions. The Irish poem, "The Lament for Art O'Leary," written by the subject's widow, Eibhlín Dhubh Ní Chonaill, clearly gives voice to the grief that any woman might feel on the death of her husband, especially one who was killed at a relatively young age under tragic circumstances:

> There is no woman in Ireland
> Who had slept beside him
> And borne him three children
> But would cry out
> After Art O'Leary
> Who lies dead before me
> Since yesterday morning.[31]

---

[30] Art Mac Comhaigh (1991), "Úirchillan an Chregáin," translated by Seamus Deane in (1991), *The Field Day Anthology of Irish Writing: Volume I*, edited by Seamus Deane. Derry: Field Day, p. 294.

[31] Eibhlín Dhubh Ní Chonaill, "The Lament for Art O'Leary," translated by Frank O'Connor in (*The Field Day Anthology of Irish Writing: Volume I*, (1991), edited by Seamus Dean. Derry: Field Day, p. 310.

Women poets writing in English included Mary Barber, Laetitia Pilkington, and Mary O'Brien. Barber, who wrote mostly in the 1730s, offered her own perspective on matrimony in the advice she gave to her son on marriage in "The Conclusion of a Letter to the Rev. Mr. C—." She held out hope that a wife could become "a companion and friend," if only her husband would treat her well and give her no cause for complaint. Such she claimed was "the true end of marriage." Pilkington addressed the theme of marriage in "The Happy Pair, a Ballad," which contrasts sincere, mature love to the feelings associated with courtship, which is driven by passion. But she also wrote poems on contemporary politics, as did O'Brien, whose 1790 poem, "The Freedom of John Bull," satirizes stereotypes of the typical Englishman while also casting aspersions on William Pitt the Younger, the youthful prime minister of the time, as an enemy of freedom. Irish poetry in the eighteenth century, whether by men or women, could be quite diverse and included works such as Andrew Cherry's (1762–1812) "The Green Little Shamrock of Ireland," which linked the mythical plant to St Patrick and fed the traditional Irish symbolism that has become so ubiquitous today.

In considering eighteenth-century prose, we again must start with Jonathan Swift whose *Modest Proposal* and *Gulliver's Travels* have already been mentioned. Swift's other classic novel, *A Tale of a Tub* (1704), was actually his earliest. This makes it no less important or illuminating of Swift's thought and his reaction to the times in which he lived. Written during the period in which Swift was residing in England, the novel's plot revolves around the ways in which three sons have misinterpreted their father's will, with the father representing God and his sons the Roman Catholic, the Anglican, and the Presbyterian churches. However, the book also contains lengthy asides in which Swift takes aim at what he considered to be the ill-conceived purposes to which learning and education had been put in his age. In this novel, Swift took on both the intellectual and religious establishments of the early eighteenth century. Taking up the seventeenth-century debate over whether ancient writers were superior to modern ones, Swift challenged the prevailing—and what he saw as the stagnating—intellectual climate of his age by coming down decidedly on the side of the Ancients. Concerning religion, Swift took aim at the hardening of religious opinions that led to closed-mindedness and mutual hostility between people of rival faiths, particularly between the two prominent groups outside the Church of England/Ireland: the Presbyterians and the Catholics, who, as far as Swift was concerned, should have been sympathetic to one another as fellow dissenters. In *A Tale of a Tub*, Swift first announced his intention to speak his mind even if it brought him influential enemies, something that he would consistently do for the rest of his life.

William Chaigneau (1709–81) claims the distinction of writing the first novel that takes place primarily in Ireland. *The History of Jack Connor*, written in 1752, established a pattern that a number of other Irish novels would follow—that of a main character that leaves Ireland to establish an alternate identity, in this case changing his name to John Conyers before coming home to discover the place where he belonged all along. Chaigneau also provided future Irish authors with an example of how to use the voices of Irish characters to teach English readers about Ireland and, perhaps, to see the Irish situation through Irish eyes. Amory's John Buncle is another such character—a young man who was raised from infancy in Ireland and leaves for England to pursue a university education. He marries a series of seven educated women who happen to all be Unitarian and whose intelligent conversations with the main character take up most of the novel. The novel treats a diversity of subjects, including Ireland, without becoming ponderous. Amory uses Buncle to expose the English reader to Irish history and culture; another indication that interest in Irish history had become an extremely important aspect of the literary and intellectual landscape of eighteenth-century Ireland.

As should be apparent from this section, the frequently made claims that *Castle Rackrent* by Maria Edgeworth was the first Irish novel are inaccurate, but otherwise Edgeworth's novel, along with her other masterpiece, *Ennui* (1809) deserve all of the attention that they receive. Largely critical of Ireland's social structure and the frequent neglect of the Irish peasants by Anglo-Irish landowners, these novels also reveal Edgeworth's preference for Irish independence before and immediately after the 1801 Act of Union. Her novels hardly romanticized the Irish peasantry and she was not above criticizing the hold that the Catholic Church had over them. In one incident from *Castle Rackrent*, a maid who had fainted during Lent and was revived with a morsel of roast beef (standard fare for the lord of the manor, even during Lent) was made to do penance for it after the incident was reported to the local priest. Mostly, Edgeworth was a keen observer of Irish life, largely sympathetic to the people but always observing them from the perspective of a woman of the upper class. In many ways, she was uniquely positioned to present both perspectives. She attacks specific abuses of the landlord class, including rack-renting (hence the title of *Castle Rackrent*), the practice of raising the rents of tenants for improvements that they themselves had made on the lands they rented. But the larger theme of both *Castle Rackrent* and *Ennui* is a more timeless one stated in the preface to the former: "That the great are not as happy as they seem, that the external circumstances of fortune and rank do not constitute felicity." As applied to Ireland's historical situation at the time, however, this reflected Edgeworth's desire to see Ireland happy, which she did not foresee occurring as a result of union with England. The contrast between England and Ireland was pursued more systematically in *Ennui*, written after the Act of Union, which shows how unprepared the English aristocracy was to rule a land of which they were so ignorant. The novel is in many ways a warning to the aristocracy that the land was still fertile for rebellion at that time, and would continue to be in the future unless the root causes of it—lack of educational opportunities for the peasants, social injustice, and religious discrimination, for example—were eradicated. These issues had already caused a good deal of social unrest in the eighteenth century, particularly after 1760.

The beginnings of social unrest

Some manifestations of social unrest can be found in most periods of history, and eighteenth-century Ireland is no exception. Even at the beginning of the century, Dublin experienced waves of violent protest against the importation of foreign goods in the wake of the British Woolen Act and other legal hindrances to Irish trade. One such demonstration in 1711 began with a march through Dublin and ended in the mock execution of foreign fabrics that were hung from makeshift gallows.[32] Dubliners angered at the importing of foreign cloth physically attacked merchants and those wearing their imported fabrics in the 1730s. In addition, in the first half of the eighteenth century, food riots accompanied periods of famine and shortages, something that Ireland had in common with Britain and much of the rest of Europe in this period. But in the course of the eighteenth century, the Irish became more adept at organizing opposition to British authority, and the political and social injustices that they believed were perpetrated under the prevailing political system. And such was the nature of British rule in Ireland during the eighteenth century that Protestants were as upset about their lack of autonomy and the restrictions on Irish trade as the Catholics were about the denial of their rights under the penal laws, perhaps more so; by the end of the century, Irish Protestants would be using much the same language of universal rights that was employed in both the American and the French Revolutions.

But for most of the century, the most serious disturbances came from peasants in the countryside who in hard times found no one on the side of the government willing to come to their assistance. Economic hardship, exacerbated by population growth, contributed to an increasing number of rural uprisings in Ireland in the second half of the eighteenth century. The Seven Years War had caused something of an economic crisis for the British with ripple effects throughout the empire; it was the British demand that the Americans pay their share for their own defense in the aftermath of this war—known as the French and Indian War in North America—that had initiated the crisis that ultimately led to the War for Independence. The imposition of additional taxes had rankled the American colonists, whose discontent began to manifest itself in the 1760s. In Ireland, also, the earliest signs of social unrest came about 1760 with the emergence of the "Whiteboy" gangs that began to cause disruption in the Irish countryside.

Named for the white linen shirts that they wore, the Whiteboys formed a formidable and intimidating force that terrified landlords and the ruling class in rural Ireland. The activities of the Whiteboys ranged from theft to arson and even murder. The first outbreaks occurred in Tipperary in County Munster and in the north of County Waterford in early 1760 when gangs

---

[32] Powell, *Politics of Consumption*, p. 173.

of outlaws began frequent attacks on property under cover of darkness; antienclosure riots in Munster followed in 1761. Peasants in Ireland, as in England, opposed the "enclosure" of what had been common lands—to which they had previously had access—within fenses so that the land could be used by landlords in whatever means that they deemed most profitable. Peasants were also upset by heavy payments demanded by the Church of Ireland, which included the main tithes on income and on more commercial products such as hay, wheat, or wood, in addition to lesser tithes on produce grown for personal use, including potatoes.

Meanwhile, in 1763, Presbyterian dissenters calling themselves the "Hearts of Oak" or the "Oakboys" initiated a wave of protests in Ulster against the landlords who raised their rents. Although the increases were ostensibly justified by the need for estate improvements, such as better roads, the peasants saw even these as benefiting the landlord and not themselves. They were also upset with the established Protestant Church of Ireland, which their landlords supported with the higher rents and taxes imposed on their tenants. A similar movement led by rebels calling themselves the "Steelboys" shook the North in the 1770s. Also known as the "Hearts of Steel," the Protestant Steelboys also protested against higher rents, unfair evictions, and rising food prices, mustering a force of at least 500 men for an invasion of Belfast in December 1770.

Agrarian disturbances during this period provided an outlet for discontent with English rule that had been largely restricted to the Jacobite movement in the first half of the eighteenth century. Peasants who joined bands like the Whiteboys swore oaths of allegiance to one another to create a feeling of solidarity within the group. Furthermore, the Whiteboys had a central organization, which made them even more formidable and gave them a certain amount of authority over the peasant classes at the same time that they caused many sleepless nights among their social superiors. Such activity fed the worst fears of the English, especially when they were at war with France, because what the English authorities feared most of all was French intervention in Ireland. These disturbances became both more radical and more widespread following the American Revolution. Both Catholics and Protestants elevated their anti-English rhetoric, but this led to a split among Irish Protestants, some of whom recoiled at the prospect of greater levels of violence and the further radicalization of Irish politics. This split led those politicized Anglicans known as the Patriots, who sought greater freedoms from the British, to seek allies for their cause among the Protestant dissenters in Ireland, though not the Catholics. The rising levels of rural violence played into the hands of the Patriots who could use them as a threat if the British refused to negotiate with them. (A similar alliance between a parliamentary party and a violent rural organization would be formed in Ireland in the second half of the nineteenth century). A new group of radicals calling themselves the Rightboys wreaked havoc throughout the countryside from 1784 to 1786.

The Catholic cause, fortified by higher levels of commitment and the emergence of new leaders from the Catholic middle class, received new life when a national Catholic Convention met in Dublin in 1792. At the time, however, Catholics aimed lower than the Protestants did. Catholics were more concerned with the repeal of the penal laws and gaining political rights than with complete independence, which was more of a Protestant aim. When Catholics who possessed holdings worth 40 shillings were granted the right to vote in 1793, this had the effect of draining Catholic support for rebellion at the same time that it convinced many Protestants of the need for drastic action to distance themselves further from British rule.

Given the corruption of the British government and the power that resided in a landed aristocracy that often showed no concern for the people living under their rule, it is not surprising that there would be social unrest in eighteenth-century Ireland. But once it became inspired by more positive ideals than just an anti-English reaction, Irish discontent acquired the potential to become truly revolutionary. In fact, as the century drew to a close, Catholics tended to become more politically quietist, while Protestants grew increasingly disenchanted with the political and economic relationship between England and Ireland. Restrictions on Catholics had been loosened while Britain's overall grip on Ireland had been tightened. As we have seen, many of the agrarian rebels of the period had been Protestant. By the 1780s, Irish Protestants had begun demanding greater autonomy putting pressure on both Westminster and Dublin to address Ireland's constitutional status. Catholics have no monopoly on Irish nationalism in Ireland's history. In the last decade of the eighteenth century, the influence of the French Revolution and the spread of works such as Thomas Paine's *The Rights of Man* would help to transform social unrest into outright political rebellion. Once again, larger European developments impinged on the history of Ireland and set it on a different course. Earlier efforts at reform and calls for legislative independence coming from politicians like Henry Grattan would be supplanted by the formation of the United Irishmen and the more radical vision for a united Ireland of Theobald Wolfe Tone (1763–98). But the French Revolution, which would end up embroiling England in yet another war with France, meant that England would once again become preoccupied with Ireland and more determined to keep it in the empire. At the same time, the specter of revolution meant that any further talk of parliamentary reform in England or Ireland would be indefinitely postponed. It would be up to William Pitt the Younger to navigate the dangerous political waters surrounding the Irish situation. Pitt had a king (George III) whose bouts of madness threatened to undo his political future and to exacerbate the uneasy situation in Ireland. As the French Revolution began in 1789, Ireland's political future was already as uncertain as ever.

CHAPTER NINE

The Rebellion of 1798 and the impact of the French Revolution

When once a Government becomes contemptible in the public eye, its strongest pillar is shaken.

– THEOBALD WOLFE TONE, April 1790

The impact of the French Revolution

The dramatic events that took place in Ireland in the 1790s occurred against the backdrop of even more dramatic events that were occurring in France and across Europe. At first, the French Revolution of 1789 provoked nearly unbridled enthusiasm in both Britain and Ireland. It was easy to think in 1789 that France was merely moving in the direction of constitutional monarchy, such as that which already existed in Britain. Britain even stood to benefit from political instability in the governance of its archrival. But it soon became clear that the implications of the French Revolution for Ireland were much different than they were for Britain.

As a stimulus to revolutionary ideas and action upon those ideas, the French Revolution had the potential to galvanize the Irish people to throw off the British yoke and assert their right to self-government. In Ireland, there was a marked and almost immediate renewal of interest in parliamentary reform. If the French could change their government from an absolute monarchy that had existed in one form or another for a thousand years, then certainly political reform within Ireland was not inconceivable. Political societies began to spring up, especially in Dublin and Belfast. In Dublin, hopes for Catholic emancipation were renewed and became intertwined with radical politics. In Belfast, enthusiasm for the French Revolution culminated in the Bastille Day celebrations held there on 14 July in 1791 and 1792 to commemorate the 1789 fall of the fortified prison in central Paris that had come to symbolize the beginning of the revolution and the downfall of the old regime. Against the backdrop of the French Revolution, groups of mostly middle-class men began assembling in Dublin and Belfast to form a debating society that would adopt the name of the "United Irishmen" in 1791. Inspired by events in France, the United Irishmen advocated a more democratic form of government based on universal suffrage. And news from France was sweeping across the island. In 1793, a Fermanagh resident told the United Irishman Thomas Russell that support for the French Revolution was so widespread in his region that it existed even "in mountains where you could not conceive that any news could reach."[1]

However, the French Revolution also provoked a reaction against it in Ireland, as well as Britain, best exemplified by Edmund Burke's 1790 book, *Reflections on the Revolution in France*. Burke had been born in Ireland in 1729, the product of a mixed marriage between his Catholic mother and Protestant father. By 1750, he had moved to England, where he began a career as a well known philosopher and politician, writing an important book on aesthetics (*A Philosophical Enquiry into the Origin of Our Ideas of the Sublime and the Beautiful*, 1757) and the American crisis (*Conciliation with America*, 1775). Burke's *Reflections* became the bible of conservatives who disdained the French Revolution but was itself disdained by liberals more sympathetic to the revolutionary cause. Whereas liberals saw in the revolution hope for the future and viewed change as a positive thing that would improve the lot of humankind, conservatives only saw the threatened end of a civilization centuries in the making. Liberals welcomed freedom of thought; conservatives feared the end of religion. Liberals welcomed political reform based on abstract principles such as liberty and equality; conservatives believed that politics needed to be based on tradition and experience. Liberals believed that change could be harnessed and steered in a positive direction; conservatives predicted that any significant political change would only end up in chaos and instability. In 1792, the conservative archbishop of Dublin, John Troy lamented that "we live . . . in wretched times, when too many of our people are ignorant of or forget their real principles, or, what is worse, are ashamed to profess them."[2]

---

[1] Quoted in Stephen Howe (1999), "Speaking of '98: History, Politics and Memory in the Bicentenary of the 1798 United Irish Uprising." *History Workshop Journal*, 47, 222.

[2] Quoted in S. J. Connolly (1982), *Priests and People in Pre-Famine Ireland, 1780–1845*. Dublin: Gill and Macmillan, p. 74.

In both Ireland and England, the leaders of the Whig Party found themselves trapped between the liberals who were enthusiastic about the revolution and the conservatives who ardently opposed it. The Whigs had already stumbled politically in the late 1780s during what became known as the *Regency Crisis*. This crisis had resulted from the temporary insanity of George III (r. 1760–1820), which led the Whigs to align themselves with his son George, the Prince of Wales and heir to his father's throne, in hopes of recapturing control of the government. To their embarrassment, George III recovered, and the Whigs found themselves at a disadvantage in their rivalry with the Tory Prime Minister, William Pitt the Younger (1759–1806). After the start of the French Revolution, the Whigs found themselves at an even greater political disadvantage since the conservative Tories could now more effectively pose as defenders of the established order. If the Whigs emphasized their own more liberal values, they risked being categorized with those who sympathized with the revolution, but if they sided with the conservatives, they would risk losing their own identity. This was especially problematic in Ireland because of the number of people there who drew inspiration from the French Revolution in their challenge to the political status quo.

The French Revolution provided Irish nationalists with the hope that they could unite, put an end to British rule, and achieve their own nationhood. Thus, in Ireland the revolution was viewed favorably by a wide range of people. James Caulfield (1728–99), the first earl of Charlemont and the first president of the Royal Irish Academy in Dublin, was among those who attempted to balance his Whig principles with support for the French Revolution. In Belfast, the leading Whig politicians William Bruce and Henry Joy did the same. But, if Burke is excluded, Arthur O'Connor may have been the most original Irish thinker to respond to the French Revolution. For example, O'Connor believed that the establishment of an Irish monarchy was one way to establish equality between Ireland and England, although like other reformers of the period, he continued to support universal suffrage.[3] Not many Irish patriots in the 1790s were monarchists, but even O'Connor no longer saw the British monarch as the legitimate head of Ireland.

The French Revolution had one other important implication for Irish history: it had brought down a Catholic monarchy and in doing so had shifted European politics in a more secular direction. This raised the possibility that Catholics and Protestants in Ireland could unite politically without their religious differences interfering. The revolution had thus seemed to make the penal laws obsolete. Catholics in Ireland were given renewed hope for the dismantling of the legal restrictions against them because the French Revolution had rallied liberal Protestants to their cause.

---

[3] Jacqueline Hill (2001), "Convergence and Conflict in Eighteenth-Century Ireland." *Historical Journal*, 44, 1058.

Many people thought, however, that the events that unfolded in France in the course of the 1790s increasingly seemed to prove that Burke was right. The execution of the king in January 1793, the Reign of Terror, in which thousands of French aristocrats and other suspected opponents of the revolution lost their heads to the recently invented guillotine, and an atrocity-filled civil war had turned France into a bloodbath. France was dragged into a war with Austria and Prussia and was now seen as threatening the peace of Europe, even though at first they were placed on the defensive. The war allowed the French to pose as the defenders of revolution not only in France but also throughout Europe as they encouraged other peoples desiring liberation to join them. In February 1793, the French declared war on the British. There was talk among the Irish of negotiating their own peace treaty with the French. Meanwhile, the British government, spooked by the terrible events occurring in France, engaged in a series of repressive measures designed to crush revolutionary activity or political dissent. Burke's outrage at the threatened horrors of the revolution provided a theoretical justification for repression by the state.

These developments dampened the enthusiasm of Whigs such as Bruce and Joy, but Charlemont and others retained their convictions and their French sympathies. By the mid-1790s, the Irish reform movement was too far along on what a growing number of people thought was their own path toward freedom. The reform movement had unified radicals of all religious stripes: Catholics, Presbyterians, and Anglicans. The United Irishmen had widespread support and had started their own newspaper. Other revolutionary societies, such as the Catholic Defenders, had started to form. Furthermore, by this time, Irish radicals had reason to believe that France might intervene on their behalf if necessary. The French Revolution had created a great divide in the history of Ireland, as in the larger history of Europe, and had won enough adherents that there was no turning back. Supporters of revolution were also fortified by the ideological arguments put forth in one of the most important books to respond to the developments in France: Thomas Paine's *The Rights of Man*.

Ireland and *The Rights of Man*

Thomas Paine's 1776 pamphlet *Common Sense* had played a significant role in riling up the Americans in support of their revolution. *The Rights of Man* was Paine's response to the French Revolution—and Edmund Burke's criticism of it. It became so popular in Ireland—where it almost immediately went through seven editions—that the Irish revolutionary Theobald Wolfe Tone, a Protestant barrister and leading advocate of reform, referred to it as "the Koran of Blefescu [Belfast]."[4] Paine himself guessed that more than

---

[4] Theobald Wolfe Tone (1998), *The Life of Theobald Wolfe Tone*, edited by Thomas Bartlett. Dublin: Lilliput Press, p. 119.

40,000 copies of Part I of his book had been sold in Ireland by November 1791. Even if Paine overestimated by 6,000, that would still have meant that the Irish sales of his book were double the number of copies sold in England and Scotland combined.[5] The government did nothing to stop the publication of Paine's book, apparently convinced that the book was expensive enough at three shillings that it would be kept out of the hands of the dangerous rabble.[6] It is possible that Burke's *Reflections on the Revolution* was at least as popular, based on the eight editions of that work that had been published in Dublin in its first year of publication.[7] But Paine's success was the more significant, given its revolutionary implications. On 5 June 1792, the Protestant publisher of *The Rights of Man*, Randal McAlister, and a Catholic bookseller named James Moore nominated Paine for an honorary membership in the Dublin Society of United Irishmen.[8]

Building on the legacy of Enlightenment thought and the ideals of the American and French Revolutions, Paine emphasized that men enjoyed certain natural and egalitarian rights that were the only rational basis for civil society. He saw the American and French Revolutions as restoring those rights. Paine attacked the English monarchy in particular as not being rooted in the support of the people; he did not regard the English parliament as a truly representative body. In fact, he regarded any form of government as illegitimate that was not selected or ratified by the people living under it: no government had the right to bind posterity to it until "the end of time." The government was "for the living, not for the dead, it is the living only that has any right in it," he wrote.[9]

To illustrate this point, Paine cited the ways in which the American and French Revolutions had already eclipsed the principles established by the Revolution of 1688. Paine advised his readers that:

> As it is not difficult to perceive, from the enlightened state of mankind, that hereditary governments are verging on their decline, and that revolutions on the broad basis of national sovereignty, and government by representation, are making their way in Europe, it would be an act

---

[5] Stephen Small (2002), *Political Thought in Ireland 1776–1798: Republicanism, Patriotism, and Radicalism*. Oxford: Clarendon Press, p. 188.

[6] Stella Tillyard (1997), *Citizen Lord: The Life of Edward Fitzgerald, Irish Revolutionary*. New York: Farrar, Straus and Giroux, p. 115.

[7] R. B. McDowell (1979), *Ireland in the Age of Imperialism and Revolution, 1760–1801*. Oxford: Clarendon Press, p. 352.

[8] David Dickson (1993), "Paine and Ireland," in D. Dickson, D. Keogh and K. Whelan (eds), *The United Irishmen: Republicanism, Radicalism, and Rebellion*. Dublin: Lilliput Press, p. 135.

[9] Quoted in John Killen (ed.) (1997), *The Decade of the United Irishmen: Contemporary Accounts, 1791–1801*. Belfast: The Blackstaff Press, p. 15.

of wisdom to anticipate their approach, and produce revolutions by reason and accommodation, rather than commit them to the issue of convulsions.[10]

Paine sought to build on the ideas of Jean-Jacques Rousseau, which to his mind had not provided enough of a practical plan for achieving the liberty that people now demanded.

Paine regarded action as necessary in order to bring out the latent principles that each man naturally cherishes but that otherwise lie dormant. It was time for people to take matters into their own hands. *The Rights of Man* was a clarion call for political change that inspired the Irish aristocrat Lord Edward Fitzgerald (1763–98) to become a revolutionary. Fitzgerald knew Paine personally, having met him in Paris in the early stages of the French Revolution. Fitzgerald, his modern biographer points out, began to act and even look the part of a revolutionary, complete with "fashionably democratic cropped hair, and ostentatiously flaunting a Republican red cravat."[11]

Not everyone, of course, was so enthralled with *The Rights of Man* or its author. Charlemont, who was no supporter of Burke, wished that neither Burke's nor Paine's books had been published. Charlemont confessed himself "to the last degree partial to the English constitution."[12] Taking their cue from Burke, conservative Irish Protestants regarded Paine and his radical adherents as more dangerous than the Catholics. Even the future revolutionary Thomas Russell thought that *The Rights of Man* went too far and might lead to a premature revolution when it might not be necessary. A writer of a 1791 pamphlet called it "a panegyric upon innovation, a ridicule of establishments, a justification of rebellion, a libel upon the government and religion of their country."[13] Other attacks were published in the *Dublin Journal*, a conservative publication, which took special aim at Part II of *The Rights of Man* when it was published in April 1792. The *Belfast Newsletter* was equally hostile, and even Wolfe Tone dismissed Paine's *Age of Reason* as "damned trash."[14]

But through the publication of his *The Rights of Man*, thousands more were influenced by Paine's ideas, including the book clubs and other affiliates of the United Irishmen. A proclamation of the Maghera freemasons defended the "rights of men" and condemned "taxation without representation."[15] Paine had provided Irish radicals with a convincing argument for change within the larger context of the Enlightenment and the age of reason.

---

[10] Thomas Paine (1791), *The Rights of Man*, I in P. S. Foner (ed.), (1945), *The Complete Writings of Thomas Paine*. New York: Citadel Press, Vol. I, p. 344.

[11] Tillyard, *op. cit.*, p. 143.

[12] Small, *op. cit.*, p. 188.

[13] "Remarks on Mr. Paine's Pamphlet called *The Rights of Man*. In a Letter to a Friend," quoted in Ibid., p. 189.

[14] Dickson, *op. cit.*, p. 145.

[15] Petri Mirala (2007), *Freemasonry in Ulster, 1733–1813: A Social and Political History of the Masonic Brotherhood in the North of Ireland*. Dublin: Four Courts Press, p. 178.

He believed that revolution and the actions of the people were the only remedies for the injustices that an oppressive and unjust government foisted upon them. In Ireland, Paine's confidence in the people and their ability to recognize their natural rights were shared by Wolfe Tone. Tone became convinced of the need for liberty for all after he became secretary of the Catholic Association in 1791. In July, he wrote:

> In the present era of great reform when unjust governments are falling in every quarter of Europe, when religious persecution is compel'd to abjure her tyranny over conscience, when the rights of man are ascertained in theory and that theory substantiated in practice, when antiquity can no longer defend absurd and oppressive norms against the common sense and common interests of mankind, when all government is acknowle[d]ged to originate from the people and to be so far only obligatory as it protects their rights and promotes their welfare, we think it our duty as Irishmen to come forward and state what we feel to be our heavy grievance and what we know to be its effectual remedy. . . . With a reformed parliament, everything is easy; without it nothing can be done, unless by means too violent for the good people of this country, if not provoked beyond human sufferance even to think on.[16]

Such sentiments led him to become one of the leading figures in the United Irishmen.

The United Irishmen

The name "United Irishmen" was appropriate since the organization contained both Catholics and Protestants, although Presbyterians predominated among the membership in Belfast. Broadly influenced by the ideas of the Enlightenment that downplayed the significance of religion, the United Irishmen advocated for an end to the religious disadvantages of both Catholics and Protestant Dissenters. But they adopted a platform that in many ways was rooted in the principles of the Patriot Party of the 1780s and traditional grievances of the Irish against English rule. At first, the United Irishmen, like the Patriots, were interested in reform, not revolution. Like the Patriots, they sought a greater measure of independence for Ireland. O'Connor's idea for the establishment of an Irish monarchy would have appealed to the Patriots. The Patriots had even made a nod in the direction of supporting Gaelic culture in their support for Irish nationalism. For example, Henry Flood (1732–91) helped to found the Royal Irish Academy

---

[16] Theobald Wolfe Tone (1791), "Resolutions enclosed with Tone's letter to Thomas Russell," in *The Writings of Theobald Wolfe Tone*, edited by T. W. Moody, R. B. McDowell and C. J. Woods, Oxford: Clarendon Press, I: 106–7.

and was among those who sought to stimulate greater interest in the Irish past. Thus, the United Irishmen provided a place for Irish Protestant Patriots to go, once the Patriot party of Grattan and Flood had been discredited, which it largely was by 1790.

Wolfe Tone, who became the main spokesperson for the United Irishmen, believed that the key to Irish liberty was an end to religious discrimination and the equal application of the principles of liberty to all citizens, regardless of their religious affiliation. He said as much in a 1791 pamphlet called *An Argument on behalf of the Catholics of Ireland.* Tone argued for the

FIGURE 9.1 *Edward Delaney's Statue of Wolfe Tone, St Stephen's Green, Dublin. The memory of the 1798 rebellion has loomed very large in Irish history. Photo by Stephen Saks. Courtesy of Getty Images.*

enlightened principle that each citizen of a society is only free so long as all members of that society are free. Tone became secretary of the Catholic Committee in 1792, a further recognition of his commitment to the cause of equality for Catholics. In fact, that same year, he joined 231 other delegates of the Catholic Committee on a mission to London to ask the king directly to address the Catholic plight in Ireland.

But Tone was equally sympathetic to Protestant Dissenters such as the Presbyterians, whom he once praised as "sincere and enlightened republicans" who "oppose the usurpations of England, [and] whose protection . . . they did not, like the Protestant aristocracy, feel necessary for their existence."[17] When Tone spoke these words in a presentation to the government of France in 1796, they seemed to reflect a real opportunity at that time for Irish Catholics and Protestants to recognize their common interests; Tone saw this as the benefit that the French Revolution had bestowed upon Ireland with its emphasis on the common rights of all men. His friend and fellow United Irishman, Thomas Russell, was a Presbyterian businessman who shared his commitment to liberty and equality. Tone emphasized his own Protestant background on more than one occasion and thought himself in a good position to argue for Catholic liberty because of it. When sectarian violence broke out in Ulster in July 1792, Tone did not exonerate the Catholics for provoking it by a military-style march, even though he acknowledged that the Protestants were the aggressors. He also pointed out to those who opposed ending restrictions on Catholics that Protestant Dissenters and Quakers suffered from the same disadvantages. He addressed *An Argument on Behalf of the Catholics of Ireland* to the Dissenters "to convince them that they and the Catholics had but one common interest."[18]

Wolfe Tone helped found a newspaper, the *Northern Star* so that the United Irishmen could reach their constituents on a regular basis. The paper also served as an outlet for other groups with similar goals. For example, in 1792, the paper printed a list of resolutions passed by the Belfast Reading Society advocating political reform and the repeal of the penal laws.[19] Later that year, the paper printed an address calling for the Dublin Volunteers to take up arms to support the cause of liberty for Catholics and political reform, which landed the paper's publisher in hot water with the authorities. The *Northern Star* was published in Belfast; its attacks on the Protestant Ascendancy appealed to the Presbyterians there. The paper made the ideas of Thomas Paine available to those readers who had not read *The Rights of Man*. The paper's support for both the Catholic and the Presbyterian

[17] Theobald Wolfe Tone (1796), "First Memorial on the Present State of Ireland, delivered to the French Government," in *The Writings of Theobald Wolfe Tone, op. cit.*, II: 64.
[18] Sean Cronin (1991), *For Whom the Hangman's Rope was Spun: Wolfe Tone and the United Irishmen*. Dublin: Repsol, p. 25.
[19] Nancy J. Curtin (1994), *The United Irishmen: Popular Politics in Ulster and Dublin, 1791–1798*. Oxford: Clarendon Press, p. 145.

cause reflected the extent to which the United Irishmen were becoming a truly national party. The paper also gave special emphasis to developments in France, making it clear to its readers that the events taking place there should be of immense concern to those interested in European affairs and the future of Ireland. Though for the most part the paper simply reported the news, it did so in a way that made what was happening in France seem acceptable. The paper supported the execution of Louis XVI, which was also condoned by Wolfe Tone, among others. The paper remained in print only until 1797, however, when the government closed it down.

The closure of the *Northern Star* is just one example of how the events of the 1790s ended up affecting the United Irishmen as much as the association contributed to the unfolding of events. Perhaps the most significant event to impact the United Irishmen was the war between Britain and France, which officially began on 7 February 1793. War with France always affected the attitude of the British government toward Ireland because of long-standing fears that Ireland could provide a launching pad for a French invasion of Britain. The British were even more afraid in the mid-1790s because the parliamentary reforms of the 1780s had given the Irish parliament the right to vote on the number of troops it would supply to the British. Furthermore, as a result of the rise of the United Irishmen and their open sympathy toward France, Ireland became an even greater concern. With agitation increasing on the part of the United Irishmen, the government now feared that the French could inspire—or, even worse, support—a revolution in Ireland. A statement issued by the Irish viceroy, Lord Camden, in August 1796 conveyed the concern "that considerable danger is to be apprehended from the organized system which has been established at Belfast, which aided by the general disaffection that prevails may alone lead to outrage and insurrections" and that if such an insurrection were "assisted by the actual cooperation of France *even to a small degree*, the danger is infinitely magnified."[20] These fears were not entirely unfounded, but the repressive measures that the British used to prevent a revolution only made one more likely to occur.

The British parliament began by passing the Convention Act of 1793, which made representative assemblies, such as the United Irishmen, illegal. They then called for the establishment of local militias throughout Ireland, which resulted in a series of militia riots that resulted in an estimated 230 deaths.[21] The Insurrection Act of 1796 suspended habeas corpus and authorized magistrates to arrest anyone without cause. The United Irishmen had to contend with local authorities as well. For example, a police raid in Dublin in May 1794 resulted in the capture of the papers of the society.

---

[20] Marianne Elliott (1982), *Partners in Revolution: The United Irishmen and France*. New Haven: Yale University Press, pp. 106–7.

[21] Thomas Bartlett (1996), "Defence, Counter-insurgency and Rebellion: Ireland, 1793–1803," in T. Bartlett and K. Jeffery (eds), *A Military History of Ireland*. Cambridge: Cambridge University Press, p. 254.

These efforts on the part of the government severely hampered the ability of the United Irishmen to openly advocate for parliamentary reform. These measures also did as much as anything to transform the United Irishmen into an organization bent on revolution rather than reform, though the exact timing and extent of this change is a subject of debate among Irish historians. By 1795, the United Irishmen had been forced to go underground in Ulster, which became the center of the revolutionary movement. It is true that this process may have been a gradual one, with the revolutionary potential of the organization present from its founding. But one thing is clear: by 1796, talk of revolution was in the air.

In February 1796, Wolfe Tone arrived in France to negotiate a military alliance between the Directory, the new five-man executive body charged with running the country, and the United Irishmen. In order to attract the support of the French, Wolfe Tone had to assure them that the Irish were serious about fighting the British. He even accepted a commission in the French army and was promised a role in a French invasion of Ireland.

By this time, Tone had become a serious revolutionary willing to take drastic measures in support of his goals. The government's policy of repression had made a marked impression on him. He had now become convinced that parliamentary reform was not enough and that Ireland needed complete independence from Britain. Not all Protestant revolutionaries were as enthusiastic about enlisting the French as Tone was. But his main goals remained the same. He assured the French that his support for the Catholics had not wavered. He told them that:

> The Protestants, who are almost entirely the descendants of Englishmen, forming so very small a minority as they do of the whole people, have yet almost the whole landed property of the country in their hands; this property has been acquired by the most unjust means, by plunder and confiscation during repeated wars, and by the operation of laws framed to degrade and destroy the Catholics, the natives of the country. England ... has rewarded them [the Protestants] ... by distributing among them all the offices and appointments in the church, the army, the law, the revenue and every department of the state, to the utter exclusion of the other two sects and more especially of the Catholics. By these means the Protestants, who constitute the aristocracy of Ireland, have in their hands all the force of the Government; they have at least five sixths of the landed property; they are devoted implicitly to the connection with England, which they look upon as essential to the secure possession of their estates; they dread and abhor the principles of the French Revolution, and, in case of any attempt to emancipate Ireland, I should calculate the opposition which it might be in their power to give.[22]

---

[22] Wolfe Tone (1796), *op. cit.*, II: 62.

Tone, a Protestant, speaking to France's secular executive body, had largely made the case for the coming rebellion on the basis of support for the rights of Catholics in Ireland.

A French naval expedition left for Ireland in December of 1796 carrying 15,000 men. Only a portion of the 43-ship fleet made it to Ireland, landing on Christmas in Bantry Bay in the southwest. Most of the ships had to turn back because of rough weather. But, more importantly, the British had been unable to prevent the invasion, a cause of great alarm for them. The threatened invasion shook the British government out of whatever complacency it retained in regard to Ireland and led to harsher measures of repression, including the arrest of a number of prominent United Irishmen. These measures did little to diminish the appeal of the organization, however, which was rapidly gaining a wider appeal outside of Belfast and Dublin.

The British government might have attempted reform measures to forestall the appeal of revolution and lessen the chance of a successful French invasion. Instead, it had become uncompromisingly hostile to reform in the face of the French Revolution, as is indicated by a government-sponsored handbill distributed in Exeter in 1794:

> ... as for them that do not like ... the present CONSTITUTION, let them have their deserts, that is a HALTER and a GIBBET, and be burnt afterward, not as PAINE hath been, in effigy, but in body and person.[23]

The Irish parliament might have taken further measures to address the plight of the Catholics, but, in the repressive atmosphere after 1793, the possibility never went beyond the discussion stage.

Meanwhile, Wolfe Tone and the United Irishmen had been gaining the support of a plethora of local radical groups that had proliferated throughout rural Ireland. Indeed, the United Irishmen had not been the only revolutionary group to form in Ireland in the 1790s that was inspired by events in France. Workers in Dublin and Belfast formed their own groups, more concerned about social change than political reforms. The Ulster freemasons, although they were not a new organization and contained conservative elements, had some chapters come down on the side of political change. For example, the lodge at Maghera acknowledged that government in Ireland had become infected by "gross corruptions."[24] The United Irishmen also drew support from book clubs that had formed in East Ulster in the previous decade. But it was mainly the United Irishmen that spread the message to the people through *The Northern Star*, other publications, and word of mouth that the

---

[23] Quoted in E. P. Thompson (1966), *The Making of the English Working Class*. New York: Vintage Books, p. 115.
[24] Mirala, *op. cit.*, p. 178.

French Revolution was not to be feared and that Ireland could only benefit by following its example and giving equal rights to all of its citizens.

North and South

The French Revolution had helped to prepare the way for the United Irishmen in part because it had involved the overthrow of a Catholic monarch, making its ideals more acceptable for Protestants, including the Presbyterians most of whom resided in the north. Presbyterians, in particular, rejoiced at the downfall of the French monarchy, seeing it as a sign of the eventual demise of the papacy itself in preparation for the Second Coming. They tended to see divine judgment in the French Revolution and attributed to it a role in the unfolding of God's plan as laid out in the Book of Revelation.[25] It is unclear why they would now become more receptive to toleration for Catholics in Ireland, given their continued hostility to popery, but Wolfe Tone and others appealed to them on the grounds that Catholics were not enemies of liberty, as demonstrated by those of the Roman faith who had participated in the French Revolution. Furthermore, in February 1798, the Directory occupied the city of Rome and stripped Pope Pius VI of his temporal authority. In his diary, Wolfe Tone wrote that this event was "of a magnitude scarce, if at all, inferior to that of the French Revolution." He believed in the idea of "providence guiding the affairs of Europe . . . turning everything to the great end of the emancipation of mankind from the yoke of religious and political superstition under which they have so long groaned."[26] But while some Protestants remained well disposed toward the French Revolution, owners of property and businesses had become more leery of the United Irishmen the more they talked about revolution because they had the most to lose.

Tensions had been high in the north even before 1789, particularly in County Armagh, and they intensified thereafter. Episodes of violence between Catholics and Protestants were not uncommon. Reforms granting Catholics greater property rights upset many Protestants in Ulster and helped to precipitate some of the anti-Catholic violence of the period. About 10,000 Catholics fled Ulster in fear of their lives in the mid-1790s, many of them (about 4,000) settling in Connacht.[27]

Catholics in the north responded with their own secret society known as the *Defenders*. The United Irishmen welcomed an alliance with the new

---

[25] Kevin Whelan (1998), *Fellowship of Freedom: The United Irishmen and 1798*. Cork: Cork University Press, p. 22.

[26] Theobald Wolfe Tone (1798), "Diary," in *The Writings of Theobald Wolfe Tone*, edited by T. W. Moody, R. B. McDowell and C. J. Woods. Oxford: Clarendon Press, III: 208.

[27] James Lydon (1998), *The Making of Ireland from Ancient Times to the Present*. London and New York: Routledge, p. 263.

society, but the Defenders operated more in the form of a traditional rural secret society and were fiercely anti-Protestant besides. Tensions erupted on 21 September 1795, when the Catholic Defenders fought the Protestant Peep O'Day Boys at what became known as the "Battle of the Diamond" in County Armagh. Shortly thereafter, a group of Protestant landlords took the initiative and formed the Orange Order, a Protestant society that pledged its loyalty to the Church of Ireland and the British king. This would prove to have a great appeal among other Protestant landlords and their Protestant tenants. Over 170,000 members had joined the order by 1800. These developments further raised the political consciousness of Irish Catholics, though they did not necessarily make them more optimistic about a "united Ireland." In fact, tales of the hostility directed against Catholics by the Orange Order were repeated throughout Ireland, initiated by those who had been most directly affected by it. Support for the Defenders soon grew outside of Ulster with chapters springing up in Leinster and Connacht.

Not all Protestants joined the Orange Order. Many remained committed to the cause of the United Irishmen, especially in Antrim, which had a high literacy rate and where Presbyterians were still hostile to the Ascendancy. Of course, there were also fewer Catholics in Antrim and Down than in Armagh and Tyrone, where religious prejudice remained strong. Wolfe Tone believed that the Presbyterians' fears of international Catholicism had been mitigated by the French Revolution and that they now saw the Catholics of Ireland in a different light on the basis of their shared disdain for the Protestant aristocracy. That Tone's hopes were premature might have been indicated by the episodes of violence directed at Catholics throughout the north shortly after the founding of the Orange Order.

Presbyterians may have been conflicted, torn between their enlightened attitudes on political participation as reflected in the democratic nature of their church on the one hand and their long-standing hostility to Catholicism on the other. One of the strongest critics of the Ascendancy was a Presbyterian minister from County Down named Samuel Barber (c. 1738–1811), who also supported Catholic emancipation. Barber attacked the principle of an established church. He objected to the assessment of tithes on both Catholics and Presbyterians who did not belong to it. Barber realized that these groups formed a natural alliance against the established church, even if they might be reluctant to join forces with one another. Sympathy for Catholics and the cause of the United Irishmen and its goals was strongest among Protestants in Belfast and less so among those who lived in the more rural areas of the north. In County Armagh, a yeomanry corps was formed in 1796 with support from the government as an added precaution against the threat of a French invasion.

Catholics were torn between their allegiance to their church, which consistently condemned violence and revolution, and their desire to achieve emancipation and overthrow the Protestant Ascendancy. In Dublin, the

United Irishmen clung to their initial commitment to a "sincere and hearty union of all the people," believing that this was the only hope for Ireland's future. Their top priority was Ireland, which they hoped to strengthen by ending the long-standing religious divisions that had characterized its history of the previous 250 years. Such an ideal proved difficult to create in practice, however. The meeting that took place in Dublin in 1795 failed to produce a consensus among Protestant Dissenters, Catholics, and Grattan's Whig Party.[28] Grattan could not find his way to support a movement that was becoming increasingly radical, even though he was still sympathetic to Catholic emancipation. Efforts to introduce reform measures granting political equality to Catholics were summarily dismissed. This effectively ended any cooperation between the Whigs and the radicals. It also drove some Dublin radicals more in the direction of revolution and put them in the forefront of the United Irishmen at that time. After the members of the Leinster provincial committee of the United Irishmen were arrested in Dublin on 12 March 1798, it seemed as if revolution might be the only option left. The committee had been betrayed by one of its own members, Thomas Reynolds from County Kildare. Tone called the episode "news of the most disastrous and afflicting kind, as well for me, individually, as for the country at large."[29] To be sure, these arrests would deprive the United Irishmen of necessary leadership when rebellion did break out later in the year.

Despite the best efforts of the United Irishmen and the growing sentiment in favor of Catholic emancipation, then, the North and South remained divided in many respects. The question for the United Irishmen in the mid-1790s was whether or not Ireland was ready to embrace the cause of Irish unity at the expense of the historical divide between the largely Protestant North and the mainly Catholic South. The United Irishmen had high ideals, but religious animosities still simmered underneath the surface. Tensions remained high between Catholics and Protestants in Ulster and elsewhere, with sectarian violence a constant threat. Many Presbyterians retained their prejudice against Catholics, while Catholics had a difficult time believing in the sincerity of Protestants, given even their most recent history. This made some Catholics reluctant to join the United Irishmen, while others stayed away because of the conservative attitude of their church. What most unified North and South in the 1790s was not a set of political ideals, but growing resentment over the repressive measures imposed by the British to prevent rebellion. When the time for rebellion came, it was not a unified Ireland that opposed the British, but isolated uprisings in different parts of Ireland that were largely independent of one another.

---

[28] Thomas Bartlett (1992), *The Fall and Rise of the Irish Nation: The Catholic Question, 1690–1830*. Savage. MD: Barnes and Noble, p. 205.
[29] Tone, *op. cit.*, III: 208.

The Rebellion of 1798

With fears of a rebellion and a French invasion escalating, the militia in 1797 destroyed the offices of the *Northern Star* in Belfast, which effectively shut down the paper. In March 1798, the government took action in Dublin. Most of the leading members of the United Irishmen in the city and its immediate environs were placed under arrest. The United Irishmen had set up a secret hierarchical network of revolutionary committees that extended out into the counties in an attempt to prepare for just such a contingency. The time seemed right for the United Irishmen to launch a revolution that would live up to their name by bringing Catholics and Protestants together in the struggle to gain Ireland its complete independence.

It was not to be. Events ran ahead of them. Spontaneous uprisings occurred in Antrim, Down, and Wexford, but they were isolated and independent of one another. The leaders of the United Irishmen were not prepared to coordinate or assert control over them. They did exercise some control over the rebellion in the northern counties of Antrim and Down. But in the south, the grievances of Catholic rebels against Protestant landlords gave the movement more of a religious dimension that was antithetical to the goals and objectives of the United Irishmen.

Like most revolutions in history, this one was to take the form of a civil war. Many Irish had joined the militia and others were being recruited into the British army itself. The rebellion began in May after the government sent out troops of militia organized by landlords and consisting of tenants and local farmers to patrol their areas in search of rebel activity. On 15 May, Lord Edward Fitzgerald, the most prominent aristocrat to join the rebellion, had a £1000 reward placed on his head. Authorities ascertained his location in Dublin within a few days and sent a contingent of soldiers to arrest him. On 20 May, Fitzgerald was wounded while resisting arrest and captured, dealing a serious blow to the rebellion. It took the authorities less than a week to put down an aborted uprising in Dublin. But if the British government thought that repression was going to prevent rebellion in Ireland—and why else would they have engaged in that strategy—they were quickly disabused of that notion on 23 May 1798. Simultaneous attacks on landlords and government troops in Mayo, Wexford, and Wicklow left authorities in Ireland reeling. In Wicklow, they faced the threat that the rebels might retake Dublin itself. Wicklow was also important as a test case because of the presence there of a Catholic middle class and Protestant landlords who were sympathetic to the cause of the United Irishmen. The largest landowner in Wicklow was Lord Fitzwilliam, who had been dismissed from his position as Lord Lieutenant for Ireland by Pitt in March 1795 because he was deemed too sympathetic to the Catholic cause and uncooperative with government policies. Even though Fitzwilliam had a reputation of being a good landlord, the rebels burned his house anyway, before the rebellion there spent itself.

FIGURE 9.2 *Murder of Robert Emmett and other members of the United Irishmen prior to the Rebellion of 1798. Illustration by George Cruikshank (1792–1878). Courtesy of Getty Images.*

Wexford proved particularly troublesome. On 26 May, government troops managed to win an important victory over rebel troops at Tara. But the next day, about 100 members of the North Cork militia joined battle with some 4,000 rebel troops at Oulart Hill, 9 miles outside of Wexford. The resulting victory by the rebels was predictable, but it still took the authorities by surprise. Even though another rebel contingent suffered a setback at Ballyminaun about the same time, the victory at Oulart Hill attracted additional support. Rebel numbers increased by an additional 2,000, and they prepared to move on the town of Wexford itself. Elsewhere, on 29 May, the army of General James Duff marched on Kildare in an effort to clear open the way to Dublin. Duff reported that between 200 and 300 rebels were killed in a skirmish that only resulted in three deaths and a few wounded men on his side. On 30 May, Wexford town fell to the rebels. But this proved to be the highpoint of the rebellion.

One of the leaders of the Wexford rebellion was a Protestant landlord and member of the United Irishmen named Bagenal Harvey. Another was a Catholic priest, Father John Murphy, who was not the only priest to actively participate in the rebellion. By 5 June, the rebel troops had managed to oust the opposing army from northern Wexford, forcing them to retreat in the direction of Wicklow. However, on that date in the southern part of the county, government forces inflicted a decisive defeat on the rebels at the Battle of New Ross, which proved to be a turning point. In the aftermath of this defeat, the rebels became desperate. One of the worst episodes of the rebellion was the massacre of over 100 men, women, and children whom the rebels had detained in a barn at Scullabouge in County Wexford. Thinking that they were taking reprisals for a massacre of rebel soldiers, those who fled the Battle of New Ross set the barn on fire and proceeded to shoot and stab anyone who attempted to flee.

On 6 June, Harvey gave orders to his troops to bring in "all men found loitering or delaying at home" and to kill anyone who refused to obey. This attempt to maintain control of the rebellion failed. Harvey was dismissed from his command in the aftermath of the New Ross debacle, and would later lose his life in the reprisals taken by the government in the aftermath of the rebellion. Meanwhile, the rebels in county Kildare were experiencing the wrath of the Limerick militia and cavalry, which proceeded to burn down a number of houses in the area, many of which they found deserted. It was not, however, so easy to subdue the Wexford rebels, who held out until 21 June. On that date, General Gerard Lake and his 13,000 men routed the rebel forces at the Battle of Vinegar Hill, leaving the defeated survivors to flee to the Wicklow Mountains as the rebellion finally disintegrated.

The rebellion confirmed the worst fears of the British who now faced the prospect of a French invasion of Ireland, something that they had expected ever since the war started. But the small French fleet that landed in Mayo on 22 August was hardly worth the name of an invasion. The rebels in Mayo were certainly counting on the landing of a larger French force. They would not have taken up arms if they had known in advance how little support they were going to receive from the French. In addition, the French landing further illustrates the lack of coordination and disjointedness that characterized the 1798 rebellion. The French invasion was both too late and too far away to help the rebel forces who had taken up arms in Ulster and Wexford. After some initial minor victories under their commander, General Jean Humbert, the French troops suffered defeat on 8 September at Ballinamuck in County Longford. There was one significant outcome of the French invasion: Wolfe Tone, who did accompany the fleet as part of the invasion force, was captured by the British; in November, he cut his own throat and, though he survived initially, he died shortly after inside a Dublin prison.

The rebellion was substantial enough to put a real scare into the British. The success of the rebellion—and of most revolutions throughout history—depended on whether the armed forces could be won over to the side of the rebels. In 1798, the insurrection never showed enough signs of success to encourage either a mass uprising or the disloyalty of the armed forces. The French invading force was too small, the organization of the United Irishmen was too weak, and the government troops were too strong. Of the two most charismatic leaders, Edward Fiztgerald was captured before the rebellion really got under way, and Wolfe Tone arrived with the French after it was essentially over. In the north, rebels came out in Antrim and Down, but the government maintained control of Belfast, as they had of Dublin in the south. Other factors in the defeat of the rebels included a lack of adequate training, a shortage of military discipline, and an insufficient amount of artillery. But a case could be made that the real problem was to be found in the deeply rooted divisions in the island that could not be overcome in such a short time.

In the end, about 30,000 people lost their lives in the violence that accompanied the rebellion. Sporadic violence continued throughout Ireland in the aftermath. With the rebellion crumbling, atrocities were committed by both sides. About 30 additional killings related to the divisions caused by the rebellion took place in Wicklow in December 1799. Father John Murphy and other accused traitors were brutally executed. Supporters of the United Irishmen and the rebellion kept quiet or went into hiding for fear of reprisals. Many rebels who were arrested swore that they had been forced to participate in the rebellion. This was especially true in Ulster, where Protestants quickly developed a collective amnesia when it came to recalling their role in the rebellion. Former rebels did not exactly step forward elsewhere; since the government never got its hands on any lists of United Irishmen in Wexford, the rebel leader Edward Hay famously stated that "there were fewer United Irishmen in Wexford than any other part of Ireland." Yet, hostilities lasted longest in County Wexford, where the sentiments of the people were most divided during the rebellion. Families split over the rebellion, with brothers sometimes supporting opposite sides. The uprising had lasted a matter of months, but it was to leave a lasting impact on Irish history.

Its meaning and significance in history

The immediate impact of the Rebellion of 1798 was the effect that it had on the urgency that William Pitt the Younger now felt regarding the need to abolish the Irish parliament and bring Ireland into total union with Great Britain. Locked in a struggle with France that was likely to become protracted, Pitt could not afford to station excess troops in Ireland, nor could he risk allowing Ireland the freedom to determine its own foreign policy. Pitt had actually been looking for an excuse to propose a union between Ireland and Britain; the 1798 rebellion provided him with that opportunity. He thought that government in Ireland had been somewhat lax in the 1790s, especially considering the circumstances of the French situation. His need to dismiss Fitzwilliam as Lord Lieutenant was an indication to him that he could not rely on the Irish aristocracy to continue to rule in British interests forever. The 1798 rebellion had made Ireland a top priority for the British government. For Pitt, achieving union between Ireland and Great Britain was a key component of his strategy for defeating the French and preventing revolution from infecting the Isles. Pitt entrusted the task of bringing about a union between Great Britain and Ireland Pitt entrusted to Lord Cornwallis, the new lord lieutenant of Ireland; the man who had played a key role in the loss of Britain's American colonies was now charged with ensuring that Ireland did not go the same way.

The rebellion also confirmed the Tory Party conservatives in their general fear of revolution, although government authorities reacted surprisingly leniently toward the rebels themselves. Many of the leaders were, of course, executed. Of the 1,019 individuals put on trial through November 1798, 336 received the death sentence and 158 were acquitted. Others received sentences that included imprisonment, corporal punishment, or deportation. Of the 659 persons tried between May and December 1799, 231 were sentenced to die and 152 received acquittals. Close to 25 per cent of those sentenced to die had their sentences commuted.[30] The Rebellion of 1798 also provided the impetus for another wave of Irish emigration. Lambkin and Fitzgerald argue that the mass emigration that occurred after the rebellion, most of it to the United States, established a pattern for Irish migration that lasted the rest of the nineteenth century.[31] This pattern included a steady outflow of people from Ireland that sharply accelerated following a major event such as a war, revolution, or natural disaster. But the émigrés that left in the immediate aftermath of the 1798 rebellion are significant for another reason. Revolutionaries who had the most to fear from staying tended to be the ones who left. They took their radical ideas and hatred of the British with them. Irish nationalism and radicalism abroad thus predates the mass exodus that followed the Great Famine of the mid-nineteenth century.

The long-range consequences of the rebellion are more complex, but they start with the extent to which it was remembered and commemorated in Irish history through ballads and other literary and historical compositions. Kevin Whelan, a contemporary Irish historian, has commented on the divisions that have existed in Ireland over the rebellion: "the 1798 rebellion was fought twice: once on the battlefields and then in the war of words which followed in those bloody footprints."[32] The Rebellion of 1798 completely colored the debates over the proposed Act of Union. Because the Act of Union followed so closely on the heels of the 1798 rebellion, the two would become inextricably linked for future generations; how one felt about one greatly influenced how one felt about the other. As early as 1801, Sir Richard Musgrave had produced an account of the rebellion as part of his *Memoirs of the Various Rebellions in Ireland, from the arrival of the English*, which took a decidedly loyalist stance in support of the Act of Union. 1798 was a turning point in the attitudes of Presbyterians to union as well. Many Presbyterians who had joined with the United Irishmen and supported the rebellion now found themselves being wooed by Anglican loyalists who once again stressed their shared hostility to the Catholics and

---

[30] Roy Foster (1988), *Modern Ireland, 1600–1972*. London: Allen Lane, p. 281.
[31] Patrick Fitzgerald and Brian Lambkin (2008), *Migration in Irish History, 1607–2007*. London: Palgrave Macmillan, p. 148.
[32] Quoted in Peter Collins (2004), *Who Fears to Speak of '98? Commemoration and the Continuing Impact of the United Irishmen*. Belfast: Ulster Historical Foundation, p. 3.

Catholicism. In their embrace of unionism, many began to act as if they had never supported the rebellion in the first place. But the effects of the rebellion were even more long lasting. One's treatment of or attitude toward 1798 would carry political overtones for the next 200 years, often with little regard for the actual facts associated with the rebellion itself.

In two of the main counties—Antrim and Down—where uprisings had occurred, the rebellion was hardly spoken of afterward by those who no longer wanted to be associated with a lost cause. There was an element of self-interest involved in this, of course; they wanted to prevent reprisals, especially against relatives who had actually fought in the rebellion. Yet, the Catholic response in many areas was very different. While Protestant participants generally turned their backs on their revolutionary past, surviving Catholic soldiers who had participated returned home to continue to nurse their grievances. The sympathy that they gained from their neighbors and relatives after the rebellion made it seem like the rebellion had more widespread Catholic support than it did. Thus, there emerged the myth that the '98 was a Catholic uprising, which it decidedly was not in actuality. Therefore, the Rebellion of 1798 was to have a much greater impact on Irish history beyond what happened during the short-lived and ill-fated event itself.

The background to the Act of Union

The aftermath of the 1798 rebellion made for a highly charged atmosphere in which preparations for an act of union were taking place. Reports were received in Dublin in January 1799 of trees being cut down in Down, Armagh, and Galway, among other places, for the making of pikes with which to revive the rebellion. Cornwallis wrote to Major-General Ross in Dublin that the proposed union was bound to face a determined opposition that would not abate any time soon. He also indicated, as a practical matter, that any attempt to link union with relief for Catholics would only rile up further Protestant opposition and make the whole idea "impracticable" for the foreseeable future. Musgrave, who was working on his Anglican, pro-loyalist history of the rebellion, was outspoken in his opposition to Catholic emancipation. Outbreaks of violence continued to occur, dispersed throughout the country, including incidents in Clare, Cork, Limerick, Louth, Mayo, and Tipperary. In August 1800, Lord Castlereagh, Cornwallis's chief secretary, was still receiving reports of attempted atrocities in County Wexford; there was a real feeling that something needed to be done quickly to quell the "assassinations, arms raids, brigandage and quasi-agrarian outrages across the country."[33]

---

[33] Ruán O'Donnell (2001), D. Keogh and K. Whelan (eds), *Acts of Union: The Causes, Contexts and Consequences of the Act of Union*. Dublin: Four Courts Press, p. 216.

Cornwallis managed the competing demands of Catholics and Protestants as best as he could. But in the attempt to gain the support of leading Protestants, especially those whose votes would be necessary for parliamentary approval for the union, he could not do much to encourage the support of the Catholics. This proved to be a disappointment—to both Pitt and the Irish Catholics. Pitt had been making overtures to the Catholics since 1791. The Roman Catholic Relief Act of 1791 opened the legal profession to Catholics and removed several other disabilities. A 1793 act gave Catholic property owners the right to vote in parliamentary and municipal elections. It also conferred the right of Catholics to hold office and attend universities, although it did not remove an oath of allegiance that was offensive to many Catholics. Pitt had a sense that for the union to be successful, the government needed to deal successfully with the Catholic question. The extension of the franchise had been a move in that direction.

It is too easy in retrospect to think of the Act of Union as something foisted upon the Irish against their will. Thomas Bartlett argues that in the context of the 1790s, it was not too late for the Irish to enter into a shared national identity with the British, citing the willingness of Irishmen to join the British army in this period as an example.[34] The fact is that there was a great deal of support for union among both Protestants and Catholics who had not supported the 1798 rebellion, including the Catholic archbishop of Dublin, John Troy and the Protestant earl of Clare, John Fitzgibbon. Catholic leaders knew that they were not operating from a position of strength in negotiations over the proposed union. Still, they tried to mitigate the impact of the rebellion by stressing their loyalty and the lack of support given to the rebellion by the church hierarchy. The Irish Tory George Ogle (1742–1814), a former patriot, supported the Act of Union while representing Dublin in the Irish House of Commons. Like the rebellion itself, the Act of Union divided families; for example, Viscount Gosford of Armagh supported the union while his son was adamantly opposed.[35]

The main case for the union was put forth in a 1798 pamphlet written by Edward Cooke, the undersecretary for Ireland, titled "Arguments for and against an Union between Great Britain and Ireland Considered." Cooke argued that Ireland under such a union would owe a greater obligation to England than vice versa since the former stood to benefit more from the arrangement. He compared the union to a business merger in which a larger and more profitable firm undertook to rescue a merchant who had proved incapable of conducting business on his own. But even Cooke, writing on behalf of the prime minister, thought that the union would not work if the end

---

[34] Thomas Bartlett (2001), "Britishness, Irishness and the Act of Union," in D. Keogh and K. Whelan (eds), *Acts of Union: The Causes, Contexts and Consequences of the Act of Union*. Dubin: Four Courts Press, p. 257. In this he challenges the perspective put forth in Linda Colley (1992), *Britons: Forging the Nation, 1707–1837*. New Haven: Yale University Press.

[35] Lydon, *op. cit.*, p. 276.

result was the subjection of Ireland to England. Cooke's treatise provoked further opposition to the idea, which had already started to form even prior to its publication. In a 1795 editorial, for example, the *Northern Star* argued that a comparison between Scotland and Ireland would quickly show a basic geographical difference that made the act of union with Scotland an inappropriate precedent for one with Ireland. In short, Scotland and England are connected; England and Ireland are not. Ireland and England could only be united on the basis of "mutual affection, a mutual intercourse of trade, and a mutual interchange of good offices."[36] But another key difference was that, unlike Ireland, Scotland was a sovereign nation at the time of its act of union. Ireland thus operated at a disadvantage that Scotland did not have during its negotiations that led to its union with England.

Furthermore, Ireland had an additional problem in that proponents of the union found it easier to achieve their desired result after 1798; at the very least opponents of union now argued from a weakened position. Sir Jonah Barrington, the Irish politician and historian who voted against the union as an MP in 1799 and again in 1800, later reflected that:

> Mr. Pitt had now reduced Ireland to a state fitted to receive the union. The loyalists were still struggling through the embers of a rebellion, scarcely extinguished by torrents of blood which had been poured upon them; the insurgents were artfully distracted between the hopes of mercy and the fear of punishment; the Catholics were seduced by delusive hopes of emancipation; and, whilst the [Protestant] [C]hurch [of Ireland] was assured of its ascendancy, protection was held out to the sectarians.[37]

The main outlines of Barrington's argument are correct, but that does not mean that the union sailed through quite so easily without opposition. James Kelly challenges the notion that one can attribute the successful passage of the act of union to the low esteem in which the Irish parliament had fallen at the time. In fact, the Irish parliament voted against the union in January 1799 and had rejected an earlier proposal for a commercial union in 1785.[38] Many resentful politicians in the Irish parliament were not so keen to give back the autonomy they and their predecessors had fought to gain in the preceding decades. Henry Grattan was among them; he believed that the relationship between Ireland and Britain had already been satisfactorily defined in 1782. Others were bitter about the amount of control still exercised from Britain,

---

[36] *The Northern Star* (20–25 April 1795), quoted in Killen (ed.), *op. cit.*, p. 59.

[37] Jonah Barrington (1835), *Historic Memoirs or Ireland Comprising Secret Records of the National Convention, the Rebellion, and the Union.* London: Henry Colburn, Vol. II, p. 252.

[38] James Kelly (2001), "The Act of Union: Its Origin and Background," in D. Keogh and K. Whelan (eds), *Acts of Union: The Causes, Contexts and Consequences of the Act of Union.* Dublin: Four Courts Press, p. 48.

arguably in violation of previous legislation. A vote in the Irish Bar on 9 December 1799 resulted in a tally of 166 to 32 votes against the proposed union.[39] Meanwhile, in Ulster, the union faced opposition from Protestants who distrusted the British to rule in their interests without pandering to the Catholic majority.

Still, the Act of Union ended up passing, and it was not because the Irish were clamoring to enjoy the rights and liberties of Englishmen under the "ancient constitution."[40] The Protestant Ascendancy simply could not rely on the Irish parliament to uphold their position as much as they could depend on the British. The Protestant leaders in Ireland may not have started out favoring a union, but in the course of the 1790s, they had become convinced that it was necessary if they were going to be able to continue to count on British support. They, too, had been affected by the uprising of 1798. The self-interests of the Protestant ruling class trumped their sense of Irish nationalism. It was as if they suddenly realized that, given the trend toward growing democracy in the eighteenth century, they would always be outnumbered by Catholics in Ireland, but not if Ireland were joined with Britain. If one were looking to answer the question "who benefited from the Act of Union?" then one need look no further than the Protestant Ascendancy.

Certainly, the Irish Catholics did not. But it is important to realize that they did not know that at the time. Cornwallis and Lord Castlereagh (1769–1822), the secretary for Ireland, had sought to reassure Catholic bishops in Ireland that the British parliament would be more favorable to their cause than a Protestant-dominated Irish parliament would be. That, however, did not turn out to be the case, at least in the short term. George III refused to consider Catholic emancipation, which led Pitt and Castlereagh, among others, to resign in protest. This is a major reason why the history of the 1798 rebellion was rewritten as a Catholic uprising, even though it had been condemned by the Catholic church and many of its leaders were Protestant. This historical revisionism helped to reinforce the advantages of Protestants and the disadvantages of Catholics in the nineteenth century since the Catholics were cast as traitors and the Protestants as loyalists.

Of course, the British benefited as well. After granting some concessions to Ireland giving it a measure of self-rule in the preceding decades, the British government was about to regain its authority over Irish affairs. This they regarded as imperative following the Rebellion of 1798. However, S. J. Connolly suggests that the critical year for understanding the background to the Act of Union was not 1798 but 1782. Once Britain had agreed to abolish

---

[39] Lydon, *op. cit.*, p. 276.

[40] James Livesey (2001), "Acts of Union and Disunion: Ireland in Atlantic and European Context," in D. Keogh and K. Whelan (eds), *Acts of Union: The Causes, Contexts and Consequences of the Act of Union*. Dublin: Four Courts Press, p. 100.

the Declaratory Act and Poynings' Law, he argues, it had demolished the old system by which Ireland was governed without an adequate substitution to put in its place.[41] The relationship between Britain and Ireland was already untenable, even before the French Revolution. Then, in the 1790s, Grattan and the Whigs had failed to prevent either the coercive measures that the government took to stamp out opposition or the rise or the popularity of the United Irishmen movement. Pitt had thus come to the realization that an Act of Union was necessary prior to 1798; the first attempted French invasion of 1796 would have already heightened his conviction. If Connolly's argument is correct (and it is plausible at the very least), then the 1798 rebellion was not the cause of the Act of Union; indeed both were products of an unworkable relationship that had to move in one direction or the other—toward total independence or union.

The Act of Union

If the goal of the Rebellion of 1798 had been complete independence for Ireland, in the end, it had the opposite effect. Rumors spread about an impending act of union in the autumn of 1798. The first proposal for union was made on 22 January 1799, only 7 months after the beginning of the rebellion. The measure failed the first time around partly because it did nothing to address the issue of Catholic emancipation. Furthermore, the Whigs were still reluctant to give up on the idea of an autonomous Irish parliament; that idea still had a strong appeal among the remnants of the Patriot Party. Patrick Geoghegan has suggested that the main factor was the failure of the government to compensate Irish parliamentary seat-holders for the abolition of their seats under the union.[42] The measure may have simply been premature; the Irish House of Commons objected to a statement supporting union in a speech made by Cornwallis at the beginning of the session in January. But support for union seemed to be growing; Cornwallis heard a number of prounion speeches in Dublin and Munster in the late summer of 1799. But as momentum started to gather toward another vote in the winter opposition started to mount as well, leading some to fear a renewal of violence.

Several factors led to the passage of the bill when it was reintroduced in 1800. British politicians gave more private assurances to Protestant leaders such as Lord Clare that Britain would uphold their interests under

---

[41] S. J. Connolly (2000b), "Reconsidering the Irish Act of Union." *Transactions of the Royal Historical Society*, Sixth Series, 10, 399–408.

[42] Patrick Geoghegan (2001), "The Making of the Union," in D. Keogh and K. Whelan (eds), *Acts of Union: The Causes, Contexts and Consequences of the Act of Union*. Dubin: Four Courts Press, p. 38.

the new union. The government had learned from the defeat of the first bill the importance of compensation to the owners of boroughs. Cornwallis and Castlereagh held out the hope of additional peerages should the union be approved. The government was also prepared to distribute additional largesse in compensation for votes. It is now known that the British secret service covertly channeled illegal funds to Ireland for the purposes of influencing the vote on the act the second time around.[43] The act probably would have passed anyway, but this revelation does no credit to the process through which it occurred. This activity also displays a certain sense of desperation on the part of the government to make sure that the act did not fail the second time around. Accusations of corruption, which was widely suspected, were common at the time.

The final passage of the Act of Union in the Irish parliament occurred with remarkably little fanfare. Opponents in the Irish House of Commons who attempted to rally support by publicizing unpopular aspects of the bill were largely unsuccessful. Yet, the margin of votes by which the Act of Union passed in 1800 did not reflect a comparable level of support for the act among the Irish people. If there was no widespread opposition, there was no marked enthusiasm either. The bill passed largely because opposition to it was so divided; regional differences meant that few MPs feared a strong public reaction to their votes. The south was largely supportive, the north largely indifferent. Only in Dublin, Galway, and the Midlands was there significant hostility toward it.[44] Even there, Catholics who opposed the union were not likely to be too vocal in the aftermath of the 1798 rebellion, especially the common people.

If there was going to be a fight, it would have to come from the middle and upper classes. Some public opposition groups did form to make their voices heard. In the months after the issue was first raised, antiunion pamphlets had outnumbered those in favor by 2-1.[45] Much of the press came out in opposition, attempting to overcome the lack of large-scale demonstrations against the measure.[46] Yet, in the end, opponents of the union who could not hope to rally popular protests in the political circumstances of the time and lacking support in parliament were left with no recourse but to appeal directly to the king. Pitt feared this enough to ask the administration in Ireland to organize "counter-demonstrations" to show the king how much

[43] See David Wilkinson (1997), "'How did they Pass the Union?': Secret Service Expenditure in Ireland, 1799–1804." *History*, 83, 223–51.

[44] James Kelly (2000), "Popular Politics in Ireland and the Act of Union." *Transactions of the Royal Historical Society*, 4th series, X, 270.

[45] Daniel Mansergh (2001), "The Union and the Importance of Public Opinion," in D. Keogh and K. Whelan (eds), *Acts of Union: The Causes, Contexts and Consequences of the Act of Union*. Dubin: Four Courts Press, p. 128.

[46] Kelly, "Popular Politics," p. 283.

support there was for the Act of Union among the Irish people.[47] But this, too, was unnecessary.

The Act of Union created the United Kingdom of Britain and Ireland and provided for Ireland to send 100 representatives to the House of Commons in Westminster. Ireland was to send 26 peers to the House of Lords there as well. The act abolished the Irish parliament. Those peers who would sit for Ireland were to be determined by the House of Lords in England; those who lost their seats had the option of running for election to the House of Commons. The king retained the option to create additional peers in Ireland, just as he had the capacity to do in Britain. The act also formally unified the established churches of Britain and Ireland to form the United Church of England and Ireland.

In the aftermath of the union, as we have seen, Pitt could not keep his end of the bargain. He had sought Catholic support for union in exchange for his commitment to Catholic emancipation. But King George III proved unwilling to honor the assurances of Cornwallis and Castlereagh and protect the interests of Irish Catholics. Catholics in Ireland were now at the mercy of Britain and it would be to Britain that they would need to appeal for change, not to an Irish parliament, which in the later decades of the eighteenth century had proven remarkably sympathetic to their cause. Given that history, it was unlikely that the British parliament was going to be more sympathetic than the Irish parliament had been. Furthermore, by eliminating the Irish parliament and its demands for reform, the Act of Union contributed to the further freezing of prospects for parliamentary reform that characterized the 1790s and the succeeding decades. In many respects, then, the Act of Union did not mark so much the end of a period of Irish history as much as it did the beginning of a new one. For, efforts to get the Act of Union repealed became a dominant theme of Irish history through the next century and beyond.

---

[47] Ibid., 284.

CHAPTER TEN

Union, the Famine, and the rise of Irish nationalism

. . . The Irishman no longer knows any need now but the need to eat, and indeed only the need to eat potatoes—and scabby potatoes at that, the worst kind of potatoes . . .

– KARL MARX, *The Economic and Philosophic Manuscripts of 1844*

Ireland under the Union during the Napoleonic wars

Most accounts of nineteenth-century Irish history focus on a few central developments: the struggle for Catholic Emancipation in the early decades of the century, the potato famine of the 1840s, the rise of nationalism, and the struggle for independence or what later in the century would be called Home Rule. Each one of these developments had their roots in a single political reality that defined them and influenced how they would be interpreted by later generations: the fact that during this period Ireland was officially part of the United Kingdom of Great Britain and Ireland. Although it has become fashionable to regard Ireland as a colony of England and a victim of British imperialism, legally that was not, in fact, the case. Theoretically, the Irish should have been on an equal footing with all other inhabitants of the United Kingdom and enjoyed equal rights, but one must look to history to understand both why Ireland has so frequently been viewed as a subject colony and the problems that exist with such an interpretation.

As we saw in the previous chapter, the Act of Union that joined Britain and Ireland into a single commonwealth came about in the context of the

Napoleonic wars that followed in the aftermath of the French Revolution. This meant, first and foremost, that Ireland was not invited into the union for its own benefit so much as to close a back door through which Napoleon might invade England. In fact, the defeat of the 1798 rebellion turned out to be the last such scare of the wars. From 1801 until the wars ended in 1815, the Irish remained not only peaceful but also many of them enlisted in the army and played an important role in the eventual victory over Napoleon. Benjamin Harris, a private in the 66th Foot Regiment, casually remarked in his memoirs that he had observed Irishmen recruiting for the wars while stationed in Dublin. The 87th and 89th Regiments would become known as the Royal Irish Fusiliers, while the Royal Irish Rifles comprised the 83rd. Irish troops were well represented in every arena of the war, including at the Battle of Waterloo in June 1815 where the British commander, the duke of Wellington, the younger son of a minor Anglo-Irish aristocrat, secured the final defeat of Napoleon largely, according to the duke himself, because his Irish troops had managed to hold the center of the British line. As it turned out, the numbers of Irish soldiers who fought in the wars represented the most significant effect that the Napoleonic wars had on Ireland after 1801. In November 1806, Napoleon had issued his Berlin Decree calling for a naval blockade of the British Isles, which caused some short-term disruption of British trade but left Ireland largely unaffected. In fact, Irish imports to Britain increased, leading to a period of general prosperity for the Irish.

Daniel O'Connell—the great Liberator

Yet opposition to the Act of Union started almost immediately, and even in the army there were signs that the Irish were not always treated with the utmost respect. In January 1812, a Catholic lawyer named Daniel O'Connell (1775–1847) received a letter from an Irish soldier named James Larkin who was stationed on the Isle of Wight. Larkin complained about the great reluctance on the part of the officers to permit Catholic soldiers to go to Mass, even though the officers were under order to allow it. But he would not have troubled O'Connell, or so he said, had it not been for a particular incident in which a soldier named John Moore was dragged "through a channel into the street head over heels, not leaving a stitch of clothes but were bedaubed with dirt" for merely requesting that a Catholic sergeant accompany the men instead of a Protestant, as was the norm.[1] O'Connell was powerless to improve conditions in the British army, which were notoriously harsh for all soldiers, not just the Irish, but he would go on to lead the fight for Catholic Emancipation under the auspices of a popular political

---

[1] Maurice R. O'Connell (ed.) (1973), *The Correspondence of Daniel O'Connell: Volume I: 1792–1814.* Dublin: Irish University Press, p. 278.

organization called the Catholic Association. It has recently been argued that O'Connell's top priority all along was the dissolution of the union, even in the earliest years of his political career at the beginning of the nineteenth century.[2] For O'Connell, the two issues were in fact inseparable because the union had left the Protestant Ascendancy in Ireland intact. But he needed to fight to get the last remaining vestiges of discrimination against Catholics overturned first so as to give Catholics a voice and a vote that could bring political pressure to bear on the issue of Irish independence.

O'Connell, known in Irish nationalist mythology as *the Liberator*, founded his first Catholic Association in 1815. He immediately called

FIGURE 10.1 *Daniel O'Connell addresses a meeting in Trim, County Meath, 1843. Courtesy of Getty Images.*

---

[2] Patrick Geoghegan (2009), "Daniel O'Connell and the Irish Act of Union, 1800–29," in James Kelly, John McCafferty and Charles Ivar McGrath (eds), *People, Politics and Power: Essays on Irish History 1660–1850 in Honour of James I. McGuire.* Dublin: University College Dublin Press, 2009, pp. 175–89.

attention to his cause but the prospects of success appeared dim at that time, despite the optimism of some of his supporters who thought Parliament would be convinced by the justness of their cause. The first incarnation of the Catholic Association lasted only 2 years because of a lack of support. The issue of Catholic emancipation did attract some political sympathy, but the Conservative Party controlled Parliament under the leadership of the arch-reactionary, Lord Liverpool (1770–1828), of whom it was once remarked that he was so opposed to change that if he would have been present at the Creation, he would have asked God to preserve the chaos. When the Earl of Donoughmore presented a resolution in the House of Lords in May 1819 calling for a consideration of the remaining penal laws, Wellington reacted by arguing that the allegiance that the Irish Catholics felt toward the pope precluded allowing them to sit in Parliament.

Wellington and the repeal of the penal laws

Throughout Europe, similar issues related to national self-determination and political rights for the people lingered in the aftermath of the French Revolution and Napoleonic Wars after 1815. The Congress of Vienna, which met in 1815 to address the numerous territorial issues that Napoleon's conquests had created and to establish a framework for international peace for the coming decades, redrew much of the map of Europe without any regard whatsoever for the hopes and aspirations of the peoples of Europe. In the Low Countries, Belgium was united with the Netherlands to create a larger buffer state on France's northern border, while the newly created and loosely organized German Confederation did not address German hopes for a unified nation and left Prussia and Austria as both member states and independent countries. The ruling classes of Britain viewed the Act of Union in much the same way—as a political expedient to which the idea of national self-determination, if it occurred to them at all, was clearly secondary. Furthermore, the continental powers committed themselves to preventing further revolution, which translated into a period of political repression and hostility to any type of reform movement. Again, the British authorities shared this conservative agenda. In 1819, Parliament passed the infamous Six Acts imposing further restrictions on public assembly, the right to bear arms, and freedom of the press because of fears engendered by a huge public gathering that took place in St Peter's Field in the northern English industrial city of Manchester. The Peterloo Massacre, as it was called in reference to the Battle of Waterloo, involved 11 deaths and hundreds of injuries when the army intervened. The event served as a reminder that the Irish were not alone in enduring a general atmosphere of repression in the early decades of the century.

Ireland did have its own set of unique circumstances, however, starting with the religious hegemony of the Protestant church of Ireland in a land that was still predominantly Catholic. Combined with the land question and the inability of Catholics to sit in Parliament, the fact that Irish Catholics paid to support the established church outweighed any positive efforts the government made to improve administrative efficiency, education, or public health. The Church of Ireland comprised only about 10 per cent of the population, while Catholics constituted 80 per cent. (Protestant Dissenters such as Presbyterians accounted for the additional 10 per cent.) In addition, Catholics complained about the so-called Orange societies, Protestant organizations that flaunted the favored position of the Protestant establishment. However, Catholics did have the right to vote, which gave some legitimacy to the Catholic Association founded by O'Connell, which was able to operate within the system in contrast to the revolutionary organizations such as the Italian *Carbonari* (literally, "charcoal burners") that were springing up in other parts of Europe.

The main purpose of the Catholic Association was to lobby for the repeal of the remaining penal laws that discriminated against Roman Catholics in the United Kingdom and secure for Catholics the right to sit in Parliament. O'Connell financed the Catholic Association through voluntary contributions and a penny tithe known as *Catholic rent*, which was put into effect in May 1823. O'Connell wrote to an MP named William Plunket in April 1822, calling his attention to the "exemplary conduct" of the educated Catholics and the Catholic clergy, especially given the miserable state to which the Irish had been reduced.[3] O'Connell asked Plunket, however, to consider how the current state of Ireland might change should the leaders of the Catholic Church and community decide to stir up agitation over the just claims of the Irish people. He stated that he did not intend this as a threat, but given conditions in Ireland in 1822, it would have been hard to interpret this in any other way. The early 1820s had witnessed a surge in popular violence and threats at the local level in a loosely organized movement under the mythical leadership of "Captain Rock."

The emergence of Captain Rock in Ireland paralleled similar movements in England during the first half of the nineteenth century associated with the equally mythical Ned Ludd, for whom the anti-industrial, machine breaking Luddites were named, and Captain Swing, whose name was associated with the agrarian Swing Riots in southeastern England in 1830. In southern Ireland, landlords and wealthy farmers received threatening letters from Captain Rock and lived in fear for their lives and property. Thomas Moore (1779–1852), a Catholic writer and poet, composed and published the *Memoirs of Captain Rock, the Celebrated Irish Chieftain* in 1824. Notices appeared on church doors, such as that appended to a chapel door in Kerry in January 1822, calling for the clergy and their parishioners to join in the

---

[3] Maurice R. O'Connell (ed.) (1972), *The Correspondence of Daniel O'Connell: Volume II: 1815–1823*. Dublin: Irish University Press, p. 367.

struggle of the people to recover their lost rights so that they might "shake off the galling yoke of slavery and claim that independence so natural to us . . ."[4]

The British responded with the passage of an Insurrection Act that same year in the hopes of curtailing the violence and eliminating an atmosphere of terror. But the British are not to be credited with the restoration of order; on the contrary, the decline of the Captain Rock movement seems proportional to the growth in influence of O'Connell's Catholic Association from the mid-twenties forward, although violence never entirely ceased and O'Connell was not averse to using the threat of renewed violence in order to press his demands—a common tactic in Irish history, as well as that of many other countries.

O'Connell's message strongly resonated with the Irish Catholics, but the man who needed to be convinced was Wellington, who became Prime Minister in 1828, Lord Liverpool having been felled by a stroke the previous year. A Catholic Emancipation bill had failed in 1825, leading to renewed and growing unrest in Ireland. At the time, Wellington was serving the government as Master General of the Ordnance and preparing for the possibility of a civil war in Ireland. In 1824, he had confessed to his associate, the Home Secretary Sir Robert Peel (1788–1850), that such a conflict must come "sooner or later." But a shift in the perspective of Conservative leaders such as Peel and Wellington had occurred as a result of the violence of the Captain Rock movement, the revival of the Catholic Association in the mid-twenties, and the growing support that it began to receive from Irish priests. In Ireland, a pattern of popular terrorism supplemented with legitimate political lobbying began that would recur again and again throughout the next two centuries. As subscriptions mounted and O'Connell's popularity grew, the Conservative government in Westminster began to feel the political heat. Already under pressure from Protestant Dissenters in England to repeal the discriminatory Test and Corporation Acts, which dated back to the 1660s, Peel and Wellington could not afford to allow the further deterioration of the situation in Ireland. Peel and Wellington, in fact, both had Irish connections. Peel had served as secretary for Ireland from 1812 to 1818; Wellington, who was born in Dublin, served in the army in Ireland in the 1790s before going on to his great military career in the Napoleonic wars. So both men knew of the potential problems that Ireland could cause for British interests. Meanwhile, O'Connell, an eloquent and persuasive orator, campaigned for Parliament in the late 1820s, saying that he was willing to go to jail in the cause of Catholicism and liberty.

The election of candidates favoring emancipation in several Irish constituencies in 1826, including Waterford, contributed to the growing

---

[4] Stephen Randolph Gibbons (ed.) (2008), *Captain Rock: Night Errant: The Threatening Letters of Pre-Famine Ireland, 1801–1845*. Dublin: Four Courts Press, p. 126.

momentum for the measure, followed by the election of O'Connell himself to a seat representing Clare in 1828. At that point, Wellington and Peel realized that they would need to choose either emancipation or repression. They chose emancipation. Perhaps only someone of Wellington's immense prestige as the hero of the Peninsular War and the Battle of Waterloo could have carried enough Conservative votes to get the measure through and even so he caused a huge rift within his party. Many Conservatives shared the sentiments of Dr Howley, the archbishop of Canterbury, who lamented that Catholic emancipation "would entirely alter the character of the Constitution,"[5] which he, of course, considered to be Protestant. Still, the measure passed in 1829 and Catholics now had the right to sit in Parliament and could serve in any civil positions saving those of Lord Chancellor of England and Lord Lieutenant of Ireland.

In his speech in support of the Roman Catholic Relief Bill, as it was called, Wellington basically argued that conditions in Ireland had deteriorated to the point where it had become impossible to uphold law and order there. He believed that sending an English army to enforce order in Ireland would result in civil war. Significantly, he doubted that even an English victory in civil war would bring the desired result. The duke had reached the point in his life where he had grown tired of war, and to make this point, he stated that he would even be willing to sacrifice his own life if it meant avoiding entanglement in civil war. The bill attempted to mitigate the effects of Catholic emancipation with provisions forbidding priests from sitting in Parliament, calling for Jesuits to leave the country, allowing for fines and imprisonment for members of any Catholic orders engaged in proselytizing, and even outlawing the wearing of Catholic clerical vestments except in church. Furthermore, Catholics were prohibited from joining lay corporations and the act actually resulted in a net decrease in the number of Catholics who had the right to vote![6]

Reaction to the bill was mixed; if it was a step forward, it satisfied almost no one. Editorial writers were unconvinced by Wellington's arguments regarding the likelihood of civil war in Ireland and blamed the Catholic Association for causing whatever problems did exist. The Liberal Party, which finally regained a parliamentary majority as a result of the divisions among the Tories caused in large part by Catholic Emancipation, moved on to the general issue of parliamentary reform, and the first tentative steps toward social reform aimed at curbing the worst aspects of the exploitation of factory workers. From his new position in the House of Commons, O'Connell continued to hammer away at English injustice in Ireland. He did work with the government on Irish issues such as the passage of a new

---

[5] Quoted in Hugh F. Kearney (2007), *Ireland: Contested Ideas of Nationalism*. New York: New York University Press, p. 66.

[6] I am grateful to an anonymous reviewer for suggesting emphasis on this point.

poor law for Ireland in 1838. "The Act for the More effectual Relief of the Destitute Poor in Ireland" allowed commissioners to divide Ireland into districts for the purposes of providing workhouses into which the poor might go if they had no other place to live and no means of sustenance. Unfortunately, it provided no other means of relief, a fateful (and fatal) omission, as would become clear in the 1840s. By then, O'Connell's demands for Home Rule for Ireland had become increasingly strident and included economic arguments such as the necessity for an Irish parliament to support Irish industry, commerce, and agriculture.

The background to the Famine

In the background of the political struggles of O'Connell and the Catholic Association, the Irish people, since at least the end of the eighteenth century, were facing significant economic challenges. The growing Irish population and the pressures it placed on employment opportunities at home had led large numbers of people to emigrate, some as far away as the United States, Canada, and Australia, more to England and Scotland through the ports of Liverpool and Glasgow. Michael Lynch estimates that Irish colliers may have comprised as much as 70 per cent of those working in the mines of Lanarkshire in 1840.[7] Over 200,000 Irish immigrated to the United States in the 1830s, up from about 50,000 the previous decade.[8] Those in Ireland who had been engaged in domestic production of cloth had been adversely affected by the Industrial Revolution in England, which had placed cheap manufactures in competition with local industry, even though Irish industry was not yet sufficiently developed for the impact to have thrown large numbers of workers out of jobs (see Chapter 11).[9] For this reason, despite the competition from England, Irish textile manufacturers were slow to adopt the power loom. Most weavers still worked with handlooms in the 1830s and 1840s. Still, the Irish population continued to grow, increasing from approximately 4 million in 1800 to around 8.5 million in 1840. The growth in the population of Ireland might have combined with the growth of domestic manufacturing to create the conditions for an Industrial Revolution that followed the English model, but at the time, this population growth was generally not seen as a positive development.

While traveling in Ireland in 1835, Alexis de Tocqueville, who that same year published his first-hand analysis of the new United States as *Democracy in America*, asked the bishop of Kilkenny what he regarded as the main cause of the poverty of the Irish people. Dr Kinseley replied

---

[7] Michael Lynch (1992), *Scotland: A New History*. London: Pimlico, p. 395.

[8] http://www.dhs.gov/xlibrary/assets/statistics/yearbook/2004/Yearbook2004.pdf

[9] Frank Geary (1995), "The Act of Union, British-Irish Trade, and Pre-Famine Deindustrialization." *Economic History Review*, 48, (1), 68–88.

that Ireland simply had too many people and that Ireland "cannot furnish a constant employment for our population."[10] Kinseley went on to state that he regarded the consequences of absentee landlords as exaggerated and blamed the state and the church for not providing sufficient tax incentives to encourage landlords to clear and cultivate additional lands. Toqueville's close friend and fellow countryman, Gustave de Beaumont thought that the landlords were largely to blame and was extremely critical of the Irish aristocracy. To Beaumont, the Irish tenants had no choice but to resort to terrorist activities and secret associations because the deck had been so strongly stacked against them in the form of an alliance among landlords, government, and the military.[11] These respective positions have found echoes in the differences among modern historians, some of whom see the landlord class as declining in power and influence during this period and the Irish economy showing signs of life and others who see the social and economic inequities as the background for an inevitable crisis.

Either way, Daniel O'Connell continued to take the position that Ireland needed the repeal of the Act of Union in order for the country to move forward and fulfill its destiny. O'Connell's campaign for political reform through Parliament continued to coexist with more ardent pressure from below for the landed classes to address the people's social and economic grievances. We must be wary of viewing Ireland solely in terms of such a simple dichotomy, partly because there continued to be overlaps between these two approaches and partly because union did carry with it some economic benefits that encouraged the growth of an Irish middle class.

Within the Irish nationalist movement, however, the return to power of the Conservative Party under Robert Peel in 1841 created a greater sense of urgency that contributed to the formation of the group known as Young Ireland. The Whigs had made some concessions to the Irish Catholics by converting tithes to a rent charge, so at least it no longer seemed as if the Catholics were directly subsidizing the Protestant church and its numerous sinecures. Young Ireland was a more secular nationalist movement that was inspired by O'Connell but that was cofounded by a Protestant, Thomas Davis (1814–45) and a Catholic, Charles Gavan Duffy (1816–1903). Davis placed a great emphasis on nationalism for its own sake. His thought shares much with the rising tide of political nationalism in nineteenth-century Europe, as can be seen in this appeal to England:

Though you were to-morrow to give us the best tenures on earth—though you were to equalize Presbyterian, Catholic, and Episcopalian—though

---

[10] Emmet Larkin (trans. and ed.) (1990), *Alexis de Toqueville's Journey in Ireland, July-August 1835*. Washington, DC: The Catholic University of America Press, p. 63.

[11] See Tom Garvin and Andreas Hess (2009), "Gustave de Beaumont: Ireland's Alexis de Toqueville," in Séamas Ó Síocháin (ed.), *Social Thought on Ireland in the Nineteenth Century*. Dublin: University College Dublin Press, pp. 9–26.

you were to give us the amplest representation in your Senate—though you were to restore our absentees, disencumber us of your debt, and redress every one of our fiscal wrongs—and though, in addition to all this, you plundered the treasuries of the world to lay gold at our feet, and exhausted the resources of your genius to do us worship and honour—still we tell you—we tell you, in the names of liberty and country—we tell you, in the name of enthusiastic hearts, thoughtful souls, and fearless spirits—we tell you, by the past, the present and the future, we would spurn your gifts, if the condition were that Ireland should remain a province. We tell you, and all whom it may concern, come what may—bribery or deceit, justice, policy, or war—we tell you, in the name of Ireland, that Ireland shall be a Nation![12]

Barbara Suess has made the interesting argument that Davis's nationalism, because it was of a more materialist and progressive nature, supported industrialization at the expense of the natural and historical legacy that had made the concept of Ireland so beloved among its inhabitants.[13] Be that as it may, the main cause of the split between Young Ireland and O'Connell's movement in 1846 was over the former's growing exasperation over O'Connell's peaceful and gradual approach to independence for the island.

As it turned out, that division would occur at a time during which the disadvantages of union seemed to be exacerbated by what was undoubtedly the worst social, economic, and demographic crisis in Irish history. The humble potato had become a staple of the diet of a significant portion of the Irish population over the course of the previous half century. In the 1840s, its importance was growing because it alone seemed capable of sustaining the kind of population growth that Ireland was continuing to experience. In 1729, Jonathan Swift had satirically suggested in his *Modest Proposal* that poor Irish families eat their own children as a practical means of solving the twin problems of poverty and overpopulation. The population of Ireland continued to grow despite extremely poor harvests and food shortages in 1740, 1782–84, 1795–96, 1810–11, 1816–17, and as recently as 1822. Much of this population growth depended upon the potato, which could be grown virtually anywhere and kept for long periods of time. Families did not require large areas of land in order to grow enough potatoes to feed a family. Furthermore, the potato contains enough vital nutrients that it alone can provide for the maintenance of good health. Approximately one-third of the population almost entirely depended upon it. Little did they know

---

[12] Thomas Davis (1915), *Selections from his Prose and Poetry*. New York: Frederick A. Stokes Company, p. 261.

[13] Barbara Suess (2011), "Revolutions, Political and Scientific in Young Ireland," presented to the Mid-Atlantic Conference on British Studies, Abington, PA.

that they were sitting on a time bomb, for which the government of the United Kingdom had made no contingency plan. A case can be made that such a plan should have been put in place because crops failed on a quite regular basis. There had been some lean years in the 1830s, and the 1840s witnessed a series of bad harvests across Europe, which contributed to the wave of revolution that swept across the Continent later in the decade. Even in England, the decade became known as the "hungry forties," which formed part of the context for the apparent lack of sympathy the English would display toward conditions in Ireland—they had their own problems and with so many already living in poverty throughout England there is actually little wonder that leaders of the government were not planning for a catastrophe in Ireland.

The great Famine

In 1845–46, a blight carried by the wind destroyed almost the entire potato crop across Europe, but with particularly devastating effects in Ireland. Additional crop failures led to severe food shortages across the Continent, raising the price of American corn, the supply of which was quickly bought up. The administrative machinery at Dublin Castle simply did not possess the knowledge or the wherewithal to deal with such a crisis, even though the Irish very much wanted to blame the government. As much as O'Connell had tried to keep Ireland on the agenda at Westminster, the famine that resulted from the failure of the potato crop suddenly placed Ireland at the forefront of British politics, where it would remain for the rest of the century and beyond. The immediate effects over the next few years included perhaps a million deaths from starvation or diseases such as typhus that devastated an already weakened populace and the emigration of at least an additional million more people from the island. The health of the population declined dramatically as the Famine progressed; an estimated 50,000 people died in fever hospitals, while many more died without hospitalization.[14]

During the administration of Robert Peel, the Conservative prime minister had come under increasing pressure from an English middle-class organization known as the Anti-Corn Law League to repeal the Corn Laws. A Tory-dominated Parliament had passed the Corn Laws in the aftermath of the Napoleonic wars to tax foreign grain imports and thus protect the economic interests of the landed aristocracy who had benefited from higher wartime prices. With the failure of the potato crop in Ireland, Peel realized that the Corn Laws needed to go, even at the risk of alienating his own political base among the aristocracy. Peel asserted his own power by

---

[14] Noel Kissane (1995), *The Irish Famine: A Documentary History*. Dublin: National Library of Ireland, p. 107.

suspending the Corn Laws, in effect committing political suicide. Although O'Connell had once dubbed him the "Orange Peel" because of his support for Irish Protestants during Peel's time as secretary for Ireland, as prime minister, Peel sacrificed his own political career in order to do the right thing by Ireland. Peel remained active in English politics until his death from a riding accident 4 years later as the leader of a splinter group of the Conservative Party known as the *Peelites*, who supported the free trade policies that Britain would follow for the rest of the century. But the repeal of the Corn Laws, coming in the midst of the crisis, did little in the short run to alleviate it. A total of 350,000 people died of typhus in 1846–47. Irish immigrants brought it with them to Britain, where it became known as *Irish fever*. Throughout Ireland, starving tenants who could not pay their rents found themselves evicted from their lands, leading to an almost total breakdown of social order similar to that which had accompanied the Black Death in 1348.

The conditions of Ireland during the Famine left a lasting mark on the memory and consciousness of the people who lived through it. Evicted tenants witnessed the destruction of their cottages by the unscrupulous agents of absentee landlords. They roamed the countryside until they could find temporary relief or shelter or make their way to places like Liverpool with whatever they could carry of their remaining possessions. Many, of course, did not make it and died along the road to be buried wherever was most convenient with little fanfare. Elizabeth Smith recorded in her diary for 3 May 1846 a visit to the cottage of an elderly couple, "neither of them able to move. She swelled and breathless on one side of the fire, he worn to a skeleton, crippled and deformed by rheumatic gout upon the other."[15] Four weeks later, she visited a family with six children who had had no potatoes to eat for a fortnight and was living on one meal a day. The *Times* for 10 February 1846 cited the *Southern Reporter* as stating that in the county of Cork:

> reports of inquests held on persons who have died of starvation [have] now become so frequent, and such numbers are daily reaching us from every part of the county, that the limits of our space to [sic] not admit of their publication.[16]

But numbers alone do not do justice to the suffering of the victims of the Famine. Men buried their wives, only to watch helplessly as their children starved to death. People entering an afflicted home could not always tell the living from the dead. A shortage of coffins prevented thousands from receiving a proper burial. Those desperate to survive looked in vain for any

---

[15] Elizabeth Smith (1980), "Journal, May 1846," in David Thomson and Moira McGusty (eds), *The Irish Journals of Elizabeth Smith, 1840–1850*. Oxford: Clarendon Press, p. 326.

[16] http://xroads.virginia.edu/~hyper/sadlier/irish/Southern.htm, Accessed 19 April 2011.

source of nourishment; by autumn 1846, there were reports of people eating grass, nettles, and weeds in an attempt to quiet their hunger pangs and stay alive. Diseases such as typhus fever, dysentery, influenza, and scurvy ravished a drastically weakened population and contributed to the high death toll.

Not surprisingly, during the immediate crisis, the main concern of the people was some sort of relief from whatever source would provide it. Workhouses and soup kitchens were quickly organized, while the Catholic clergy took the lead in appealing to the government for further assistance. Starving peasants were put to work building stone "famine walls" as a means of earning their food and clearing the land. But without potatoes to get the people through the winter and no money with which to purchase food, even if it had been available, by the time that the authorities started to respond, it was simply too late for many people.

English responses

The developments in Ireland during the late 1840s could be seen as either a vindication of the ideas of Thomas Malthus, who in his 1798 *Essay on Population* had warned about the dangers of population outstripping food supply, or as an avoidable catastrophe whose effects could have been largely mitigated by a more determined effort on the part of the British government. Again, any consideration of the situation in Ireland must be understood in connection with the situation in Britain, where the government was also hampered by a shortage of doctors, nurses, and hospital beds and had difficulty coping with its own high mortality rate from typhus and the like. In addition, it is perhaps easy to criticize the new Liberal Prime Minister, Lord John Russell, for failing to intervene, without taking into consideration the extent to which he had to weigh carefully the political ramifications of his decisions, especially in light of what had just happened to Peel and the Conservative Party. To some extent, it would be accurate to say that the leading politicians were hampered in dealing with the crisis by their own ideology of laissez-faire economics, much as the Republican Party in the United States was constrained under Herbert Hoover during the early years of the Great Depression decades later. However, many people in Ireland thought that the repeal of the Corn Laws was just not enough, nor were the half-hearted attempts at poor relief in the first 2 years of the famine.

The government finally decided to apply the English Poor Law to Ireland in August 1847, which represented their most determined effort to address the crisis up to that point. This meant a combination of setting up workhouses for those strong enough to get to them and work and soup kitchens that mostly provided a watered-down concoction of corn, rice, and oats. The government also devised a scheme to put those in need of relief to work on public construction projects, primarily repairing roads or constructing new ones. Additionally, the government made provision for conversion of houses or available buildings into fever hospitals, based on the numerous incidences of fever that had accompanied famines in the past. But the results of these efforts were still uneven. Though Poor Law Boards brought relief in some areas, they still did not solve the crisis any more than Franklin Roosevelt's early New Deal policies ended the Depression in the United States in the 1930s. Furthermore, the government continued to take what seemed a particularly hard-hearted approach to appeals for further aid, such as the response that a group of Catholic bishops received in October 1847 in which the government reminded them that England had its own problems, since "trade and credit are disastrously low, with the immediate prospect of hundreds of thousands being thrown out of employment or being as destitute of the means of existence as the poorest peasant in Ireland."[17]

The English responses to the Famine were multifaceted and cannot be captured in a single quote, no matter how telling they were. However, one does not get the sense in any of the literature from the period that the English considered Ireland's interests as synonymous with their own. At best, they regarded Ireland as a younger sister under their protection, as can be seen in various cartoons in the English magazine *Punch* during this period.[18] Still, their response did indicate a fatal flaw in the Act of Union and did much to vindicate the nationalist sentiments of both O'Connell and Young Ireland. Ireland, although it contained about a third of the population of the United Kingdom, seemed to comprise a secondary interest on the part of the government that represented them, a kind of additional burden that it had taken on as opposed to an integral part of the whole. Historians still debate whether in fact the Act of Union benefited Ireland economically or not; the question was a matter of great contention in the first half of the nineteenth century. But it was easy in the midst of the Famine to get the impression that England did not care much about Ireland. Charles Trevelyan, the Assistant Secretary of the Treasury, unfortunately contributed much to this impression with his patronizing attitude and his refusal to raise the wages of those employed on public works, despite being kept abreast of the numbers dying of starvation in Ireland. So did editorials such as that which appeared in the *Economist* on 16 January 1847. In defense of the free market, it argued that: "To convert a period of distress, arising from natural causes, into one of unusual comfort and ease, by the interference of government money, or of private charity, is to paralyze the efforts of the people themselves."[19]

---

[17] Quoted in Christine Kinealy (1995), *This Great Calamity: The Irish Famine, 1845–52*. Boulder, CO: Robert Rhinehart, p. 346.

[18] I am grateful to an anonymous reviewer for pointing this out to me. See Edward G. Lengel (2002), *The Irish Through British Eyes: Perceptions of Ireland in the Famine Era*. Westport, CT: Praeger Press.

[19] Quoted in Cormac Ó Gráda (2000), *Black '47 and Beyond: The Great Irish Famine in History, Economy, and Memory*. Princeton: Princeton University Press, p. 77.

According to this view, the Irish Famine was indeed an inevitable Malthusian crisis that could not have been averted. One is also reminded of the attitude of Josiah Bounderby in Charles Dickens's *Hard Times* who liked to complain that if you gave anything to the workers they would not be satisfied until they were eating turtle soup from a golden spoon. Of course, not everyone was so hard-hearted; many volunteers came from England to assist with relief work, particularly religious organizations of which the Quakers stood out in particular, while others gave serious thought to viable long-range solutions. In 1852, Harriet Martineau observed that improvements on the land, whether they came from the landlords or the tenants, needed to occur in order to provide a permanent remedy to the problem of poverty in Ireland.[20] During the Famine, landlords varied in their response, with some digging deep into their own pockets to provide for their tenants at a time of crisis. But mass starvations and the expulsion of tens of thousands of people from their homes completely overshadowed these efforts.

Recent historians have tended to view the Famine against the background of the general economic history of the period, which, it is argued, did much more to prolong and exacerbate the crisis than anything the government in Westminster did or did not do. For example, a sharp decline in wheat imports in 1845 could be seen as mainly the result of the failure of the European wheat harvest, though the import of maize or American corn increased even more sharply at around the same time. Brunt and Cannon have shown that the estimated amounts of maize consumed by poultry increased steadily from 1847 to 1912, but that human consumption of maize only increased significantly when the potato crop failed, indicating that the increase in maize imports did not really reduce Ireland's reliance on the potato.[21]

The focus on economic history has also included attention to enduring, semipermanent aspects of Irish land use, tenant rights, and agricultural efficiency, all of which had profound effects on the larger patterns of the rural economy of nineteenth-century Ireland that contributed to the Famine. We have already seen that crop failures recurred throughout the eighteenth and nineteenth centuries on a regular if unpredictable basis. Patrick Brantlinger has examined the twin accusations that the Irish Famine either was the result of Malthusian inevitability or British culpability, as well as the revisionist historiographical trend of the 1980s and 90s based on economic history that would place the blame on neither. He concludes that the Famine does not deserve to be classified as a genocide on the part of the British, but he refuses to let the British off the hook entirely because

---

[20] Harriet Martineau (2001), *Letters from Ireland*, in Glenn Hooper (ed.), Dublin: Irish Academic Press, pp. 112–13.

[21] Liam Brunt and Edmund Cannon (2004), "The Irish Grain Trade from the Famine to the First World War." *Economic History Review*, LVII, (1), 33–79.

of their prejudicial views about Ireland and their tendency to view the Irish problem as of secondary importance, despite clear knowledge of the dire conditions there.[22] One thing is clear and that is that historically the Famine strongly influenced Anglo-Irish relations for some time to come. Tony Blair acknowledged as much when he decided to issue a statement of regret regarding the Famine in 1997:

> That one million people should have died in what was then the richest and most powerful nation of the world is something that still causes us pain as we reflect on it today. Those who governed in London at the time failed their people through standing by while a crop failure turned into a massive human tragedy. We must not forget such a dreadful event.[23]

More recently, when the British failed to send a representative to the National Famine Commemoration Ceremony in May 2010, it served as a reminder to some of past insensitivity to the crisis and helped to keep alive unresolved issues over the Famine between the two countries.

Irish responses

The Irish response to the Famine was also multifaceted but included two predominant and related forms: the first among those who had left their homeland and considered their emigration a form of exile and the second involving a renewed commitment to Home Rule among those who stayed. One of the reasons that approximately 80 per cent of the emigrants migrated to the United States was because many did not want to move to another British commonwealth. Even many of those who did immigrate to Canada chose to move from there to the United States once in North America. Many of those who left Ireland believed that the British had driven them out through a combination of oppression, incompetence, and neglect. In 1845, Lord Stanley had commented that the Irish people were so attached to their local region that anyone forced to leave would experience their move as an unbearable hardship.[24] Emigration was a constant during the Famine years, with over 150,000 leaving Ireland each year between 1847 and 1854. Furthermore, although emigration continued on a lesser scale for the rest of the century, it was enough to cause a further decline in Ireland's population to about 3.9 million in 1900.

---

[22] Patrick Brantlinger (2004), "The Famine." *Victorian Literature and Culture*, 32, 193–207.
[23] http://rootsweb.ancestry.com/~irlker/famemig.html, Accessed 20 April 2011.
[24] Ignatius Murphy (1996), *A Starving People: Life and Death in West Clare, 1845–1851.* Dublin: Irish Academic Press, p. 80.

Cecil Woodham Smith called the emigration movement "the most important event of the Famine," and wrote that:

> It was the famine emigrants—leaving their country with hatred in their hearts for the British and the British Government—who built up communities across the ocean, above all in the United States, where the name of Britain was accursed and whose descendants continued to be Britain's powerful and bitter enemies, exacting vengeance for the sufferings their forbears endured.[25]

From this point forward, Irish-Americans could afford to be more critical and less accommodating in their nationalism from their vantage point away from the hurly-burly of everyday Irish life and politics.

At home, in some ways, the Famine initially weakened Irish nationalism, since the Irish depended now on British assistance to a greater degree than ever and since starvation had weakened the will as well as the bodies of a large portion of the population. Still, the editors of the Young Ireland publication, the *Nation*, railed against the inadequacy of Britain's response to the famine and Young Ireland began to reconsider reviving the alliance with O'Connell's repeal movement. A gang of Young Irelanders did lead a brief, botched attempt to replicate the 1848 revolution in France (which inspired a wave of copycat revolutions throughout Europe) that ended in a shootout at a widow's farm in County Tipperary. One of the leaders, William Smith O'Brien (1803–64), was a Protestant who sympathized with the Catholics and believed in the nationalist cause but faded from the political scene after serving 5 years in Tasmania following his arrest. Protestant nationalists, including John Mitchel and John Martin, tended not only to take a secular approach to Irish nationalism, but also showed a strong affinity for the French revolutionary tradition.[26] These secular revolutionaries not only downplayed the religious aspects of Irish nationalism but the cultural and linguistic dimensions of the movement as well. In imitation of the French, the Irish nationalists adopted a tricolor flag in this period, with the color green representing the Gaelic heritage of Ireland, Orange the Protestant, and white the hope for peace among all the Irish.

During the decades following the Famine, however, this international, secular element to Irish nationalism would substantially disappear, largely as a result of a growing attachment to the church during the Famine years. During the crisis, the Catholic Church focused on relief efforts instead of involving itself in politics. But this contributed to a renewed respect for

---

[25] Cecil Woodham-Smith (1962), *The Great Hunger: Ireland 1845–49*. New York: Harper and Row, p. 206.

[26] Matthew Kelly (2010), "Languages of Radicalism, Race, and Religion in Irish Nationalism: The French Affinity, 1848–1871." *Journal of British Studies*, 49, (4), 801–25.

the church, as did the natural tendency for individuals to seek religious consolation in such a troubled time. When the Italian revolutionary Giuseppe Garibaldi and the Piedmontese army challenged the pope's political power in central Italy during the wars for Italian unification less than 10 years after the Famine ended, a thousand Irish volunteers fought in Italy to defend the Papal States while Garibaldi, widely revered as a hero across the Continent and even in America, found little sympathy in Catholic Ireland.[27]

In the long run, memories of the Famine bound the Irish together in much the same way that later generations in a number of countries would embrace a common identity based on the shared experience of the Great Depression or World War II. In one memoir, Hugh Dorian recalled that at first the Famine highlighted the differences between those who had money and those who did not or those who owned more livestock than others, but that after a couple of years, all classes suffered under the grip of hunger and poverty that enveloped the island.[28] It deserves emphasis that in the midst of the crisis people were more interested in surviving than they were with making sure that the Famine was remembered or with turning it to a political end. In one recent article on the visual arts, the author could discover only one painting by an Irish artist on the subject of the Famine from the 1840s.[29] In a sense, the Irish were forced into greater cooperation with Britain, and even concerns for cultural nationalism or the preservation of the Irish language became of secondary importance.

This did not mean, however, that the Irish people were content to sit by idly and accept their fate. Nor did it mean that the Famine would not contribute significantly to shaping Irish nationalism in the long run. At the beginning of the Famine in April 1846, food riots threatening the social order erupted in many places throughout Ireland. Cork, Waterford, Clonmel, and Carrick-on-Suir all experienced disturbances or raids on stocks of food. Meanwhile, the increasingly radical leaders of Young Ireland, whose movement culminated in the attempt at revolution in 1848, placed much of the blame for the calamity at the feet of the British. In 1847, Devin Reilly, a friend of John Mitchel, wrote a letter to the *Nation* accusing the British government of murder. Mitchel would continue the excoriation of British treatment of Ireland in a series of books in the 1860s, including *The Last Conquest of Ireland* (1860), *An Apology for the British Government in*

---

[27] Lucy Riall (2007), *Garibaldi: Invention of a Hero*. New Haven: Yale University Press, pp. 302–3.

[28] Hugh Dorian (2000), *The Outer Edge of Ulster: A Memoir of Social Life in Nineteenth-Century Donegal*, edited by Breandán Mac Suibhne and David Dickson. Notre Dame: University of Notre Dame Press, p. 214.

[29] Catherine Marshall (2010), "History and Memorials: Fine Arts and the Great Famine in Ireland," in Ciara Breathnach and Catherine Lawless (eds), *Visual, Material and Print Culture in Nineteenth-Century Ireland*. Dublin: Four Courts Press, pp. 20–9. The painting is "the Irish Peasant Family Discovering the Blight of their Store" by Daniel McDonald.

Ireland (1860), and his *History of Ireland* (1869).[30] Perhaps as many as 20,000 people attended a demonstration in Dublin on 21 March 1848 to show their support for the likes of O'Brien and Mitchel, both of whom addressed the crowd. But this was the highpoint of the revolution, if it can be called that. Irish radicals became disillusioned, not only with the failure of their own revolution, but also with the lack of support from France—moral or otherwise. They reconsidered their tactics and decided on a reunion with O'Connell's Repeal Association, which took the form of a new organization known as the Irish League. Representing a temporary triumph of moderate nationalists, the Irish League stood for constitutional change, even though the decision to allow the formation of a National Guard signified tacit approval for the use of violence as a means to an end. However, not everyone in the league was comfortable with this, making for an uneasy alliance at best.

The failure and demise of Young Ireland may be attributed to their almost farcical attempt at revolution and the arrest and transportation of their leaders, including Mitchel, but recent scholars have tended to view their long-term impact on Irish nationalism and history more favorably. In the midst of the worst and most enduring crisis of nineteenth-century Ireland, the leaders of Young Ireland had left a legacy of being willing to challenge the authorities who they held responsible for the debacle. There may be reason to doubt whether the crisis would have been averted, or even significantly lessened, if the Irish had control over their affairs in the 1840s or if the British leaders had not felt so constrained by the orthodoxy of laissez-faire economics. But British hypocrisy had been exposed because throughout the crisis, the government had treated Ireland as of secondary importance, acted as if relief sent there should be considered foreign aid given at the expense of meeting other dire emergencies at home, and, in an act reminiscent of the crisis that led to the American War for Independence, placed a separate tax on Ireland in 1850 to help pay for relief efforts there. The leaders of Young Ireland had called for national unity, had included both Protestants and Catholics, and had appealed to both urban and rural Ireland. Although deep divisions would remain within Irish society, Ireland in some ways emerged from the Famine more unified than ever before.

In the second half of the nineteenth century, however, the tensions between the moderate or constitutional nationalists and those nationalists who favored direct action, a synonym for terror, would continue, although the efforts of the two groups often supplemented one another. The former, the heirs of O'Connell, continued to campaign for the repeal of the Act of Union and Home Rule for Ireland. Ironically, their leader would be a Protestant lawyer and former opponent of O'Connell who served as the defense attorney for William Smith O'Brien after the 1848 insurrection. His name was Isaac Butt (1813–79) and his gradual conversion to Home Rule

---

[30] Kearney, *Ireland: Contested Ideas of Nationalism and History*, 271.

would eventually lead him to found the Home Government Association in 1870. The "direct action" nationalists considered themselves the heirs of the martyrs who had died in the rebellion of 1798. They cultivated and developed a romantic mythology of Irish nationalism according to which the deaths of those who had previously fought for independence, as well as those who suffered in the Famine, needed to be avenged and Ireland freed from British tyranny. They also followed in the tradition established under the name of Captain Rock, although by the 1860s, they would be known by a new name that derived from a Gaelic word for a band of warriors—the Fenians. The critical role that the Fenians would play in Irish history will be treated at greater length in the following chapter, but it is significant to point out here that both of these movements had their roots in the pre-Famine period and were greatly influenced by the period of the Famine itself and in their own way by the Young Ireland movement. With chapters founded simultaneously in the United States and in Ireland, the Fenian movement would also illustrate the role that Irish émigrés would continue to play in the history of Ireland.

Although O'Connell appeared moderate next to the radical turn that Irish nationalism started to take in the 1840s, the British press seems to have unwittingly contributed to that turn by their repeated attempts at discrediting O'Connell and their failure to recognize the legitimacy of his movement. Leslie Williams has suggested that the "killing remarks" directed toward O'Connell by British newspaper writers and editorialists may have contributed to the tepid response of the British government and people toward the Famine crisis.[31] When all of the constraints on the British are taken into consideration, a lasting perception was left that they could have done more, a perception that was going to contribute significantly to the next generation of Irish rebels. The English, for their part, continued to regard Ireland more as a colony the interests of which were not their primary responsibility, despite the Act of Union, which had united Britain and Ireland into a single nation. It is no wonder that in an age of cultural nationalism the Irish would react to their secondary status in the United Kingdom with their own romantic brand of nationalism. The Irish who had emigrated kept Irish nationalism alive throughout the world, especially in the United States. Ironically, emigration seems to have contributed to an increase in living standards among those who stayed in Ireland, similar to that which accompanied the depopulation of Europe associated with the Black Death in the fourteenth century.[32] Those who remained in Ireland also contributed to a decline in population by marrying later and therefore reducing the birth

---

[31] Leslie Williams (2003), *Daniel O'Connell, the British Press, and the Irish Famine: Killing Remarks*. Aldershot, England; Burlington, VT: Ashgate.

[32] See especially Kevin Rourke (1995), "Emigration and Living Standards in Ireland since the Famine." *Journal of Population Economics*, 8, (4), 407–21.

rate in the second half of the nineteenth century. Examined from any angle, it is hard to escape the conclusion that the Famine was a watershed in the history of nineteenth-century Ireland.

But this does not mean that we should not question old assumptions about the Famine or the impact that it had. Thomas Carlyle, for example, has recently been exonerated of the accusation that he held racist attitudes toward the Irish when he blamed their own lack of leadership and inadequate social morality for contributing to the Famine. Carlyle also discerned the same faults among the English and actually exercised a significant influence among the leaders of Young Ireland who borrowed from his ideas.[33] In a 2001 article, Eileen Moore Quinn asked, "Can new scholarship and an eschewal of representational ideologies combine to render new interpretations of the Famine possible?"[34] In other words, is it possible to develop a treatment of the Famine that neither portrays the Irish as victims nor serves as a justification for British imperialism? I would say yes, because each generation has the ability to interpret history anew based on a different understanding of the relationship between the past and the present. However, any interpretation of the Famine must still take into account the scale of the tragedy and to attempt to come to grips with the role that the British government played in exacerbating the crisis. Interpretations that completely deny British culpability risk distorting the past in the service of challenging the nationalist version of Irish history. Interpretations that remain rooted in nineteenth-century notions of nationalism and seek only to use the past to assess blame risk charges of bias and have the weaknesses of all monocausal explanations for significant historical developments. To steer a middle course risks charges of taking a political stance under the guise of neutrality. But to ignore the Famine altogether poses greater risks than any of those alternatives.

---

[33] John Morrow (2008), "Thomas Carlyle, 'Young Ireland' and the 'Condition of Ireland Question'." *The Historical Journal*, 51, (3), 643–67.

[34] Eileen Moore Quinn (2001), "Entextualizing Famine, Reconstituting Self: Testimonial Narratives from Ireland." *Anthropological Quarterly*, 74, 73.

CHAPTER ELEVEN

The Land War, Parnell, and Home Rule

I believe security of tenure and the fruits of his industry to be equally necessary to do justice to the tenant, and to promote the prosperity of the whole community.

– CHARLES STEWART PARNELL, 2 April 1875

Industrial expansion in Nineteenth-century Ireland

Nineteenth-century Ireland is generally thought of as poor and relatively underdeveloped, largely because of the images associated with the Famine. The picture of an impoverished, largely rural people struggling to feed themselves stands in stark contrast to the image most people associate with England in the same period, where the Industrial Revolution was booming and the urban population was increasing at an exponential rate. These stereotypes, whatever elements of truth they contain, can be misleading, however. There was plenty of poverty and hunger in England, which also experienced "the hungry forties" and where at mid-century there were still as many people living in rural areas as in urban centers. Meanwhile, industrial expansion and urban growth did occur in Ireland, although not nearly to the extent that they did in England. In 1841, an estimated 20 per cent of Irish workers were employed in the textile industry, with another 12 per cent working in construction and other industries, while only about 53 per cent of the three and a half million workers in Ireland at that time were employed in agriculture.[1] Industrialization in Ireland was largely confined to the North, which helps to explain the increase in the size of Belfast, whose growth—from 37,000 in 1821 to about 350,000 by the end of the century[2]—rivaled the rate of increase of any of the industrial centers in England. The York Street linen mill opened in Belfast in 1828; within 20 years, there were over 60 such mills in the city.[3] Almost 8,000 workers labored in the 35 linen mills that were operating in or around Belfast in 1839.[4] The areas around Belfast experienced significant growth as well; for example, the neighboring town of Lisburn had a population of about 12,000 in 1891, nearly twice the size that it had been 50 years earlier.[5] Bangor and Newry also grew to about 12,000 people by that date, while Derry/Londonderry, the next largest city in Northern Ireland after Belfast, had a population of over 33,000.[6]

In 1840, the vast majority of the labor force in the textile industry in and around Belfast still worked with handlooms, the use of which had already decreased significantly in Scotland and England. But once the Famine dramatically reduced the labor supply, Irish mill owners began to react. The expansion in the use of power looms after 1850 in Irish textile factories made it easier for them to keep up with rising demand. In the 1860s, the Irish linen industry benefited greatly from the increased demand created by the American Civil War, which interrupted the supply of cotton from the United States to the textile mills of northern England.

By that time, Irish manufacturers had also started a significant retail business instead of just selling wholesale to English merchants.[7] The Irish retail business was aided by Ireland's participation in the transportation revolution of the nineteenth century. Railroad mileage increased from 65 to 2,000 between 1842 and 1872.[8] In addition to aiding retail trade, the

[1] Frank Geary and Tom Stark (2004), "Trends in Real Wages during the Industrial Revolution: A View from across the Irish Sea." *Economic History Review*, VII, 375.

[2] Hugh F. Kearney (2006), *The British Isles: A History of Four Nations*, 2nd edn. Cambridge: Cambridge University Press, p. 235.

[3] Fergal Tobin (2003), "Industrial Revolution," in Brian Lalor (ed.), *The Encyclopedia of Ireland*. New Haven and London: Yale University Press, p. 518.

[4] D. George Boyce (2005), *Nineteenth-Century Ireland: The Search for Stability* (revised edn). Dublin: Gill and Macmillan, p. 108.

[5] Patrick Fitzgerald and Brian Lambkin (2008), *Migration in Irish History, 1607–2007*. London: Palgrave Macmillan, p. 186.

[6] T. W. Freeman (1977), "Irish Towns in the Eighteenth and Nineteenth Centuries," in R. A. Butlin (ed.), *The Development of the Irish Town*. London: Croom Helm, p. 133.

[7] Alastair Durie and Peter Solar (1988), "The Scottish and Irish Linen Industries Compared, 1780–1860," in R. Mitchison and P. Roebuck (eds), *Economy and Society in Scotland and Ireland, 1500–1939*. Edinburgh: John Donald, p. 219.

[8] Garth Stevenson (2006), *Parallel Paths: The Development of Nationalism in Ireland and Quebec*. Montreal: McGill-Queen's University Press, p. 137.

construction of the railroads also provided jobs and made it easier for laborers to migrate to manufacturing centers where other jobs were to be had. Towns that were accessible by rail, such as the linen-manufacturing center of Portadown near Armagh in the north or Waterford in the south, were in the best position to attract workers. Dublin also became even more accessible as a result of the railroads. Its population swelled, but less as a manufacturing center than as a thriving metropolis.

Dublin was smaller than London, but like London it was dominated by the service and retail industries that required large numbers of workers to supply the needs of the middle and upper classes. Women in particular who sought work in Dublin had little choice but to take service jobs. There were fewer jobs in the service industry following the Famine, of course, because of the overall decline in the population. The Irish Poor Law of 1838 had set up a system of workhouses to provide a place to live for those who could not find work, as well as a rudimentary education for children forced to go there. In exchange, residents were expected to engage in manual labor, as the name "workhouse" implies. Anna Clark has shown that girls predominated over boys at these workhouses because of the greater difficulty they had finding jobs on the street. There they encountered a harsh environment in which girls from the age of 15 were treated as adults; this meant that they were given hard work and subjected to harsh discipline for breaking rules, which young adolescent girls are often prone to do.[9] The very existence of workhouses in nineteenth-century England testifies to the fact that even there the Industrial Revolution did not provide enough work to provide for everyone in an expanding population. Youth and geography worked against everyone simply moving to factory towns, where jobs also became increasingly hard to get in the 1840s and 1850s. Dublin had to resort to workhouses to an even greater extent because it lacked the industrial jobs that were more plentiful in Ulster.

Industrial growth in Northern Ireland was not just restricted to textile manufacturing. Tobacco, brewing, and food processing industries also thrived there in the nineteenth century. Iron and steel industries developed by the early twentieth century. It was in the second half of the nineteenth century that Belfast became a center of the shipbuilding industry, starting when the Thompson and Kirwan Company began operations in 1851. Thompson and Kirwan soon floundered, however; it took the innovative genius of a young engineer from Yorkshire to transform Belfast into a major shipbuilding center.

---

[9] Anna Clark (2005), "Wild Workhouse Girls and the Liberal Imperial State in Nineteenth-Century Ireland." *Journal of Social History*, 39, 391–2.

In 1854, Edward Harland (1831–95) took a job as yard manager for Robert Hickson, who had taken over for Thompson and Kirwan in 1853 after previously starting a successful ironworks factory. Harland had just finished a five-year apprenticeship at Robert Stephenson and Company in Newcastle, England. Within 4 years he had purchased the company from Hickson and went on to form a partnership with a merchant named Gustave Wolff. Harland and Wolff, whose first choice had been to build a shipyard in Liverpool, greatly enhanced Belfast as a manufacturing center. They became famous for developing the modern ocean liners that contributed further to the transportation revolution of the nineteenth century. They were responsible for the later construction of the ill-fated *Titanic*, which sunk in the North Atlantic in 1912. Another prominent shipbuilder, Workman Clark, opened for business in 1880.

There was some other shipbuilding in Ireland, most notably at Waterford in the southeast where the Neptune works constructed 40 steamships between 1847 and 1877. Not only was the first steam icebreaker built in Waterford, but also a Waterford-built steamer was the first to transport live cattle from the United States to England.[10] Derry/Londonderry also had a shipbuilding industry, though it was known for a variety of industries, of which shirtmaking was one of the most prominent. Derry/Londonderry joined Belfast as a major shipping center. Nor was the linen industry exclusively confined to Belfast and its vicinity. Linen mills could be found as well in Mayo, Roscommon, and Sligo, for example, where they coexisted along with woolen manufacturing. Still, northeastern Ireland dominated Irish industry in the same way that northern England had dominated the Industrial Revolution there.

Among the many effects that the Famine had on Irish society, the resulting decline in the population meant that there would be something of a labor shortage in the second half of the nineteenth century. Geary and Stark have argued that real wages in both agriculture and industry increased for Irish workers in the post-Famine period. They have also argued that this increase occurred earlier and was larger than had previously been thought.[11] Railroads had made it easier for workers to migrate to Irish cities to fill the new jobs that were created by industrialization. Unfortunately, those jobs were mainly to be found in Belfast and its surrounding area. Unlike Britain—even Wales, where conditions most closely approximated those of Ireland—Ireland did not become industrialized enough to stop the continued emigration that resulted in a constant drain on the Irish population and its labor supply.

---

[10] Julian Walton (1995), "From *Urbs Istasta* to Crystal City: Waterford, 1495–1995," in Howard B. Clarke (ed.), *Irish Cities*. Dublin: Mercier Press, p. 215.
[11] Geary and Stark, *op. cit.*, 389.

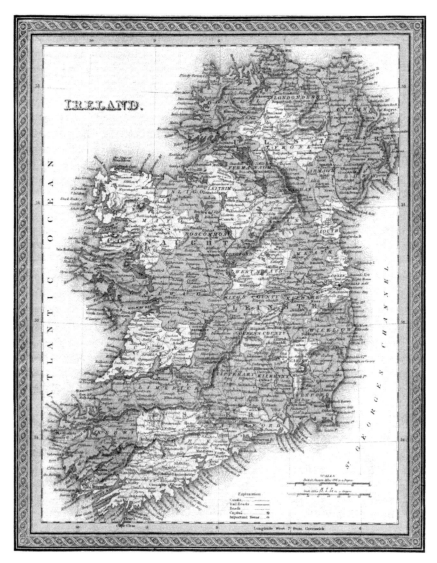

FIGURE 11.1 *Map of Ireland, 1849. Illustration by S. Augustus Mitchell. Courtesy of Getty Images.*

Irish migration to America and overseas

The pattern of migration out of Ireland—that had predated but had been greatly accelerated by the Famine—continued in the second half of the nineteenth century. In other words, the end of the Famine did not mean the end of emigration. It is estimated that over 3 million Irish people emigrated between 1855 and 1900. Post-Famine emigration may have been less dramatic than that of the Famine years, but it was steady: at least 30,000 people left in every single year between 1855 and the end of the century.

By the end of the nineteenth century, there were probably as many people who had been born in Ireland living abroad as lived in Ireland itself. Ireland was certainly not alone in experiencing emigration; 26 million people emigrated from Europe as a whole between 1840 and 1890.[12] Seen from that perspective, Irish emigration becomes part of a much larger pattern and a relatively small percentage of the total numbers leaving Europe in that period. But Irish migration after the Famine did not follow the same pattern as emigration from Britain or other European countries. After mid-century, compared to other countries, a disproportionate number of young single persons chose to leave Ireland, while most families chose to remain. This was even a departure from the pattern of emigration during the Famine years, when many families had left Ireland together. Furthermore, about 50 per cent of those who left were young women. By contrast, males made up the vast majority of emigrants leaving other European countries during this period. After the Famine, younger sons with no hope of inheriting land that families could no longer afford to divide among their children had little choice but to leave Ireland. Young women would be left with little hope of finding a husband, given the large numbers of young men who were leaving. However, this is not to say that this was the only reason that young women decided to leave; in fact, women in their late teens or early twenties mainly left to find work.

Most of those who left Ireland never returned, although the return rate increased in the 1860s and 1870s as travel became cheaper aboard the new steamships traversing the seas. For obvious geographical reasons, those who migrated to Britain found it easier to return than those who went to the United States, while those who went to America were more likely to return than those who moved to Australia or New Zealand. Even more returned from the United States during the hard economic times of the 1890s, even as numerous people were leaving Europe at the same time for similar economic reasons. No doubt many who did not return to Ireland wished that they could. Many of the Irish who settled in the cities along the eastern seaboard of the United States during the nineteenth century endured miserable working and living conditions. The large numbers of people who continued to emigrate from Ireland after the Famine is partly accounted for the perception that better opportunities awaited them elsewhere. Parents with large families came to expect that some of their children would emigrate in the hopes that they would help to support the family from abroad. They had not counted on such economic hardship that would drive some to return and leave others living in slums and working for pennies a day.

Awareness of these conditions prompted some more successful Irish-American businessmen to encourage new Irish immigrants to move

---

[12] Fitzgerald and Lambkin, *op. cit.*, p. 190.

westward during this period of American expansion. In October 1873, an Irish convention in St Louis heard accounts of the shockingly low standard of living and quality of life of Irish immigrants in the cities. Attendees at this assembly entertained a proposal that information about the soil and climate of the western states be sent to Ireland for distribution among prospective emigrants. Robert Johnston, the Irish-American owner of a dry goods business, visited Ireland later in the decade and was so appalled by the poverty he encountered there that he returned to the United States and organized the Fermanagh Relief Association to help those in Ireland who wished to leave. In 1880, the *State of Alabama* sailed from Glasgow to New York carrying among its passengers 200 people from Ireland whose fares had been paid by Johnston's association. They were promised additional funds if they wished to migrate to the American West.

The lure of the American West for some Irish settlers was matched by that of Australia. The first Irish settlers to arrive in Australia did so as convicts transported there in 1791. After the Famine, Australia became an attractive destination for those leaving Ireland because of the gold rush that began in the early 1850s. Over the course of the decade, about 84,000 Irish moved to Australia, compared to the approximately 15,000 that had arrived there between 1846 and 1852.[13] Mainly because of distance, a move to Australia or New Zealand tended to be a permanent decision, even for those who had been lured there by the hopes of finding gold. Australia also did more to attract immigrants from Ireland than any other country of destination, even factoring in the assistance that some aid societies in the United States provided for those willing to move westward. They targeted certain areas of Ireland to offer assistance, which made a big difference in the composition of those who decided to emigrate there. The same was true of emigrants to New Zealand, although Irish immigrants did not begin to arrive there in significant numbers until after the Gold Rush had ended in Australia. The Irish experience in New Zealand was vastly different from that of the large numbers of Irish who had migrated to Britain and the United States, most of which had settled in urban environments. New Zealand was sparsely inhabited and plenty of land was available, allowing the new immigrants to take up farming and enjoy a rural life. Meanwhile, at home, Irish rural society was undergoing a transformation that made it significantly different from that which the inhabitants of the Irish countryside had known before the Famine.

Irish rural society after the Famine

The growth of Belfast, Dublin, and smaller manufacturing towns and the continued overseas migration of significant numbers of Irish people led to

---

[13] Donald Harman Akenson (1996), *The Irish Diaspora: A Primer*. Toronto: P. D. Meany, p. 96.

the further depopulation of the countryside. One can imagine the impact that this depopulation had on rural villages, some of which simply did not survive. With industry concentrated in the north and Dublin occupying increasing numbers of people, western and southern Ireland remained almost completely undeveloped, especially the west. There is no getting around the fact that most of Ireland was still overwhelmingly rural, or the fact that those rural regions had suffered a severe drain on their population during and after the Famine years. Garth Stevenson has drawn some interesting parallels between rural society in Ireland and rural society in Quebec during the nineteenth century. Land reform came earlier in Quebec (1854) and was less controversial because the laws that were abolished were already seen as obsolete. Quebec thus became a territory in which small family-owned farms predominated, in contrast with Ireland where aristocratic landlords still owned much of the land and most people who worked it did so as tenants, even after there were fewer people to work the land.

But many of the Irish landowners of the 1850s and 1860s were different men than those who had owned land in the 1830s and 1840s. With the depopulation and poverty of the countryside, many landowners had chosen to sell their land at cheap prices. This was made easier by the Encumbered Estates Act of 1849, which simplified the legal process of sale of estates encumbered with debt. At the same time, the depopulation of the countryside and a decline in agricultural prices made it more profitable for these new landowners to convert their property to grazing, which frequently meant the eviction of even more tenants.

Landowners even had an economic incentive to evict their poorer tenants, since they did not want to pay taxes on farms valued at less than £4. Almost 28,000 evictions took place in the years 1849 and 1850 alone and remained common occurrences in the following years.[14] The Irish Poor Law was still in place, leaving workhouses the only viable option for those evicted besides emigration. Agricultural prices dropped after 1846 when Britain repealed the Corn Law, which had placed tariffs on imported grain to benefit native landowners. Irish landowners benefited from the Corn Law since Ireland was part of the United Kingdom and they were hurt by its repeal. Prices declined still further later in the century when steamships lowered the price of imported American grain. The amount of wheat and American corn (maize) imported into Ireland increased considerably in the second half of the century, especially in the years between 1850 and 1875.

Ireland exported little to no grain in the two decades following the end of the Famine and not much more in the ensuing decades. The number of acres devoted to growing beans, oats, peas, and rye all declined in the second half of the nineteenth century. What was grown was almost entirely for

---

[14] James Lydon (1998), *The Making of Ireland from Ancient Times to the Present*. London and New York: Routledge, p. 304.

FIGURE 11.2 *Sketch of Brigit O'Donnell,* Illustrated London News, *22 December 1849. Brigit reported that she had been forced off her land because of her inability to pay the rent. Afterwards, she endured a number of hardships, suffering from fever at the house of a neighbor. One child was stillborn; her 13-year-old son died of starvation while she was sick.*

internal consumption.[15] The Irish economy became increasingly based on livestock, mainly dairy, beef, and pork products. Ireland continued to export oats into the twentieth century, but at levels at least 75 per cent lower than during the pre-Famine years.[16] In this economic environment, unlike that

---

[15] Liam Brunt and Edmund Cannon (2004), "The Irish Grain Trade from the Famine to the First World War." *Economic History Review,* LVII, 36.

[16] Ibid., 40–1.

which prevailed in Quebec, the small family farm became virtually extinct as available land fell into the hands of wealthy entrepreneurs. In Ireland, there were three times as many estates of over 30 acres and twice as many estates of between 15 and 30 acres as before the Famine.[17] At the same time, the size of the land worked by tenants or small landowners was shrinking. This was part of the incentive for families to have fewer children or for those who continued to have large families to encourage some of their children to emigrate. These conditions help to explain why so many young men and women did emigrate during this period.

In one rural village in County Galway, after 1871, the majority of young men decided to emigrate even though it meant that no male heir would even be left to inherit their family farms.[18] In this particular locale, families without a male heir began to seek husbands for their daughters from outside the village, but in some places, holdings simply were left without tenants. The absence of tenants sometimes created problems for landlords, who wanted the rent that they provided even though they were quick to evict tenants when it suited them. In one such instance, a landlord named Joynt in County Mayo placed a man named Murphy and his family on a farm that had been left without a tenant. In this case, however, Joynt attempted to reclaim the land from Murphy's wife, after her husband had gone to America and left her behind. Mrs Murphy, as the papers reported, refused to leave the farm. When Joynt came to personally evict her, he left, as one reporter put it, with "a severed artery in his head and a more or less fractured skull." Although this incident occurred in 1880, it was not the first time that Irish tenants had taken matters into their own hands, individually or collectively. Their grievances were long-standing and the land problem became even more acute during the 1870s.

According to a law of 1851, tenants who paid less that £50 a year in rent could be evicted if their rent was in arrears. One of the main demands of the Irish tenants was that they at least receive compensation for improvements that they made on the land if they were evicted. Irish tenants were haunted by the Famine and were seeking protections that did not exist when that disaster struck. In fact, tenant-right was more of an issue in places where improvements had been made than in the poorer areas of the west or north of Ireland where the soil was too poor or the geography too mountainous to grow much besides potatoes. The Landlord and Tenant Law Amendment Act of 1860, also known as Deasy's Act, affirmed the right of landlords to take possession of any property they owned if rent was in arrears by a year. Deasy's Act was also significant

---

[17] Jurgen Kramer (2007), *Britain and Ireland: A Concise History*. London: Routledge, p. 155.
[18] Gabriel O'Connor (1998), "Cloanfish, County Galway," in P. Connell, D. A. Cronin and B. Ó Dálaigh (eds), *Irish Townlands: Studies in Local History*. Dublin: Four Courts Press, 1998, p. 81.

because it specified that transactions between buyers and sellers of land be put into writing. This was a reasonable enough stipulation for any society seeking to place a greater emphasis on law. The problem was that Irish tenants believed in a higher principle than law: the right of those who worked the land to own it, or at least have security in their possession of it. They objected to landlords being able to simply sell their land to the highest bidder without any kind of security for the share of it that they possessed. D. George Boyce explains:

> This did not amount to a claim on the tenant's part that he could deprive his landlord of the right to terminate a lease if he, the landlord, wished to do so; but it provided for a set of securities that enabled the tenant to make good his belief, or claim, that he had an interest in the soil and that this gave him certain benefits.[19]

By mid-century, some leaders had begun to seek a political solution to the Irish problem of tenant-right. It was actually an Ulster landlord named William Sharman Crawford who in 1847 put forth a bill that would have legalized the rights of tenants to sell their interest in the land. Unfortunately—for both landlords and tenants, it could be argued—Crawford's bill was defeated. Crawford then helped to found the Ulster Tenant Right Association, although it was now clear that he did not speak for his entire class. In 1850, Charles Gavan Duffy, one of the leaders of the Young Ireland movement, turned his attention from revolution to the land problem and founded the Tenant Right League with support from the Ulster Association. Others sought more violent and revolutionary means to address their complaints in their attempt to find a long-range solution to the land problem. The resentment that many felt toward the aristocracy as a result of the Famine gave these demands a greater sense of urgency and did not portend well for the future of the Protestant Ascendancy. As one writer put it in 1868:

> Many Catholics and Protestants consider . . . that by bribery your fathers bought up the Lords and Commons at the beginning of this century, saddled the country with an undue proportion of debt, and drew money out of it by taking the landlords to the London Parliament House to spend rents acquired in Ireland. Finally, that by yourselves, perhaps by cold-blooded calculation, certainly by Saxon apathy, [you] starved hundreds of thousands in the famine year, and drove yet a greater number into exile.[20]

---

[19] Boyce, *op. cit.*, p. 111.
[20] *A Saxon's Remedy for Irish Discontent*, London: Tinsley Brothers, 1868, pp. 142–3. http://books.google.com/books/reader?id=-U4XAAAAYAAJ&num=13&printsec=frontcover&output=reader&pg=GBS.PR3.

The second half of the nineteenth century would see such challenges to the Protestant Ascendancy become more frequent. It became increasingly clear that the status quo in Ireland could not be maintained in the face of the social, economic, and cultural changes that followed in the aftermath of the Famine.

The decline of the Protestant Ascendancy and the rise of the middle class

The transfer of land to new landowners in Ireland after the Famine came at the expense of many of the larger estates and long-time members of the Protestant aristocracy that had dominated Ireland since the eighteenth century, or earlier. Many landowners had been forced to sell because of excessive debts and encumbrances, but even those who did not sell frequently carried these forward. The transfer of lands that took place in the aftermath of the Famine essentially led to the rise of a kind of rural Irish middle class, most of whose members came from the regions where they bought their land. But, although there were more relatively small landlords, about half the land was still owned by about 800 landlords in 1876.[21]

The precarious economic climate of the post-Famine period led most landlords to look for short-term profits rather than long-term investments, no matter what the size of their estate was. They did not invest in industry and largely remained disconnected from what urban and industrial growth was occurring in the nineteenth century. When a widespread agricultural depression hit Ireland in the 1870s, the economic position of even the new landlords was adversely affected. These economic problems only exacerbated the decline of a landed aristocracy that was detested by many of the inhabitants of the Irish countryside. On estates where landlords were not directly involved in their operations, their agents were often more hated than the landlords themselves because of their harsh treatment of the tenants.

Of course, it did not help that most landlords were still Protestants who were regarded as foreigners by the majority of their tenants, who were Catholic. The English background of many landlords had combined with the establishment of Anglicanism as the state religion of Ireland to intensify Irish demands for independence or Home Rule. Welsh tenants, many of whom were Protestant Dissenters, felt the same way about their English landlords, but political independence was not as high on the Welsh agenda. Protestant landlords in Northern Ireland had an advantage over their counterparts in Wales and the rest of Ireland: their Protestant tenants, whatever their other

---

[21] Roy Foster (1988), *Modern Ireland, 1600–1972*. London: Allen Lane, p. 375.

grievances, tended to share with them a commitment to Unionism for fear of becoming a religious minority in a Catholic-dominated Ireland.

And what was the response of Anglo-Irish landlords in Catholic areas to the economic, religious, and political dissatisfaction of their tenants? In most cases, it was one of intransigence. These landlords made a determined effort to maintain their economic and political power. They frequently showed a willingness to evict any tenants who fell too far behind on their rent or offered any challenge to the authority of the landowning class. This helps to explain why the security of their right to remain on the land became an even more obsessive focus of the tenant class after the Famine. Tenant right was the issue most likely to put them at odds with their landlords. This heightened the effect of expulsions when they did occur, even if they were no longer as numerous as they had been during the Famine years.

Some qualifications need to be offered to this picture of a declining aristocracy that was intransigent in the face of the challenges they faced from the economy and their tenants. Landownership was still the single most important factor in the exercise of political power in nineteenth-century Ireland. The defeat of Crawford's bill speaks to the continuing influence of the landlord class and helps to explain the continuing suspicions that most landlords were not to be trusted by their tenants. One of the reasons that tenants were so upset with their landlords, especially in the North, was a tendency of landlords to deprive tenants of selling their interest in the land, which by custom they believed was their right to do.

Furthermore, tenant-landlord relations were not always as hostile as they seem on the surface. Many tenants knew that they were ultimately dependent on their landlords and thus remained susceptible to landlord influence, even over their politics. This helps to explain why in 1859 of the 103 Irish candidates elected to Parliament, 57 of them represented the Conservative Party. But this influence would decline dramatically once voting by secret ballot was introduced in 1872. It is also important to note that not all landlords were unsympathetic to the plight of their tenants. The rate of evictions did decline in the decades following the end of the Famine, even if the numbers were still large enough to continue to evoke public outcry against them. If a landlord were not sympathetic for humanitarian reasons, the negative publicity alone might be enough to make him think twice about evicting his tenants. In addition, rents did not increase exorbitantly in the post-Famine decades and generally were proportionate with agricultural prices during this period.

Finally, Irish landlords, like their counterparts in England and on the European continent, constituted a culturally elite class whose education, lifestyle, and leisure time set them apart from those beneath them on the social scale. They still lived in large manor houses such as Kylemore Abbey in Connemara, which provided employment and poured money into the local economy, in some places as one of the only sources. They needed not only tenants to work their fields, but also servants to work at the manor house, local craftsmen to work on the house, and local merchants, traders, and craftsmen to keep the house supplied. To their minds, their importance to the local economy justified their decisions to take their own financial status into consideration when determining rents and evicting tenants who could not pay them. Still, we must not paint too rosy a picture of landlords or of their goodwill toward their tenants. This would not square very well with the Land War between them that was to erupt at the end of the 1870s. Moreover, the general trend in both agricultural prices and debt accumulation was not in the landlords' favor, and it was unlikely that in the long run they would acquiesce in their economic decline by granting more rights to their tenants without a fight. The aristocracy was still the dominant class, but many of its individual members were struggling.

In fact, the challenges to the Protestant Ascendancy in the nineteenth century did not just come from Catholic tenants or as a result of the Famine and the falling agricultural prices that followed it. They also came from the Irish middle class of merchants, professionals, shopkeepers, and successful farmers whose demands for greater political power met with a favorable reception from the British government. One indication that the Irish middle class was gaining in power was the passage of the Municipal Corporation Act for Ireland in 1843. This act called for municipal commissioners to be elected and was a major change from the outdated form of town government that was steeped in favoritism and elitism. The Catholic middle class did not just originate after the repeal of the penal laws. Dating back to the eighteenth century, many Catholics who were prohibited from pursuing a career in politics or the law became successful merchants or cattle farmers. But by the 1840s, a younger, better educated Catholic middle class was beginning to emerge among those who had benefited from the improved educational opportunities for Catholics that accompanied the repeal of the penal laws. These individuals had provided a base of political support for Daniel O'Connell and generally displayed a rising level of political consciousness. The growth of a literate, Catholic middle class even allowed Irish writers, such as John and Michael Banim, to begin writing more for an Irish than an English audience.[22]

The emergence of the Catholic middle class illuminates a number of other key developments in Irish history. Politically, the Catholic middle class often supported the Whig Party, which was known for its sympathies to the interests of business and its commitment to free trade. Those who did so followed the party they deemed more supportive of their economic interests instead of adopting a nationalist ideology that might have been counterproductive to their business success. In this way, they were not all that different from Catholic landlords who usually aligned themselves

---

[22] Melissa Fegan (2011), "'Isn't it your own country?': The Stranger in Nineteenth-Century Irish Literature." *The Yearbook of English Studies,* 34, 43–5.

politically with Protestant landlords who shared their economic interests rather than with their Catholic tenants or the middle class. After 1801, the members of the Catholic middle class were not content to wait in hope for the end of the Union at some unknown date in the distant future. Instead, they adapted themselves to their circumstances and focused on their day-to-day business activities. But by building up Irish commerce and industry, they were helping to establish the necessary components of an autonomous state whenever independence for Ireland would come about.

The culmination of the growing political power of the Irish bourgeoisie came with the passage of the Irish Local Government Act in 1898, making local government in Ireland more consistent with English practices. The British government hoped that this act would help to appease nationalist sentiments by transferring power in local areas to elected representatives, thus giving the Catholic majority more of a say in their governance in most of Ireland. But the prosperity of the Catholic middle class in Ireland contributed to another key development shaping Ireland's history in the second half of the nineteenth century: the growing prestige of the Roman Catholic Church. The growing strength of the Catholic Church in Ireland and the rising confidence and pride of the Catholic laity are more intangible than factors such as land sales or agricultural price indices. But in the end, they may have done more than anything else to undermine the position of the Protestant Ascendancy in late nineteenth-century Ireland.

Irish religious developments in the second half of the nineteenth century

When the Young Ireland leader Charles Gavan Duffy founded the Tenant Right League in 1850, he wanted it to include tenant-farmers from all parts of Ireland and tenants of all religious denominations. After the Famine, the land issue became increasingly connected to the issue of religion, which was becoming more, not less, important in nineteenth-century Ireland. The Irish had experienced the most devastating natural catastrophe in their history just as the Roman Catholic Church was undergoing a transition that included the desire of the papacy to exercise more control over the church, especially in Ireland. The Famine helped to make the Irish more receptive to that goal.

The papal initiative was largely successful. When Mary Kenny wrote her book *Goodbye to Catholic Ireland* in the 1990s, she was mainly referring to a religious identity that was forged in the second half of the nineteenth century.[23] In the past, Irish spiritual practices had been tinged with magic

---

[23] Mary Kenny (1997), *Goodbye to Catholic Ireland: A Social, Personal and Cultural History from the Fall of Parnell to the Realm of Mary Robinson*. London: Sinclair-Stevenson.

based on a belief in the practical efficacy of charms, holy water, and living one's life according to the rhythms of the Christian calendar. It was during the nineteenth century that Irish Catholics, with the support and encouragement of the papacy and its representatives in Ireland, adopted many of devotional practices and a spiritual sensibility that is characteristic of modern Catholicism. These included the recitation of the rosary, identification and visitation of holy shrines, and participation in religious processions and retreats. Mass attendance rose. Lay religious societies flourished. After the Famine, communion was much more likely to be celebrated in church, a number of which were newly built in this period, rather than in private homes. It would certainly be an exaggeration to say that all of these developments originated in Ireland during the post-Famine years. New churches were built in the first half of the century and Catholic priests already enjoyed a great deal of influence and prestige. But after 1850, there was clearly a more concerted effort on the part of the papacy and the church hierarchy in Ireland to foster these developments and to bring about a transformation of Irish Catholicism. In short, the papacy wanted to make the Catholic Church in Ireland, as one contemporary source put it, "more Roman and less Irish."[24]

Irish Catholics, both at home and abroad, were greatly impacted by the developments that dominated the Catholic Church in the middle decades of the nineteenth century, particularly those associated with the rise of what was known as *ultramontane Catholicism*. Ultramontane (meaning "beyond the mountains," referring to the Alps) Catholicism looked to the papacy for leadership in the revival of a unified vision for the Catholic Church in the nineteenth century, one that would combat the rising tide of secularism and revolution that had accompanied the French Revolution and its aftermath. The chief representative of ultramontane Catholicism—and, by definition, of papal interests—in Ireland was Paul Cullen. Cullen's father was a successful farmer from County Kildare. Although both his parents were Catholic and came from families that had provided priests to the church, Cullen was educated at a Quaker school before he attended seminary at Propaganda Fide University in Rome. He was ordained in 1829 and remained in Rome serving as rector of the Irish College there before being appointed archbishop of Armagh in 1850.

The pope with whom Cullen was closely aligned was Pius IX (r. 1846–78). PioNono, as he was also known, was an Italian who had begun his career within the church as a reformer but who became an arch-conservative following the revolutions that swept across Europe in 1848. A revolution led and inspired by the nationalist leader Giuseppe Mazzini—whose Young Italy movement bore a strong resemblance to Young Ireland—had resulted in the establishment of a republic in Rome for a brief time, which turned Pius against both republicanism and nationalism. Among his many efforts to

---

[24] "The Roman Propaganda in Ireland." *The New York Times*, 24 October 1855.

enhance papal authority, Pius IX was responsible for the restoration of the church hierarchy in England and Wales in 1850 and the formal proclamation of the doctrine of papal infallibility in 1870. After being made archbishop of Dublin from 1852, Cullen oversaw the administrative restructuring and centralization of the Catholic Church in Ireland.

Cullen's activities and the Catholic revival in Ireland did not go unnoticed in England. The British Parliament responded to the restoration of the church hierarchy with the passage of the Ecclesiastical Titles Act of 1851, forbidding any church from using ecclesiastical titles that were already being utilized by the Church of England (or the Church of Ireland). Anglican archbishops and bishops were not to have Catholic counterparts or competitors, making the Catholic hierarchy illegal. Within 3 weeks, in August 1851, a group of leading Catholics in Dublin had formed a new organization devoted to the protection of Catholic interests in Ireland called the Catholic Defense Association.

Cullen, for his part, tried to ensure that his bishops and clergy toed the papal line, partly through rigorous oversight of the appointment process. But Cullen was concerned not just with the clergy; he also was worried about the Catholic laity, especially the kind of education that they were receiving in the national system of public schools that had been put in place in 1831. Cullen stressed that the clergy needed to exercise "supervision and control of every system of education proposed or instituted for the children of the Catholic Church."[25]

This was an abrupt reversal of position for the Catholic hierarchy in Ireland. Before 1860, it had been the Protestant Church of Ireland that had been most concerned with public education; Anglicans had even started a Church Education Society in 1839 to support the founding of their own schools. However, just as Anglicans were abandoning their challenge to the school system in the late 1850s, Cullen launched his attack on public education as "a dreadful engine" that threatened to subvert Catholic values in Ireland.[26] Cullen viewed the battle over education as a struggle for the hearts and minds of the Irish people. He was not just worried about Protestantism; atheism now seemed just as large a threat. He even became suspicious of liberal Catholics, especially English ones. Although some priests became heads of national schools, Cullen's goal was not so much to work within the system as it was to go around it. He became embroiled in a controversy over the issue in the 1860s. In 1863, Reverend Edward Rowan resigned as manager of the schools in Callan, Newtown, and Coolagh. Controversy erupted in the market town of Callan in County Kilkenny when Rowan's successor, Father Robert O'Keefe, attempted to establish a national school there. O'Keefe ran

---

[25] Quoted in Joseph Doyle (2011), "Cardinal Cullen and the System of National Education in Ireland," in D. Keogh and A. McDonnell (eds), *Cardinal Paul Cullen and his World*. Dublin: Four Courts Press, p. 190.

[26] Brian Jenkins (2006), *Irish Nationalism and the British State: From Repeal to Revolutionary Nationalism*. Montreal: McGill-Queen's University Press, p. 122.

afoul of his bishop, Edmund Walsh, who saw to his dismissal. O'Keefe in turn sued his ecclesiastical superiors for libel and loss of income in a civil suit. He defied church authority, even that of Paul Cullen, who was later named in one of the suits. In November 1871, Cullen suspended O'Keefe from performing any ecclesiastical functions. After a protracted correspondence and court case that failed to vindicate O'Keefe, he finally agreed to do penance and was admitted back into the good graces of the church before he died in 1881. The fact that the hierarchy of the Catholic Church could interfere with the running of the national school system was at the heart of the controversy, which became something of a cause célèbre about the same time that the Vatican was approving the doctrine of papal infallibility; both seemed at odds with the rise of modern secularism.

Cullen also opposed Irish nationalism, especially a new revolutionary movement led by an organization called the Irish Republican Brotherhood, also known as the Fenians. He opposed the Fenians both because of their advocacy of secular goals and because of the sanction that they gave to violence. Irish Catholics had emerged from the Famine needing a new identity to help them overcome the traumatic experiences of the 1840s and the loss of so many of their coreligionists to exile and death. Revolutionary nationalism provided an opportunity for Catholics to take action in this world in an attempt to gain a measure of control over their own destiny, something which so many of them had manifestly lacked in the 1840s. At the same time, a new spiritual identity provided consolation and hope that did not depend on political solutions and allowed Irish Catholics to take pride in a faith and devotional identity that was a product of, as much as it was a reaction to, the nineteenth century. At times, these two identities fused and supported one another, but the attitude of the Catholic Church was generally hostile to revolution, as it had been in 1798.

Even if the church hierarchy was at odds with Irish nationalism, many Protestants in Britain and Ireland were alarmed at the growing influence of the Catholic Church. Greater control over the church by Rome extended all the way to Australia during this period, most notably with the appointment of James Quinn as the first bishop of Brisbane in 1861. In the same year, the first seminary school in Australia was established by the Sisters of Mercy. As in Ireland, appointing bishops sympathetic to the cause of Rome and providing opportunities for more Catholics to enter the priesthood or religious orders were two ways in which Rome sought to strengthen its influence. Rome very much tried to control the type of seminary education that priests and members of religious orders received during this period. The church's effectiveness in achieving its goals in this period is obvious. There were 3,700 nuns in Ireland in 1870 compared to 120 in 1800.[27]

---

[27] Myrtle Hill (2011), "Culture and Religion, 1815–1870," in D. Ó Corráin and T. O'Riordan (eds), *Ireland, 1815–70*. Dublin: Four Courts Press, p. 53.

Protestants were also appalled at the presumption of the Catholic hierarchy to interfere in the realm of education and other matters that were becoming increasingly the concern of civil authorities. Yet at the same time there was a growing awareness that further attacks on the church or Catholics would only make the growing problems between Britain and Ireland worse. For example, the board that oversaw the system of education calculated that 84 per cent of the pupils in its schools were Catholic, a fact that they could hardly ignore when deciding on curriculum and other matters.[28]

It was because of the importance of religion to the Irish people that one of the first steps that Parliament made toward addressing their grievances was the disestablishment of the Church of Ireland in 1869. The Irish Church Act meant that the Protestant Church of Ireland would no longer be supported by the state, with the payment of tithes to support the church being no longer a requirement. Power to administer the act was vested in a board of commissioners who received the authority to oversee the tenants on the church lands that were now being transferred from the church to the state. This move represented yet another blow to the influence of the Protestant Ascendancy in Ireland. The Irish Church Act was followed by the repeal of the Ecclesiastical Titles Act in 1871. But these could only be first steps, because it was also becoming increasingly clear that no peace would exist in Ireland without some resolution of the land issue.

The Fenians, agricultural depression, and the Land War

Those who had left Ireland in the late 1840s and early 1850s blamed Britain both for the Famine and for the fact that they had to leave their homeland. Irish-Americans therefore became highly politicized, often much more so than those who had remained. Some, such as the former Young Irelander Thomas Francis Meagher, came to America with the intention of plotting rebellion at home. The Irish Republican Brotherhood came into existence on 17 March 1858, founded by a group of Irish nationalists meeting in Dublin and by some disgruntled Irishmen who had been forced to leave their country for the United States. The Fenians, as they were more commonly known, were highly dependent on support from Irish-Americans, especially those who had migrated because of the Famine. Furthermore, the Fenian cause was assisted by the sympathetic treatment that it received from some American newspapers, especially the *New York Tribune*. The continued influx of Irish immigrants in the second half of the nineteenth century reinforced ties and connections with the homeland, as did the tendency of the young men and

---

[28] Doyle, *op. cit.*, p. 194.

women who left Ireland to keep in touch and send money back home to their families. Many Irish-Americans fought in the American Civil War and were anxious to use their military training in order to fight for their homeland.

The founder of the Fenians was a man named James Stephens (1824–1901), who like Meagher had cut his teeth on rebellion in the Young Ireland movement. After a period in America organizing support for Irish nationalism, he went back to Ireland and founded the IRB with the intention of overthrowing British rule. He made it clear that his goal was nothing less than the establishment of an Irish democratic republic. Stevens claimed not to seek leadership of the organization, but he viewed himself as uniquely qualified because of his combination of practicality and devotion to the Irish people. Once Ireland was free, he said, no one could force a position of power upon him. Stephens attempted to maintain command over the organization, but he did not have the wherewithal to completely control the independent local Fenian organizations that formed across Ireland. He ultimately failed as a nationalist leader; the IRB renounced his leadership in 1866. But he had helped to stir up nationalist sentiment and to give the movement some momentum, while providing a bridge between Young Ireland and the nationalist leaders of the late nineteenth century.

The Fenians were not the only organization committed to Irish nationalism. On 17 March 1861, Thomas Neilson Underwood, Dennis Holland, Clinton Hoey, and Thomas Ryan formed the National Brotherhood of St Patrick. Within 2 months this new organization, which was also devoted to Irish nationhood, had 23 branches in Ireland and Britain.[29] The National Brotherhood of St Patrick was not so much a revolutionary organization as it was one that just wished to lend its support for the cause of Irish independence and to encourage unity among different groups of Irish nationalists. The reason that the Fenians receive more attention is because they were revolutionary nationalists who favored direct action over constitutional negotiation in order to achieve their objectives. They drew their inspiration from the Rebellion of 1798, not from the legislative triumphs of Daniel O'Connell. They embodied a more emotional, romantic nationalist tradition and believed that the blood of their martyrs would be the seeds of a future independent Irish republic. In this respect, they differed from the heirs of O'Connell who wanted Home Rule and greater autonomy within the British Commonwealth.

The Fenian rebellion of 1867 was almost as spectacularly unsuccessful as the feeble attempt at revolution undertaken by Young Ireland in 1848. After the rebellion, in March 1867, the *New York Times* proclaimed the Fenian movement "a total failure." At this point it was difficult to see where all of the money that was being donated in America was going. The leaders of the

---

[29] Marta Ramón (2007), *A Provisional Dictator: James Stephens and the Fenian Movement.* Dublin: University College Dublin Press, p. 110.

movement were suspected of lining their own pockets without accomplishing anything for the rural poor in Ireland. But, as would be the case later in the Easter Uprising of 1916, the arrests of the daring nationalists that undertook it stirred up a good deal of publicity and sympathy for the cause. The Prime Minister, William E. Gladstone (1809–98), even granted amnesty to some of the prisoners in order to staunch public reaction to their treatment.

The Fenians received an unexpected boost when three of their members—William Philip Allen, Michael Larkin, and Michael O'Brien— were executed in November 1867 in Manchester, England. These men, who became known as the Manchester Martyrs, had attacked a police carriage that contained two arrested members of the brotherhood and a police officer named Charles Brett. Brett was killed in the attack, the first police officer in Manchester to die in the line of duty. But to the Irish, including those living in Manchester, Allen, Larkin, and O'Brien were the heroes, not Brett. These men were seen as martyrs to the cause of Irish nationalism. The pre-execution speeches of the men were published and their cry of "God save Ireland" appealed to those who had months earlier despaired over the failure of the Fenian rebellion. Priests prayed for the souls of the martyrs; the requiem masses held on their behalf seemed to indicate that the Catholic Church in Ireland was beginning to change its position on revolutionary nationalism. In February 1868, a mob did battle with police in the city of Cork. Fresh donations came pouring in from American sources. Developments in Ireland began to conjure up associations with the wave of earlier nineteenth-century revolutions that had repeatedly threatened disorder and anarchy in the minds of established authorities. Perhaps, the most celebrated success of the Fenians occurred after several members recruited an American whaling captain named George Smith Anthony to captain a ship, the *Catalpa*, whose covert mission was the rescue of Irish Fenians imprisoned in Western Australia. The ship left New Bedford, Massachusetts, on 29 April 1875 and arrived in the coastal waters of Australia in March 1876. Six men escaped while on work duty outside the prison and boarded a rowboat provided for their rescue. The rowboat had to survive a storm and outrace a pursuing police boat to reach the *Catalpa*, which successfully reached New York Harbor on 19 August. News of the rescue provided a boost to the morale of Fenian supporters in both Ireland and the United States.

Meanwhile, a new Irish political party had reemerged concomitant with the rise of the Fenians. This party was the heir of Daniel O'Connell's in its commitment to achieving Home Rule for Ireland through peaceful, constitutional means. The unlikely leader of the party was the Dublin-educated attorney, a former professor of political economy at Trinity College, Isaac Butt. Butt had been a political opponent of O'Connell in the 1840s, but the Famine and the rise of Fenianism seem to have led him to lose confidence in the ability of the British to govern Ireland. He first became convinced of the need to repeal the Act of Union when he defended two Young Irelanders in 1848. He based his defense on the notion that their rebellion was not aimed against the Crown but against the union; therefore, he argued, by legal definition they could not be guilty of sedition. However, Butt feared revolutionary organizations such as the Fenians. If change had to come to Ireland, he wanted to be in a position to control it. The Fenians, in turn, were suspicious of the conservative Butt, who wanted to preserve Irish society and protect the rights of Protestants. Butt saw Home Rule as the best means to do that.

Meanwhile, in Britain, leading politicians were becoming convinced that something needed to be done about what was being referred to as the "Irish Question," even if the government was not willing to countenance violence or revolution and was determined to crush the Fenians. No one was more prominent or more serious about the need to address the Irish situation than Gladstone, who in 1868 announced his intention "to pacify Ireland." After successfully putting through Parliament the act that disestablished the Church of Ireland, Gladstone next turned to the land question and managed to get a Land Act through Parliament the very next year. The Land Act of 1870 met one of the most important demands of the tenants, their ability to sell their interest in the land to ensure that they would receive some compensation if they were facing eviction. But Gladstone's measures were not enough. Agricultural depression made conditions in the Irish countryside worse. Agrarian unrest culminated in a wave of attacks on landowners and their property beginning in 1879 that became known as the Land War. It was going to take more than the disestablishment of the Church of Ireland and the Land Act of 1870 to "pacify Ireland."

In his early reform measures, there is a sense in which Gladstone acknowledged the failure of the English to ever really assimilate Ireland and its people into the United Kingdom. In fact, both parties seemed to recognize this fact and were beginning to talk about Home Rule for Ireland. For a time it even appeared a possibility that the Conservative Party might adopt Home Rule before the Liberals did, just as it had co-opted the issue of political reform in 1867, when the Second Great Reform Act had been passed by a Conservative government headed by Benjamin Disraeli. The Conservatives decided that it would be too dangerous to their own political interests. But the Irish Party was about to become a much more influential player in parliamentary politics and its demands for Home Rule more insistent.

Parnell and Home Rule

In 1878, leadership of the Irish Party passed to Charles Stewart Parnell (1846–91). Under Butt's leadership, the party had managed to send 59 members to Parliament in 1874 (out of 105 seats allotted for Ireland). Butt had difficulty maintaining the unity of his party in the House of Commons and he particularly alienated the Fenians through his moderation and inaction. He also failed in his attempt to gain the support of Protestants that would have made his party a truly national one and would have allowed him to put more pressure on the government. Parnell, the half-American, Protestant son of a County Wicklow landlord, joined the Irish Party in 1874 at the age of 27. In April 1875, Parnell had won election to Parliament as a representative of the Irish Party from County Meath. The causes of his conversion to the Home Rule movement have long been a subject of debate. He was accused of trying to take advantage of the misery and hardship endured by the Irish people for his own political ends. At first, the Fenians were as wary of Parnell as they had been of the man whom John Mitchel had once called "Anything Butt." It is certainly true that Parnell was clearly trying to gain control of the movement for Irish independence and to steer it more in a more legal and constitutional direction. He knew that he had to distance himself from the Fenian tradition in order to gain the support that he needed for Home Rule. But it was a common sentiment by this time that relief efforts to feed the hungry would not solve the long-term problems of Ireland. Those problems were rooted in the system of land ownership that still favored the rights of the landlords. Parnell silenced his critics by fighting an effective war on two fronts. In Parliament, he used a tactic known as "parliamentary obstruction" to delay legislation in the House of Commons by violating rules of procedure and in doing so forcing it to consider the demands of the Irish Party. In Ireland, he gave his support to the Land League.

In August 1879, the radical journalist Michael Davitt (1846–1906) had formed the National Land League of Mayo in an effort to organize the tenant farmers who were fighting for their rights and living in fear of an impending famine that conjured up images of the 1840s. The Land League arose out of protests that Davitt had helped to organize in Mayo in the summer of 1878. Davitt wanted to move tenant farmers from random violence to a well-coordinated strategy to maximize pressure on the landlords. In 1880, under Davitt's leadership, Irish agricultural laborers refused to work on the estates of a landowner named Captain Charles Boycott. Boycott was completely ostracized by those supporting the worker's cause, transforming his name into a new word in the English language. Parnell supported Davitt because he knew that a land war would force the British government to work with him. In October, Parnell and Davitt organized the Irish National Land League, which was going to prove a more formidable opponent than the Fenians ever were. Parnell was a political pragmatist who believed that parliamentary legislation was the only way to achieve his ultimate objective, but he was not above using the threat of violence and deteriorating stability of social relations in Ireland to achieve it. At the same time, he made sure that the demands of the Land League were reasonable enough that he could defend them in Parliament. He benefited from contacts he had in America and the support of the American Land League, which was formed in 1880 to work in conjunction with the Land League in Ireland. In fact, Parnell had attended a meeting at the New York Hotel in March 1879 to set up the American Land League and Michael Davitt attended its first convention in 1880. In February 1880, Parnell gave a speech to the U.S. House of Representatives in which he said:

> ... up to the present moment scarcely any ray of light has ever been let in upon the hard fate of the tillers of the soil in that country. But many of us who are now observing the course of events believe that the time is fast approaching when the artificial and cruel system of land tenure prevailing in Ireland is bound to fall and be replaced by a more natural and a more just one.[30]

That same year, the Land League called for a rent strike that spread throughout Ireland. Gladstone had already been accused by his enemies of being too soft on Ireland and of granting too many concessions to the Irish. His political foes saw Gladstone's Irish policy as a transparent effort to extend his own political career and time in power. He was also accused of capitulating to terror and not demanding good behavior by the Irish before he put forward reforms on their behalf. But by 1881, even Gladstone, who had returned to power in 1880 after stepping down as prime minister in 1874, had had enough. Land reform he was willing to grant. But he was not willing to tolerate the rent strike or acquiesce to the violence that was running rampant through rural Ireland. The Land League had circumvented legal and constitutional means of redress for its grievances. It had become virtually an absolute authority in the Irish countryside. It was known to have support from many industrial workers and members of the lower middle class as well.

Gladstone responded by introducing the Protection of Person and Property Act of 1881, more popularly known as the Coercion Act. The Coercion Act permitted police in Ireland to arrest and detain suspected criminals without trial, including those who encouraged tenants not to pay their rents. Parnell himself was arrested under the act in October. In December, two leaders of the Land League were arrested in Cork. Michael Davitt asked Parnell's sister, Anna (1852–1911) to set up a Ladies' Land League, which she did with her sister Fanny (1848–82), who was an ardent supporter of Irish nationalism well known for her poems and writings. The Ladies' Land League was to run the Land War if it should become necessary due to the arrest of the leaders of the Land League. One of the leaders of the Ladies' Land League, Hanna Reynolds, was herself arrested and charged with participating in a

---

[30] Charles Stewart Parnell's speech to the House of Representatives of the United States, 2 February 1880, in A. O'Day and J. Stevenson (eds), (1992), *Irish Historical Documents Since 1800*. Dublin: Gill and Macmillan, p. 94.

conspiracy to prevent the payment of rents. However, the league received such tremendous support from the Irish people that the government was unable to crush it. In response, landlords and their urban allies organized the Property Defense Association.

Ireland was on the verge of revolution and Gladstone (and, increasingly, other English politicians) realized that additional measures were going to be necessary to avert it. In the end, though, it was not the Coercion Act or the Property Defense Association that put an end to the Land War, but rather additional concessions on the issue of land reform, starting with the Ashbourne Purchase Act of 1885 and concluding with the Irish Land Act or Wyndham Act of 1903. The Ashbourne Act represented the attempt of the Conservative Prime Minister, Lord Salisbury, to bribe the Irish to abandon demands for Home Rule in exchange for a more radical approach to land reform. He was also interested in the support of Parnell and his constituents to help the Conservative Party stay in power. To this end, Salisbury went much further in the direction of land reform than Gladstone had ever been prepared to go. Under the terms of the act, the British government gave Irish tenant farmers the opportunity to borrow money to buy their land at the modest interest rate of 4 per cent. Purchasers had 49 years to repay the loan, which was to be based on seventeen and a half years of the annual rent paid on the property. It has been said that Salisbury was trying to kill Home Rule with kindness, but demands for Home Rule simply were not going away. The end of the Land War was crucial to Parnell's hopes for Home Rule because as long as Irish landlords and their tenants were fighting each other, there could be no unified front against Britain. The landlords were bound to remain unionist as long as they thought the British supported them. With the passage of the Ashbourne Purchase Act of 1885, they had no longer had any vested interest in resisting Home Rule. Perhaps Parnell had seen this all along; perhaps, as a landlord, this vision had influenced his own conversion to Home Rule.

As it turned out, Parnell was willing to support Salisbury temporarily in order to get a more comprehensive land act passed. But he was not willing to support Salisbury after this because Parnell remained committed to Home Rule as his ultimate objective. He therefore helped to bring down Salisbury's government and bring about another term for Gladstone at the head of yet another Liberal government in 1886. Meanwhile, Herbert Gladstone while campaigning for his father had announced that his father had become convinced of the necessity and morality of a Home Rule bill for Ireland. William Gladstone, 76 years old at the time, was more determined than ever to solve the "Irish problem" before he ran out of time and chances. His Government of Ireland bill, usually referred to as the First Home Rule bill, came to a vote before the House of Commons on 8 June 1886. The House voted the bill down 343 to 313. It had failed despite the Liberal majority in the House of Commons, meaning that a significant number of Liberals (93) had voted against the single-most important political initiative of the party leadership. Gladstone had failed to get his Home Rule act and had split his own party in the process. His biographer Philip Magnus writes that "Gladstone had once again allowed the best policy to become an enemy of the good, and he had failed to educate his Party at a time when the tide of liberalism was already on the ebb."[31] Gladstone seemed to be discredited and was accused of being swayed by needing the votes of Parnell's party. With the exception of a three-year interlude from 1892 to 1895, the Conservative Party would dominate the British government for the next two decades.

What did this failure signify for Parnell and his Irish Party? On 8 January 1885, Parnell gave a speech at Thurles in County Tipperary urging his party to remain united. He spoke with confidence that if Home Rule was not achieved then, it was inevitable that it would be in the future. Some historians have seen Parnell as an atypical nationalist who lacked the passion and romantic attachment to his ideal that many nineteenth-century European nationalist leaders possessed. But there is no mistaking the passion with which he spoke in the months leading up to the vote on the First Home Rule Bill. For example, at a St Patrick's Day banquet in London in 1885, he regaled his audience in the following terms:

Ireland a nation! Ireland has been a nation; she is a nation; and she shall be a nation. England will respect you in proportion as you and we respect ourselves. They will not give anything to Ireland out of justice or righteousness. They will concede you your liberties and your rights when they must and no sooner. . . . We can none of us do more than strive for that which may seem attainable to-day; but we ought at the same time to recollect that we should not impede or hamper the march of our nation; and although our programme may be limited and small it should be such a one as shall not present hereafter the fullest realization of the hopes of Ireland; and we shall, at least keep this principle in mind, have this consolation, that while we may have done something to enable Ireland in some measure to retain her position as a nation, to strengthen her position as a nation, we shall have done nothing to hinder others who may come after us from taking up the work with perhaps greater strength, ability, power and advantages than we possess, and from pushing to that glorious and happy conclusion which is embodied in the words of the toast which I now ask you to drink—"Ireland a nation!"[32]

---

[31] Philip Magnus (1954), *Gladstone: A Biography*. New York: E. P. Dutton, p. 346.
[32] Charles Stewart Parnell (2009), *Words of the Dead Chief: Being Extracts from the Public Speeches and Other Pronouncements of Charles Stewart Parnell from the Beginning to the Close of his Remarkable Life*, edited by Donal McCartney and Pauric Travers. Dublin: University College Dublin Press, p. 103.

After the defeat of the First Home Rule Bill, Parnell calmly proclaimed that "we are going to have a Home Rule Bill." Parnell retained the confidence of his numerous supporters in Ireland. Once again, an act of repression intervened to revive sympathy for the Irish cause. On 9 September 1886, in Mitchelstown in County Cork, police shot three men in the aftermath of a Land League Rally that had brought 8,000 people to the small town. The "Mitchelstown Massacre" was yet another reminder of the unresolved and volatile situation in Ireland, which had not been helped by the defeat of the First Home Rule Bill.

The defeat of the 1886 Home Rule bill had serious consequences not only for Irish history but also for British history. Home Rule had split the Liberal Party and caused a major realignment in British politics. Liberal and radical politicians worried about the consequence of continued repression in Ireland and of Britain's refusal to consider self-government for a people that were surely not going to stop demanding it. Home Rule at that time did not even mean complete independence; Ireland was merely demanding the same degree of autonomy that Britain had already granted to Canada, Australia, and South Africa. Canada had even granted Quebec a greater degree of autonomy in 1867, which did much to mitigate aggressive nationalism there.[33] Once the bill was rejected, anti-imperialist Liberals and those who were attracted to the forerunners of the British Labor Party looked askance at what this meant for the continued power of the British state to ignore the demands of the people that it governed at home and elsewhere.

In Ireland, there were a number of signs that nationalism was not going to go away, even if for the time being it was channeled into new directions. Several men assembled in the billiards' room at Lizzie Hayes' Hotel in County Tipperary on 1 November 1884 in order to discuss the formation of a new Gaelic Athletic Association. The presence of several Fenians at the meeting linked the GAA to the Irish revolutionary tradition from the onset. Parnell himself hosted a series of games at his estate in County Wicklow on 31 October 1886. Douglas Hyde founded the Gaelic League (Conradh na Gaeilge) in 1893 to promote the Gaelic (Irish) language. He founded the League based on the belief "that if Ireland is to become a really cultured country, and an artistic country, she must cease to imitate, and must take up the thread of her own past, and develop from within upon native lines."[34] In other words, Hyde saw the Gaelic League as a means of promoting education in Ireland and allowing the Irish people to achieve their true artistic, literary, and intellectual potential. In addition, W. B. Yeats and Augusta Gregory (1852–1932) led a literary revival that promoted Irish cultural nationalism.

---

[33] Stevenson, *op. cit.*, p. 140.
[34] "The Gaelic League and Native Culture, 1902," in O'Day and Stevenson, *op. cit.*, p. 134.

This included support for the Gaelic League (Lady Gregory herself learned Gaelic and translated two anthologies of Irish literature), but encouraged English-language writing on Irish themes as well. The GAA was more popular than the Gaelic League or the associated literary revival, but they all indicated receptiveness to new forms of nationalist expression that went beyond politics but were not mutually exclusive from demands for independence.

As for Parnell, he lost control over the Home Rule movement because of a personal scandal. Captain William O'Shea was a shadowy character who was suspected of having links with both the Fenians and the government. He suddenly became a man of importance when his wife, Katherine O'Shea, began an extramarital relationship with Parnell in 1880. It seems that O'Shea knew about the relationship and chose, for reasons at which we can only guess, not to say or do anything about it—at least at first. Whatever the truth of the rumors that circulated about him, it is clear that he was not above exploiting his wife's relationship with Parnell for his own personal gain. Then O'Shea, who was either fed up with his wife's indiscretion or convinced that he had no more to gain from staying married to her, filed for divorce on 24 December 1889. He accused his wife of adultery and named Charles Stewart Parnell as corespondent in the case. O'Shea must have known about the affair for at least 5 years at that point because in 1885 Katherine had given birth to a child that he knew could not have been his. Still, in the eyes of the law and of society, Katherine was in the wrong and she chose not to contest the divorce.

The trial began on 15 November 1890 and 2 days later it was over. At that point, Gladstone and the Liberals would not touch Parnell. The cause of Home Rule had been dealt yet another blow with no hope for recovery in sight. If it had been up to Parnell, who cared little for the middle class values that made such an affair so scandalous, he might have gone public with his relationship with Mrs O'Shea years earlier. Torn between personal happiness and what he considered his public duty, Parnell held out in the hopes that Home Rule would pass, after which he could retire from politics and settle down for the rest of his life with Kitty. It was not to be.

Home Rule had failed. Parnell's career was ruined by the scandal. Paul Bew has concluded that "Nothing else at the time could have undermined his leadership."[35] Parnell died shortly after in October 1891. But his legacy proved to be much longer lasting. Revered by many Irish people while he was alive, he was perhaps even more so after his death. But others had come

---

[35] Paul Bew (2011), *Enigma: A New Life of Charles Stewart Parnell*. Dublin: Gill and Macmillan, p. 165.

FIGURE 11.3 *Statue of Charles Stewart Parnell, O'Connell Street, Dublin. Courtesy of Getty Images.*

to revile him in a way that bitterly divided Irish society. Before the scandal, Parnell alone seemed to have the ability to relate to the common people, the leading citizens of Ireland, and the most powerful politicians in Britain. As time passed, his legacy as a proponent of Home Rule overshadowed the end of his life. The memory of Parnell has never died among the Irish; the events of the early twentieth century would prove that Home Rule was not really dead either.

CHAPTER TWELVE

The Easter Uprising and the Anglo-Irish Treaty of 1921: Ireland in the first half of the twentieth century

People call us dreamers because we fought for what appeared to be a forlorn hope, but now that the victory is won, the Irish people are soberly making the most of it.

– W. B. YEATS, 1932

The Home Rule issue at the beginning of the twentieth century

In September 1897, Prince George, the grandson of Queen Victoria, became the first member of the British royal family to visit Ireland since the second decade of the century. The Irish people, including Catholics, celebrated his visit, leaving George with the impression that they were content to remain loyal subjects of the Crown.[1] But the issue of Home Rule had not died with Parnell in 1891; it just lay dormant until it could be revived under a new leader who could reunite the members of the Irish Party who sat

---

[1] Miranda Carter (2009), *George, Nicholas, and Wilhelm: Three Royal Cousins and the Road to World War I.* New York: Vintage Books, p. 200.

in the House of Commons in Westminster. That person turned out to be John Redmond (1856–1918), the son of an MP who first sat in Parliament himself in 1881 as a member of Parnell's party.

In the meantime, leading Irish intellectuals of the age had moved away from a political preoccupation with Home Rule toward the emphasis on literary and cultural nationalism that had started to emerge in the late nineteenth century. The disillusionment with politics that set in with the fall of Parnell discouraged some men and women coming of age in the 1890s from devoting themselves to a political solution to Ireland's problems.

For example, support for the Gaelic Athletic Association and the Gaelic League was growing at the turn of the century. The Gaelic Athletic Association, the product of that famous meeting in the billiard room in Thurles headed by Michael Cusack and Maurice Davin, focused on support for native Irish sports such as Gaelic football and hurling. In addition to promoting the study of the Irish language, the Gaelic League promoted the study of Irish history and participation in cultural activities such as Irish dancing. The Gaelic League published its own newspaper, *An Claidheamh Soluis* ("the Sword of Light"), which gave authors who wrote in Irish an outlet for their prose and poetry. The Gaelic revival was infused with a kind of cultural nationalism that celebrated Ireland's literary heritage, which its founder, Douglas Hyde, believed would be lost if the Irish language disappeared. The revival largely succeeded as well at changing people's attitudes toward spoken Irish which was no longer seen as a sign of backward ignorance and instead was regarded as a national treasure of which people in the countryside and small towns could be justifiably proud. Meanwhile, those who would focus on Irish culture could celebrate the founding of the Abbey Theater in Dublin, over which W. B. Yeats and Lady Gregory came to preside.

The Abbey Theater provided a vehicle for Irish playwrights, although their work was not always well received or particularly flattering to Irish sensibilities. This was especially the case with J. M. Synge's play, *The Playboy of the Western World*, which provided a rather harsh and depressing depiction of life and relationships in a village in rural Ireland. The response to Synge's play demonstrated the ways in which nationalism clashed with new cultural forces associated with the rise of modernism. A spontaneous outburst by the audience at the first performance yielded to organized riots on the play's second night. Yeats and Lady Gregory had their own nationalist agenda, but it was attached to their vision of a certain kind of Ireland and not to something as prosaic as the right of the island to govern itself. It was over the issue of political nationalism that they split with the Gaelic League, whose support for Irish culture was closely linked to a belief that a people with a great culture also deserved its own identity as a nation.

The Catholic Church did not offer much support to Redmond's party either. Its leaders were concerned about nationalism replacing religion as a top priority among the Irish people.

And yet for Irish nationalists such as D. P. Moran (1869–1936), Catholicism was an important part of what it meant to be Irish. Many Catholics supported his weekly newspaper, *The Leader*, which he began publishing in Dublin in 1900. In 1902, the Catholic Association (not to be confused with the nineteenth-century organization led by Daniel O'Connell) was founded with Moran's support for the express purpose of combating Protestant influences and including Catholicism as part of its definition of what it meant to be Irish. Moran's nationalism, however, like that of the more secular Yeats, was not political in nature, and he did not endorse Redmond's party. Moran had little use for Redmond's party and believed that chasing after Home Rule distracted Ireland from the larger meaning of nationalism and the Gaelic movement.

However, to some, the lesson of Parnell's failure was that in the future the party needed to be even better organized and prepared to adopt more effective tactics in order to achieve Home Rule for Ireland. Redmond's party had certain advantages that it had lacked under Parnell. First, it had the ability to pay its members, thanks to donations from the United States that were funneled through the American chapter of the Land League. Second, the Liberal Party after 1900 was desperate to regain power and even more in need of the 81 members of the House of Commons that had united under Redmond's leadership. Third, the followers of Parnell who had divided after his death realized in the decade that followed the necessity of unifying behind one leader and were unlikely to split the party as readily a second time. But Redmond was not the leader that Parnell was, nor did he generate the same kind of passionate enthusiasm from his followers that Parnell had. In addition, one disadvantage of allying with the Liberals, who had adopted a platform that included more significant social reform, was that such an alliance further alienated many within the Catholic Church, especially the church hierarchy.

Still, most Catholics supported Redmond's party, not the least because his movement was fairly conservative in that it aimed for achieving autonomy for Ireland without leaving the British Empire. In 1900, Ireland was still governed by a British administration that was installed in Dublin Castle and oversaw approximately 30 administrative departments. Many advocates of Home Rule would have simply been content to see British administrative officials replaced by a comparable Irish administration.

Support for Home Rule was by no means unanimous in Ireland. Unionists existed in both the North and the South. They were opposed to any move in the direction of political autonomy for Ireland. They had their own party—the Irish Unionist Party—and they usually managed to occupy about 20 seats in the House of Commons. Unionism, however, had much more support from the Protestant middle and working classes in Ulster than in the South. It was on the verge of becoming primarily a Northern phenomenon.

The commitment to unionism in the North coincided with the rise of Sinn Féin ("Ourselves Alone") in the South. Sinn Féin was a political movement seeking outright independence for Ireland as opposed to the achievement of dominion status that Home Rule would have entailed. The Irish revolutionary Desmond Fitzgerald (1888–1947) would later write that "those of us who thought of Home Rule as something utterly inadequate were a very small minority without influence, impotent."[2] But Fitzgerald and others did not believe that a parliamentary party was adequate for achieving the true nationhood for Ireland that they desired.

Meanwhile, in Britain, the Conservative Party had regained power in 1895. In 1893, Gladstone had put forward a new Home Rule Bill, but its defeat only further divided the Liberals. The Liberal Prime Minister Lord Rosebury had an agenda that revolved around social reform and curbing the rising tide of militarist aggression that was already threatening the peace of Europe in the 1890s rather than achieving Home Rule for Ireland. The Liberal Party, therefore, would have been of little use to the Irish Home Rule movement, even if it had been stronger in the 1890s. Given the division in the Liberal Party over Home Rule and the support that the Conservatives received from the Liberal supporters of the union, it seemed unlikely in 1895 that the Conservatives would relinquish power any time soon. The visit that Prince George made to Ireland in 1897 seemed to reassure unionists in both England and Ireland that the Home Rule issue was effectively dead. And so it seemed to be—until the Liberals regained power 9 years later.

The Liberals and Home Rule 1906–1914

The Liberal Party that assumed power in December 1905 was headed by Henry Campbell-Bannerman, who would prove himself the heir of Gladstone by declaring his support for Home Rule for Ireland. But once in office, after 11 years in the wilderness, the Liberal Party had no desire to risk relinquishing their hold on power as a result of divisions that might be caused by the introduction of a new Home Rule bill. They did make a half-hearted attempt to conciliate Redmond's party with an Irish Council Bill in 1907, but Redmond refused to support anything less than Home Rule. Campbell-Bannerman died in 1908, to be replaced by H. H. Asquith, a wealthy, Oxford-educated lawyer who had previously served as home secretary (1892–95) and Chancellor of the Exchequer (1905–08).

For his Chancellor of the Exchequer, Asquith chose David Lloyd George (1863–1945), a Welsh solicitor and political outsider who was determined to carry out a reform program that included imposing land and inheritance taxes on the wealthy in what was known as the "people's budget," which he

---

[2] Desmond Fitzgerald (1968), *Desmond's Rising: Memoirs 1913 to Easter 1916*. Dublin: Liberties Press, p. 37.

introduced in 1909. The House of Lords was by nature a conservative body of the British elite that was becoming increasingly politicized as a result of the Liberal Party's reform agenda. Retaining veto power over legislation passed by the House of Commons, the Lords had allowed some significant reform legislation through, including an Old-Age Pensions Act in 1908. When Lloyd George proposed the people's budget, however, the House of Lords, which traditionally did not interfere with government finances, overstepped its bounds in many people's eyes and vetoed the budget. The ensuing national election became a popular referendum on the Lords' veto and the budget, but it ended with the Liberals and the Conservatives deadlocked and without the majority necessary to form a government. The election results made it clear to Lloyd George that he would need the support of the Irish MPs to get his budget passed, as well as legislation designed to curtail the power of the House of Lords. That meant recommitting the Liberal Party to Home Rule. With the help of Irish votes—and a threat by the king to create additional lords if they failed to cooperate—both the House of Commons and the House of Lords passed the Parliament Act of 1911. This act restricted the House of Lords to the ability to postpone legislation for 3 years, after which any bill passed by the House of Commons would become law. Keeping their promise to their Irish supporters, the Liberals successfully steered the Third Home Rule Bill through the House of Commons in 1912, only to have it rejected by the Lords. In January 1913, the House of Lords once again vetoed a Home Rule bill after the House of Commons had approved it. At that point, however, everyone knew—under the terms of the Parliament Act—that the Lords were out of vetoes.

This did not mean, however, that Home Rule for Ireland was a fait accompli. Ulster unionists were well organized behind their leader and spokesperson, Sir Edward Carson (1854–1935), a formidable speaker who had made his reputation defending the Marquess of Queensbury against a criminal libel charge filed by the gifted Irish writer, Oscar Wilde. In September 1912, Carson went on a speaking tour throughout the North that drew large crowds of enthusiastic Ulstermen eager to defend their right to remain a part of the United Kingdom. On 28 September, unionists signed "a Solemn League and Covenant" committing them to a defense of their "cherished position of equal citizenship in the United Kingdom."[3] Carson had no illusions about the illegality of the actions with which he was involved. By 1914, Ulster unionists had an army—the Ulster Volunteer Force—of 100,000 men. In April, they imported perhaps as many as 50,000 rifles and approximately 3 million rounds of ammunition.

The fact that they were able to carry out such an operation spoke volumes about the preparedness and organizational skills of the UVF's military

---

[3]   Phillip Orr (2008), *The Road to the Somme: Men of the Ulster Division Tell Their Story*, 2nd edn, Belfast: Blackstaff Press, p. 4.

leaders.[4] Despite the questionable quality of their weapons, the unionists were showing that they meant business and were prepared to resist Home Rule, which they called *Rome Rule*, even if it meant civil war. Unlike the case in most civil wars, however, they would be fighting to remain in a country, not to secede from it. The support that they received from the Conservative Party leaders in Britain made them even more confident in their chances of success. It was still an open question whether they were fighting to keep the nine Northern counties of Ulster in the United Kingdom or all of Ireland, since there were plenty of unionists in the South as well.

Either way, the leaders of the Liberal government in Westminster now found themselves in a completely untenable position. They had promised to pass a Home Rule Bill in exchange for the support of Redmond's Irish Party. There were now no legal or political obstacles to passing such a bill into law. But they had somehow not reckoned with the threat of armed resistance by those opposed to the bill. The militant aggression of the unionists has tended to obscure the nature of their main grievance, which was that they were being forcefully denied citizenship in what they saw as their country of origin against their will. Meanwhile, on 25 November 1913, Irish nationalists formed their own paramilitary organization, the Irish Volunteers, which quickly recruited about 75,000 members prepared to fight for Irish independence as a counter against the pressure of the Unionists. Two additional factors made the position of the Liberal government even more tenuous. One was the passive response of the police force in Ulster to the illegal gunrunning activities of the unionists and the probable unreliability of that force should it be called upon to defend the government. The second was the active support to the Unionist cause provided by the English Conservative Party.

In his 1935 book, *The Strange Death of Liberal England*, George Dangerfield referred to the willingness of the Conservatives to defy the ruling government—by force, if necessary—over the issue of Ulster as "the Tory Rebellion." He generally excoriated the Conservatives, led by Andrew Bonar Law (1858–1923), a Scottish iron magnate with strong unionist sympathies, for the threat that they posed to England's political stability. More recent historians have been more sympathetic toward Bonar Law and the Conservatives, including the author of the definitive biography of Bonar Law, R. J. Q. Adams.[5] Conservative opposition to Home Rule also needs to be seen in the context of the previous attacks upon their world view undertaken by the Liberal Party, especially the Parliament Act of 1911 that had curtailed the power of the House of Lords. In Dangerfield's words,

---

[4] Charles Townshend (2006), *Easter 1916*. Chicago: Ivan R. Dee, p. 51.

[5] R. J. Q. Adams (1999), *Bonar Law*. Edinburgh: John Murray. See also Jeremy Smith (2000), *The Tories and Ireland, 1910–1914: Conservative Party Politics and the Home Rule Crisis.* Dublin: Irish Academic Press and the discussion of the revisionist treatment of Dangerfield's thesis in Thomas C. Kennedy (2007), "Troubled Tories: Dissent and Confusion concerning the Party's Ulster Policy." *Journal of British Studies*, 46, 571.

these were "earnest men and men of good-will, who, gazing back in spirit to the mellow vistas of a pastoral England, truly believed that the country was better off under the guidance of men of birth."[6] The Conservatives, like the Unionists, may have been doing what they believed in their hearts to be right and politically necessary, but they were playing a dangerous game with potentially disastrous consequences.

It appeared that the government was going to have to make a decision one way or the other—to implement Home Rule and risk civil war or to delay it once again and violate their pledge while at the same time yielding to the unconstitutional tactics of the opposition. Given that the government delayed implementing the legislation when it should have taken effect in June 1914, it seems likely that they were prepared to abandon Redmond and their Irish political allies before they risked a military confrontation in Northern Ireland without the support of the Conservative Party. Lloyd George had already proposed a compromise solution favorable to the Unionists in February.

Negotiations that took place that summer seemed likely to end in an extremely watered-down version of Home Rule, if any. In July, Redmond was actually willing to see four Northern counties excluded from the Home Rule Bill, but not six. But this was not about to suffice for unionists, who could not even settle on agreeing to the exclusion of only six counties as opposed to the nine that constituted the historical region of Ulster. Meanwhile, knowing that the delay in Home Rule would give added fuel to the nationalist paramilitary organization known as the Irish Volunteers who were not under his control, Redmond negotiated a truce with them and successfully placed 25 of his men on their executive committee.[7] It appeared that Bonar Law's political strategy might succeed in forcing the Liberals to back down without a civil war; if it had succeeded, it might now be seen in a very different light. However, the Liberals were spared from having to make such a decision because of the outbreak of a general European war in August 1914.

Ireland and World War I

Britain's decision to declare war on Germany on 4 August 1914 had the potential to inflame the Irish situation because of the likelihood of disloyalty from unionists should Home Rule become law and the possibility of disloyalty from Irish nationalists if Home Rule continued to be delayed.

---

[6] George Dangerfield (1980; first published 1935), *The Strange Death of Liberal England*. New York: Perigree, p. 49.

[7] The Earl of Longford and Thomas P. O'Neill (1971), *Eamon de Valera*. Boston: Houghton Mifflin, p. 22.

But Britain's entry into the war also had the potential to defuse the Irish situation since it called for the people of both the North and the South to fight on the same side. As it turned out, the outbreak of war had several immediate effects on the Irish situation. The Conservative Party, which had the potential to split over the extremity of Bonar Law's position on the Ulster crisis, was reunited. Tensions among the Conservatives died down in the face of a common enemy, even if they were not forgotten. Furthermore, on 3 August, John Redmond announced that he would unconditionally support the war, one day before the British even declared war on Germany. In doing so, he had effectively agreed to postpone consideration of Home Rule until after the war, even though it had legally been scheduled to take effect that year. Home Rule was postponed, the issue unresolved and set aside for the duration of the war. Redmond and Carson were now on the same side.

The Irish response to World War I was hardly monolithic. Serious nationalists opposed the war from the beginning and were angered by the thought of Irishmen dying in the armies of the British Empire. The leaders of Sinn Féin disagreed with the whole premise of Home Rule because they were interested in complete independence; their quarrel was with Britain, not with Germany. Pacifists existed in Ireland (and indeed in all countries). The unionists followed the lead of the Conservative Party in Britain and enthusiastically went to fight for the country of which they were so desperate to remain a part. If Britain was the enemy that the Ulster Volunteer Force was preparing to fight before the war, after its outbreak the UVF quickly changed its target to Germany. They were permitted to form their own division (the 36th Ulster). Philip Orr's description of the 36th could apply to any number of units that marched off to war in 1914: "a bunch of ordinary men drawn together by extraordinary circumstances and manifesting all kinds of military shortcomings, particularly during the early years when it was being turned from a crowd of civilians into a fighting unit."[8]

Thousands of other Irishmen also voluntarily joined the British army, including Catholics in both the North and the South. Catholics in Ulster seemed to support the war just as much as Protestants did. The Catholic press throughout Ireland supported the war; Mary Kenny has found numerous prayers for "our brave Irish Tommies" in their publications.[9] The arrival of war refugees from the German invasion of Belgium increased support for the British decision to intervene. Irish recruits had been important to the British army since the Napoleonic wars and had been vital in the turn-of-the-century war that the British had fought against the Dutch Boers in South Africa. The British needed the loyalty of the Irish because they could hardly afford to keep troops stationed in Ireland for the duration of the war when they were

---

[8] Orr, *op. cit.*, p. xiii.
[9] Mary Kenny (1997), *Goodbye to Catholic Ireland: A Social, Personal and Cultural History from the Fall of Parnell to the Realm of Mary Robinson.* London: Sinclair-Stevenson, p. 60.

so badly needed on the Western Front. Most of the 30,000 or so British troops stationed in Ireland when the war broke out were deployed elsewhere by the third week of August.[10] The British military deployed approximately 58,000 Irishmen in all in the early weeks of the war. One estimate put the total participation of Irishmen in the war at 206,000, excluding those of Irish descent who fought in the British or American armies.[11] If the latter were included, that number might total closer to 500,000.[12]

Not all of the Irishmen who joined the army did so for patriotic reasons, of course. As elsewhere, the army was a popular option for unemployed young men or those who were employed in work they found dull. Many of these young men saw war as an opportunity for adventure in a foreign land. Many others enlisted in the armies during World War I because they wanted to fight alongside their buddies or out of peer pressure from friends and relatives. Other Irishmen from both the North and the South migrated to find work in British factories that were geared up for wartime production but short on labor.

For his part, Redmond thought that the Irish Volunteers could serve as a home defense force, but the British rejected the idea. They also rejected the idea that the Irish Volunteers be allowed to join the British army as a unit, although they had no such qualms about the Ulster Volunteer Force. Still, Redmond gave a passionate speech in Co. Wicklow on 20 September, while soldiers in France were digging in for what would become a long and horrifically bloody war:

> The interests of Ireland—of the whole of Ireland—are at stake in this war. This war is undertaken in the defense of the highest principles of religion and morality and right, and it would be a disgrace forever to our country and a reproach to her manhood and a denial of the lessons of her history if young Ireland confined their efforts to remaining at home to defend the shores of Ireland from an unlikely invasion, and to shrinking from the duty of proving on the field of battle that gallantry and courage which has distinguished our race all through its history.[13]

Redmond tried to sell his support for the war to his constituents on the basis that Irish freedom was at stake too, but for nationalists who desired freedom from the British, this claim sounded hollow. He seemed to be confident that the service of Irish soldiers during the war would make Britain more

---

[10] Catriona Pennell (2012), *A Kingdom United: Popular Responses to the Outbreak of the First World War in Britain and Ireland*. Oxford: Oxford University Press, p. 165.

[11] Catherine Switzer (2007), *Unionists and Great War Commemoration in the North of Ireland, 1914–1918*. Dublin: Irish Academic Press, p. 9.

[12] Jeremy Black (1997), *A History of the British Isles*. New York: St. Martin's, p. 272.

[13] Quoted in Denis Gwyn (1971; 1932), *The Life of John Redmond*. Freeport, NY: Books for Libraries Press, p. 391.

predisposed to grant Home Rule when the war ended. By the end of the war 4 years later, Redmond would be dead. But his dream of being the one to usher in Home Rule for Ireland had already died in 1914. Home Rule had now been indefinitely postponed.

Even though unionists supported the war, they had not changed their stance with regard to the British over the issue of Home Rule and were still prepared to fight them, if necessary, at war's end. As David Fitzpatrick put it, "The immediate effect of the war was to divert the most active section of Ireland's paramilitary organizations to the European conflict, without achieving lasting reconciliation between the parties left at home."[14] "They were," Thomas Bartlett points out, "permitted, indeed encouraged, to preserve their prewar identity and were allowed to retain their own officers and colors."[15] The UVF was, of course, depleted by the deployment of the 36th overseas and by enlistments in the British army, especially as a result of those who had previously served being recalled to active duty. Given the high death rate of officers during the war as a result of the role they played in leading their troops "over the top" of the trenches into the deadly barrage of shells and machine gun bullets that exploded and flew across the hell known as no-man's-land, the UVF was unlikely to regain many of its officers who had departed for France or Turkey. In effect, their leadership was almost totally inept.[16] But the British recognized that they now owed something to the unionists for their support. Given the government's previous commitment to Home Rule, the only possible solution seemed to be partitioning the island to allow Northern unionists to remain within the United Kingdom while granting Home Rule to the rest of Ireland.

The war took its toll on Ireland's people, as it did to the people of every combatant country. Millions were dying for purposes that became murkier as the war progressed. Commemorative church services began to remind people at home of how many of their countrymen had died in the war. The enthusiastic support that many people were prepared to offer at the beginning of the war gave way to war-weariness and in some cases to outright opposition. The British would find it increasingly difficult to entice Irishmen to enlist during the course of the war, partly because those most supportive of it had already done so. In addition, the Irish shared in the food shortages and other forms of deprivation that were caused by a war that demanded industrial production to be geared almost exclusively to the war instead of toward consumer items.

As the war dragged on, a small, committed group of Irish nationalists determined that the British would never give Ireland its independence

---

[14] David Fitzpatrick (1989), "Ireland Since 1870," in Roy Foster (ed.), *The Oxford Illustrated History of Ireland*. Oxford: Oxford University Press, pp. 234–5.

[15] Thomas Bartlett (2010), *Ireland: A History*. Cambridge: Cambridge University Press, p. 380.

[16] Timothy Bowman (2007), *Carson's Army: The Ulster Volunteer Force, 1910–1922*. Manchester: Manchester University Press, p. 163.

unless they were forced to do so because of armed insurrection. Led by Eamon de Valera (1882–1975), they determined that no time might be more advantageous than to strike the British while they were already embroiled in a massive world war. Nationalists such as de Valera and Desmond Fitzgerald did not want to wait *in case* the British did grant Home Rule, which they were afraid would suffice for a large majority of the Irish people but would fall short of their ultimate goal of independence. They need not have worried about that, as support for Home Rule within Parliament had steadily dwindled during the course of the war. But, as Irish nationalists, they believed that the Irish nation referred to the entire island, and it was becoming increasingly clear that the British might consider partition a viable option—if they were to consider granting Home Rule at all.

The Easter Rising and the Anglo-Irish Treaty of 1921

Irish nationalists began to prepare for revolution much as had their unionist counterparts in the North: by importing weapons. Prior to the war, sympathizers in Ireland and England had provided the Volunteers with arms so that they would not be at such a distinct disadvantage if a war should break out with the UVF.[17] Dublin Castle was aware of the activities of the nationalists and closely monitored them. Those areas that had contributed smaller number of recruits for the British army became particularly suspect. The British had already had several run-ins with nationalists who were trying to smuggle guns into the hands of the Volunteers. In one famous incident on Bachelor's Walk in Dublin in July 1914, British troops fired upon a group of civilians, killing several, who taunted them after a successful gun-running operation from Howth. A similar operation is portrayed in David Lean's film *Ryan's Daughter* (1970), which portrays anti-British feeling during the war on the Dingle Peninsula in County Kerry in the Southwest. According to Desmond Fitzgerald, however, "in West Kerry the people seemed to be interested in the Volunteers as an item of news in the papers rather than as an organization that they might join in themselves."[18] Yet, the scene in the film does approximate the arrival of weapons aboard a German ship intended for the Volunteers that the British managed to intercept in west Kerry on 21 April 1916.[19] Such incidents inflamed anti-British sentiment but at the same time helped the Volunteers to attract additional recruits.

---

[17] Eoin Neeson (2007), *Myths from Easter 1916*. Aubane, Co. Cork: Aubane Historical Society, p. 51.
[18] Fitzgerald, *op. cit.*, p. 42.
[19] Michael Tanner (2012), *Troubled Epic: On Location with Ryan's Daughter*. Cork: The Collins Press, p. 19.

The Volunteers drew support from both moderates who merely wanted to put more pressure on the British to grant Home Rule and radical nationalists who were determined to make a clean break with Britain and set up an independent country. Thousands of men enlisted in the organization, providing a sense of confidence in its prospects for success and a belief that it enjoyed widespread support. Not that this would have mattered; the organizers of Sinn Féin were determined to challenge both Home Rule and the British government even if they died trying. Sinn Féin might be considered the political wing of the Volunteers in the same way that it would be later for the Irish Republican Army. The party had been founded in 1905, about the same time that a Russian revolutionary who adopted the name of Lenin had split his own Marxist party over his belief that revolution would be better served by a small band of professional revolutionaries than by a broad political party that tried to win the support of the masses. Meanwhile, the Irish Republican Brotherhood, which had been active in the nineteenth century during the Land War, experienced a revival in 1907 and managed by 1916 to gain leadership positions within the Irish Volunteers. Among those leaders were Patrick Pearse and James Connolly. Pearse was a poet and a member of the Gaelic League who joined the Irish Republican Brotherhood in 1913 and had become the director of military operations for the Volunteers by the time of the Easter Rising. Connolly was a union organizer and one of the founders of the Irish Labor Party who was motivated to join the Volunteers as a result of Redmond's support for the war, which ran counter to his own nationalist sentiments.

The Rising was originally announced for Easter Sunday, April 23, but Holy Week was full of confusion, rumors, and conflicting messages. On 19 April, a forged document calling for the suppression of the Volunteers that was intended to stir sympathy lacked credibility and failed to have the desired effect. The Volunteers counted on German arms and hoped for the arrival of German troops if they were to have any chance at a successful rebellion, but those efforts were ill-coordinated. Roger Casement (1864–1916) had spent time in Berlin since joining the Volunteers in 1916 attempting to recruit German aid for their cause. The capture of the arms shipment in Kerry—and of Casement—left the rebels with a shortage of arms and leadership.

Despite this setback and a general state of confusion, the Rising did commence on Easter Monday (24 April). Pearse read a proclamation stating that

> In every generation the Irish people have asserted their right to national freedom and sovereignty; six times during the past three hundred years they have asserted it in arms. Standing on that fundamental right and again asserting it in arms in the face of the world, we hereby proclaim the Irish republic as a sovereign independent state.[20]

---

[20] Richard English (2003), *Armed Struggle: The History of the IRA*. Oxford: Oxford University Press, p. 4.

The proclamation was addressed to "Irishmen and Irishwomen" and claimed to speak for Ireland in summoning "her children to her flag" to have the support of "her exiled children in America" and gallant allies in Europe.[21] But the plans and actions of the revolutionaries were not sufficient to allow them to achieve their ideals. They seized the General Post Office on Sackville (now O'Connell) Street, which was hardly the equivalent of the Bolsheviks storming the Winter Palace in Petrograd the following year. They occupied other public buildings as well, but did not choose locations of strategic or political significance. Instead of striking at the British, they used sandbags as barricades and prepared to defend themselves from attack.

About 1,200 rebels participated in the Easter Uprising, which could easily have led the British to believe that the rebellion was the work of a fanatical minority that did not have the support of the Irish people. To some extent, they would have been correct. The uprising itself lasted less than a week and ended with 450 people dead and 2,500 wounded.[22] The Catholic press did not react favorably to the rebellion. But there are reasons why the Easter Rising is considered one of the turning points in Ireland's history. Whereas many Irish Protestants turned their back on Irish nationalism after the abysmal failure of the 1798 rebellion, many Irish Catholics became more attracted to Irish nationalism after the ignominious collapse of the Easter Rising. In that sense, the nationalists who sponsored and led the uprising were able to turn failure into success and gain the support of the Irish people—after the fact.

Robin Higgins has recently asserted that 1916 remains for many people "the most vivid symbolic representation of the nation."[23] Whether this is what the organizers of the rebellion intended all along is still up for debate. Not all of the leaders of the Irish Volunteers supported it, including the history professor Eoin Mac Neill (1867–1945), who was among the most important leaders of the Volunteers. Mac Neill actually tried to countermand the order to begin the Rising by sending out a message that the rebellion had been cancelled. At the time of the Rising, the nationalists did not have the support that they needed among the Irish people, and they had virtually no chance of defeating the British. What little chance they did have they squandered with an ill-conceived military operation in which they made numerous tactical errors, including their failure to "block the communication route for British reinforcements from Kingstown to the center of Dublin."[24]

---

[21] Alan O'Day and John Stevenson (eds) (1992), *Irish Historical Documents Since 1800*. Dublin: Gill and Macmillan, p. 160.

[22] Maurice Walsh (2008), *The News from Ireland: Foreign Correspondents and the Irish Revolution*. London: I. B. Tauris, p. 51.

[23] Robin Higgins (2012), *Transforming 1916: Meaning, Memory and the Fiftieth Anniversary of the Easter Rising*. Cork: Cork University Press, p. 5.

[24] Michael Hopkinson (2002), *The Irish War of Independence*. Montreal and Kingston: McGill-Queen's University Press, p. 13.

The shift toward sympathy for their cause happened partly as a result of the shrewd public relations campaign undertaken by the nationalists in the years immediately following the Rising, partly as a result of the negative reaction that many people had to the execution of 16 nationalists (Roger Casement, plus 15 captured rebels including Pearse and Connolly), and partly as a result of the dramatic success that the Irish nationalist army began to enjoy in its guerilla campaign against the British authorities. Furthermore, Easter is a symbol of rebirth and the timing of the rebellion was a reminder to a Catholic population of the necessity of sacrifice prior to the resurrection, religious imagery transformed in support of a secular cause. Martyrdom has a powerful and emotional appeal for people steeped in the Christian tradition and it was easy in retrospect to consider those who had died as brave heroes sanctified by their blood. Pearse, in particular, had fostered such a view; in 1915, he had said as part of a funeral oration for Jeremiah O'Donovan Rossa: "Life springs from death; and from the graves of patriot men and women spring living nations."[25]

Michael Collins (1890–1922), who had fought in the rebellion himself and been imprisoned afterward, was released and became one of the leading spokespersons for the movement following the rebellion. He hammered away at the theme that freedom was not the possession of Britain to give but the right of the Irish people to take. At this point, de Valera, Collins, and Sinn Féin seemed to realize that they could not achieve success without popular support—at home and abroad.

Ireland had been placed under martial law following the Rising, which Lloyd George decided to end in February 1917, though he did so too late to save what remained of Redmond's party. Sinn Féin trounced the Irish Parliamentary Party in the 1918 election by 73 seats to 7. Those elected on the Sinn Féin ticket refused to occupy the seats they won because of their principled refusal to acknowledge British authority over Ireland, but they had gained a huge symbolic victory. Sinn Féin employed this policy of abstention from British politics from 1918 to 1920 as an act of protest, but at the cost of removing the voice of its members from the discussion about the future of Ireland. At home, they escalated their attacks on the British through guerilla warfare with the intent of driving them from Ireland.

Following the war with Germany, the British dispatched soldiers to Ireland wearing military uniforms that gave them their nickname of the "Black and Tans." They behaved brutally, but D. M. Leeson has recently argued that they did so because of the inherently brutal situation into which they had been cast and not because they had become inured to violence and bloodshed on the Western Front, as is often thought.[26] Either way, the

---

[25] Quoted in Liz Curtis (1994), *The Cause of Ireland: From the United Irishmen to Partition.* Belfast: Beyond the Pale Publications, p. 266.

[26] D. M. Leeson (2011), *The Black and Tans: British Police and Auxilliaries in the Irish War of Independence, 1920–1921.* Oxford: Oxford University Press.

FIGURE 12.1 *Soldiers inspecting the ruins of Dublin's General Post Office Following the Easter Rising, 3 May 1916. Courtesy of Getty Images.*

British soldiers who were sent to Ireland had been assigned a role for which they were psychologically unprepared. Nonetheless their actions did much to turn public opinion against them, not only in Ireland but also in Britain and the United States. To some extent, the struggle of Sinn Féin became a worldwide cause célèbre at the same time that the US President Woodrow Wilson was championing the cause of self-determination for smaller nations at the Paris Peace Conference that followed the end of the war. Wilson's position gave de Valera a platform from which to launch his appeal to the American people on an 18-month visit to the United States in 1919–20.

The British simply saw themselves as fighting fire with fire and, it could be argued, after 4 years of a wartime mentality, were more and not less disposed to seek a military solution in Ireland. But the British were acutely aware of the need for propaganda as well. In 1920, the military commander in charge, General Tudor, appointed a Press Officer of the Information Section of Police Authority and a Secretary to the Information Section. The former, Captain H. B. C. Pollard, would later describe the successor of the Volunteers, the newly formed Irish Republican Army as "a group of moral decadents leading a superstitious minority into an epidemic of murder and violent crime," a problem that he believed was "rooted in the racial characteristics of the people themselves."[27]

---

[27] H. B. C. Pollard (1922), "The Secret Societies of Ireland: Their Rise and Progress," quoted in Brian P. Murphy, (2006), *The Origins and Organisation of British Propaganda in Ireland, 1920.* Aubane, Co. Cork: Aubane Historical Society, p. 22.

The situation escalated. Collins was not averse to terror. On a single day, 21 November 1920, his men killed 14 men who were suspected of conducting espionage for the purposes of derailing Collins and his organization. British forces were quick to retaliate. British troops indiscriminately shot and killed 12 spectators at a football match in Croke Park in Dublin, including one of the players, Michael Hogan of Tipperary. The British also executed three republican prisoners on the same day, allegedly because they were attempting to escape. It looked perhaps as if Sinn Féin had met its match, but most of its members were determined to fight on.

Meanwhile, a Fourth Home Rule Bill was introduced in 1919, calling for Home Rule—in both the North and the South with two separate parliaments. The bill passed into law as the Government of Ireland Act of 1920. The first elections under the terms of the new treaty took place in May 1921. In the Southern legislature, the Dáil Éireann, the only four seats not occupied by representatives of Sinn Féin were held by representatives of Trinity College. Unionists, of course, dominated the Northern parliament.

At this point, the British were ready to negotiate with the South rather than prolong the violence. The British thought that they could work with de Valera, but de Valera chose not to negotiate and to send Collins as the head of a republican delegation instead. Collins negotiated the 1921 Anglo-Irish Treaty, which included a provision that the Irish would still be responsible for part of Britain's national debt and one that prohibited Ireland from placing tariffs on British goods, while asserting that Britain would remain responsible for the defense of Ireland. The 1921 Anglo-Irish Treaty called for a boundary commission to be established to "determine in accordance with the wishes of the inhabitants, so far as may be compatible with economic and geographical conditions, the boundaries between Northern Ireland and the rest of Ireland."[28] In the meantime, the partition of the island would continue. Collins found himself in no position to argue with such language and returned to Ireland having secured a greater measure of autonomy for Southern Ireland, which became officially known as the Irish Free State.

Collins thought that half a victory was better than total defeat, but de Valera rejected the treaty and prepared his troops to continue fighting for an independent, unified Ireland. Northern Unionists were not happy either. They had not asked for Home Rule or their own parliament, only to remain under British rule. They did not want Home Rule or the Anglo-Irish Treaty to be seen as an intermediate step toward an independent Ireland. In the South, independence quickly gave way to civil war as the IRA refused to accept partition or the idea that any boundary between the North and South could be "compatible with economic and geographic conditions." Collins took control of the government forces, now with military aid from Britain,

---

[28] http://treaty.nationalarchives.ie/document-gallery/anglo-irish-treaty-6-december-1921/
anglo-irish-treaty-6-december-1921-page-4/

FIGURE 12.2 *Eamon de Valera, upon his return to Ireland from the United States, 1 July 1921. Courtesy of Getty Images.*

which was also committed to defending the treaty. Collins was assassinated in West Cork on 22 August 1922, a casualty of the bad blood between the pro- and anti-treaty factions that would ebb, but not entirely disappear in the years that followed.

Ireland in the interwar years

The civil war had deep implications for Northern Ireland. It led to suspicions of Northern Catholics by unionists who worried about the potential implications of an IRA victory. The activity of the IRA thus not only created more of a division between North and South, but also between Catholics and Protestants in the North. De Valera, who was in the process of gradually and strategically engineering his rise to power, was largely oblivious to this fact. He claimed to represent all of Ireland, but it should have been clear that all of Ireland did not want him to represent them.

Some Southerners boycotted Northern goods in the early 1920s in retaliation for the unionists' unwillingness to be included in the Irish Free State. But by 1923, many of the Irish people had had enough of violence and were unprepared to support de Valera's uncompromising stand. In the general election of 1923, the opposition Cumannan Gaedheal gained 63 seats in the Dáil to 44 for de Valera's Republican Party.

Still, 1916 continued to cast a shadow over Irish politics in the years that followed. The Irish Free State found numerous ways to commemorate what it saw as its seminal moment, ranging from films and plays to school essay contests. The Civil War would not be soon forgotten either, although politically both sides tried to move forward and put the past behind them. In 1924, Dorothy Macardle's *Tragedies of Kerry* appeared to keep fresh the wounds inflicted on the Republicans through its detailed descriptions of the deaths that they had suffered fighting for their cause. Her book represented a certain strain of thought that continued to excoriate those who had agreed to the treaty and then betrayed their allies by using the might of the state against them. In 1926, Sean O'Casey's bleak and tragic play about the Easter Rising, *The Plough and the Stars* was performed at the Abbey Theater in Dublin against a background of controversy and riots because it did not fit with the celebratory mood that accompanied most remembrances of the rebellion.

The two main parties after 1926, Fianna Fáil and Cumannan Gaedheal, both claimed the Easter Rising as part of their heritage. Fianna Fáil was still committed to working against the Anglo-Irish Treaty, taking votes away from the Labor Party as a result. De Valera had always believed that Ireland was destined to become a nation; nothing had happened to convince him otherwise.

But the new leaders of the Free State had other concerns to which they needed to attend. They now had responsibility for formulating domestic policies for which they would be held accountable. Ireland experienced a further decline in its population that augured against it becoming the great nation that it aspired to be. Irish people continued to emigrate in order to find work because the government was committed to Ireland's rural identity and refused to support policies that would foster urbanization and industrial growth to any significant degree. In doing so, it contributed to the drain on the countryside without providing any alternatives for those living within Ireland. Mary Daly points out that, in addition to this, the Irish practice of encouraging large families actually worked against population growth because it delayed marriages for so many people until they inherited land or could afford to support a large family.[29]

Culturally, the 1920s were characterized by an increased interest in sports, as evidenced by the growth of the Gaelic Athletic Association, which started intercounty leagues across Ireland in 1926 and expanded to 1,600 clubs by 1935. Football celebrities such as Larry Stanley and Joe Keohane and hurling stars such as Larry Meagher and Mick Mackey attracted huge followings.[30] While in other ways Ireland did not keep in tune with the spirit of what was known in the United States as the "Roaring Twenties," with its flappers, free-flowing dances like the Charleston, and looser sexual morals, it did see a significant increase in the numbers of women who played sports.[31]

---

[29] Mary E. Daly (2006), *The Slow Failure: Population Decline and Independent Ireland, 1922–1973.* Madison: University of Wisconsin Press, p. 18.

[30] Mike Cronin, Mark Duncan, and Paul Rouse (2009), *The GAA: A People's History.* Cork: Collins, p. 50.

[31] Ibid.

Religiously, the Irish Free State was a Catholic nation, which was revealed in diverse ways. It was becoming clear that any political party that ignored the Catholic sensibilities of the populace was going to suffer in the polls as a result. Even the Labor Party moderated its stance in an effort not to turn away Catholic voters who might find socialism inimical. Women continued to find themselves marginalized by a religious culture that valued them primarily in their roles as mothers and caretakers. The death of Pope Pius XI in 1939 caused an outpouring of grief in Ireland, where the pontiff was particularly beloved. Speaking to the Dáil Eierann on 10 February, de Valera praised Pius in particular for opposing "violence and materialism and all those evils which are fast bringing the world back to the edge of a new catastrophe."[32]

The Irish Free State was also a new nation that was focused, to a large degree, on its past. The Folklore of Ireland Society, founded in 1927 as an offshoot of the Gaelic League, dedicated itself to the preservation and publication of Irish folklore. The government of the Free State created its own Irish Folklore Institute in 1930. In 1935, its name was changed to the Irish Folklore Commission, and it was placed under the auspices of the Department of Education. At this time, the majority of the people in some remote parts of the country still spoke Gaelic, which had come to be seen as something of a national treasure. In 1934, Irish nationalists reacted negatively when budget considerations led the government to cut grant money designated to support the teaching of Gaelic.

Ireland in the interwar years was also a divided land that had not successfully come to terms with that division. Factional strife caused divisions in both Northern Ireland and the Irish Free State. Violence and terror were not unknown in the 1930s. Private militia began drilling just in case another civil war should break out. The IRA did not disband at the end of the civil war. In an interview with S. J. Woolf of *The New York Times* published in November 1932, W. B. Yeats expressed his disappointment that the Irish literary revival that he had done so much to foster had not been able to heal those divisions:

> I felt that the two opposing forces [Protestant and Catholic] might be brought together if a national literature could be developed which would make Ireland beautiful in memory yet freed from provincialism by an exacting criticism.[33]

---

[32] "Catholic Ireland Pays Its Tribute," *The New York Times*, 11 February 1939. http://bluehawk. monmouth.edu:2141/hnpnewyorktimes/docview/102733333/13ACC97C3FC23E68262/1?a ccountid=12532.

[33] S. J. Woolf, "Yeats Foresees an Ireland of Reality," *The New York Times*, 13 November 1932. http://bluehawk.monmouth.edu:2141/hnpnewyorktimes/docview/99534936/13A707B1D7 023DE617F/6?accountid=12532.

Yeats stressed that he believed in a national literature, not a nationalistic literature. But politicians in the South were not willing to let the matter drop. In March 1936, W. T. Cosgrave, the president of the Fine Gael party, which had become the second largest party in Ireland in 1933 out of the merger of the right-wing National Guard and the National Center Party, called for the unification of Ireland in his annual speech to party members, saying that the issue "overshadows every other political question, and ought to command the most earnest attention of all parties of the State."[34] On 30 September 1938, nationalists sitting in the parliament of Northern Ireland called for the immediate reunification of the two Irelands, claiming that "no boundary in Europe is more outrageous than that which divides the historic territory of Ireland and separates more than a million Irishmen from a national government's just and beneficent rule."[35] Of course, that statement ignored the fact that the majority of the population in Northern Ireland did not feel that way and would have felt just as aggrieved at being separated from Britain. De Valera and others, however, continued to look at the unionists of Northern Ireland as a minority within greater Ireland. De Valera said that he did not wish to coerce Protestants to live in a Catholic country, but that he regarded it as unfair that Protestants should coerce Catholics in Northern Ireland to remain in the United Kingdom against their will. He continued to pressure the British government to end partition. The prime minister of Northern Ireland, Viscount Craigavon responded that he did not believe that partition resulted in any serious problems.

If each of the above-mentioned qualities made the Irish experience somewhat unique in the 1930s, in other ways, the people of Ireland shared in the general experience of the economic depression that afflicted so many countries. The Irish Free State experienced a 20.2 per cent decline in external trade in 1933 alone, in comparison with the previous year.[36]

Almost quietly, Ireland adopted a new constitution in 1937, which changed the name of the Irish Free State to Éire or Ireland (the two names are interchangeable, thus it is perfectly appropriate to use Ireland when writing in English since they mean the same thing). Under the new constitution, the main executive authority would be known as the Taoiseach, based on an ancient Gaelic word for "chief," while the president would be the official and ceremonial head of state. De Valera resigned the presidency of the executive council and became Ireland's first Taoiseach. De Valera specifically expressed the desire that the state reflect the unique characteristics of the Irish people. The constitution redefined Ireland's relations with the United Kingdom. While it did not at that time end the connection with Britain, it did declare that Ireland would henceforth participate in the British Commonwealth as an

---

[34] *The Irish Times*, 6 March 1936.
[35] *The New York Times*, 1 October 1938.
[36] *The Irish Times*, 3 February 1934.

equal and independent member that would make its own decisions on foreign policy. Ireland, in fact, stopped sending representatives to Commonwealth conferences at that point. At that time, no proposal was made to abolish the parliament in Belfast or to change the relationship between Britain and Northern Ireland. And the External Relations Act of 1936 still recognized Ireland's connection to the British monarchy.

Relations between the United Kingdom and the Irish Free State

Throughout the 1920s and 1930s, the relationship between the United Kingdom and the Irish Free State was tentative, ill-defined, and filled with underlying tension on both sides, neither of which was quite sure of the other's sincere desire for friendship. In 1932, the Irish Minister for Finance, Ernest Blythe defined that relationship as one of "friendship and co-operation, so far as co-operation was possible."[37] Britain showed little interest in the situation in Ireland, after Irish concerns had dominated British politics to a large degree for the previous 50 years. Britain's control over certain naval bases in Ireland was one reminder that the Free State had not yet achieved total independence. There did remain some sticking points in the relationship between the two. The leaders of the Free State resented the fact that she was still required to repay money loaned decades earlier to help Irish tenants to buy their own lands. This had been a provision included in the Anglo-Irish Treaty of 1921. De Valera unilaterally decided to cease making these annual payments of about £3 million in 1933. Britain retaliated with a 20 per cent value-added tax on all produce imports from Ireland and an even higher tariff on cattle. This set off a chain of retaliatory measures on both sides that came to be known as the *economic war*. Irish farmers were hurt economically, but they soon compensated by growing more produce that could be sold at home instead of concentrating on raising cattle for the export market. Coming in the midst of depression, inflation caused by the economic war hurt the Irish consumer.

Ireland and the United Kingdom were still tied together economically, whether they liked it or not. The Irish printed their own money, but its value was tied to that of the British pound sterling. The United Kingdom remained Ireland's primary trading partner. In 1933, 69.9 per cent of imports into the Free State came from Britain or Northern Ireland, while 94.1 per cent of the Free State's exports went to the United Kingdom, up from an already high 88 per cent in 1924.[38] Both sides eventually recognized that the economic

---

[37] *The Irish Times*, 4 January 1932.
[38] *The Irish Times*, 3 February 1934 and Roy Foster (1988), *Modern Ireland, 1600–1972*, London: Allen Lane, p. 522.

war was in neither one's interests and they reached a compromise agreement in 1938 in which Britain cancelled the annual payments required of Ireland in exchange for a negotiated payoff amount.

As for relations with Northern Ireland, some organizations—such as sports leagues and the Irish Trades Union Congress—simply ignored the boundary. But the issue of Northern Ireland remained the stickiest aspect of the relationship between Ireland and the United Kingdom. It did not help that in the North Craigavon still had a connection with the paramilitary organization known as the Ulster Special Constabulary. It did not help that anti-Catholic prejudice remained high in the North nor that Catholics found it difficult to get jobs from unionist employers. Some issues thus remained unresolved when, in September 1939, the relationship between Britain and Ireland would change again when Britain declared war on Germany in response to an invasion of Poland that marked the beginning of World War II.

Ireland during World War II

De Valera and Ireland chose to remain officially neutral during World War II, which was known there as *the Emergency*. The Irish people in the South, including most Protestants, were largely behind de Valera's decision to keep Ireland out of the war, as were most other Irish political leaders. The one prominent exception was James Dillon, who opposed neutrality largely on moral grounds based on his hostility to fascism. De Valera no doubt saw the war as another opportunity to sever the historical links between Britain and Ireland and to affirm Ireland's ability to chart its own course. He did not see what Ireland had to gain by its involvement in the war, perhaps remembering all of the Irish soldiers who had died for the British Empire in World War I and other past wars with no tangible gain for Ireland.

Irish neutrality posed some problems for Britain, especially at the beginning of the war. British intelligence officers worried about the possibility that neutral Ireland might be fertile ground for active hostility against the British because of the past history of anti-British sentiment and the continuing controversy over partition. The IRA was a particular concern, since it could potentially be supported and used by a foreign power against the British. Exaggerated reports from loyalist contacts in Ireland did nothing to alleviate their concerns. On at least one occasion, the British considered military intervention in Ireland on the basis of these reports.

But neutrality did not mean total apathy or indifference in Ireland about who won the war. On the one hand, there were some far right pro-German groups that formed in secret during the war, providing some justification to British paranoia about Ireland. The IRA actually did have contacts with

Germany during the war and still considered Winston Churchill more of an enemy than Adolf Hitler. But R. M. Douglas argues that these groups were more motivated by political discontent at home than by formal links with Fascists or Nazis on the European continent.[39] On the other hand, Alvin Jackson estimates that 50,000 Irishmen and women voluntarily joined the British armed forces during the war.[40] Others went to Britain to work, as they had in World War I.

The more dominant theme of the Irish response to the war, however, centered on the efforts of the Irish government and people to cooperate and even assist Britain as the war went on, despite never relinquishing their official neutrality. British and Irish intelligence agencies cooperated to ensure Ireland's security from foreign invasion and to constrain the activities of the IRA.[41] The Irish people at the time had no knowledge of this, or much else about the war and Ireland's connection to it because of political censorship, which Mary Kenny describes as "so misleading about actual events as to be effectively mendacious."[42] But de Valera supported this co-operation and privately knew that the world would be better off if Britain won. De Valera shared with Dillon a sincere devotion to the Catholic faith and his hostility to fascism. If he would not actively assist the British, he would make sure that his country would do nothing to hinder their victory. And, as Alvin Jackson points out, in some instances, active assistance was provided. For example, the Irish made available a strip of land known as the Donegal Corridor for British military aircraft, which were needed to protect allied ships from German U-boats. Lough Foyle was used as a safe haven for allied vessels as needed and served as the site for the scuttling of German U-boats after the war. Yet, because of the intense atmosphere of political censorship, Dillon was excoriated for his pro-British views and was rejected by his own party, while de Valera remained the fierce protector of Irish neutrality and independence in the public mind. This does not mean, however, that de Valera was actually a secret agent working for the British, as a recent book has claimed.

The fact that Northern Ireland could be relied upon to protect the Atlantic sea-lanes to Britain actually made it less imperative to both Britain and Ireland that the South enter the war in its own right. Convoys arriving from the United States could be diverted around Northern Ireland instead of taking the southern route to the Irish Sea. By contrast, the efforts of both

---

[39] R. M. Douglas (2006), "The Pro-Axis Underground in Ireland, 1939–1942." *Historical Journal*, 49, 1155–83. http://www.jstor.org/stable/4140154.

[40] Alvin Jackson (2010), *Ireland, 1798–1998: War, Peace and Beyond*, 2nd edn. Oxford: Wiley-Blackwell, p. 299.

[41] Michael Kennedy (2008), *Guarding Neutral Ireland: The Coast Watching Service and Military Intelligence, 1939–1945*. Dublin: Four Courts Press, p. 310.

[42] Kenny, *op. cit.*, p. 191.

sides to draw either Spain or Portugal, both of which were also neutral, into
the war—or at least to prevent them entering on the opposite side—was a
much greater priority than Ireland because the Iberian Peninsula occupied
such a strategic location that if either Spain or Portugal had entered the war
it could have tilted the balance one way or the other.

Prior to the start of the war, the leadership of Northern Ireland displayed
no desire to see war break out in Europe. Prime Minister Craigavon sent a
congratulatory message to Neville Chamberlain on his return from Munich in
September 1938 after he had reached an agreement with Hitler and famously
proclaimed "peace in our time." But, as in World War I, Northern Ireland once
again proved completely loyal to Britain once war came. The war fostered
an even closer relationship between Northern Ireland and Britain. At the
same time, the war exacerbated the tense relations between the South and
Northern Ireland. There was some resentment in the North toward the policy
of neutrality in the South, perhaps best exemplified by Louis MacNeice's
poem, *Neutrality*, which refers to an island that preferred to face the Atlantic,
while ignoring to the east "A continent, close, dark, archetypal sin." But
support for the war in Northern Ireland was not unanimous or as strong as
it was in Britain, sometimes to the great frustration of Sir Basil Brooke after
he became prime minister in 1943.[43] Northern Ireland experienced a level
of political censorship that rivaled that in any other country though, so any
opposition to the war was likely to go unreported. Nationalists in Northern
Ireland, of course, were not nearly as likely to be as sympathetic to the
war as Protestant unionists. As a belligerent, Northern Ireland shared with
Britain the experience of coming under aerial attack and the destruction of
lives and property by enemy bombs. According to one report, only 51,127
houses in Northern Ireland did not need repairs costing more than £200,
out of a total of 323,052 homes.[44] One by-product of the bombings was the
flight of thousands of Belfast residents into the countryside, where these city
dwellers experienced something of a culture shock. The rural communities
had difficulty accommodating them all, and the government in Stormont
was reluctant to provide much assistance because they disapproved of the
response of those who had fled. Some went so far as to cross the border into
Southern Ireland, where they received immediate assistance, perhaps to the
dismay of the authorities in the North. The South also dispatched firemen
to assist their counterparts in Belfast, while an *Irish Times* editorial of April
1941 commented that "the people of Ireland were united under the shadow
of a national blow."

---

[43] Brian Barton (1995), *Northern Ireland in the Second World War*. Belfast: Ulster Historical
Foundation, p. 120.
[44] Diarmaid Ferriter (2004), *The Transformation of Ireland*. Woodstock and New York: The
Overlook Press, p. 445.

Northern Ireland thus ended the war, like much of the rest of Europe, battered and much in need of economic and physical recovery. The South was not as badly damaged and, despite its policy of neutrality, had found ways to contribute to the Allied victory. The fact that it had maintained that policy throughout the war helped to prepare the way for what came next in its evolving relationship with the United Kingdom.

CHAPTER THIRTEEN

The two Irelands in the post-war period

In the Name of the Most Holy Trinity, from Whom is all authority and to Whom, as our final end, all actions both of men and States must be referred, We, the people of Éire, humbly acknowledging all our obligations to our Divine Lord, Jesus Christ, Who sustained our fathers through centuries of trial, gratefully remembering their heroic and unremitting struggle to regain the rightful independence of our Nation, and seeking to promote the common good, with due observance of Prudence, Justice and Charity, so that the dignity and freedom of the individual may be assured, true social order attained, the unity of our country restored, and concord established with other nations, do hereby adopt, enact, and give to ourselves this Constitution.

– Preamble to the Irish Constitution of 1937

1949—The creation of the Republic of Ireland

The Irish Republic officially came into existence in 1949 with the repeal of the Executive Authority Act. Also known as the External Relations Act, the Executive Authority Act had affirmed the ties between the Irish Free State and the British monarchy in the wake of Edward VIII's abdication crisis in 1936. Surprisingly, it was not Eamon de Valera, and his Fianna Fáil party, who presided over the birth pangs of the Republic, but John Costello of the opposing and more conservative Fine Gael party. In 1948, when the Fianna

Fáil party of de Valera did not gain enough seats in the Dáil Éireann to form a government, Costello was selected to head a coalition government as a compromise candidate for the position of Taoiseach. It was this coalition that introduced the bill to repeal the External Relations Act in the Dáil Éireann in 1948, with de Valera helping to pave the way by suggesting that the act could be repealed simply by introducing a new bill.

The only indication that such a bill was forthcoming, however, was a speech that Costello had made on a visit to Ottawa that September. But this measure had already been preceded by a virtual declaration of independence in the form of the Constitution of Ireland adopted on 1 July 1937. The new government accepted wholesale the 1937 Constitution. Article 1 of that document declared that "The Irish nation . . . affirms its inalienable, and sovereign right to choose its own form of Government, to determine its relations with other nations, and to develop its life, political, economic, and cultural, in accordance with its own genius and traditions."[1] Of course, this formulation could mean different things to different people. To some, it meant exclusive use of the Gaelic language and the forsaking of English in schools and the public arena. Knowledge of Gaelic was already an entrance requirement at the National University of Ireland, meaning that the vast majority of its students were Catholics. But while some looked to the past and emphasized the preservation of Irish traditions, others looked to the future and stressed the intent to "develop" its political, economic, and cultural life. If the creation of the republic was almost universally accepted as the natural outcome of the events that had preceded it, this did not mean that the future course of the history of the republic was a historical inevitability as well.

Despite varying opinions about the future, the creation of the new republic did not mean an immediate alteration of the circumstances of most people's daily lives. The government of the new republic did undertake some initiatives that would contribute to change in the future, if not immediately. For example, the creation of an Industrial Development Authority eventually drew interest from foreign investors after an initial period of inefficient administration. In addition, a series of public health measures was introduced that virtually wiped out tuberculosis as a major threat within a few years. However, in several important ways, the 1937 constitution had set the tone for an attempt to preserve a relatively static society, particularly in the areas of religion, family life, and the role of women.

First, religion remained a foundation of the new Irish state. The creation of the Irish republic did not usher in an age of religious equality or promote a religiously pluralist society. Secondly, the constitution went so far as to affirm the rights of the family as "inalienable and . . . superior to all positive law," while recognizing it as the "primary and fundamental unit group of society."

---

[1] Constitution of Ireland (1937), http://www.constitution.ie/reports/ConstitutionofIreland. pdf.

It furthermore committed the Irish republic to "protect the family . . . as the necessary basis of social order." This emphasis on the inviolability of the family led to a political controversy concerning those at the Department of Health who advocated imitating Britain's creation of a National Health Service and moving toward a welfare state. Costello, in fact, would oppose public health proposals for Ireland put forward by the physician Nöel Browne (1915–97), who as minister of health from 1948 until 1951 wanted to introduce free medical services for mothers and children. Thirdly, 1949 did nothing to create a new role for women, whose place was in the home, according to the constitution itself, which stated that "by her life within the home, woman gives to the State a support without which the common good cannot be achieved." That document committed the state to ensuring that mothers, in particular, "shall not be obliged by economic necessity to engage in labor to the neglect of duties in the home."

So what, if anything, did 1949 mean to the people of Ireland? Did the Irish people, as the *Lowell Sun* in Massachusetts reported on 19 April of that year, become "at long last . . . a totally free people?" The creation of the Republic was of special interest in places like Lowell, which had a sizeable Irish-American population. In fact, the 1937 constitution had gone so far as to recognize "a special affinity with people of Irish ancestry living abroad." Therefore, the declaration of the republic had reverberations around the world.

But were its effects exaggerated? The Republic of Ireland had officially severed its ties with the British Commonwealth, but did this involve a new birth of freedom or merely a formal recognition of a fait accompli?

De Valera himself gave a speech in the Dáil on 24 November in which he emphatically stated that "We here today are *not* proclaiming a republic anew; we are *not* establishing a new state . . . We are simply giving a name to what exists—that is, a republican state."[2] Furthermore, de Valera went on to accuse Costello of calling too much attention to the republic, at the risk of provoking opposition in England and Northern Ireland, by making the repeal of the External Relations Act seem more significant than it actually was. In fact, 1949 can be viewed as both an end and a beginning in Irish history. On the one hand, it marked the culmination of nationalist aspirations for independence that dated at least back as far as O'Connell. On the other hand, it created a new set of problems, with the most obvious one being the position of the new government toward the counties of Northern Ireland that had remained within the United Kingdom. Irish leaders needed to decide whether the republic would focus on its own internal affairs and on smoothly making the transition into the European and international community of nations or whether they would imitate Italy at the end of World War I and focus on Ireland *irredenta* (unredeemed Ireland).

---

[2] Maurice Moynihan (ed.) (1980), *Speeches and Statements by Eamon de Valera*. Dublin: Gill and Macmillan, p. 508. (italics mine).

Liberalism and nationalism had been closely aligned in the first half of the nineteenth century in the age of O'Connell. In the second half of the nineteenth century, however, these two forces had divided revolutionaries and proven to be unreliable allies. The leaders of the new Irish republic had the benefit of the hindsight of history, including the destructive uses to which nationalism had been put in the world wars of the twentieth century. They knew that an uncompromising commitment to nationalism and the unification of the island could jeopardize everything that they had waited so long to gain. Furthermore, the republic had even more to lose in the form of aid and recognition from the United States as part of the postwar recovery assistance program known as the Marshall Plan. The United States was not prepared to give the republic carte blanche to continue on a path of isolation and neutrality in the early stages of the Cold War between the United States and the Soviet Union. One indication that Ireland was moving out of its isolationist phase was the adoption of a liberal policy toward accepting refugees from the European continent, despite the reservations of some government officials, specifically in the departments of justice and industry and commerce.[3] This policy had been foreshadowed during the war by de Valera's expressed willingness to accept French, Jewish, and Dutch child refugees, even if only on a temporary basis. Between the beginning of 1946 and the middle of 1947, 462 child refugees arrived in Ireland, including 421 German children.[4] But it was the decision to accept a loan as part of the Marshall Plan (see below) that gave Ireland something more in common with other Western European nations and did the most to bring the new republic out of its isolation. This process continued in 1955 when Ireland joined the United Nations, once again under Costello's leadership. In 1958, the republic sent unarmed troops to Lebanon in its initial participation in a UN peacekeeping mission.

Therefore, on the one hand, the new leaders of the Irish government seemed to understand that the interests of the republic were probably best served by not stirring up the thorny issue of partition at that time. By not doing so, not only would their international relations benefit in a way that would have positive economic repercussions for the new state, but the government would be free to concentrate on internal improvements and solving its own problems. If Ireland wanted to become part of Europe, it would have to overcome the stigma of remaining embroiled in a nineteenth-century nationalist conflict that seemed out-of-date to many outsiders in the new postwar Europe. On the other hand, the republic had accepted the 1937 constitution, which recognized everyone born on the island as belonging to the Irish nation. This verbiage gave little satisfaction to the republican

---

[3] Dermot Keogh (1998), *Jews in Twentieth-Century Ireland: Refugees, Anti-Semitism and the Holocaust.* Cork: Cork University Press, p. 207.

[4] Ibid., p. 209.

nationalists in Northern Ireland who refused to accept the 26-state republic because it did not include them or the whole island. The constitution provided for the creation of a united Ireland, but only if it occurred "by peaceful means with the consent of a majority of the people, democratically expressed, in both jurisdictions of the island." In other words, the question was left wide open and completely unresolved.

Meanwhile, in Westminster, the British parliament once again found itself navigating through the narrow waters of recognizing the nationalist aspirations of the Irish people without alienating or abandoning the unionists in Northern Ireland who wished to remain part of the United Kingdom. The British Parliament initially responded to the creation of the Republic of Ireland with the Ireland Act of 1949, a curious piece of legislation that refused to recognize Ireland as a foreign country or its citizens as aliens within the UK. More significantly, the act affirmed Northern Ireland's position within the UK until such time as its own parliament would decide otherwise. This law stunned the newly formed Irish government.

In response, various parties in the republic formed the Mansion House Committee to oppose partition, but with little effect. Costello believed that the committee's ineffectiveness was partly the result of de Valera's half-hearted support for an initiative in which he was not in the lead.[5] De Valera's public statements, however, were all in favor of ending partition. He even gave a speech in the Dáil supporting a resolution proposed by Costello denouncing the British parliament's Ireland Act. Yet nationalist republicans had little success mounting a political challenge to the unionists in the North. In 1949, the unification of Ireland seemed as far away as ever, based on the positions of the governments in both Dublin and Westminster. But it was the issue of partition that was at the forefront of people's minds in the early years of the republic. It was not going to go away any time soon.

Comparison between the situation in Ireland and British problems in India and the Middle East

When approached exclusively from an Irish perspective, the British response to partition might seem conservative, even reactionary, in attempting to hold on to Northern Ireland at a time when they had already begun divesting themselves of colonial responsibility elsewhere. From the British perspective, it was their experiences with that process of divestment, particularly in India and the Middle East, which helps to explain their handling of the Irish

---

[5] John Bowman (1982), *De Valera and the Ulster Question, 1917–1973*. Oxford: Clarendon Press, p. 273.

situation. Ireland itself had reached a stalemate over the issue of partition by 1949. The end of partition did not have majority support in Northern Ireland, and neither the British nor the Irish republic itself was willing to support unification without that majority support. Political remedies in Northern Ireland seemed doomed to failure.

In Britain, the new Labor government headed by Clement Attlee had many important items on its agenda after it took power in 1945; the British position in Northern Ireland was not at the top of its list. The Labor Party had prevailed in the 1945 election primarily because after World War II people who had grown weary of international commitments were ready for a government to focus on domestic policy. The Attlee government respected that mandate, but still had to preside over the transition to independence in India and to manage or wind down British commitments in the Middle East. Other British colonies such as those in Africa could wait, but Indian independence was not only widely anticipated in India, but was also on the postwar agenda of the two emerging superpowers—the United States and the Soviet Union.

The main job of the Attlee government was to ensure that the new India would not be hostile to the many British people who still lived and hoped to remain there nor to British interests in general. Conservative opposition to independence remained intense until the very end, but they had no effective base from which to challenge the Attlee government in the immediate aftermath of the war.[6] The central problem with the transition was the presence of a sizeable Muslim minority who did not wish to be ruled in a democratic state that would always guarantee a Hindu majority on the basis of demographics. The British preferred that India remain united; the problem was what to do about those Muslim areas, such as Hyderabad and Junagadh that were not located at a distance from a proposed Muslim state in the north. Lord Mountbatten (1900–79), the British viceroy in India at the time, dismissed the notion that either Hyderabad or Junagadh might unite with Pakistan as "just stupid."[7] The British did not want to leave India in a state of violence, but remaining in power there was no longer a choice.

Events in India had begun to take on a life of their own. In order to facilitate strong relations with the new Indian government, Attlee favored cooperation with the majority Hindu Congress Party, which was poised to take over. But this alliance angered the Muslim minority, as Attlee's critics in the Conservative Party were quick to point out. The Muslims rebelled, leading to a civil war that left the country divided into two states, a predominantly

---

[6] See Nicholas Owen (2003), "The Conservative Party and Indian Independence, 1945–1947." *Historical Journal*, 46, 403–36.

[7] Ian Copland (1991), "The Princely States, the Muslim League, and the Partition of India in 1947." *International History Review*, 13, 40.

Hindu India and Pakistan, where Muslims constituted a majority of the population. The British had been unable to leave India in peace or to negotiate a settlement that would have saved hundreds of thousands of lives. In the end, however, Atlee's hopes were rewarded when both India and Pakistan opted for remaining within the British Commonwealth, though Pakistan did not join until 1953.

So, when the issue of partition started to gather steam in Ireland in 1948 after the formation of the coalition government and de Valera's fall from power, the British were wary. The repeal of the External Relations Act at first caught Attlee off guard, and his initial response was to guarantee the presence of Northern Ireland within the United Kingdom unless the parliament in Belfast voted otherwise. This guarantee was important against the background of Britain's recent withdrawal from India where Hindus and Muslims were left to fight a civil war that ended in partition and the situation in Palestine, where Britain could be seen as having abandoned the Palestinians as a permanent minority within the newly created state of Israel. When republican nationalists began to employ violence directed at British rule in Northern Ireland, the British were not inclined to simply go away, as they more or less had in India and Palestine.

In fact, the trend toward decolonization favored British withdrawal from Northern Ireland. But, for all their similarities, there were important differences between Northern Ireland and India or the Middle East. Both Muslims and Hindus in India were undeniably Indian, and no one could claim that Palestinians did not belong in the Middle East. However, the Protestants of Northern Ireland had an identity crisis rooted in their claims to be both British and Irish that did not exist in these other parts of the world. As Stephen Howe put it, there is "no direct Middle Eastern equivalent for the ambivalences displayed by both British and Irish about the relationship of Irishness to Britishness."[8] The line between Arab and Jew, or even Hindu and Muslim, was drawn much more sharply than that between Irish and British in Northern Ireland.

India had remained a member of the British Commonwealth after 1947, bound by long historical ties but now with an opportunity to forge a new relationship that placed the two nations on a more equal footing. The same opportunity existed for the Irish republic, but an even longer history, closer proximity, and the thorny issue of the continued presence of Northern Ireland within the United Kingdom all greatly complicated relations between the United Kingdom and the new Irish republic. Ironically, Irish nationhood was finally achieved in 1949 at a time when the whole concept of nationalism was becoming increasingly outdated in the context of the European situation following World War II. The Irish writer James Cousins (1873–1956), who had spent time in both Ireland and India, became a leading proponent of

---

[8] Stephen Howe (2000), "The Politics of Historical Revisionism." *Past and Present*, 168, 242.

internationalism that put him at odds with many of his fellow countrymen.[9] To Cousins, assertions of Irish nationalism were not the appropriate response to an end to colonialism, a cause which he very much supported. Cousins had seen important parallels between India and Ireland, even if his ideas were not fully embraced in either place. Unlike India, Ireland did not choose to remain within the British Commonwealth, but that decision did not mean that the republic could cut all ties with the United Kingdom, any more than Scotland or Wales could have if they had become independent. In addition, the powerful ideals of international cooperation in Europe exercised a centripetal force on both Ireland and the UK.

Relations between the United Kingdom and the Irish Republic

The first step in this direction came with Ireland's participation in the Marshall Plan. This was regarded as critical by the British government because of Ireland's importance to the British economy. From the treasury department, Otto Clark, who headed the finance division, said in January 1948 that: "It is pretty well the truth to say that it is more important to us that Eire should receive adequate aid than it is for Eire herself."[10] The decision of the republic to accept Marshall Plan aid led it in the direction of furthering a relationship with the United States, the United Kingdom, and the British Commonwealth. The Republic of Ireland then joined the Committee for European Economic Cooperation as a first tentative step toward greater integration into Europe after the decision to accept Marshall Plan aid. The next big foreign policy decision for the republic came when it faced a decision on whether or not to join the newly formed North Atlantic Treaty Organization (NATO) in 1949.

At first, the leaders of the republic balked at joining NATO, a defensive alliance primarily formed in response to the growing power of the Soviet Union in Eastern Europe. Costello attempted to make the desire to unify the island a point of negotiation, even as de Valera opposed joining under any circumstances based on his firm commitment to Irish neutrality. In addition, the people of the republic were not prepared to see the nation relinquish much of its sovereignty so soon after becoming fully independent. On the other side, Ireland had to overcome the resentment on the part of some

---

[9] Gauri Viswanathan (2004), "Ireland, India, and the Poetics of Internationalism." *Journal of World History*, 15, 7.

[10] Quoted in Daniel Davies (2004), " 'It is more important to us that Eire should receive adequate aid than it is for Eire herself': Britain, Ireland and the Marshall Plan," in T. Geiger and M. Kennedy (eds), *Ireland, Europe and the Marshall Plan*. Dublin: Four Courts Press, 66.

in Britain and the United States over the fact that Ireland had benefited from the Allies' defense of the island and ultimate victory in World War II, despite Eire's position of neutrality in the war.[11] Winston Churchill certainly felt this way, but he had been voted out of office, so it was easier for Ireland to overcome this opposition. In the end, Ireland did not join NATO, but the leaders of the new Irish government remained fully aware of the importance of Britain to the Irish economy. The British also continued to recognize the importance of Ireland as a trading partner.

In short, neither the Irish republic nor the British government wished to cut all ties with each other, primarily for economic reasons. In addition, the people of Ireland and Britain spoke the same language, had in common a number of cultural similarities, and possessed, in many respects, a shared history. The British Nationality Act of 1948 had placed Irish citizens of the UK in an entirely separate category from British subjects or aliens. This was important because Irish immigrants continued to flood into Britain after World War II, roughly 55,000 a year between 1946 and 1961. By 1966, about one million people born in Ireland resided in Britain, more than any other external nationality at that time.[12] On the one hand, the Nationality Act could have been seen as an affront to Irish residents of Britain, but on the other hand, it reflected the recognition that Britain had a special relationship with Ireland that it was unwilling to either dissolve or define very clearly.

In March 1956, however, under the initiative of the minister of finance, Gerard Sweetman, the republic began to impose higher import duties. The goal, as reported by Ireland's ambassador to Britain at the time, Frederick Boland, was to redress the unequal balance of payments between the two nations through higher taxes on British goods entering Ireland.[13] The fact that the British parliament had committed itself in 1949 to Northern Ireland remaining in the UK ensured that relations with the republic would be strained at best for the foreseeable future, despite their mutual economic interests. Tensions always simmered just below the surface. Sweetman's initiative was a unilateral attempt to change the nature of the republic's economic relationship with Britain. It demonstrated that the republic—no longer a member of the British Commonwealth—was capable of pursuing its own economic policy at the expense of Britain. But even this policy had its roots more in the stagnant nature of the Irish economy in the 1950s than in any animus that was still felt toward Britain. Furthermore, this policy did not prove such a boon to the Irish economy as was expected; by the end

---

[11] Michael Kennedy and Eunan O'Halpin (2000), *Ireland and the Council of Europe.* Strasbourg: Council of Europe Publishing, p. 17.

[12] Kathleen Paul (1996), "A Case of Mistaken Identity: The Irish in Postwar Britain." *International Labor and Working Class History*, 49, 11.

[13] Gary Murphy (2003), *Economic Realignment and the Politics of EEC Entry: Ireland, 1948–1972.* Dublin: Maunsel and Company, p. 50.

of the decade, the finance ministry was looking for new ways to improve the economy. These included the possibility of establishing an even stronger economic relationship with Britain.

When Seán Lemass (1899–1971), who had already abandoned his previously held isolationist views, took over as Taoiseach in 1959, he immediately began to explore closer economic ties with Britain as a first step toward greater integration with Europe.[14] In fact, Lemass's main foreign policy initiative in the early 1960s consisted of the talks with the UK that would lead to the Anglo-Irish Free Trade Agreement of 1965. The close economic relationship between the republic and the United Kingdom ensured that if the UK joined the European Economic Community (EEC), then the republic would likely follow. It is no coincidence that both applied for membership for the first time in 1961 or that they would both join at the same time at the beginning of 1973. The rejection of their applications in 1961 only made it more important that the two nations cooperate economically and form an important part of the background to the Free Trade Agreement of 1965.

Only in the 1970s did the economic interests of Britain and Ireland begin to diverge. But the spirit of cooperation, which had lasted for decades and was best exemplified in the Anglo-Irish Free Trade Agreement, had paved the way for harmonious relations on other issues in the future, including the problem of Northern Ireland. The Republic of Ireland had, in effect, charted its own course in foreign and economic policy independent of the goals of the nationalists whose main priority was the end of the division of the island. Nationalist sentiment, however, only increased as a result of the republic's apparent acceptance of the status quo, which continued to be characterized by a stark division between the North and the South.

The legacy of Eamon de Valera

As long as Eamon de Valera was alive and at the center of Irish politics, the Ulster question would remain at least in the background, if not at the center, of Irish politics. De Valera, who had become the leader of Sinn Féin in 1917—the same year that Lenin carried out the Bolshevik Revolution in Russia—would serve as president of the republic until 1973. But de Valera knew, perhaps better than anyone, the difficulties involved in ending partition and finding a solution that would allow for the unification of Ireland. He was not willing to let those difficulties get in the way of the establishment of an independent Irish republic, with or without Ulster. Even though the independence of the republic had become official while he was out of office,

---

[14] D. J. Maher (1986), *The Tortuous Path: The Course of Ireland's Entry into the EEC, 1948–73.* Dublin: Institute of Public Administration, p. 93.

most people knew the role that he had played in bringing it about. De Valera himself had this to say on 24 November 1948:

> We did not believe in the blowing of trumpets, and we did our work quietly in most of these matters because we wanted to achieve the results; and if the Government today can blow trumpets on the position which obtains, they may thank those who worked quietly and were prepared to do the work without the fanfare.[15]

Shortly after the independence of the republic had become official, however, in June 1951, de Valera once again found himself at the head of a minority government. He was 69 years of age at the time. He resumed office in the midst of a controversy over the forced resignation of Noel Browne, the minister of health. Browne's proposed "mother and child" legislation was too upsetting for some members of the recently founded Clann na Poblachta Party ("Party of the Republic") and its leader Seán MacBride (1904–88), former chief of staff of the IRA. The party's withdrawal of support for the government helped to lead to its collapse. However, others bristled that Browne had been forced to resign over the issue. Browne had simply wanted to make free medical care available to all children (under the age of 16) and their mothers. De Valera's government followed the lead initiated by Browne and guaranteed hospital care not only for mothers and children but also for about 85 per cent of the population that fell beneath a certain income threshold.[16] The Health Act of 1953 drew the ire of the Vatican and the hierarchy of the Catholic Church. The church ostensibly objected to the state's assumption of the responsibility for the health of mothers during childbirth and removing fathers and the family from the decision-making process.[17] But the real opposition to the Health Act came from a blind reaction against a proposal that seemed to resemble communism, despite the fact that socialized medicine was becoming widely accepted throughout the rest of Western Europe. Most notably, in Britain, the National Health Service seemed to be working just fine under the new Labor government without any signs of an imminent communist takeover. Undeterred by the criticism, the Irish government went one step further in 1957 by establishing a Voluntary Health Insurance Board, through which people could purchase insurance providing extra coverage that would allow them to select their own physician and make up the difference in what was not covered under the 1953 Health Act.

---

[15] Moynihan (ed.), *op. cit.*, p. 510.

[16] Ruth Barrington (2003), "Governance in the Health Services," in D. de Buitleir and F. Ruane (eds), *Governance and Policy in Ireland: Essays in Honour of Miriam Hederman O'Brien*. Dublin: Institute of Public Administration, p. 106.

[17] Dermot Keogh (1995), *Ireland and the Vatican: The Politics and Diplomacy of Church-State Relations, 1922–1960*. Cork: Cork University Press, pp. 337–8.

Despite failing eyesight and advancing age, de Valera still displayed the stamina and discipline to function effectively as Taoiseach. Nonetheless, in 1954, de Valera, who was unwilling to form a coalition government, was once again replaced by John Costello. The *New York Times* labeled this a "serious defeat" for de Valera, even though his party still had the largest representation in the Dail. Costello did form a coalition government that promised financial assistance to workers and farmers, while lowering taxes and increasing social benefits. But Ireland's economy did not permit the achievement of these ambitious goals. One might have thought de Valera's career over, but he regained office in 1957, at which time he announced his support for European integration. Knowing that Ireland was not quite ready for such a step, however, he introduced the concept of a "two-speed Europe," according to which Ireland would be among those who would join the European Community later. He also continued to speak out against partition, telling the Dáil in 1958 that it was "an injustice to a large section of the Irish people if not to the whole nation."[18] But this did not mean that he supported the IRA raids across the border with Northern Ireland. In fact, he had become unpopular with university students and others who sympathized with the IRA because of a proposal to change the basis of representation in the Dáil in a way that was likely to reduce the number of representatives from Sinn Féin. On 17 June 1959, de Valera announced his resignation from the position of Taoiseach and his candidacy for the presidency of the republic. When he stepped down as Taoiseach, there was a sense among some, the nationalists in particular, that he had left his job unfinished because Ireland remained partitioned.

After he became president in 1959, de Valera no longer exercised control over the day-to-day affairs of the country, but his past experience, leadership, and reputation gave his presence in office a great symbolic importance. Furthermore, his voice would still matter on the larger issues confronting the country. His continued support for European integration was particularly important and made it easier for the government to apply for membership in the Common Market. He remained optimistic, telling a reporter in October 1962 that he thought the future of Ireland looked brighter than at any other time in his "conscious 75 years of life." His hope for Ireland at that time was that it would become "a tiny piece of cosmopolitanism."[19] Irish politics had lost something with de Valera largely out of the picture though, despite his occupancy of the presidency. Comparing de Valera with his successor as Taoiseach, Dermot Keogh has written that:

Lemass was a good manager, but he was not a particularly good personnel manager. He lacked de Valera's infinite patience and father-confessor

---

[18] Moynihan (ed.), *op. cit.*, p. 586.
[19] "De Valera, at 80, Says Outlook for Ireland is Best in Memory," *New York Times*. 14 October 1962.

skills, which kept backbenchers happy and feeling as if they were an important part of the team and not just lobby fodder.[20]

But de Valera also remained a controversial figure, only winning reelection as president in 1966 (at the age of 83) by a narrow margin (just over 10,000 votes out of more than a million cast) over the Fine Gael party candidate, Thomas F. O'Higgins. De Valera's legacy is, in fact, a complicated one. At times supportive of the IRA and its members, he was much more willing to compromise for the sake of political expediency, to consolidate gains even if he could not achieve everything he hoped for. In the past, he had sanctioned violence when it served his purposes, but he had come to the conclusion that violence was not the way to end partition and bring about the unification of Ireland. In World War II, he refused to support the British, but drew the line at accepting financial support and arms from Hitler, a stance that angered those in the IRA who did just that. He always regarded partition as wrong, but after independence, he refused to press the issue despite his earlier insistence on enshrining this as a goal in the Irish constitution. This was partly because of his renunciation of violence and partly because of his desire that Ireland's problems be solved by the legal authority of the Irish government and not by paramilitary freelancers, of whom he said that they "were not authorized to act on behalf of the Irish nation." He opposed the extremist tendencies of the IRA and had even imprisoned some of its members and executed others in the late 1950s. These actions made him the target of hunger strikes, a tactic that would be later used with great effect against the British government in Northern Ireland. His principles extended to his refusal to exploit his prominence in Irish politics for personal gain. He lived modestly, while demonstrating personal integrity in office. He did not look kindly on those who did not live up to his standards. Even as president, he took a more active role in politics than was expected from someone holding the position at that time. But, as his narrow victory in the 1966 election demonstrated, many people in Ireland were ready to move beyond the political issues that had brought de Valera to prominence dating back to the Easter rebellion.

The Irish Republic in the 1960s

As the Republic of Ireland entered the 1960s, new cultural forces were beginning to challenge traditional social, economic, and religious views. Ireland was ready to move forward, partly by rejecting its identity as a rurally based, agricultural society. Ireland and East Germany had been the

---

[20] Dermot Keogh and Andrew McCarthy (2005), *Twentieth-Century Ireland: Revolution and State Building* (revised edn). Dublin: Gill and McMillan, p. 258.

only countries in Europe in which the size of the population had actually declined during the baby boom period of the 1950s, although in the case of Ireland this was almost entirely because of emigration.[21] The 1950s had largely been depressing years for the new republic, tempering some of the enthusiasm that had accompanied independence. But the 1960s opened amid a new wave of optimism, based on signs that the economy was improving due to a healthy combination of increased tourism, industrial growth, and a rise in overseas investment in the country.

As we have seen, economic growth was one of the top priorities of Seán Lemass, who started to view government as essential to its promotion. If Ireland was going to stop losing population because of its inability to employ its people, then more jobs needed to be created first, after which the additional workforce would become consumers that would help sustain economic growth. Lemass had introduced his five-year Program for Economic Expansion, otherwise known as the Whitaker Report, in 1958. Industrial growth averaged 8½ per cent a year in 1961 and 1962, followed by another 5 per cent increase in 1963.[22] Most of this growth occurred in the industrial sector, but the Agricultural Institute had also been created to promote research that would help Irish farmers make the transition to commercial farming. Ireland's main export commodity in the mid-1960s was beef. Irish society was undergoing a profound transformation within a relatively short period of time. Tourism received a boost in July 1965, when the Tourist Boards of the North and the South united to promote Ireland as a whole as a desirable destination for tourists from around the world. This had seemed inconceivable just a year before, prior to the rapprochement between Lemass and Terence O'Neill, prime minister of Northern Ireland. The new Irish republic was starting to grow in strength and confidence.

Lemass's government would still face challenges, however, and cultural change could not be achieved overnight. Resistance to his government came from a variety of sources. For example, Ireland's participation in a UN peacekeeping mission in the Congo in 1960 signaled its involvement in world affairs, but sending two battalions of Irish soldiers created a firestorm within the country among those who cherished Ireland's tradition of neutrality and were upset about Ireland's involvement in such a mission. This crisis led Lemass to call a premature election in October 1961 in order to gain a vote of confidence that would allow him to continue in office. Then, in 1962, a Council of Education report stated that the primary goal of the curriculum was to foster "the religious, moral, and cultural development of the child,"[23] a policy not entirely consistent with the government's modernizing agenda.

---

[21] Mary E. Daly (2006), *The Slow Failure: Population Decline and Independent Ireland, 1922–1973*. Madison: University of Wisconsin Press, p. 183.

[22] Paul Bew and Henry Patterson (1982), *Seán Lemass and the Making of Modern Ireland, 1945–66*. Dublin: Gill and Macmillan, p. 165.

[23] Finnegan and McCarron, *op. cit.*, p. 107.

Furthermore, when the government decided to add fluoride to the public water supply in Dublin, a woman named Gladys Ryan, who had given birth to five children born between 1950 and 1960, challenged the decision in court. She appealed to the Supreme Court of Ireland in 1965 on the grounds that it was her personal responsibility to manage the health of her children and that forced medication was a violation of her own personal integrity. She lost her case, but voiced a traditional resistance that many people had to government interference in people's lives. Also in 1965, the prominent economic commentator Garret Fitzgerald (1926–2011) wrote an article questioning the government's attempt to regulate the economy, arguing that Ireland had adopted "a vocational-bureaucratic system of government" that had empowered civil servants at the expense of parliamentary democracy.[24] Lemass's policies faced opposition from the Labor Party as well. Ireland lost more working hours to strikes in 1964 than any other country in the world.

Furthermore, social and cultural progress remained tied to the success of the Irish economy, which did not yet have a completely firm foundation. First, one problem was that it would take some time to build or attract a skilled labor force adapted for the jobs required in a modernized economy. Secondly, Ireland remained too reliant on trade with Britain. In 1964, Britain, in an effort to address its own trade imbalance, raised tariffs to 15 per cent, hurting Irish exports. The British decreased the tariff to 10 per cent in 1965, but this was still too high for many Irish industries. The economy experienced another downswing in 1966, largely as the result of a British seaman's strike, which hurt both trade and tourism. And Lemass could only do so much without the cooperation of the Dáil, which was not always forthcoming. Lemass tried to convince the Dáil and others that the government was attempting to improve the economy without forcing people to do anything against their will, but he sometimes faced an uphill battle. Nonetheless, Ireland under Lemass did make significant economic strides and emerged from the 1960s both a more urban and a more industrial nation. He had the support of the middle class and, in time, the trade union leaders came around. Lemass had taken a country that even in the 1950s identified nationalism with the right of the individual to own land and the promotion of local industry and made it a more prosperous and economically developed state. And he had done it largely through the employment of Keynesian strategies (named after the English economist John Maynard Keynes) by which the government promoted industrial growth in export industries without interfering directly with the free market economy.

Significant strides were made in education as well. A new commission on education was appointed in 1962; 3 years later, the commission released its report, "Investment in Education," which has been called "one of the most important documents in the history of modern Ireland." Before change

---

[24] Bew and Patterson, *op. cit.*, p. 145.

could be made, it was first important to recognize that there was a problem, which was made evident in this study, which revealed the high percentage (45 per cent) of classes in secondary schools that had more than 45 students. Irish classrooms were overcrowded despite the fact that many children in the countryside did not attend school because they lacked transportation to get there. The latter problem was rectified by the new minister for education, Donagh O'Malley, who was appointed in 1966 and who initiated a series of reforms that included sending buses into rural areas and increasing the mandatory age for attendance from 13 to 14.[25] Progress on reducing class size occurred more gradually; in 2006, the average primary school class in Ireland contained 24 students, but this was still one of the largest numbers among European countries, and many classes still had over 30 students.

Among the new cultural forces of the 1960s was the beginning of a women's movement in Ireland similar to others that were emerging throughout Western Europe and the United States at the same time. The Irish manifesto for the new feminism might have been Edna O'Brien's 1960 novel, *The Country Girls*, which detailed the lives of young single Irish women striking out on their own in the big cities of Dublin and London. In 1968, a group of Irish women responded to an initiative by the United Nations Commission on the Status of Women by petitioning the government to examine discrimination against women in Ireland. The government responded by forming its own commission, preparing the way for a number of social and legal reforms that benefited women in the 1970s (see Chapter 15).

Also in keeping with the times, there was the beginning of a new openness about sexuality, perhaps best reflected in John McGahern's 1965 novel, *The Dark*, which centered on the struggles of a young Catholic boy to navigate the passages of adolescence without a mother. But Irish officials did not respond as favorably to this development. McGahern's novel was banned and led to his dismissal from his teaching position. Still, exploring the legacy of Catholic culture and its effects on people, which had been a theme in Irish literature since James Joyce (1882–1941), had been given new life by McGahern, who would become one of Ireland's most accomplished novelists, even though he left Ireland for England and, eventually, the United States.

In the republic, then, the 1960s was a decade of progress and change, but the main political issue remained its relationship with Northern Ireland. The leaders of the Fianna Fáil Party divided over the issue of Northern Ireland, where increasing violence associated with protests demanding civil rights for Catholics ushered in a period that would become known simply as *the Troubles*. The partition question had never really gone away, despite the different historical paths that the "two Irelands" had taken in the postwar period.

---

[25] Brian Fallon (1998), *An Age of Innocence: Irish Culture, 1930–1960*. New York: St. Martin's Press, p. 109.

The North-South divide

The growth of a more militant nationalism would eventually manifest itself in Ireland in the late 1950s and 1960s. People who are committed to an idea often become desperate once they see any hope for the fulfillment of that idea slipping away. Terrorism is usually an act of desperation—a last resort. Once the republic had become official without Northern Ireland being a part of it, nationalists feared that if this boundary were accepted now, it might become permanent. Furthermore, the formal division of Ireland between the North and the South only widened the differences between them. This realization was probably what led to an increase in activity on the part of the IRA in the mid-1950s, though they had carried out an arms raid on Ebrington Barracks in Derry/Londonderry as early as June 1951. This new wave of activity started with a stunningly successful raid on Gough Barracks in June 1954 (in which an IRA member posed as a guard while arms were loaded on a truck[26]) and culminated in the border campaign lasting from 1956 to 1962 known as *Operation Harvest*.

Operating out of centers in the south, such as Wexford, the IRA members would surreptitiously vanish for a week or more to participate in the raids on the North. It would have been fairly obvious to friends and neighbors who belonged to the IRA, though most said nothing about it and would not have admitted it openly to anyone. Others knew little and cared less, occupied with their own problems and day-to-day struggles. Northern Ireland was rapidly becoming another country, which was exactly the problem as members of the IRA and their supporters saw it.[27]

In 1948, when he became prime minister, John Costello had offered the unionists in the North "any reasonable guarantee" if they would agree to support the unification of Ireland.[28] The unionists, however, had their own agenda and viewed 1948 as an opportunity to affirm their commitment to staying within the United Kingdom—and to seek a reciprocal guarantee from the British government. Far from being interested in obtaining guarantees that would allow them to comfortably join the republic, they were interested in clarifying the relationship between the North and the South in light of the developments of 1948–49. The creation of the Irish republic had galvanized unionist political sentiment in the North at exactly the same time that nationalist sentiment in both the North and the South was becoming more divided. The unionists made it clear that Ulster was "not for sale." When

---

[26] Tim Pat Coogan (2003), *Ireland in the Twentieth Century*. New York: Palgrave Macmillan, p. 462.
[27] John Banville (2004), "Memory and Forgetting: The Ireland of de Valera and Ó Faoláin," in D. Keogh, F. O'Shea and C. Quinlan (eds), *The Lost Decade: Ireland in the 1950s*. Cork: Mercier Press, p. 22.
[28] Bowman, *op. cit.*, p. 267.

the IRA raids began in the early fifties, the unionists became even more defensive and looked to Britain for protection. Basil Brooke (1888–1973), who dominated politics in Northern Ireland for two decades as prime minister from 1943 to 1963, was not averse to appealing to the fears of Protestants by taking a hard line against those who supported unification. Liam O'Dowd has observed that the creation of a national boundary between the North and the South led each to develop "homogenized and antagonistic official cultures—one Protestant, British and proimperial, the other Catholic, Gaelic and anti-imperialist."[29]

Not only did the unionists of the North resist unification with the South for fear that they would become a Protestant minority in a predominantly Catholic country, they cited economic reasons as well. The North liked to portray itself as more economically prosperous and implied that union would be a drain on the Northern Irish economy that would cost workers jobs. Since the start of World War II, the South had experienced an economic downturn characterized by higher unemployment rates and more people emigrating to seek jobs elsewhere. In this respect, Northern politicians could convince themselves that Catholic workers in Ulster were better off than they would have been under the republic. Brooke, a Protestant, did not believe in giving the Catholic minority any special consideration.

Since the nineteenth century, Northern Ireland had been more heavily industrialized than the South and had become even more so during World War II. Factories in the North worked at full tilt to meet wartime demand. In 1950, only one of every six workers in Northern Ireland did agricultural labor.[30] The South was not only more rural, but its population tended to be less educated, partly because Northern Ireland benefited from the Education Act of 1944, which provided free secondary education for all young people throughout the United Kingdom. The participation of the Northern Irish economy in the postwar boom of the 1950s contrasted with the sluggish economic performance of the republic during the same period. Northern Ireland benefited economically from its membership in the UK, with its broad international trading connections, while the republic struggled economically despite its tentative steps toward integration in the European Community. For the republic, rejoining the UK was out of the question, but closer ties with the UK and Europe were not. Of course, this meant some degree of acceptance of the partition of Ireland and reconciliation with the fact that Northern Ireland was an independent political entity. Therefore, the reversal of the isolationist economic policy of the republic in the late 1950s had

---

[29] Liam O'Dowd (2005), "Republicanism, Nationalism and Unionism: Changing Contexts, Cultures and Ideologies," in J. Cleary and C. Connolly (eds), *The Cambridge Companion to Modern Irish Culture*. Cambridge: Cambridge University Press, p. 88.

[30] Diarmaid Ferriter (2004), *The Transformation of Ireland*. Woodstock and New York: The Overlook Press, p. 453.

political overtones as well and helped to reinforce the division of Ireland between North and South.

The problem with just letting the North go its own way was that Catholics there were subjected to a form of discrimination that one prominent Irish historian has compared to the system of apartheid that prevailed in South Africa at that time.[31] Protestant politicians sought to isolate the Catholic minority by gerrymandering electoral districts in such a way that ensured control of the government by the Ulster Unionist Party and using their influence to orchestrate a stronger police presence in Catholic areas. In May 1955, the UUP announced that it would oppose any attempt by a member of the Sinn Féin party to take a seat in the House of Commons, even if they won an election.

Strong sentiment for unifying the island existed overseas, especially among Irish-Americans who believed that a strong injustice had been committed with the political division of the island. Many of them wished to see all of the Irish people united as one. John Kelleher, a professor of Irish Studies at Harvard University, argued in *The Atlantic Monthly* in April 1954 that partition was holding back both the North and the South and preventing Ireland from developing a healthy society. In Ireland, in the absence of strong leadership from the politicians on the issue of union, the IRA attempted to bridge the North-South divide, operating in both places.

On 14 January 1965, Seán Lemass travelled to Northern Ireland to meet with its prime minister, Terence O'Neill. This was a significant development, because only a year earlier Lemass had angered O'Neill by visiting Britain and making a statement which said, in effect, that he had the impression that the British government was ready to drop its commitment to partition. But their first meeting went well and the two met again in Dublin several weeks later, on 9 February. The talks with O'Neill were connected to Lemass's attempts to strengthen the Irish economy that led to the Anglo-Irish Trade Agreement that same year. For his part, O'Neill sought both a rapprochement with the republic and a diminution of tensions between Catholics and Protestants in Northern Ireland. About 3 years later, Lemass's successor, John Lynch (1917–99) and O'Neill held another round of talks in each other's capitals, once again looking to improve the relationship between the two states and promote increased trade and tourism between them. Better political and cultural relations and closer economic ties between the North and the South, of course, did not preclude the possibility of creating a more liberal, tolerant society that had the potential to improve the lot of Catholics in Northern Ireland. But by then, the rupture between Catholics and Protestants in Northern Ireland had become too great to be quickly overcome.

---

[31] Coogan, *op. cit.*, p. 298.

Cultural divisions within Northern Ireland

Partition had thus reinforced the cultural divide in Northern Ireland at the same time that it contributed to the political division of both North and South. While what was known as *the Ulster question* lingered as a political issue in the republic, the Protestant leaders of the Ulster Unionist Party showed no interest in bridging the gap between the two cultures in Northern Ireland. Their primary concern was to prevent the spread of republican ideals in the North, which led them to regard any Catholic as a potential enemy of the state. Segregation of Protestants and Catholics was rigidly enforced, not only as a result of blind prejudice but because it made it easier to monitor and contain any rebel activity. To advocate for Irish unification was still tantamount to treason against Northern Ireland and the United Kingdom in the eyes of the unionists. Catholics, for example, were not even permitted in the 1950s to commemorate the Easter Rebellion with any kind of public demonstration or to wear symbols, such as an Easter lily, associated with it. Furthermore, in 1955, the Unionist Party made clear that it would oppose the legality of any elections won by members of the Irish Republican party, Sinn Féin. In fact, Sinn Féin had actually made it clear that its members would not sit in the House of Commons even if they were elected to do so. Sinn Féin was committed to a policy of demonstrating that they did not regard the British government in Northern Ireland as legitimate. Unionists had reason for concern because Sinn Féin was gaining support from nationalists in areas where Protestants were not in the majority, such as Fermanagh in the southwest.

At the same time, the Unionist Party sought to keep Protestants of different classes united by giving them a feeling of all belonging to a single culture. This had become more challenging in the postwar period, however, as social divisions and economic concerns threatened to trump the unifying forces of politics and religion. The introduction of the welfare state and the labor policies of Basil Brooke helped to reinforce the notion that the Unionist government represented the interests of the working class. But this feeling became harder to maintain in the 1960s, when unemployment rose to 7.3 per cent in 1968 even though the government had continued to invest heavily in industrial development; at that time, the comparable figure for the rest of Britain was 2.4 per cent.[32] The economy of Northern Ireland had been hurt by a general economic downswing throughout the United Kingdom that had begun in 1966 when the Labor government initiated a policy aimed at reducing a deficit in the country's balance of payments with the rest of the world. But this still does not explain the wide disparity between the unemployment rates in Northern Ireland and the rest of Britain.

---

[32] John M. Lee (1968), "Unemployment Grows in Northern Ireland," *New York Times*, June 24.

That Northern Ireland was treated like a stepchild by the government in Westminster was something that rankled for some unionists, even though they were fully committed to remaining within the United Kingdom. For example, one common complaint centered on the Anglo-centric nature of most BBC programming that was aired in Ulster.[33] But unionists could not have it both ways. They could not promote Ulster's affinity with Britain and at the same time promote a stronger sense of national cultural identity that would have undermined their unionist stance. Was Northern Ireland British or Irish? Was it both? Was it neither? Since the unionists had such a hard time answering these questions, and because of the class divisions that had accompanied the growth of industry, they needed another source of cultural identity around which their supporters could rally. They found it in religion.

The Protestant clubs and orders that had proliferated in the North since partition relied on symbols and demonstrations to reaffirm their identity and their vision for Northern Ireland. Annual July marches to commemorate the anniversary of the Battle of the Boyne of 1690 gloried in the defeat of the Catholic King James II by the Protestant hero, William of Orange (William III). It seemed as if the Protestant unionists were doing everything they could to reinforce the cultural differences in Northern Ireland and to deliberately provoke Catholic resentment. Catholics who could not get jobs and depended on welfare received little sympathy, while being viewed as parasites on the Protestant state. Discrimination in the hiring of Catholics had become a major issue by the 1960s. Unemployment among Catholics was higher than among Protestants in every city of Northern Ireland.[34]

It would be misleading, however, to portray the Catholics of Northern Ireland as a passive, helpless minority just waiting for their deliverance by the IRA or the government in Dublin. The 1960s saw a growth in political consciousness on the part of Catholics that would make them an increasingly important factor in the politics of the region in the 1970s.[35] This could have been partially the result of the Education Act of 1944, which did not discriminate against Catholics. Some Catholics began to see reform within Northern Ireland as the answer instead of looking to unification with the republic as a panacea for their problems.

At that time, Catholics represented approximately 35 per cent of the population of Northern Ireland. The western part of Northern Ireland tended to contain more Catholics, while Protestants predominated in the east. Cities such as Belfast and Derry/Londonderry were divided into a hodgepodge of clearly delineated Catholic and Protestant streets and neighborhoods.

---

[33] Ferriter, *op. cit.*, p. 456.
[34] Richard B. Finnegan and Edward T. McCarron (2000), *Ireland: Historical Echoes, Contemporary Politics.* Boulder: Westview Press, p. 290.
[35] Alvin Jackson (1999), *Ireland, 1798–1998.* Oxford: Blackwell, p. 366.

Catholics and Protestants thus lived in close proximity to one another in the major cities while living in relative isolation from each other. They avoided contact as much as possible and traveled in their own social circles, but their living so close together made the isolation seem forced and peculiar. It also made some contact inevitable and an eventual conflict seem more likely.

In April 1966, Terence O'Neill worried about the possibility of open violence between Catholics and Protestants as the fiftieth anniversary of the Easter Rebellion approached. O'Neill called up 200 policemen from the reserve force of the Royal Ulster Constabulary and marshaled an additional 11,000 civilians who belonged to a group known as the Special Ulster Constabulary as insurance against mob violence. Border areas received special attention to prevent an influx of IRA members from the South. Easter passed without violence, but tensions did not abate after the holiday had come and gone. During a royal visit by Elizabeth II in July, protesters hurled a bottle of stout and a chunk of concrete at the queen's car. Then the 1966 parades on the anniversary of the Battle of the Boyne drew an estimated 50,000 Protestant marchers. Banners flew containing such slogans as "Kick the Pope" and "Rebels Keep Out."[36] This was the first year that the Reverend Ian Paisley (b. 1926), who had recently formed his own Free Presbyterian Church, introduced to the world at large his particularly vitriolic blend of unionist politics and religious fundamentalism. Paisley denounced the Catholic Church as an international power still intent on destroying the Protestant faith. He had no use either for the moderate policies of Terence O'Neill or the ecumenical movement within Christianity that had begun to gain ground in the 1960s. He contributed to a growing atmosphere of fear and distrust that erupted into open violence 2 years later.

On 12 July 1968, protesters disenchanted with O'Neill's leadership of the Unionist Party disrupted a speech by George Forrest, a member of the British parliament from Northern Ireland. They knocked him unconscious when they stormed the stage from which he was speaking. Forrest was speaking in favor of O'Neill's moderate policies when he was attacked. The political atmosphere was becoming tense and O'Neill's hopes for moderation seemed to be losing ground.

The situation was made worse by how hard hit the western part of the country was by the economic downturn. At that time, Derry/Londonderry had an unemployment rate of 14.5 per cent, about twice the national average. This was partly the result of the priority that the government had attached to stimulating economic and industrial growth and improvements to the infrastructure of the east, particularly Belfast, where unemployment was actually lower than the national average. Since the end of World War II, 69,000 new jobs had been created in Northern Ireland, most of them in the 250 new factories, the largest number of which were located in Belfast.

---

[36] Dana Adams Scmidt (1966), "Northern Ireland is Tense as Elizabeth Leaves," 6 July.

In the decade leading up to 1968, 72,000 jobs had disappeared, many of them in agriculture and older industries such as shipbuilding and linen manufacturing.[37]

By October, open violence—the worst since the 1920s by some reports—erupted between Catholics and Protestants in Derry/Londonderry. Police openly clashed with Catholic protesters who had begun to demonstrate for civil rights, leaving about 100 people injured. O'Neill's worst fears that had dated back to 1966 had at last become a reality. Northern Ireland was on the verge of a dark and troubled time.

---

[37] Lee, *op. cit.*

CHAPTER FOURTEEN

The Troubles: Northern Ireland, 1969–2000

*Dreaming in the night, I saw a land where no one had to fight
Waking in your dawn, I saw you crying in the morning light . . .*

– PHIL AND JUNE COLCLOUGH, "Song for Ireland"

Northern Ireland and civil rights

The Troubles that afflicted Northern Ireland from 1969 until the end of the twentieth century have certainly become part of common knowledge about the island, and it would be easy to assume that they are merely part of a continuous history of violence and revolutionary activity that have come to be associated with a sad land. In many respects and upon close examination, however, there is a marked discontinuity between the history of Northern Ireland before and after the late 1960s. Furthermore, recent developments have provided hope that this period will eventually come to be seen as an anomaly and not as the rule for the six northern counties that remained part of the United Kingdom when the Republic of Ireland gained full independence in 1948. Nonetheless, for the generations that lived through the sectarian strife that afflicted Northern Ireland in the last three decades of the twentieth century, the Troubles seemed interminable and deeply rooted in the problems and deep divisions within their society. Those divisions were complicated by the presence of the British army, seen by many Catholics as a hostile, occupying force. Meanwhile, the more extreme Protestants in Northern Ireland saw the army as entirely too neutral in the Armageddon that was unfolding between bitter enemies, however much they wanted to remain part of the United Kingdom.

The world was changing in the 1960s, and it was perhaps inevitable that the winds of change would reach Northern Ireland, where Catholics still felt like second-class citizens in a Protestant-dominated society. Real discrimination existed, although, as the political activist Bernadette Devlin McAliskey has pointed out, if Catholics had held more positions of authority in business and government, then they would have discriminated against Protestants equally. Devlin accused both Catholics and Protestants of using "religion to divide and rule the working class."[1]

The Civil Rights movement sweeping the United States inspired persecuted minorities around the world, and in Northern Ireland, it aroused the Catholics to seek social and economic change. Marches for civil rights in 1968 attempted to call attention to the need for electoral reform, which was deemed necessary to address the social and economic grievances of the Catholic working class. The electoral system in Northern Ireland favored wealthy businessmen who had the right to cast multiple votes based on the size of their companies. Ireland still had a restricted franchise that was at odds with the "one-person, one-vote" standard common in most democracies; some had more than one vote while those who did not own or rent property (or were not married to someone who did) had no right to vote at all. This system disenfranchised poor Protestants as well as Catholics, but Catholics took greater offense since most businessmen were Protestants and the system excluded a higher percentage of Catholics. As in the United States, middle-class liberals and students joined the Civil Rights movement, exhibiting a profound belief that they could bring about a positive change in the world, starting with their own society. But in Northern Ireland, another group joined the movement with something of an ulterior motive. Although the nationalists sincerely supported civil rights for Catholics, they believed that the cause was linked to a larger problem: the continuing presence of Northern Ireland within the United Kingdom, which was preventing the six northern counties, often collectively referred to as Ulster, from uniting with the predominantly Catholic Republic of Ireland in the south.

However, the Protestant unionists vehemently opposed the nationalist agenda, which their more radical leaders, such as Reverend Ian Paisley, believed amounted to nothing more than a popish plot designed to enslave free Protestants under the tyranny of Rome and a Catholic Ireland. Beginning in the 1960s, Paisley used his pulpit in his Free Presbyterian Church of Ulster to radicalize opposition against any initiative designed to compromise union with Britain, as well as to launch his own political career. Many members of the Protestant working class, who otherwise might have shared the social and economic grievances of Catholic workers, became strong supporters

---

[1] Bernadette Devlin (1969), *The Price of My Soul*. New York: Alfred A. Knopf, p. 54.

of Paisley's anti-Catholic stance. Their employers, who were frequently Protestant, benefited from this lack of unity among their employees. Thus, they had had good reason not to oppose Paisley even if they did not actively support him.

In this way, the Civil Rights movement in Ireland became about much more than civil rights. Although it started with peaceful protest marches on the model of those sponsored by the Reverend Dr Martin Luther King in the southern United States, it quickly degenerated into clashes between Catholics and Protestants. Both sides were guilty of perpetuating violence. Paisley had openly stated his opposition to any concessions to Catholics and had previously initiated a riot in June 1966 aimed at Catholics in Belfast. Riots in Derry/Londonderry beginning in the fall of 1968 and continuing in 1969 marked a significant turning point in this regard. In Derry/Londonderry, Catholics had even more reason to resent discrimination because they constituted a majority of the population in that city. Many of them lived in squalid conditions in an area beyond the walls of the old city known as the Bogside. Inspired by the Civil Rights movement, they reacted hostilely to the Protestant marches moving through the city that seemed to flaunt their privileged position.

Once the British army intervened to quell the violence, the nationalist call for separation from Britain and denunciation of the Stormont regime that governed Northern Ireland seemed to take precedence over the original civil rights agenda. This was not necessarily intentional on the part of the nationalists, because events had a logic of their own. The British army arrived in Northern Ireland with a charge of maintaining peace on all sides. Army intervention stood to benefit the Catholics more than the Protestants because as of mid-August 1969 of those killed in the riots 4 out of 5 had been Catholic; Catholic-owned homes had accounted for more than 80 per cent of those destroyed or damaged.

Britain intervenes

In Northern Ireland, the riots of 1968–69 and the subsequent intervention by British forces led to the creation of a new organization that fused socialist and nationalist demands, the Social Democratic and Labour Party (SDLP). In many respects, it replaced the Northern Ireland Civil Rights Association (NICRA), which had become increasingly radical since its founding at the International Hotel in Belfast on 29 January 1967. Some nationalists had never quite accepted the NICRA because they had no desire to be linked by association with the African-American Civil Rights movement, either because of racial prejudice or because they wanted their cause to be viewed on its own terms. In addition, by 1970, the frequency of clashes between Protestants and Catholics in the Catholic area of West Belfast led to the revival of the Irish Republican Army, a paramilitary organization formed at first to protect Catholics against Protestant thugs. In response, Protestant loyalists created their own paramilitary group in 1971, the Ulster Defense Association (actually an amalgamation of several smaller vigilante groups already in existence) leaving Belfast essentially divided into two armed camps.

The IRA soon evolved into a terrorist organization and its goal shifted to ousting the British from Northern Ireland. It split into two factions in 1969: the Provisional IRA, which was more committed to revolutionary violence, and the "Official" IRA, which wanted to put pressure on the British to end partition without causing a civil war in Northern Ireland. Meanwhile, the Ulster Defense Association evolved in the same direction as the PIRA, with the goal of intimidating the Catholics and keeping Northern Ireland within the United Kingdom. The IRA's campaign against British rule corresponded with the concomitant occupation of the province by the British army, which was necessitated by the ineffectiveness of the Northern Irish police force, the Royal Ulster Constabulary (RUC) in the face of increasing sectarian violence.

The military presence of the British army, however, did not put an end to the bloodshed and strikes that were becoming increasingly commonplace and disrupting any semblance of normal life in Northern Ireland. Violence claimed the lives of 174 people in 1971, including some British soldiers, up from 25 deaths in the preceding year. In addition, bombings increased from 170 to 1,515, and the number of shootings rose from 213 to 1,756.[2] British paratroopers were stationed in Derry/Londonderry to maintain peace and order. In January 1972, they were called out to prevent a banned march from taking place. On 30 January 1972, a date that would henceforth be known as *Bloody Sunday*, several of them shot and killed 14 unarmed people. On 1 February, Brian Faulkner (1921–77), the head of the Northern Irish government at Stormont said:

> What is absolutely clear to all concerned is that, from the start, Sunday's events had potential for tragedy. Here was a city—Londonderry—in which policemen had been done to death only days before; in which gunmen were known to be active; which for many months had been subject to almost every kind of physical violence. Yet, in this situation, it was thought proper to encourage the assembly of many thousands of people to take part in a calculated defiance of the law ... It has been proven times without number that assemblies of this kind, including, no doubt, people of genuine and honest conviction, also inevitably attract a large hooligan element spoiling for a confrontation with the security forces ...[3]

---

[2] Gary McMichael (1999), *An Ulster Voice: In Search of Common Ground in Northern Ireland*. Boulder: Robert Rhinehart, p. 5.
[3] *The Stormont Papers* (1972), 84, 17–18. http://stormontpapers.ahds.ac.uk/index.html.

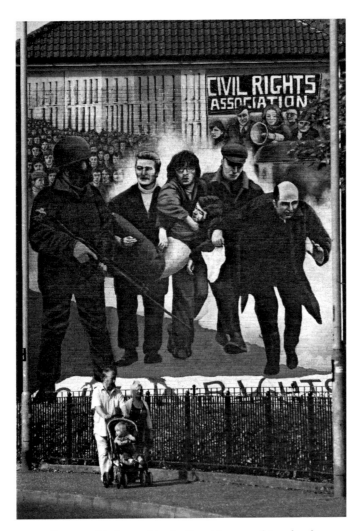

FIGURE 14.1 *This mural is located in the Bogside area of Londonderry near where the Bloody Sunday killings took place in 1972. Courtesy of Getty Images.*

Despite Faulkner's attempt to exonerate the army, from this point forward, Catholics perceived the British army as sympathetic to the loyalists and hostile to the nationalists, making it a target of future IRA attacks. In 1972, violence claimed the lives of almost 500 people in Northern Ireland, a figure that would never again be equaled for the rest of the period known as the Troubles.[4]

---

[4] David McKittrick and David McVea (2002), *Making Sense of the Troubles: The Story of Conflict in Northern Ireland.* Chicago: New Amsterdam Books, p. 76.

In 1969, the Home Secretary in the Labor government in Britain, James Callaghan (1912–2005) had proposed a way out of the crisis by granting Northern Ireland independence, but the idea was rejected because of the strong likelihood that civil war would ensue. In 1947, as was discussed in the previous chapter, the British had faced a similar decision in both India and Palestine and in both cases withdrew their forces, allowing India and Israel to gain their independence. In India, a civil war between Hindus and Muslims led to a horrendous death toll, while Israel was left to fight against the Arabs in the first Arab-Israeli war of 1948. The British decided against withdrawal in Northern Ireland at least in part because they did not wish to see a repeat of these similar situations so close to home. Furthermore, British withdrawal from Northern Ireland was complicated by the fact that, unlike India or Palestine, Northern Ireland was neither a colony nor a protectorate but, as Algeria had been to France, an actual province of the United Kingdom.

The Algerian War of Independence from 1954 to 1962 provides some additional interesting parallels with the situation in Northern Ireland. Against a backdrop of decolonization, the French found themselves in an untenable position in Algeria. In 1954, the French suffered a military defeat in their colony of Indochina (Vietnam) at Dien Bien Phu, a French military post near the border with Laos. After abandoning Vietnam, the French threw their military resources into defending their position in Algeria against the revolutionary organization, the FLN, or National Liberation Front. When the FLN began a terrorist campaign accompanied by an attempt at a general strike in Algiers in 1956, the French army intervened when the police called for assistance to maintain order. The French army attempted to crush the FLN by making mass arrests and using torture to extract information on the whereabouts of the organization's leaders. Finding themselves accused of using tactics similar to those that the Nazis had employed during World War II, French military authorities defended their tactics as necessary to bring an end to terrorism and to save innocent lives. At first, the French refused to give in to Algerian demands for independence out of consideration for the million or so Europeans who had made Algeria their home and based on the belief that the FLN spoke for only a minority of the Algerian people.

The British found themselves in a similarly untenable position in Northern Ireland in the 1970s because no matter what they did, they were going to make enemies of one side or the other. The British government had attempted to calm tensions with the passage of a Prevention of Incitement to Hatred Act in 1970, but this had obviously not worked. In stationing the British army in Northern Ireland, the best outcome the British could hope for was to maintain order long enough for a peaceful and democratic solution to emerge. In 1971, the Northern Ireland government headed by Faulkner had introduced, with the support of the British Prime Minister Ted Heath, a Special Powers Act that allowed British soldiers to arrest suspected terrorists and to detain them indefinitely without trial. But this left open the possibility of abuse of power. During the 1970s, the government of Northern Ireland would continue its policy of holding suspected terrorists without trial, while the British simply beefed up their military presence following the Bloody Sunday debacle. In August 1971, the British implemented an internment policy that was kick-started by "Operation Demetrius," an ill-fated spree of sweeping arrests that led to the imprisonment of 342 people. Not only were most of those arrested innocent of any terrorist activity, but the British based the arrests on faulty intelligence that left the new Provisional IRA largely untouched. The raids were aimed almost entirely at Catholics, leading thousands to flee their homes and others to turn to rioting in protest at this biased and inherently flawed policy—one that the British did not officially abandon until 1975.

In Algeria, when Charles de Gaulle, the heroic leader of the Free French during World War II and president of the newly formed Fifth French Republic, realized that independence did in fact have widespread support within Algeria and that France's honor and reputation were suffering internationally from what had become known as the *dirty war*, he came to the conclusion that France needed to leave Algeria. The problem for the British was that independence for Northern Ireland did not have the support of the majority of the population in Northern Ireland. Still, they knew that repression alone would not work and so attempted to foster a resolution of the grievances of all parties through a power-sharing arrangement that would include Catholics and Protestants—the so-called Sunningdale Agreement of 1973. Although representatives of the Unionist Party attended the negotiations that led to the agreement, the Ulster Unionist Council refused to endorse it. When the Ulster Workers' Council called a strike in May 1974, the resignation of the Northern Ireland Executive doomed the agreement and put the British and Northern Ireland governments back to square one.

The 1970s

In the meantime, Gerry Adams (b. 1948) had emerged in the leadership of the more militant Provisional IRA. Unlike the Official IRA, which was led by experienced leftists such as Roy Johnston, Toma MacGiolla, Cathal Goulding, and Sean Garland, the Provisional IRA appealed to a younger, action-oriented group that included Adams. The Provisional IRA refused to acknowledge the legitimacy of the governments of the Republic of Ireland or Northern Ireland because they did not accept the historical partitioning of the island. Adams described the events of the early 1970s as leading to "an increasing militarization of a problem that was essentially political." As for the Provisional IRA, Adams would write that it "organized, trained, adapted to changing circumstances, and developed a military stalemate with one of the most powerful and experienced armies in the world."[5] He described the relationship between the IRA and the Catholic people of Northern Ireland in the following terms:

> Closely knit with the Nationalist community, it was made up of the sons and daughters of ordinary people, its members indistinguishable from the rest of the community. Whether people in the Nationalist areas agreed or disagreed with the IRA and all its actions, they recognized it as their Army, knew for the most part which of the neighbors were members, and referred to it simply as the "RA".[6]

Even in 1972 at the height of the internment policy in Northern Ireland, the British seemed to recognize that any future settlement would need to include the Provisional IRA, just as the French were forced to negotiate with the FLN after they failed to crush that terrorist organization, following its defeat in the Battle of Algiers in 1956. In a shocking reversal of policy, the British government arranged for Adams's release from prison in June 1972, only months after his arrest, and invited him to London for clandestine negotiations.

The negotiations with Adams failed, and the remainder of the 1970s was characterized by increasing resentment by the Catholics of Northern Ireland toward the government there, particularly toward its policy of internment without trial. Their bitterness was fueled by the fact that Catholics interned under this policy overwhelmingly outnumbered Protestants (1,981 to 107) and by a contemporary report that largely exonerated prison authorities of abusive treatment of prisoners. "One could hardly allow an animal to remain in such conditions, let alone a human being," was the conclusion of Cardinal Ó Fiaich after he was permitted in August 1978 to visit the main prison where suspected terrorists, including Adams, were interned.[7]

Nor did it help that Paisley continued to turn up his pro-Unionist, anti-Catholic rhetoric, since 1970 as a Member of Parliament. Nonetheless, the number of large-scale demonstrations and protests decreased in 1973, possibly to avoid further conflict with the British army after the 1972 Bloody Sunday debacle and the escalation of tensions that continued for the rest of that year. On 5 October 1973, only 30 people showed up for a planned march to commemorate the fifth anniversary of a major civil rights protest march.[8] But this did not change the facts that Northern Ireland had become

---

[5] Gerry Adams (2003), *A Farther Shore: Ireland's Long Road to Peace*. New York: Random House, p. xxxiii.

[6] Ibid., p. 35.

[7] Ibid., p. 11.

[8] Anthony Craig (2010), *Crisis of Confidence: Anglo-Irish Relations in the Early Troubles, 1966–1974*. Dublin and Portland, OR: Irish Academic Press, p. 167.

divided into armed camps, negotiations with the IRA had collapsed, and no workable solution to the divisions was in sight.

The Provisional IRA had taken over the leadership of the nationalist movement, while the populist wing of the Protestant Orange movement had asserted itself as unwilling to cooperate with the British or Northern Ireland governments if it meant any kind of agreement that would allow Catholics a share of power. In a speech that he made shortly after Bloody Sunday, Paisley advocated that "the strongest possible measures be taken against the terrorists" or else Northern Ireland would experience "an escalation of violence which could bring this country down to the very depths."[9] By December 1974, however, the Provisional IRA was ready to make at least a gesture toward peace. On 20 December, the organization released a statement declaring "a suspension of offensive military actions in Britain and Ireland for the Christmas period." Merlyn Rees, the British Secretary of State for Northern Ireland, having learned of the proposed cease-fire from Protestant clergymen who had secretly met with representatives of the IRA, responded with a statement that "the Government has received . . . what it understands to be the Provisional IRA's proposal for a permanent ceasefire."[10] In response, Rees informed the British Prime Minister, Harold Wilson, that the government of Northern Ireland was releasing 20 internees and granting parole to an additional 50 prisoners. The IRA responded on 2 January with the statement that "while recognizing some minor developments as regards political prisoners and the role of Crown forces," they would extend the cease-fire only for another fortnight after which time it would expire. There would be no permanent cease-fire.

Behind the proposed cease-fire, however, was a growing realization among the leadership of the Provisional IRA that violence alone would not bring the desired result but had to be combined with other tactics. The Provisional IRA drew its political support from Provisional Sinn Féin, which broke from Official Sinn Féin in 1970, around the same time as the Provisional IRA had split from the Official IRA. Just as the Provisional IRA had eclipsed the Official IRA, Provisional Sinn Féin would surpass Official Sinn Féin in influence and importance during the 1970s. The SDLP, having withdrawn from participation in the government at Stormont in July 1971, also declined in influence with the rise of Provisional Sinn Féin. In general, Sinn Féin served as the political wing of the IRA and followed its lead, but they always remained two separate organizations. However, the leader of Provisional Sinn Féin in the 1970s, Ruairí Ó Brádaigh, was reputed to be a founding member of the Provisional IRA as well. In 1974–75, the Provisional IRA made it clear that they were willing to negotiate and they publicized

---

[9] *The Stormont Papers* (1972), 84, 133–4. http://stormontpapers.ahds.ac.uk/index.html.

[10] Public Record Office (1975), *Summary of Political Events in Northern Ireland for the Period 19 December 1974–9 January 1975.*

their demands, which included freedom of movement for its members, the end of all government-sponsored raids on Catholic buildings, homes, and lands, and a progressive withdrawal of all troops to barracks. Any cease-fire needed to be mutual and the army needed to act in good faith. The main goal of the British, however, was to secure a cease-fire agreement from the IRA without appearing to give in to terrorism, a goal that was going to be extremely difficult to achieve. Still, on 20 February 1975, Foreign Secretary James Callaghan sent a top secret telegram to the British ambassador to the Republic of Ireland indicating the government's willingness to gradually release those who had been detained without charge. By the end of the year, the policy of detention without trial had ended.

The 1970s were not without signs of hope. In 1976, Mairead Corrigan (b. 1944) and Betty Williams (b. 1943) received the Nobel Peace Prize for organizing the Community of Peace People in an attempt to bring about an end to the Troubles. Their organization brought Catholics and Protestants together in an attempt to find common ground that would further the cause of peace in Northern Ireland. But a mere desire for peace, no matter how sincere and well intentioned, was not enough to bring it about. The movement quickly dissolved over financial issues, organizational difficulties, and its failure to propose a realistic solution to the actual issues that divided the two sides.

The unionist movement was rather more divided than that of the nationalists, with a larger number of groups competing to represent the Protestant interest. Paisley's Democratic Unionist Party was merely the best known of the groups that split from the Unionist Party. Protestants in the countryside generally tended to be more liberal than those in the cities who had more frequent exposure to the tirades of politicians and lived in closer proximity to the declared enemy. But in the course of the Troubles, many Protestants, including a number of former members of the established Church of Ireland, migrated to the rabidly anti-Catholic party of Ian Paisley.

The IRA and Sinn Féin simply attempted to bypass the unionists to deal directly with the British government. Their ultimate goal was to force British withdrawal from Northern Ireland, but their more immediate goal was to get the British to acknowledge that the IRA was a political enemy fighting a war, not merely a gang of criminals. By 1977, not only had the British failed to live up to their promise to release imprisoned IRA members, but also they had begun a new campaign aimed at treating IRA terrorists as common criminals. The authorities, employing the same tactics that the French had used in their attempt to crush the FLN, began to use torture in the interrogations of prisoners at the new prison at Long Kesh—better known as the Maze—in an attempt to obtain incriminating information against other IRA members. Numerous arrests and convictions followed. Judges sentenced prisoners at clandestine trials during which no jury was present. Prisoners at the Maze protested against their treatment as common criminals, at first by refusing to wear prison uniforms. They used their blankets to cover themselves and became known as the blanket-men. They also refused to budge from their cells. They coated the walls of their cells in their own feces. None of this did much good, while on the outside, the Provisional IRA had been severely crippled by the new antiterrorism campaign, at least temporarily.

Suddenly, on 27 August 1979, the IRA began a new chapter in their campaign against the British when they carried out the assassination of Lord Louis Mountbatten, a retired World War II hero and member of the royal family, while he was aboard his boat off the coast of County Sligo. Eighteen British soldiers were killed on the same day. By the end of the year, the death toll from terrorism in Northern Ireland had risen to 125. Politically, 1979 was also extremely significant because in that year, the Conservative Party once again took power in Britain, now under the leadership of Margaret Thatcher (1925–2013). After the assassination of Lord Mountbatten, Thatcher, who assumed power with a no-nonsense approach to the myriad problems confronting the United Kingdom at that time, became even more determined to deal harshly with terrorism in Northern Ireland. A strong unionist, who had no desire to see Northern Ireland separate from the United Kingdom, she had once remarked that "Ulster is as British as Finchley," her constituency in north London. Her solution was to provide additional arms to the Royal Ulster Constabulary, a policy for which she sought the approval of the US President Ronald Reagan in February 1981. She also made it clear that she would not compromise with the demands of the blanket-men inside the Maze.

Margaret Thatcher and policy toward Northern Ireland

In October 1980, IRA prisoners had decided to employ a hunger strike as their main weapon to gain sympathy for their cause and force concessions from the authorities. As a consequence of the hunger strike, the British did agree to open negotiations over the issue of whether or not the IRA prisoners deserved "special category" status, which would distinguish them from other criminals. Their demands included the right to wear their own clothing, freedom from prison-related work, the right to associate freely with one another and to receive weekly visits and letters. But what was really at stake, as Gerry Adams reiterated in a speech in Derry in 2005, was the IRA's refusal to allow the British to define the terms of the struggle by criminalizing their opponents.

The British hoped somehow to end the hunger strike, but again without granting major concessions. Furthermore, they wanted the prisoners to end their hunger strike before negotiations could begin. The prisoners ended their hunger strike on 18 December, but on 1 March 1981, the IRA announced that prisoners at the Maze and at Armagh prison would resume their hunger strike until they were convinced that the British were acting in good faith.

The hunger strike resulted in a wave of popular support for the Provisional IRA and for the prisoners, particularly the 26-year-old Bobby Sands, who was elected to Parliament in a by-election that April. Before it was over, ten people had died, including Sands and six other members of the Provisional IRA.

The British responded to the hunger strikes by establishing a new assembly in Northern Ireland in 1981 to study the possibility of devolution of power, the idea of James Prior, the new Secretary of State for Northern Ireland. The Ulster Defense Association, however, had stepped up their attacks on Catholics and prominent supporters of Irish unification. It is important to remember that the problem in Northern Ireland was not one involving just the IRA and the British government. Danger and violence continued to stalk the people of Northern Ireland as the attitudes of all parties—the British government, the IRA and Sinn Féin, and the Protestant Loyalists—hardened. But in the mid-1980s, a couple of developments provided a glimmer of hope for the future. First, Gerry Adams, who was a little more open to dialogue even as he remained committed to the goals of the IRA, was elected president of Sinn Féin and gained election to the House of Commons in 1983. He refused to take his seat, practicing the old Sinn Féin policy of abstention as an additional form of protest. The second development was even more dramatic and led to a softening of the intransigent attitude of Margaret Thatcher.

In October 1984, the IRA exploded a bomb in Room 629 of the Grand Hotel in Brighton, where the prime minister had been staying during the Conservative Party Conference. She narrowly escaped death and seemed to emerge from the experience a changed woman. Actually, Thatcher had never sympathized with unionist extremists any more than she did with the IRA, but now she became convinced that repression and heightened security alone could not end the conflict in Northern Ireland. The IRA released a statement saying that "Mrs. Thatcher will now realize that Britain cannot occupy our country and torture our prisoners and shoot people in their own streets and get away with it."[11] The prime minister was not one to back down in the face of such threats; in fact, she continued to deplore the IRA and to work assiduously to undermine its bases of support. But she did understand that, however much she abhorred the IRA's tactics, their demands were rooted in legitimate grievances on the part of the Catholic minority. She may have simply reflected on what her legacy was going to be in Northern Ireland, but whatever the reasons, she decided to take an entirely different tack, with encouragement from Sir Robert Armstrong, a member of her Cabinet.

The desire of Margaret Thatcher and Garret Fitzgerald, the Taoiseach in the Republic of Ireland, to find a solution to the Troubles led to a series of talks that produced the Anglo-Irish Agreement in 1985. During the talks, the Secretary of State for Northern Ireland, Tom King, sought to reassure the Protestants in Ulster that Northern Ireland would remain part of the United

---

[11] Adams, *op. cit.*, p. 33.

Kingdom until such time as a majority of the people desired to become united with the republic. Although such a provision was written into the agreement, the British government had agreed to support legislation that would lead to the unification of Ireland should a majority in Northern Ireland vote in favor, a significant move away from Thatcher's previously strong commitment to unionism.

The Anglo-Irish Agreement, instead of locking Northern Ireland into a set timetable for independence, allowed for a gradual process in which the territory could acquire responsibilities for governance in stages. The agreement committed the British and Irish governments to continued meetings, the first of which were to focus on "relations between the security forces and the minority community in Northern Ireland," "ways of enhancing security cooperation between the two governments," and "seeking measures which would give substantial expression to the aim of underlining the importance of public confidence in the administration of justice."[12] Both the British government and the Republic of Ireland foreswore violence as a means of resolving the Troubles, Fitzgerald committing the republic to a condemnation of violence or the threat of violence as tactics that do not lead to success. Fitzgerald also made it clear that the agreement did not take sides in the dispute but recognized the validity of both the Catholic and Protestant traditions in Northern Ireland. In her speech to the House of Commons on 26 November, Thatcher acknowledged the death toll during the Troubles— then standing at about 2,500—and said that, although the deep divisions within Northern Ireland were real and could not be ignored, ending the violence had to be the country's top priority and that this could best be achieved by an agreement that recognized the rights of both communities. The commitment to end the violence was reaffirmed at the first Anglo-Irish Intergovernmental Conference held in Belfast on 11 December.

Such hopes, however, depended on the consent of the two opposing sides in the conflict, which was conspicuously missing from the Anglo-Irish Agreement. Thatcher expected the unionists to simply trust her on the basis of her past support for unionism. Her expectations were disappointed when the incumbent unionist Members of Parliament resigned to demonstrate their opposition to the agreement. Sinn Féin rejected the Agreement as well, and the IRA remained convinced that unionist intransigence made violence still necessary in order to achieve its objectives. After the discovery of over 100 Soviet- and East-German-made guns and 18,000 rounds of ammunition in Counties Sligo and Roscommon in February 1986, it was clear that the IRA was still at war. The only major party in Northern Ireland that did support the Agreement was the SDLP, headed by John Hume, who was willing to enter into negotiations to begin the process of devolution.

---

[12] British Information Services (1985), *Policy Statement: Northern Ireland: Anglo-Irish Agreement*. 15 November 1985.

Thatcher met with unionists, including Ian Paisley and James Molyneaux, the leader of the Democratic Unionist Party, in late February 1986 in an effort to include them in discussions about how to move forward. In March, she met with Church of Ireland bishops, at which time she expressed her hopes that unionists would participate in the process of devolution but stated emphatically that she was totally committed to the Anglo-Irish Agreement, unionist dislike notwithstanding. A general strike called by unionists two days later resulted in violence and intimidation and ended with disturbances that lasted into the night and resulted in injuries to 47 policemen and 57 arrests. These events led Sir Geoffrey Howe, the Secretary of State for Foreign and Commonwealth Affairs, to assert that "attempts to bring [the agreement] down by force cannot and will not be allowed to succeed. Those critics who condone bully-boy tactics, while at the same time proclaiming their attachment to democratic principles, seriously undermine their own credibility."[13] In the meantime, Thatcher found herself dealing with growing proof of increased support for the IRA from Libya and its military dictator, Muammar Gaddafi. A statement by Gerry Adams condemning US raids on Libya later that spring seemed to offer further confirmation of a strong connection between the two. Adams's new alliance may have had something to do with the conciliatory tone that Thatcher began to strike regarding the unionist opposition to the agreement at around the same time, despite how appalled she was privately at how little support unionists had given her and her Anglo-Irish Agreement.

Following the signing of the agreement, the Thatcher administration continued to try various means to bring the situation in Northern Ireland under control and to find solutions to the problems there. Tom King was dispatched to the United States in May 1986 to seek economic assistance for Northern Ireland and an agreement on terrorism and extradition policies. The Anglo-Irish Intergovernmental Conference continued to meet, focusing on issues of border cooperation and the administration of justice. The conference could do little to stem the violence that afflicted Northern Ireland beyond condemning it, however. The Republic of Ireland continued to support the Anglo-Irish agreement and to condemn those on both sides in the North who opposed it. In a speech at the Patrick Mc-Gill Summer School, Gemma Hussey, the Minister for Social Welfare, spoke forcefully about "both sets of extremists [who] fear and hate the Agreement . . . because they see that it has the capacity to deprive them of securing their only ambition which is to take and to hold power entirely in their hands." It seemed clear that talk alone was not going to bring an end to the Troubles without progress toward addressing the problems that led to them in the first place. In June, the Northern Ireland Assembly, which had been formed in 1981 to study the

---

[13] British Information Services (1986), *Policy Statement: Northern Ireland: Anglo-Irish Agreement*, 14 March 1986.

issue of devolution, was now dissolved because of lack of support from the unionist parties, Sinn Féin, or even the SDLP.

Despite the focus in the news on continued violence and the lack of an agreement, progress was made in some areas during the 1980s, and the government had taken some steps to address remaining problems. In July 1986, British Information Services reported that between 1980 and 1985, the number of Catholics employed in the Northern Ireland Civil Service had increased almost 6 per cent, although Protestants still comprised 59 per cent of the civil servants. It was an encouraging sign, too, that 48 per cent of civil servants between the ages of 20 and 24 were Catholics.[14] In September 1986, the British government endorsed "equality of opportunity of employment in Northern Ireland" and called for an end to discrimination of any sort, asking companies to sign a Declaration of Practice to that effect. Failure to do so would exclude them from the possibility of obtaining any government contracts. At the same time, the United Kingdom and the Republic of Ireland agreed to establish an International Fund for Ireland, which drew support from both the United States and Canada and was intended to support further economic and social development in both Northern Ireland and the republic. But the unemployment rate among Catholics was still double that of Protestants, with women in particular confined to low-paying and frequently part-time jobs.

Politically, Thatcher imposed a test oath on candidates for the Northern Ireland parliament at Stormont and for local offices in January 1989. Candidates were asked to foreswear support for terrorism or any organizations that used it. But this, too, did nothing to actually bring about an end to violence and the decade ended with little progress having been achieved toward a permanent solution for the Troubles in Northern Ireland.

In retrospect, the major shift that had occurred in British policy toward Northern Ireland during the 1980s was the beginning of a permanent commitment to devolution. While both major parties in Britain shared this commitment, the Labor Party was more open to devolution as a step toward the unification of Ireland and to forging a stronger relationship with the government of the republic. Furthermore, nationalists in Ireland were not the only ones interested in devolution from the United Kingdom at the beginning of the 1990s. Devolution had become a popular topic in Wales and Scotland as well.

Parallels with Scotland and Wales

The history of devolution in Scotland and Wales provides some perspective on the constitutional position of Northern Ireland within the United Kingdom.

---

[14] British Information Services (1986), *First Report on Religious Affiliations within the Northern Ireland Civil Service*. 29 July 1986.

The National Party of Scotland had first raised the issue in 1928, but at that time, the party consisted of disparate elements that lacked unity. In 1934, it merged with the Scottish Party to form the Scottish National Party. But the SNP failed to achieve significant electoral gains in the 1930s and ceased to play a major role for the next two decades. In the mid-1960s, however, nationalist parties in both Wales and Scotland began to garner attention and elected their first representatives to Parliament. These movements led Prime Minister Harold Wilson to establish a Royal Commission in 1968 to study the possibility of devolution for these two regions. In 1973, the Commission advocated separate legislative assemblies and executive authorities in Scotland and Wales in its report.

However, by then, the problems in Northern Ireland had swamped the government, while interest in devolution waned in both Scotland and Wales during the 1970s. The Welsh Nationalist party, Plaid Cymru, did gain some seats in Parliament in a 1974 election, but never really caught on with a majority of the Welsh population, most of whom were content to remain part of the United Kingdom. The SNP gained 11 seats that same year, but a 1979 poll did not show widespread support in Scotland for independence. For almost the next two decades, the ruling Conservative Party froze the issue, but the unpopularity of the Conservative government in Scotland led to a renewal of interest in devolution among many Scots, particularly after the introduction of a controversial poll tax in 1989. When the Labor Party finally regained power in 1997, the issue was reopened. In fact, devolution had constituted a major plank in the party platform during the election campaign. But the Labor Party always stopped short of supporting independence for Scotland, which would not have had a wide enough appeal in either England or Scotland.

Northern Ireland, which actually experienced devolution from 1920 to 1972, could have provided a precedent for any decision of the British government to grant greater authority to regional governments in Scotland and Wales. But in 1972, the British government reversed its position in Northern Ireland and once again imposed direct control over the government at Stormont. Meanwhile, the Labor Party saw no reason not to consider such a move for Scotland and Wales, leading to the recreation of the Scottish Parliament in Edinburgh and the creation of the first elected parliament in Welsh history. In both places, devolution undercut much of the support for their nationalist parties while solidifying support for the Labor Party in both places.

Therefore, in some respects, support for devolution in Northern Ireland was consistent with growing support for it elsewhere in the United Kingdom. However, there are several important and obvious differences between the nationalist movements in Scotland and Wales and that supported by Sinn Féin and the IRA in Northern Ireland. Perhaps the most obvious difference was the presence at any one time of between 10 and 12 infantry battalions of the British army in Northern Ireland. The ostensible purpose of the army's presence there was to maintain the peace, but to the Irish nationalists it constituted an occupying force. Scotland not only did not experience England as an occupying power, but also had historically always retained its own church and educational and legal systems. Furthermore, the majority of the Scots and the Welsh did not live under a regional government that was dominated by a minority, such as what the Catholics experienced under the Protestant government of Northern Ireland. Both Wales and Scotland had also retained much of their distinct cultural identities, which helped to assuage nationalist sentiment and channel it away from demands for political independence. Nor was there a part of Wales or Scotland that was independent and had its own government. Therefore, even the goals of the Scottish National Party (SNP) and Plaid Cymru differed significantly from those of Sinn Féin.

Sinn Féin and the IRA

It is perhaps worth pausing here to provide further explanation regarding the IRA and Sinn Féin and what they were trying to achieve. The main goal of Provisional Sinn Féin was to achieve the unification of Ireland, without recognizing the authority of the government in Dublin. The group which had become known as Republican Sinn Féin did not recognize the government of the established republic and wanted to see a new Irish government created on a four-province model, until 1986 when it recognized the republic and began to participate in the government of the republic. Both groups were intensely nationalist and therefore opposed to Irish membership in the European Union. Both were also interested in the promotion of Gaelic culture. Finally, they also both saw the nationalist cause as essentially a military one that necessitated armed conflict.

The military counterpart of Provisional Sinn Féin, the Provisional IRA, took the cause seriously and took the time to explain to its recruits the history of the republican nationalist movement in Northern Ireland. The PIRA provided them a "Green Book" that included rules of engagement, techniques to employ during interrogations, and the general duties and responsibilities of PIRA members.[15] The leadership of the organization was not interested in random killing or violence for its own sake. The leaders of the Provisional IRA recognized terror as a tactic in a larger struggle and not an end in itself. They sought to instill this attitude in their members. The organization of the Provisional IRA had become more centralized in the course of the decades-long struggle, an important shift that made it more disciplined but also more dangerous. The leaders, who generally lived ordinary lives with families and jobs outside of their involvement in the Provisional IRA, gained expertise at conducting covert operations aimed at strategic targets designed to force

---

[15] Eamon Collins and Mick McGovern (1997), *Killing Rage*. London: Granta Books, p. 66.

Britain out of Ireland. In the south, the main difference in the leadership of the Provisional IRA and that of the Official IRA was geographical, with the Provisionals residing more in the rural areas and in western Ireland, whereas the Officials were centered in Dublin.[16]

As the IRA refused to back down and end its campaign, so too did the Protestant forces, who believed that the activities of the IRA were part of a larger international Catholic plot to destroy Protestantism. In Northern Ireland, a murderous campaign against Catholics and Republicans was carried out from 1989 to 1991 under the authority of high-ranking police officers in the Royal Ulster Constabulary. The main purpose of this campaign was to prevent the Provisional IRA from achieving its objective of separating Northern Ireland from the United Kingdom. Its main tactics were assassination and attacks on members of the IRA and its supporters.[17]

This was just the latest episode in what had become known as Ireland's own *dirty war* in which violence increasingly begat more violence and attacks from one side continually provoked attacks from the other. It had gotten to the point where violence had almost become an end in itself and revenge had become a stronger motive than achievement of the original political goals of either side. Retaliatory bombings and shootings on both sides took the lives of innocent civilians along with the terrorists' intended targets. Since the Protestant terrorists in a group known as the Ulster Freedom Fighters could not distinguish who was and was not a member of the IRA, they began to retaliate against the IRA with random killings to which any ordinary Catholic might be susceptible. Furthermore, the IRA took the struggle to England, employing a bombing campaign similar to that used by the Basque separatist movement, the ETA, against Spain. In the 1970s, the IRA began a letter bombing campaign, sending their explosive deliveries primarily to government offices. The campaign produced no deaths but dozens of injuries. But the IRA also began to leave bombs in public or residential areas. The bombing of two pubs in Guildford on 5 October 1974 killed five people and wounded another 65. The arrest and conviction of two separate groups, known as the Guildford Four and the Maguire Seven, which did not follow proper judicial procedure, resulted from the British desire to hold someone accountable. But when the cases against the accused were brought to light and their convictions overturned in the late 1980s and early 1990s, it became clear that the British had compounded one tragedy by perpetrating another. The IRA bombing campaign continued sporadically into the 1990s. For example, in 1993, a bomb planted by the IRA led to the deaths of two young boys in an apartment building in Warrenton, England.

---

[16] Robert W. White (2006), *Ruairí Ó Brádaigh: The Life and Politics of an Irish Revolutionary.* Bloomington and Indianapolis: Indiana University Press, pp. 152–3.

[17] Sean McPhilemy (1998), *The Committee: Political Assassination in Northern Ireland.* Niwot, CO: Roberts Rinehart, p. 1.

Northern Ireland in literature and film

It is not surprising that a conflict of such length and complexity as that which afflicted Northern Ireland for three decades would attract significant attention from writers and filmmakers. Novels and films dealing with Northern Ireland generally fall into one of two categories: those that merely use the Troubles as a backdrop to plots that sensationalize violence and concentrate on action and intrigue on the one hand and, on the other hand, those that explore the Troubles in ways that reflect upon the human tragedy of people caught up in circumstances beyond their control or take a serious look at the larger political or social context of the conflict and its meaning in the unfolding of a complex history. The former include British films such as *Hennessey* (1975) and *A Prayer for the Dying* (1988), the American film *The Devil's Own* (1997), and novels such as the American writer Tom Clancy's *Patriot Games* (1987), which was also made into a film. In the latter category belong films such as Bill Miskelly's *The End of the World Man* (1985), a serious children's film presenting a parable about the efforts of children to assist in saving the last tree on earth that is threatened by government bulldozers. A novel particularly representative of the second category is Belfast-born Brian Moore's *Lies of Silence* (1991), in which the protagonist is presented with a moral dilemma very much against his will revolving around the IRA's attempt to force him to commit a terrorist act.

It has been argued that short stories are particularly effective at reflecting the difficulty of coming to grips with the human problems that led to and resulted from the Troubles.[18] For example, "The Cry," written by John Montague in 1964, sheds light on the period immediately preceding the Troubles through a Catholic protagonist who feels the repressive atmosphere that led to the Civil Rights movement. But novels, too, can capture any of multiple viewpoints that challenge the prevailing narratives on either side of the conflict.

Even without the Troubles, life in Belfast and changes in society in Northern Ireland in the late twentieth century would likely have attracted the novelist's eye and called forth a rich literature. Jennifer Johnston (b. 1930) is perhaps the most accomplished and well-known writer dealing with these social realities and, in particular, their effect on the women of Northern Ireland in novels such as *Shadows on Our Skin* (1977). Johnston's novel deals with a troubled teen trying to make sense of growing up in a divided society amid the growing military presence in the 1970s, while his mother tries to keep him from buying into nationalistic rhetoric that is only likely to get him killed. In *Love and Sleep* (2003), *The Swing of Things* (2005), and his other works, Sean O'Reilly examines the difficulties of individuals whose

---

[18] Ronan McDonald (2005), "Strategies of Silence: Colonial Strains in the Short Stories of the Troubles." *Yearbook of English Studies*, 35, 249–63.

lives have been scarred by the Troubles, even after they manage to extricate themselves from direct involvement in the conflict.

Eoin McNamee (b. 1961) also demonstrates the points at which history intersects with the lives of individuals, but his novels are in many ways even bleaker. The plot of *The Blue Tango* (2000) revolves around the murder of a young woman with a reputation for promiscuity who is the daughter of a local judge. The public becomes fascinated with learning the lurid details of the crime, even though most of what they hear is based on speculation or blatant untruths. The novel portrays the seamier side of politics and prejudice in the late twentieth century. His *Resurrection Man* (1994) is about a sociopathic murderer who operates within the convenient context of the Troubles. McNamee's compelling prose makes his novels must-reads for those interested in contemporary Irish literature. Maurice Leitch (b. 1933) is another important twentieth-century novelist who examines the actions of paramilitary groups in *Silver's City* (1981) and the religious motivations of Ulster Protestants in *Gilchrist* (1994). Poets such as Derek Mahon have also tried to evoke some of the feelings stirred up in natives of Belfast caught up in the Troubles, essentially victims of those who "stand on a corner stiff with rhetoric, promising nothing under the sun," as he writes in his 2000 poem "Ecclesiastes."

Some of the best films dealing with Northern Ireland explore the culture of violence and the clash between Catholics and Protestants in subtle and complex ways that go beyond a simple morality tale of good versus evil. For example, Jim Sheridan's 1997 film *The Boxer* shows how difficult it can be for a person who had once been a loyal member of the IRA to live a normal life and to escape from the legacy of violence in which he had once participated. Boxing is promoted as an outlet substituting for more lethal violence for the main character, played by Daniel Day-Lewis, who also starred in Sheridan's exposé of the British justice system, *In the Name of the Father* (1993). *High Boot Benny* (1994) is a very somber drama about the Troubles directed by Joe Comerford that essentially depicts the violence in Northern Ireland as senseless. It does not portray anyone in a good light and does not seem to suggest any solutions. The main character is a slow-witted young man who seems to be in trouble with both the British police and the IRA, who tar and feather him at one point. When IRA gunmen shoot the Catholic priest and Protestant headmistress of the school where Benny works, British soldiers refuse to send for help because their superiors wanted the couple, who had apparently been having an affair for years, dead as well. There are even hints at complicity between the British army and the IRA in the murders because they would rather force people to take sides than to allow them to stay neutral in the conflict. *High Boot Benny* was filmed entirely in County Donegal, giving it a tremendous aura of authenticity. It is not a particularly entertaining film, probably because it does such a good job of reflecting a reality that is so depressing. *Harry's Game* (1982), a BBC miniseries based on the novel by Gerald Seymour, tells the story of an undercover agent sent to infiltrate the IRA to discover the identity of the assassin who had murdered a British cabinet minister. The agent, Harry Brown, was chosen both because of his past success as an agent passing for a native in Yemen and because of his familiarity with Belfast, where he had grown up as an orphaned Catholic boy before joining the British army. Harry thus returns to his roots and even the viewer/reader can have trouble discerning the good guys from the bad guys and what side Harry is really on. Ken Loach's *Hidden Agenda* (1990), written by Ken Allen, represents a film that spreads responsibility for the continued escalation of violence in Northern Ireland to the highest levels of the British government in a conspiracy based thriller that loosely resembles the actual conspiracy in which the Royal Ulster Constabulary surreptitiously carried out the murder of leading Catholics and IRA defenders. Though more sympathetic to the IRA than the above films ("and you call me a terrorist while you look down your gun," an IRA supporter sings in one pub scene), it still reflects why the conflict in Northern Ireland was called the Troubles. Finally, in 2008, the film *Hunger*, directed by Steve McQueen (b. 1969), provided a sympathetic but grim look at the six-week hunger strike conducted by IRA prisoners in 1981 in a protest over the conditions of their incarceration.

In Tatjana Soli's 2010 novel, *The Lotus Eaters*, about a woman photographer caught up in the complexities of the Vietnam War, the main character Helen says at one point that "Every good war picture is an anti-war picture."[19] The same might be said of books and films as well. It is in them that we perhaps experience more of the tragedy and futility of the conflict and experience it in its human dimensions than through the endless reports of yet another bombing, riot, or assassination on television, in the newspapers, or, now, on the internet. Films, novels, poems, and short stories all have the ability to force sustained reflection in a way that brief news reports do not. Literature and films have the ability to both reflect and to help change the realities with which they deal, although their full impact can never be precisely measured.

The peace movement

The peace process finally started to gain momentum during the 1990s. In June 1992, Ian Paisley and other leading Protestants agreed to meet for the first time with representatives of the Republic of Ireland in London to discuss ways to end the violence in Northern Ireland. This created an opening on which the Conservative government led by John Major failed to capitalize. Major did, however, establish closer relations with Irish Prime Minister John Bruton—much too close for the IRA's liking—and

---

[19] Tatjana Soli (2010), *The Lotus Eaters: A Novel*. New York: St. Martin's Press, p. 316.

their talks led to a proposal for an autonomous parliament in Northern Ireland. Furthermore, the leaders of the United States finally began to take an interest, particularly during the administration of Bill Clinton, whose presidency lasted from 1993 to 2001. Prior to the 1990s, US presidents had generally stayed out of the conflict in Northern Ireland, not supporting either side and trying to dissuade US citizens from getting involved and from supporting terrorism. Bill Clinton dispatched George Mitchell in 1995 as Special Envoy to Northern Ireland to negotiate with all parties in an attempt to end the violence. Mitchell secured a pledge from each of them to that effect. On 30 November of that year, Clinton became the first serving US president to visit Northern Ireland.

When Tony Blair took over as British Prime Minister in 1997, he made his first official visit to Belfast. In his autobiography, Blair demonstrated a good grasp of the effects of terrorism and its role in prolonging the strife that had characterized Northern Ireland for three decades. He wrote:

> Terrorism causes chaos and death, but also hatred of the perpetrators among the group targeted by them; human nature being what it is, the victim group regards the perpetrator group, not just the perpetrators, as responsible; the perpetrator group becomes the victim, and so the ghastly spiral continues.[20]

Blair was also the first prime minister to unequivocally state that he was open to dealing directly with the IRA, but no progress toward peace could be made until both Protestant loyalists and Sinn Féin were ready to come to the table. The IRA had made it abundantly clear that they were not going away, but its leaders also realized that they had to be ready to negotiate in order to achieve their goals. The IRA has also seen much of its support erode in the Republic and Northern Ireland as a backlash against the killing of Protestant civilians, such as the 11 who died at a bombing in Enniskillen in 1987. For his part, Blair was ready to negotiate with terrorists without holding the past against them if they were willing to renounce the bomb and the gun in the future. He also acknowledged the British role in the escalation of the Troubles. For example, the Report of the Bloody Sunday Inquiry that he convened in 1998 concluded that "it does not appear that any of the offences for which civilians were arrested on Bloody Sunday was an arrestable offence."[21] He did not neglect the concerns of the unionists, but made it clear that they would not operate from a privileged position vis-à-vis the nationalists.

---

[20] Tony Blair (2010), *A Journey*. New York: Alfred A. Knopf, p. 154.
[21] Report of the Bloody Sunday Inquiry, Chapter 196.11. http://webarchive.nationalarchives. gov.uk/20101103103930/http://report.bloody-sunday-inquiry.org/.

Efforts toward peace in Northern Ireland culminated in the Good Friday Agreement of 1998 which did not resolve all of the issues causing division but did establish a mechanism and a process for doing so. Although it might have appeared to represent a dramatic leap forward, it was preceded by decades-long efforts of community nongovernmental organizations (NGOs) and grass roots campaigns to end the cycle of hatred between generations of Catholics and Protestants. The significance of the Good Friday Agreement was its proposal for cross-border councils, which represented a new approach based on international parliamentary institutions.[22] The Northern Ireland Bill that followed called for a North-South Ministerial Council and a British-Irish council. The agreement also contained very specific language on human rights, that included a commitment from all sides to recognize the right to free political thought, freedom of religion, "the right to pursue democratically national and political aspirations," and, perhaps most significantly given how the Troubles began, "the right to equal opportunity in all social and economic activity, regardless of class, creed, disability, gender, or ethnicity." In early 2000, Northern Ireland Secretary Peter Mandelson announced significant changes to the Royal Ulster Constabulary, including changing its name to the Police Service of Northern Ireland (PSNI), in an effort to create a new police force that was both smaller and more representative of the population. Violence had not entirely eased by then, and there were splinter groups, such as that calling itself the Real IRA, that refused to recognize the agreement. However, visible signs of progress by 2000 included the replacement of armored Land Rovers with regular patrol cars and the appearance of police on foot or bicycles in some districts.

Perhaps the greatest irony of the period is that the Troubles began with demands for civil rights and yet resulted in greater security measures and the abrogation of the rights of so many people, from the victims of violence to the suspension of civil liberties as a strategy by the British in the fight against terrorism. But it is also ironic that in their desire to unify Ireland, the IRA created a greater divide between the North and the South as many Catholics in the republic gradually tired of the havoc wreaked by the IRA in the North. This is not to say that the IRA was wholly responsible for the Troubles; revolutions arise because the existing structure has not proven flexible enough to accommodate or address the grievances of a significant portion of the population. By the late 1960s, the Catholic minority in Northern Ireland had aspirations that simply would not allow them to accept the status quo. In their determination to defend the status quo without compromise, rival Protestant organizations did much to prevent an atmosphere of conciliation that might have undermined the goals of the more extreme Nationalists.

---

[22] Kristen P. Williams and Neal G. Jesse (2001), "Resolving Nationalist Conflicts: Promoting Overlapping Identities and Pooling Sovereignty: The 1998 Northern Irish Peace Agreement." *Political Psychology*, 22, p. 571.

Unfortunately, Protestants believed such a defense was necessary in order to ensure their own survival and that of their faith. They saw the IRA as "the armed wing of the Roman Catholic Church whose real aim was to annihilate Protestantism" despite official pronouncements condemning terrorism emanating from numerous Catholic Church leaders.[23] It would take time to change such perceptions, but if the Protestants of Ulster had paid more attention to what was going on south of their border during the Troubles, their fears may have been allayed much sooner.

[23] John D. Brewer and Gareth I. Higgins (1998), *Anti-Catholicism in Northern Ireland, 1600–1998*. Houndmills, England: MacMillan, p. 109.

CHAPTER FIFTEEN

The Republic of Ireland and the European Union, 1973–2000

Life is short; life is precious. If we want to leave something to our children, we can leave them money. Not all the shouting and fighting and disagreeing and all that baloney.

– OLIVE CURRAN, office manager, County Westmeath, 1998

General directions in Irish politics

In the late 1960s and 1970s, Fine Gael moved to the left under the leadership of Garret Fitzgerald and Declan Costello (1926–2011). Costello was the author of a political manifesto adopted by Fine Gael called *Toward a Just Society*, which advocated greater government intervention to ensure a greater degree of economic fairness and social justice. In January 1973, Fitzgerald, in keeping with Costello's views, criticized Irish trade unions for pursuing political objectives restricted to industrial relations alone at the expense of wider social concerns. Fitzgerald's rebuke of the unions proved to be in keeping with a society that was starting to undergo social and economic change. In March, Fianna Fáil, which had held power since 1957, lost a general election amid concerns about an inflationary economy, rising unemployment, and the government's failure to address the problems in Northern Ireland in a meaningful way. Like other countries in Europe, as well as the United States, Ireland was affected by a rise in oil prices caused by the manipulation of the market by the Middle Eastern oil cartel known as OPEC (Organization of Petroleum-Exporting Countries). As for Northern Ireland, Fianna Fáil had moved so far away from de Valera's original position on partition that it now seemed mainly concerned that the "Troubles" in the North did not spill over to the South.

The result of Fianna Fáil's defeat was a new coalition government between Fine Gael and the Labor Party. However, the new government, headed by Liam Cosgrave (b. 1920), proved no more willing to develop a proactive policy toward the North, especially after the Sunningdale Agreement had failed to produce a lasting settlement there. This policy of nonengagement did not inoculate the Republic against terror, as demonstrated by a number of car bombings that occurred in Dublin and Monaghan on 17 May 1974 that resulted in the deaths of 34 people and injuries to another 300. While most people in the Republic shared the indifference shown by the government to Northern Ireland, some politicians and people still sympathized with the IRA and were angered by it. The Irish historian and journalist Tim Pat Coogan has identified "parts of Kerry, Mayo, the border counties, Laois, and Offaly in the southeastern midlands, and Dublin itself" as areas where such sympathies were more prevalent. But he also notes that, except during hunger strikes, Republican voting figures remained basically the same throughout the decade.[1]

Cosgrave did do more to intervene in the economy, however, primarily through increased public spending. Some signs of recovery started to appear by 1975, but the government continued its policy of deficit spending. The only other countries that increased their national debt to the same extent as Ireland during this period were Greece, Italy, and Portugal.[2] The rate of spending and the growth of the debt were key reasons why the coalition government lasted only until 1977, when Fianna Fáil regained power. The fall of Cosgrave's government was also due in part to divisions within both of the coalition parties.

The economic downswing continued until the end of the seventies. The news got worse when another oil shortage caused a spike in prices in 1979; this time the economy did not recover until the mid-1990s. Ireland took refuge in greater coordination with Europe, joining the European Monetary Union in 1979, a move that in the short run caused an additional problem. When Britain decided not to join the union, Irish bank clerks refused to handle transactions in British pounds because of the additional work involved. On 22 November 1979, Irish depositors withdrew the equivalent of $217 million, about 25 per cent of the total assets of the four largest banks in the Republic. The banks closed the following day to prevent a further run, even though it was a scheduled payday for most people. In the

---

[1] Tim Pat Coogan (2003), *Ireland in the Twentieth Century.* New York: Palgrave Macmillan, p. 519.

[2] Cormac Ó Gráda (1997), *A Rocky Road: The Irish Economy since the 1920s.* Manchester: Manchester University Press, p. 30.

long run, the Irish pound did not gain in value against the British pound, as had been expected, leading to yet more inflation.

On 5 December 1979, Jack Lynch, who had succeeded Sean Lemass as head of Fianna Fáil in 1966 and served as Taoiseach in each of his party's administrations since then, resigned his leadership of the party. He was replaced by Charles Haughey (b. 1926), who had served as Minister for Justice, Agriculture, and Finance in previous Fianna Fáil administrations. Unfortunately for Haughey, the debt carried over into the 1980s, as did the problems of unemployment and the crisis in Northern Ireland. Haughey and Fianna Fáil did not have a majority of seats after the February 1982 election, but they were able to enlist enough support from other parties to form a government. Though this government lasted only eight months, Haughey and Fianna Fáil returned to power at the head of another minority government in 1987. Another coalition government between Fine Gael and the Labor Party had formed in the meantime. In the second Fianna Fáil government of the eighties (1987–89), Haughey and his Finance Minister, Ray McSharry presided over a series of budget cuts, including a canceled pay increase for senior civil servants, that earned McSharry the nickname, "Mac the Knife." Revelations that under Haughey's watch the government had tapped the phones of two journalists might now be seen as part of a larger pattern that has culminated in the phone-hacking scandal that came to light in the United Kingdom in 2011.

In the 1980s, Ireland began to experience some of the same problems inherent in other modern democratic capitalist societies, notably the increased influence of special interests in the political system. As elsewhere, politicians proved reluctant to raise taxes or reduce spending if either were deemed politically unpopular. Allegations of political corruption became commonplace as politicians routinely left office much wealthier than when they had entered. Tax evasion and the manipulation of property prices were among the most frequent charges. Yet, the indignation felt by some did not translate into a public outcry for reform or do much to change the voting patterns of the electorate. This negative trend culminated in the resignation of Bertie Ahern from the position of Taoiseach in May 2008 amid allegations of fiscal malfeasance. The investigation focused on the amount of cash that was funneled through his accounts, including a two-year period in the mid-1990s when that amount totaled over three times his annual salary.[3]

By the time a referendum on the Good Friday Agreement was reached in May 1998, the Irish public seemed to be largely indifferent, perhaps burned out on the subject after such a lengthy process. The popular talk show host Gay Byrne reported that on the morning of the referendum, his listeners were more interested in talking about a school shooting in Oregon and the

---

[3] Michael Clifford and Shane Coleman (2009), *Bertie Ahern and the Drumcondra Mafia.* Dublin: Hachette Books Ireland, p. 15.

potential ban faced by Irish Olympic swimmer Michelle Smith after she had failed a drug test.[4] The public showed little more interest in Irish politics, as the two leading parties became virtually indistinguishable from one another. But in many ways, domestic politics took a back seat in the 1980s and 1990s to Ireland's changing relationships with Britain and Europe.

Relations with the United Kingdom during the Thatcher years

Relations between the Republic of Ireland and the United Kingdom began to improve almost as soon as Margaret Thatcher became prime minister in 1979. In December 1980, Thatcher and the Irish Taoiseach, Charles Haughey, agreed to charge their civil servants to review the "totality of relationships between the two islands."[5] In November 1981, Thatcher and Garret Fitzgerald agreed to create an Anglo-Irish Inter-Governmental Conference, which Thatcher described in her memoirs as "really the existing ministerial and official contacts under a new name."[6] The Fine Gael-Labor coalition led by Fitzgerald collapsed in February 1982. But his previous agreement with Thatcher had paved the way for better relations between the two countries when Fitzgerald once again became Taoiseach in November 1982. Representatives from Fianna Fáil, Fine Gael, the Irish Labor Party, and the SDLP from Northern Ireland assembled in May 1983 in a newly created body called the New Ireland Forum. In November 1984, Fitzgerald agreed to a joint statement with Thatcher that supported the principle that "the identities of both the majority and the minority communities in Northern Ireland should be recognized and respected and reflected in the structures and processes of Northern Ireland in ways acceptable to both communities."[7] Fitzgerald also helped to pave the way for a new agreement with the United Kingdom by agreeing to recognize Irish unification as an "aspiration" and not a claim of law. Fitzgerald had originally hoped to gain British support for Irish unification as a result of his negotiations with Thatcher, but he ended up acknowledging that a majority of the people of Northern Ireland would need to support this in order for it to become a reality, a position that was acceptable to the British as well.

---

[4] James F. Clarity (1998), "For Some in the Republic: The Vote? What Vote?." *The New York Times*, 23 May.

[5] J. H. Whyte (2011), "Ireland, 1966–82," in T. W. Moody, F. X. Martin and Dermot Keogh with Patrick Kiely (eds), *The Course of Irish History*, 5th edn. Lanham, MD: Roberts Rhinehart, p. 316.

[6] Margaret Thatcher (1993), *The Downing Street Years*. New York: HarperCollins, p. 393.

[7] Richard English (2011), "Ireland: 1982–94," in T. W. Moody, F. X. Martin and Dermot Keogh with Patrick Kiely (eds), *The Course of Irish History*, 5th edn. Lanham, MD: Roberts Rhinehart, p. 318.

Thatcher's relationship with the leaders of the Republic had some rocky moments, however. Thatcher and the British were particularly upset by the lack of support that they received from Dublin during their Falkland Islands War with Argentina in 1982. When Thatcher made some premature comments in November 1984 about her joint efforts with the Republic toward finding a solution to the violence in Northern Ireland, she drew a strong rebuke. Fitzgerald called Thatcher's remarks "gratuitously offensive," referring especially to her statement ruling out unification as a possible solution to the situation in Northern Ireland. Even after the Anglo-Irish Agreement, Dublin angered British leaders when it refused to extradite a Catholic priest named Patrick Ryan who was accused of assisting the IRA with money and weapons. The Irish expressed their concern that Father Ryan, who was charged with possessing explosives and conspiracy to commit murder, would not receive a fair trial if extradited because of excessive negative publicity regarding his case. Their failure to extradite him still greatly offended the British.

There were those on both sides of the Irish Sea who were unhappy about the closer relationship between Ireland and Britain. Thatcher did not even have the full support of her own cabinet. Ian Gow, her Treasury Minister of State, resigned in November 1985 because the Anglo-Irish Agreement had provided the Republic of Ireland with a "consultative role" in the governance of Northern Ireland. Fitzgerald had his own nationalist critics in Ireland. Dublin shops suffered from a decline in business after Protestant extremists in the North threatened a bombing campaign to force the Irish government to back out of the accord. Bomb threats made police dogs sniffing for explosives a common site on the streets of Dublin. Fitzgerald sought to defuse the bombing campaign and his critics by stressing that:

> . . . the Irish Government's approach has been to seek ways of securing recognition of and respect for the rights and aspirations of both traditions in this island, a process which must of its nature contribute also to better relations between the peoples of Ireland and Britain.[8]

All in all, there was surprisingly little criticism in the Republic of the agreement, the first anniversary of which in 1986 passed with little notice besides some concern about terrorist threats. One of the goals of the agreement had been to foster better relations between the two governments in Ireland and to facilitate cross-border cooperation, particularly with regard to stopping terrorism. The agreement also called for a "conference" that would include cabinet ministers from both Britain and Ireland to facilitate discussion on security and other issues. It helped to set the stage for the Belfast Agreement

---

[8] British Information Services, *Policy Statement: Northern Ireland: Anglo-Irish Agreement*, 15 November 1985.

of 1998. Thatcher and Fitzgerald had found common ground in the desire to outflank extremists on both sides of the dispute in Northern Ireland.

The negotiations between the British and Irish governments over Northern Ireland were one of two major developments that changed the relationship between them since the 1970s. The other was the decision of both countries to join the European Economic Community in 1973 and the subsequent participation of both countries in the movement in the direction of the unification of Europe.

Ireland, Britain, and the European Union

In February 1972, Terence O'Raifeartaigh, representing the Irish Higher Education Authority, warned that Ireland faced "eventual cultural annihilation" if it did not join the European Economic Community.[9] By contrast, the outspoken writer and politician, Conor Cruise O'Brien (1917–2008) suggested that membership in the EEC would expose Ireland to the secular influences of the European continent and undermine Ireland's identity as a Christian nation.[10] Either way, Ireland was about to take one of the most significant steps in its history. It was understandable that some people would be enthusiastic and that others would be apprehensive. The Republic of Ireland joined the European Economic Community in 1973 with overwhelming support from its people, with about 80 per cent voting in favor in a 1972 referendum. By contrast, in 1974, the new Labor government in Britain held a referendum to ascertain the level of national support for membership in the EEC there; 17,300,000 voters cast ballots in favor of membership compared to 8,400,000 who voted *no*.[11]

The major political parties of Fianna Fáil and Fine Gael have been especially indistinguishable in their policies toward European integration. The British parties tended to be more divided on the issue. The Conservative prime minister, Edward Heath (1916–2005) led Britain into the EEC. Heath believed strongly that the best future for Britain lay with closer integration with Europe. At that time, it was the British Labor Party that expressed reservations about restrictions on British sovereignty as a result of joining the European Community. The issue for the Labor Party was whether or not its goals of moving Britain more in the direction of a socialist state could be achieved faster inside or outside of the Community. In contrast with Ireland, where support for EEC membership remained strong, a

[9] Diarmaid Ferriter (2012), *Ambiguous Republic: Ireland in the 1970s*. London: Profile Books, p. 407.

[10] Ibid., p. 309.

[11] Tony Judt (2005), *Postwar: A History of Europe Since 1945*. New York: Penguin, p. 526.

"Get Britain Out" movement had developed on the other side of the Irish Sea within two years.

The attitude of the two main British parties toward Europe began to shift in the 1980s. One of the major planks of Margaret Thatcher's Conservative Party platform was to cut the proportion of the budget allotted for the EEC. Thatcher succeeded in doing so at the same time that she reasserted Britain's independent foreign policy in the Falklands War. The British Labor Party simultaneously began to favor a stronger relationship with Europe. But views on the issue in Britain did not just break down along party lines. There were divisions within each party as well. Thatcher almost split the Conservative Party over the extent of her hard-line opposition to Europe in the late 1980s.

One of the factors that accounts for the differences between Irish and British reaction to the European Community was the extent to which Irish agriculture benefited from European subsidies. Individual farmers received a higher rate of assistance than was offered to farmers in the United Kingdom. From 1973 until 1991, Ireland received a total of about £14 billion from the EEC. In addition, Ireland attracted additional investment from overseas, particularly from the United States, as a result of its EEC membership.[12] However, not all segments of the Irish economy benefited equally from membership in the EEC. While some industries benefited from access to European markets, others—especially in and around Cork—lost out in competition with European manufacturers, leading some factories to shut down by the early 1980s.

Garret Fitzgerald had argued from the outset that that membership in the EEC would make Ireland less economically dependent on Britain. Fitzgerald also believed that being joint members of a larger political structure would ease the tensions between the Republic and Northern Ireland. One interesting result of Ireland and the United Kingdom joining the EEC at the same time is that Irish voters in both North and South, when they voted for representatives to the European parliament in 1979, voted in the same election for the first time since 1918.

There were times when Ireland was at odds with the European Community. On occasion, the Community encroached upon Irish sovereignty, as, for example, in cases involving European oversight of how development funds were distributed. European supervision did have the positive effect of encouraging the central government in Dublin to work more closely with local communities to ensure that the funds were used appropriately.[13] There have been other times when Ireland did not support all of the initiatives of the European Union, especially those that involved committing troops.

---

[12] Alvin Jackson (1999), *Ireland, 1798–1998*. Oxford: Blackwell, p. 385.
[13] Richard B. Finnegan and Edward T. McCarron (2000), *Ireland: Historical Echoes, Contemporary Politics*. Boulder: Westview Press, p. 382.

Ireland has historically valued its position as a neutral nation, which was also reflected in its refusal to join NATO even though the country benefited from its military protection. A third area of conflict, including very recently, has been over the issue of abortion, where Irish laws are prohibitive in contrast to Europe's more liberal attitude toward the issue.

For these reasons, there were some people in Ireland who developed ambiguous feelings about the EEC by the late 1970s. But this has hardly dimmed general enthusiasm for membership in Europe. The Irish have particularly taken pride in the central role that they have played at the heart of the affairs of the European Community. It is generally accepted that Ireland has had more influence in the European Community in proportion to its size than virtually any other country. At home, membership in the European Community opened the door to political careers for more people than would have been feasible in the Republic alone.

In December 1978, the Taoiseach Jack Lynch announced that Ireland would join the European Monetary System scheduled to go into effect in January 1979, giving the Irish a different currency than the British for the first time in 152 years. Ireland negotiated additional subsidies and loans in exchange for agreeing to participate. But an underlying current of dissatisfaction has revealed itself in the increase in the number of anti-Europe votes in a series of referenda that have been put before the Irish public since 1987. Whereas 83 per cent had voted in favor of joining the EEC in 1972, only 70 per cent voted for the Single Europe Act (SEA) in 1987 and 69 per cent for the Maastricht Treaty in 1992.[14] The Single Europe Act had sought to eliminate remaining trade barriers among European nations and to bring their domestic and foreign policies into greater harmony, while the Maastricht Treaty put Europe on a schedule for the adoption of a single currency and approval for a new Social Charter, which focused on such issues as worker's rights, gender equality, and health care. Irish concerns about Maastricht were nothing compared to the reaction against it in Britain, especially among the Conservatives where the anti-European wing was becoming even more vociferous. Thatcher was out of office, but the deeply held beliefs about British independence into which she had tapped remained. Billboards were erected during one anti-European campaign that said "Brussels Spouts," in reference to the location of the European government.

By the 1990s, even the Irish were growing increasingly skeptical about whether further steps toward integration in Europe were to their benefit and in the best interests of their country. A majority of Irish voters actually rejected the Nice Treaty in 2001, which called for approval to changes in the European Union related to the proposed entry of additional countries in Eastern Europe. The Nice Treaty was approved in a second referendum a year later with only 37 per cent voting against on that occasion. The first

---

[14] Finnegan and McCarron, op. cit., p. 380.

vote may have been as much directed at the Irish government as it was at the treaty itself.[15] But six years later, when the Lisbon Treaty—which mainly had to do with governance issues but which proposed that a Charter on Fundamental rights be legally binding—was put before the Irish voters, 53 per cent voted against it.

Ireland adopted the euro in 1999, one of the first countries to do so. In the late nineties, however, as the Irish economy began to boom, Ireland suddenly became less willing to allow the European Union to have a say in its economic affairs. Ireland was reluctant to put the brakes on its thriving economy, which signaled a more independent attitude than that to which the EU was accustomed. It seemed to some as if Ireland had been willing to accept large subsidies from the EU when its economy needed them, but once their economy was booming, the Irish were less willing to subsidize poorer European countries such as Greece, Spain, or Portugal. The tax breaks offered by the Finance Minister, Charlie McGreevy (b. 1949), to foreign investors between 1997 and 2004 were of particular concern because they threatened to undermine the economies of other countries that were supposed to be part of a single market. McGreevy subsequently came under heavy criticism for policies that encouraged financial speculation, especially on property values, that contributed to the collapse of the Irish economy by 2009.

Another reason for Britain's reluctance to become more integrated into Europe was the "special relationship" that the British believed they had with the United States. This was especially true under Margaret Thatcher, who had a close personal relationship with and a strong political affinity for Ronald Reagan, the US president from 1981 to 1989. Tony Blair would affirm this relationship in the late 1990s and early 2000s, especially with his decision to support George W. Bush on the US invasion of Iraq in 2003. Ireland, however, had something of its own special relationship with the United States. The large number of Irish-American voters who retained some interest in Irish affairs helped to ensure that the United States would maintain good relations with the Republic. US involvement in the peace process in Northern Ireland was welcomed by the Republic and helped to strengthen the good will between the two countries. In a way, Ireland can claim an even more "special" relationship with the United States because the United States does not make the same kinds of demands on Ireland that it does on Britain, especially those involving foreign policy initiatives like the invasion of Iraq. Ireland was largely free to go its own way, but social changes within Irish society combined with certain pressures from the European community led to significant changes in the later decades of the twentieth century.

---

[15] Maura Adshead and Jonathan Tonge (2009), *Politics in Ireland: Convergence and Divergence on a Two-Polity Island*. Houndmills: Palgrave Macmillan, p. 213.

Social change

The American writer John Hawkes begins his 1997 novel, *An Irish Eye*, which is narrated by a young Irish orphan girl, with the suggestion that all Irish girls are, in fact, orphans.[16] His narrator goes on to explain that boys are the "sons of Ireland," but that daughters, even if they have parents, do not really know where and to whom they belong in Irish society. I am not sure that all Irish women would agree with this statement, but it can serve as a useful starting point for a discussion of the role of women in modern Irish society. Violence is mostly perpetrated by men, with women left to grieve for those killed in the conflict that raged in the North and sometimes affected the South. Men were responsible for organized crime. Men had determined so much of the political history of the land, including the provisions in the Irish constitution that identified a woman's role as primarily centered on the home and family.

Men passed laws on abortion and contraception and other issues related to women's health and bodies. Only men were permitted to serve as Catholic priests and led the church that dominated Irish culture and society for so much of the twentieth century. Some of those men scarred hundreds of lives by taking advantage of their power and position to abuse the children with whose spiritual and physical well-being they had been entrusted.

Beginning in the 1970s, however, a number of changes did occur that improved the lives of Irish women and gave them greater opportunities for participation in public life. The government finally lifted a ban on married women in public service jobs and passed other legislation related to women's equality, including an equal pay act and a law legalizing contraception. The latter was a particularly controversial issue at the time. In 1970, a group in favor of legalized contraceptives formed the Irish Family Planning Rights Association. In May 1971, a group of women protested against the law against contraceptives by publicly displaying those which they had purchased in Belfast in front of customs officials and the press, who had been previously notified. The legalization of contraceptives followed a legal challenge by a 27-year-old Catholic woman named Mary McGee. McGee already had given birth to four children, but when pregnant she suffered from a condition known as toxemia, which was potentially fatal and likely to become increasingly life threatening if she became pregnant again. She had ordered contraceptives from abroad, but customs officials had confiscated them. A young activist attorney named Mary Robinson (b. 1944) represented McGee in a case that made it to the Supreme Court, which ended up ruling in her favor on 19 December 1973 on the grounds that she possessed a right to privacy within her marriage.[17]

---

[16] John Hawkes (1997), *An Irish Eye*. New York: Viking, p. 1.
[17] Diarmaid Ferriter (2009), *Occasions of Sin: Sex and Society in Modern Ireland*. London: Profile Books, pp. 418–19.

Ireland responded to pressure from the European Community when it passed the Anti-Discrimination Act (Pay Act) of 1974. This became part of a wave of changes, largely in response to European Community directives, many of which significantly affected women. In 1976, women finally gained the right to serve on juries, from which they had been excluded since 1927, thanks to a case brought to the Supreme Court by Mairín de Burca and Mary Anderson. In 1977, Ireland established an Employment Equality Agency to enforce the Employment Equality Act, which sought to end discrimination on the basis of sex or marital status. The Irish government also created a Health and Safety Authority to conform to EEC directives.

Of course, some issues took longer to address. In November 1982, the Holy Faith Convent School in New Ross fired a young woman named Eileen Flynn, who taught Irish and History at the school, because her "lifestyle . . . ran counter to Catholic morals and principles."[18] She argued in her appeal that her pregnancy and her relationship with a married man who had separated from his wife were her own private business. She lost all of her appeals, but her case has remained controversial and a cause célèbre for privacy advocates. At the same time, a reduction in public expenditure on education in the 1980s made it harder for other young teachers to get a job at all. Ireland lagged behind in the area of sex education, which remained a controversial topic there into the 1980s. Beginning in about 1992, however, most schools started to offer at least some sex education.

The improvement in the status of women, though, is perhaps best symbolized by the elevation of Mary Robinson of the Labor Party to the presidency in 1990, followed by the presidency of Mary McAleese (b. 1951) in 1997. Both Robinson and McAleese had impressive legal credentials and both had served as Reid professor of Law at Trinity College Dublin, a position that Robinson had attained by the age of 25, McAleese at the age of 24. They are both strong, successful women who excelled while in office, helping to raise the profile of the presidency at the same time that they became important role models for other women seeking leadership positions.

In 1977, Mary Robinson had represented a man named David Norris in an attempt to challenge legislation dating back to the nineteenth century that made male homosexuality a criminal offense. The influence of the Catholic Church, which viewed homosexuality as a challenge to the natural order of God's creation, had previously inhibited much public discussion on the issue, despite the existence of a gay community in Dublin. The law was on the side of the church. In the early 1970s, dozens of men were sentenced for "gross indecency." The Irish Gay Rights Movement started about that time. Public discussion raised awareness, while academics such as the psychiatrist Anthony Clare (1942–2007) challenged the church's position that regarded

---

[18] John Cunningham (2009), *Unlikely Radicals: Irish Post-Primary Teachers and the ASTI, 1909–2009*. Cork: Cork University Press, p. 225.

homosexuality as abnormal behavior. Finally, in 1993, the Irish government decriminalized homosexuality. Two acts—the Employment Equality Act of 1998 and the Equal Status Act of 2000—combined to make discrimination on the basis of sexual orientation illegal. The Republic of Ireland legalized same-sex civil unions in 2010 with support from both parties. Same-sex marriages are still not recognized by the state, though this could change in the near future as a result of pressure from the European Union.

In the 1980s, the Republic began to address the problem of racism in Irish society, most notably through an attempt to better accommodate the Irish ethnic group known as Travellers. The Travellers were previously known as Gypsies, though they are not related to the Roma, people on the European continent who used to be known by the same name. The Irish have had an ambivalent relationship with the Travellers. On the one hand, they have been considered as exemplars of what it means to be Irish and as being more in touch with ancient Celtic traditions than most Irish people. On the other hand, the Travellers are outsiders, yet ones who frequently interact with Irish people and are never that far removed from mainstream society. In the 1970s, Travellers in the town of Ennis were frequently prosecuted for violating health codes or for parking illegally. Attempts at increased accommodation in the 1980s did not prevent continued harassment by the authorities through fines and evictions.[19]

One of the most important trends in these decades was the continuation in the rise of immigration rates in Ireland. As a result, Irish society has become much more multiethnic. It is estimated that a quarter of a million people migrated to Ireland between 1995 and 2000, many of them from diverse ethnic, racial, and cultural backgrounds.[20] The changing composition of the Irish population has forced Ireland to confront anew the question of what it means to be Irish. It was becoming more difficult to assert an uncompromising Irish nationalism in the face of an increasingly large number of residents who had come from other countries, especially since the Irish economy seemed to be so heavily dependent upon them. State support for those seeking political asylum posed a different kind of challenge to the Irish people's self-conception. As Steve Garner put it, "if asylum-seekers are 'spongers' because they (are forced to) live off welfare, what does that say about the thousands of Irish nationals who do so without the same constraint?"[21]

This was all happening against a backdrop of plans to commemorate the bicentennial of the 1798 rebellion and the negotiations that led to the Good Friday Agreement in Northern Ireland. The government of the Republic

---

[19] Bryan Fanning (2002), *Racism and Social Change in the Republic of Ireland.* Manchester: Manchester University Press, p. 118.

[20] Patrick Fitzgerald and Brian Lambkin (2008), *Migration in Irish History, 1607–2007.* London: Palgrave Macmillan, p. 228.

[21] Steve Garner (2004), *Racism in the Irish Experience.* London: Pluto Press, p. 227.

established a "1798 Commemoration Committee," which was instructed to downplay the theme of nationalism and to emphasize instead themes such as democracy and internationalism.[22] Numerous public events, media programs, and books marked the occasion without the strong nationalist overtones that had previously been associated with the rebellion.

In many ways, Ireland was emerging as a successful modern society. Another important change involved the shift in occupation distribution. In 1985, about 25 per cent of the workforce comprised "professionals, managers, and salaried employees," up from 10 per cent in 1951.[23] The overall standard of living increased, despite problems with the Irish economy. Religious attitudes in Ireland became more ecumenical and open-minded. The cumulative effect of the changes discussed above was a more equal and less insular society.

Other changes from the period did not seem so positive, however. The gap between the poor and the wealthy appeared to be widening. Racism seemed to be increasing in conjunction with increased immigration. Ireland experienced an increase in drug abuse and the rise of organized crime that generally accompanies the existence of a drug culture. In 1996, young investigative journalist named Veronica Guerin was murdered following a series of articles on Dublin's criminal underworld, after she had previously been shot in the leg and had her house fired upon. Her death shook Ireland badly and became an international scandal, as well as the subject of a feature film (*Veronica Guerin*, 2003) directed by Joel Schumacher and starring Cate Blanchett as Guerin. In addition, suicide rates rose during this period, especially among young men. In 1999, there was a slight drop in the suicide rate in Ireland for the first time in 40 years, and still 340 men and 90 women took their own lives.[24] Perhaps most alarming, was the extent of the child abuse epidemic that shook Ireland during this period, including a disquieting number of sexual abuse cases involving the Catholic clergy.

In *Goodbye to Catholic Ireland*, Mary Kenny argues that the sexual abuse scandal did not cause changes in Irish attitudes toward the church so much as it resulted from changing Irish attitudes toward the church. In 1993, the Vatican issued a statement placing some of the blame for the sex abuse scandal in the church on a society that had become too permissive. The Vatican spokesperson, Dr Joaquin Navarro-Valle said that "One would have to ask if the real culprit is not a society that is irresponsibly permissive, hyperinflated with sexuality [and] capable of creating circumstances that induce even people who have received a solid moral formation to commit

---

[22] Garth Stevenson (2004), "The Politics of Remembrance in Irish and Quebec Nationalism." *Canadian Journal of Political Science*, 37, 913.

[23] Richard Breen, Damian F. Hannan, David B. Rottman and Christopher T. Whelan (1990), *Understanding Contemporary Ireland: State, Class, and Development in the Republic of Ireland*. New York: St. Martin's Press, p. 59.

[24] http://www.irishhealth.com/article.html?id=508

FIGURE 15.1 *Lise Hand, friend of late investigative reporter Veronica Guerin who was gunned down execution-style, standing outside the flower-strewn gate of the Parliament. Photo by Ken Goff. Courtesy of Getty Images.*

grave moral acts."[25] But Kenny emphasizes the importance of the liberal reforms enacted by the church at the Second Vatican Council, which met in Rome from October 1962 to December 1965. Vatican II, as it is popularly known, gave increased recognition to the role of the laity. Thus, according to Kenny, the church had unwittingly decreased the number of people who thought that they needed to enter the priesthood in order to fulfill a religious vocation.[26]

An International Consultation on Mixed Marriage meeting in Dublin in September 1974 called for an end to the refusal of the Catholic Church to recognize marriages performed in other churches and gave support to those seeking to change the law requiring that all mixed religious marriages be conducted in a Catholic Church. In 1981, a majority of people polled said that they favored legalized divorce, whereas only 22 per cent had been in favor only a decade earlier.[27] Church attendance declined and significantly fewer people entered the priesthood or religious orders. But the willingness to blame society instead of its own priests for committing abuse and members of the church hierarchy for turning a blind eye and even covering it up

---

[25] Philip Pullella (1993), "Church Says Society to Blame for Scandals." *The Irish Times*, 24 June.

[26] Mary Kenny (1997), *Goodbye to Catholic Ireland: A Social, Personal and Cultural History from the Fall of Parnell to the Realm of Mary Robinson*. London: Sinclair-Stevenson, p. 346.

[27] Tom Garvin (2011), "Turmoil in the Sea of Faith: The Secularization of Irish Social Culture, 1960–2007," in Thomas E. Hachey (ed.), *Turning Points in Twentieth-Century Irish History*. Dublin: Irish Academic Press, p. 161.

showed a degree of insensitivity that made people even angrier toward the church. Veronica Guerin had summed up many people's changing attitudes toward the Catholic Church when she said, "I'm not anti-church but I do think the church has some gall if it thinks that because it's the church it can mislead and be a law unto itself."[28]

Ireland at the end of the twentieth century was a much more secular society. Furthermore, the growth of secularization had come at the expense of the Catholic Church, which had dominated virtually all aspects of Irish society since the mid-nineteenth century. Ireland was in a position to embrace the modern world and opportunities that the favorable global economic climate had to offer in the 1990s. As the twentieth century drew to a close, Ireland entered a period of economic growth that was practically unprecedented in its history, earning it the nickname of the "Celtic Tiger." Per capita GDP surpassed that of both Britain and Northern Ireland.[29] But all changes come with costs as well as benefits.

Environmental and health issues

Irish medicine in the last three decades of the twentieth century shared many of the same characteristics as that practiced throughout the western world. The dominant approach throughout the west in the 1970s was to treat the body as a machine and to view the role of medicine as to fix whatever part of the body was broken. But starting in the United States and the United Kingdom, some physicians were beginning to take an interest in holistic medicine, which developed a bit more slowly in Ireland.[30] The American Holistic Medical Association was founded in 1978. The Association of Natural Medicines was founded in the United Kingdom in 1983. Ireland followed suit in 1986 with the establishment of Irish Association of Holistic Medicine. The Irish medical establishment was also only just beginning to become aware of the hidden dangers of silent killers such as high blood pressure. The Dean of the Faculty of Medicine of University College Dublin, D. K. Donovan, published an article in the early seventies in the *Journal of the Irish Medical Association* warning of the dangers of hypertension and chastising Irish doctors for their conservative approach to the problem. Ireland also seemed backward compared to many places because of the conservative approach to contraception that placed physicians and health care providers in an awkward position over the issue.

---

[28] "Duty to Expose Stories that Others Would Prefer Not to Be Told," *The Irish Times*, 27 June 1996.

[29] Coogan, *op. cit.*, p. 697.

[30] Tony Farmar (2004), *Patients, Potions, & Physicians: A Social History of Medicine in Ireland, 1654–2004*. Dublin: A. and A. Farmar in association with the Royal College of Physicians of Ireland, p. 184.

Despite a vast increase in the amount of money spent by the government on public health from the seventies through the nineties, many believed that health care in Ireland was getting worse, not better. This belief received confirmation when a 2001 report came out announcing that Ireland had the lowest life expectancy and the highest infant mortality rate of the 15 European states included in the study on which the report was based. The Irish were also found to have higher rates of cancer and respiratory diseases, as well as of those afflicting the circulatory system.[31]

A main issue that continues to confront the Irish health care system is the inequity between public and private patients. In her 2009 book, *Irish Apartheid: Healthcare Inequality in Ireland*, Sara Burke criticizes the tendency of the government to put more money into private health care, while failing to provide resources for a quality public health program. Burke also points out that the health care system in Ireland can be hard to navigate for many patients because of its division into public, private, and voluntary (charitable) providers.[32] Whatever the intentions behind the health care system of providing universal health care, the poor simply do not have the same access to quality healthcare. Immigrants from other countries in the 1990s and early twenty-first century have brought with them some of their own healing culture, which in some cases has included more alternative approaches than are covered under the health care provided by the state. This has led to a process of negotiation between patients and the system as patients seek biomedicines as needed but seek alternative therapies when they might be more appropriate.[33] In many places, Ireland has a strong tradition of folk healing and alternative medicine, which has survived into the twenty-first century. In addition, Ireland's Catholic religious tradition has provided hope and consolation for the infirm and the aged, as is evidenced by the popularity of the Marian shrine at Knock in County Mayo as a pilgrimage site.

Environmental concerns in Ireland date back to the 1970s. In 1973, a road built without governmental permission aroused public ire because it threatened to disturb the ecology of North Bull Island, which had been declared a bird sanctuary in the 1930s. A citizens' movement to preserve Dublin Bay had already been assured by politicians that the sanctuary would not be disturbed. Another cause for concern was the planned expansion of the use of nuclear energy. In 1978, a proposed nuclear power plant at Carnsore Point in County Wexford was accompanied by assurances from a minister of state that nuclear power technology was "tried and tested." While engineers

---

[31] Adshead and Tonge, *op. cit.*, p. 204.

[32] Sara Burke (2009), *Irish Apartheid: Healthcare Inequality in Ireland*. Dublin: New Island, pp. 12–13.

[33] Anne MacFarlane and Tomas de Brún (2010), "Medical Pluralism in the Republic of Ireland: Biomedicines as Ethnomedicines," in Ronnie Moore and Stuart McClean (eds), *Folk Healing and Health Care Practices in Britain and Ireland: Stethscopes, Wands, and Crystals*. New York: Berghan Books, pp. 194–5.

derided the antinuclear movement as "a sociological phenomenon" and "a crusade," concerned citizens looked at the issue more critically.[34] A series of demonstrations generated immense publicity. The Irish singer Christy Moore (b. 1945) contributed his support to the antinuclear movement with concert appearances and a television appearance in 1979 where he performed "The House Down in Carne (The Ballad of Nuke Power)," written by Jim Whelan. Public pressure led to the appointment of an inquiry in February 1980 and, eventually, the abandonment of the Carnsore Point project. Today, the site is the home of wind-generated power stations.

Environmental controversy erupted in the 1980s over a story related by Tim Pat Coogan in his book, *Ireland in the Twentieth Century*. It involved a woman, Mary Hanrahan, who lived in County Tipperary who believed that her son and her livestock had been made ill by emissions from a chemical factory near her farm. She took the large international company that owned the factory, Marck, Sharp, and Dohane, to court in 1985. When she lost her case, she was forced to sell her farm, but the farm was now unsellable because of the negative publicity surrounding the environmental dangers of the property. She was forced to go on living on the farm until she won her case on appeal to the Supreme Court in July 1988.[35]

Ireland as a predominantly rural country has not had to deal with the same amount of urban cleanup of abandoned industrial areas that other countries have, including the United Kingdom. It was only in the 1970s that a majority of the Irish people lived in towns and cities, a landmark that was reached in Britain in the 1850s. By the end of the twentieth century, however, there were some significant "brownfields," as such areas are known, that demanded attention. In fact, urban growth in the 1990s and early 2000s has brought Ireland problems all too familiar in many other countries, including traffic congestion, noise pollution, and housing shortages. By the twenty-first century, river pollution was also increasing, even though as of 2002 about two-thirds of Ireland's rivers and streams were considered unpolluted.[36] Waste has increased as well. But Ireland has had a number of environmental successes, including the virtual elimination of pollution caused by fermented grass, also known as silage, which is deadly to fish if the toxins it produces get into the water supply.[37] Another positive development has been a shift from bituminous coal to natural gas in the course of the seventies and eighties that resulted in a significant improvement in Dublin's air quality. The establishment of an Integrated Pollution Control Licensing System in 2003 has since contributed to a dramatic decrease in emissions throughout Ireland. Furthermore, a 2002 strategic report issued by the

---

[34] "Alternative Nuclear Energy." *The Irish Times*, 6 February 1980.

[35] Coogan, *op. cit.*, p. 405.

[36] Peter Clinch, Frank Convery and Brendan Walsh (2002), *After the Celtic Tiger: Challenges Ahead*. Dublin: The O'Brien Press, p. 139.

[37] Ibid., p. 139.

Department of Energy stated "counter-urbanization" as one of its goals for the period ending in 2020, particularly the prevention of a megalopolis along the east coast of the Republic.[38]

Irish literary, cultural, and musical trends

Irish literature, culture, and music have all had a great influence not only on Ireland but also throughout the world. Modern Irish writers have had a rich cultural heritage from which to draw. Perhaps the most influential modern Irish writer was James Joyce (1882–1941), although a case could be made for W. B. Yeats, Oscar Wilde, and several others. Joyce is considered to be one of the creators of modern fiction. He is known for his exploration of aesthetic theory in *The Portrait of the Artist as a Young Man* (1916), for experimenting with stream of consciousness and other literary techniques in *Ulysses* (1922), and for the stark realism of *Dubliners* (1914), which comprises a collection of stories that depict scenes in the everyday lives of mostly troubled characters. Joyce has remained an influential figure because, although in some ways he reflected his times, he largely ignored the nationalistic struggle and contemporary political developments that might have dated his work. He concentrated on more universal themes using modern literary approaches. *Dubliners* might also help to account for the strong tradition of short-story writing in Ireland that continued throughout the twentieth century and was the preferred genre of writers such as Liam O'Flaherty (1896–1984), Sean O'Faolain (1900–91), and Frank O'Connor (1903–66). Ita Daly's 1980 collection, *The Lady with the Red Shoes* portrays the ill-effects on different women of the stereotypical gender roles in which they are trapped. The stories in Mary Lavin's *A Family Likeness and Other Stories* (1985) portray, in the words of literary scholar Heather Ingman, "mothers and daughters who fail to disentangle themselves from social and religious pressures to conform to notions of self-sacrificing feminity."[39]

In her novels, Jennifer Johnston (see also Chapter 14) addresses a wide variety of themes, mostly centered on human relationships, set amid the moral and ethical dilemmas of the times. Some of her books reflect the debate that went on in the South over the issues that were dividing people in the North. This is perhaps best exemplified in her 1985 novel, *The Railway Station Man*, in which the fight for freedom is reduced by one character to the simple matter of people dying without accomplishing anything.[40] The past often

---

[38] Niamh Moore (2005), "Re-greening Brownfields: Land Recycling and Urban Sustainability," in N. Moore and M. Scott (eds), *Renewing Urban Communities: Environment. Citizenship, and Sustainability in Ireland*. Aldershot: Asghate, p. 37.

[39] Heather Ingman (2009), *A History of the Irish Short Story*. Cambridge: Cambridge University Press, p. 227.

[40] Jennifer Johnson (1985), *The Railway Station Man*. New York: Viking, p. 16.

looms over characters in Johnston's books, perhaps most notably in her first novel, *The Captains and the Kings* (1972). The same can be said of Colm Toíbín's novels, particularly *The Heather Blazing* (1993), which is about a prominent Irish judge whose troubled childhood during the period of the Easter Rising and the War of Independence provides the key to unlocking the reasons for his feelings of alienation from society. In *The Blackwater Lightship* (2000), a young man dying of AIDS brings his family together but in the process forces them to confront the history of their rocky relationships. But nowhere does Toíbín explore the relationship between past and present more successfully than in his novel, *Brooklyn*. In this novel, which won the Costa Novel of the Year Award for 2009, the main character, Eilis Lacey, moves from Ireland to the United States to find work but soon finds herself torn between her adopted and original homeland. The novel provides great insight into the experience of the Irish immigrant in general.

Whether to concentrate on the past or the present was a choice that confronted Irish filmmakers in the 1980s and 1990s as well. Luke Gibbons has attributed the cultural success of the Irish film industry in this period to several factors, including:

> . . . the emergence of a disparate group of highly gifted directors, actors, and other related personnel; the capacity of visual expression to come out from the shadow of a powerful literary tradition; the success of Irish popular culture, particularly rock music, at a global level; and the impact of a successive range of measures taken by the government to support the film industry.[41]

The Commitments (1991) was a film directed by Alan Parker (b. 1944) about a working-class Dublin rock band that turned away from traditional Irish musical genres to cover African-American soul classics such as "Mustang Sally" and "Midnight Hour," the latter by the legendary soul singer Wilson Pickett, who makes a short cameo appearance at the end of the film. Referring to the Irish as "the blacks of Europe," the film uses soul to express the underlying passion and heart of a segment of Irish society from inner-city Dublin. Neil Jordan's *Michael Collins* (1997) turned to one of the most controversial periods in the Irish past, covering the Easter Rising, the war for independence, and the civil war. The film was a great success in Ireland, less so outside of the Republic even though it featured superstars such as Liam Neeson and Julia Roberts, contained plenty of action, and included a romantic tear-jerking love story. But it also proved controversial in Ireland, mainly because the film does not provide a positive portrayal of Eamon de Valera.

---

[41] Luke Gibbons (2005), "Projecting the Nation: Cinema and Culture," in J. Cleary and C. Connolly (eds), *The Cambridge Companion to Modern Irish Culture*. Cambridge: Cambridge University Press, p. 211.

It even implied that he was behind the plot to assassinate Collins, something which de Valera had always emphatically denied.

Any assessment of Ireland's cultural history and role in the world in the late twentieth century must include some discussion of the global popularity and influence of Irish music and musicians. The rock group U2 achieved global popularity with its fourth studio album, *The Unforgettable Fire*, released in 1984, not least because of the powerful social content of songs such as "Pride (In the Name of Love)," which was the first single released from the album and became one of their most popular songs. The title of the album itself was inspired by a museum exhibit on the atomic bombings of Hiroshima and Nagasaki. The band remained at the center of its times by recording their album *Achtung Baby* in Germany in 1990 when that country was beginning the process of reunification at the end of the Cold War. By that time, however, the group had moved away from politically charged songs such as 1983's "Sunday Bloody Sunday."[42]

Irish music became even more popular in the 1990s, led by the hauntingly beautiful music of Eithne Ní Bhraonáin, better known as Enya (b. 1961). Her music on albums such as *Shepherd Moon* (1991) and *The Memory of Trees* (1995) evoked a blend of New Age and traditional Celtic spirituality. Sinéad O'Connor (b. 1966) also achieved international success, particularly with her 1990 recording, "Nothing Compares to You." She can also be heard performing "The Foggy Dew" with the Chieftains on their 2002 compilation, "The Wide World Over," celebrating that group's four decades as cultural ambassadors bringing Irish music to the world and world music to Ireland.

Although male groups such as the Saw Doctors were popular in Ireland in the eighties and nineties, two groups featuring talented female lead singers emerged to dominate Irish popular music in the 1990s: Dolores Ó Riordain (b. 1971) of the Limerick band the Cranberries and Andrea Corr (b. 1974) of the family based group named the Corrs from Dundalk in County Louth. In 1994, the Cranberries' song "Zombie" was the most played song on alternative radio in the United States, even though it was not released there as a single.[43] As of this writing, their 1994 album *No Need to Argue* has sold more than 17 million copies worldwide. The Corrs have also achieved global popularity, although some critics attributed this to their happy pop sound and not to their Irish roots. Indeed, the music that they learned from their parents was more likely to be by American groups from the seventies such as the Eagles and the Carpenters than traditional Irish folk music. However, Andrea Corr, lead singer and songwriter for the group, took umbrage at the suggestion that their music was too shallow to be taken seriously. In a 1995

---

[42] Joshua Clover (2009), *1989: Bob Dylan Didn't Have This to Sing About*. Berkeley: University of California Press, p. 131.

[43] *The Irish Times*, 22 August 1995.

interview, she pointed to the profound sadness inherent in a song like her "Forgiven Not Forgotten," which she described as about a woman who "has lost her beloved and she knows it's her own fault . . . so she lives with grief and disillusionment, constantly." She sees this as reflected in the music as well as the words, as "when the minor gives way to the major."[44] The Corrs have managed to blend Irish folk music and traditional instruments with a pop sound in a way that has led to global success.

Mary Black's (b. 1955) popularity has spanned the period from the mid-1980s to the present. She has recorded music from an eclectic range of songwriters, not all of them Irish. But she has managed to incorporate so many songs of a traditional Irish nature or that deal with themes from Irish history into her repertoire that she still comes across as quintessentially Irish. In the latter category, songs such as "Ellis Island" (1995) by Noel Brazil and "Leaving the Land" (1994) by Eric Bogle speak to the emigration experience of so many people from Ireland throughout the centuries. An example of the first category would be the poignant tragedy of the traditional Irish ballad "Anachie Gordon," which appeared on her first solo album in 1983. Her performance of the song, especially when performed live, leaves one's heart aching for the women and men in traditional landed society who were expected to put their family's interest ahead of their own and lacked the power to choose their own marriage partners.

Space precludes the inclusion of many fine Irish writers and musicians, but not even a short discussion of Irish musical trends would be complete without mentioning Tommy Makem and the Clancy Brothers and Christy Moore (b. 1945). Tommy Makem and the Clancy Brothers became very popular in the 1960s for their simple rendition of Irish ballads, developing a particular strong following in the United States after an appearance on "The Ed Sullivan Show" in 1961. But they continued performing periodically well into the 1990s. Moore's career has also spanned decades and made him an icon of Irish folk music. In a 1994 review of one of Moore's concerts, Luke Clancy wrote that "people don't just like or enjoy Christy, they love him. That's just the way it is." When he sings the line "Let the music keep your spirits high" from Jackson Browne's "Before the Deluge," it is impossible not to get the impression that Moore is trying to do just that. He sings songs from any era and imbues them all with present relevance and universal significance. To cite just one example, in "Ordinary Man," listeners feel and empathize with the sense of helplessness and despair that comes from being downsized out of a job after years of hard work and loyalty to a company.

Finally, the genre known as "country and Irish music," Ireland's response to American country music, has enjoyed a large popular following as well. Daniel O'Donnell (b. 1961) from Donegal has attained immense popularity in Britain and Ireland. Other country and Irish stars include The Willoughby

---

[44] "Irish to the Corrs," *The Irish Times*, 22 December 1995.

Brothers from County Wicklow, Louise Morrissey (b. 1961) from County Tipperary, and Lisa McHugh (b. 1988), who was actually born in Scotland but has been dubbed "Ireland's sweetheart of country music." American country music is also popular in its own right in Ireland. It is not unusual to walk into an Irish pub today and hear Johnny Cash's "Ring of Fire" or to hear his songs being played in music stores.

In their book on Irish migration, Lambkin and Fitzgerald provide an interesting juxtaposition of three cultural phenomena in different genres that have caused controversy in the late twentieth century.[45] "Riverdance," the brainchild of Irish musician Bill Whelan (b. 1950), a sensational dance show, has been exported to the world as an Irish cultural phenomenon, but traditionalists object to its amalgamation of different styles and the choreography of the American Michael Flatley to the point where they no longer consider the dancing truly Irish. *Angela's Ashes*, Frank McCourt's 1996 best-selling memoir of growing up poor in Ireland has aroused similar objections to those addressed at Synge's *Playboy of the Western World* earlier in the century, namely that it cast modern Ireland in a poor light, complete with the stereotypes reinforced by McCourt's drunken, absent father. Along the same lines, Shane McGowan's enormously popular and captivating 1987 song "Fairy Tale of New York," performed by the Pogues with Kirsty MacColl, is about a young Irishman who ends up in a drunk tank in New York City on Christmas eve, perhaps in the 1940s, that leads to a brilliant exploration of the lost dreams that accompany a failed relationship. These examples and the controversies surrounding them all speak to Irish creativity, Ireland's lack of insularity, and the continuing efforts to redefine what it means to be Irish as the Republic of Ireland moved into the twenty-first century.

---

[45] Lambkin and Fitzgerald, *op. cit.*, p. 279.

CHAPTER SIXTEEN

Conclusion

There is a music in the soul of Ireland that can still be heard, except that nobody knows they are hearing it because there is so much other noise . . . But, sometimes, through the fog of prejudice and irony and rage and self-hating, we hear the music and are moved by it in spite of ourselves.

– JOHN WATERS, *Was It For This? Why Ireland Lost the Plot*, 2012

Role of political and cultural nationalism in an age of globalization

Nationalism has proven to be a surprisingly resilient force in an age that has witnessed the unification of Europe and the wider phenomenon of globalization. For example, in the 1990s, nationalism reemerged in a particularly violent and deadly way in the Balkans following the fall of communism and the collapse of the multiethnic country of Yugoslavia. As recently as 25 November 2012, the people of Catalonia voted into power a party committed to separating from Spain as an independent nation. At the same time, the British are threatening withdrawal from the euro zone that Angela Merkel, the chancellor of Germany, is trying so hard to hold together. Within Britain itself, a distinct possibility exists that Scotland will eventually withdraw from the United Kingdom; to this point, the process of devolution has been remarkably peaceful. Nationalism has continued to play a strong role in Ireland as well. The Republic celebrates the history of the struggle for independence from Britain, while nationalists in Northern Ireland continue to oppose partition and seek to unite with the Republic. The Sinn Féin leader

Gerry Adams still seeks an eventual vote on the unification of Ireland. Sinn Féin not only favors the end of partition but also remains more opposed to further European integration than any other party in the Republic. Loyalists in Northern Ireland continue to assert their "Britishness," retaining their own particular brand of nationalist sentiment. They oppose leaving the United Kingdom.

However, there are signs that these nationalistic divisions, which have torn Northern Ireland apart in the past, are no longer as intense as they once were. For example, celebrations to commemorate the 100th anniversary of the signing of the 1912 Ulster Covenant, which was designed to ensure that Northern Ireland remain British, occurred without any violent backlash from nationalists. Furthermore, despite the survival of several splinter groups from the IRA who still oppose the power-sharing agreement between Catholics and Protestants in Northern Ireland, the number of incidents of violence and killing has been dramatically reduced. Similarly, Basque separatists demanding independence from Spain have renounced terrorism and turned to conventional politics as the appropriate means through which to attempt to achieve their goals. The terrorist attacks conducted by al-Qaeda in the United States on 11 September 2001 have gone a long way toward discrediting terrorism globally, something that the IRA and the ETA (the Basque Separatist group) presumably have taken into consideration.

Other developments indicate that issues of national identity remain problematic, however. In December 2012, a controversy arose in Belfast over a decision made by the city government to limit the number of days on which it would fly the Union Jack. Flags are powerful symbols that have the ability to unite or divide a people. For example, a controversy erupted in July 2011 when Governor Nikki Haley of South Carolina announced that she supported the continued flying of the Confederate flag over the state house. A few months later, in September, protestors flocked to the South Carolina home of a woman named Annie Chamber Caddell to demonstrate against the flag of the Confederacy that flew from her porch. At the same time, others were protesting the flying of a Confederate flag in an Atlanta cemetery. Caddell defended the flying of the Confederate flag as part of her "Southern heritage."[1] But it is hard to ignore the political meaning of such an act.

Nationalism has mainly to do with how people see themselves belonging to a larger group based more on history than anything else. At the center of the flag-flying controversy in Belfast is the issue of the national identity of the people of Northern Ireland. Loyalists see 1912 as the beginning of a new identity for them of which Britishness is an extremely important component. Loyalists have for a long time considered themselves British, but at the same

---

[1] Karen Freeman (2011), "Confederate Flag at Center of Controversy, Again," http://www.washingtonpost.com/blogs/blogpost/post/confederate-flag-at-center-of-controversy-again/2011/09/27/gIQA3T891K_blog.html, 27 September.

time, they have a separate Irish identity. They presumably see themselves as both British and Irish. A third alternative, which seems to have made headway in recent years, is a separate identity that is neither British nor Irish, but rather Northern Irish. However, none of these categories need to be mutually exclusive. After loyalists disrupted Christmas shopping in Belfast as a result of their protests against the decision to restrict the flying of the Union Jack, Peter Robinson (b. 1948), Northern Ireland's first minister, warned them that "Britishness will not be progressed by acts of violence. Anyone engaging in wanton violence or intimidation does not defend our national flag, but disgraces it."

The flag-flying controversy shows that divisions still remain in Northern Ireland at the end of 2012. These divisions can also be seen in the urban landscape of Belfast, Derry/Londonderry, and Portadown, where the so-called "peace walls" that had been erected during the Troubles to separate Protestants and Catholics still stand. According to a poll conducted by the University of Ulster in 2012, over two-thirds of the people who live near them do not want to see them removed.[2] This result would seem to indicate that many people in these cities still fear the sectarian violence that the walls were originally intended to prevent. However, the vast majority (78 per cent) of people in Northern Ireland as a whole said that they wanted to see the peace walls removed.[3] This is a clear indication that most people in Northern Ireland are ready to move forward into a more peaceful, less divisive future (see below).

Political nationalism has declined even more in the Republic of Ireland, and it is no wonder since Ireland has benefited so much from membership in the European Union, from globalization, and from its relationship with the United States. The republic has also benefited from the security provided by NATO, even though it never became a member. Of course, these benefits fluctuate from time to time, based largely on the global economy. In 2004, Ireland was named the most globalized country in the world by *Foreign Policy* magazine for the third consecutive year. The recession that hit in 2007 hindered the future globalization of the Irish economy and brought the Celtic Tiger to a screeching halt. Ireland found itself in competition for resources and investment with Eastern European nations such as Romania, which benefited from remaining outside the euro zone. Like other countries affected by recession, Ireland turned inward and sought to protect its national economy. But at the same time, Irish leaders have continued to seek the benefits of membership in the European Union, to which the country remains committed.

---

[2] Douglas Dalby (2012), "Tension, Though No Violence, as Protestants Parade in Belfast." *The New York Times*, 29 September.

[3] Henry McDonald (2012), "No end in sight for Belfast 'Peace Walls'," *The Guardian*, 25 September. http://www.guardian.co.uk/uk/2012/sep/26/belfast-peace-walls-republicans-loyalists.

Cultural nationalism would seem to have a more promising future than political nationalism. The people of Ireland still take great pride in their cultural and literary heritage. The Republic of Ireland is promoting 2013 as a year for people of Irish descent around the world to return to Ireland in a tourism campaign called *the Gathering*. Yet the prominent actor, director, and cultural ambassador, Gabriel Byrne (b. 1950), criticized the initiative as "a scam." He suggested that the campaign was designed to take advantage of people's association with Ireland merely in order to attract their money.

Is that, in fact, what Irish cultural nationalism has been reduced to in the twenty-first century? Even if it is so, it could be argued that it is not necessarily a bad thing to expose people from around the world to the richness of Irish culture at the same time that Ireland derives an economic benefit from what it has to offer to those who do visit the country. In addition, those people of Irish descent who choose to attend the Gathering will find a much more peaceful atmosphere in Northern Ireland if they decide to visit there as well.

Northern Ireland: A lasting peace?

On the brink of 2013, the leaders and people of Northern Ireland have demonstrated a commitment to move forward together. It is no longer enough to just accept the power-sharing agreement reached between nationalists and loyalists in 2007, as momentous a step as that was. A real desire for peace has obviously developed among the major parties involved in the past conflict. But not all went smoothly immediately following the signing of the Belfast Agreement in 1998. On 15 August 1998, the splinter group known as the Real IRA carried out a bombing in Omagh that killed 29 people and injured more than 200 others. The Sinn Féin leader Martin McGuinness denounced the bombing, saying "it was carried out by those opposed to the peace process." The IRA continued to operate for a time, most spectacularly in a daring robbery of the Northern Bank in Belfast in late December 2004 that resulted in the theft of about £30 million. At first, extremists in the IRA and the Democratic Union Party staked out their positions for fear of losing power to the moderates within their organizations. It took until the St Andrews Agreement was reached in August 2006 for the major parties involved to affirm the principles behind the Belfast Agreement of 1998.

In May 2007, Tony Blair, the British prime minister who helped negotiate the Belfast Agreement, returned to Stormont Castle in Belfast to attend a ceremony returning executive authority to Northern Ireland under a power-sharing agreement. The negotiations that led up to that agreement were stalled by negotiating ploys that showed a reluctance at the time which, if it has been largely overcome, had at its heart the main issue that still divides Sinn Féin from the Democratic Unionist Party. Ian Paisley was installed as first minister in a power-sharing arrangement between the DUP and Sinn

FIGURE 16.1 *Reverend Ian Paisley (center) and Martin McGuinness (left) with Alex Salmond, First Minister of Scotland in May 2008.*

Féin, represented by Martin McGuiness (b. 1950), a former IRA commander who became deputy first minister. Blair captured the significance of this event best when he wrote in his memoirs that "people who wanted to kill each other were now wanting to work together."[4] The impact of this was (and still is) truly astounding and makes some people wonder why so much bloodshed had been necessary to reach this point. To see the two of them together on television being interviewed and speaking so respectfully to one another must have evoked a variety of emotions in the people who had lived through the history of the previous 40 years. Paisley and McGuiness, in fact, got along so famously that people in Ireland refer to them as *the chuckle twins* (or *chuckle brothers*) because they laughed so much in each other's company.

Despite the close personal relationship between Paisley and McGuiness, however, total harmony between the two parties does not yet exist. They are still fundamentally divided on the future of Northern Ireland. Peter Robinson, who replaced Paisley in January 2010 as first minister, has not been particularly popular or successful at bringing the two sides closer together. He did propose the creation of a single school system for Protestants and Catholics, but has not yet brought the Catholics on board with the idea. Recently, Northern Ireland has launched a strategy designed to bring down the peace walls and end segregation called "CSI," which stands for cohesion, sharing, and integration. Unfortunately, the Alliance Party and the DUP withdrew from the committee when they became frustrated by

---

[4] Tony Blair (2010), *A Journey*. New York: Alfred A. Knopf, p. 199.

a lack of progress. Still, nationalists and loyalists have begun to speak the same language, with words such as Northern Ireland and even the issue of the name of Derry/Londonderry becoming less politically charged than in the past.

When Tony Blair visited Northern Ireland, he took satisfaction from the fact that the protests he met with had to do with the war in Iraq and not the presence of a British prime minister in Belfast.[5] In July 2007, the British military operation in Northern Ireland had officially ended. The meeting and handshake between Martin McGuiness and Queen Elizabeth II in June 2012 became a real symbol of change and goodwill that had a huge public relations effect. The people of the North have felt the difference in the political atmosphere, but still live with reminders of the Troubles. In 2011, Ashlean Burke, a college student living near the border with the Republic, summed up the situation well by relating that "although the trouble may not be as widespread today, bomb scares are still heard of, and minorities experience exclusion and violence due to their political and religious views . . . to some extent the troubles were resolved through the agreements but there are still remnants of the past in Northern Irish society today."[6]

One key development that could affect the situation in Northern Ireland in the future is the shifting balance in the population there. One of the premises on which the current peace in Northern Ireland has been constructed is that Northern Ireland will remain part of the United Kingdom until a majority of the population would vote otherwise. Census data from 2011 reveals that the Catholic population of Northern Ireland has increased within the past decade. The percentage of Catholics rose from 44 per cent in 2001 to 45 per cent in 2011. The percentage of Protestants declined during the same decade from 53 per cent to 48 per cent, making them a minority in Northern Ireland for the first time. Furthermore, Catholics were already a majority among school-age children in 2001. It is conceivable that Catholics could become a majority in Northern Ireland in the foreseeable future.

This possibility raises two important questions. If Catholics did become a majority, would they automatically vote to leave the United Kingdom to become part of the Republic? This might not necessarily be the case. Many Catholics have forged their own Northern Irish identity. One survey, cited by Peter Robinson in November 2012, indicated that only a third of the Catholics in Northern Ireland actually supported Irish unification.[7] Secondly, if a majority ever did vote for unification, would Protestants accept the results of the referendum or would they resort to threats of violence or actual violence in an attempt to prevent the secession of Northern Ireland

[5] Ibid., p. 199.
[6] Burke Ashlean (2011), Interview by Terence B. Bodak, Jr. Online Correspondence, 4 May.
[7] Hugo Mac Neill (2012), "People of the North Must Lead Building of a New Society." *The Irish Times*, 29 November.

from the United Kingdom, as they have in the past? Just as there may always be extremist nationalists such as those who have not yet accepted the peace agreement in Northern Ireland, there may also always be Protestant loyalists who would never accept the unification of Ireland.

The demonstrations in Belfast over the flag issue demonstrate how strongly committed to the union with Britain many people still are at the end of 2012. In early December, 18 people were injured in street fighting that accompanied a loyalist demonstration over the city council's decision regarding the flag. In the face of this violence, some despair that the Troubles are not yet over. It may be hard to envision these sectarian divisions ever dying down, given how deeply rooted they are in centuries of history, but that does not mean that it is impossible. If the situation improves in the next ten years as much as it has in the past decade, the Troubles may become another part of Irish history relegated to a bygone day. If so, it will be left to writers and filmmakers to remind the people of this part of their past and explore its meaning and effects, as some twenty-first century artists have already been doing.

Recent Irish cultural, literary, and musical trends

The Troubles and their aftermath have continued to provide material for filmmakers wishing to explore this aspect of Northern Ireland's recent history, though the most well-known films have been made by non-Irish directors. The English director Paul Greengrass's *Bloody Sunday* (2002) received critical acclaim for its reexamination of that fateful day 30 years after the day for which the film is named. *Bloody Sunday* was filmed in much the same way that Gillo Pontecorvo filmed *The Battle of Algiers* (1966)—by making the film resemble a documentary to provide the viewer with the impression that the events were actually unfolding as they were being filmed. Greengrass said of the film that he was "essentially making it for all of our island."[8] Pete Travis, who is also from England, directed *Omagh* in 2004, a film about the events surrounding a 1998 IRA bombing from the perspective of the father of one of the victims. In 2009, the German director Oliver Hirschbiegel made a suspense thriller about a former loyalist, played by Liam Neeson, seeking forgiveness for past deeds from his former enemies. To say that it conveys the difficulty of reconciliation between them would be an understatement. Northern Irish directors have generally steered clear of the subject; the Northern Irish director Brendan Foley set his 2007

---

[8] Brian Lavery (2002), "In Ulster, Reliving Its Day of Infamy." *New York Times*, 29 September.

independent thriller, *The Riddle*, which deals with a series of murders that follow the discovery of an unpublished novel by Charles Dickens without any reference to the Troubles.

In addition to *Bloody Sunday*, 2002 also saw the release of Peter Mullan's *The Magdalene Sisters*, which deals with the harsh conditions in institutions known as Magdalene Asylums and the despair experienced by the disgraced girls sent to them because of their sexual indiscretions. This dark secret of Irish society, which had previously been the subject of a 1994 song, "The Magdalene Laundries," by the Canadian singer Joni Mitchell, was also brought to the attention of a wide audience through a BBC film called *Sinners* broadcast on Irish television in 2002. There was no attempt in either film to downplay the abject horror associated with these institutions; Robert Cooper, who was in charge of BBC drama for Northern Ireland at the time, described the subject as "harrowing."[9] These films dovetail with the numerous documentaries on the sexual abuse scandal in the Catholic Church that have appeared in the past decade. In each instance, Ireland continues to confront the dark aspects of its past in an attempt to move past them.

The actual teachings of the church have also been challenged, perhaps most notably by Colm Tóibín, who has remained at the center of Irish cultural trends with his 2012 historical novel, *The Testament of Mary*. In this novel, Tóibín provides a retelling of the life of the mother of Jesus in her own words. Tóibín is not the first novelist to reexamine the lives of the central figures of the New Testament through the imagined eyes of the participants. For example, *Paul: A Novel* (2000), by Walter Wangerin Jr., examines the life of St Paul in a way that is consistent with his letters and recent Biblical scholarship. In *Jesus: A Story of Enlightenment* (2008), Deepak Chopra looks at the missing years of Jesus' life in a way that is intended to make him a sympathetic figure to Christians and non-Christians alike. By contrast, Tóibín's Mary bears little resemblance to the woman depicted in the Gospels and is at odds with their account of her son's life. It challenges the central message of the Gospels as we see Jesus through the eyes of a mother unconvinced that her son's sacrifice was necessary. In the novel, Mary describes the authors of the Gospels as propagandists out to further their own agenda instead of telling the truth, especially about her. Tóibín is known for exploring mother and child relationships in much of his fiction. It is well documented that he had a strained relationship with his own distant mother who left him and his brother in the care of relatives at a young age. *The Testament of Mary* has not quite received the critical acclaim of *Brooklyn*, but it has added to Tóibín's literary legacy and is a highly creative, original, and thought-provoking novel in its own right.

There are a slew of fine contemporary Irish novelists (see the website associated with the book for additional recommendations), but John

---

[9] Jeremiah Bailey (2002), "Airing Our Dirty Laundry." *The Irish Times*, 23 March.

Banville (b. 1945) might be the second-most critically acclaimed after Toíbín. Having received a great deal of attention for *The Book of Evidence* (1989), Banville has continued to produce outstanding work, most recently in *Ancient Light* (2012), a novel about a man recalling a youthful love affair with an older woman that blurs the boundary between memory and reality. Glenn Patterson (b. 1961) is considered one of Northern Ireland's finest contemporary novelists; four of his seven novels have been published in the twenty-first century. His most recent work, *The Mill for Grinding Old People Young* (2012), is set in nineteenth-century Belfast and deals with a city that is facing the future through industrialization with an eye on the past and the lingering effects of the Rebellion of 1798.

In other genres, the poetry of Dermot Bolger (b. 1959), who comes from the Dublin suburb of Finglas, is considered particularly moving and profound. Northern Ireland's Sinead Morrissey (b. 1972) has published four books of poems since 1996. Her most recent collection is *Through the Square Window* (2010), which one reviewer praised for its "incisive imagery and taut rhythms," saying that "the poems come to us with the intimacy of whispered secrets."[10] Kevin Barry (b. 1969) is keeping the Irish short story tradition alive; his work has been published in two highly praised collections: *There Are Little Kingdoms* (2007) and *Dark Lies the Island* (2012). But he is hardly the only one; *News from Dublin: New Irish Short Stories* is a collection edited by Joseph O'Connor that includes stories by Roddy Doyle and Colm Toíbín among others. It is the third such anthology published since 2004.

It should also be noted that Irish historians continue to publish important work that is aimed at a broad audience of the Irish reading public. Diarmaid Ferriter has written a number of works that are both scholarly and accessible, most recently *Ambiguous Republic: Ireland in the 1970s* (2012), a must-read for anyone interested in the Republic during that transitional decade. In addition to Tim Pat Coogan's recent book on the Famine, *The Atlas of the Great Irish Famine* (2012), edited by John Crowley, William J. Smith, and Mike Murphy is based on up-to-date scholarship and is an impressive volume that stands out among the many works that have been devoted to that subject. Readers interested in understanding events in Dublin in the period of the War for Independence from a social perspective would be well served by Padraig Yeates's *A City in Turmoil: Dublin, 1919–1921* (2012). (Again, see the book's website for additional suggestions.)

Irish traditional music remains alive in the twenty-first century; a traditional music festival in Listowell in County Kerry in August 2002 drew about 10,000 performers and more than 200,000 people. The festival was

---

[10] Paul Batchelor (2010), "Review of Sinead Morrissey's *Through the Square Window*," *The Guardian*. 12 March. http://www.guardian.co.uk/books/2010/mar/13/through-square-window-sinead-morrissey.

sponsored by the organization Comhaltas Ceoltóirí Eireann, which was founded in 1951 and still refers to itself as "the largest group involved in the preservation and promotion of traditional Irish music."[11] By 2008, traditional Irish folk music (along with the learning of Gaelic) was even undergoing a revival in Northern Ireland, showing a greater level of comfort by people there with their own Irish roots. The annual festival of Comhaltas, called the "Fleadh Cheoil," is held on an annual basis; the 2013 festival will take place in May in Ballycastle in County Antrim.

In addition to traditional acts, new Irish musical groups and artists arrive on the rock and pop musical scene every year. Recent albums such as "Little Sparks" by Delorentos, "Cover and Flood" by Katie Kim, and "The Brutal Here and Now" by The Spook of the Thirteenth Lock all provide evidence of the vitality and creativity of contemporary Irish music. The Spook of the Thirteenth Lock, which the group's website says is "named after a poem about a haunted canal lock" describe their music as a cross between "Irish folk and traditional sounds with more modern experimental rock sounds."[12] By contrast, Katie Kim's lilting voice and acoustic guitar playing on a song such as "Your Mountains, My Mountains" is simpler but completely mesmerizing. Delorentos, based in Dublin, claim a varied musical lineage that they say draws on "most genres of music and virtually every decade since the 1950s."[13] Among Northern Irish bands, Snow Patrol, which released their sixth album, *Fallen Empires* in 2011 continues a tradition of rock and alternative music from Northern Ireland, following the success in previous decades of Northern Irish artists such as Van Morrison and bands such as The Undertones, The Divine Comedy, and, more recently, Ash, whose last studio album was *Twilight of the Innocents* (2007). There is no question that the rich literary output and the continued vitality of different genres of Irish music have done much to enrich the quality of life in Ireland, but there are, of course, other aspects to that as well, not all quite so positive.

Quality of life issues

In December 2012, the Economic and Social Research Institute released a 2010 report showing that 22 per cent of households in the Republic of Ireland did not contain a working adult, a higher proportion than in any of the 31 other European countries included in the study. The average number of households without a working adult in those other nations was 10 per cent.[14] Although Ireland also had a relatively high percentage of such

---

[11] http://comhaltas.ie/about/
[12] http://thirteenthlock.net/bio
[13] http://www.delorentos.net/index.php/bio
[14] Dan O'Brien (2012), "Ireland Tops European League of Jobless Households." *The Irish Times*, 11 December.

households even before the recession of 2007, these later figures seemed dire at the time that they were released in 2012. That is because at the same time the sagging economy led the government to engage in substantial budget cuts that threatened to weaken social services. Ireland has faced a paradoxical choice with which every government whose country is in recession has to deal: to introduce austerity measures to reduce the debt and cut social services at the time in which they are most needed or provide relief and pump money that it does not have into the economy in the hope of stimulating a recovery. Government leaders, led by Taoiseach Enda Kenny (b. 1951), responded by attempting to make the economy more competitive and to assuage European leaders concerned about the viability of Ireland remaining in the euro zone.

Because of the latter concern, Kenny's government refused to consider any reversals of the budget cuts scheduled for 2013 despite an outcry against those cuts when they were announced. 3500 positions in the health service department were scheduled to be cut in 2013 alone. The health budget was scheduled to be reduced by some €800 million. In the course of a 12-month period prior to December 2012, 60,000 people canceled their health insurance policies. The number of people with health insurance declined from 2.297 million people in 2008 to 2.109 million in 2012.[15]

Such cuts did not sit well with Irish public intellectuals who had witnessed the erosion of the values on which they believed that Irish society had been based before the Celtic Tiger years. Some Irish commentators have been quite critical of the free market economy. The Celtic Tiger economy had convinced many people in Ireland to respect market forces, a belief which has not sustained the Irish people in the aftermath of the economic collapse. In late 2012, the environmental activist John Gibbons wrote in *The Irish Times* that "consumption-based capitalism is now an unsustainable model for wealth creation."[16] About the same time, the columnist John Marsden wrote that "a valueless secular autonomy cannot provide the kind of civic culture that resists the evident pathologies of contemporary market economics."[17] And, in a speech following his induction into the Royal Irish Academy, President Michael Higgins (b. 1941) spoke of the "moral choice" confronting Irish leaders "to be part of a passive consensus that accepts an insufficient and failed model of life and economy or to seek to recover the possibility of alternative futures."[18]

---

[15] Conor Pope (2012), "Large Drop in People with Health Insurance." *The Irish Times*, 1 December.

[16] John Gibbons (2012), "'Steady as She Goes': Global Climatic Denial Guarantees Chaotic Future For All." *The Irish Times*, 30 November.

[17] John Marsden (2012), "Religion Can Provide Early Warning System Against Excesses of the Market." *The Irish Times*, 4 December.

[18] Joe Humphreys (2012), "Higgins Calls for 'Independent Thought'." *The Irish Times*, 27 November.

Another issue that remains of great concern, particularly for women, is the abortion debate and the ways in which Irish law is seen as placing women's health beyond their control. The death of Savita Halappanavar at the age of 31 in November 2012 sparked enormous outrage and controversy, bringing the issue once again to the center of Irish politics. Ms Halappanavar had been admitted to a hospital in Galway as she was experiencing a miscarriage when she was 17 weeks pregnant. According to her husband, she repeatedly requested that the pregnancy be terminated, but doctors refused her request for three days because they could still hear a fetal heartbeat. She was told that Ireland was a "Catholic country" and that it was irrelevant that she was not Catholic. She died of septicemia as a result of the doctors' refusal to perform an abortion.

The death of Ms Halappanavar was preceded by a 2009 case argued by Julie Kay before the European Court of Human Rights involving a woman suffering from cancer who had been forced to obtain an abortion in England when doctors in Ireland would not discuss the risks to her body caused by her pregnancy. She not only won her case, but the court found Ireland in violation of the European Convention on Human Rights and insisted that Ireland reform its abortion laws.[19] In 2002, the UN Committee on Human Rights had already expressed its concern that Ireland restricted the access of women to legal abortions and did not have clear guidelines on which circumstances might make abortion lawful. Despite these warnings, and other previous rulings against it, the Halappanavar case was what finally forced the government to discuss the issue. At first, the government expressed its regret and sorrow over the death of Ms Halappanavar and affirmed its position that abortion was legal in Ireland to save the life of the mother. However, by the end of 2012, the government announced that new legislation would be introduced to clarify the circumstances under which pregnancies could be legally terminated to comply with the rulings against Ireland in the European Court of Human Rights. The most controversial aspect of the proposal was that it included risk of suicide among those conditions considered life-threatening for the mother. Representatives of the Catholic Church in Ireland immediately expressed concern that this would create a loophole that would in effect legalize abortion. Defenders of the bill denied that was the case, and noted that abortion would still not be permitted for extenuating circumstances such as rape or incest.

The fact that the Constitution still defines women's duties as being primarily in the home has remained a source of unhappiness for many Irish women. Thus the abortion issue actually tapped into much larger concerns by women about the ways in which the law and the constitution are out of sync with the realities of women's (and men's) lives in the twenty-first century.

---

[19] Julie F. Kay (2012), "Time for an Abortion Law to Stop Irish Women Suffering." *The Irish Times*, 22 November.

The legacy of the past

William Faulkner famously wrote in *Requiem for a Nun* that "The past is never dead. It is not even past." If this is true in general, it seems to be even more so for Ireland. For example, at the request of the British government, Sir Desmond da Silva conducted an investigation into the February 1989 murder of a Belfast solicitor named Pat Finucane (1949–89). In the early 1980s, Mr Finucane had represented prominent members of the IRA, including Bobby Sands, one of the leaders of the hunger strike by IRA prisoners. It had long been suspected that the British government had been complicit in Finucane's death. Da Silva's report concluded that employees of the British government "actively furthered and facilitated his murder" and then attempted to cover up the involvement of the state.

This admission, however, brought little consolation to Mr Finucane's widow, Geraldine, or the rest of his family. Furthermore, it did not go far enough to satisfy those with intimate knowledge of the situation, such as the respected journalist Ed Moloney (b. 1948), who had made a career covering the Troubles and the Provisional IRA. Moloney claimed to have first-hand knowledge that the British knew in advance of threats to three prominent solicitors. He also asserted knowledge that the British had neither informed them nor took active measures to prevent the killings. The family of Mr Finucane had long called for a public inquiry into the murder, which they believed they had been promised by Tony Blair. Following the release of the da Silva report, Enda Kenny voiced his support for a public inquiry in which documents and witness testimony would be available to the family and the general public. He vowed the cooperation of his government if such an inquiry were to be held. To Geraldine Finucane and her family, da Silva was a "lawyer with strong links to the Conservative Party," which had been in power at the time of the murder. David Cameron (b. 1966), the British prime minister, did issue an apology for the actions of the government, one which Geraldine Finucane grudgingly accepted without toning down her condemnation of the report. She dismissed the report as "a sham," "a whitewash," "a confidence trick," and "not the truth." She said, "At every turn, it is clear that this report has done exactly what was required: to give the benefit of the doubt to the state, its cabinet, to the Army, to the intelligence services, to itself."[20]

This case, of course, symbolizes how recent is the history of the Troubles in Northern Ireland. There are many people alive today who have been directly impacted by them and there will be for quite some time. For some, like Geraldine Finucane, the wounds are still fresh. It is reasonable to assume that her demands for a public inquiry were made out of a desire to know

---

[20] Kevin Rawlinson (2012), "British Agents 'Facilitated the Murder' of Belfast Solicitor Pat Finucane." *The Belfast Telegraph*, 13 December.

the full truth of her husband's murder in the hopes of possibly achieving her own peace of mind. That she is open to reconciliation with the truth is at least a step in the right direction. The case could perhaps provide a model for how the legacy of the past will—or will not—be dealt with.

In the Republic, the past continues to manifest itself in different ways. The Fianna Fáil and Fine Gael parties have been contesting for power since the 1930s and continue to do so. Fianna Fáil is noted for its opposition to abortion and its defense of the conservative nature of the Irish constitution. The journalist John Waters has written that "the myth creation and the conservatism are equally vital elements of Fianna Fáil's spiritual dynamic, and together form the unassailable moral resource so envied by outsiders" and called the party "the living political conscience of the Irish nation."[21] But he also notes that that conscience was on short display during the administrations of Charles Haughey in the 1980s and early 1990s and Bertie Ahern from 1997 to 2008. The backlash against Fianna Fáil led to Fine Gael's return to power following the beginning of the recession and Ahern's fall.

Sinn Féin, another reminder of the past, remains a voice in the Republic calling for a united Ireland, a goal that it restated as soon as the power-sharing agreement was reached in Northern Ireland in 2007. In April 2006, the Republic held a military parade through the streets of Dublin to commemorate the anniversary of the Easter Rising for the first time since the 1970s. For 25 years, the Republic had chosen not to put on a display that might be construed as showing sympathy for the IRA. The decision by Bertie Ahern to hold the event was controversial nonetheless. There is still no consensus in Ireland on how the 1916 rebels should be remembered.

The legacy of the past is even more obvious in the North, where there is still a fear that violence can break out at any time and enough recent examples to justify that fear. Riots occurred in north Belfast in September 2001, and sporadic incidents of violence recurred in the months that followed. The IRA officially renounced violence in 2005, but splinter groups have not. In March 2009, Irish nationalist extremists threw gasoline bombs at police in retaliation for the arrest of three IRA dissidents, including Colin Duffy, considered one of the leaders of the IRA, who were suspected of the murder of two British soldiers. Incidents of violence are likely to occur from time to time for the foreseeable future. Criminals will even use political terrorism as a cover for their illicit activities. But as long as these incidents and crimes are the acts of sociopathic outliers and not sanctioned by a larger community, they will no longer be part of the legacy of the past but only one of the many present problems that confront police on a regular basis and that are a result of the depravity of individuals rather than the forces of history.

---

[21] John Waters (2012), *Was It For This? How Ireland Lost the Plot*. London: TransWorld Ireland, p. 116.

The promise of the present
and the hope for the future

Both the Republic of Ireland and Northern Ireland stand at a crossroads in 2013. Although that might sound like a cliché that could be said of any year for any country, a strong argument can be made for that assertion nonetheless.

The republic is six years into a recession and faces difficult decisions about how to strengthen the economy. If it can take lessons from the hubris of the Celtic Tiger years and yet remain optimistic about the future—with assistance from Europe, the United States, and a successful tourism campaign—it can start to build steadily to a solid and happy future, even if it is not accompanied by the spectacular successes of the boom years of the late twentieth and early twenty-first century. Most of the Irish people in 2012 still seem to consider their future with Europe, even as Britain threatens to break away. If the British do withdraw from the European Union, they would be pulling away from Ireland as well. But that might have the effect of bringing Ireland and the United States even closer together. In December 2012, the US ambassador to Ireland, Daniel M. Rooney, wrote a column in *The Irish Times* affirming that the US-Irish relationship is stronger than ever and pointing to the €145 billion that American companies have invested in Ireland.[22] To some degree, the hope for Ireland is the challenge that all modern capitalistic economies face: balancing regulation with free enterprise and avoiding the extreme lows of the economic cycle even if it means foregoing the extreme highs. But Ireland has unique problems too. In particular, it must find a way to see that more of its citizens receive higher education and reduce the number of households with no working adults. In addition, the suicide rate for adult males is still extremely high. But the present is not all bleak. To talk to people in Ireland is not to get the impression of a depressed society.

In Northern Ireland, 15 years after the Belfast Agreement, a half dozen years after the power-sharing arrangement between nationalists and loyalists, the hope is that the momentum toward peace will be sustained and that extremists on both sides will continue to dwindle in number, if they do not entirely disappear. As Gerry Moriarty wrote in *The Irish Times* in November 2012, "The North hasn't quite crossed the line to some brave, new, harmonious world, but there is hope, and people are moving on."[23] Perhaps, in a fairer, less discriminatory, and less prejudiced Northern

---

[22] Daniel M. Rooney (2012), "US-Irish Relationship 'the Strongest It Has Ever Been'." *The Irish Times*, 14 December.

[23] Gerry Moriarty (2012), "Northern Ireland's Quiet Revolution." *The Irish Times*, 17 November.

Ireland, Catholics will not only accept but cling to their Northern Irish identity, rendering the fears of Protestants obsolete. If the unionists can make a case for continued allegiance to Britain that is not based on their Protestant identity and tone down their anti-Catholic rhetoric, then such a possibility would be more likely. Perhaps, Protestants will embrace their Irish identity and, with the Republic shaken by the abuse scandals in the Catholic Church and no longer willing to give it as much power, lose their fear of unification and accept an eventual majority vote to secede from the United Kingdom. From an outsider's perspective, either would seem a satisfactory solution to a land that has experienced so much strife for the past century. There is a chance, however, that class divisions could replace religious ones as sources of violence, even if they retain older religious overtones.

One thing is certain: unless the peace process continues to take hold and the power-sharing agreement works, any discussion of unification would be out of the question. Hugo O'Neill put it best when he wrote: "A stable Northern Ireland is . . . an essential prerequisite for any closer constitutional relationship with the South. Without stability, the people of the South have no interest."[24]

As for the religious future of Ireland, spirituality has been such an important part of Irish history that it is difficult to envision a future in which it does not continue to play a significant role. If Catholic Ireland is largely gone, as Mary Kenny suggested, that does not necessarily mean that the Irish people have completely rejected the spiritual roots that are deeply embedded in their history. Within the past year, President Michael Higgins said "I don't believe spirituality is lesser or has been rejected in Ireland at all. I think it has been given a different expression."[25]

There have been expressions of revulsion against the crass materialism associated with the Celtic Tiger years and the administrations of Haughey and Ahern. John Waters described Haughey as a man who "preached the deep tradition of a peasant Catholicism and yet lived the life of a Renaissance prince" and who "tried to simulate the impression of a visionary based on parodying ancient values and their adherents, even while he was up to his oxters in the green slime of the material world."[26] In 2011, Patrick Kiely and Dermot Keogh wrote that the choice facing the political leaders of each main party in the republic was "to return to the idealism of the founding generation of the state and restore Ireland to a position of dignity internationally and its rightful place among the nations of the world," a phrase that echoed

---

[24] Hugo O'Neill (2012), "People of the North Must Lead Building of a New Society." *The Irish Times*, 29 November.

[25] Patsy McGarry (2012), "A Year in the Áras: 'I'm Not Inventing a Different Version of Michael D. Higgins'." *The Irish Times*, 3 November.

[26] Waters, *op. cit.*, pp. 118–19.

the words of the Irish nationalist Robert Emmet before his execution for treason in 1803.[27]

It seems to me that there is no shortage of idealism in contemporary Ireland and that Ireland's recent admission to membership on the United Nations Human Rights Council has given positive affirmation of the place that it occupies among "the nations of the world." In addition, environmental consciousness is on the rise and Ireland can already point to a number of environmental successes. During the Celtic Tiger years, there was perhaps a greater reluctance to enforce or improve environmental standards for fear of slowing down the economy. The new, less-materialistic Ireland is not as concerned about that. Environmental concerns still remain; in December 2012, Ireland was fined €3.5 million for failure to regulate the installation of septic tanks and inadequate waste water management. Larger issues, such as climate change, are of course not Ireland's problem alone. But there seems to be willingness on the part of the government to redress or address these issues as best and as quickly as it can. Overall, the administration of Enda Kenny has also contributed to signs of recovery of the goodwill of the Irish people toward their political leaders. However, at the end of 2012, budget cuts and the controversy over abortion were threatening to undermine that and are likely to remain potential sources of further division.

What Irish history can teach the rest of the world

In May 2011, Queen Elizabeth II, on an invitation from President Mary McAleese, paid a four-day visit to the Republic of Ireland. This was the sign of a mature society secure enough to no longer need to define itself by its opposition to Britain. If the people of Ireland were able to embrace the queen of their former enemy, then surely this is a lesson of the possibilities for peace and reconciliation elsewhere in the world. If Ian Paisley and Gerry Adams, the bitterest of enemies during the Troubles, can reach a power-sharing agreement in Northern Ireland, then this could inspire others locked in similar struggles to negotiate sooner and to see the humanity in those they regard as an enemy. The Troubles provide evidence that violence begets more violence, and there is only one way out of the cycle: for enemies to lay down their arms and negotiate their way to peace.

That is not to minimize how difficult peace was to achieve in Northern Ireland or the long and arduous efforts that led to it. But those engaged in conflict resolution around the globe might learn something from that as well.

---

[27] Patrick Kielyand Dermot Keogh (2011), "Turning Corners: Ireland 2002–11," in T. W. Moody, F. X. Martin and Dermot Keogh, Patrick Kiely (eds), *The Course of Irish History*, 5th edn. Lanham, MD: Roberts Rhinehart, p. 397.

Yet, I hope that this book has demonstrated that Irish history has much more to teach us than even these important lessons. Every period of the past has the ability to speak to us directly in the present. James A. Garfield, the twentieth president of the United States, said:

> There is nothing in all the earth that you and I can do for the Dead. They are past our help and past our praise. We can add to them no glory, nor can we give them immortality. They do not need us, but forever and forever we need them.[28]

The Irish past constitutes an important part of the human story with all of its achievements and wisdom as well as its suffering and tragedy. Ireland's history is varied and complex and has all the more to teach us because of that. Ireland's history teaches us that we need to be careful about how history is interpreted and not to take the subject lightly or receive a handed-down version on blind faith. Nationalism can create pride, but pride can lead to prejudice. Revisionist historians have made a great contribution in challenging handed-down versions of the Irish past, as well as turning our attention to other dimensions of it that are left out of most popular accounts. In fact, the dangers of viewing history from a monolithic perspective— nationalist or loyalist, Catholic or Protestant—is one of the many lessons that Irish history has to teach the rest of the world.

There are, however, also limits to revisionism. Some actions are heroic, some injustices wrong. John Waters writes that when we listen "we hear again the unconditional bravery of some great patriot and not even the collective efforts of legions of revisionists can talk us out of seeing it for what it is."[29] Nationalism, patriotism (British and Irish), the struggle for Irish independence, and the struggle of Irish women for greater rights are all part of Ireland's history, sometimes for worse but sometimes for better.

Ireland's history demonstrates other important aspects of the past that bear keeping in mind. Irish history cannot be understood in a vacuum and demonstrates the interconnectedness that any land shares with many others. In this conclusion, I have attempted to bring the story up to the time at which I am writing, but if Ireland's past shows anything, it is that history does not stop and at no point can history be considered final. Ireland's history also seems to me to be particularly well suited to demonstrate, through the lessons that the Irish have had to sometimes painfully learn, that the meaning of life is not just found in economics and technological advance, as important as these are. Ireland's rich traditions and contemporary creativity in the areas of culture, music, literature, and criticism are one way in which

---

[28] Quoted in Candice Millard (2011), *Destiny of the Republic: A Tale of Madness, Medicine, and the Murder of a President*. New York: Doubleday, p. 247.

[29] Waters, *op. cit.*, p. 300.

Irish history reflects that truth. The Irish have also found meaning in their spiritual traditions, which need not decline even if the reputation of the organized Catholic Church has suffered as a result of recent scandals. Ireland remains a unique place and its history and culture continue to have a claim on the world's attention. In the end, a study of Ireland's past provides myriad lessons that can be applied by anyone studying the past of their own—or any other—country.

BIBLIOGRAPHY

Primary sources

http://www.1641.tcd.ie/index.php.

Adams, Gerry (2003), *A Farther Shore: Ireland's Long Road to Peace*. New York: Random House.

Adomnán (1991), *Life of Columba*, edited by Alan Orr Anderson and Marjorie Ogilvie Anderson. Oxford: Clarendon Press.

The Agreement Reached in the Multiparty Negotiations (10 April 1998). http://cain.ulst.ac.uk/events/peace/docs/agreement.htm#rights.

The Annals of Connaught (1970), edited by A. Martin Freeman. Dublin: The Dublin Institute for Advanced Studies.

The Annals of the Four Masters, http://www.ucc.ie/celt/published/T100005B/index.html.

The Annals of Innisfallen, http://www.ucc.ie/celt/published/T100004/index.html.

The Annals of Ireland by Friar John Clyn (2007), edited and translated, with an Introduction by Bernadette Williams. Dublin: Four Courts Press.

The Annals of Loch Cé, http://www.ucc.ie/celt/published/T100010A/index.html.

The Annals of Tigernach, http://www.ucc.ie/celt/published/T100002A/index.html.

The Annals of Ulster, http://www.ucc.ic/celt/published/T100001C/index.html.

Banville, John (2004), "Memory and Forgetting: The Ireland of de Valera and Ó Faoláin," in D. Keogh, F. O'Shea and C. Quinlan (eds), *The Lost Decade: Ireland in the 1950s*. Cork: Mercier Press, pp. 21–30.

Barrington, Jonah (1835), *Historic Memoirs or Ireland Comprising Secret Records of the National Convention, the Rebellion, and the Union*, 2 vol. London: Henry Colburn.

Bede (1994), *Ecclesiastical History of the English People*, edited by Edith McClure and Roger Collins. Oxford: Oxford University Press. http://books.google.com/books?id=UussAAAAYAAJ&printsec=frontcover&source=gbs_ge_summary_r&cad=0#v=onepage&q&f=false.

Blair, Tony (2010), *A Journey*. New York: Alfred A. Knopf.

A Bloody Battell: Or the Rebels Overthrow, and Protestant Victorie (1641), London: Joseph Greensmith. http://bluehawk.monmouth.edu:2213/openurl?ctx_ver=Z39.88-2003&res_id=xri:eebo&rft_id=xri:eebo:image:125544.

British Information Services (1985), *Policy Statements*.

Bruce, William and Joy, Henry (2005), *Belfast Politics: Thoughts on the British Constitution*, edited by John Bew. Dublin: University College Dublin Press.

Calendar of State Papers Related to Ireland, of the reigns of Henry VIII, Edward VI, Mary . . . http://www.archive.org/stream/1887calendarofstatep03greauoftpage14/mode/2up.

Clifford, Brendan (ed.) (1998), *Lord Downshire and the United Irishmen: A Selection from the Downshire Papers, 1793–1799, with a Historical Review of the British Constitution*. Belfast: Athol Books.

Coles, Robert (1980), "Ulster's Children: Waiting for the Prince of Peace," *Atlantic Monthly Online*. http://www.theatlantic.com/past/docs/unbound/flashbks/ireland/coleul.htm.

Collins, Eamon and McGovern, Mick (1997), *Killing Rage*. London: Granta Books.

Columbanus. *Letters*, translated by G. S. M. Walker, electronic edition compiled by Ruth Murphy. http://143.239.128.67/celt/published/T201054/index.html.

Constitution of Ireland (1937), http://www.constitution.ie/reports/ConstitutionofIreland.pdf. http://www.craigavonhistoricalsociety.org.uk/rev/luttonyeomanry.html.

Cromwell, Oliver (1904), *The Letters and Speeches of Oliver Cromwell with Elucidations by Thomas Carlyle*, edited by S. C. Lomas. London: Methuen. http://openlibrary.org/books/OL7102295M/The_letters_and_speeches_of_Oliver_Cromwell.

Cunningham, Bernadette (ed.) (2010), *Calendar of State Papers, Ireland: Tudor Period, 1568–1571*. Dublin: Irish Manuscripts Collection.

Davis, Thomas (1915), *Selections from his Prose and Poetry*. New York: Frederick A. Stokes Company.

Dean, Seamus (ed.) (1991), *The Field Day Anthology of Irish Writing: Volume I*. Derry: Field Day.

Devlin, Bernadette (1969), *The Price of My Soul*. New York: Alfred A. Knopf.

Dorian, Hugh (2000), *The Outer Edge of Ulster: A Memoir of Social Life in Nineteenth-Century Donegal*, in Breandán Mac Suibhne and David Dickson (eds), Notre Dame: University of Notre Dame Press.

Firth, C. H. and Rait, R. S. (1911), *Acts and Ordinances of the Interregnum, 1642–1660*. London: Wyman and Sons.

Fitzgerald, Desmond (1968), *Desmond's Rising: Memoirs 1913 to Easter 1916*. Dublin: Liberties Press.

Foner, Philip S. (ed.) (1945), *The Complete Writings of Thomas Paine*, 2 vol. New York: Citadel Press.

Gerald of Wales (1863), *The Historical Works of Giraldus Cambrensis*, edited by Thomas Wright. London: H.G. Bohn.

Gookin, Vincent (1655), *The Great Case of Transplantation in Ireland Discussed*. London: I.C. http://bluehawk.monmouth.edu:2213/openurl?ctx_ver=Z39.88-2003&res_id=xri:eebo&rft_id=xri:eebo:image:197848.

Greene, David H. (1954), *An Anthology of Irish Literature*, Volume I. New York: New York University Press.

Harris, Benjamin (2011), "Recollections," in Rafe Blaufarb and Claudia Liebeskind (eds), *Napoleonic Foot Soldiers and Civilians: A Brief History with Documents*. Boston: Bedford/St. Martin's.

Holinshed, Raphael (1808, 1965), *Holinshed's Chronicles of England, Scotland, and Ireland: Volume VI: Ireland*. London: J. Johnson; New York: AMC Press.

Hood, A. B. E. (ed. and trans.) (1978), *St. Patrick: His Writings and Muirchu's Life*. London: Phillimore.

Hughes, Paul L. and James F. Larkin (eds) (1964), *Tudor Royal Proclamations: Volume I: The Early Tudors (1485–1553)*. New Haven and London: Yale University Press.

— (1969), *Tudor Royal Proclamations: Volume II: The Later Tudors (1553–1587)*. New Haven and London: Yale University Press.

Hyde, Douglas (1906), *Religious Songs of Connacht*. London: T. Fisher Unwin.

Jeffares, A. Norman and Van De Kamp, Peter (eds) (2006), *Irish Literature in the Eighteenth Century*. Dublin: Irish Academic Press.

Johnson, Jennifer (1985), *The Railway Station Man*. New York: Viking.

Jonas (1975), "Life of St. Columbanus," in W. C. McDermott (ed.), *Monks, Bishops and Pagans: Christian Culture in Gaul and Italy, 500–700*. Philadelphia: University of Pennsylvania Press, pp. 75–113.

Keating, Geoffrey, *History of Ireland*. http://www.ucc.ie/celt/published/T100054/index.html.

Kelleher, John V. (1954), "Can Ireland Unite?." *The Atlantic Monthly*, 193, 58–72. http://www.theatlantic.com/past/docs/unbound/flashbks/ireland/kelle.htm.

Killen, John (ed.) (1997), *The Decade of the United Irishmen: Contemporary Accounts, 1791–1801*. Belfast: The Blackstaff Press.

Kissane, Noel (1995), *The Irish Famine: A Documentary History*. Dublin: Leabharlann Náisiúnta na hÉireann.

Knighton, Henry (1995), *Knighton's Chronicle, 1337–1396*, edited and translated by G. H. Martin. Oxford: Clarendon Press.

Knutson, Jeanne M. (1984), "Toward a United States Policy on Northern Ireland: An Addendum on Terrorism." *Political Psychology*, 5, 295–8.

Lynch, John (1848), *Cambrensis Eversus*, Volume I, translated and edited by Matthew Kelly. Dublin: Celtic Society.

MacAlister, R. A. Stewart (ed. and trans.) (1938–), *Lebor Gabála Érenn: The Book of the Taking of Ireland*. Dublin: Irish Texts Society.

Mac Carthaigh's Book, http://www.ucc.ie/celt/published/T100013/index.html.

Martineau, Harriet (2001), *Letters from Ireland*, edited by Glenn Hooper. Dublin: Irish Academic Press.

McPhilemy, Sean (1998), *The Committee: Political Assassination in Northern Ireland*. Niwot, CO: Roberts Rinehart.

Meehan, E. P. (ed.) (1884), *The Poets and Poetry of Munster: A Selection of Irish Songs*, translated by James Clarence Mangan. 4th edn. Dublin: James Duffy and Sons. http://www.archive.org/stream/poetspoetryofmun00manguoft#page/n5/mode/2up.

Molyneux, William (1770; first published 1698), *The Case of Ireland's Being Bound by an Act of Parliament in England, Stated, with a New Preface*. London: J. Almon. http://oll.libertyfund.org/index.php?option=com_staticxt&staticfile=show.php%3Ftitle=1769&layout=html.

Moore, Thomas (2008), *Memoirs of Captain Rock, the Celebrated Irish Chieftain with some Account of his Ancestors*, edited and introduced by Emer Nolan, with annotations by Seamus Deane. Dublin: Field Day.

Moynihan, Maurice (ed.) (1980), *Speeches and Statements by Eamon de Valera*. Dublin: Gill and Macmillan.

http://www.nationalarchives.ie/index.html.

http://www.nationalarchives.ie/topics/1798/1798.pdf.

O'Connell, Maurice R. (ed.) (1972), *The Correspondence of Daniel O'Connell: Volume II: 1815–1823*. Dublin: Irish University Press.

— (1973), *The Correspondence of Daniel O'Connell: Volume I: 1792–1814*. Dublin: Irish University Press.

O'Daly, John (1844), *Reliques of Irish Jacobite Poetry*. Dublin: Samuel J. Machen. http://archive.org/stream/reliquesirishja00odagoog#page/n5/mode/2up.

O'Day, Alan and Stevenson, John (eds) (1992), *Irish Historical Documents Since 1800*. Dublin: Gill and Macmillan.

Parnell, Charles Stewart (2009), *Words of the Dead Chief: Being Extracts from the Public Speeches and Other Pronouncements of Charles Stewart Parnell from the Beginning to the Close of his Remarkable Life*, edited by Donal McCartney and Pauric Travers. Dublin: University College Dublin Press.

Petty, William (1691), *The Political Anatomy of Ireland with the Establishment for that Kingdom when the late Duke of Ormond was Lord Lieutenant . . .: to Which is Added Verbum Sapienti, or, An Account of the Wealth and Expences of England, and the Method of Raising Taxes in the most Equal Manner. . . .* London: D. Brown and W. Rogers.

Report of the Bloody Sunday Inquiry, http://webarchive.nationalarchives.gov. uk/20101103103930/http://report.bloody-sunday-inquiry.org/.

The Report of the Independent Commission on Policing for Northern Ireland, http://www.nio.gov.uk/a_new_beginning_in_policing_in_northern_ireland.pdf.

Smith, Elizabeth (1980), *The Irish Journals of Elizabeth Smith, 1840–1850*, edited by David Thomson and Moira McGusty. Oxford: Clarendon Press.

Spenser, Edmund (1997), *A View of the State of Ireland*, edited by Andrew Hadfield and Willy Maley, From the printed edition of 1633. Oxford: Blackwell.

Stephens, James (2009), *The Birth of the Fenian Movement: American Diary, Brooklyn 1859*, edited by Marta Ramón. Dublin: University College Dublin Press.

The Stormont Papers, http://stormontpapers.ahds.ac.uk/index.html.

Temple, Sir John (1698), *The Irish Rebellion, or, An History of the Beginnings and First Progress of the General Rebellion Raised within the Kingdom of Ireland upon the Three and Twentieth day of October in the year 1641 together with the Barbarous Cruelties and Bloody Massacres which ensued Thereupon.* Dublin: Andrew Crook. . . . and are to be sold by William Norman and Eliphal Dobson. http://bluehawk.monmouth.edu:2213/openurl?ctx_ver=Z39.88-2003&res_id=xri:eebo&rft_id=xri:eebo:image:47155.

Thackeray, William Makepeace (1984), *The Memoirs of Barry Lyndon, Esq.*, edited by Andrew Sanders. Oxford: Oxford University Press.

Thatcher, Margaret (1993), *The Downing Street Years*. New York: HarperCollins.

Toqueville, Alexis de (1990), *Alexis de Toqueville's Journey in Ireland, July–August 1835*, translated and edited by Emmet Larkin. Washington, DC: The Catholic University of America Press.

Tone, Theobald Wolfe (1998), *The Life of Theobald Wolfe Tone*, edited by Thomas Bartlett. Dublin: Lilliput Press.

— (1998–2007), *The Writings of Theobald Wolfe Tone*, 3 vol, edited by T. W. Moody, R. B. McDowell and C. J. Woods. Oxford: Clarendon Press.

Treadwell, Victor (ed.) (2006), *The Irish Commission of 1622: An Investigation of the Irish Administration, 1615–1622, and its Consequences, 1623–1624.* Dublin: Irish Manuscripts Commission.

(1972), *The True Reporte of the Prosperous Success which God gave unto our English Souldiours against the Forraine Bands of our Romaine Enemies, lately Arrived . . . in Ireland, in the yeare, 1580.* Amsterdam: Teatrum Orbis Terrarum.

Tucker, Josiah (1798), *Arguments for and against an Union between Great Britain and Ireland*. London: John Stockdale.

Twiss, Richard (2008; 1776), *A Tour of Ireland in 1775*, edited by Rachel Finnegan. Dublin: University College Dublin Press.

Secondary sources

Aalen, F. H. A. (2011), "The Irish Landscape: Synthesis of Habitat and History," in F. H. A. Aalen, K. Whelan and M. Stout (eds), *Atlas of the Irish Rural Landscape*, 2nd edn. Cork: Cork University Press, pp. 4–30.

Abrams, Lesley (2010), "Conversion and the Church in Viking-Age Ireland," in John Sheehan and Donnchadh Ó Corráin (eds), *The Viking Age: Ireland and the West*. Dublin: Four Courts Press, pp. 1–10.

Adshead, Maura (2003), "European Union Politics and Ireland," in Brian Lalor (ed.), *The Encyclopedia of Ireland*. New Haven and London: Yale University Press, pp. 364–5.

Adshead, Maura and Tonge, Jonathan (2009), *Politics in Ireland: Convergence and Divergence on a Two-Polity Island*. Houndmills: Palgrave Macmillan.

Akenson, Donald Harman (1996), *The Irish Diaspora: A Primer*. Toronto: P. D. Meany.

Andrews, J. H. (2011), "A Geographer's View of Irish History," in T. W. Moody, F. X. Martin and Dermot Keogh, Patrick Kiely (eds), *The Course of Irish History*, 5th edn. Lanham, MD: Roberts Rhinehart, pp. 15–26.

Andrews, J. H. (2005), "The Geographical Element in Irish History," in D. Ó Cróinín (ed.), *A New History of Ireland: Volume I: Prehistoric and Early Ireland*. Oxford: Oxford University Press, pp. 1–31.

Ansell, Richard (2010), "The Revolution in Ireland and the Memory of 1641," in M. Williams and S. P. Forrest (eds), *Constructing the Past: Writing Irish History, 1600–1800*. Woodbridge: The Boydell Press, pp. 73–93.

Antpohler, Werner (2000), *Newgrange, Dowth & Knowth: A Visit to Ireland's Valley of the Kings*. Cork: Mercier Press.

Armitage, David (1998), "Literature and Empire," in Nicholas Canny (ed.), *The Oxford History of the British Empire: Volume I: The Origins of Empire: British Overseas Enterprise to the Close of the Seventeenth Century*. Oxford: Oxford University Press, pp. 99–123.

— (2000), "The Political Economy of Britain and Ireland after the Glorious Revolution," in J. H. Ohlmeyer (ed.), *Political Thought in Seventeenth-Century Ireland: Kingdom or Colony*. Cambridge: Cambridge University Press, pp. 221–43.

Barnard, T. C. (1998), *The Oxford History of the British Empire: Volume I: The Origins of Empire: British Overseas Enterprise to the Close of the Seventeenth Century*, edited by Nicholas Canny. Oxford: Oxford University Press, pp. 309–27.

— (2004), *Irish Protestant Ascents and Descents, 1641–1770*. Dublin: Four Courts Press.

— (2010), "Writing in Publishing Histories in Eighteenth-century Ireland," in M. Williams and S. P. Forrest (eds), *Constructing the Past: Writing Irish History, 1600–1800*. Woodbridge: The Boydell Press, pp. 95–112.

Barrington, Ruth (2003), "Governance in the Health Services," in D. de Buitleir and F. Ruane (eds), *Governance and Policy in Ireland: Essays in Honour of Miriam Hederman O'Brien*. Dublin: Institute of Public Administration, pp. 105–22.

Barry, Terry (2002), "Review of *The Irish Ringfort* by Matthew Stout." *Speculum*, 77, 1399–401.

Bartlett, Robert (1993), *The Making of Europe: Conquest, Colonization, and Cultural Change, 950–1350*. Princeton: Princeton University Press.

Bartlett, Thomas (1996), "Defence, Counter-insurgency and rebellion: Ireland, 1793–1803," in T. Bartlett and K. Jeffery (eds), *A Military History of Ireland*. Cambridge: Cambridge University Press, pp. 247–93.

Bartlett, Thomas (1992), *The Fall and Rise of the Irish Nation: The Catholic Question, 1690–1830*. Savage, MD: Barnes and Noble.

— (2001), "Britishness, Irishness and the Act of Union," in D. Keogh and K. Whelan (eds), *Acts of Union: The Causes, Contexts and Consequences of the Act of Union*. Dubin: Four Courts Press, pp. 243–58.

— (2010), *Ireland: A History*. Cambridge: Cambridge University Press.

Barton, Brian (1995), *Northern Ireland in the Second World War*. Belfast: Ulster Historical Foundation.

Beiner, Guy (2007), *Remembering the Year of the French: Irish Folk History and Social Memory*. Madison: University of Wisconsin Press.

Bennett, Matyn (2000), *The Civil Wars Experienced: Britain and Ireland, 1637–1661*. London: Routledge.

Berrington, Hugh (1998), "Britain in the Nineties: The Politics of Paradox," in H. Berrington (ed.), *Britain in the Nineties: The Politics of Paradox*. London: Frank Cass, pp. 1–27.

Berrington, Hugh and Hague, Rod (1998), "Europe, Thatcherism and Traditionalism: Opinion, Rebellion and the Maastricht Treaty in the Backbench Conservative Party, 1992–1994," in H. Berrington (ed.), *Britain in the Nineties: The Politics of Paradox*. London: Frank Cass, pp. 44–71.

Bew, Paul (2011), *Enigma: A New Life of Charles Stewart Parnell*. Dublin: Gill and Macmillan.

Bew, Paul and Patterson, Henry (1982), *Seán Lemass and the Making of Modern Ireland, 1945–66*. Dublin: Gill and Macmillan.

Biagini, Eugenio F. (2007), *British Democracy and Irish Nationalism, 1876–1906*. Cambridge: Cambridge University Press.

Bitel, Lisa M. (1994), *Isle of the Saints: Monastic Settlement and Christian Community in Early Ireland*. Ithaca: Cornell University Press.

— (1998), *Land of Women: Tales of Sex and Gender from Early Ireland*. Ithaca: Cornell University Press.

Black, Jeremy (1997), *A History of the British Isles*. New York: St. Martin's.

Blackstock, Allan (2000), "The Union and the Military, 1801–c.1830." *Transactions of the Royal Historical Society*, Sixth Series, 10, 329–51.

Bossy, John (1970), "The Counter-Reformation and the People of Catholic Ireland, 1596–1641." *Historical Studies*, 8, 153–70.

Bourke, Angela (2001), *The Burning of Bridget Cleary*. New York: Penguin.

Bowman, John (1982), *De Valera and the Ulster Question, 1917–1973*. Oxford: Clarendon Press.

Bowman, Timothy (2007), *Carson's Army: The Ulster Volunteer Force, 1910–1922*. Manchester: Manchester University Press.

Boyce, D. George (2005), *Nineteenth-Century Ireland: The Search for Stability* (revised edn). Dublin: Gill and Macmillan.

Bradley, Ian (1999), *Celtic Christianity: Making Myths and Chasing Dreams.* New York: St. Martin's.

Bradley, Richard (2007), *The Prehistory of Britain and Ireland.* Cambridge: Cambridge University Press.

Bradshaw, Brendan (1979), *The Irish Constitutional Revolution of the Sixteenth Century.* New York: Cambridge University Press.

Brady, Ciaran (1999), "Shane O'Neill Departs from the Court of Elizabeth: Irish, English, Scottish Perspectives and the Paralysis of Policy, July 1559 to April 1562," in S. J. Connolly (ed.), *Kingdoms United? Great Britain and Ireland since 1500: Integration and Diversity.* Dublin: Four Courts Press, pp. 13–28.

Brantlinger, Patrick (2004), "The Famine." *Victorian Literature and Culture*, 32, 193–207.

Bréadún, Deaglán de (2001), *The Far Side of Revenge: Making Peace in Northern Ireland.* Cork: The Collins Press.

Breathnach-Lynch, Síghle (2007), *Ireland's Art, Ireland's History: Representing Ireland, 1845 to Present.* Omaha: Creighton University Press.

Breen, Richard, Hannan, Damian F., Rottman, David B. and Whelan, Christopher T. (1990), *Understanding Contemporary Ireland: State, Class, and Development in the Republic of Ireland.* New York: St. Martin's Press.

Brewer, John D. and Higgins, Gareth I. (1998), *Anti-Catholicism in Northern Ireland, 1600–1998.* Houndmills, England: MacMillan.

Brigden, Susan (2000), *New Worlds, Lost Worlds: The Rule of the Tudors, 1485–1603.* New York: Penguin.

Brouillette, Sarah (2007), "The Northern Irish Novelist in Ronan Bennett's 'The Catastrophist'." *Contemporary Literature*, 48, 253–77.

Brown, Peter (2003), *The Rise of Western Christendom: Triumph and Diversity, A.D. 200–1000*, 2nd edn. Malden, MA: Blackwell.

Brown, Stewart J. (2008), *Providence and Empire: Religion, Politics and Society in the United Kingdom, 1815–1914.* Harlow: Pearson, 2008.

Brunt, Liam and Cannon, Edmund (2004), "The Irish grain trade from the Famine to the First World War." *Economic History Review*, LVII, 33–79.

Buckley, Maria (2001), *Celtic Spirituality.* Cork: Mercier Press.

Burke, Sara (2009), *Irish Apartheid: Healthcare Inequality in Ireland.* Dublin: New Island.

Byrne, F. J. (2005a), "Church and Politics, c. 750–c. 1100," in D. Ó Cróinín (ed.), *A New History of Ireland: Volume I: Prehistoric and Early Ireland.* Oxford: Oxford University Press, pp. 656–79.

— (2005b), "The Viking Age," in D. Ó Cróinín (ed.), *A New History of Ireland: Volume I: Prehistoric and Early Ireland.* Oxford: Oxford University Press, pp. 609–34.

— (2011), "Early Irish Society: 1st–9th Century," in T. W. Moody, F. X. Martin and Dermot Keogh, Patrick Kiely (eds), *The Course of Irish History*, 5th edn. Lanham, MD: Roberts Rhinehart, pp. 38–52.

Byrne, Sean (2001), "Constitutional and Civic Society Approaches to Peacebuilding in Northern Ireland." *Journal of Peace Research*, 38, 327–52.

Bryant-Quinn, M. (2002), Review of *Celtic Spirituality*, by Oliver Davies, with the collaboration of Thomas O'Loughlin. *Mystics Quarterly*, 28, 37–40.

Cahalan, James M. (1993), *Modern Irish Literature and Culture: A Chronology*. New York: G.V. Hall and Co.

Cahill, Mary (1983), "Irish Prehistoric Goldworking," in Michael Ryan (ed.), *Treasures of Ireland: Irish Art 3000 B.C.–1500 A.D.* Dublin: Royal Irish Academy, pp. 18–23.

Cahill, Thomas (1995), *How the Irish Saved Civilization: The Untold Story of Ireland's Heroic Role from the Fall of Rome to the Rise of Medieval Europe*. New York: Doubleday.

Capern, Amanda L. (1996), "The Caroline Church: James Ussher and the Irish Dimension." *The Historical Journal*, 39, 57–85.

Campbell, Bruce M. S. (2008), "Benchmarking Medieval Economic Development: England, Wales, Scotland, and Ireland, c. 1290." *Economic History Review*, 61, 896–945.

Campbell, Malcolm (2008), *Ireland's New Worlds: Immigrants, Politics, and Society in the United States and Australia, 1815–1922*. Madison: University of Wisconsin Press.

Canny, Nicholas (1976), *The Elizabethan Conquest of Ireland: A Pattern Established, 1565–76*. New York: Barnes and Noble.

— (1988), *Kingdom and Colony: Ireland in the Atlantic World, 1560–1800*. Baltimore: Johns Hopkins University Press, 1988.

— (1989), "Early Modern Ireland, c. 1500–1700," in Roy Foster (ed.), *The Oxford Illustrated History of Ireland*. Oxford: Oxford University Press, pp. 104–60.

— (1995), "What Really Happened in Ireland in 1641?," in Jane H. Ohlmeyer (ed.), *Ireland From Independence to Occupation, 1641–1660*. Cambridge: Cambridge University Press, pp. 24–42.

— (2001), *Making Ireland British 1580–1650*. Oxford: Oxford University Press.

— (2003), "Writing Early Modern History: Ireland, Britain, and the Wider World." *Historical Journal*, 46, (3), 723–47.

Cantor, Norman F. (1993), *The Civilization of the Middle Ages*. New York: HarperPerennial.

Carey, Vincent P. (2002), *Surviving the Tudors: The "Wizard" Earl of Kildare and English Rule in Ireland, 1537–1586*. Dublin: Four Courts Press.

Carlin, Norah (1993), "Extreme or Mainstream?: the English Independents and the Cromwellian Reconquest of Ireland, 1649–1651," in A. Hadfield and W. Maley (eds), *Representing Ireland: Literature and the Origins of Conflict, 1534–1660*. Cambridge: Cambridge University Press, pp. 209–26.

Carney, James (2005), "Language and Literature to 1169," in D. Ó Cróinín (ed.), *A New History of Ireland: Volume I: Prehistoric and Early Ireland*. Oxford: Oxford University Press, pp. 451–510.

Carpenter, Christine (1997), *The Wars of the Roses: Politics and the Constitution in England, c. 1437–1509*. Cambridge: Cambridge University Press.

Carpenter, David (2003), *The Struggle for Mastery, 1066–1284*, Oxford: Oxford University Press.

Carter, Miranda (2009), *George, Nicholas, and Wilhelm: Three Royal Cousins and the Road to World War I*. New York: Vintage Books.

Casey, Christine (ed.) (2010), *The Eighteenth-Century Dublin Town House: Form, Function, Finance*. Dublin: Four Courts Press.

Childs, John (1996), "The Williamite War, 1689–1691," in Thomas Bartlett and Keith Jeffery (eds), *A Military History of Ireland.* Cambridge: Cambridge University Press, pp. 188–210.

Chrimes, S. B. (1973), *Henry VII.* Berkeley: University of California Press.

Clarke, Aidan (1976), "The Irish Economy, 1600–60," in T. W. Moody, F. X. Martin and F. J. Byrne (eds), *A New History of Ireland III: Early Modern Ireland 1534–1691.* Oxford: Clarendon Press, pp. 168–86.

— (2011), "The Colonisation of Ulster and the Rebellion of 1641: 1603–60," in T. W. Moody, F. X. Martin and Dermot Keogh, Patrick Kiely (eds), *The Course of Irish History*, 5th edn. Lanham, MD: Roberts Rhinehart, pp. 163–75.

Clarke, Aidan, R. Dudley Edwards (1976), "Pacification, Plantation, and the Catholic Question, 1603–23," in T. W. Moody, F. X. Martin and F. J. Byrne (eds), *A New History of Ireland III: Early Modern Ireland 1534–1691.* Oxford: Clarendon Press, pp. 187–232.

Clark, Anna (2005), "Wild Workhouse Girls and the Liberal Imperial State in Nineteenth-Century Ireland." *Journal of Social History*, 39, 389–409.

Clarke, Howard B. and Philips, R. S. (eds) (2006), *Ireland, England and the Continent in the Middle Ages and Beyond: Essays in Memory of a Turbulent Friar, F.X. Martin, O.S.A.* Dublin: University College Dublin Press.

Cleary, Joe (2005), "Introduction: Ireland and Modernity," in J. Cleary and C. Connolly (eds), *The Cambridge Companion to Modern Irish Culture.* Cambridge: Cambridge University Press, pp. 1–21.

Clifford, Michael and Coleman, Shane (2009), *Bertie Ahern and the Drumcondra Mafia.* Dublin: Hachette Books Ireland.

Clinch, Peter, Convery, Frank and Walsh, Brendan (2002), *After the Celtic Tiger: Challenges Ahead.* Dublin: The O'Brien Press.

Clover, Joshua (2009), *1989: Bob Dylan Didn't Have This to Sing About.* Berkeley: University of California Press.

Collins, A. E. P. (1981; 1994), "The Flint Javelin Heads of Ireland," in D. Ó Corráin (ed.), *Irish Antiquity: Essays and Studies Presented to Professor M. J. O'Kelly.* Dublin: Four Courts Press, pp. 111–33.

Collins, Kritin Bornholdt (2010), "The Dunmore Cave [2] Hoard and the Role of Coins in the Tenth-Century Hiberno-Scandinavian Economy," in John Sheehan and Donnchadh Ó Corráin (eds), *The Viking Age: Ireland and the West.* Dublin: Four Courts Press, pp. 19–46.

Collins, Peter (2004), *Who Fears to Speak of '98? Commemoration and the Continuing Impact of the United Irishmen.* Belfast: Ulster Historical Foundation.

Comerford, R. V. (2009), "Ireland's Nineteenth Century," in Séamus Ó Síocháin (ed.), *Social Thought on Ireland in the Nineteenth Century.* Dublin: University College Dublin Press, pp. 1–8.

Connolly, S. J. (1982), *Priests and People in Pre-Famine Ireland, 1780–1845.* Dublin: Gill and Macmillan.

— (1992), *Religion, Law, and Power: The Making of Protestant Ireland, 1660–1760.* Oxford: Clarendon Press.

— (1996), "The Defence of Protestant Ireland, 1660–1760," in Thomas Bartlett and Keith Jeffery (eds), *A Military History of Ireland.* Cambridge: Cambridge University Press, pp. 231–46.

— (2000a), "Precedent and Principle: The Patriots and their Critics," in S. J. Connolly (ed.), *Political Ideas in Eighteenth-Century Ireland*. Dublin: Four Courts Press, pp. 130–58.

— (2000b), "Reconsidering the Irish Act of Union." *Transactions of the Royal Historical Society*, Sixth Series, 10, 399–408.

— (2000c), "A Woman's Life in Mid-Eighteenth-Century Ireland: The Case of Letitia Bushe." *Historical Journal*, 43, 433–51.

— (2007), *Contested Island: Ireland, 1460–1630*. Oxford: Oxford University Press.

— (2008), *Divided Kingdom: Ireland 1630–1800*. Oxford: Oxford University Press.

— (2009), Review of Alan Ford, *James Ussher: Theology, History, and Politics in Early Modern Ireland and England*. *Journal of British Studies*, 48, 201–2.

Connors, Thomas G. (2001), "Surviving the Reformation in Ireland (1534–80): Christopher Bodkin, Archbishop of Tuam, and Roland Burke, Bishop of Clonfert." *Sixteenth Century Journal*, 32, 335–55.

Byrne, Francis John (2001), *Irish Kings and High-Kings*. 2nd edn, Dublin: Four Courts Press.

Conway, Stephen (2000), *The British Isles and the War of American Independence*. Oxford: Oxford University Press.

— (2006), *War, State, and Society in Mid-Eighteenth-Century Britain and Ireland*. Oxford: Oxford University Press.

Coogan, Tim Pat (1987), *Disillusioned Decades: Ireland 1966–87*. Dublin: Gill and Macmillan.

— (1996), *The Troubles: Ireland's Ordeal 1966–1996 and the Search for Peace*. Boulder: Robert Rhinehart.

— (2001), *Wherever the Green is Worn: The Story of the Irish Diaspora*. New York: Palgrave.

— (2002), *The IRA*. New York: Palgrave.

— (2003), *Ireland in the Twentieth Century*. New York: Palgrave Macmillan.

Cooney, Gabriel (2000a), *Landscapes of Neolithic Ireland*. London and New York: Routledge.

— (2000b), "Reading a Landscape Manuscript: A Review of Progress in Prehistoric Settlement Studies in Ireland," in Terry Barry (ed.), *A History of Settlement in Ireland*. London and New York: Routledge, pp. 1–49.

Cope, Joseph (2003), "The Experience of Survival in the 1641 Irish Rebellion." *The Historical Journal*, 46, 295–316.

Copland, Ian (1991), "The Princely States, the Muslim League, and the Partition of India in 1947." *International History Review*, 13, 38–69.

Cosgrove, Art (1993), "Ireland Beyond the Pale, 1399–1460," in A. Cosgrove (ed.), *A New History of Ireland: II: Medieval Ireland, 1169–1534*. Oxford: Clarendon Press, pp. 569–90.

Coward, Barry (2003), *The Stuart Age: England, 1603–1714*, 3rd edn. London: Longman.

Craig, Anthony (2010), *Crisis of Confidence: Anglo-Irish Relations in the Early Troubles, 1966–1974*. Dublin and Portland, OR: Irish Academic Press.

Crooks, Peter (2010), "Representation and Dissent: Parliamentarianism and the Structure of Politics in Colonial Ireland." *English Historical Review*, 125, 1–34.

Cronin, Mike, Duncan, Mark and Rouse, Paul (2009), *The GAA: A People's History*. Cork: Collins.

Cronin, Sean (1991), *For Whom the Hangman's Rope was Spun: Wolfe Tone and the United Irishmen*. Dublin: Repsol.

Cunningham, Bernadette (2010), "Seventeenth-century Constructions of the Historical Kingdom of Ireland," in Mark Williams and Stephen Paul Forrest (eds), *Constructing the Past: Writing Irish History*. Woodbridge: The Boydell Press, pp. 9–26.

Cunningham, Bernadette and Raymond Gillespie (2003), *Stories from Gaelic Ireland: Microhistories from the Sixteenth-Century Irish Annals*. Dublin: Four Courts Press.

Cunningham, John (2009), *Unlikely Radicals: Irish Post-Primary Teachers and the ASTI, 1909–2009*. Cork: Cork University Press.

Cunningham, Michael (2001), *British Government Policy in Northern Ireland, 1969–2000*. Manchester: Manchester University Press.

Curtin, Nancy J. (1994), *The United Irishmen: Popular Politics in Ulster and Dublin, 1791–1798*. Oxford: Clarendon Press.

Curtis, Liz (1994), *The Cause of Ireland: From the United Irishmen to Partition*. Belfast: Beyond the Pale Publications.

Daly, Mary E. (2006), *The Slow Failure: Population Decline and Independent Ireland, 1922–1973*. Madison: University of Wisconsin Press.

Daly, Mary K. and Hoppen, K. Theodore (2011), *Gladstone: Ireland and Beyond*. Dublin: Four Courts Press.

Daly, Paul (2008), *Creating Ireland*. Dublin: Hachette Books Ireland.

Dangerfield, George (1976), *The Damnable Question: A Study in Anglo-Irish Relations*. Boston: Little, Brown and Company.

— (1980; first published 1935), *The Strange Death of Liberal England*. New York: Perigree.

Daniels, Philip (1998), "From Hostility to 'Constructive Engagement': The Europeansation of the Labour Party," in H. Berrington (ed.), *Britain in the Nineties: The Politics of Paradox*, London: Frank Cass, pp. 72–96.

Dargan, Pat (2011), *Exploring Celtic Ireland*. Dublin: The History Press Ireland.

Davies, Daniel (2004), "'It is more important to us that Eire should receive adequate aid than it is for Eire herself': Britain, Ireland and the Marshall Plan," in T. Geiger and M. Kennedy (eds), *Ireland, Europe and the Marshall Plan*. Dublin: Four Courts Press, pp. 65–80.

Davies, Norman (1999), *The Isles: A History*. Oxford: Oxford University Press.

Davies, R. R. (1990), *Domination and Conquest: The Experience of Ireland, Scotland and Wales, 1100–1300*. Cambridge: Cambridge University Press.

— (2000), *The First English Empire: Power and Identities in the British Isles, 1093–1343*. Oxford: Oxford University Press.

— (2009), *Lords and Lordship in the British Isles in the Late Middle Ages*, edited by Brendan Smith. Oxford: Oxford University Press.

Davis, Richard (1987), *The Young Ireland Movement*. Dublin: Gill and MacMillan.

Denby, David J. (2005), "The Enlightenment in Ireland." *Eighteenth-Century Studies*, 38, 385–91.

De Paor, Liam (1986), *The Peoples of Ireland: From Prehistory to Modern Times*. London: Hutchinson.

Devenney, Andrew D. (2010), "Joining Europe: Ireland, Scotland, and the Celtic Response to European Integration, 1961–1975." *Journal of British Studies*, 49, 97–116.

Dickson, David (1993), "Paine and Ireland," in D. Dickson, D. Keogh, and K. Whelan (eds), *The United Irishmen: Republicanism, Radicalism, and Rebellion*. Dublin: Lilliput Press, pp. 135–50.

— (2000), *New Foundations: Ireland, 1660–1800*. Dublin: Irish Academic Press.

Dixon, Paul (2008), *Northern Ireland: The Politics of War and Peace*, 2nd edn. Houdmills, UK: Palgrave Macmillan.

Doherty, Charles (1998), "The Vikings in Ireland: A Review," in Howard Clark, Máire Ní Mhaonaigh, and Raghnall Ó Floinn (eds), *Ireland and Scandinavia in the Early Viking Age*. Blackrock: Four Courts Press, pp. 288–330.

Donnelly, James S., Jr. (2009), *Captain Rock: The Irish Agrarian Rebellion of 1821–1824*. Cork: The Collins Press.

Donohue, Laura K. (1998), "Regulating Northern Ireland: The Special Powers Acts, 1922–1972." *Historical Journal*, 41, 1089–120.

Douglas, R. M. (2006), "The Pro-Axis Underground in Ireland, 1939–1942." *Historical Journal*, 49, 1155–183.

Doumitt, Donald P. (1999), *Voices of Ulster: A Cry from the Heart*. Huntington, NY: Kroshka Books.

Doyle, Joseph (2011), "Cardinal Cullen and the System of National Education in Ireland," in D. Keogh and A. McDonnell (eds), *Cardinal Paul Cullen and his World*. Dublin: Four Courts Press, pp. 190–204.

Dryburgh, Paul (2009), "Roger Mortimer and the Governance of Ireland, 1317–1320," in Brendan Smith (ed.), *Ireland and the English World in the Late Middle Ages*. London: Palgrave Macmillan, pp. 89–102.

Duffy, Seán (1997), *Ireland in the Middle Ages*. Houndmills and London: Macmillan.

— (2002), "The Bruce Invasion of Ireland: A Revised Itinerary and Chronology," in Seán Duffy (ed.), *Robert the Bruce's Irish Wars: The Invasions of Ireland, 1306–1329*. Stroud, England: Tempus, pp. 9–44.

Duncan, A. A. M. (1988), "The Scots' Invasion of Ireland," in R. R. Davies (ed.), *The British Isles, 1100–1500: Comparisons, Contrasts, and Connections*. Edinburgh: John Donald, pp. 100–17.

Dungan, Myles (2009), *The Captain and the King: William O'Shea, Parnell and Late Victorian Ireland*. Dublin: New Island.

Durie, Alastair and Solar, Peter (1988), "The Scottish and Irish Linen Industries Compared, 1780–1860," in R. Mitchison and P. Roebuck (eds), *Economy and Society in Scotland and Ireland, 1500–1939*. Edinburgh: John Donald.

Edwards, David (2001), "Collaboration with Anglisation: The MacGiollapadraig Lordship and Tudor Reform," in P. J. Duffy, D. Edwards and E. Fitzpatrick (eds), *Gaelic Ireland, c.1250–c.1650: Land, Lordship and Settlement*. Dublin: Four Courts Press, pp. 77–97.

Edwards, Nancy (2005), "The Archaeology of Early Medieval Ireland, c. 400–1169: Settlement and Economy," in D. Ó Cróinín (ed.), *A New History of Ireland: Volume I: Prehistoric and Early Ireland*. Oxford: Oxford University Press, pp. 235–300.

Edwards, R. Dudley (1935), *Church and State in Tudor Ireland: A History of Penal Laws against Irish Catholics, 1534–1603*. London: Longmans, Green and Co.

— (1977), *Ireland in the Age of the Tudors: The Destruction of Hiberno-Norman Civilization*. London: Croom Helm.

Elliott, Marianne (1982), *Partners in Revolution: The United Irishmen and France*. New Haven: Yale University Press.

Ellis, Steven G. (1998), *Ireland in the Age of the Tudors, 1447–1603: English Expansion and the End of Gaelic Rule*. London and New York: Longman.

English, Richard (2003), *Armed Struggle: The History of the IRA*. Oxford: Oxford University Press.

— (2011), "Ireland: 1982–94," in T. W. Moody, F. X. Martin and Dermot Keogh, Patrick Kiely (eds), *The Course of Irish History*, 5th edn. Lanham, MD: Roberts Rhinehart, pp. 317–32.

Fallon, Brian (1998), *An Age of Innocence: Irish Culture, 1930–1960*. New York: St. Martin's Press.

Fanning, Bryan (2002), *Racism and Social Change in the Republic of Ireland*. Manchester: Manchester University Press.

Farmar, Tony (2004), *Patients, Potions, & Physicians: A Social History of Medicine in Ireland, 1654–2004*. Dublin: A. and A. Farmar in association with the Royal College of Physicians of Ireland.

Fegan, Melissa (2011), "'Isn't it your own country?': The Stranger in Nineteenth-Century Irish Literature." *The Yearbook of English Studies*, 34, 31–45.

Ferguson, Niall (1999), *The Pity of War*. New York: Basic Books.

Ferriter, Diarmaid (2004), *The Transformation of Ireland*. Woodstock and New York: The Overlook Press.

— (2009), *Occasions of Sin: Sex and Society in Modern Ireland*. London: Profile Books.

— (2012), *Ambiguous Republic: Ireland in the 1970s*. London: Profile Books.

Finnegan, Richard B. and McCarron, Edward T. (2000), *Ireland: Historical Echoes, Contemporary Politics*. Boulder: Westview Press.

FitzGerald, Garret (2003), "Eamon de Valera: The Price of His Achievement," in G. Doherty and D. Keogh (eds), *De Valera's Irelands*. Cork: Mercier Press, pp. 185–204.

Fitzgerald, Maurice (2000), "The Anglo-Irish Free Trade Area Agreement, 1965," presented to the Western Conference on British Studies. Denver, Colorado.

Fitzgerald, Patrick and Brian Lambkin (2008), *Migration in Irish History, 1607–2007*. London: Palgrave Macmillan.

Fitzpatrick, David (1989), "Ireland Since 1870," in Roy Foster (ed.), *The Oxford Illustrated History of Ireland*. Oxford: Oxford University Press, pp. 213–74.

— (1996), "Militarism in Ireland, 1900–1922," in Thomas Bartlett and Keith Jeffery (eds), *A Military History of Ireland*. Cambridge: Cambridge University Press, pp. 379–406.

Flanagan, Laurence (1998), *Ancient Ireland: Life before the Celts*. Dublin: Gill and Macmillan.

Flanagan, Marie Therese (1996), "Irish and Anglo-Norman Warfare in Twelfth-Century Ireland," in Thomas Bartlett and Keith Jeffery (eds), *A Military History of Ireland*. Cambridge: Cambridge University Press, pp. 52–75.

— (2010), *The Transformation of the Irish Church in the Twelfth and Thirteenth Centuries*. Woodbridge: The Boydell Press.

Flynn, Roderick and Brereton, Patrick (2007), *Historical Dictionary of Irish Cinema*. Lanham, MD: The Scarecrow Press, Inc.

Foster, Roy (1988), *Modern Ireland, 1600–1972*. London: Allen Lane.

— (1989), "Ascendancy and Union," in Roy Foster (ed.), *The Oxford Illustrated History of Ireland*. Oxford: Oxford University Press, pp. 161–212.

— (2010), "Introduction," in M. Williams and S. P. Forrest (eds), *Constructing the Past: Writing Irish History, 1600–1800*. Woodbridge: The Boydell Press, pp. 1–5.

Frame, Robin (1981), *Colonial Ireland*. Dublin: Helicon.

— (1990), *The Political Development of the British Isles*. Oxford: Oxford University Press.

— (1993), "'Les Engleys Nées in Irlande': The English Political Identity in Medieval Ireland." *Transactions of the Royal Historical Society*, Sixth Series, Volume 3, pp. 83–103; reprinted in Frame (1998), *Ireland and Britain, 1170–1450*. London and Rio Grande: The Hambledon Press, pp. 131–50.

— (2006), "The Wider World," in Rosemary Horrox and W. Mark Ormond (eds), *A Social History of England, 1200–1500*. Cambridge: Cambridge University Press, pp. 435–54.

Fraser, Lyndon (2002), "To Tara via Holyhead: The Emergence of Irish Catholic Ethnicity in Nineteenth-Century Christ Church, New Zealand." *Journal of Social History*, 36, 431–68.

Freeman, Philip (2004), *St. Patrick of Ireland: A Biography*. New York: Simon and Schuster.

Froude, James Anthony (1895), *The English in Ireland in the Eighteenth Century*, 3 vol. London: Longmans, Green, and Co.

Garner, Steve (2004), *Racism in the Irish Experience*. London: Pluto Press.

Garvin Tom and Andreas Hess (2009), "Gustave de Beaumont: Ireland's Alexis de Toqueville," in Séamas Ó Síocháin (ed.), *Social Thought on Ireland in the Nineteenth Century*. Dublin: University College Dublin Press, pp. 9–26.

Garvin, Tom (2011), "Turmoil in the Sea of Faith: The Secularization of Irish Social Culture, 1960–2007," in Thomas E. Hachey (ed.), *Turning Points in Twentieth-Century Irish History*. Dublin: Irish Academic Press, pp. 155–66.

Gash, Norman (1973), *The Age of Peel*. London: Edward Arnold.

Geary, Frank (1995), "The Act of Union, British-Irish Trade, and Pre-Famine Deindustrialization." *Economic History Review*, 48, (1), 68–88.

Geary, Frank and Stark, Tom (2004), "Trends in Real Wages during the Industrial Revolution: A View from across the Irish Sea." *Economic History Review*, VII, 362–95.

Genet-Rouffiac, Nathalie (2010), "The Irish Jacobite Regiments and the French Army: A Way to Integration," in Paul Monod, Murray Pittock and Daniel Szechi (eds), *Loyalty and Identity: Jacobites at Home and Abroad*. Houndmills: Palgrave Macmillan, pp. 206–28.

Geoghegan, Patrick (1999), *The Irish Act of Union: A Study in High Politics, 1799–1801*. Dublin: Gill and Macmillan.

— (2001), "The Making of the Union," in D. Keogh and K. Whelan (eds), *Acts of Union: The Causes, Contexts and Consequences of the Act of Union*. Dublin: Four Courts Press, pp. 34–45.

— (2009), "Daniel O'Connell and the Irish Act of Union, 1800–29," in James Kelly, John McCafferty and Charles Ivar McGrath (eds), *People, Politics and Power: Essays on Irish History 1660–1850 in Honour of James I. McGuire*. Dublin: University College Dublin Press, pp. 175–89.

Gibbons, Luke (2005), "Projecting the Nation: Cinema and Culture," in J. Cleary and C. Connolly (eds), *The Cambridge Companion to Modern Irish Culture*. Cambridge: Cambridge University Press, pp. 206–24.

Gibbons, Stephen Randolph (ed.) (2008), *Captain Rock: Night Errant: The Threatening Letters of Pre-Famine Ireland, 1801–1845*. Dublin: Four Courts Press.

Gilbert, Bentley Brinkerhoff (1996), *Britain, 1914–1945: The Aftermath of Power*. Wheeling, IL: Harlan Davidson.

Gillespie, Raymond (1999), "Differing Devotions: Patterns of Religious Practice in the British Isles, 1500–1700," in S. J. Connolly (ed.), *Kingdoms United? Great Britain and Ireland since 1500: Integration and Diversity*. Dublin: Four Courts Press, pp. 67–77.

— (2006), *Seventeenth-Century Ireland: Making Ireland Modern*. Dublin: Gill and Macmillan.

Githens-Mazer, Jonathan (2006), *Myths and Memories of the Easter Rising: Cultural and Political Nationalism in Ireland*. Dublin: Irish Academic Press.

Goodman, Anthony (2006), "The British Isles Imagined," in Linda Clark (ed.), *The Fifteenth Century VI: Identity and Insurgency in the Late Middle Ages*. Woodbridge: The Boydell Press, pp. 1–14.

Graham-Campbell, James (2011), *The Cuerdale Hoard and Related Viking-Age Silver and Gold from Britain and Ireland in the British Museum*. London: The British Museum.

Gray, Jane (2003), "The Irish, Scottish, and Flemish Linen Industries during the Long Eighteenth Century," in B. Collins and P. Ollerenshaw (eds), *The European Linen Industry in Historical Perspective*. Oxford: Oxford University Press, pp. 159–86.

Green, David (2008), "Lordship and Principality: Colonial Policy in Ireland and Aquitaine in the 1360s." *Journal of British Studies*, 47, 3–29.

Grenham, John (1997), *An Illustrated History of Ireland*. Dublin: Gill and Macmillan.

Gwynn, Aubrey, S. J. (1992), *The Irish Church in the Eleventh and Twelfth Centuries*, edited by Gerard O'Brien. Dublin: Four Courts Press.

Gwyn, Denis (1971; 1932), *The Life of John Redmond*. Freeport, NY: Books for Libraries Press.

Hachey, Thomas E. and McCaffrey, Lawrence J. (2010), *The Irish Experience Since 1800: A Concise History*, 3rd edn. Armonk, NY: M. E. Sharpe, Inc.

Hadfield, Andrew and Willy Maley (1993), "Introduction: Irish Representations and English Alternatives," in B. Bradshaw, A. Hadfield and W. Maley (eds), *Representing Ireland: Literature and the Origins of Conflict, 1534–1660*. Cambridge: Cambridge University Press, 1993, pp. 1–23.

Hadfield, Andrew (1993), "Translating the Reformation: John Bale's Irish *Vocacyon*," in B. Bradshaw, A. Hadfield and W. Maley (eds), *Representing Ireland: Literature and the Origins of Conflict, 1534–1660*. Cambridge: Cambridge University Press, 1993, pp. 43–59.

Hall, Dianne (2003), *Women and the Church in Medieval Ireland, c. 1140–1540*. Dublin: Four Courts Press.

Hancock, Landon E. (2008), "The Northern Irish Peace Process: From Top to Bottom." *International Studies Review*, 10, 203–38.

Harbison, Peter (1976), *The Archaeology of Ireland*. New York: Charles Scribner's Sons.

— (1988), *Pre-Christian Ireland: From the First Settlers to the Early Celts*. London: Thames and Hudson.

Harrington, Christina (2002), *Women in a Celtic Church: Ireland 450–1150*. Oxford: Oxford University Press.

Hayes, McCoy, G. A. (1976a), "The Completion of the Tudor Conquest, and the Advance of the Counter-Reformation, 1571–1603," in T. W. Moody, F. X. Martin and F. J. Byrne (eds), *A New History of Ireland III: Early Modern Ireland 1534–1691*. Oxford: Clarendon Press, pp. 94–141.

— (1976b), "Conciliation, Coercion, and the Protestant Reformation, 1547–71," in T. W. Moody, F. X. Martin and F. J. Byrne (eds), *A New History of Ireland III: Early Modern Ireland 1534–1691*. Oxford: Clarendon Press, pp. 69–93.

— (1976c), "The Royal Supremacy and Ecclesiastical Revolution, 1534–47," in T. W. Moody, F. X. Martin and F. J. Byrne (eds), *A New History of Ireland III: Early Modern Ireland 1534–1691*. Oxford: Clarendon Press, pp. 39–68.

Hazlett, W. Ian P. (2003), *The Reformation in Britain and Ireland: An Introduction*. London: T&T Clark.

Heal, Felicity (2003), *The Reformation in Britain and Ireland*. New York: Oxford University Press.

Hederman, Miriam (1983), *The Road to Europe: Irish Attitudes, 1948–1961*. Dublin: Institute of Public Administration.

Helleiner, Jane (2003), *Irish Travellers: Racism and the Politics of Culture*. Toronto: University of Toronto Press.

Henry, Françoise (1970), *Irish Art in the Romanesque Period (1020–1170 A.D.)*. Ithaca: Cornell University Press.

Herren, Michael and Brown, Shirley Ann (2002), *Christ in Celtic Christianity: Britain and Ireland from the Fifth to the Tenth Century*. Woodbridge, UK: Boydell and Brewster.

Herron, Thomas (2007), *Spenser's Irish Work: Poetry, Plantation, and Colonial Reformation*. Aldershot: Ashgate.

Higgins, Robin (2012), *Transforming 1916: Meaning, Memory and the Fiftieth Anniversary of the Easter Rising*. Cork: Cork University Press.

Hill, Jacqueline (1997), *From Patriots to Unionists: Dublin Civic Politics and Irish Protestant Patriotism, 1660–1840*. Oxford: Clarendon Press.

— (2001), "Convergence and Conflict in Eighteenth-Century Ireland." *Historical Journal*, 44, 1039–63.

Hill, Myrtle (2011), "Culture and Religion, 1815–1870," in D. Ó Corráin and T. O'Riordan (eds), *Ireland, 1815–70*. Dublin: Four Courts Press, pp. 43–57.

Hirst, Derek (1999), *England in Conflict: 1603–1660*. London: Arnold.

Holmes, Richard (2011), "James Arbuckle: A Whig Critique of the Penal Laws," in J. Bergin, E. Magennis, L. Ní Mhunghaile and P. Walsh (eds), *New Perspectives on the Penal Laws: Eighteenth-Century Ireland/Iris an dá chultúr, Special Issue No. 1*. Dublin: Eighteenth-Century Ireland Society, pp. 93–114.

Hood, Adrienne D. (2003), "Flax Seed, Fibre, and Cloth: Pennsylvania's Domestic Linen Manufacture and its Irish Connections, 1700–1830," in B. Collins and P. Ollerenshaw (eds), *The European Linen Industry in Historical Perspective*. Oxford: Oxford University Press, pp. 139–58.

Hopkinson, Michael (2002), *The Irish War of Independence*. Montreal and Kingston: McGill-Queen's University Press.

Hoppen, K. Theodore (2011), "Gladstone, Salisbury and the end of Irish assimilation," in M. K. Daly and K. T. Hoppen (eds), *Gladstone: Ireland and Beyond*. Dublin: Four Courts Press, pp. 45–63.

Houston, R. A. (1992), *The Population History of Britain and Ireland, 1500–1750*. Houndmills: Macmillan.

Howe, Stephen (1999), "Speaking of '98: History, Politics and Memory in the Bicentenary of the 1798 United Irish Uprising." *History Workshop Journal*, 47, 222–39.

— (2000), "The Politics of Historical Revisionism." *Past and Present*, 168, 227–53.

Hughes, Eamonn (1996), "'Town of Shadows': Representations of Belfast in Recent Fiction." *Religion and Literature*, 28, 141–60.

Hughes, Kathleen (1966), *The Church in Early Irish Society*. Ithaca, NY: Cornell University Press.

— (2005a), "The Church in Irish Society, 400–800," in D. Ó Cróinín (ed.), *A New History of Ireland: Volume I: Prehistoric and Early Ireland*. Oxford: Oxford University Press, pp. 301–30.

— (2005b), "The Irish Church, 800–c.1050," in D. Ó Cróinín (ed.), *A New History of Ireland: Volume I: Prehistoric and Early Ireland*. Oxford: Oxford University Press, pp. 635–55.

Hurley, Maurice F. (2010), "Viking Elements in Irish Towns: Cork and Waterford," in John Sheehan and Donnchadh Ó Corráin (eds), *The Viking Age: Ireland and the West*. Dublin: Four Courts Press, pp. 154–64.

Ingman, Heather (2007), *Twentieth-Century Fiction by Irish Women: Nation and Gender*. Aldershot: Ashgate.

— (2009), *A History of the Irish Short Story*. Cambridge: Cambridge University Press.

Jackson, Alvin (2010), *Ireland, 1798–1998: War Peace and Beyond*, 2nd edn. Oxford: Wiley-Blackwell.

Jackson, Kenneth Hurlstone (1964), *The Oldest Irish Tradition: A Window on the Iron Age*. Cambridge: At the University Press.

Jackson, Ruth (2004), *Viking Age Dublin*. Dublin: Town House.

Jardine, Lisa (1993), "Encountering Ireland: Gabriel Harvey, Edmund Spenser, and English Colonial Ventures," in B. Bradshaw, A. Hadfield and W. Maley (eds), *Representing Ireland: Literature and the Origins of Conflict, 1534–1660*. Cambridge: Cambridge University Press, pp. 60–75.

Jefferies, Henry A. (2010), *The Irish Church and the Tudor Reformations*. Dublin: Four Courts Press.

Jenkins, Brian (2006), *Irish Nationalism and the British State: From Repeal to Revolutionary Nationalism*. Montreal: McGill-Queen's University Press.

Johnston, Kevin (2010), *Home or Away: The Great War and the Irish Revolution*. Dublin: Gill and Macmillan.

Jones, Norman (1993), *The Birth of the Elizabethan Age: England in the 1560s*. Oxford: Blackwell.

Judt, Tony (2005), *Postwar: A History of Europe Since 1945*. New York: Penguin.

Kaufmann, Eric P. (2007), *The Orange Order: A Contemporary Northern Irish History*. Oxford: Oxford University Press.

Kearney, Hugh F. (2006), *The British Isles: A History of Four Nations*, 2nd edn. Cambridge: Cambridge University Press.

— (2007), *Ireland: Contested Ideas of Nationalism*. New York: New York University Press.

Kelly, James (1998), *Henry Flood: Patriots and Politics in Eighteenth-Century Ireland*. Notre Dame: University of Notre Dame Press.

— (2000), "Popular Politics in Ireland and the Act of Union." *Transactions of the Royal Historical Society*, 4th series, X, 259–87.

— (2001), "The Act of Union: Its Origin and Background," in D. Keogh and K. Whelan (eds), *Acts of Union: The Causes, Contexts and Consequences of the Act of Union*. Dublin: Four Courts Press, pp. 48–61.

— (2011), "The Historiography of the Penal Laws," in J. Bergin, E. Magennis, L. Ní Mhunghaile and P. Walsh (eds), *New Perspectives on the Penal Laws: Eighteenth-Century Ireland/Iris an dá chultúr, Special Issue No. 1*. Dublin: Eighteenth-Century Ireland Society, pp. 27–52.

Kelly, Matthew (2010), "Languages of Radicalism, Race, and Religion in Irish Nationalism: The French Affinity, 1848–1871." *Journal of British Studies*, 49, (4), 801–25.

Kennedy, Liam (1989), *The Modern Industrialization of Ireland, 1940–1988*. Dunkalk: The Economic and Social History Society of Ireland.

Kennedy, Michael (2008), *Guarding Neutral Ireland: The Coast Watching Service and Military Intelligence, 1939–1945*. Dublin: Four Courts Press.

Kennedy, Michael and O'Halpin, Eunan (2000), *Ireland and the Council of Europe*. Strasbourg: Council of Europe Publishing.

Kennedy, Thomas C. (2007), "Troubled Tories: Dissent and Confusion concerning the Party's Ulster Policy." *Journal of British Studies*, 46, 570–93.

Kenny, Mary (1997), *Goodbye to Catholic Ireland: A Social, Personal and Cultural History from the Fall of Parnell to the Realm of Mary Robinson*. London: Sinclair-Stevenson.

Kenyon, John P. and Ohlmeyer, Jane (1998), "The Background to the Civil Wars in the Stuart Kingdom," in J. P. Kenyon and J. Ohlmeyer (eds), *The Civil Wars: A Military History of England, Scotland, and Ireland, 1638–1660*. Oxford: Oxford University Press, pp. 3–40.

Kenyon, John P. (1985), *Stuart England*, 2nd edn. Harmondsworth: Penguin.

Keogh, Dáire and McDonnell, Albert (eds) (2011), *Cardinal Paul Cullen and his World*. Dublin: Four Courts Press.

— (1990), *Ireland and Europe, 1919–1989*. Cork and Dublin: Hibernian University Press.

— (1995), *Ireland and the Vatican: The Politics and Diplomacy of Church-State Relations, 1922–1960*. Cork: Cork University Press.

— (1998), *Jews in Twentieth-Century Ireland: Refugees, Anti-Semitism and the Holocaust*. Cork: Cork University Press.

Keogh, Dermot and McCarthy, Andrew (2005), *Twentieth-Century Ireland: Revolution and State Building* (revised edn). Dublin: Gill and McMillan.

Kiberd, Declan (1989), "Irish Literature and Irish History," in R. Foster (ed.), *The Oxford Illustrated History of Ireland*. Oxford: Oxford University Press, pp. 275–337.

Kiely, Patrick and Keogh, Dermot (2011), "Turning Corners: Ireland 2002–11," in T. W. Moody, F. X. Martin and Dermot Keogh, Patrick Kiely (eds), *The Course of Irish History*, 5th edn. Lanham, MD: Roberts Rhinehart, pp. 358–97.

Kilfeather, Siobhán (2005), "Irish Feminism," in J. Cleary and C. Connolly (eds), *The Cambridge Companion to Modern Irish Culture*. Cambridge: Cambridge University Press, pp. 96–116.

Kilroy, Patricia (2008), *The Fall of the Gaelic Lords, 1534–1616*. Dublin: Éamonn de Búrca for Edmund Burke.

Kinealy, Christine (1995), *This Great Calamity: The Irish Famine, 1845–52*. Boulder, CO: Robert Rhinehart.

— (2002), *The Great Irish Famine: Impact, Ideology and Rebellion*. Houndmills, Basingstoke, Hampshire: Palgrave.

— (2009), *Repeal and Revolution: 1848 in Ireland*. Manchester: Manchester University Press.

Kishlansky, Mark (1996), *A Monarchy Transformed: Britain, 1603–1714*. Penguin: London.

Kissane, Noel (1995), *The Irish Famine: A Documentary History*. Dublin: National Library of Ireland.

Knott, Eleanor and Murphy, Gerard (1966), *Early Irish Literature*. New York: Barnes and Noble.

Kramer, Jürgen (2007), *Britain and Ireland: A Concise History*. London: Routledge.

Laffin, Martin and Thomas, Alys (1999), "The United Kingdom: Federalism in Denial?." *Publius*, 29, 89–107.

Lake, Peter (1996), "Retrospective: Wentworth's Political World in Revisionist and Post-Revisionist Perspective," in J. F. Merritt (ed.), *The Political World of Thomas Wentworth, Earl of Strafford, 1621–1641*. Cambridge: Cambridge University Press, pp. 252–83.

Lalor, Brian (ed.) (2003), *The Encyclopedia of Ireland*. New Haven and London: Yale University Press.

Larkin, Emmett (2011), "Paul Cullen: The Great Ultramontane," in D. Keogh and A. McDonnell (eds), *Cardinal Paul Cullen and his World*. Dublin: Four Courts Press, pp. 15–33.

Leeson, D. M. (2011), *The Black and Tans: British Police and Auxilliaries in the Irish War of Independence, 1920–1921*. Oxford: Oxford University Press.

Lengel, Edward G. (2002), *The Irish Through British Eyes: Perceptions of Ireland in the Famine Era*. Westport, CT: Praeger Press.

Lenihan, Pádraig (2011), "The Impact of the Battle of Aughrim (1691) on the Irish Catholic Elite," in Brian Mac Cuarta (ed.), *Reshaping Ireland, 1550–1700: Colonization and its Consequences: Essays Presented to Nicholas Canny*. Dublin: Four Courts Press, pp. 300–25.

Lennon, Colm (1995), *Sixteenth-Century Ireland: The Incomplete Conquest*. New York: St. Martin's Press.

Little, Patrick (2001), "The Irish 'Independents' and Viscount Lisle's Lieutenancy of Ireland." *The Historical Journal*, 44, 941–61.

— (2009), "Cromwell and Ireland before 1649," in P. Little (ed.), *Oliver Cromwell: New Perspectives*. New York: Palgrave Macmillan, pp. 116–41.

Livesey, James (2001), "Acts of Union and Disunion: Ireland in Atlantic and European Context," in D. Keogh and K. Whelan (eds), *Acts of Union: The Causes, Contexts and Consequences of the Act of Union*. Dublin: Four Courts Press, pp. 95–105.

Longford, The Earl of and O'Neill, Thomas P. (1971), *Eamon de Valera*. Boston: Houghton Mifflin.

Lloyd, T. O. (1996), *The British Empire, 1558–1995*, 2nd edn. Oxford: Oxford University Press.

Lockey, Brian (2004), "Conquest and English Legal Identity in Renaissance Ireland." *Journal of the History of Ideas*, 65, (4), 543–58.

Longford, Elizabeth (1975), *Wellington: Pillar of State*. St. Albans: Panther Books.

Lucas, A. T. (1973), *Treasures of Ireland: Irish Pagan and Early Christian Art*. Dublin: Gill and Macmillan.

Lydon, James (1987a), "The Expansion and Consolidation of the Colony, 1215–54," in A. Cosgrove (ed.), *A New History of Ireland: II: Medieval Ireland, 1169–1534.* Oxford: Clarendon Press, pp. 156–78.

— (1987b), "The Years of Crisis, 1254–1315," in A. Cosgrove (ed.), *A New History of Ireland: II: Medieval Ireland, 1169–1534.* Oxford: Clarendon Press, pp. 179–204.

— (1997), "Parliament and the Community of Ireland," in J. Lydon (ed.), *Law and Disorder in Thirteenth-Century Ireland.* Dublin: Four Courts Press, pp. 125–38.

— (1998), *The Making of Ireland from Ancient Times to the Present.* London and New York: Routledge.

Lynch, Ann (1981; 1994), "Astronomical Alignment or Megalithic Muddle," in D. Ó Corráin (ed.), *Irish Antiquity: Essays and Studies Presented to Professor M. J. O'Kelly.* Dublin: Four Courts Press, pp. 23–7.

Lynch, Michael (1992), *Scotland: A New History.* London: Pimlico.

Lynch, Patrick (2011), "The Irish Free State and the Republic of Ireland: 1921–66," in T. W. Moody, F. X. Martin and Dermot Keogh, Patrick Kiely (eds), *The Course of Irish History,* 5th edn. Lanham, MD: Roberts Rhinehart, pp. 283–98.

MacCartney, Donal (2011), "From Parnell to Pearse," in T. W. Moody, F. X. Martin and D. Keogh (eds), *The Course of Irish History,* 5th edn. Lanham, MD: Roberts Rinehart, pp. 273–82.

MacCulloch, Diarmaid (2003), *The Reformation: A History.* New York: Penguin Books.

MacFarlane, Anne and de Brún, Tomas (2010), "Medical Pluralism in the Republic of Ireland: Biomedicines as Ethnomedicines," in Ronnie Moore and Stuart McClean (eds), *Folk Healing and Health Care Practices in Britain and Ireland: Stethscopes, Wands, and Crystals.* New York: Berghan Books, pp. 181–99.

MacInnes, Allan I. (2000), "Covenanting Ideology in Seventeenth-Century Scotland," in J. H. Ohlmeyer (ed.), *Political Thought in Seventeenth-Century Ireland: Kingdom or Colony.* Cambridge: Cambridge University Press, pp. 191–220.

MacKenzie, Kirsteen M. (2009), "Oliver Cromwell and the Solemn League and Covenant of the Three Kingdoms," in P. Little (ed.), *Oliver Cromwell: New Perspectives.* New York: Palgrave Macmillan, pp. 142–67.

Mac Uistin, Liam (1999), *Exploring Newgrange.* Dublin: The O'Brien Press.

Mallory, J. P. and McNeill, T. E. (1991), *The Archaeology of Ulster from Colonization to Plantation.* Belfast: The Institute for Irish Studies.

Malone, Kelli Ann (2010), *Discovering Ancient Ireland.* Dublin: History Press Ireland.

Mansergh, Daniel (2001), "The Union and the Importance of Public Opinion," in D. Keogh and K. Whelan (eds), *Acts of Union: The Causes, Contexts and Consequences of the Act of Union.* Dublin: Four Courts Press, pp. 126–39.

Martin, F. X. (1993a), "Allies and an Overlord, 1169–72," in Art Cosgrove (ed.), *A New History of Ireland: II: Medieval Ireland, 1169–1534,* 2nd edn. Oxford: Oxford University Press, pp. 67–97.

— (1993b), "Overlord Becomes Feudal Lord, 1172–85," in Art Cosgrove (ed.), *A New History of Ireland: II: Medieval Ireland, 1169–1534,* 2nd edn. Oxford: Oxford University Press, pp. 98–126.

McCormack, Anthony M. (2005), *The Earldom of Desmond, 1463–1583: The Decline and Crisis of a Feudal Lordship.* Dublin: Four Courts Press.

McCourt, Malachy (2004), *Malachy McCourt's History of Ireland.* Philadelphia: Running Press.

McCulloch, David, Willis (ed.) (2000), *Wars of the Irish Kings: A Thousand Years of Struggle from the Age of Myth through the Age of Queen Elizabeth I*. New York: Crown.

McDonald, Ronan (2005), "Strategies of Silence: Colonial Strains in the Short Stories of the Troubles." *Yearbook of English Studies*, 35, 249–63.

McDowell, R. B. (1970), *The Irish Convention, 1917–18*. London: Routledge and Kegan Paul.

— (1979), *Ireland in the Age of Imperialism and Revolution, 1760–1801*. Oxford: Clarendon Press.

McHugh, Jason (2011), "'For our owne defence': Catholic Insurrection in Wexford, 1641–2," in Brian Mac Cuarta (ed.), *Reshaping Ireland, 1550–1700: Colonization and its Consequences: Essays Presented to Nicholas Canny*. Dublin: Four Courts Press, pp. 214–40.

McKittrick, David and McVea, David (2002), *Making Sense of the Troubles: The Story of Conflict in Northern Ireland*. Chicago: New Amsterdam Books.

McMichael, Gary (1999), *An Ulster Voice: In Search of Common Ground in Northern Ireland*. Boulder: Robert Rhinehart.

Maher, D. J. (1986), *The Tortuous Path: The Course of Ireland's Entry into the EEC, 1948–73*. Dublin: Institute of Public Administration.

Maginn, Christopher (2004), "The Baltinglass Rebellion, 1580: English Dissent or a Gaelic Uprising?." *Historical Journal*, 47, 205–32.

Marshall, Catherine (2010), "History and Memorials: Fine Arts and the Great Famine in Ireland," in Ciara Breathnach and Catherine Lawless (eds), *Visual, Material and Print Culture in Nineteenth-Century Ireland*. Dublin: Four Courts Press, pp. 20–9.

McConnell, James (2011), "Remembering the 1605 Gunpowder Plot in Ireland, 1605–1920." *Journal of British Studies*, 50, 863–91.

McGarry, Fearghal (2010), *The Rising: Ireland, Easter 1916*. Oxford: Oxford University Press.

McGurk, John (1997), *The Elizabethan Conquest of Ireland: The 1590s Crisis*. Manchester and New York: Manchester University Press.

McMahon, Sean (2001), *Wolfe Tone*. Cork: Mercier Press.

McNeill, John T. (1974), *The Celtic Churches: A History A.D. 200 to 1200*. Chicago: University of Chicago Press.

Mirala, Petri (2007), *Freemasonry in Ulster, 1733–1813: A Social and Political History of the Masonic Brotherhood in the North of Ireland*. Dublin: Four Courts Press.

Mitchell, G. F. (2011), "Prehistoric Ireland," in T. W. Moody, F. X. Martin and D. Keogh (eds), *The Course of Irish History*, 5th edn. Lanham, MD: Roberts Rinehart, pp. 27–37.

Moore, Niamh (2005), "Re-greening Brownfields: Land Recycling and Urban Sustainability," in N. Moore and M. Scott (eds), *Renewing Urban Communities: Environment. Citizenship, and Sustainability in Ireland*. Aldershot: Asghate, pp. 29–48.

Moore, Sean D. (2010), *Swift, the Book, and the Irish Financial Revolution: Satire and Sovereignty in Colonial Ireland*. Baltimore: Johns Hopkins University Press.

Moorhouse, Geoffrey (1997), *Sun Dancing: A Vision of Medieval Ireland*. San Diego: Harcourt Brace and Company.

Morgan, Hiram (2004), "'Never Any Realm Worse Governed': Queen Elizabeth and Ireland." *Transactions of the Royal Historical Society*, Sixth Series, 14, 295–308.

Morley, Vincent (2002), *Irish Opinion and the American Revolution, 1760–1783*. Cambridge: Cambridge University Press.

Morrill, John, Manning, Brian and Underdown, David (2000), "What was the English Revolution?," in P. Gaunt (ed.), *The English Civil War: The Essential Readings*. Oxford: Blackwell, pp. 14–32.

Morrow, John (2008), "Thomas Carlyle, 'Young Ireland' and the 'Condition of Ireland Question'." *The Historical Journal*, 51, (3), 643–67.

Munck, Ronnie (1992), "The Making of the Troubles in Northern Ireland." *Journal of Contemporary History*, 27, 211–29.

Murphy, Brian P. (2006), *The Origins and Organisation of British Propaganda in Ireland, 1920*. Aubane, Co. Cork: Aubane Historical Society.

Murphy, Gary (2003), *Economic Realignment and the Politics of EEC Entry: Ireland, 1948–1972*. Dublin: Maunsel and Company.

Murphy, Ignatius (1996), *A Starving People: Life and Death in West Clare, 1845–1851*. Dublin: Irish Academic Press.

Murphy, Kathleen S. (2000), "Judge, Jury, Magistrate and Soldier: Rethinking Law and Authority in Late Eighteenth-century Ireland." *American Journal of Legal History*, 44, 231–56.

Murray, James (2009), *Enforcing the English Reformation in Ireland: Clerical Resistance and Political Conflict in the Diocese of Dublin, 1534–1590*. New York: Cambridge University Press.

Murray, Paul (2011), *The Irish Boundary Commission and Its Origins: 1886–1925*. Dublin: University College Dublin Press.

Myers, Benjamin (2006), "'Such is the Face of Falshood': Spenserian Theodicy in Ireland." *Studies in Philology*, 103, 383–416.

Neal, Frank (1998), *Black '47: Britain and the Famine Irish*. Houndsmills and London: MacMillan.

Neeson, Eoin (2007), *Myths from Easter 1916*. Aubane, Co. Cork: Aubane Historical Society.

Ní Bhrolcháin, Muireann (2009), *An Introduction to Early Irish Literature*. Dublin: Four Courts Press.

Ní Mhaonaigh, Máire (1998), "Friend and Foe: Vikings in Ninth- and Tenth-Century Irish Literature," in Howard Clark, Máire Ní Mhaonaigh and Raghnall Ó Floinn (eds), *Ireland and Scandinavia in the Early Viking Age*. Blackrock: Four Courts Press, pp. 381–402.

Novick, Ben (2001), *Conceiving Revolution: Irish Nationalist Progaganda during the First World War*. Dublin: Four Courts Press.

O'Brien, Dan (2009), *Ireland, Europe and the World*. Dublin: Gill and Macmillan.

O'Brien, Gillian (2001), "Camden and the Move towards Union, 1795–1798," in D. Keogh and K. Whelan (eds), *Acts of Union: The Causes, Contexts and Consequences of the Act of Union*. Dublin: Four Courts Press, pp. 106–25.

O'Byrne, Emmett (2007), "The MacMurroughs and the Marches of Leinster, 1170–1340," in Linda Doran and James Lyttleton (eds), *Lordship in Medieval Ireland*. Dublin: Four Courts Press, pp. 160–92.

O'Callaghan, Chris (2004), *Newgrange: Temple to Life*. Cork: Mercier Press.

O'Carroll, Ciarán (2008), *Paul Cardinal Cullen: Portait of a Practical Nationalist: Paul Cullen and his Relationship with the Independent Irish Party of the 1850s and the Fenian Movement in Ireland of the 1860s*. Dublin: Veritas.

Ó Ciardha, Éamonn (1999), "The Stuarts and Deliverance in Irish and Scots-Gaelic Poetry, 1690–1760," in S. J. Connolly (ed.), *Kingdoms United? Great Britain and Ireland since 1500*. Dublin: Four Courts Press, pp. 78–94.

— (2002), *Ireland and the Jacobite Cause, 1685–1766: A Fatal Attachment*. Dublin: Four Courts Press.

Ó Clabaigh, Colmán N. (2002), *The Franciscans in Ireland, 1400–1534: From Reform to Reformation*. Dublin: Four Courts Press, 2002.

O'Connell, Maurice R. (2007; 1965), *Irish Politics and Social Conflict in the Age of the American Revolution*. Philadelphia: University of Pennsylvania Press.

O'Connor, Frank (1967), *A Short History of Irish Literature: A Backward Look*. New York: G. P. Putnam's Sons.

O'Connor, Gabriel (1998), "Cloanfish, County Galway," in P. Connell, D. A. Cronin and B. Ó Dálaigh (eds), *Irish Townlands: Studies inh Local History*. Dublin: Four Courts Press, 1998.

O'Connor, Fr. Tom (2003), *Turoe and Athenry: Ancient Capitals of Celtic Ireland*, edited by Kieran Jordan. Midleton: Litho Press.

Ó Corráin, Donnchadh (1989), "Prehistoric and Early Christian Ireland," in R. Foster (ed.), *The Oxford Illustrated History of Ireland*. Oxford: Oxford University Press, pp. 1–52.

Ó Cróinín, Dáibhí (2005a), "Hiberno-Latin Literature to 1169," in D. Ó Cróinín (ed.), *A New History of Ireland: Volume I: Prehistoric and Early Ireland*. Oxford: Oxford University Press, pp. 371–404.

— (2005b), "Ireland c. 800: Aspects of Society," in D. Ó Cróinín (ed.), *A New History of Ireland: Volume I: Prehistoric and Early Ireland*. Oxford: Oxford University Press, pp. 549–608.

— (2005c), "Ireland, 400–800," in D. Ó Cróinín (ed.), *A New History of Ireland: Volume I: Prehistoric and Early Ireland*. Oxford: Oxford University Press, pp. 182–234.

O'Donnell, Ruán (2001), D. Keogh and K. Whelan (eds), *Acts of Union: The Causes, Contexts and Consequences of the Act of Union*. Dubin: Four Courts Press, pp. 216–42.

O'Dowd, Liam (2005), "Republicanism, Nationalism and Unionism: Changing Contexts, Cultures and Ideologies," in J. Cleary and C. Connolly (eds), *The Cambridge Companion to Modern Irish Culture*. Cambridge: Cambridge University Press, pp. 78–95.

Ó Giolláin, Diarmuid (2005), "Folk Culture," in J. Cleary and C. Connolly (eds), *The Cambridge Companion to Modern Irish Culture*. Cambridge: Cambridge University Press, pp. 225–44.

Ó Gráda, Cormac (1997), *A Rocky Road: The Irish Economy since the 1920s*. Manchester: Manchester University Press.

— (2000), *Black '47 and Beyond: The Great Irish Famine in History, Economy, and Memory*. Princeton: Princeton University Press.

O'Halloran, Clare (2005), *Golden Ages and Barbarous Nations: Antiquarian Debate and Cultural Politics in Ireland, c. 1750–1800*. Notre Dame: University of Notre Dame Press.

Ó Halpin, Eunan (2008), *Spying on Ireland: British Intelligence and Irish Neutrality during the Second World War*. Oxford: Oxford University Press.

O'Hearn, Denis (1994), "Innovation and the World System Hierarchy: British Subjugation of the Irish Cotton Industry, 1780–1830." *American Journal of Sociology*, 100, 587–621.

Ohlmeyer, Jane H. (1996), "The Wars of Religion, 1603–1660," in T. Bartlett and K. Jeffery (eds), *A Military History of Ireland*. Cambridge: Cambridge University Press, pp. 160–87.

— (1998), "'Civilizing of those rude partes': Colonlization within Britain and Ireland, 1580s–1640s," in Nicholas Canny (ed.), *The Oxford History of the British Empire: Volume I: The Origins of Empire: British Overseas Enterprise to the Close of the Seventeenth Century*. Oxford: Oxford University Press, pp. 124–47.

O'Kelly, Michael J. (1989), *Early Ireland: An Introduction to Irish Prehistory*. Cambridge: Cambridge University Press.

— (2005a), "Ireland before 3000 B.C.," in D. Ó Cróinín (ed.), *A New History of Ireland: Volume I: Prehistoric and Early Ireland*. Oxford: Oxford University Press, pp. 49–68.

— (2005b), "Neolithic Ireland," in D. Ó Cróinín (ed.), *A New History of Ireland: Volume I: Prehistoric and Early Ireland*. Oxford: Oxford University Press, pp. 69–97.

— (2005c), "Bronze-Age Ireland," in D. Ó Cróinín (ed.), *A New History of Ireland: Volume I: Prehistoric and Early Ireland*. Oxford: Oxford University Press, pp. 98–133.

Ó Laoire, Lillis (2005), "Irish Music," in J. Cleary and C. Connolly (eds), *The Cambridge Companion to Modern Irish Culture*. Cambridge: Cambridge University Press, pp. 267–84.

O'Loughlin, Thomas (2000), *Celtic Theology: Humanity, World and God in Early Irish Writings*. London and New York: Continuum.

Oppenheimer, Stephen (2006), *The Origins of the British: A Genetic Detective Story: The Surprising Roots of the English, Irish, Scottish and Welsh*. New York: Carroll and Graf.

O'Reilly, Edward (1970), *A Chronological Account of nearly Four Hundred Irish Writers with a Descriptive Catalogue of their Works*. Introduction by Gearóid S. MacEoin. New York: Barnes and Noble.

Orpen, Goddard Henry (2005), *Ireland under the Normans, 1169–1333*. Dublin: Four Courts Press.

Orr, Phillip (2008), *The Road to the Somme: Men of the Ulster Division Tell Their Story*, 2nd edn. Belfast: Blackstaff Press.

Ó Siochrú, Mícheál (2005), "The Duke of Lorraine and the International Struggle for Ireland, 1649–1653." *The Historical Journal*, 48, 905–32.

Otway-Ruthven, A. J. (1968), *A History of Medieval Ireland*. London: Ernest Benn.

— (2008), "The Chief Governors of Medieval Ireland," in Peter Crooks (ed.), *Government, War and Society in Medieval Ireland: Essays by Edmund Curtis, A.J. Otway-Ruthven, and James Lydon*. Dublin: Four Courts Press, pp. 79–89.

Owen, Nicholas (2003), "The Conservative Party and Indian Independence, 1945–1947." *Historical Journal*, 46, 403–36.

Packenham, Thomas (1970), *The Year of Liberty: The Story of the Great Irish Rebellion of 1798*. Englewood Cliffs, NJ: Prentice-Hall.

Parkes, Peter (2006), "Celtic Fosterage: Adoptive Kinship and Clientage in Northwest Europe." *Comparative Studies in Society and History*, 48, 359–95.

Paul, Kathleen (1996), "A Case of Mistaken Identity: The Irish in Postwar Britain." *International Labor and Working Class History*, 49, 116–42.

Pawlisch, Hans (1985), *Sir John Davies and the Conquest of Ireland: A Study of Legal Imperialism*. Cambridge: Cambridge University Press.

Pennell, Catriona (2012), *A Kingdom United: Popular Responses to the Outbreak of the First World War in Britain and Ireland*. Oxford: Oxford University Press.

Perceval-Maxwell, M. (1994), *The Outbreak of the Irish Rebellion of 1641*. Montreal: McGill-Queen's University Press.

Pittock, Murray G. H. (1994), *Poetry and Jacobite Politics in Eighteenth-Century Britain*. Cambridge: Cambridge University Press.

Powell, Martyn J. (2003), *Britain and Ireland in the Eighteenth-Century Crisis of Empire*. New York: Palgrave Macmillan.

— (2005), *The Politics of Consumption in Eighteenth-Century Ireland*. Houndmills: Macmillan.

— (2010), "The *Volunteer Evening Post* and Patriotic Print Culture in Late Eighteenth-Century Ireland," in M. Williams and S. P. Forrest (eds), *Constructing the Past: Writing Irish History, 1600–1800*. Woodbridge: The Boydell Press, pp. 113–35.

Quinn, D. B. and K. W. Nicholls (1976), "Ireland in 1534," in T. W. Moody, F. X. Martin and F. J. Byrne (eds), *A New History of Ireland III: Early Modern Ireland 1534–1691*. Oxford: Clarendon Press, 1976, pp. 1–38.

Puirséil, Niamh (2007), *The Irish Labour Party, 1922–73*. Dublin: University College Dublin Press.

Quinn, Eileen Moore (2001), "Entextualizing Famine, Reconstituting Self: Testimonial Narratives from Ireland." *Anthropological Quarterly*, 74, (2), 72–88.

Raftery, Barry (2005), "Iron-Age Ireland," in D. Ó Cróinín (ed.), *A New History of Ireland: Volume I: Prehistoric and Early Ireland*. Oxford: Oxford University Press, pp. 134–82.

Ramón, Marta (2007), *A Provisional Dictator: James Stephens and the Fenian Movement*. Dublin: University College Dublin Press.

Ranelagh, John O'Beirne (1983), *A Short History of Ireland*. Cambridge: Cambridge University Press.

Riall, Lucy (2007), *Garibaldi: Invention of a Hero*. New Haven: Yale University Press.

Richter, Michael (1988), *Medieval Ireland: The Enduring Tradition*. New York: St. Martin's Press.

— (1999), *Ireland and Her Neighbours in the Seventh Century*. New York: St. Martin's Press.

Riggs, Pádraigín and Vance, Norman (2005), "Irish Prose Fiction," in J. Cleary and C. Connolly (eds), *The Cambridge Companion to Modern Irish Culture*. Cambridge: Cambridge University Press, pp. 245–66.

Robbins, Caroline (1961), *The Eighteenth-Century Commonwealthman: Studies in the Transmission, Development and Circumstance of English Liberal Thought from the Restoration of Charles II until the War with the Thirteen Colonies*. Cambridge, MA: Harvard University Press.

Robbins, Keith (2006), *Britain and Europe, 1789–2005*. London: Hodder Arnold.

Ronan, Miles V. (1926), *The Reformation in Dublin, 1536–1558*. London: Longmans, Green, and Co.

— (1930), *The Reformation in Ireland under Elizabeth, 1558–1580*. London: Longmans, Green, and Co.

Rourke, Kevin (1995), "Emigration and Living Standards in Ireland since the Famine." *Journal of Population Economics*, 8, (4), 407–21.

Rowley-Conwy, Peter (2007), *From Genesis to Prehistory: The Archaeological Three Age System and Its Contested Reception in Denmark, Britain, and Ireland*. Oxford: Oxford University Press.

Ruggles, Clive (1999), *Astronomy in Prehistoric Britain and Ireland*. New Haven and London: Yale University Press.

Ryan, Michael (1983), "The Iron Age ca. 300 B.C.–450 A.D.," in Michael Ryan (ed.), *Treasures of Ireland: Irish Art 3000 B.C.–1500 A.D.* Dublin: Royal Irish Academy, pp. 23–30.

Ryan, Ray (2000), "Introduction: State and Nation: The Republic and Ireland, 1949–99," in R. Ryan (ed.), *Writing the Irish Republic: Literature, Culture, and Politics, 1949–1999*. Houndsmills and London: Macmillan Press, pp. 1–13.

Scally, Robert James (1995), *The End of Hidden Ireland: Rebellion, Famine, and Emigration*. New York: Oxford University Press.

Schama, Simon (2002), *The History of Britain: The Fate of Empire, 1776–2000*. New York: Hyperion.

Shagan, Ethan (1997), "Constructing Discord: Ideology, Propaganda, and English Responses to the Irish Rebellion of 1641." *Journal of British Studies*, 36, 4–34.

Sher, Richard B. (2007), *The Enlightenment and the Book: Scottish Authors and Their Publishers in Eighteenth-Century Britain, Ireland, and America*. Chicago: University of Chicago Press.

Simms, Katherine (1987), *From Kings to Warlords: The Changing Political Structures of Gaelic Ireland in the Later Middle Ages*. Woodbridge: Boydell Press.

— (1989), "The Norman Invasion and the Gaelic Recovery," in Roy Foster (ed.), *The Oxford Illustrated History of Ireland*. Oxford: Oxford University Press, pp. 53–103.

— (2009), *Medieval Gaelic Sources*. Dublin: Four Courts Press.

Small, Stephen (2002), *Political Thought in Ireland 1776–1798: Republicanism, Patriotism, and Radicalism*. Oxford: Clarendon Press.

Smyth, Alfred P. (1999), "The Effect of Scandinavian Raiders on the English and Irish Churches: A Preliminary Reassessment," in Brendan Smith (ed.), *Britain and Ireland, 900–1300: Insular Responses to Medieval European Change*. Cambridge: Cambridge University Press pp. 1–38.

Smith, Brendan (1999), *Colonisation and Conquest in Medieval Ireland: The English in Louth, 1170–1330*. Cambridge: Cambridge University Press.

— (2007), "Lordship in the British Isles, c. 1320–c. 1360: the Ebb Tide of the English Empire?," in Huw Price and John Watts (eds), *Power and Identity in the Middle Ages: Essays in Memory of Rees Davies*. Oxford: Oxford University Press, 153–63.

— (2011), "Late Medieval Ireland and the English Connection: Waterford and Bristol, ca. 1360–1460." *Journal of British Studies*, 50, 546–65.

Soli, Tatjana (2010), *The Lotus Eaters: A Novel*. New York: St. Martin's Press.

Spurlock, R. Scott (2010), "Cromwell and Catholics: Towards a Reassessment of Lay Catholic Experience in Interregnum Ireland," in M. Williams and S. P. Forrest (eds), *Constructing the Past: Writing Irish History, 1600–1800*. Woodbridge: The Boydell Press, pp. 157–79.

Squatriti, Paolo (2001), "How the Irish Sea (May Have) Saved Civilization: A Review Article." *Comparative Studies in Society and History*, 43, 615–30.

State, Paul F. (2009), *A Brief History of Ireland*. New York: Checkmark Books.

Stephens, Philip (2004), *Tony Blair: A Biography*. New York: Viking.

Stevenson, Garth (2004), "The Politics of Remembrance in Irish and Quebec Nationalism." *Canadian Journal of Political Science*, 37, 903–25.

— (2006), *Parallel Paths: The Development of Nationalism in Ireland and Quebec*. Montreal: McGill-Queen's University Press.

Stout, Geraldine (2003), *Newgrange: The Bend of the Boyne*. Cork: Cork University Press.

Stout, Matthew (2007), *The Irish Ringfort*. Dublin: Four Courts Press.

Suess, Barbara (2011), "Revolutions, Political and Scientific in Young Ireland," presented to the Mid-Atlantic Conference on British Studies, Abington, PA.

Switzer, Catherine (2007), *Unionists and Great War Commemoration in the North of Ireland, 1914–1918*. Dublin: Irish Academic Press.

Thompson, E. P. (1966), *The Making of the English Working Class*. New York: Vintage Books.

Tillyard, Stella (1997), *Citizen Lord: The Life of Edward Fitzgerald, Irish Revolutionary*. New York: Farrar, Straus and Giroux.

Townshend, Charles (2006), *Easter 1916*. Chicago: Ivan R. Dee.

Tristram, Kate (2010), *Columbanus: The Earliest Voice of Christian Ireland*. Dublin: The Columba Press.

Valante, Mary A. (2008), *The Vikings in Ireland: Settlement, Trade and Urbanization*. Dublin: Four Courts Press.

Vance, Rob (2003), *Secret Sights: Unknown Celtic Ireland*. Dublin: Gill and Macmillan.

Viswanathan, Gauri (2004), "Ireland, India, and the Poetics of Internationalism." *Journal of World History*, 15, 7–30.

Walker, Graham (2010), "Scotland, Northern Ireland, and Devolution, 1945–1979." *Journal of British Studies*, 49, 117–42.

Wallace, Patrick F. (2005), "The Archaeology of Ireland's Viking-Age Towns," in D. Ó Cróinín (ed.), *A New History of Ireland: Volume I: Prehistoric and Early Ireland*. Oxford: Oxford University Press, pp. 814–41.

Walsh, Maurice (2008), *The News from Ireland: Foreign Correspondents and the Irish Revolution*. London: I.B. Tauris.

Walsham, Alexandra (2008), "The Reformation and 'The Disenchantment of the World' Reassessed." *Historical Journal*, 51, 497–528.

Walton, Julian (1995), "From *Urbs Istasta* to Crystal City: Waterford, 1495–1995," in Howard B. Clarke (ed.), *Irish Cities*. Dublin: Mercier Press.

Warley, Christoper (2002), "'So Plenty Makes Me Poore': Ireland, Capitalism, and Class in Spenser's *Amoretti* and *Epithalamion*," *English Literary History*, 69, 567–98.

Warren, W. L. (1973), *Henry II*. Berkeley and Los Angeles: University of California Press.

Waters, John (2012), *Was It For This? How Ireland Lost the Plot*. London: TransWorld Ireland.

Whelan, Kevin (1998), *Fellowship of Freedom: The United Irishmen and 1798*. Cork: Cork University Press.

— (2011), "Facing the Future," in F. H. A. Aalen, K. Whelan and M. Stout (eds), *Atlas of the Irish Rural Landscape*, 2nd edn. Cork: Cork University Press, pp. 114–55.

White, Robert W. (2006), *Ruairí Ó Brádaigh: The Life and Politics of an Irish Revolutionary*. Bloomington and Indianapolis: Indiana University Press.

White, Timothy J. (1997), "The Changing Social Bases of Political Identity in Ireland," in Susan Shaw, Sailer (ed.), *Representing Ireland: Gender, Class Nationality*. Gainesville: University of Florida Press, pp. 113–32.

Whyte, J. H. (2011), "Ireland, 1966–82," in T. W. Moody, F. X. Martin and Dermot Keogh, Patrick Kiely (eds), *The Course of Irish History*, 5th edn. Lanham, MD: Roberts Rhinehart, pp. 299–316.

Wilkinson, David. (1997), "'How did they Pass the Union?': Secret Service Expenditure in Ireland, 1799–1804." *History*, 83, 223–51.

Williams, J. E. and Ford, Patrick K. (1992), *The Irish Literary Tradition*. Cardiff: University of Wales Press.

Williams, Kristen P. and Jesse, Neal G. (2001), "Resolving Nationalist Conflicts: Promoting Overlapping Identities and Pooling Sovereignty: The 1998 Northern Irish Peace Agreement." *Political Psychology*, 22, 571–99.

Williams, Leslie (2003), *Daniel O'Connell, the British Press, and the Irish Famine: Killing Remarks*. Aldershot, England; Burlington, VT: Ashgate.

Woodham-Smith, Cecil (1962), *The Great Hunger: Ireland 1845–49*. New York: Harper and Row.

Woolf, S. J. (1932), "Yeats Foresees an Ireland of Reality." *New York Times*, 13 November. http://bluehawk.monmouth.edu:2141/hnpnewyorktimes/docview/99 534936/13A707B1D7023DE617F/6?accountid=12532.

INDEX

Page references in *Italics* refers to the Figures.